*The Jossey-Bass*
Social and Behavioral Science Series

The Study of Organizations

Findings from Field and Laboratory

Daniel Katz

Robert L. Kahn

J. Stacy Adams

EDITORS

The Study of Organizations

Jossey-Bass Publishers

San Francisco • Washington • London • 1980

THE STUDY OF ORGANIZATIONS
Findings from Field and Laboratory
by Daniel Katz, Robert L. Kahn, and J. Stacy Adams, Editors

Copyright © 1980 by: Jossey-Bass Inc., Publishers
433 California Street
San Francisco, California 94104
&
Jossey-Bass Limited
28 Banner Street
London EC1Y 8QE

Library of Congress Cataloging in Publication Data

Katz, Daniel, 1903-
   The study of organizations.

   Includes bibliographical references and index.
   1. Organization. 2. Organizational effectiveness.
I. Kahn, Robert Louis, 1918-   joint author.
II. Adams, J. Stacy, joint author. III. Title.
HM131.K352   302.3'5   80-15488
ISBN 0-87589-464-X

Manufactured in the United States of America

JACKET DESIGN BY WILLI BAUM

FIRST EDITION

Code 8025

~~&~~ Preface

Social studies become social sciences when their substantive core derives from research investigations rather than from untested theory and uncontrolled observation. Our purpose here is to strengthen the research orientation of organizational psychology by providing a volume devoted exclusively to reports of recent experiments and field studies. The articles included deal with significant issues in the field and demonstrate ways in which complex and difficult questions can be translated into researchable terms.

Research is especially important in organizational psychology because it links the world of knowledge to the world of practice. We can check the validity of our generalizations if we put them into practice and test the results. Such linkages are desirable for the social sciences in general, but they are indispensable in organizational psychology, since we cannot study systems in isolation from their function in the real world. Hence, both scientists and practitioners must be research oriented if they are to be maximally effective in understanding and changing organizations.

Speculations about the nature of human organizations and advisory writings to their leaders go back to ancient times, and there have been organizational guidebooks for generations. Quantitative research and experimentation in organizational settings are more recent; their major growth has developed within the past fifteen years. That growth has taken the direction of empirical investigation and hypothesis testing and has conferred on the field of organizational study some of the distinguishing features of a science. This book presents the research that is bringing about such changes. The literature of organizational research is widely scattered. Studies of organizations are conducted by research workers in many different fields and published in the journals of many disciplines. As a consequence, anyone interested in organizational theory and practice has had to rely on review chapters and other secondary sources to supplement their own study.

This book is designed to give readers direct contact with the organizational research that is leading and shaping the field. It is only through reading the specifics of an actual investigation that one comes to understand the meaning of research. Summaries of

ix

research literature, as in review articles and handbooks, are too cryptic to allow readers to learn how techniques of investigation are applied to theoretical issues and practical problems. In this volume, readers can see how investigators actually go about the operations of doing research and how their findings are transforming the organizational field.

To represent the broad range of organizational research, selections were chosen from psychology, sociology, management, and the health sciences. Specific criteria in the selection process were fivefold: (1) relevance to significant theoretical issues, (2) informative contributions to practical problems, (3) coverage of a wide range of research techniques, (4) ingenious use of research methods, and (5) currency of the study. To give additional perspective on this extensive collection, the editors have written introductory and concluding chapters as well as essays to introduce each of the eight sections into which the research selections have been grouped.

The eight parts are themselves chosen and presented in a sequence that facilitates an understanding of the field as a whole. They begin with the environment, the larger technological and social context in which organizations must function. The second section includes articles that deal with organizations themselves as entities—their major types, their characteristics, and the roles that constitute them. The next sections present research on organizational effectiveness and on one of its major determinants, motivation. Two of the key processes of organizational life—communication and decision making—make up the next sections, and the final sections bring together research on some important unintended aspects of organizational life: the effects of work on health and the nature of organizational conflict and change.

The selections represent a wide array of research settings and methods. Among the settings are the classic laboratory, simulated work environments, public educational and health institutions, and multi-plant industries. Choice of methodologies ranges from survey questionnaires, participant observation, and archival search to biomedical assay. The analytic procedures employed are as diverse.

The Study of Organizations is well suited for the bookshelf of the professional concerned with organizational science. It will also be useful either by itself or in conjunction with various texts or other works in a number of fields—psychology, sociology, public administration, social work, education, and business administration and management —in advanced undergraduate and graduate level courses on organizations. The selection of readings contains special relevance to these disciplines either because of the authors' disciplines, populations, or organizations studied or because of the problems investigated and the wide range of methodologies employed.

We are indebted to the Institute for Social Research for institutional support in the preparation of this volume. We are grateful to members of its secretarial staff, namely, Marie Klatt, Janice MacKenzie, Cheryl Peck, and Josephine Wilsman, who cooperated in preparing the manuscript under the able guidance of Grace Stribley and Marjorie MacKenzie. Special thanks are due to Faith O'Neal for her great assistance to Stacy Adams at the North Carolina part of the enterprise. We also acknowledge the helpful suggestions of Linda Argote, Mark Peterson, Graham Staines, Lorraine Uhlaner, and Eser Uzun.

We wish, too, to thank the following publishers for permission to reprint articles and excerpts: Academic Press; American Association for the Advancement of Science; American Psychological Association; American Sociological Association; Cornell University; Mississippi State University; National Training Laboratory Institute; Pergamon Press;

Personnel Psychology, Inc.; Plenum Publishing Company; Sage Publications, Inc.; Charles C Thomas, Publisher; and University Associates, Inc.

June 1980

Daniel Katz
Robert L. Kahn
Ann Arbor, Michigan

J. Stacy Adams
Chapel Hill, North Carolina

Contents

Part VIII: Conflict and Change   465

∾ The Editors

Daniel Katz is professor emeritus of psychology at the University of Michigan and faculty associate at the university's Institute for Social Research. He received his B.A. degree (1925) in sociology from the University of Buffalo and his M.A. degree (1926) and his Ph.D. degree (1928) in social psychology from Syracuse University.

Katz has served on the board of directors of the American Psychological Association (APA) and on the Fulbright Committee on the International Exchange of Persons. He is a former president of the Society for the Psychological Study of Social Issues and of Division 1 (general psychology) of the APA. He has been a fellow of the Center for Advanced Study in the Behavioral Sciences, a Fulbright research fellow to Norway, and a visiting professor at the University of Aarhus, Denmark. In 1965, Katz received the Kurt Lewin Memorial Award, which honors those who have made outstanding contributions to the integration of research and social action.

His writing and research include the areas of methodology, ethnic stereotypes, attitude change, and morale and motivation in organizational settings. Katz was the editor of the *Journal of Abnormal and Social Psychology* from 1962 to 1964 and of the *Journal of Personality and Social Psychology* from 1964 to 1967. He is the coauthor or co-editor of *Student's Attitudes* (1931), *Social Psychology* (1938), *Research Methods in the Social Sciences* (1953), *Public Opinion and Propaganda* (1954), *Political Parties in Norway* (1964), and *The Social Psychology of Organizations* (with R. L. Kahn, 1966, rev. ed. 1978). His numerous journal articles include such topics as psychological barriers to communication, the reflection of interviewers' biases in poll results, the impact of nationalism in international conflict resolution, and satisfactions and deprivations in industrial life.

Robert L. Kahn is program director of the Survey Research Center and professor of psychology at the University of Michigan. He received his B.A. degree (1939) and M.A. degree (1940) in English and his Ph.D. degree (1952) in social psychology, all from the University of Michigan.

Kahn is past president of the Society for the Psychological Study of Social Issues and has held other offices in professional societies. He is a fellow of the APA and the American Statistical Association and a member of Phi Beta Kappa and Sigma Xi.

Among the books of which he is author or coauthor are *The Dynamics of Interviewing* (1957), *Participation in Union Locals* (1958), *Organizational Stress* (1964), *Power and Conflict* (1964), *Justifying Violence* (1973), and *Bureaucratic Encounters* (1975). His research interests have long centered on large-scale organizations, in terms of their productivity and their effects on individual well-being. Recently he has been working on social-psychological measures of the quality of life, including the tendency to justify violence, the treatment of individuals by service agencies, and the nature of social support systems.

J. Stacy Adams is the R. J. Reynolds Industries Professor of Applied Behavioral Science in the Graduate School of Business Administration and research professor in the Department of Psychology at the University of North Carolina, Chapel Hill, where he has taught since 1967. Adams received his B.A. degree (1948) in psychology from the University of Mississippi and his M.A. degree (1955) and Ph.D. degree (1957) in psychology at the University of North Carolina.

Adams was previously on the faculties of Stanford University and Columbia University. He has been a member of General Electric Company's Behavioral Research Service and was deputy director of the Attitude Research Branch, U.S. Army, in Europe. He is a fellow of Division 8 (personality and social psychology) of the APA and a member of the Academy of Management.

As a member of editorial boards, Adams has served the *Journal of Applied Social Psychology, Journal of Experimental Social Psychology, Sociometry, Journal of Personality and Social Psychology,* and *Applied Behavioral Science.* Articles by Adams have appeared in such journals as *Public Opinion Quarterly, Psychological Review, Child Development, Journal of Abnormal and Social Psychology, Industrial Relations,* and *Organizational Behavior and Human Performance.* He has also contributed to several books, including *Decisions, Values, and Groups* (1962), *Studies in Communication* (1962), *Advances in Experimental Social Psychology* (1965), *Handbook of Industrial and Organizational Psychology* (1976), and *Research in Organizational Behavior* (1980). In the past few years, Adams' research has focused on organization boundaries and organizational boundary roles.

The Study of Organizations

*Findings from Field
and Laboratory*

∞ Introduction

In this volume we seek to bring together disparate approaches to the study of organizational behavior, which is now a fractionated field. We want to show that research and methodology are the common meeting ground of students of organizations, whether they come from psychology, sociology, or administration and whether their interest is in science or in practice. We include comments on methods and techniques and show that methodological lessons can be learned from the hits and misses of others. Finally, we indicate the state of our knowledge in various subareas of organizational study, with some account of how we got there and some attention to the direction that future research should take.

The study of organizations has many residences but no single home. Its problems cut across a number of disciplines, both basic and applied, and make difficulty for the traditional separations between psychology, sociology, administrative science, public administration, social work, educational administration, and business management. In any given university, research and training may be housed in various administrative units. Increasingly, interdisciplinary programs have been launched in institutes, but the teaching and degree granting are generally under the direction of individual academic departments or professional schools. A problem for graduate students is the professional identity they hope to achieve: will they be primarily industrial psychologists, social psychologists, sociologists, educational administrators, public administrators, or management specialists? Whichever route they take, they would be well advised to have a firm grounding in research methods, for research is where the various interests will converge.

Such convergence is demonstrated in the journals that publish research studies about organizational behavior. Articles can appear in a wide variety of periodicals, such as the *Journal of Applied Psychology, Personnel Psychology, American Sociological Review, American Journal of Sociology, Harvard Business Review,* and *Policy Sciences.* For the last few years, however, these disciplinary jurisdictions have been breached by such journals as *Administrative Science Quarterly, Academy of Management Journal, Organizational Behavior and Human Performance,* and *Human Relations*—periodicals concerned primarily with research in organizational behavior.

Not only is the study of organizations multidisciplinary, as this array of journals suggests; it is increasingly interdisciplinary as well. As a result, scholars engaged in research on organizational problems, whatever their home discipline, must read across disciplinary lines in order to be current on the problems they propose to study. The press of

1

research has begun to overcome the parochial effects of departmental training and thinking. Today it is clear that the results of empirical investigations concerned with the functioning of social systems are of direct and immediate interest to workers in many of the social sciences and to practitioners as well.

Science and Practice

Some fields of investigation can afford the luxury of long separations between science and practice. Organizational study cannot. Its investigations generally go beyond the laboratory. And any field study or field experiment becomes a form of practice in that it involves interference or intervention with ongoing activities. Actually operationalizing concepts in the field involves the application of knowledge or theory. The action orientation of the researcher may differ from the action orientation of the practitioner, but they do overlap in influencing people and observing the outcomes.

In some fields, science has become so abstract that it seems to have little relevance for social practice. In organizational study, for most purposes we lack models of such abstraction. Moreover, even if we had them, it is unlikely that they would be directly helpful in dealing with concrete problems in real-life organizations—problems of motivation and productivity, for example. We need models that, while less general, include relationships between variables that are identifiable and measurable in ongoing human organizations and that specify conditions under which such organizations must operate. For example, a mathematical model of decision making based on a rational man is less useful than the theory formulated by Cyert and March (1963), which points toward the organizational constraints to be considered. There may be two points here, rather than the single point of abstraction. The concept of bounded rationality may be as abstract as the concept of perfect rationality, but it is a better abstraction because it is truer to the phenomena to be explained and predicted. All theories and concepts must meet that test.

In addition, we are interested in theories that meet the predictive and explanatory test specifically for organizational life. That is an issue of abstraction. We want a theory of bounded rationality that is specifically concerned with the limits to rationality that are inherent in organizations. And similarly with respect to motivation. If those theories also fit other life domains, so much the better, but the first concern is the organizational context. This is an example of Merton's (1957) old point about theories of the middle range.

Abstract models play a part in physical science, but it is premature to give them emphasis in the social sciences. We do need theory, but theory that concerns itself with substance as well as form. For example, we not only need to know that there is a tendency toward balance and dissonance reduction; we also need to know the nature of the imbalances and the apparent resolution of the conflict. The substance or content of issues, as well as their formal properties, needs study. A general theory of motivation which does not specify the nature of motives is not helpful. One reason for the popularity of Maslow's (1954) need hierarchy is that it directs us toward different kinds of motives and the conditions for their arousal. The use of abstraction without empirical referents can be overdone. In econometrics there is an overuse of abstract models, with insufficient attention to the data measures fed into those models. Hence, the predictive power of these models for the real world has often been poor.

Another example of excessive abstraction is found in *The Limits to Growth* (Meadows and others, 1972), based on Forrester's (1971) *World Dynamics*. The principal factors considered in the model are population, resources, capital, and pollution; omitted from consideration as factors are human values and responses to the levels of the other factors. It is already clear, however, that human responses at the individual and societal level have altered the conclusions drawn from the model. Fertility rates have decreased, environmental protection legislation has been passed, resource consumption is being managed, material recycling—resulting in purer throughput systems—is acquiring impetus. A related point, derivable from this critique of the Meadows/Forrester model, is that man-made models influence the very phenomena under study. In social system theory and research, theories and research results must be incorporated in the models—in social systems there *are* Maxwell demons! Freudian theory had profound effects on child rearing; Keynesian economic theory influences economic policies; and the classical organizational theories of Max Weber, Luther Gulick, and Frederick Taylor determine even today the policies and practices of managers. In contrast, physical theories do not affect the fundamental phenomena under study—the "big-bang" theory of cosmologists docs not influence the universe. Biological theory falls nearer to social theory in its effects, but with a difference: the effects are second-order ones. Communication of social theory influences behavior directly; biological theory changes biological phenomena (for example, DNA structure) indirectly through human intervention. Organizations are entirely human creations, and organizational theory and research have particular potential for influencing organizational design, behavior, and performance because, once discoveries and ideas become known to organizational heads, these leaders have the legitimate power to initiate changes.

If the preceding analysis is tenable, it follows that organizational models must include organizational theories and research findings *as system components.*

As we move away from abstract models to more substantive theories, the overlap between science and practice increases. The concepts and findings of substantive research can be readily applied because they deal with variables that can be manipulated in practice. Though there is a commonality in the interests of practitioner and researcher, their roles are still not identical. The practitioner has to make decisions about policies and their implementation without reference to the confirmation of hypotheses dictated by substantive science. The data from science are often inadequate; therefore, organizational leaders must utilize their own experiences, observations, and intuitions in making decisions. Organizational theories and research comprise a relatively modest proportion of the complexities of organizational life. Researchers, for their part, should be responsive to the needs of the practitioner and, in designing their studies, should take account of the practitioner's insights and wisdoms. Thus, interaction between the researcher and practitioner is called for.

The present stage of development of the field argues for a strenuous commerce between the domains of science and of practice. As that develops, the boundaries of the two domains become obscured. Lewin (1951) anticipated this outcome in his action research movement in social psychology. The potential of this doctrine has still to be realized in the study of organizational behavior. As Sanford (1970) has observed, Lewinian action research never became part of the mainstream of social psychology because of the institutional separation of science and practice in established funding agencies and the established professions. Based on the analogy of the differences between engineering and science in the physical sciences, psychology split into two branches in divorcing research from practice. The study of organized groups is, however, the natural place for bringing science and practice together.

Is substantive research another name for applied research, and are we abandoning the notion of basic research in the study of organizational behavior? The answer to both questions is in the negative. Basic research is concerned with the discovery of relationships between variables, with the reasons for them, their generality, and the conditions under which they hold. Applied research is concerned with the facts and relationships that characterize a particular setting. It is also concerned more with the possibilities of successful intervention than with explanation as such. Basic science does not have to be at the highest level of abstraction. It can include substantive investigations that achieve some generality. For example, research results suggest that in organizational structures an increase in formal communication is accompanied by an increase in informal communication. This finding, if it holds up in replications, seems, to us, basic. If it holds under some organizational conditions and not under others, the task is to identify the contingent conditions under which it holds. The basic finding, then, includes one or more contingency statement. Applied research would differ from basic substantive work in that it attempts little of generality. When applied research goes beyond immediate problems and specific settings, it cannot be distinguished from basic research. We are dealing with a dimension of generality and abstraction. At one extreme formal and mathematical models, which typically incorporate simplifying assumptions. At the other extreme is the aesthetician's emphasis on the uniqueness of the phenomena observed. Between these extremes lie substantive research and the practices based on it.

Some organizational students take the artist's approach, insisting that every organization is unique and that consultation with it and intervention in its practices must derive from that system alone. This problem of generalization and of uniqueness has been well analyzed by Allport (1937), who pointed out that social phenomena have two aspects: the idiographic and the nomothetic. They have uniqueness, and they also have commonality, since some common characteristics can be abstracted. Thus, the artist seeks to capture the uniqueness of the thing in itself, and the scientist seeks to discover relationships that generalize across people and situations. Though Allport's interest was in personality study, the idiographic and nomothetic approaches apply to the study of organizations. We reject the idiographic, not because organizations lack unique aspects but because scientific study is committed to the discovery of general principles. Scientists believe that uniqueness ultimately can be reduced to probability statements, but for the present they give their attention to the generalizable aspects of phenomena.

Integration of Knowledge

In a multifaceted discipline, physically separated and psychologically divided, how do we put it all together? Three types of linkages can bind together the fragmented parts of the field: common problems, common methods and techniques, and common theory. If workers from different sciences are seeking answers to the same problem, there is a fair probability of communication among them. In part this probability depends on their definition of the problem. If the problem can be stated in terms of substantive issues rather than abstract models or unique qualities, the probability increases. It is important, then, for researchers to think not only in terms of their professional specialization but also in terms of broad problems. Even though their own investigations yield but partial answers, these partial answers can be considered in relation to the findings of others. At the present stage of development, problem definition is important so that investigators from different backgrounds can see similarities in their interests. It will help, too, if researchers translate their own verbal labels into older currency. An idiosyncratic terminology impedes communication, and science rests on a publicly accepted language.

A common methodology is a second major way of tying together the work of the different scientists. Here there is a community of techniques to begin with. Experimental and survey technology are the same whether the investigator is an administrative scientist, a sociologist, or a psychologist. In one discipline some techniques (such as sampling) may have reached a more refined development than in another, but the basic tools do not differ. Methods of data collection and measurement determine the character and the interpretation of findings. Comparisons across studies therefore can be made even though the field is segmented. Because of the use of similar techniques, a fair amount of integration is possible once we develop standard measures for use by investigators of different persuasions. In the tradition of psychology, we have seen a profusion of measuring instruments, many of them directed at the same phenomena. In place of standard instruments of known psychometric properties, researchers have employed their own scales and their own nomenclature. We would be much further ahead if we were less inventive at this level of creativity and showed a greater willingness to utilize existing measures of organizational variables and measures of individual behavior in organizations. The reason for focusing on standard instruments is that researchers can readily tie their work to what has gone before, and, in fact, are almost forced to consider what others are doing. If the same measures are used by the management researcher as by the social psychologist, there is no problem in crossing disciplinary boundaries when one is integrating results.

The third method of integration is through unifying theory. This is the ideal but most difficult road. Social science has been more successful in developing single-concept theories for limited subareas than in producing a comprehensive theory that embraces various types of phenomena. Single-concept theories work themselves out because they deal with an extremely limited territory. When the central area is exhausted and we reach the boundaries and problems of relationships with other concepts, the theory loses its force. Unfortunately, this has been the history of a great many promising doctrines in social psychology. For example, both status congruence and dissonance reduction have languished while field theory has flourished. When comprehensive theories are lacking in social psychology, sociology, and administrative sciences, it is probably too much to expect to find an overall theory for organizational behavior, which is closely allied to these fields. Miller (1978) has made the most ambitious attempt in applying open-system theory to seven hierarchical levels of living systems, of which organization is one. But explanation should be attempted at the organizational level before we try to develop it across all levels. Miller's new conceptual language may inspire organizational scientists to unify their findings, but Miller himself does not translate many of the traditional organizational concepts into his own set of terms. Nor does he provide a new theory of organizational functioning. He rightfully notes that the field lacks a large body of empirically established facts. Open-system theory, in line with Miller's example, is the approach to take to achieve unity, but it is still more of an approach than a developed theory. It directs us to important types of variables but does not give specifications about their lawful interactions.

Open-System Theory

Open-system theory conceives of organizations as interdependent, with an environment for constant renewal through inputs and for the disposal of products and services. We cannot develop an internal system of mechanics to describe organizational functioning without reference to its ongoing commerce with its surroundings. Burns and Stalker (1961) highlighted this problem by distinguishing between mechanistic and organic conceptions of organizations. The organic conception, with its emphasis on flexibility and adaptability, is an open-system approach.

Since every living system runs down (entropy) without the constant importation of energy, open-system theory suggests detailed consideration of maintenance inputs to preserve the structure, as well as production inputs to get the work done. The recent interest in human resources accounting—in which the skills, training, and experience of an organization's members are evaluated as an asset—does recognize the importance of maintenance as well as production inputs. The traditional assumption, however, is that the organization, when set in motion, will somehow keep going and that its structure is self-maintaining. Consequently, measures of absenteeism, turnover, and productivity have been considered as hard data on organizational performance, rather than in the frame of reference of structural maintenance.

By calling attention to the input, throughput, and output aspects of energy exchange, open-system theory suggests three major types of subsystems of organization: procurement arrangements for materials and personnel; production structures; and disposal procedures, such as marketing and advertising. Each of these subsystems develops its own logic and its own dynamics around its specialized function.

The differentiation of structures calls for mechanisms of regulation and control. Von Bertalanffy (1956) speaks of progressive mechanization, or the development of rules and regulations to replace the dynamic interactions of system components. To the three basic subsystems is added a managerial structure for coordination of all activities.

The energy exchange of open systems and their environments calls attention to the dependence of a system upon inputs. This dependence does not indicate a complete openness and fluidity such that systems have no boundaries or characteristic forms of their own. Change is less ubiquitous than stability, and systems seek to preserve a steady state. They utilize feedback from the environment to stay on target. But the equilibrium of forces is not a static balance, in that there is a tendency to overreact. One way of protecting against competition is to control more of the market. In general, the organization tries various ways of controlling the instability of its environment—sometimes through direct incorporation, at other times through indirect manipulation. In this process it develops adaptive subsystems to fully utilize feedback from its operations. As the organization's environment increases in complexity and as environments acquire turbulent field characteristics (Emery and Trist, 1973), the need for adaptive activities increases, perhaps exponentially.

Open-system theory also suggests permeable boundaries of organizations, since they affect and are affected by their environments. It is but a step from the nature of permeable boundaries to a consideration of boundary roles. The function of such roles is the mediation and translation of influences between systems or subsystems. Thus, these roles may have built into them conflicts of various sorts. The linkages between system components are usually the weakest parts of systems. We find this differential weakness in physical man-made systems and in social systems but not in biological systems, which have survived evolutionarily.

Marxian theory predicts social change as the working out of internal contradictions in the social structure. Open-system theory would predict change as the response to external forces. Without environmental modifications that interfere with the flow of maintenance and production inputs, organizations will not change. The reforms attempted by the organizational interventionist or change agent need the support of environmental influences; that is, some source of organizational support in the world outside the organization needs to be driving the organization toward the proposed changes.

Open-system theory suggests a hierarchical arrangement of subsystems with respect to dependence on other structures. If one follows the cycle of transactions that maintain an organized form, one can ascertain that there is a hierarchy of dependencies. In a public university, for example, a department depends on the college for its teaching budget, the college depends on the university, and the university depends on the state legislature. This does not mean that we can assume a simple pattern of dependence in a society. We need to know how one structure impinges on another and the relative autonomy of any given subsystem. The general rule is that the more comprehensive structures may have greater significance for the problem under consideration than we realize. If we are dealing with a business enterprise, we want to know the industry of which it is a part and the degree of independence of the companies within it. This takes us beyond economic dependence and gets into political issues of control, about which open-system theory is not explicit. Miller (1978) has gone beyond it in his analysis of information inputs and feedback.

Errors of Reductionism and Uniqueness

There are two forms of error to guard against in organizational psychology, especially when one is attempting integration of various approaches. One is the *reductionist error* of attempting to account for the variance in complex groupings through individual psychological variables. Reductionism is marvelously attractive and takes many forms. The equating of authoritarian organizations with authoritarian personalities is an extreme example. More subtle instances involve, for example, the explanation of organizational degrees of integration in terms of intragroup cohesiveness or individual identification. The study of organizational behavior becomes the study of behavior *in* organizations rather than the study *of* organizations. Such organizational variables as differentiation of structure, power distribution, horizontal and vertical communication, and characteristics of boundary roles are ignored. Leadership becomes the study of a personal style rather than a structured influence process. It is as if the individuals in the system were acting in parallel or in concert, rather than interacting. An adequate science of organization cannot be based on a simplistic reductionism.

The reductionist error has various aspects. It loses information because it misses the explanatory power of variables that are apparent at successively higher levels of organization. And it misses the two-way or reciprocating (dialectical, interdependent) nature of causal relations, especially in organizational life. The attributes of individuals and of groups *do* indeed affect the properties of the larger organization, but the properties of the organization as such also affect the groups and individuals that comprise it. Reductionist explanations give us one-way glasses to negotiate traffic on a two-way street —a dangerous practice.

The second type of error is the *uniqueness-of-data approach*. Organizational and individual variables are viewed as of such a different order that appropriate relationships are not established. There is a belief in the purity of levels and the desirability of not mixing psychological and structural measures. This error arises from the failure to conceive of organizations as systems (1) nested within and linked to larger systems and (2) containing smaller subsystems that are, in turn, linked to them. The belief in the purity of levels ignores the fact that at the point of data collection there is a marked similarity in the types of data collected. Our data come for the most part from the behavior and perceptions of individuals, and the issue of levels arises from the way the data are handled, not in the uniqueness of the phenomena observed. The psychological approach would take the perceptual responses of individuals and relate them to attitudes and behavior of the same individuals. The structural approach would aggregate these perceptions to characterize a given system or subsystem.

In Tannenbaum's work, for example, individual perceptual data are summated to give the steepness of hierarchical control curves for different structures (Tannenbaum and others, 1974). The same perceptions, individually considered, can be used for psychological analysis. This is also true where individual measures are aggregated to characterize larger units, such as departments, as in the case of high productive or low productive sections. The characterization of structures thus can derive from aggregating measures of individual perception or behavior; but they can also derive from observation or records of the product of group effort, as in the instance of number of cars produced. When dealing with the products of group interaction, we do have a type of datum that is independent of psychological measurement. While we do not want to confuse our levels of measurement, there is no problem in relating one to the other in analysis. In fact, we avoid some of the circularity of conclusions drawn when all measures come from a single source.

Social scientists may also gather psychological data other than those gathered by industrial psychologists because of their different theoretical orientation. They may be more concerned with group norms about productivity than about achievement motivation. But they still rely on measures of individuals to ascertain group norms, since group norms are found only in the perceptions, attitudes, and actions of people. Since the social sciences, with the exception of group products, share the same phenomena, they can also share the same data. Care must be exercised, however, in the use of individual measures to characterize larger structures. If we are taking the perceptions of organization members as our method, we should include members at different ranks and seek for consensus. If we are using summated attitudes from individuals to characterize the climate of a department, there should be representative and adequate sampling of that department. With proper precautions, there are advantages to comparing measures at different levels. We can look at the dissatisfied worker in a satisfied group, or the nonparticipant in a participative group. We can compare different echelons in the organization on an individual or on a group basis. Finally, we can relate measures of group outcome to individual and group variables.

One caution is frequently ignored in the use of group and organizational variables. The N is no longer the number of individuals studied but the number of groups or departments or organizations. Because the aggregated data come from individuals, analysts forget that they are now treating a higher level of unit and still use the number of individuals as the basis for computing the significance of differences. A more pressing reason for this error is that it is difficult to obtain data from an adequate number of higher units, such as departments or organizations.

Strategy of Research

We have been contending that we cannot reduce concepts at a higher level to some miniature individual model as if the organization had the goals of its leader. Since many individuals are involved, we need concepts that take account of social interaction and role systems rather than personal qualities. But in avoiding the error of reductionism, we do not avoid data and measures at the individual level (the uniqueness error). We seek other measures than assessments of single personalities and turn to such complex measures as indicators of consensus and reciprocity. For example, we look for measures of system norms in the agreement of members about system requirements.

Of the two mistakes, the more crippling bias has been the reductionist error. To study variables suggested by individual psychological theory is not so much an error as it is poor strategy. Organizational variables may account for the greater part of the variance, and hence we need to start there in a research program. Organized activities in their nature place constraints on individual behavior, and we need to know the character of these constraints. Before we study departures from roles, we need to know what the roles are, whether formal or informal. We need to know as well the type of organization, the type of technology it employs, and the conflicted versus cooperative interrelationships among its subgroups (for example, labor and management).

Tannenbaum and his associates (1974) have presented evidence to indicate that the influence patterns within organizations are generally hierarchical. How should this finding about hierarchical levels affect our research strategy? We would maintain that just as we consider organizational variables before individual variables in accounting for variances, so should we turn first to the next-higher level in the system in dealing with a problem identified at a given level. The problem may persist at that level, and so we pursue the issue up the organization. Thus, worker dissatisfaction may stem from an ineffectual supervisor, but it may also be a function of a higher level in the company, such as the department or even the company itself. One can also follow the matter to the larger society, but that is likely to introduce many factors irrelevant to the organization. For practical purposes, the next-higher relevant level is the place to start inquiries. That is because the organization is hierarchical, and influence and information dominantly flow downward and not upward.

The articles which follow have been selected because they are current illustrations of a quantitative approach, because they show the interplay of practice and of science, and because they demonstrate the interdisciplinary character of this field. Many of them, moreover, are derived from or are consistent with open system theory.

References

Allport, G. W. *Personality: A Psychological Interpretation.* New York: Holt, Rinehart and Winston, 1937.

Burns, T., and Stalker, G. M. *The Management of Innovation.* London: Tavistock, 1961.

Cyert, R. M., and March, J. G. *A Behavioral Theory of the Firm.* Englewood Cliffs, N.J.: Prentice-Hall, 1963.

Emery, F. E., and Trist, E. L. *Toward a Social Ecology.* New York: Plenum, 1973.

Forrester, J. W. *World Dynamics.* Cambridge, Mass.: Wright-Allen Press, 1971.

Lewin, K. *Field Theory in Social Science.* (D. Cartwright, Ed.) New York: Harper & Row, 1951.

Maslow, A. H. *Motivation and Personality.* New York: Harper & Row, 1954.

Meadows, D. H., and others. *The Limits to Growth.* New York: Universe Books, 1972.

Merton, R. K. *Social Theory and Social Structure.* New York: Free Press, 1957.

Miller, J. G. *Living Systems.* New York: McGraw-Hill, 1978.

Sanford, N. "Whatever Happened to Action Research?" *Journal of Social Issues,* 1970, *26,* 3-23.

Tannenbaum, A. S., and others. *Hierarchy in Organizations: An International Comparison.* San Francisco: Jossey-Bass, 1974.

Von Bertalanffy, L. "General Systems Theory." *General Systems. Yearbook of the Society for General Systems Theory,* 1956, *1,* 1-10.

PART I

Technology, Environment, and Growth

There has been wide debate about a technological imperative in organizations and society —namely, the assumption that technology determines the forms that organizations take, as well as the social values of the society. In its broadest form, the technological imperative would be used to account for the pragmatic direction the Chinese have taken in repudiating some of Mao's doctrines and seeking technical help from the West. In a more narrow framework, technology has been used to account for the structure of industrial organizations. Specifically, Woodward (1965) found strong relationships between the technology of production and number of levels of authority, ratio of managers to total personnel, and span of control of first-level supervisors. She distinguished among small-batch, mass-production, and process-production plants and found that, with increasing technical complexity, some structural characteristics, such as levels of authority and size of administrative component, increased. Other characteristics, however, showed a U-shaped relationship with complexity. Her conclusion was that the more appropriate forms of structure for complex technology are organic or flexible, whereas mechanical or rigid social forms are more appropriate for simpler technology.

Her findings were not confirmed by the Aston group (Hickson, Pugh, and Pheysey, 1969), who found that size rather than the technical variable showed a linear relationship with structural characteristics. Speculations about this failure to confirm the plausible Woodward findings have led to the hypotheses that in small organizations the relationships hold (Woodward's sample was predominantly of small factories) and that her results would also be true of production sections and production-linked sections rather than for the more remote organizational substructures. *Blau* and his colleagues find, however, that these hypotheses were not supported in their study of 110 manufacturing plants in which the Aston group's results about the size relationships were confirmed. *Blau** did find, however, a clear U-shaped relationship between technical complexity and structural characteristics, in that mass-production plants showed less differentiation than either small-batch production factories or process-production industries. The move toward mass production did increase the span of control, but as firms became more involved in process production, the span of control decreased (or number of supervisors increased). This finding is consistent with Woodward's findings in that, in addition

*Names in italic indicate authors of selections appearing in this volume.

10

to linear relationships for some characteristics, she reported a curvilinear relationship for span of control. Thus, there is technological determinism. It is the character of the technology, however—and not the dimension of technological complexity as such—that is the determining factor.

Robey's review of the effects of computer technology reveals a similar set of findings. In some organizations and under certain conditions, computer technology can lead to centralization, but this is not an inevitable outcome of the use of computers. Where the task environment is complex and unstable, computerization leads to decentralization; in a more simple, placid environment, however, computer use is accompanied by centralization. This is consistent with the work of Lawrence and Lorsch (1967), who reported a more flexible or organic structure in coping with an uncertain environment than with a predictable environment.

New developments in computerization have been described by Noyce (1977), in his account of the microelectronic revolution. Small and reliable sensing and control devices at ever lower cost are increasing the capacity of the computer to store, process, and display information at a phenomenal rate. Annual usage of transistors has doubled eleven times in the past seventeen years. And applications of technical advances are in their infancy. The automobile engine can now be controlled by the computer, but the extension of intellectual power by microelectronics can, in the future, radically transform educational and social institutions. As *Robey* indicates, it is difficult to predict the effects of electronics on the social structures of organizations without more specification of their functions in relation to the nature of the task environment.

An old issue in organizational sociology is the effect of growth on the component substructures of a system. Do they all grow at the same rate, or does the supportive component increase at a different rate than the production component? Parkinson (1957) has assumed that the administrative sector of the organization increases more rapidly than the production sector. The assumption is that the demands for coordination are greater in the larger organization, and Parkinson also assumes an empire-building tendency in administration. An opposing thesis is that economy of scale permits a decrease in administration and an increase in span of control for the supervisor of production workers. Blau (1970), for example, does make this point. In general, the research supports Blau and not Parkinson. It is true that, as industry has grown, the proportion of people in direct production has decreased, but this is due in good part to other supportive functions than administration.

Freeman and *Hannan* have thrown new light on this problem by showing that the relationships between components are not the same in growth as in decline. Most previous studies have been cross-sectional in nature and have looked at size at one point in time. Thus, the organization with a large administrative component may be in a declining rather than a growing period. Their general hypothesis is that the number of production workers will increase or decrease as the demand for their services varies, but that the size of the administrative staff will not decline as much in a slack period as it increases in a boom period. They tested their theory in school districts by a longitudinal study in which the number of teachers was compared over time with the number of people playing supportive roles. The hypothesis was supported in that both the supportive component and the production component increased in periods of growth, but the supportive component did not fall off as much as the production component in periods of decline. Their study clearly demonstrates the inadequacy of the cross-sectional approach in dealing with problems of growth.

As technology grows, as organizations multiply, as we approach the physical limits of the natural environment in raw materials and forms of energy, the environmental field takes on a complex, dynamic character. Emery and Trist (1973) have described shifts in the milieu from a random, placid state to a turbulent environment. The stability and dependability for organizational programming are often lacking. It is small wonder that environmental uncertainty has become a central concept in the study of organizational functioning. The very notion of organization assumes some degree of planned coordinating effort, yet the unpredictability of external happenings can wreck the best-laid plans. Bennis and Slater (1968) have argued accordingly that organizations should be set up as temporary, flexible arrangements instead of permanent, fixed structures. In a laboratory experiment, *Mericle* tested four hypotheses: (1) that subjects in changing environments will report higher environment dynamism and uncertainty; (2) that subjects in environments characterized by large numbers of heterogeneous organizations will report perceptions of greater complexity; (3) that subjects in uncertain environments will allocate more resources to such boundary activities as information seeking, representing, negotiating, coding, and filtering; (4) that subjects in complex environments will allocate more resources to boundary activities. Three of these hypotheses were supported. Only the third hypothesis, that more resources would be allocated to boundary activities under the condition of environmental uncertainty, was not substantiated. In this experiment, business students were assigned the role of a manager of a company and were fed information about environmental factors, such as prices of raw materials, annual sales of competitors, and union wage demands. They were then asked to allocate a million dollars in corporate funds among thirteen company activities. How much this ingenious simulation went beyond the experiential background of the subjects is a question. Experimental simulation of this sort has great advantages in employing laboratory techniques to problems difficult to study in a field setting, but the simulation can be more meaningful if the contrived situation is not too remote from the experience of the subjects. Thus, simulation using managers from industry would, in this case, have added strength to the study.

Another aspect of organizational environment, seldom investigated, is that of scarcity-munificence. *Staw* and *Szwajkowski* imaginatively tested the hypothesis that the scarce environment will produce more effort by the organization to wring resources from that environment—specifically, that less prosperous firms will be more likely to be cited for unfair market practices and restraint of trade than will more prosperous firms. The volume *Trade Acts* was consulted for companies engaging in legally questionable activities and *Fortune* for its list of the 500 largest firms and their financial performance. The companies cited for illegal activity were less prosperous than the companies not cited. The study demonstrates how ingenuity can be used to find secondary sources of data to describe relationships. The difficulty is that causes are not readily established. The flourishing companies may have used their resources to stay out of litigation.

References

Bennis, W. G., and Slater, P. E. *The Temporary Society.* New York: Harper & Row, 1968.

Blau, P. M. "A Formal Theory of Differentiation in Organizations." *American Sociological Review,* 1970, *35,* 201-218.

Emery, F. E., and Trist, E. L. *Toward a Social Ecology.* New York: Plenum, 1973.

Hickson, D. J., Pugh, D. S., and Pheysey, D. C. "Operations Technology and Organization Structure: An Empirical Reappraisal." *Administrative Science Quarterly,* 1969, *14,* 378-397.

Lawrence, P. R., and Lorsch, J. W. *Organization and Environment.* Boston: Graduate School of Business Administration, Harvard University, 1967.

Noyce, R. N. "Microelectronics." *Scientific American,* 1977, *237* (3), 63-69.

Parkinson, C. N. *Parkinson's Law.* Boston: Houghton Mifflin, 1957.

Woodward, J. *Industrial Organization: Theory and Practice.* London: Oxford University Press, 1965.

1

$\mathscr{ }$ Technology and Organization
in Manufacturing

Peter M. Blau
Cecilia M. Falbe
William McKinley
Phelps K. Tracy

Few would question the impact of technology on society. Technological developments have caused the movement of people from farms to cities and from industrial to service occupations. They have stimulated the evolution of the modern economic organization, altered class structures, and affected political institutions. Technological change today occurs primarily in large organizations, both public and private. Yet research on the structural implications of technology for the organization of work has uncovered few unambiguous patterns.

In one of the pioneering attempts to examine these implications with comparative data from many organizations, Woodward's (1958, 1965) study of 100 firms in England reported systematic differences in structure accompanying various types of production technology. But in another carefully designed research effort involving forty-six British organizations a decade later, Hickson, Pugh, and Pheysey (1969) failed to replicate Woodward's findings. Their study found few associations between production technology and the organization of work. Its results indicated that differences in organizational structure depend not so much on technology as on the size of a firm. Since the publication of these two classic studies, several attempts have been made to replicate them in different industrial and economic contexts, but so far the debate between the proponents of size and technology as prime determinants of structure remains largely unresolved.

Child and Mansfield (1972) applied the Aston questionnaire (Pugh and others, 1968) to a national sample of eighty-two British firms, while Hickson and his colleagues (1974) extended their original research to United States and Canadian corporations. In each case, organizational size rather than production technology appeared to exert the more significant influence on the division of labor and organization of work. During this period, Zwerman (1970) followed Woodward's basic approach in his study of fifty-five Minnesota firms and reported patterns inconsistent with the Aston-type findings. Organizational size was associated with number of levels and the average span of control of the chief executive officer, but, apart from these results, his findings largely supported Woodward's conclusion that technology is most influential.

The inconsistency in these findings suggests the need for further study. Research, however, should not stop with an examination of production technology. Technological innovation in factories used to be confined largely to production, substituting machines for manual labor, but the recent development and spread of computer systems now also substitutes automated operations for white-collar work. Like its blue-collar counterpart a half-century ago, administrative work is becoming increasingly mechanized and automated, leading to structural changes which are also widely debated. Studies of the impact of computers on organizational structure and decision making are following a course similar to that taken by research on production technologies, with impressionistic observations preceding more systematic comparative efforts and yielding inconsistent findings and disagreements.

For example, Whisler (1970a, 1970b) and Argyris (1970) noted strong parallels between technological displacement of labor in blue-collar and white-collar work, with more formal centralized control and less individual skill and autonomy. These conclusions are supported by Mumford and Banks's (1967) study of a British banking firm. A more extensive report by Withington (1969), which drew upon impressionistic evidence in manufacturing, government, and service organizations, came to opposite conclusions. While acknowledging that computers may provide opportunities for greater centralized control, he indicated that this has occurred only in routine areas. Withington's observations agreed with those made earlier by Bavelas (1960) that computers, by and large, do not alter the evolution toward increasingly more specialized and complex managerial structures.

This article clarifies the influence of technology on the structure of white-collar and blue-collar work in factories by analyzing data obtained from interviews with key executives in 110 American manufacturing establishments. To ensure comparability with earlier empirical research, the concept of technology employed here refers to the substitution of mechanical equipment for human labor, and therefore does not take direct account of other dimensions of technology—knowledge, strategies, techniques, and skills—discussed by such theorists as Thompson (1967) and Perrow (1967). After a description of research procedures, the influence of the production technology and of automation of support functions on the organization of work is discussed. The last section preceding the conclusions examines and compares the relationships of mechanization and automation to the decentralization of authority in manufacturing plants.

Research Procedures

Data were collected from a random sample of 331 New Jersey manufacturing establishments employing 200 or more persons. New Jersey was selected as the location of the study because its wide variety of manufacturing firms are representative of American industry as a whole. All the two-digit Standard Industrial Classification codes, for instance, are found in this state. One third of the plants in the original random sample agreed to participate in the study. Reliability checks indicated that the 110 plants participating did not differ significantly from the sample of 331 in terms of size (number of employees), product type (two-digit SIC code), or whether the manufacturing organization was a single-site company or a branch of a larger firm. Although these findings do not preclude the existence of significant differences in other areas, they suggest that the data are fairly representative of larger New Jersey manufacturing concerns, and probably typical of manufacturing establishments in the country.

Information was collected at each of the 110 plants with a structured questionnaire administered to senior managers; these included the chief executive officer (plant manager), the head of production, and the personnel manager. Data were gathered at the site on day-to-day operations, including information on decision making, personnel breakdowns, computer usage, and mechanization of production machinery. All the data obtained refer to attributes of a plant's social structure and objective conditions, such as size, personnel distributions, production technology, and automation. No information was gathered on psychological attitudes.

The unit of analysis was the manufacturing site at a particular location, not the entire corporation that owned the site. If a plant had a parent company—as all but 11 of the 110 establishments did—some information was collected on the larger corporate structure, but it was kept separate from data pertaining to the site, even when the site was located at parent company headquarters. The mean number of employees in the 110 plants was 497 in 1973, but more than half of them had fewer than 360. Personnel totals ranged from less than 100 to more than 4,000, and the standard deviation of plant size was 553, indicating a highly skewed distribution. On the average, plants were smaller than those studied by Hickson, Pugh, and Pheysey (1969), Child and Mansfield (1972), or Zwerman (1970), but larger than Woodward's (1958, 1965). The corporations owning the New Jersey manufacturing establishments employed an average total of 38,480 persons.

A majority of the plants surveyed experienced a decline of 5 percent or more in their labor force from 1967 to 1973. There was some decrease in size for 60 percent of the 110 factories, while only 27 percent were larger in 1973 than in 1967. The average factory in 1973 was composed of 57 percent direct production workers, 18 percent workers in indirect production, and 21 percent nonproduction—white-collar—workers, including supervisors, other exempt staff, and clerks. The average plant was differentiated horizontally into five major subunits or divisions with heads reporting directly to the chief executive officer, and vertically into five administrative levels. The mean span of control of the plant manager (CEO) was seven—five division heads and two assistants—and the spans of control of first-line supervisors averaged twenty-one for foremen in direct production, twelve for those in indirect production, and five for white-collar supervisors.

The two main independent variables were production technology and the automation of functions through computers. Several measures of production technology refer to the degree of mechanization of manufacturing equipment, which is defined according to Amber and Amber's (1962) automaticity scale. Their scheme measures the extent to which human energy and control over the production process are replaced by machines; it distinguishes five levels of automaticity, ranging from powered machine tools—all work is mechanized but control is dependent on the operator—to computerized equipment—both labor and control functions are taken over by the machine. Estimates of the percentage of total production machinery operating at each of these levels and equivalent figures for the percentage of machines basic to the manufacturing process—the core technology—were obtained. From these data, two principal measures were computed: MechIII, the percentage of total production equipment operating at or above Amber level 3—self-feeding machines which repeat cycles automatically; and MechIIIB, the percentage of basic machines at the same stage of mechanization. Another index of the production technology is

Woodward's (1958, 1965) eleven-point score of the technical complexity of the production process; a seven-point version of the Woodward score, eliminating her two mixed types and combining her first two and last two categories, was used. The three main types of manufacturing Woodward derives from combinations of her score—complex units and small-batch, large-batch and mass production, and process production—were also used. Straightforward measures were preferred to complex scales or scales based on factor analysis, like Hickson, Pugh, and Pheysey's (1969) technology index, "work-flow integration," but since the major component of their index is also based on the Amber and Amber classification, their measure is roughly comparable to the present mechanization score.

The second dimension of technology was the automation of various functions by using a computer. Since some plants have their own data-processing facilities at the site, while others have most of their computer work done elsewhere—at corporate headquarters or by time-sharing services—separate measures of automation were devised. AutII is the number of different functions for which a computer at the site is used; AutOut is the number of functions automated by off-site computer systems. A third index, AutIII, refers to total computer use, the number of functions in which a computer is used either on or off the site. In addition, AutI, a dummy variable, indicates whether a plant has its own data-processing facilities. Parallel measures were provided for the estimated minutes per day a computer is used at the site, off the site, and both combined.

Major dependent variables to be related to mechanization and automation were structural differentiation, personnel components, and spans of control of supervisors at various levels of a plant's administrative hierarchy. Vertical differentiation was measured by the number of managerial levels; horizontal differentiation was indicated by the number of divisions—units whose heads report to the plant manager—or sections—subunits of divisions whose managers were not first-line supervisors. Three measures of the division of labor were the number of job titles, an index of occupational diversity, and the Aston measure of functional specialization. Detailed information furnished by the personnel manager made it possible to calculate the percentages of three main personnel components—direct and indirect production workers and employees performing white-collar jobs—and to divide the last group into three subcomponents: the percentage of full-time supervisors, salaried staff, and clerical workers. Finally, average subordinate-supervisor ratios—spans of control—were obtained for various ranks of supervisors, including the chief executive officer, the division heads who report to that officer, section managers, and first-line supervisors, who oversee work-flow operations and represent the lowest administrative level.

To measure decentralization of decision-making authority, information was gathered on the administrative level at which twenty-five key decisions are made, and intermediate scores were given for decisions made jointly by managers on two different levels. These data were combined into two composite indices, one measuring decentralization of operational decisions, and the other decentralization of authority in personnel matters. Although the decision as to which items to include in the two measures was guided by factor analysis, the actual weighting of components was based on arbitrary loading rather than factor scores. The first index refers primarily to marketing decisions, but includes such other decision-making areas as purchasing, production control, and budget allocations. In these areas, authority is rarely decentralized below the plant manager's level, and most decisions are made at divisional and company headquarters, or even by the corporate board of directors. The second index pertains to personnel decisions—the authority to hire, promote, or fire employees at various hierarchical levels. Decentralization of personnel authority is considerably more pronounced than decentralization of operational authority; middle managers—section or division heads—can often hire or fire employees up to the level immediately below them, although decisions on promotion are usually made in consultation with the plant manager.

Mechanization of Production Operations

In manufacturing, differences in production technology are largely, though not entirely, reflected in the type of equipment used and the degree of its mechanization. The central thesis of the Woodward (1958, 1965) study—that the degree of technical complexity is the critical factor in explaining variation in organization structure—is not supported by the work of Hickson, Pugh, and Pheysey (1969). In contrast to Woodward, they found that the operations technology is not strongly associated with organizational structure. Child and Mansfield (1972), using a national British sample, arrived at the same conclusion: production technology is not a major determinant of organizational structure. These two studies in the Aston tradition challenge Woodward's notion of a technological imperative.

The data from the New Jersey sample of manufacturing concerns uphold the general conclusions of Hickson, Pugh, and Pheysey, while contradicting those of Woodward. The degree of mechanization (MechIII) is not related to the six dimensions of structural differentiation (Table 1, column 1, rows 1-6), nor is there a significant zero-order correlation between mechanization and the five indicators of spans of control (Table 1, column 1, rows 17-21). Furthermore, among the personnel components (column 1, rows 7-16), only two of the ten reveal a significant relationship with degree of mechanization. The Woodward scale (Table 1, column 2) exhibits a similar pattern: absence of a significant association with aspects of differentiation and, with a few exceptions, an overall lack of association with either spans of control or personnel components.

The degree of technical sophistication in production does not determine the structure of factories as predicted by Woodward. Specifically, the data do not support Woodward's (1965, pp. 51-60) claims that an advanced technology increases the number of levels in the organization (Table 1, row 1), widens the chief executive officer's span of control (row 17), increases the ratio of managers and supervisors (row 8), raises the proportion of clerical and administrative staff (rows 9-10), and enlarges the proportion of college graduates among the staff (row 12). Although the findings generally do not support Woodward, there are some exceptions. Mechanization is associated with a larger proportion of workers in indirect production (Table 1, row 13), specifically with workers in maintenance (row 14). A positive association between the maintenance component and operations technology was also found by Child and Mansfield (1972, p. 380); Hickson, Pugh, and Pheysey, however, observed a ∩-shaped relationship between the proportion of maintenance workers and production technology. In the Woodward study, an advanced technology narrowed the span of control of middle managers; the present findings support this conclusion for one level of middle management, division heads (row 18), though not for another, section heads (row 19).

In contrast to mechanization, size exerts a considerable influence on the structure of factories. The size of the labor force (log 10 of the number of employees) exhibits substantial correlations with five of the six measures of differentiation (Table 1, column 3). Thus, the larger an organization, the more it is divided into vertical levels, horizontal subunits, and occupational specialties. Although the associations of size with personnel components (column 3, rows 7-16) and with spans of control (rows 17-21) are generally

Table 1. Selected Measures of Association Between Size, Indices of Technology, and Dimensions of Plant Structure

	1 MechIII	2 Woodward Score	3 Size (Log)	4 Size (Log)/[a] w/Controls	5 Woodward Production Types	6	7 Pattern of Relation	8 AutII
					Eta	Eta Controlling Size (Log)		
	r	r	—	Beta	Eta			r
Differentiation								
1. Number of levels	.10	.10	.49[b]		.04	.08	∪	.27[b]
2. Number of divisions	.03	.01	.41[b]		.06	.14	∪	−.14
3. Number of sections	.08	.14	.68[b]		.13	.25	∪	.19[b]
4. Number of job titles	−.08	−.10	.62[b]	.43[b]	.13	.15	∪	.21[b]
5. Occupational diversity	.02	.09	.06	−.26	.28[b]	.30	∪	.30[b]
6. Functional specialization	−.01	.11	.25[b]	.01	.07	.12	∩	.56[b]
Personnel components (%)								
7. Nonproduction	−.08	.01	−.06	−.59[b]	.21	.20	∪	.33[b]
8. Supervisors	.04	.14	−.28[b]	−.88[b]	.35[b]	.30	∪	.22[b]
9. Staff	−.04	−.07	−.04	−.40[b]	.17	.18	∪	.30[b]
10. Clerks	−.15	.02	−.01	−.34[b]	.09	.09	∩	.27[b]
11. Professionals	−.04	−.01	.16	−.38[b]	.17	.20	∪	.19
12. College graduates	.07	.12	−.08	−.56[b]	.23	.23	∪	.09
13. Indirect production	.24[b]	.34[b]	−.01	−.09	.32[b]	.33	±/	−.24[b]
14. Maintenance	.24[b]	.43[b]	−.04	−.31[b]	.49[b]	.50	±/	−.18
15. Direct production	−.09	−.21[b]	.05	.56[b]	.33[b]	.33	∩─	−.15
16. Craftsmen	.11	.01	−.03	−.11	.26[b]	.26	∪	.03
Spans of control								
17. Chief executive officers	.08	.06	.15	−.21[b]	.20	.24	∪	−.19[b]
18. Division heads (X̄)	−.18	−.25[b]	.01	.35[b]	.20	.20	─	−.04
19. Section heads (X̄)	−.12	−.01	.08	.41[b]	.25	.25	∩	.23[b]
20. FLS–All (X̄)	−.06	−.09	.25[b]	.79[b]	.24[b]	.20	∩	−.22[b]
21. FLS–Direct production (X̄)	−.13	−.03	.24[b]	.71[b]	.36[b]	.32	∩	−.02

[a] Controlling levels, divisions, and sections.

[b] Significant at .05 level (significance levels are not presented for the eta under controls—column 6—but they can be inferred from the eta in column 5).

weak, these zero-order correlations are misleading, because the effects of size on most personnel components and spans of control are concealed by the opposite influences of structural differentiation on them, as previous research indicated (Blau, 1972). When the three main forms of structural differentiation—number of levels, divisions, and sections —are controlled (Table 1, column 4), size is revealed to exert strong influences on nearly all personnel components and spans of control. The only exceptions are that the proportion of indirect production workers is unrelated to size, but correlated positively with mechanization, and that the proportion of skilled craftsmen is unrelated to either size or mechanization.

Thus, large factories have complex, differentiated structures, and their large work force reduces the proportionate size of most supportive components and widens the spans of control of middle managers and first-line supervisors—whereas their differentiated structures have the opposite effects. These findings parallel those in other types of organizations, including government agencies, department stores, and universities and colleges (Blau, 1972). Furthermore, the findings are similar to those of Hickson and his associates (1969, p. 387), who reported that correlations of structural variables with size are considerably stronger than those with technology. Although some of the Aston measures differed from those of the present study and not all of the results are identical—compare Table 1 in the present study with Table 8 in Hickson, Pugh, and Pheysey (1969, p. 386)—the overall conclusion in both cases is that the structure of factories, like that of other organizations, depends greatly on their size.

In spite of these findings, it is not plausible that a factory's structure is affected as little by its production technology as the data reveal so far. Hickson and his colleagues (1969, pp. 393-395), in attempting to reconcile their conclusions with those of Woodward, suggested two hypotheses to explain the conflicting results. The first was that the technology of an organization affects only production-linked aspects of the administrative structure, such as the maintenance component. In order to test this hypothesis, correlations were computed for both degree of mechanization and Woodward scores with a number of variables within the production sector only of the factories. None of these correlations is appreciably greater than zero or larger than the corresponding correlation for the entire manufacturing plant. For example, within the production sector only, the proportion of supervisors is correlated with MechIII .09 (and with the Woodward score, .07); that of staff, .02 (.03); that of clerks, −.09 (−.07); the span of control of division heads, −.15 (−.17); of section heads, −.17 (−.17); and of first-line supervisors, −.13 (−.03). These weak associations are quite similar to the corresponding ones for the total plant (Table 1, columns 1-2). The hypothesis that structural variables directly linked to production will reveal stronger associations with degree of mechanization is not confirmed by these data.

The second hypothesis advanced by the Hickson study is that the smaller size of the manufacturing concerns in Woodward's sample is responsible for the difference in findings. Specifically, Hickson, Pugh, and Pheysey suggested that the technology will exert more influence on the administrative structure in small manufacturing concerns because administration is less removed from production than in large concerns. To test this hypothesis, separate correlations of MechIII with the variables in Table 1 were computed for the smallest quartile of the sample—the 28 manufacturing concerns with fewer than 233 employees—and for the remainder of the 110 plants. The results show that only four variables have a correlation coefficient of .20 or more in either size category, and two of these four negate the hypothesis. The proportion of workers in indirect production is correlated with mechanization in large (.23), as well as small (.29), manufacturing concerns. In addition, the proportion of maintenance workers is correlated only in large (.30), and not in small (.06), factories. The two remaining variables with correlations above .20 support the hypothesis: mechanization reduces the number of divisions in small manufacturing concerns (−.23) but not in large ones (.11), and mechanization narrows the span of control of division heads only in small (−.47), and not in large (−.06), factories.

In general, the current data do not support the size hypothesis, for only 10 percent of the comparisons indicate that mechanization exerts a stronger influence in small than in large organizations. Furthermore, Child and Mansfield's (1972, p. 384, Table 6) findings provided only weak support for Hickson, Pugh, and Pheysey's proposition regarding the influence of technology on administrative structure in small organizations. The hypothesis may yet prove tenable in very small organizations; that is, concerns with a work force under 100 employees. The quartile *small* in the present study contains only one plant with fewer than 100 members, and the mean of the group is 172. More important, however, is that the technology is associated with the structure of factories independent of their size, though these effects become apparent only if types of technical systems are distinguished and procedures are employed that reveal curvilinear relationships.

Type of Production Technology

In her study of industrial organizations in South Essex, Woodward (1965, p. 38) combined the categories in her score to distinguish three types of production technology according to degree of technical advancement. The three types of production are (1) unit and small-batch, the least technologically advanced; (2) large-batch, assembly, and mass production, an intermediate category; and (3) process production, the most technologically advanced. Although these three types of production exhibit linear differences in mechanization, their influence on the factory tends to be curvilinear. These curvilinear effects were observed by Woodward (1965, pp. 60-67), as well as by Hickson, Pugh, and Pheysey (1969, pp. 392-393) and Child and Mansfield (1972, pp. 381-383). For example, all found the span of control of first-line supervisors in direct production to have a curvilinear relation to production technology; but this observation did not alter the main conclusion of the two latter studies, that technology does not have important effects on administrative structure. Neither Hickson, Pugh, and Pheysey nor Child and Mansfield realized the pervasiveness of this curvilinear pattern, partly because their principal measures of association—zero-order and partial correlation coefficients—only indicate linear relationships.

Mass-production plants are generally larger—with a mean work force of 631—than small-batch plants—with 421; and process plants tend to be smaller than either—with 326. These differences in size are accompanied by differences in skills and in administrative structure that are independent of plant size. To reveal this pattern, the correlation ratio (eta) of the three production types with the variables in Table 1 is presented (Table 1, column 5); since size has been shown to be strongly related to many of these variables, the eta with size (log) controlled is also shown (column 6). Because the eta, which has no sign, indicates a linear relationship as well as a nonlinear one, only a value of eta substantially greater than the Pearsonian correlation coefficient provides evidence of curvilinearity; the pattern of relationship is illustrated in column 7. Table 2 presents a comparison of means for these variables that discloses their curvilinear relationships with the three types of technology, both without controls (columns 2-4) and controlling log size (columns 5-7).

Table 2. Means of Structural Dimensions for Three Woodward Production Types

	1 Grand Mean	2 Unit and Small-Batch	3 Mass	4 Process	5 Unit and Small-Batch	6 Mass	7 Process
		Unadjusted Means			Adjusted for Log Size		
Differentiation							
1. Number of levels	5.14	5.11	5.17	5.18	5.14	5.08	5.35
2. Number of divisions	4.95	5.03	4.80	5.09	5.10	4.61	5.44
3. Number of sections	2.88	2.73	2.73	3.19	2.91	2.23	5.12
4. Number of job titles	125.14	135.15	120.74	94.80	139.04	108.83	121.76
5. Occupational diversity	.70	.71	.66	.76	.71	.66	.76
6. Functional specialization	12.38	12.17	12.50	13.12	12.22	12.21	13.78
Personnel components (%)							
7. Nonproduction	.25	.26	.22	.30	.26	.22	.30
8. Supervisors	.09	.09	.08	.12	.09	.08	.12
9. Staff	.07	.08	.06	.08	.08	.05	.08
10. Clerks	.09	.09	.08	.10	.09	.08	.10
11. Professionals	.04	.05	.03	.05	.05	.03	.06
12. College graduates	.05	.05	.04	.09	.05	.04	.09
13. Indirect production	.19	.18	.18	.28	.18	.18	.28
14. Maintenance	.08	.07	.07	.19	.07	.07	.19
15. Direct production	.56	.56	.60	.42	.56	.60	.42
16. Craftsmen	.18	.20	.14	.22	.20	.14	.22
Spans of control							
17. Chief executive officers	7.15	7.33	6.60	8.27	7.37	6.48	8.50
18. Division heads ($\bar{X}$)	6.14	6.58	5.88	4.94	6.58	5.86	4.97
19. Section heads ($\bar{X}$)	5.65	5.26	6.50	4.66	5.25	6.51	4.65
20. FLS—All ($\bar{X}$)	14.72	14.55	16.13	10.30	14.71	15.76	10.91
21. FLS—Direct production ($\bar{X}$)	21.22	19.63	25.40	13.46	19.82	24.94	14.23

The data indicate that mass-production plants contrast most sharply with process-production plants, with small-batch-production concerns occupying the intermediate position. While not all of the relationships are statistically significant, the consistency of the pattern is impressive. For example, as one moves from the least mechanized small-batch to the more mechanized mass-production and on to the most mechanized process plants, there is first an increase and then a sharper decrease in the proportion of workers in direct production (Table 2, row 15) and in the spans of control of first-line supervisors and of middle managers (rows 19-21).

Spans of control, with one exception, exhibit a curvilinear relationship with type of technology, but the relationship gradually changes as one moves from the top of the pyramid to the production floor. For the chief executive officer's span, the relationship is ∪-shaped (row 17), while the relationship with division head span is linear and negative (row 18). For the spans of section heads and first-line supervisors, the association is ∩-shaped (rows 19-20), and it is most pronounced for the foremen in direct production (row 21). Production foremen generally have wider spans of control than first-line supervisors in either indirect production or the white-collar sector, since the large volume of routine work in direct production enables foremen to supervise many persons. Work in mass production is more routine than that in small-batch factories, while work in process production is the least routine (Blauner, 1964, pp. 132-142). These differences are reflected in the pronounced ∩-shaped relationship of the spans of control of production foremen with the three types of technology (row 21). Parallel differences are observable for middle managers on lower levels (row 19), but not for higher managers far removed from the production floor (rows 17-18). These findings lend some support to the hypothesis of Hickson, Pugh, and Pheysey that production-linked aspects of structure are most influenced by the technology of the organization, but the hypothesis is substantiated only for curvilinear relationships, not for linear associations.

Thus, the nature of work in mass production and in process production differs in opposite ways from that in the technically least advanced small-batch production, and this is reflected in ∪-shaped relationships with specialization and nonproduction components. Specialized training and skills of both white-collar and blue-collar workers are less frequent in mass production, but more frequent in process production than in small-batch production (Table 2, rows 11-12 and 16). The proportionate size of the nonproduction component reveals the same ∪-shaped curve (row 7); the differences are substantial, however, only for the proportion of managers and supervisors (row 8); they are less for the proportion of staff and virtually nil for the proportion of clerks (rows 9-10). The proportions of indirect production workers and of those in maintenance do not differ in small-batch and mass production, but are substantially higher in process production (rows 13-14), which accounts for the positive correlations of these variables with the technology score, and which shows that the positive slopes curve sharply upward.

These ∪-shaped differences in specialization and in the nonproduction component give rise to corresponding differences in occupational diversity. The work force is less diverse in mass production and more diverse in process production than in small-batch production (Table 2, columns 2-4, row 5). The Aston measure of functional specialization (row 6) reveals no such differences, however, nor do most of the other measures of differentiation (rows 1-4), except for very slight curvilinear tendencies. The dominant influence of size on differentiation in the structure obliterates the influence of technology. But when size is controlled, some curvilinear effects of the technology on differentiation become apparent, as observed in the comparison of means adjusted for log size (Table 2, columns 5-7, rows 1-5).

To summarize, advances in production technology do not have linear, but do have curvilinear, relationships with various aspects of plant structure. As one moves from small-batch to mass production, the nature of manufacturing tasks becomes more uniform, which is reflected in an increase in routine work, a lower skill level of the labor force, and reductions in support components. The data indicate that these trends are reversed in advanced production technologies. Thus, production jobs are least standardized in process plants, since they generally involve maintenance of complex equipment or responsible monitoring functions there. Process plants usually have not only the most highly skilled blue-collar work force but also the largest proportion of white-collar jobs requiring specialized skills.

Computer-Automated Support

The use of automated data processing is prevalent in the 110 plants in the sample: nine tenths of them employ computers [for some functions]. Yet nearly two thirds (sixty-eight) of the plants do not have data-processing facilities at their own site. The reason for this disparity is the extensive use of off-site computers at divisional or corporate headquarters, or time-sharing services. Of the sixty-eight sites which do not maintain a separate computer installation, most have access to off-site systems for at least some of their data-processing work. In addition, many of the plants with their own systems also use off-site computers, because for some functions, such as payroll and accounting, it is more efficient to take advantage of the standardized programs offered by time-sharing contractors than to create one's own software. As would be expected, on- and off-site computer use are inversely correlated (for automation of functions, $-.62$; for minutes per day, $-.44$). Data from this study also show that branch plants are the most likely to utilize off-site computer systems, since they usually have one available at their parent company's headquarters. Total computer use, whether on- or off-site, however, hardly differs for branch plants and independent factories. On the average, eight functions in branch plants and 8.4 in others are automated. This finding indicates that the demand for automated data processing is determined by functional requirements of manufacturing establishments and not by geographical location or structural position within the parent company hierarchy.

Even factories that have an in-house computer rarely use it to automate the production process itself. For example, only five of the plants in the sample had any computer-controlled production equipment (Amber level 5) in 1973, and none of the machinery basic to the manufacturing operation—the core technology—was computerized. These observations are corroborated by the lack of a significant positive relationship between mechanization of production and the indices of computer use. Thus, the correlation between MechIII and AutII, the number of functions using on-site computers, is $-.03$, and MechIII's association with AutIII, the number of functions with any computer use, is .07. By the same token, the number of minutes per day of on-site computer time is correlated $-.07$ with MechIII, while total computer use in minutes per day actually has a significant negative relationship ($-.26$) with this mechanization index. From these data, it can be concluded that the automated factory is still a rare exception, and the tentative inference can be drawn that extensive mechanization of production machinery may discourage instituting automated data processing.

Although computers are used very little in direct control of manufacturing equipment, they are employed widely in administrative support of production, as well as in marketing and distribution. The functions which are most frequently automated are accounting, billing and paying, payroll, inventory control, and sales. Computers are also often used in immediate support of the manufacturing operation itself, notably in production scheduling. In the current sample, thirty plants applied their on-site computer in production control, and thirty-nine others used an off-site computer for the same purpose. Thus, production control is automated in almost two thirds of the 110 manufacturing concerns surveyed. Withington (1969) also emphasized the role of computers in production scheduling, citing several detailed case studies that showed how automated data transmission and analysis allow managers to control the flow of supplies on the factory floor and thereby improve the cost-effectiveness of tool and raw material distribution. It might be inferred from Withington's examples and the present data that most production-related computer use involves analysis of ongoing operations, while actual implementation of manufacturing tasks remains essentially in the hands of human operators. Moreover, these data may help explain the negative correlation between MechIII and total minutes of computer use, inasmuch as production scheduling consumes much computer time and mechanization, which makes the production process less flexible, and reduces the need for detailed scheduling.

In recent years, there has been much conjecture about the effects of automation on the administrative structure of formal organizations. For example, Whisler (1970a, pp. 3-6, 30-45, and 68), basing his claims on other sources as well as on his own research, stated that computer use leads to consolidation of departments and hence fewer departments, a smaller number of levels in the managerial hierarchy, and narrower spans of control on lower supervisory levels. Withington (1969, pp. 82-83) noted that the introduction of automated data-processing methods tends to enlarge the administrative component and reduce supervisory spans of control. These propositions, however, are only partially supported by the present study, as the correlations between AutII and the various structural indices (Table 1, column 8) demonstrate. The automation of plant functions with on-site computer systems does narrow the span of control of all first-line supervisors (Table 1, row 20), though it has a negligible effect on the span of control of direct production foremen (row 21). This is not surprising, since automation is largely confined to support functions and very rarely involves direct production itself. The data in Table 1 also show that computer use has no influence on the span of control of division heads (row 18), and that it widens the span of control of their subordinates, section heads (row 19). The negative association between in-house automation and the chief executive officer's span of control is spurious. Thus, the findings contradict past predictions that computer use will reduce subordinate-supervisor ratios throughout the administrative hierarchy.

Neither is there any evidence that automation of plant functions by on-site computers leads to the consolidation of departments—in the present study's terms, sections or divisions—and a reduction in their number. The correlation between AutII and number of divisions (row 2) is negative but insignificant, while automation has a positive effect on the number of sections. If any shrinkage of the administrative structure occurs, it is on the level just below the chief executive officer, and not in the lower middle-management ranks, as has been claimed. Contrary to Whisler's assumption, moreover, computer use tends to increase rather than decrease the number of administrative levels in the plant hierarchy (Table 1, row 1). The reason probably is that a computer system serves as an impersonal mechanism of control, which makes it less disadvantageous for top management to be separated from the work flow by many hierarchical levels. By establishing guidelines for the computer's design and programming, high-level executives can direct ongoing operations without passing directives down a human chain of command, which often delays the directives' execution. Automation also provides a shortened feedback loop, furnishing immediate information to management about work in progress, thereby reducing dependence on hierarchical channels of communication, reporting, and accountability. The tendency of automation to be associated with an increased number of administrative levels has also been observed in government agencies (Blau and Schoenherr, 1971, pp. 74-77). The influence of automation on vertical differentiation in manufacturing concerns persists when size (log) is controlled; the beta weight is .21, which is more than twice its standard error.

Computer use at the site increases the proportion of nonproduction workers (Table 1, row 7) and each of its three subcomponents—supervisors, salaried staff, and clerks (rows 8-10). This finding supports the observation of Withington (1969, pp. 82-83) that automated operations generally require more administrative personnel and a larger white-collar staff. Since automation of plant functions enlarges the white-collar support component, it must necessarily reduce the proportion of workers engaged in direct and indirect production activities (rows 13-15). In-house computer use has mixed effects on the training and skill of employees: it raises the percentage of professionals somewhat (row 11), but it does not increase appreciably the need for college graduates (row 12), nor does it affect the proportion of skilled craftsmen.

The technical complexity of automation is associated with greater structural complexity in manufacturing plants. Computer use (AutII) is positively related to most forms of differentiation (Table 1, column 8, rows 1-6), the only major exception being number of divisions. These relationships raise the possibility that correlations observed between AutII and other variables in Table 1 are spurious, owing to the influences of differentiation, for the three major forms of differentiation—levels, divisions, and sections—are also associated with many of the variables in rows 7-21. To check this, these three forms of differentiation were controlled through multiple regression techniques; that is, each of the remaining variables in Table 1 was regressed on size (log), number of levels, number of divisions, number of sections, and on-site computer use. Most of the beta weights for AutII derived from this analysis closely resemble the corresponding zero-order correlations (column 8), and all the correlations above .20 have matching beta weights that are more than twice their standard error. Only three of the regression coefficients differ as much as .05 from the simple correlation with AutII. The beta weight for staff is .25 (r = .30), for section head span .28 (r = .23), and for chief executive officer's span −.09, revealing the zero-order correlation of −.19 to be spurious. Thus, the influences of automation discussed are observable even when size and differentiation are controlled.

The automation of support functions creates a more differentiated structure in factories, and it exerts additional influences that parallel and reinforce those of structural differentiation. Independently, both automation and differentiation enlarge the proportion of all kinds of administrative personnel, narrow the spans of control of first-line supervisors, and raise the professional skills of the salaried staff. Since automation also increases differentiation, part of its effects on the variables in rows 7-21 is mediated through differentiation. Thus, automation influences the composition of the work force in part directly and in part by engendering differentiation, which affects it further. In particular, both technological and structural complexity expand the administrative apparatus in manufacturing plants, and their effects on it are cumulative.

A process technology in production and the automation of support functions by on-site computers also exert numerous parallel influences on the administrative structure (compare columns 7-8 in Table 1). Both process production and automation enlarge a plant's administrative apparatus (rows 7-10), particularly the supervisory and staff components. In addition, both promote the division of labor into diverse, specialized occupations (rows 4-5) and somewhat raise professional skills (row 11). Finally, through their positive influence on white-collar components, computer use and process manufacturing both narrow the average span of control of first-line supervisors (row 20), since the ratio of first-line supervisors to subordinates is higher in specialized white-collar work than in more routine production operations. Most variables that do not exhibit parallel relationships with the two technologies fall into one of two categories. As might be expected, ratios of production personnel (rows 13-16 and 21) are influenced by manufacturing technology, but only weakly by automation of support functions. In addition, spans of control of middle and senior managers (rows 17-19) do not reveal parallel influences.

In sum, process production generates changes in factories that reverse the trends mass production has introduced. Whereas mass production routinizes work and simplifies the administrative structure, process manufacturing leads to the development of specialized skills and a complex administrative apparatus. The automation of support functions produces changes that continue these new trends; it is tempting to infer that automation of the production process itself will accelerate these changes in the future.

Technology and Authority

Whereas the influences of automation on administrative structures at first appeared to far outweigh those of production technology, these initial findings obscured important curvilinear relationships between type of production system and structure. When probing further by comparing structural characteristics in less mechanized mass-production plants with those in plants utilizing advanced process technologies, many similarities with automation appeared. But despite these parallels, there is one important area in which the influences of production technology and of automation are very different; namely, the distribution of authority over important operational and personnel decisions.

Highly mechanized production technologies reduce the autonomy of plant managers and discourage decentralization. The index of decentralization of marketing and production decisions is negatively correlated with the Woodward scale ($-.27$). The corresponding eta, which lacks a sign, is similar to the zero-order correlation, whether or not size (log) is controlled (.28 in both cases). This implies that the negative relationship is linear. The average decentralization score for operational decisions, independent of size (log) differences, is .78 for small-batch plants, .57 for mass production, and .41 for process plants. These data suggest that the more highly mechanized production is, the more likely is it that the final authority for making key production and marketing decisions rests above the plant manager's level (scored 0) than at his level (scored 1) or below (scored 2 or more, depending on the level). In the present sample, as one proceeds from small-batch to mass-production and then to process plants, the autonomy of the plant manager to make major operational decisions decreases and authority becomes more centralized at corporate headquarters.

For decisions involving the hiring, promotion, and dismissal of plant personnel, however, delegation of authority is little correlated with the Woodward score ($-.07$). But the corresponding eta is substantially larger (.42) than the zero-order correlation, disclosing a curvilinear relationship between production technology and the decentralization of personnel decisions. Contrary to the stereotypical view of mass-production plants as being most regimented, personnel decisions, controlling for size (log), are most decentralized in mass production (2.05), even slightly more than in small-batch production (1.85), and substantially more than in process plants, which have the lowest decentralization score

(1.30). Hence, in process plants, which have the most advanced production technologies, both personnel and operational decisions tend to be most centralized. Generalizations from these findings must be made with extreme caution, but some conjectures interpreting the results in terms of the economic character of the plants in the sample may be permissible.

Of the 110 plants in the random sample of New Jersey manufacturing establishments, all but eleven belong to larger corporate units. This accounts for the great discrepancy between the average plant size of 500 employees and the average size for the parent company, which is nearly 40,000. In other words, most plants analyzed here are not fully independent economic units, but must rely upon resources provided by the parent company. The more corporate resources are invested in expensive, mechanized plant equipment, which must be depreciated over many years, the more caution one would expect corporate managements to exercise in delegating authority over production and marketing decisions to plant managers. Large capital investments must be protected against unpredictable events, and delegating autonomy to plant managers, though it may yield unforeseeable benefits, undoubtedly lessens predictability. Besides, corporations own many plants—the average number owned by the parent companies in this sample was forty-six—and the coordination of operations in many establishments fosters centralization at corporate headquarters. The most highly mechanized establishments are most likely to be owned by large corporations, since large capital investments are required for their equipment, which may explain why authority is most centralized in them. Another factor may contribute to the delegation of personnel decisions in mass-production plants. Since employees in mass-production factories are least specialized and skilled, personnel decisions assume less import there and are perhaps for this reason more likely to be delegated in these than in other factories.

In contrast to the centralizing influence of an advanced production technology, an in-house computer to automate support functions promotes decentralization, though primarily in the form of granting autonomy to the plant manager. The correlation of AutI, indicating the presence of an on-site computer, with decentralization of operational decisions is strong and positive (.59). Its correlation with decentralization of personnel decisions is weak (.13). The implication is that on-site computers foster decentralization to the level of plant managers, but hardly below this level.

These results at first seem to contradict the argument that large investments in capital equipment foster centralization. But the cost of a computer relative to expenditures for production machinery is apparently small. The measure of capital invested in equipment per employee for the forty plants where data are available is negatively correlated with AutI (−.21), which agrees with statements by industry experts that the amount of money invested in computer technologies is small when compared with that invested in production machinery ("The Office of the Future," 1975). The findings, based upon data from 110 manufacturing plants in many different industries, are particularly significant in light of the ongoing debate about the implications of computers for the locus of organizational decision making.

In an early article addressing the future consequences of computers for middle-level and senior management, Leavitt and Whisler (1958) predicted that the spread of automation would "extend the thinking range" of top executives by providing them with immediate access to current information about ongoing operations. The authors forecasted loss of autonomy for many middle-management positions and a recentralization of control to more senior levels. A decade later, Whisler (1970b), in a study of nineteen insurance agencies, found some support for his arguments that computers reduce clerical and middle-managerial positions, and that their introduction facilitates the recentralization of decision-making authority. Although case studies by Mumford and Banks (1967) and Argyris (1970) arrived at parallel conclusions, there is still disagreement on the broader implications of Whisler's results for firms outside the insurance industry.

Withington's (1969) examination of a broad variety of organizations in both the public and the private sector led him to conclude that automation, while it may result in centralized data processing, tends to promote decentralization of line responsibilities for a variety of reasons. Since few senior managers have sufficient first-hand information to specify data-processing requirements, he pointed out that attempts to recentralize decision making often result in the generation of huge amounts of output which quickly overburden top management and encourage delegation. Automation of record keeping does permit the development of large, centralized information files, but Withington noted that this readily available information reduces top management's monopoly on company-wide data and enhances the decision-making capability of middle managers. For more routine accounting and budgeting purposes, which are generally some of the first functions to be automated, Withington agreed with Whisler that computers do displace some clerical employees. This does not result in the elimination of hierarchical levels or the recentralization of control, however, because the easy access to extensive information which computers provide to managers on all levels strengthens the authority of junior managers.

The finding in the present study that on-site computer use is associated with decentralization of operational decisions supports Withington's predictions and contradicts those of Whisler and others. But further analysis of those plants that utilize time-sharing facilities linked to off-site computers indicates that the influences of automation may be more complex than either Withington's or Whisler's arguments suggested. Seventy of the 110 plants use off-site computers, and the correlation between outside computer use and the decentralization of operational decisions is strongly negative ($-.55$). While data are not available to determine whether these time-sharing facilities are supplied by corporate headquarters or by an outside contractor, most are probably located at the parent company headquarters. If this is the case, the data imply that the location of computer facilities governs the locus of decision-making authority. If a plant has its own computer, its management is likely to have much autonomy, but if a plant uses an off-site computer, presumably in most cases at corporate headquarters, chances are that authority is centralized there.

Inasmuch as on-site and off-site computer use have opposite implications for decentralization, it is of interest to ascertain the factors associated with a plant's having its own data-processing facilities. The extent to which factories handle their own sales activities is an important condition associated with the presence of on-site computers. In plants that do not have their own computer, sales personnel constitute only 1 percent of all employees, while in those plants that do have their own computer system, the sales force is four times as great. The correlation between AutI and the percentage of sales personnel is .46. Although these findings are not surprising, since sales is one of the two functions for which on-site computers are most often used—accounting is the other—they have important implications. Plants that must process their own orders and invoices as well as perform their own sales analyses and market research greatly benefit from having a computer on the premises. But the size of the sales force is also strongly correlated with the decentralization of both operational (.62) and personnel decisions (.30), and this raises the possibility that the relationships noted earlier between on-site computer use and decentralization may be spurious.

Regression analysis reveals, however, that this is not the case and that in-house computers as well as extensive selling foster decentralization. AutI (beta weight, .41) and percent of personnel in sales (.40) exert independent influences on the decentralization of marketing and production decisions, and they account for nearly half (47 percent) of the variance in this decentralization measure. The demands of the market constrain corporations to enlarge the autonomy of managers of plants that are much involved in market transactions and to furnish them with on-site computers to facilitate adjusting to market demands. And the location of a computer at a plant further strengthens the autonomy of its management and lessens centralized corporate authority.

The costs of installing on-site computers include not only the initial capital investment, but additional organizational expenses resulting from structural changes. Plants using on-site systems must hire or retrain specialists to develop the software capabilities necessary for automation. The current study's findings suggest that costs do not end there. For automated factories exhibit higher levels of functional specialization, narrower spans of control, and greater differentiation, all of which increase administrative overhead. Nevertheless, avoiding these costs by centralizing computer facilities at corporate headquarters carries perhaps an even greater long-run cost; namely, that of reduced ability to adjust quickly to changing environmental conditions at the plant. With the recent advent of inexpensive minicomputers, it is likely that many more plants will acquire their own computer facilities in the near future. If the patterns observed here continue to apply, this trend will not lead to recentralization, but foster greater structural complexity and more autonomy at the plant level.

Concluding Conjectures

One important reason for the disagreement over the implications of technology for organizational structure is that the technical developments of the last century have not affected factory structures in any simple, unilinear fashion. Some plants utilize the mass-production methods first instituted in the early decades of this century, while others continue to use small-batch technologies reminiscent of earlier days, and still others employ process technologies which rose to prominence prior to World War II. Since all these different production techniques are in wide use today, their historical influences, as well as those of more recent computer technologies, can be inferred from the present cross-sectional comparison.

The rise of mass-production technology at the turn of the century relied heavily upon the routinization of work and provided attractive employment for untrained migrants moving to industrial centers. Mass-production plants were much larger than small-batch factories, providing work for many but few opportunities for upward mobility into the ranks of craftsmen or supervisors. Thus, routinization and its structural consequences in mass-production plants contributed to frustration, thereby stimulating the growth of the industrial labor movement. The development of the technically more advanced process-production methods in the 1930s started a reversal of the trends in factory structure. While corporations grew larger, as did investments in process equipment, which was changing rapidly, the size of plants was reduced and process production fostered the specialization of responsibilities in both blue-collar and white-collar work. The more diverse work force made coordination at the plant level and above more complex and required more supervisors, managers, and staff experts. This in turn provided greater opportunities and discouraged alienation, as Blauner's (1964) study has shown.

Whereas the impact of the computer is quite recent and cuts across industries with very different production technologies, automation appears to reinforce the trends begun by process technologies. Computers are most frequently used for routine data-processing operations in accounting and sales, yet their influence extends far beyond the clerical level. Automation, like process production, promotes specialization and increases ratios of supervisory and staff personnel. In addition to reinforcing changes initiated by the advent of process technologies, automation also has effected changes of its own. Computers in factories encourage the development of multilevel hierarchies and decentralization of authority from corporate headquarters to plant managers.

These changes in factory structure are not simply the result of advances in technology, however. The technology interacts with contemporary social conditions in complex ways. Mass-production methods, for example, were first developed when the majority of the labor force had little education or technical training. It is doubtful that the level of technical knowledge at the turn of the century predetermined the nature of mass-production factories. What seems more likely is that the low level of available skills influenced the manner in which this knowledge was applied to the organization of work. Mass-production techniques simply made it possible to produce complex products with a large unskilled work force. Efficiencies generated by the development and spread of mass production made it possible to shorten the years people must work and extend their years of schooling, thus raising the education of the labor force.

The better-educated labor force, in turn, affected the ways in which advances in technical knowledge were translated into production methods. It permitted designing process-production procedures that require most workers to assume considerable responsibility. As education expands further and growing proportions of the labor force acquire technical and professional competence, the adaptation of computer technologies to production and office work will undoubtedly take these higher skills into account. While it is possible to automate many operations without raising the skills workers use, a highly trained labor force makes this increasingly unnecessary. Hence, one can expect the growing automation of factories to raise the level of skill and responsibility of workers.

References

Amber, G. S., and Amber, P. S. *Anatomy of Automation.* Englewood Cliffs, N.J.: Prentice-Hall, 1962.

Argyris, C. "Resistance to Rational Management Systems." *Innovation,* 1970, *10,* 28-35.

Bavelas, A. "Communication and Organization." In G. Shultz and T. Whisler (Eds.), *Management Organization and the Computer.* New York: Free Press, 1960.

Blau, P. M. "Interdependence and Hierarchy in Organizations." *Social Science Research,* 1972, *1,* 1-24.

Blau, P. M., and Schoenherr, R. A. *The Structure of Organizations.* New York: Basic Books, 1971.

Blauner, R. *Alienation and Freedom.* Chicago: University of Chicago Press, 1964.

Child, J., and Mansfield, R. "Technology, Size and Organization Structure." *Sociology,* 1972, *6,* 369-393.

Gibbs, J. P., and Martin, W. T. "Urbanization, Technology and the Division of Labor." *American Sociological Review,* 1962, *27,* 667-677.

Hickson, D. J., Pugh, D. S., and Pheysey, D. C. "Operations Technology and Organization Structure: An Empirical Reappraisal." *Administrative Science Quarterly,* 1969, *14,* 378-397.

Hickson, D. J., and others. "The Culture-Free Context of Organization Structure: A Trinational Comparison." *Sociology,* 1974, *8,* 59-80.

Leavitt, H., and Whisler, T. "Management in the 1980's." *Harvard Business Review,* 1958, *36,* 41-48.

Mumford, E., and Banks, O. *The Computer and the Clerk.* London: Routledge and Kegan Paul, 1967.

"The Office of the Future." *Business Week,* June 30, 1975, No. 2387.

Perrow, C. "A Framework for the Comparative Analysis of Organizations." *American Sociological Review,* 1967, *32,* 194-208.

Pugh, D. S., and others. "Dimensions of Organization Structure." *Administrative Science Quarterly,* 1968, *13,* 65-105.

Starbuck, W. H. "Organizational Growth and Development." In J. March (Ed.), *Handbook of Organizations.* Chicago: Rand McNally, 1965.

Thompson, J. D. *Organizations in Action.* New York: McGraw-Hill, 1967.

Whisler, T. *Information Technology and Organizational Change.* Belmont, Calif.: Wadsworth, 1970a.

Whisler, T. *The Impact of Computers on Organizations.* New York: Praeger, 1970b.

Withington, F. G. *The Real Computer: Its Influence, Uses, and Effects.* Reading, Mass.: Addison-Wesley, 1969.

Woodward, J. *Management and Technology.* London: Her Majesty's Stationery Office, 1958.

Woodward, J. *Industrial Organization: Theory and Practice.* London: Oxford University Press, 1965.

Zwerman, W. L. *New Perspectives on Organization Theory.* Westport, Conn.: Greenwood Press, 1970.

2

Computers and Management Structure: Some Empirical Findings Reexamined

Daniel Robey

Ever since the computer was first applied in business organizations over twenty years ago, managers and management theorists have been intrigued by its potential effects on employment, job content, managerial work, and organization structure. Much of the early writing on this subject was pitched at a highly emotional level, with the apparent intent of wakening those involved to the evils of technology. Since the middle 1960s, fortunately, this type of approach to the issue has been gradually replaced by positive research efforts. The purpose of this paper is to examine a significant portion of these studies in an effort to understand the computer's impact on organizational structure. This particular review is limited to the dimension of centralization versus decentralization. The paper is structured so as to draw upon the contributions of recent, open-system concepts in organization theory to resolve the fundamental issues. Let us first review briefly some of the basic positions on the issue of computers and structure.

The Fundamental Issues

Although the speculative literature regarding computer effects on organizational structure is vast, the basic positions are represented best by a few writers. Four fundamental positions may be delineated: (1) computers lead to greater organizational centralization, (2) computers lead to greater decentralization, (3) computers have no effect on organization structure, and (4) the computer's impact on structure is moderated by other influences. Our discussion of these four possibilities is brief, primarily since they are reported upon rather extensively in the management literature. Readers unfamiliar with the basic arguments are urged to refer to the sources cited, where a more complete discussion is presented.

1. Computers and Centralization. The early and almost classic arguments by Leavitt and Whisler (1958) linked computerization to an increase in centralization. Reasoning that the rapid movement of information upward in an organization would permit decisions to be made with a more global perspective, they viewed the deterioration of

Reprinted from *Human Relations*, 1977, *30*, 963-976, with permission of the author and Plenum Publishing Corporation.

middle-management jobs as decision powers were removed. In effect, the computer countered the primary reason why decentralization existed at all—that is, it facilitated upward information flows and enabled complex manipulation of data once it reached the higher levels.

2. Computers and Decentralization. Dissenters to the centralization arguments quickly appeared. Both Anshen (1960) and Burlingame (1961) claimed that computerization would lead to greater decentralization of decision making. Reasoning that computer technology can assist information flows both upwardly *and* downwardly, they suggested that decisions can be pushed further down the management hierarchy. Thus, the primary reason for decentralization, better decisions being made where the problem exists, is strengthened by the organization's capability to supplement local information with additional data from above. Centralization is not increased because higher-level managers have neither the time nor the expertise to deal with local problems.

3. Computers Have No Impact. In all the writing about computers, few have taken the position that computers do not affect organization structure. Yet this view should be included and actually becomes a rather viable position when the morass of conflicting research and speculative writing on the subject is reviewed. However, a competing explanation may exist—that the computer's impact is moderated by other factors that have not yet been systematically explored. This is our fourth position.

4. Computer Impact Is Moderated. In place of claiming that computerization always has a certain effect or has no effect at all, it is useful to examine possible moderating influences. Here computer technology may be viewed as a tool which may assist management in creating a structure appropriate for various other conditions. As one author states: "The computer itself does not affect the major reasons for adopting the decentralization concept. Thus, it does not have a major impact on whether a company centralizes or decentralizes. . . . Although not the major determinant of whether a company centralizes or decentralizes, the computer is an aid in proceeding along either route" (Kanter, 1972, p. 203). If this fourth view is accepted, a question remains concerning the nature of these moderating influences. Traditional management literature suggests that centralization and decentralization are management philosophies, yet for any systematic analysis of structure we must go further to ask the question: What influences the philosophy? It is here that modern organization theory, with its emphasis on technological and environmental determinants of organization structure, can contribute. Hunt and Newell (1971) have already suggested the importance of considering technology as a moderating variable between computers and structure, citing the work of Woodward (1965). The approach of the present paper is to focus upon the task environment as a possible variable moderating the computer's impact on organization structure.

The spectrum of views presented here does little to resolve the fundamental issue. Logical arguments can only serve to stimulate and guide empirical research. Too often in the past, theoretical logic and common sense have proven misleading in the management area. The objective here, then, is to see what empirical research studies have found, to compare their findings, and to explain these findings in the light of current thinking in organization theory. Before proceeding to the studies themselves, it will be useful to review briefly some relevant concepts from modern organization theory.

Modern Organization Theory: Systems and Environments

For almost ten years it has been deemed useful to think of organizations as open systems interacting with their environments. Theorists and researchers have been intent upon drawing relationships between conditions in the task environment and the structure, functioning, and effectiveness of organizations. Although contributors to this contingency view, as it is commonly called, are many, the central ideas are well represented by the work of Thompson (1967), Lawrence and Lorsch (1967), and Pugh and associates (1963).

The term *task environment* was first used by Dill (1958) to identify environmental components relevant to goal setting and goal attainment, and includes factors such as customers, competitors, and suppliers. Thompson (1967) suggested that organizational environments can be characterized with respect to their degrees of homogeneity and stability. As environments move from homogeneous to heterogeneous and from stable to dynamic, the structure of the organization moves toward geographic and general decentralization. The propositions apply to those organizations which are governed by the norms of rationality, which means that organizations which adapt appropriately to environmental conditions are more effective. The theoretical assertions by Thompson are supported empirically by Lawrence and Lorsch (1967). They obtained data in ten organizations which showed that effective firms in dynamic environments were more differentiated than effective firms in stable environments. Their findings support the contingency view that organizational structure depends upon conditions in the task environment.

The contingency or open-systems approach has become a common and very useful way of looking at organizations. It has often been rewarding to reexamine traditional management questions in the light of modern theory. It is in this spirit that the following studies are reviewed—with the hope that the open-system conceptual scheme can help resolve the issues concerning computerization and structure.

Empirical Studies

The studies below are presented in two groups, suggested by the open-system concept mentioned above. First, studies which show the computer to be associated with centralization are presented. Second, those which support the relation between computers and decentralization are reviewed. The purpose for this division is to contrast the environmental conditions facing the organizations in each of the two groups. It is expected that greater centralization is associated with relatively stable task environments, and that the decentralized group as a whole will exhibit more complex or dynamic environments. Because of this approach, many research studies have been omitted. Only those studies are included which describe environmental factors or from which these conditions can be inferred. In virtually every case where a description of industry characteristics or market conditions is given, however, the original author has failed to tie the environment to organizational structure. Generally, the concern was to find a relation between computerization and structure. It is hoped that the structuring of this review will aid in changing this myopic preoccupation with the computer's impact and turn researchers toward more broadly based and theoretically meaningful research.

Studies Which Show Computers Associated with Centralization. At a major seminar sponsored by the University of Chicago and the McKinsey Foundation (Schultz and Whisler, 1960), five case studies were presented by managers of the companies in question. Three of these company spokesmen reported apparent centralization after computer systems were installed. The International Shoe Company, a transformer-manufacturing department of the General Electric Company, and the Atwood Vacuum Machine Company all had used computers to centralize many functions and to gain greater control over inventories, production, and marketing activities. In each case a fairly complete description of industry conditions was also given. Both the shoe manufacturer and the transformer department dealt with a single product, although both shoes and transformers are produced in a variety of styles. The task environments of both of these organizations may thus be regarded as stable. Indeed, one of General Electric's competitors in the transformer business once described the procedure of sales forecasting as getting twelve months of back orders together. Given the heavy demand for transformer equipment as the demand for power and housing steadily increases, we cannot really consider the market conditions to be dynamic or uncertain. Similarly, the demand for shoes should be stable and tied to population growth, even though styles change rather regularly.

The third company reporting centralization at the Chicago seminar, Atwood, was a smaller company making primarily original automobile parts. The company made use of a random-access computer to control its job-shop operations and to centralize production planning. Although the technology of a job shop may be somewhat more complex or uncertain than the other two cases, the company did sell its products in one industry, which was quite stable at that time. These three examples all show relatively stable task environments as well as centralized decision making, facilitated by their computer applications.

Much of the research on the computer's effect has occurred in the life insurance industry, which was a leader in EDP applications. Delehanty (1967) conducted interviews in nine companies which had converted to computers. He reports that computers per se have not affected the degree of centralization because "The hard fact is that very few decisions of any significance have ever been made below the very top echelons of life insurance companies" (p. 90). However, he does indicate that the relationship between home and field offices appears to be centralizing. Delehanty also makes clear the environmental conditions facing life insurance companies. A single service is provided, demand is related to population growth, companies do not compete in price, companies are regulated closely by state governments, industry competition is close (almost perfectly competitive due to ease of entry), and a nontechnical labor force of clerical workers and salesmen is employed. These conditions can be regarded as stable. The reason why computerization has not led to an increase in centralization is that most companies are already highly centralized. Such findings are certainly consistent with the general stance of open-system organization theory.

Another major study of twenty-three companies in the life insurance industry is reported by Whisler (1970). One finding pertains to the level of decision making. "With a small number of exceptions, companies reported that the effect of using computers is to push decisions (choice making) to a higher level in the organization" (p. 76). Although this varies slightly from Delehanty's findings, Whisler is not inconsistent with the expectations of contingency theory, given the task-environmental conditions in industry.

A case study by Siegman and Karsh (1962) of a state civil service bureau showed an increase in centralization of authority coupled with a changeover to automated office equipment. In this case, the EDP personnel assumed authority over line operations which formerly were independent. One can only guess the nature of the task environment in this study, but state agencies are probably not affected by changing technologies, competition, or other dynamic influences. The number of services provided by the agency is not reported.

Gallagher (1961) reports a case study of the American Airlines SABRE system for seat reservations. This is an excellent example of a real-time system in which decisions on seat request are effectively centralized for the entire airline. A customer making a request for reservations on any flight can get a firm reservation instantly, and the airline runs no risk of selling the same seat twice. Again, reflection on the environmental conditions of this application reveals a single service, a preset flight schedule, and a fixed capacity per flight. These are all characteristics of a stable task environment, and a centralized decision system is consistent with expectations.

In a set of three cases reported by Reif (1968), two show evidence of increasing centralization associated with computerization. One company, an electric and gas utility, showed a move toward centralization of accounting, inventory control, and some aspects of customer service. Budgets prepared centrally served to constrain local managers more than previously. In addition, plans for construction expenditures were moved up to the central office for computer analysis. The management's former policy of decentralization was thus observed to be in jeopardy in spite of many managers' believing otherwise. The task environment of utilities can generally be regarded as stable, with easily forecast long-range demand and little diversification in products.

The second organization studied by Reif which showed centralization was a medium-sized commercial bank. As was true for the life insurance industry, Reif found that most decisions were already being made at the vice-presidential level and that computerization did not change this. One cannot conclude that computers cause centralization in this case, but we may assert that they do not promote decentralization. Once again, the type of environment in which a community bank operates would lead us to expect centralization of decision making.

All of the cases reported above have three things in common. They report cases of organizations which have computerized systems and which are also centralized. They are also reports of organizations which exist in relatively stable or simple task environments. Beyond that, the studies largely differ in methodology and sometimes in basic definitions. When taken as a whole, however, and compared with the research which is reviewed next, there is support for the positions stated earlier: that task environment moderates the impact of computers on organization structure.

Studies Which Show Computers Associated with Decentralization. A case study by Wagner (1966) of the Northern Natural Gas Company in Omaha, Nebraska, provides an interesting contrast to the utility company reported by Reif. Whereas Reif's utility showed centralization, Northern Natural Gas kept its decentralization philosophy intact. The difference between the two situations, importantly, lies in the task environment. The particular computer application (a personnel system) took place as the company expanded and diversified. Thus, it was not operating in a placid environment, and the decentralized structure was appropriate to its needs.

Two case studies are available which report the experience of giant, international oil companies with computerized systems. In both of these companies, computers had not significantly affected the decentralized structure which existed. The first case, Standard Oil (New Jersey) (now Exxon), was reported by Carl H. Rush at the Chicago Seminar (Schultz and Whisler, 1960). Although there were hints of attempts at greater corporate integration in the future, the decentralized structure had remained unaffected by the introduction of linear programming models and numerous other computer applications. In view of the complex task environment of the international oil conglomerates, a decentralized structure would certainly be predicted by modern organization theory.

The second large oil company to be studied is British Petroleum, reported in depth by Stewart (1971) as one of a series of cases, all related to implementation and early experiences with computers. British Petroleum, like Exxon, is a major international oil conglomerate and a pioneer in computer usage. Of particular interest is the investment-planning model used by the firm. The model generated information useful in making decisions about capital investments. However, the effect that this computerized application had was to increase the degree of decentralization. Regional coordinators adopted decision powers previously unheld, and subsidiaries or associate companies took greater responsibility for planning, aided by the planning model's accurate and timely information. There was some evidence of greater control in the form of more clearly defined group objectives, but the general effect of computers was to increase decentralization. As in the case of Exxon, the policy is consistent with conditions in the task environment.

Another case reported by Reif (1968) involved a large manufacturer of heavy industrial equipment. In contrast to the utility and the bank he studied, the manufacturing firm was apparently able to incorporate a computer system which was consistent with its policy of decentralization. There was some evidence of central control becoming stronger with computer usage, but actual decisions were still made at the local level. The company had thirteen domestic and eleven foreign plants, which attests to the complexity of its task environment. Intimate knowledge of local conditions was essential for the effectiveness of many decisions in this organization.

To conclude, it appears that conditions in organizational task environments do affect the degree of centralization or decentralization. Since computers were evident in all the organizations, one may safely conclude that computerization does not explain the variance in structure. Instead, we may regard computerized information technology as a flexible mechanism which can facilitate either form of structure, depending on the more basic requirements which the task environment imposes.

Some Important Conceptual and Methodological Issues

In most areas of organizational analysis, there exist conceptual and methodological problems which cloud our ability to interpret research findings. To the extent that the present review is subject to these problems, it is essential to recognize them. Most of these difficulties center on differences in definitions and research methods among the studies in the area. Hopefully, future research can be guided by the discussion given to these issues here.

One of these issues concerns the distinction between the functions of decision making and control. Some of the studies reviewed above found evidence of decentralized decision making but increased central control. We also find some researchers, notably Whisler, primarily concerned with the impact of computers on control. Before any overall findings can emerge from the empirical efforts in this area, it is essential to distinguish what is meant by decentralization and centralization.

Dale (1952) has defined decentralization in terms of the number of decisions delegated, the importance of those decisions, the extent of those decisions' impact, and the amount of checking or review of those decisions. Using this definition, there comes a point where the concept of control begins to overlap with the degree of decision-making decentralization. As control or checking systems become centralized, does not decision making also become centralized? Can companies exert centralized control over decentralized operations, as many managers claim is possible? Somewhere a clearer distinction must be made if we are to understand the impact of the computer on the structured arrangement of decision making or control.

Some important insights into this problem have been provided by recent empirical work on organizational structure. Whisler and associates (1967) took three common measures of control and showed that there is no necessary correlation among them. In fact, only where the organization is engaged in a highly routine task is there high correlation. When tasks are loosely structured, no strong intercorrelation exists. In other research,

Pennings (1973) showed a lack of convergence among common measures of centralization. He concluded that centralization is a multifaceted concept and that measures cannot be used interchangeably. Since different operational measures of centralization and control measure different things, perhaps a complete reassessment of organizational dimensions is necessary.

A second conceptual problem lies in possible perceptual bias by interviewees in management positions affected by the computer. Reif (1968) is exceptionally alert in pointing out inconsistencies between respondents' claims and organizational realities. For example, affected managers in the utility company saw no evidence that the computer would lead to more centralized decision making. However, there was clear evidence that certain accounting, budget, inventory, and planning decisions were recentralized (pp. 71-74). One explanation is that the managers interviewed were defending against an unacceptable (for them) trend in company policy. It is also quite clear that companies may maintain a surface policy of decentralization while quietly centralizing many functions and decisions. The fact that so many case studies rely almost totally upon personal interviews should thus cause readers of these studies to interpret findings cautiously. There is little doubt of the value of the case-study method here, but interviews should be supplemented by more institutional types of evidence.

A third conceptual problem is the general lack of effectiveness criteria for the organizations studied. It is insufficient to assume that, because an organization adopts a particular structure, it is an effective choice. Certainly contingency theorists make a central issue of this point. However, too few researchers studying computerization attempt to assess the effectiveness of the adopting organization's structure.

Finally, and very importantly, the studies show that it is dangerous to consider an overall impact of computerization because there are so many different functions which computers can perform. An attempt to relate an overall "level of computer use" to organizational structure is beset with problems. For this reason, case-study research appears to be a more valuable research tactic than survey methods. Case studies permit detailed elaboration of the type of application, the particular functions affected, and the structural effects felt in different areas. Reif, for example, showed that, although the manufacturer he studied effectively centralized many production functions, marketing remained a local concern. In this case a critical relationship between the company salesman and the dealer existed which required responsiveness by the seller. In the utility company, "The only distinct accounting procedures which are not centralized pertain to customer accounts" (Reif, 1968, p. 99). Thus, it is clear that where task environments differ for different organizational functions, intraorganizational structural differences may also exist. As Stewart (1971) observes: "Generalizations about the impact of the computer on management are likely to be misleading. The nature of the impact can vary because of differences in the type of problem that the computer application is designed to help with, because of differences in the organization of the computerization process, and because of differences in the extent and nature of managerial involvement" (pp. 221-222). More is to be gained by taking a particularistic orientation, where contingencies and conditions are specified, than by trying to assert broad generalities.

The Computer as a Variable?

Perhaps the ultimate question to be asked is whether computerization has been or can be effectively treated as an organizational variable. Certainly the thrust of the literature reviewed in this paper is to consider it as such, yet there are severe conceptual problems. A review of a research study by Klatzky (1970), using a markedly different methodology, illustrates the point. Klatzky attempted to relate the extent of computer usage in fifty-three state employment agencies to the degree of centralization found. The results show basically that decentralization is positively related to greater computer use, as measured by the number of computers and input-output units employed by the agency. These results become somewhat difficult to explain in the context of the present paper, since the task environments of the state agencies surveyed should not be exceedingly complex. (This assumption has already been made for the Siegman and Karsh paper reviewed earlier.) How, then, can Klatzky's results be rationalized?

One clear reason for the results is the fact that only one type of decision, that of hiring for the agency, was studied. Because the computer applications in state employment agencies do not involve information relating to such decisions, the situation differs from most of the applications discussed earlier. Klatzky explains her results by suggesting that office automation frees persons lower in the hierarchy from routine tasks. Upper-level executives may then delegate more decisions to their subordinates, so that more important top-level decisions may be tackled. This argument seems plausible and is indeed supported by the data. Yet one can contend that general decentralization may not have occurred. In fact, greater centralization of decisions affected by the computer may have taken place. For instance, decisions regarding agency operations, which formerly were made by lower-level managers, may now be effectively centralized because of data processing. However, these data are not reported.

Furthermore, it is open to question whether the number of input-output units and central processing units has any meaning. Where in the sociological theory of organizations does it say anything about the number of machines? It is probably more appropriate to relate machine technology to job change via organizational variables such as work flow or specialization. As Meyer (1968) has observed, "The effects of automation on human relations should be assessed only after taking into account the changes in organizational processes which automation itself engenders" (p. 257).

There have been some worthwhile attempts to conceptualize the variable information system, so that its impact may be systematically investigated by survey methods. Galbraith (1973) has defined such systems on two dimensions: a global-local dimension and a timing (periodic-continuous) dimension. Melcher (1970) has defined information systems with respect to communication center linkage, channel density, storage/retrieval capability, and transmission time. Unfortunately, these conceptual definitions have not guided the efforts of researchers interested in the computer's impact on structure.

Summary and Conclusions

The purpose of this paper is to review and to reexamine existing studies which relate computerization to either centralization or decentralization of organizational decision making. The studies reviewed are grouped by their major findings to facilitate comparisons between task-environmental conditions in each organization. In addition, four issues are addressed which relate to conceptual or methodological problems. Of concern is the distinction between decision making and control, the perceptual bias of interviewees, the lack of effectiveness criteria, and the problem of making generalizations about computer impacts where organizational functions are differentially affected. Finally, the question is raised whether computerization is a meaningful organizational variable.

The general thrust of this paper is to shed light on a body of research which deals with the computer's impact on organizational structure—specifically, the degree of centralization in decision making. The conclusion of this paper is that structure does not primarily depend on any internal technology for information processing, but rather on the nature of the task environment. Under stable conditions, computers tend to reinforce centralization. Under dynamic conditions, computers reinforce decentralization. Earlier positions are difficult to support because they are locked into the idea that computers "cause" changes. The present review points to the value of looking beyond computers to more theoretically grounded causal variables in the organization's task environment.

References

Anshen, M. "The Manager and the Black Box." *Harvard Business Review,* 1960, *38,* 41-48.

Burlingame, J. F. "Information Technology and Decentralization." *Harvard Business Review,* 1961, *38,* 121-126.

Dale, E. *Planning and Developing the Company Organization Structure.* New York: American Management Association, 1952.

Delehanty, G. E. "Computers and Organization Structure in Life Insurance Firms: The External and Internal Economic Environment." In C. A. Meyers (Ed.), *The Impact of Computers on Organizations.* Cambridge, Mass.: M.I.T. Press, 1967.

Dill, W. R. "Environment as an Influence on Managerial Autonomy." *Administrative Science Quarterly,* 1958, *2,* 409-443.

Galbraith, J. R. *Designing Complex Organizations.* Reading, Mass.: Addison-Wesley, 1973.

Gallagher, J. D. *Management Information Systems and the Computer.* New York: American Management Association, 1961.

Hunt, J. G., and Newell, P. F. "Management in the 1980's Revisited." *Personnel Journal,* 1971, *50,* 35-43.

Kanter, J. *Management-Oriented Management Information Systems.* Englewood Cliffs, N.J.: Prentice-Hall, 1972.

Klatzky, S. R. "Automation, Size, and the Locus of Decision-Making: The Cascade Effect." *Journal of Business,* 1970, *43,* 141-151.

Lawrence, P. R., and Lorsch, J. W. *Organization and Environment.* Boston: Graduate School of Business Administration, Harvard University, 1967.

Leavitt, H. J., and Whisler, T. L. "Management in the 1980's." *Harvard Business Review,* 1958, *36,* 41-48.

Melcher, A. J. "A Systems Model." In A. R. Negandhi and J. P. Schwitter (Eds.), *Organizational Behavior Models.* Kent, Ohio: Kent State University, 1970.

Meyer, M. W. "Automation and Bureaucratic Structure." *American Journal of Sociology,* 1968, *74,* 256-264.

Pennings, J. M. "Measures of Organizational Structure: A Methodological Note." *American Journal of Sociology,* 1973, *79,* 686-704.

Pugh, D. S., and others. "A Conceptual Scheme for Organizational Analysis." *Administrative Science Quarterly,* 1963, *8,* 289-315.

Reif, W. E. *Computer Technology and Management Organization.* Iowa City: Bureau of Business and Economic Research, University of Iowa, 1968.

Schultz, G. P., and Whisler, T. L. (Eds.). *Management Organization and the Computer.* New York: Free Press, 1960.

Siegman, J., and Karsh, B. "Some Organizational Correlates of White Collar Automation." *Sociological Inquiry,* 1962, *32,* 108-116.

Stewart, R. *How Computers Affect Management.* London: Macmillan, 1971.

Thompson, J. D. *Organizations in Action.* New York: McGraw-Hill, 1967.

Wagner, L. G. "Computers, Decentralization, and Corporate Control." *California Management Review,* 1966, *9.*

Whisler, T. L. *The Impact of Computers on Organizations.* New York: Praeger, 1970.

Whisler, T. L., and others. "Centralization of Organization Control: An Empirical Assessment of Its Meaning and Measurement." *Journal of Business,* 1967, *40,* 10-26.

Woodward, J. *Industrial Organization: Theory and Practice.* London: Oxford University Press, 1965.

3

Growth and Decline Processes in Organizations

John Freeman
Michael T. Hannan

Since the original articles by Melman (1951) and Terrien and Mills (1955), researchers have most often attempted to explain variations in administrative intensity through reference to size. Administrative intensity is defined as the relative sizes of two personnel components in organizations: administrative (or "supportive") and production worker (or "direct"). In its most recent form, the linkage between this variable and size has been asserted by Blau and a number of collaborators (Blau, 1970, 1972, 1973; Blau and Schoenherr, 1971). The essential idea is that bigger organizations have more highly elaborated structures with regard to both horizontal and vertical differentiation. Size has positive effects on administrative intensity because these elaborate structures produce coordination problems for which the organization compensates by hiring additional administrators. On the other hand, bigger organizations have previously made investments in organizational patterns required to manage a higher level of work activity. As Blau (1972, p. 18) put it: "The investment of administrative time required for organizing operations is not proportionate to their volume, increasing far less than the volume of work increases." In addition, larger size makes for a more efficient use of specialized administrative effort. Skills and abilities are not infinitely divisible. So small organizations are less able to use administrative manpower efficiently. "If the volume of administrative work increases less than proportionately as the volume of operations increases, and if the volume of work governs the number of persons needed to accomplish it, in administration as well as in operations, it follows that the number of persons in administration increases less than that in operations and hence that the proportion of administrative personnel decreases as the total number of employees decreases" (Blau, 1972, p. 18).

Reprinted from *American Sociological Review*, 1975, *40* (2), 215-228, with permission of the authors and the American Sociological Association. Since its publication, Kaufman (1976) has pointed out that the assumption used to solve equation 8, namely that number of teachers changes linearly over time, is inconsistent with equation 7. However, this inconsistency does not affect any of the qualitative findings we report. See Freeman and Hannan (1976). Subsequent developments in the model and estimation are reported in Hannan and Freeman (1978).

Increases in size lead to increases in differentiation, which in turn lead to increases in administrative intensity. But increases in size also produce economies of scale, which counteract effects via differentiation. Since in most organizations the negative direct effects of size exceed the positive indirect effects, the bivariate relationship is negative.

In another recent article, Hendershot and James (1972, p. 151) found that school districts which had previously experienced more rapid growth displayed the usual negative relationship between size and administrative intensity. But districts which had experienced slow growth did not show a consistent relationship. Furthermore, districts which experienced slow growth displayed increases in administrative intensity while those which grew rapidly showed decreases. However, their inferences are based mainly on categorized interval scale data, for which subcell n's [numbers] are often quite small. Although their discussion suggests a monotonic relationship between rate of growth and change in administrative intensity, their data show a curvilinear relationship.

Hendershot and James attempt to explain the differences for rapid and slow growers by positing different lags for the relations of size (enrollment) with the administrative component and with the production worker component. We want to examine the implications of this possibility from a more general perspective.

If the numerator and denominator of the usual A/P ratio are related to size by causal lags of different lengths, two design implications follow. First, the ratios are not unitary from a theoretical perspective. Since the numerator and denominator are related to other variables in different ways, the ratio will behave erratically as the other variables vary. The implication is that one should decompose the A/P ratio into its components and study the effects of other variables on the components and on each other. The second design implication is that one should employ dynamic models to study administrative intensity. If lags in adjustment enter the process in a central way, only dynamic models estimated from longitudinal observations can clarify the nature of the relations.

It is commonplace to argue that cross-sectional analysis of the interrelation of organization dimensions will ordinarily lead to inferences quite different from those suggested by longitudinal analysis (Tsouderos, 1955; Haire, 1959; Starbuck, 1965; Meyer, 1972). There are at least three broad reasons why the two methods ought to yield such differences. One likely possibility concerns specification error in the models estimated. It is commonly the case that omitted variables in a cross section are different from those in a time series. This will ordinarily result in quite different empirical findings. A second reason for expecting a divergence of cross-sectional and longitudinal findings is that advanced by Hendershot and James, differences in the lag structures for certain variables in the model. It is certainly true that if one studies a cross section of organizations which are adjusting to equilibria such that different variables adjust at different rates, one should expect to find differences from what would be seen in a longitudinal investigation of the adjustment process.

It is notoriously difficult to induce the proper lag structure from empirical analysis of a panel of observations. For this reason it is more fruitful to consider the third possibility. This is a failure of the equilibrium assumption which underlies cross-sectional analysis (Coleman, 1968). Repeated cross sections from a panel of organizations which are out of equilibrium will ordinarily produce estimates varying considerably from cross section to cross section. Depending upon which of them one takes, the results will be closer or farther from those estimated from a time series.

Failures of equilibrium can arise for an enormous diversity of reasons. We find one possibility intriguing from a substantive point of view. This is the possibility that *the process relating the sizes of organizational components may differ in organizational growth as opposed to decline.* We argue below why we expect such differences. The bulk of literature on administrative intensity is cross-sectional. It should be apparent that, if the processes of study are not symmetric in growth and decline, cross-sectional analysis mixing growers and decliners will obscure the processes of interest.

In the next section we consider the effects of changes in demand for organizational services on various personnel categories. While the approach is intended to be general, the specifics of this theory are generated by characteristics at least partly peculiar to the organization under study—school districts. It is our position that the relationship between enrollment and the direct component (teachers) should be symmetrical in growth and decline, but this should not be the case with the supportive component. Increases in enrollment should have greater effects than declines. Underlying these expectations is a "featherbedding" logic which places emphasis on the assumption that cutbacks in the supportive component are more costly in the short run for decision makers than over-staffing. An implication of this position is that cyclical rises and falls in enrollments can lead to increases in administrative intensity.

We follow the theoretical discussion with a description of the data. A set of regression equations are used to analyze the data. These are based on representations of the processes of interest in differential equations. Weighted least squares estimates are compared for subsamples of growing and declining districts.

After discussing the empirical findings, we trace out some implications of the model for the study of administrative intensity.

Developing a Dynamic Model of Organizational Demography

The supportive and direct components of organizations may change their relative sizes, either through internal processes involving job changes or through processes based on in-and-out migration (that is, hiring and firing). Since we do not have data allowing us to distinguish between these processes, we take advantage of a characteristic of formal organizations that distinguishes them from most other units of social organization—the fact that each member of the organization's population occupies a formally designated position. We focus on expansion or contraction in the number of positions filled by members of the organization's population to model the differences between growth and decline.

The Direct Component

The direct component in school districts is composed of teachers. Although professional staff also provide services to pupils, we consider these supportive because they are less central to the mandates of most districts. Positions for teachers, like positions for direct component members in other kinds of organizations, are added and deleted because demand for services (or products) changes.

If enrollments reflect demand for services, we can expect a positive correlation with number of teachers. We can be more precise than this, however. Limited funds and competing demands for the allocation of those funds place lower limits on class sizes in school districts. Upper limits on class size also exist. We believe that these are rooted in the community served by each district. Parents expect to find small classes in areas with highly reputed schools and larger classes in less reputed areas. They often make decisions to move partly on the basis of school reputation. We believe that the result is a *norm of maximum acceptable class size.* In affluent areas we would expect parents to object if their children find themselves with forty others in most classes. This may be acceptable to parents in less affluent areas. We combine these speculations in an *assumption of constant class size*. We assume that school districts establish an equilibrium between community-based upper limits on class size and financially based lower limits. The result is that, while size of enrollment may not be proportionately related to number of teachers, *change in enrollments ought to have proportionate effects on change in number of teachers*. This norm should operate in both growth and decline situations. *So for teachers we would expect decline to be the opposite of growth.*

The Supportive Component

We expect the supportive component to respond to changes in enrollments, too. As demand for services provided by school districts expands, more students must be enrolled. There are more records to keep. More supplies have to be purchased, controlled, and disbursed. And since school districts receive part of their revenues from governmental programs, in which pupil days in class is used as the basis of funding formulas, more pupils mean more accounting. At the same time, expanded enrollment means an expanded direct component. The usual expectation is that coordination and control problems generated by larger direct components lead to expansions in the supportive component. If this is true, we can expect both the direct component and enrollment to have effects on the supportive component.

Many supportive-component members perform functions which are as much linked to the *school* as to the student. As Blau (1973, pp. 68-74) and others have pointed out, differentiation often carries with it minimal levels of support for departments. This is one of the factors producing economies of scale. For example, each school has to have a principal and a secretary. It must have a janitor.

Since we do not at present have data on number of schools over time, we must treat it as an unmeasured intervening variable. However, an important implication rests on the fact that schools represent a sizable capital investment for districts, and closing them causes inconvenience for students and their parents. Many people make house-purchasing decisions with proximity to schools in mind, just as they consider school quality. In consequence, it is probably cheaper over a two- or three-year period in both monetary and social-cost terms for districts to operate underused schools than to close them. If part of the supportive component is tied to schools as much as to enrollments, declining enrollments should not be matched (proportionately) by cuts in the supportive component. Administrators are responsible for such decisions. Cuts in the supportive component usually result in firing personnel and reduction of staffs. In each school, and at the district level, they are likely to resist cuts. If nothing else, they may *delay* cuts.

It seems reasonable to argue that larger supportive components will be more successful at resisting cuts than small ones. The bureaucratic apparatus is populated with supportive-component members. It is better able to protect its members when it is large because outside critics will find it difficult to obtain information. School district administrators, like other bureaucrats, can defend their staffs through reference to disruption of important functions which only they are in a position to realistically assess. Further, critics are likely to accept additions to both direct and supportive components. So long as the pie is expanding, allocation decisions are relatively easy to make. In decline, critics may push for allocation of those cuts to the supportive component. We argue that they will find it difficult to buttress those arguments with facts, particularly since the "court" to whom they must appeal has a stake in maintaining an "adequate" supportive staff. The bigger that staff is, the more elaborate the bureaucratic apparatus is likely to be, and the more difficult it becomes to pierce the wall of secrecy and impersonality which contributes to its defensive capability.

Both parents, whose children may have to attend a more distant school, and administrators have a community of interest in forestalling cuts. One of the implications of this position is that a *given increment of decline in enrollment will produce a smaller decline in the supportive component than the same increment of growth in enrollment.*

Disaggregating the Supportive Component

One of the serious problems pervading the administrative intensity literature is the variation in definition from study to study. Rushing's (1967) suggestion that research would be improved if more specific subcategories of the administrative (supportive) component were studied seems to be a good one.

Our data include full-time-equivalent counts of *professional staff* (who provide nonteaching services directly to students), *administrators* (who are responsible for control and finance), and a residual category which we call *nonprofessional staff.* The defining criterion for this last group is that they are not required to have special educational certificates. The category is residual in the sense that it includes a segment of the organization's population which is functionally diverse. Secretaries and clerks are lumped together with janitors and school bus drivers.

Making predictions for nonprofessional and professional staff is difficult. We have data on these more specific personnel categories covering only two years. Professional staff members perform functions which are in many ways "luxuries" for school districts. Librarians, guidance counselors, and the like, often perform tasks which can also be performed by teachers. A district in serious financial trouble may choose to abandon some of these functions altogether. On the other hand, special programs supported by state and federal money often create positions for professional staff.

Nonprofessional staff also present problems. Some members of this component (for example, secretaries and clerks) perform work for administrators. Cuts in this component would increase the burden on administrators. Others perform jobs which are tied more directly to schools than to enrollments. An underused school probably requires nearly the same janitorial staff as a fully used school. On the other hand, nonprofessional staff occupy a low level in the status hierarchy of the district. Because their skills are not scarce, they can be replaced later with relative ease. This should make it easier to fire them.

While we are unable to develop specific hypotheses pertaining to these components, we do expect the same general causal process to operate. Analyses based on administrators, professional and nonprofessional staff will be informative if only to show whether the difference between growth and decline is due to its operation in only one of them.

Cross-sectional studies intended to discover the effects of organizational size on structure are based on the assumption that decline is simply the opposite manifestation of the same causal process occurring with growth. To this point we have argued that there are theoretical reasons for questioning this often unrecognized assumption. In the next section we describe our data set and develop a strategy for analysis which displays striking differences in the two processes.

Data and Methods

The Data

The California State Department of Education gathers data on school districts every year. These data are used by the legislature in its budgetary deliberations and by other state agencies in planning for educational needs. The virtue of these data lies in the constancy of variable definition over time and across reporting organizations. These definitions are built into the State Education Code, which requires districts to report. So the number of missing cases is very small. Very small districts have been omitted from the analysis. Elementary school districts with less than 101 average daily attendance and high school districts with less than 301 average daily attendance are not reported in California data. Approximately 100 districts were omitted because they underwent unification over the period of time covered by the longitudinal analysis (1968 to 1972). This leaves 769 districts as our sample.

Following Haas, Hall, and Johnson (1963, p. 12), we define the "supportive component" (*SUP*) as "those persons engaged in activities which contribute *indirectly* to the attainment of organizational goals." The "direct component" is the number of teachers (*T*) in the district.

The supportive component is broken down into the following exhaustive categories:

1. Professional Staff (*PROF*)—a certificated employee who performs a service for pupils in direct contact with them (for example, guidance counselors, librarians, school nurses).
2. Administrators (*A*)—a certificated employee who does not provide a service directly to pupils (for example, principals, superintendants, financial officers).
3. Nonprofessional Staff (*NPS*)—employees whose jobs do not require educational certification (for example, janitors, cafeteria workers excluding dieticians, secretaries, clerks).
4. *SUP = PROF + A + NPS.*

Analysis of Growers and Decliners

Our procedure is to divide the sample into subsamples of continuous growers and decliners and to analyze each separately. Growers are those districts whose size has increased each year in the period (either 1968-72 or 1970-72, depending on the analysis) while decliners are those whose size has decreased.

In the analysis of the size of the direct component (teacher), the natural size dimension on which to separate growers and decliners is enrollment (*E*). For analysis of variations in size of the supportive component, this choice is quite conservative. There are a great many school districts which lost enrollment but gained teachers over the period. This means that the *E*-decliners subsample includes many districts where the size of the direct component increased. This fact tends to obscure possible differences between growth and decline. For these analyses, we chose to analyze the subsamples defined in terms of continuous growth or decline in number of teachers as well as those defined by enrollment.

All of our inferences concerning the symmetry or asymmetry of growth and decline depend on differences in regression estimates for the subsamples of growers and decliners. The method depends on the assumption that the two sets of subsamples differ only on the growth-decline dimension. As we will see in the empirical analysis, there are considerable size differences between growers and decliners. Those districts in which enrollment declined are half again as large as those which grew, but those in which teaching staff declined are very much larger than those in which T grew.

The size difference is troubling because the relations of interest may be nonlinear with respect to size. If the subsamples are concentrated on different segments of the size axis in such a case, we would be led to mistakenly infer that different processes characterize the growers and decliners.

We have conducted a detailed examination of possible size nonlinearities. In no case have we found any statistically significant nonlinear terms in our regression models (.05 level). These results strongly suggest that the differences we find between growers and decliners are not due to size differences between the subsamples.

The scanty data on resources and expenditures which we have gathered also show differences between subsamples. Assessed valuation per pupil is slightly higher among growers, and expenditures per pupil are higher among decliners. We have introduced both variables into each of the regression models reported. In no case do the coefficients of interest change substantially with the introduction of resources or expenditures.

Although we cannot categorically state that these or other variables do not produce the differences reported below, we are confident, on the basis of the internal consistency of our analyses, that the differences reflect the processes we have hypothesized. In the future we will have the capacity to use 1970 Census data on districts to study this problem in more depth. But the present analysis proceeds on the assumption that the only important systematic difference between the growers and decliners is just that—growth versus decline.

The Model

In developing a model to represent the theoretical ideas described above, we wish to distinguish between effects of *change* in independent variables over a specified period of time and other effects of that variable. In particular, we want to control for the effects of previous changes in that variable as well as scale factors, such as the norm of maximum acceptable class size.

Our empirical analysis concentrates on estimation of regression models of the following form:

$$Y_t = \alpha_0 + \alpha_1 Y_{t-k} + \alpha_2 X_{t-k} + \alpha_3 \Delta X_t + u_t \tag{1}$$

where $\Delta X_t = X_t - X_{t-k}$, and Y_t is the size of some personnel component at time t, Y_{t-k} is the value of the same variable measured k periods earlier, and X_{t-k} is a measure of either demand (enrollments) or of the size of the direct component.

The model in (1) is chosen for several reasons. It is perhaps the simplest model to estimate among the class of models which allow for the separation of the effects of initial size and change during some period. In addition, the model is consistent with a dynamic representation of the demographic processes. In particular, Coleman (1968) shows that (1) is a solution to the following differential equation:

$$\frac{dY}{dt} = q + rY + sX. \tag{2}$$

Equation (2) states that the rate of change in some component depends both on the existing size of the component, Y, and on some other factors, X. But (2) will yield stable equilibria only if $r \leqslant 0$ (that is, $\alpha_1 \leqslant 1$). In such a case, the rate of change in the size of the component decreases with size of the component. So the term rY contributes a self-decelerating component to the process. In most instances, such a negative feedback on the rate of change arises due to unobserved causal loops. For instance, as the size of the supportive component increases, it may give rise to political opposition, which slows down the rate of growth (Blau, 1970). Unless the net consequence of all such unobserved loops is negative, the process will not be stable. In each case we consider, the results are consistent with stability. The translation from (2) to (1) takes the following form.

$$q = \alpha_0 C/\Delta t \tag{3a}$$

$$r = 1n\alpha_1/\Delta t \tag{3b}$$

$$s = [C/2\Delta t] \; [\alpha_2 + \alpha_3 \, (\alpha_1 - 1)/(1 - C)] \tag{3c}$$

where

$$C = 1n\alpha_1/(\alpha_1 - 1). \tag{3d}$$

We employ the following estimators, suggested by Coleman:

$$\hat{q} = \hat{\alpha}_0 \hat{C}/\Delta t \tag{4a}$$

$$\hat{r} = 1n\hat{\alpha}_1/\Delta t \tag{4b}$$

$$\hat{s} = [\hat{C}/2\Delta t] \; [\hat{\alpha}_2 + \hat{\alpha}_3 \hat{C}(\hat{\alpha}_1 - 1)(1 - \hat{C})] \tag{4c}$$

$$\hat{C} = 1n \, \hat{\alpha}_1/(\hat{\alpha}_1 - 1) \tag{4d}$$

where the α's are ordinary least squares estimates from (1).

The first feature of the pair of equations (1) and (2) to notice is that they imply that for growers and decliners to follow the same process, all of the parameters of (1) must be the same for the two. It follows that the most direct test of the symmetry of growth and decline is to estimate (1) separately for growers and decliners and to test the null hypothesis that the parameters are the same for both categories. The complete estimation model is:

$$T_t = \beta_0 + \beta_1 T_{t-k} + \beta_2 E_{t-k} + \beta_3 \Delta E_t + u_t \tag{5}$$

$$SUP_t = \gamma_0 + \gamma_1 SUP_{t-k} + \gamma_2 T_{t-k} + \gamma_3 \Delta T_t + v_t, \tag{6}$$

and the differential equations are

$$\frac{dT}{dt} = a + bT + cE \tag{7}$$

$$\frac{dSUP}{dt} = d + eSUP + fT. \tag{8}$$

Equation (6) is estimated for SUP and each of its components, A, $PROF$, and NPS. In each case our main hypothesis is that growers and decliners will be identical for (5) and differ for (6).

We are also interested in testing a more refined hypothesis; namely, that administrative intensity will tend to be smaller in growth than in decline. That is, we expect a sort of supportive-component "featherbedding" in decline. The next step is to develop specific hypotheses for this proposition in terms of (6).

Our expectation is that a given increment of size (of demand or of the direct component) will produce a larger increment of *SUP* in growth than the same change, taken as a decrement, will decrease *SUP*. For example, suppose an increase of one hundred teachers yields an increase of twenty *SUP*. We expect that a decrease of one hundred teachers will tend to produce a decrease of only ten or fifteen *SUP*. Such a result can arise in a number of ways.

The proposition that growth is different from decline has to this point been formulated largely in terms of the effects of changes in the size of the direct component (net of initial size) on the supportive component. This focuses attention on γ_3, the coefficient of ΔT_t in (6). Our hypothesis is that γ_3 will be positive for both growers and decliners but that it will be greater for growers. In this case both the regression model (6) and the differential equation (8) yield the same qualitative inferences, since if γ_3 is positive and greater for growers, *f* will be greater (net of γ_1) for growers.

There is a second implication of the "featherbedding" argument that concerns γ_3 in equation (6), the "autoregression" term. Earlier we argued that large supportive components would tend to resist cuts in decline. Such resistance can be represented in terms of relative dampening of growth-decline. In the differential equation (8), *e* represents these effects. As long as *e* is negative, effects of changes in enrollments and in the direct component are dampened down over time. The larger is this negative effect, the less the long-run effects of environmental changes. In other words, high levels of resistance to cuts implies large negative values of *e*. In particular, the dampening effects ought to be greater in decline than in growth.

According to (4b), $\hat{e} = 1n\hat{\gamma}_1/\Delta t$. So if *e* is to be a larger negative quantity for decliners, γ_1 must be smaller for decliners. That is, our argument implies that the autoregression coefficient, γ_1, will be smaller in decline than growth.

In summary, we hypothesize first that (5) will be identical for growers and decliners but that (6) will be different. Second, we hypothesize that the autoregression term γ_1 will be greater for growers as will the coefficient of the change term γ_3.

Estimation

Two problems arise in the estimation of our regression models. Both concern the distributions of the disturbances u_t and v_t. Recall that for ordinary least squares (OLS) to be consistent (unbiased in large samples), the disturbances must be uncorrelated with regressors. For OLS to be efficient, the disturbances must have the same variance from observation to observation ("homoscedasticity"). There is reason to suspect that u_t and v_t fail on both counts.

The first problem, correlation of disturbances and regressors, follows from the suspected autocorrelation of the disturbances and the presence of lagged dependent variables in the models. If the omitted causes of, say, *SUP* are stable over time for districts, they will certainly be correlated with lagged *SUP*. In such cases OLS "gives credit" to the lagged dependent variable for the stable portion of the disturbances. As a result, $\hat{\beta}_1$ and $\hat{\gamma}_0$ will be upwardly biased. And, at least for three variable models (Malinvaud, 1970, p.

558), we know that OLS estimates of the coefficients of other variables will tend to be biased toward zero. Since we expect β_2, β_3, γ_2, and γ_3 to be positive, we expected their estimates to be downwardly biased.

Correction of OLS estimates for this problem requires at least four "waves" of observations. Our present data base does not furnish enough time periods of observation for us to make a correction. So the reader should keep the expected bias in mind in evaluating our results. The most important point is that there is no reason to suspect that the nature of the problem differs for the grower and decliner subsamples. Finally, given the tentative nature of the regression estimates, we will not calculate estimates of the parameters of the differential equation.

Examination of calculated residuals from OLS estimates of our models shows a fan-shaped pattern of dispersion with respect to the dependent variable. This suggests that the variance of the disturbances increases with the size of the organization. Organizational analysts ought not to find this surprising, since yearly increments in, say, *SUP* in large organizations may exceed the size of *SUP* in small organizations. We ought to expect a multiplicative error structure.

We have applied a widely used version of the generalized least squares method known as *weighted least squares* to correct this problem. Given our guess as to the nature of the problem, the appropriate weighting is achieved by dividing through each equation by the relevant size variable (Johnston, 1972, pp. 214-217). This transforms (5), for example, into

$$\frac{T_t}{E_{t-k}} = \beta_0 \frac{1}{E_{t-k}} + \beta_1 + \beta_2 \frac{T_{t-k}}{E_{t-k}} + \beta_3 \frac{\Delta E_t}{E_{t-k}} + \frac{u_t}{E_{t-k}} \tag{9}$$

Then OLS is applied to the transformed equations. Examination of the residuals calculated from the weighted least squares estimation suggests that we have eliminated the heteroscedasticity problem. We use this method throughout.

Empirical Results

Our results can be stated very simply. We proceed by personnel categories, considering both two-year and four-year growth and decline. Means and variances are presented in Table 1.

The Direct Component

We expect no differences between growers and decliners in the effects of enrollments on the size of the teaching staff. The natural time dimension for this analysis would seem to be one- or two-year lags. The results for the two-year samples, reported in Table 2, support our hypothesis. Neither the autoregression term nor the change term coefficient differ substantially between the two.

We attempted to replicate these findings with the sample of continuous four-year growers or decliners, using a four-year change score. This effort, reported in Table 2, produces some inconsistencies between the two samples. In particular, the autoregression term for growers is considerably greater than is the case for decliners. We are not sure what to make of this partially disconfirming evidence. We suspect that the long lag picks

Table 1. Means and Variances[a]

Variable	Full	Subsamples Defined by Changes in Direct Components from 1970 to 1972		Subsamples Defined by Changes in Enrollments from 1970 to 1972	
		Growers	Decliners	Growers	Decliners
Supportive component $SUP70$[b]	.0285 (.0115)	.0289 (.0102)	.0285 (.0122)	.0307 (.0123)	.0266 (.0100)
Administrative component $A70$[b]	.0032 (.0011)	.0033 (.0011)	.0032 (.0010)	.0032 (.0012)	.0031 (.0010)
Professional staff $PROF70$[b]	.0028 (.002)	.0026 (.0016)	.0021 (.0013)	.0028 (.0018)	.0022 (.0015)
Nonprofessional staff $NPS70$[b]	.0236 (.0104)	.0238 (.0094)	.0237 (.0112)	.0255 (.0112)	.0218 (.0088)
Direct component (teachers) $T70$[b]	.0430 (.0081)	0433 (.0081)	.0443 (.0080)	.0450 (.0088)	.0416 (.0063)
"A/P ratio" $SUP70/E70$	65.1 (20.5)	66.5 (19.8)	63.6 (20.4)	67.8 (21.3)	63.5 (19.7)
Student/teacher ratio $E70/T70$	23.7 (3.8)	23.6 (3.6)	23.3 (4.0)	22.9 (3.8)	24.6 (3.7)
Assessed valuation per pupil	23.6 (26.1)	24.6 (27.4)	22.1 (34.3)	27.4 (31.3)	18.5 (16.1)
Enrollment $E70$[b]	5,389.4 (24,896.6)	4,323.0 (6,506.6)	11,203.3 (64,141.2)	3,951.1 (6,166.1)	6,100.1 (10,686.0)
N	805	250	106	255	248

[a]Because of space limitations, only 1970 statistics are presented. Variances are in parentheses.

[b]Variable divided by $E70$, as entered in weighted least squares regression analyses.

Table 2. Effects of Growth and Decline in Enrollments on the Direct Component: Weighted Least Squares Estimates

Subsample

Two-Year Samples

Enrollment growers

$$T_{72} = .040 + \underset{(.035)}{.8990T_{70}} + \underset{(.002)}{.0054E_{70}} + \underset{(.003)}{.0402(E_{72} - E_{70})} \qquad \begin{array}{l} R^2 = .783 \\ N = 255 \end{array}$$

Enrollment decliners

$$T_{72} = .259 + \underset{(.036)}{.9284T_{70}} + \underset{(.002)}{.0047E_{70}} + \underset{(.005)}{.0412(E_{72} - E_{70})} \qquad \begin{array}{l} R^2 = .754 \\ N = 248 \end{array}$$

Four-Year Samples

Enrollment growers

$$T_{72} = .296 + \underset{(.089)}{1.0958T_{68}} + \underset{(.004)}{.0013E_{68}} + \underset{(.002)}{.0394(E_{72} - E_{68})} \qquad \begin{array}{l} R^2 = .736 \\ N = 179 \end{array}$$

Enrollment decliners

$$T_{72} = .392 + \underset{(.054)}{.7584T_{68}} + \underset{(.002)}{.0143E_{68}} + \underset{(.005)}{.0452(E_{72} - E_{68})} \qquad \begin{array}{l} R^2 = .661 \\ N = 138 \end{array}$$

Standard errors in parentheses.

up trends unrelated to the enrollment-teacher relations and attributes them to the lagged dependent variables.

The Supportive Component

The analysis of the entire supportive component discloses dramatic differences between growers and decliners. These differences appear when partitioning is based on enrollment changes (Table 3) and when it is based on changes in the direct component (Table 4). In each case, the differences occur for both the two-year and four-year samples.

Table 3. Effects of Growth and Decline in Direct Component on the Supportive Component: Weighted Least Squares Estimates

Subsample

Two-Year Samples

Enrollment growers

$$SUP_{72} = .178 + .9369SUP_{70} - .0030E_{70} + .1802T_{70}$$
$$\quad\quad\quad (.057) \quad\quad\quad (.003) \quad\quad (.079)$$
$$+ .4477(T_{72} - T_{70})$$
$$(.086)$$

$R^2 = .687$
$N = 255$

Enrollment decliners

$$SUP_{72} = .215 + .7618SUP_{70} + .0007E_{70} + .1834T_{70}$$
$$\quad\quad\quad (.042) \quad\quad\quad (.002) \quad\quad (.068)$$
$$+ .4503(T_{72} - T_{70})$$
$$(.092)$$

$R^2 = .686$
$N = 248$

Four-Year Samples

Enrollment growers

$$SUP_{72} = .216 + .7138SUP_{68} - .0014E_{68} + .2654T_{68}$$
$$\quad\quad\quad (.086) \quad\quad\quad (.005) \quad\quad (.158)$$
$$+ .6094(T_{72} - T_{68})$$
$$(.059)$$

$R^2 = .591$
$N = .179$

Enrollment decliners

$$SUP_{72} = .028 + .5698SUP_{68} + .0013E_{68} + .2942T_{68}$$
$$\quad\quad\quad (.071) \quad\quad\quad (.004) \quad\quad (.111)$$
$$+ .3768(T_{72} - T_{68})$$
$$(.118)$$

$R^2 = .444$
$N = 138$

Standard errors in parentheses.

Before considering the main hypotheses, we raise a subsidiary issue. This concerns the role of demand—that is, enrollments—in the determination of the size of the supportive component. Earlier we noted that there is reason to expect both "direct" effects and "indirect" effects (that is, through size of the direct component). We find absolutely no evidence of any "direct" effects of enrollments on the size of the supportive component. That is, in the regressions reported in Tables 3, 4, and 5, the effects of enrollments are always insignificant (at the .05 level).

In three of the four comparisons in Tables 3 and 4, the autoregression term is very much greater for growers, as hypothesized. In the fourth, for two-year growers and decliners defined in terms of the size of the direct component, the two estimated autoregressions are within one standard error of each other. The results for γ_3, the coefficient

Table 4. Effects of Growth and Decline in Direct Component on the Supportive
Component: Weighted Least Squares Estimates

Subsample		

Two-Year Samples

Dir. comp. growers	$SUP_{72} = .071 + .8823SUP_{70} + .0019E_{70} + .0713T_{70}$ $\quad\quad\quad(.049)\quad\quad\quad(.002)\quad\quad(.059)$ $\quad + .5722(T_{72} - T_{70})$ $\quad\quad(.070)$	$R^2 = .744$ $N = 250$
Dir. comp. decliners	$SUP_{72} = -.307 + .8101SUP_{70} - .0040E_{70} + .2799T_{70}$ $\quad\quad\quad\quad(.069)\quad\quad\quad(.004)\quad\quad(.099)$ $\quad + .1269(T_{72} - T_{70})$ $\quad\quad(.131)$	$R^2 = .761$ $N = 106$

Four-Year Samples

Dir. comp. growers	$SUP_{72} = -.431 + .7385SUP_{68} + .0058E_{68} + .0473T_{68}$ $\quad\quad\quad\quad(.070)\quad\quad\quad(.004)\quad\quad(.110)$ $\quad + .6344(T_{72} - T_{68})$ $\quad\quad(.046)$	$R^2 = .638$ $N = 199$
Dir. comp. decliners	$SUP_{72} = .859 + .5292SUP_{68} - .0026E_{68} + .4684T_{68}$ $\quad\quad\quad\quad(.137)\quad\quad\quad(.008)\quad\quad(.241)$ $\quad + .6099(T_{72} - T_{68})$ $\quad\quad(.389)$	$R^2 = .805$ $N = 25$

Standard errors in parentheses.

of the change score, are fairly similar. In two cases, four-year enrollment samples and two-year direct-component-change samples, the estimate of $\hat{\gamma}_3$ is much larger for the growers. In the case of the four-year direct-component-change samples, the estimates are close in value. However, the test of the null hypothesis that $\gamma_3 = 0$ is strongly rejected for growers but cannot be rejected for decliners. So for the aggregated supportive component, both more specific hypotheses tend to be supported by the data.

Elements of the Supportive Component

Disaggregated data on categories of the supportive component are available only for the 1970-1972 period. This limits our analysis to that of two-year growers and decliners. On substantive grounds outlined earlier, we expect variations in administrative staff (A) and nonprofessional staff (NPS) to be causally related to changes in the size of the direct component. But variations in the size of the professional staff ($PROF$), who provide services directly to pupils, should be related to changes in enrollments. The regressions reported in Table 5 take these assumptions into account.

Administrative Staff. The hypothesis of divergence of growers and decliners is supported with respect to the change term but not the autoregression. In fact, for decliners, changes in number of teachers have no effect on administrators over the two-year period.

Nonprofessional Staff. The situation for NPS is identical to that for administrative staff. Again the hypothesis of divergence of growers and decliners is supported.

Professional Staff. Finally, for the professional (or "pupil services") staff the

Table 5. Effects of Growth and Decline in Direct Component and in Enrollments on
Elements of the Supportive Component: Weighted Least Squares Estimates

Subsample		
Dir. comp. growers	$A_{72} = .096 + .4600A_{70} - .00003E_{70} + .0362T_{70}$ $\quad\quad\quad (.055) \quad\quad (.0003) \quad\quad (.007)$ $\quad\quad + .0335(T_{72} - T_{70})$ $\quad\quad\quad (.009)$	$R^2 = .499$ $N = 250$
Dir. comp. decliners	$A_{72} = -.002 + .4461A_{70} + .0003E_{70} + .0429T_{70}$ $\quad\quad\quad (.070) \quad\quad (.0003) \quad\quad (.0092)$ $\quad\quad + .0081(T_{72} - T_{70})$ $\quad\quad\quad (.011)$	$R^2 = .656$ $N = 105$
Dir. comp. growers	$NPS_{72} = -.013 + .9154NPS_{70} + .0026E_{70} + .0262T_{70}$ $\quad\quad\quad (.050) \quad\quad\quad (.002) \quad\quad (.054)$ $\quad\quad + .4750(T_{72} - T_{70})$ $\quad\quad\quad (.067)$	$R^2 = .724$ $N = 250$
Dir. comp. decliners	$NPS_{72} = -.045 + .8468NPS_{70} - .0041E_{70} + .2332T_{70}$ $\quad\quad\quad (.063) \quad\quad\quad (.003) \quad\quad (.091)$ $\quad\quad + .1036(T_{72} - T_{70})$ $\quad\quad\quad (.125)$	$R^2 = .754$ $N = 106$
Enrollment growers	$PROF_{72} = -.247 + .8925PROF_{70} - .0004E_{70} + .0155T_{70}$ $\quad\quad\quad (.063) \quad\quad\quad\quad (.0005) \quad\quad (.014)$ $\quad\quad + .0052(E_{72} - E_{70})$ $\quad\quad\quad (.001)$	$R^2 = .710$ $N = 175$
Enrollment decliners	$PROF_{72} = -.019 + .7138PROF_{70} + .0001E_{70} + .0204T_{70}$ $\quad\quad\quad (.040) \quad\quad\quad\quad (.0004) \quad\quad (.010)$ $\quad\quad + .0042(E_{72} - E_{70})$ $\quad\quad\quad (.001)$	$R^2 = .740$ $N = 178$

Standard errors in parentheses.

"featherbedding" hypothesis is supported on both counts. Both $\hat{\gamma}_1$ and $\hat{\gamma}_3$ are larger than the corresponding estimates for decliners. *PROF* responds to growth and decline in ways more like the other parts of the supportive component than like teachers. If the reverse were true, we would be tempted to consider *PROF* part of the direct component.

As we noted above, we expected to find that correlations between the supportive and direct components are partly spurious due to the effects of enrollment on both of them (for all dependent variables but *PROF*). Our results indicate that enrollment (E) has no appreciable effect when teachers (T) is controlled, suggesting that the effects of E are channeled through T.

Discussion and Conclusions

The very large empirical literature on the relationship of size and administrative intensity is almost wholly cross sectional. As a result, this research tradition has depended heavily on the assumption that the relations are symmetric in growth and decline. We have advanced a number of arguments to the contrary and have conducted empirical tests of the counterassertions. Our argument leads to a broad hypothesis that growers and decliners will be alike in the relations of size of direct (or production) component to demand for organizational products or services, but that the two will differ in the relation of supportive-component size to the direct-component size and to demand. This hypothesis is strongly supported in our analysis.

We developed more specific hypotheses concerning two parameters that describe adjustment of the supportive component to changes in the direct component. We expected direct-component changes to have smaller effects in decline. And we hypothesized that this difference would be reinforced by a stronger dampening tendency in decline. The evidence is consistent with our hypotheses, and in a large number of comparisons we find dramatic differences in the predicted directions between growers and decliners.

These results have a number of implications. Returning to issues raised at the outset, our analysis suggests that A/P ratios are too complex to be useful in many analyses and that cross-sectional analysis of organizational demography may be quite misleading. The ratios are complex because the denominator, size of the direct (or production) component, behaves similarly in growth and decline while the numerator, size of the supportive component, does not. So the ratios are not unitary from a substantive point of view. The second point, concerning cross-sectional analysis, is obvious. One's inferences concerning the relationship of supportive-component size to direct-component size should change systematically with the growth/decline composition of the study sample. In other words, cross-sectional results will not be dependable.

Our research also suggests two complications for the study of organizational structure. First, growth and decline are likely to bring about different effects on such structural variables as degree of differentiation (both horizontal and vertical), centralization, and formalization. For example, growth in manufacturing firms from 300 to 1,000 personnel may lead to an increased use of written procedural rules, but a subsequent decline of the same magnitude would probably not have a comparable effect.

Second, in the model we have developed, variations in the demand environment drive the system. The process we formulated works something like a bumperjack. When demand is increasing, the size of the direct component increases as does the supportive component. But when demand declines, the loss in direct component is not matched by loss in the supportive component. That is, the supportive component tends to increase on the upswings but decreases less on the downswings. Consequently, a turbulent environment, producing oscillations in demand for the organization's products or services, may produce an increase in administrative intensity even if there is no upward trend in the oscillations.

References

Blau, P. "A Formal Theory of Differentiation in Organizations." *American Sociological Review,* 1970, *35,* 201-218.

Blau, P. "Interdependence and Hierarchy in Organizations." *Social Science Research,* 1972, *1,* 1-24.

Blau, P. *The Organization of Academic Work.* New York: Wiley, 1973.

Blau, P., and Schoenherr, A. *The Structure of Organizations.* New York: Basic Books, 1971.

Blau, P., and Schoenherr, A. *Ratios of California Public School Non-teaching Employees to Classroom Teachers; as of November 1, 1970, 1971, and 1972.* Sacramento: California State Department of Education, Bureau of Administrative Research and District Organization, 1970-1972.

Coleman, J. "The Mathematical Study of Change." In H. Blalock, Jr., and A. B. Blalock (Eds.), *Methodology in Social Research.* New York: McGraw-Hill, 1968.

Freeman, J., and Hannan, M. T. "Reply to Kaufman." *American Sociological Review,* 1976, *41,* 748-749.

Freeman, J. H., and Kronenfeld, J. E. "Problems of Definitional Dependency: The Case of Administrative Intensity." *Social Forces,* 1973, *52,* 108-121.

Fuguitt, G. V., and Lieberson, S. "Correlation of Ratios or Difference Scores Having Common Terms." In H. L. Costner (Ed.), *Sociological Methodology 1973-1974.* San Francisco: Jossey-Bass, 1974.

Haas, E., Hall, R. H., and Johnson, N. "The Size of the Supportive Component in Organizations: A Multi-organizational Analysis." *Social Forces,* 1963, *43,* 9-17.

Haire, M. "Biological Models and Empirical Histories of the Growth of Organizations." In M. Haire (Ed.), *Modern Organization Theory.* New York: Wiley, 1959.

Hannan, M. T., and Freeman, J. "Internal Politics of Growth and Decline." In M. W. Meyer and Associates, *Environments and Organizations: Theoretical and Empirical Perspectives.* San Francisco: Jossey-Bass, 1978.

Hannan, M. T., and Young, A. A. *Estimation in Panel Models: Results on Pooling Cross-Sections and Time Series.* Stanford, Calif.: Laboratory for Social Research, Stanford University, 1974.

Hendershot, G. E., and James, T. F. "Size and Growth as Determinants of Administration-Production Ratios in Organizations." *American Sociological Review,* 1972, *37,* 149-153.

Johnston, J. *Econometric Methods.* (2nd ed.) New York: McGraw-Hill, 1972.

Kaufman, R. L. "Solution and Interpretation of Differential Equation Models." *American Sociological Review,* 1976, *41,* 746-748.

Malinvaud, E. *Statistical Methods of Econometrics.* (2nd ed.) New York: American Elsevier, 1970.

Melman, S. "The Rise of Administrative Overhead in the Manufacturing Industries of the United States 1889-1947." *Oxford Economic Papers,* 1951, *3,* 62-112.

Meyer, M. "Size and the Structure of Organizations: A Causal Analysis." *American Sociological Review,* 1972, *37,* 434-440.

Rushing, W. "The Effects of Industry Size and Division of Labor on Administration." *Administration Science Quarterly,* 1967, *12,* 273-295.

Schuessler, K. "Ratio Variables and Path Models." In A. Goldberger and O. D. Duncan (Eds.), *Structural Equation Models in Social Science.* New York: Seminar Press, 1973.

Starbuck, W. "Organizational Growth and Development." In J. G. March (Ed.), *Handbook of Organizations.* Chicago: Rand McNally, 1965.

Terrien, F. W., and Mills, D. L. "The Effect of Changing Size upon the Internal Structure of Organizations." *American Sociological Review,* 1955, *20,* 11-13.

Tsouderos, J. E. "Organizational Change in Terms of a Series of Selected Variables." *American Sociological Review,* 1955, *20,* 206-210.

4

The External Environment: Effects of Change on Environmental Dynamism and Complexity

Mary F. Mericle

It has become an undisputed tenet of organizational theorists that organizations must adapt to their "external" environments in order to survive. Yet alarmingly little has been empirically resolved about the nature of the organizational adaptation process.

While the main variables in the process have been identified as the organization's objective, "external" environment, its decision makers' perceived environment, their uncertainty, and their strategic decisions (see Downey, Slocum, and Hellreigel, 1975; Huber, O'Connell, and Cummings, 1975), the effect of environments with different characteristics on the other variables remains undiscernible in a quagmire of contradictory and incomplete research findings.

The purpose of this study is to determine the effects of different "objective" environments on those important variables in the adaptive process; that is, the perceived environment, decision-maker uncertainty, and strategic decisions. A laboratory simulation was used to test these effects.

Previous Research and Hypotheses

The external environments to which organizations are adjured to adapt have been characterized many ways by many people (see Jurkovich, 1974; Shortell, 1977). The two characteristics of environments that continue to be identified as being of major import are forms of dynamism and complexity. Dynamism is consistently defined in terms of the magnitude, rate, and regularity of change in external conditions; and complexity has been defined by the number and heterogeneity of external "objects" with which the organization must deal. Noted studies have suggested that different organizational structures and processes will be more appropriate than others in dynamic and complex environments (see Pennings, 1975). But how do these adaptive structures and processes emerge? Are

Excerpted by permission of the author from her dissertation "The Effect of Change and Complexity in the External Environment on Perceived Environmental Dynamism and Complexity, Uncertainty, and Allocations to Boundary Activities," University of North Carolina, 1979.

they a result of a form of natural selection, or do decision makers who face different environments select these different structures and processes as more appropriate than others? Do decision makers even perceive the nature of their environment accurately, so that they can make the "correct" strategic choices?

Several different strategic actions have been proposed as effective in dynamic and complex environments. One strategic response that has received considerable theoretical attention (Adams, 1976; Aldrich and Herker, 1977; Leifer and Delbecq, 1976; Miles, 1978; Thompson, 1967) but has not been empirically investigated is the strengthening or expanding of boundary-spanning activities to cope with increasingly dynamic and complex heterogeneous environments. Thompson proposed over a decade ago that, as environments become more unstable and heterogeneous, organizational boundary activities become more crucial to organizational survival. Recently Adams (1976), Leifer and Delbecq (1976), and Miles (1978) have been more specific in suggesting that, as the rate of change and heterogeneity in the environments increases, information search activity, the rate of filtering and changing organizational filters, the level of negotiating with the environment, and the degree of representation activity in which the organization must engage to maintain legitimacy increase. Boundary-spanning activity can only increase if it is supported by increased organizational resources. Therefore, one would expect that the more change in the environment and the greater the number and heterogeneity of organizations there, the more money, manpower, and energy decision makers would allocate to boundary activities such as information search, representing, negotiating, coding, and filtering.

Further research is also needed to clarify the relationship between the external environment, which is the objective stimulus, and decision makers' perceptions of it. While it is beyond the scope of this paper to discuss in detail the research findings which bear on the relationship, it can be generally stated that there is theoretical controversy (Downey and Slocum, 1975; Pennings, 1975) and empirical contradiction over the relationship between objective environmental dynamism and complexity and perceptions of dynamism, complexity, and uncertainty (Downey, Slocum, and Hellreigel, 1975; Duncan, 1972; Lorenzi, Sims, and Slocum, 1978; Pennings, 1975). Another purpose of this study is to clarify the relationship between objective characteristics of an organization's external environment and decision makers' perception of it.

To summarize, the present study investigated the effect of the change and the number and heterogeneity of organizations in the environment on decision makers' allocations to boundary activities, their perceptions of environmental dynamism and complexity, and their level of uncertainty. It is hypothesized that the greater the change and magnitude and heterogeneity of the external environment, the greater would be the levels of each of the four dependent variables.

Method

In order to meet the objectives of the study, an in-basket simulation was constructed which portrayed the external environment of an organization as being characterized by a great deal of large changes (high dynamism) or by little or no change (low dynamism) and either as containing a large number of different organizations with which it interacts (high complexity) or containing a relatively small number (low complexity). Ninety-two undergraduate students served as subjects, and twenty-three were randomly assigned to each of the four conditions in the resultant 2×2 complete factorial design.

Subjects were asked to assume the role of a manager of a company and make a series of managerial decisions. These decisions were based on information contained in a series of three bimonthly reports describing business conditions which the company faced over a six-month period. The reports, prefaced with background information about the company, were in an envelope placed in front of each subject on a conference table. Subjects were required to read the reports in the sequence in which they were stapled, without flipping back and forth. After they read the reports, subjects returned them to the envelope and received a set of decision forms to complete. One form asked them to evaluate their company's business environment based on the information in the reports. Another required that they allocate a fixed amount of company funds among various company activities.

The two levels of the independent variables, change in the environment (dynamism) and heterogeneity and number of environmental organizations (complexity), were manipulated by differing critical information in the reports. The reports were identical except that in the high-dynamism conditions the following events in the external environment changed dramatically (positively and negatively): prices of raw materials, annual sales of competitors, customers, competing companies, investigations by federal agencies, and union wage demands. In the low-dynamism conditions the above items remained unchanged or changed only slightly. In the high-complexity conditions the company's environment was described in the reports as containing nine times as many different suppliers, five times as many competitors, three times as many different kinds of customers, and many more numbers of customers than in the low-complexity conditions.

After having read the reports, all subjects completed assessment forms on which their impressions of the business conditions were recorded. Embedded in these forms were self-report items, which measured (1) their perceptions of environmental dynamism, (2) their perceptions of environmental complexity, and (3) their uncertainty about the environment. These items were used to check the manipulations of the independent variables as well as to measure the perceptions of subjects. Multiple seven-point bipolar-adjective scales and seven-point Likert-type scales were used to measure the above three dependent variables. The validity of the items used to measure each of the variables was determined by multitrait, monomethod analysis (Campbell and Fiske, 1959). The inter-scale reliabilities between the bipolar-adjective and Likert-type scales were sufficiently high (.75 to .84) to justify averaging responses on the different scales to form one index for each of the three variables. The value of each index ranged from 1 to 7. The odd-even reliabilities for these dependent measures, adjusted by the Spearman-Brown Correction Formula, ranged from .81 to .91.

After subjects recorded their assessment of the environment, they were asked to allocate, in a way that would maximally benefit the firm, $1,000,000 in corporate funds among thirteen company activities, seven of which were boundary activities (for example, advertising and public relations, lobbying, and sales) and six of which were "internal" activities (for example, manufacturing, accounting, and general management). Allocations were made in $100,000 increments, resulting in a maximum of ten out of the thirteen activities that could possibly receive allocations. Having a greater number of total activities than the maximum number that could receive allocations prevented subjects from assigning every activity the same amount. The number of $100,000 increments which subjects allocated to boundary activities served as a measure, ranging from 1 to 10, of the allocation to boundary activities.

Results

Perceived Environmental Dynamism. It was expected that decision makers facing environments characterized by different magnitudes and rates of change would have different perceptions of the dynamism of their environments. The results (see Table 1) con-

Table 1. Means and Standard Deviations[a]

		High Dynamism		Low Dynamism	
		High Complexity	Low Complexity	High Complexity	Low Complexity
Perceived dynamism[b]	M	5.017	5.038	3.446	3.304
	SD	0.682	0.583	0.813	0.844
Perceived complexity[b]	M	5.078	4.274	3.800	3.235
	SD	0.945	0.684	1.023	0.879
Decision maker un-certainty[b]	M	3.333	2.913	2.391	2.725
	SD	1.064	0.854	0.930	0.952
Allocations to boundary activities[c]	M	5.870	4.565	5.043	4.478
	SD	1.866	1.854	1.637	1.344

[a]The number of subjects in each condition was 23.

[b]Values on these variables range from 1 to 7, low to high.

[c]Values measured in $10,000.

firm these expectations in that the level of perceived dynamism reported by subjects in the high-dynamism conditions (M = 5.028) was significantly higher (F = 115.352, $p <$ .001) than that of counterparts in low-dynamism conditions. For subjects in high- and low-complexity conditions, the level of perceived dynamism was essentially equal (M = 4.232 and M = 4.171, respectively). The interaction effect was not significant.

Perceived Environmental Complexity. Analysis of subjects' responses reveals evidence supporting the hypothesized effects of a large, multifaceted environment on perceptions of complexity. It also reveals unanticipated effects of change in the environment on the perception of complexity. As hypothesized, in high-complexity conditions levels of perceived complexity (M = 4.439) were significantly higher (F = 13.471, $p <$ .001) than in low-complexity conditions (M = 3.755). Unexpectedly, subjects in changing environments perceived them to be more complex (M = 4.676) than did their counterparts in relatively unchanging environments (M = 3.518). The level of change in the environment had a greater impact on perceptions of complexity than did what has been traditionally considered as a "complex" environment, as can be seen by comparing the respective F values (F = 38.959 and F = 13.471). There were no significant interaction effects.

Decision Maker Uncertainty. The hypothesis that decision makers in changing and multifaceted environments would exhibit a higher level of uncertainty than counterparts in static and relatively simple environments was only partially supported. Uncertainty was higher (F = 8.091, $p <$ .006) under conditions where events were changing greatly (M = 3.123) than where there was little or no change (M = 2.553). However, the degree of uncertainty reported by subjects facing complex external conditions (M = 2.862) was virtually the same as their counterparts in relatively simple environments (M = 2.819). There was not a significant interaction effect, although the pattern of means revealed the lowest uncertainty in the high-complexity, low-dynamism condition.

Allocations to Boundary Activities. It was hypothesized that decision makers would respond to both increasing environmental change and larger numbers of different organizations with which the company dealt by allocating more resources to organizational activities that took place at the organization's boundary and "linked" the organization to its environment. Although the allocations of subjects in high-dynamism (M = 5.218) and low-dynamism (M = 4.761) conditions were in the predicted direction, the difference was not statistically different. Consistent with the second part of the hypothesis, subjects facing environments composed of many different organizations allocated more ($F = 7.047$, $p < .009$) to boundary activities ($M = 5.457$) than did subjects whose firms dealt with relatively few organizations ($M = 4.522$). There was no significant interaction effect.

Summary and Discussion

One view of organizational adaptation is that it is an active strategic decision process, which is stimulated by conditions in the environment. This study tested the effect of different environments on a strategic decision on allocations to boundary activities and on the perceptions of environments by using a decision-making simulation where the environment of a firm was created by a series of reports describing events external to the firm. With the manipulation of the information in the reports, the environments were portrayed as containing either a great deal of change or little-to-no change and either a large number of different organizations or relatively few homogeneous ones.

Analysis of the subjects' perceptions, their uncertainty levels, and allocation decisions in the four types of environments confirmed many of the experimental hypotheses. Subjects did vary in their perceptions of environmental dynamism depending on the amount of change in their environments. However, when subjects made decisions to allocate valuable resources between activities within the organization and activities that interfaced with the environment, the level of change in the environment had no effect on where the dollars went. Only larger numbers and more heterogeneity of environmental organizations brought larger allocations to important boundary functions.

With regard to future research, there are several implications suggested from the findings. First, because uncertainty was induced by changing environments and yet strategic decisions were the same in changing and unchanging environments, the explanation that enlarging boundary activities is a strategy to reduce uncertainty (Leifer and Delbecq, 1976) may need reconsideration. In any event, the adaptiveness of increased boundary activities in changing environments needs to be empirically determined. A second implication addresses the use of objective and subjective measures of the environment. Often, perceived environmental dynamism and complexity are used as surrogate measures for objective measures of the environment. This research suggests that environments perceived as complex may not be "objectively" complex—that is, heterogeneous and multifaceted; rather, they may simply contain a great deal of change. To the extent researchers are interested in distinguishing between the effects of the two environmental characteristics, they may want to eschew using perceptual measures, or at least test carefully the validity of perceptual measures, of the environment.

While the limitations of trying to create a firm's environment through a simulation are acknowledged, it is still proposed that more of the research on organizational adaptation needs to focus on the causal relationship between the environment and the organization. This research indicates that decision makers do make different strategic choices in different types of environments. It is very likely, however, that just as frequently decision makers make strategic choices to "engineer" the type of environment with which they deal (Weick, 1977). Without determining under what circumstances and in what degree external environments are the cause or effect, or both, we cannot make with confidence prescriptions about what strategic action firms should take to adapt to their environments.

References

Adams, J. S. "Organizational Boundary Behavior." Paper presented at 84th convention of the American Psychological Association, Washington, D.C., September 1976.

Aldrich, H., and Herker, D. "Boundary Spanning Roles and Structure." *Academy of Management Review*, 1977, *2*, 217-230.

Campbell, D. T., and Fiske, D. W. "Convergent and Discriminant Validation by the Multi-trait-Multimethod Matrix." *Psychological Bulletin*, 1959, *56*, 81-105.

Downey, H. K., and Slocum, J. W. "Uncertainty Measures, Research and Sources of Variation." *Academy of Management Journal*, 1975, *18*, 562-578.

Downey, H. K., Slocum, J. W., and Hellreigel, D. "Environmental Uncertainty: Its Construct and Its Application." *Administrative Science Quarterly*, 1975, *20*, 613-619.

Duncan, R. B. "Characteristics of Organizational Environments and Perceived Environmental Uncertainty." *Administrative Science Quarterly*, 1972, *17*, 313-327.

Huber, G., O'Connell, M. J., and Cummings, L. L. "Perceived Environmental Uncertainty: Effects of Information and Structure." *Academy of Management Journal*, 1975, *18*, 725-740.

Jurkovich, R. "A Core Typology of Organizational Environments." *Administrative Science Quarterly*, 1974, *19*, 380-394.

Leifer, R., and Delbecq, A. "Organizational/Environmental Interchange: A Model of Boundary Spanning Activity." Unpublished paper, 1976.

Lorenzi, P., Sims, H., and Slocum, J. "Perceived Environmental Uncertainty: An Individual or Environmental Attribute." Paper presented at 35th annual meeting of the Academy of Management, San Francisco, August 1978.

Miles, R. H. *Macro Organizational Behavior*. Santa Monica, Calif.: Goodyear, 1978.

Pennings, J. "The Relevance of the Structural-Contingency Model for Organizational Effectiveness." *Administrative Science Quarterly*, 1975, *20*, 393-410.

Shortell, S. "The Role of Environment in a Configurational Theory of Organizations." *Human Relations*, 1977, *30*, 275-302.

Thompson, J. *Organizations in Action*. New York: McGraw-Hill, 1967.

Weick, K. "Enactment Processes in Organizations." In B. Staw and G. Salancik (Eds.), *New Directions in Organizational Behavior*. Chicago: St. Clair Press, 1977.

5

The Scarcity-Munificence Component
of Organizational Environments
and the Commission of Illegal Acts

Barry M. Staw
Eugene Szwajkowski

Over the past decade, there has been a substantial increase in research on the interaction of the organization and environment (Cyert and March, 1963; Emery and Trist, 1965; Thompson, 1967; Terreberry, 1968; Pfeffer, 1972; Duncan, 1972; Starbuck, 1976). One focus of analysis has been the adaptation of the organization to the environment (Burns and Stalker, 1961; Bennis, 1966; Lawrence and Lorsch, 1967). In this work, the environment generally has been treated as a constraint or problematic element with which the organization must deal to be effective or increase its chances of survival. The interaction of the uncertainty component of the environment and the structural component of the organization has been of particular concern, and it has been widely posited that there exists an optimal fit between structure and environment (Lorsch and Lawrence, 1970; Galbraith, 1973).

A second focus of analysis has emphasized the organization's ability to control or change its environment. In addition to adapting its own structures to the environment, several theorists (Cyert and March, 1963; Starbuck, 1965; Thompson, 1967) have noted that organizations may act on their environments in order to reduce uncertainty. It has been shown, for example, that organizations may make their environments less uncertain by engaging in long-term contracts with other organizations (Macaulay, 1963), by absorbing elements of the environment into the organization (Selznick, 1949), by seeking external support for the organization within the environment (Litwak and Hylton, 1962; Zald, 1967), by forming temporary coalitions or joint ventures with other organizations (Aiken and Hage, 1968), or by undertaking an interorganizational merger (Pfeffer, 1972).

To date, most of the theoretical work on the interaction of the organization and environment has focused on the uncertainty element of the environment. Environmental uncertainty, however, has been viewed in several different ways. Thompson (1967),

Reprinted from *Administrative Science Quarterly*, 1975, *20* (3), 345-354, with permission of the authors and the publisher. Copyright © 1975 Cornell University.

Perrow (1970), and Pfeffer (1972) have considered organizational dependence upon external resources as an important source of uncertainty and one which the organization strives to reduce. Duncan (1972), on the other hand, has followed Emery and Trist (1965) and Terreberry (1968) in delineating two separate components of environmental uncertainty: the simple-complex dimension and the static-dynamic dimension. Duncan found that individuals in decision units with dynamic-complex environments perceive the greatest amount of uncertainty in decision making, but that the static-dynamic dimension accounts for a substantially greater proportion of the variance than does the simple-complex dimension.

Although environmental uncertainty is no doubt the most heavily researched factor in the interaction between organization and environment, it is not the only aspect of the environment relevant to this interaction. One factor which is sometimes referred to in theoretical discussions, but is rarely included in empirical research on organizations, is scarcity-munificence of the environment. March and Simon (1958), probably the first organizational theorists to specifically build this environmental dimension into a theoretical model, were concerned primarily with the effect of environmental munificence on intraorganizational conflict. They suggested that, when resources are restricted in the environment, relations among individual members and subgroups within the organization will resemble a purely competitive or zero-sum game. When organizations function within a benign or munificent environment, however, the organization need not resolve the relative merits of subgroup claims to resources. Following March and Simon (1958), it therefore can be posited that scarcity-munificence of the environment may have important effects upon several intraorganizational processes: interpersonal and intergroup conflict, differentiation of individual and subgroup goals, and felt need for joint decision making.

The scarcity-munificence component of the environment may also be an important determinant of organizational actions in the environment. Previously, Starbuck (1965) noted that organizations seek to grow, in part, to make their environments more munificent. Also, Cyert and March (1963) have considered environmental munificence to be a factor which interacts with the accumulation of slack resources to ensure organization stability and survival. Neither Cyert and March (1963) nor Starbuck (1965), however, considered environmental scarcity-munificence as an independent variable which directly affects the actions of organizations in the environment. Even Haas and Drabek (1973), who have extensively reviewed the sources of organizational stress and reactions to them, have omitted the scarcity-munificence component of the environment as a determinant of organizational action. Thus, there is a need for both theoretical and empirical research on the effects of environmental munificence on organizational action in the environment.

In the research reported here it was posited that the scarcity-munificence of an organization's environment would be associated with organizational actions designed to procure additional resources. Organizations must import resources from their environments in order to function (Katz and Kahn, 1966), and, regardless of whether there exist organizational goals of survival and growth or individual performance goals of key organizational members, it is clear that resources must be inputted from the environment. It is therefore hypothesized that the less munificent is the organization's environment, the more effort the organization will exert to obtain resources from its environment.

The effort to procure resources may take many forms, but one of the most interesting and important from a societal point of view is the commission of illegal acts. When the organization is located within a scarce environment, one method of coping with intra- and extraorganizational demands may be to perform activities which are legally questionable. Specifically, it is predicted that the more scarce the environment of a business organization, the more likely it will engage in activities which are considered unfair market practices or restraints of trade. It is hypothesized that such trade violations may be undertaken by the organization within a scarce environment in order to procure additional resources. When the organization is in a munificent environment, it is more likely to obtain sufficient resources without resorting to illegal practices.

Research Design

The goal of the research was to test the relation between the scarcity-munificence component of the environment and the occurrence of illegal corporate acts. To assemble a sample of organizations which had engaged in legally questionable activities, the authors consulted the published volume *Trade Cases*. This publication reports decisions and consent and litigated decrees entered in federal and state courts throughout the United States for cases involving possible violations of antitrust laws and the Federal Trade Commission Act. For the years 1968 to 1972, a sample was constructed of all publicly held companies involved in the following areas of litigation: price discrimination, tying arrangements, refusal to deal, exclusive dealing, franchise violation, price fixing, foreclosure of entry, reciprocity, allocation of markets, monopoly, conspiracy, and illegal mergers and acquisitions. Sampled companies included firms found guilty in litigated cases, firms which were a party to nonlitigated consent decrees, and unsettled cases in which the court found substantial merit to the cases against the cited firm. To facilitate the use of published data and provide a control for size, the final sample was restricted to companies listed by *Fortune* as one of the 500 largest firms in the United States. The final sample thus consisted of 105 large companies involved in trade litigation from 1968 to 1972.

In order to measure the degree of scarcity-munificence of the organization's environment, two approaches were taken. First, as an indirect measure of environmental munificence, the financial performance of the cited firms was contrasted to that of all firms in the *Fortune* 500 list. Since the performance of individual firms should be correlated with the scarcity-munificence of its environment, a comparison of financial performance between cited firms and all firms in the *Fortune* 500 would be relevant to the hypothesis. Second, as a more direct measure of the relation between environmental munificence and the commission of illegal acts, the financial performance of the industries in which the cited firms operated was contrasted with the financial performance of all firms (and industries) in the *Fortune* 500. Finally, firm and industry statistics were compared to observe whether cited firms differed from other firms in their industries.

Five years of financial data were collected from *Fortune* for each company in the sample. Since it was hypothesized that environmental munificence is a factor influencing the commission of illegal acts, financial data were collected for each of five years preceding the date that a formal complaint was filed by either a governmental or civil party against the firm. Because the sample was constructed from 1968-1972 trade cases the bulk of the financial data was collected for the years 1963-1971. However, it was necessary that some of the company data be collected from earlier years—for instance, 1954-1962—in order that the five-years' data precede some long-standing trade complaints.

The financial performance of the cited firms was measured by the mean return on equity and mean return on sales over the five years preceding a trade complaint. Mean returns on equity and sales were also recorded for the cited firms' industry and for all firms in the *Fortune* 500 during these years. Special attention was given to the weighting of industry and all firms' means, so that they would correspond exactly to the proportion of individual firms cited for illegal activities in the years under study. That is, since data from individual firms spanned five-year periods from 1954-1958 to 1967-1971, it was necessary to compute means for their industries and all firms in the *Fortune* 500 which would properly reflect these time periods. Thus, for each observation of an illegal corporate act, five preceding years of data were collected for the individual firm, its industry, and all firms in the *Fortune* 500. These data were subsequently averaged and prepared for comparison. Because of the temporal correspondence of the data, statistical analyses could subsequently be performed in which an average of individual firm data could be considered to be a sample mean drawn from a known population of all firms in the *Fortune* 500 or their industries.

Two other measures of financial performance were provided by *Fortune* but were more difficult to interpret: the percentage change in sales and percentage change in profits. These data were considered to be less valid indicators of financial performance than the return on equity and return on sales data, since the mean percentage change over the relevant five-year period may be highly correlated with the variability of a firm's performance. That is, if a firm showed alternate declines and advances in profits, the average percentage change would be a large increase; for example, a 50 percent decline becomes a 100 percent increase in returning to the original level. To minimize this bias, only the median industry ranks as reported in *Fortune* for change in sales and change in profits over the five years were used in the analyses. Although bias is not eliminated in these analyses, it is reduced due to the greater stability of industry over individual company data and the greater stability of median ranks over percentage change data. The change in sales and profits indicators thus serves as supplementary data to the return on equity and return on sales measures of financial performance.

Results

Table 1 shows the mean return on equity and the mean return on sales for the cited firms and all firms in the *Fortune* 500. Since the sample was drawn from a population with known mean and variance, the Z statistic was used to compare the two means. As predicted, the data showed that, for the five years preceding a trade complaint, the financial performance of cited firms was significantly below all firms in the *Fortune* 500 on both mean return on equity ($Z = -4.24$, $p < .001$, one-tailed) and mean return on sales ($Z = -1.70$, $p < .05$, one-tailed).

Table 1 also shows the contrast between the financial performance of all firms in the *Fortune* 500 and the industries in which the cited firms operated. Since the industry statistics published by *Fortune* are based only on the 500 firms in their yearly sample, the population mean for all firms is also the population mean of all the industries delineated by *Fortune*. Thus, a Z statistic was again used in contrasting the sample mean for cited industries versus the population mean of all firms. The table indicates that the financial performance of the cited industries was significantly below that of all firms in the *Fortune* 500. The difference was highly significant on both the mean return on equity ($Z = -11.10$, $p < .001$, one-tailed) and the mean return on sales ($Z = -4.98$, $p < .001$, one-tailed). It should be noted that the sample of observations for the cited industries was smaller than the sample of observations for cited firms in that some firms could not be assigned unambiguously to an industry. This loss of cases also accounts for the slight difference in the weighted averages of return on sales and return on equity for all *Fortune*

Table 1. Comparisons of the Financial Performance of Cited Firms, Their Industries, and All Firms in the *Fortune* 500 List

Comparison I	Cited Firms	All Firms	Z	p^a
Mean return on equity	$\bar{X} = 9.67$ $(N = 105)$ (range = −5.98 to 24.56)	$u = 11.45^b$ $(N = 500)$ (range = 10.16 to 12.46)	−4.24	.001
Mean return on sales	$\bar{X} = 5.46$ $(N = 105)$ (range = −1.31 to 17.91)	$u = 6.03^b$ $(N = 500)$ (range = 5.40 to 6.38)	−1.70	.05
Comparison II	**Cited Industries**	**All Firms**	**Z**	**p^a**
Mean return on equity	$\bar{X} = 9.85$ $(N = 92)$ (range = 7.40 to 12.98)	$u = 11.47^c$ $(N = 500)$ (range = 10.16 to 12.46)	−11.10	.001
Mean return on sales	$\bar{X} = 5.12$ $(N = 92)$ (range = 2.58 to 10.90)	$u = 6.05^c$ $(N = 500)$ (range = 5.40 to 6.38)	−4.98	.001
Comparison III	**Cited Firms**	**Cited Industries**	**Z**	**p^d**
Mean return on equity	$\bar{X} = 9.50$ $(N = 92)$ (range = −5.98 to 24.56)	$u = 9.85$ $(N = 92)$ (range = 7.40 to 12.98)	−.78	N.S.
Mean return on sales	$\bar{X} = 5.36$ $(N = 92)$ (range = −1.31 to 16.82)	$u = 5.12$ $(N = 92)$ (range = 2.58 to 10.90)	.70	N.S.

[a]One-tailed tests.

[b]Population mean derived from 105 observations.

[c]Population mean derived from 92 observations.

[d]Two-tailed tests.

Note: Range scores are based upon average financial performance over five years preceding trade complaint.

500 firms. Each missing case required the removal of its five-year time period from the weighting of the population means for all firms.

In addition to the comparison of cited firms and industries to the means for all firms, the contrast between cited firms and their industries can also be seen in Table 1. The financial performance of the cited firms was neither better nor worse than the average performance of its industry. There was no statistically significant difference between cited firms and their industries on mean return on equity ($Z = -.78$, N.S.) nor mean return on sales ($Z = .70$, N.S.). In these analyses, the industry data represent the population from which the cited firms were drawn.

Table 2 provides additional data on the comparison of cited industries to all firms in the *Fortune* 500. The table lists percentiles of financial performance for all the cited industries. Since the number of industries delineated by *Fortune* changed during the time periods over which data were collected, it was necessary to convert industry ranks as presented by *Fortune* to percentile scores. Table 2 thus represents percentiles converted from the median rank of cited industries for return on equity, return on sales, change in

Table 2. Percentile Distribution of Cited Industries on Four Financial Statistics[a]

	Number of Cited Industries in Each Percentile										Average Percentile	Z	Kolmogorov-Smirnov Distribution Test
	1-10	11-20	21-30	31-40	41-50	51-60	61-70	71-80	81-90	91-100			
Return on equity	5	18	30	14	2	6	16	1	0	0	32.68	−8.62[b]	D_{max} = .36[c]
Return on sales	11	9	10	13	5	11	13	5	13	2	44.02	−1.52[d]	D_{max} = .14[e]
Change in sales	0	14	20	6	33	9	7	1	1	1	38.09	−5.08[b]	D_{max} = .27[c]
Change in profits	0	11	6	20	22	16	12	1	4	0	43.00	−3.28[c]	D_{max} = .17[c]

[a]Data are divided into decile form for presentation purposes only. The average percentile scores and Kolmogorov-Smirnov tests are both based on actual percentile data.

[b]$p < .001$.

[c]$p < .01$.

[d]$p < .07$.

[e]$p < .05$.

sales, and change in profits. As shown in the table, the cited industries were rated below average on each of the four financial indicators. On three of these indicators—mean return on equity, change in sales, change in profits—there was a highly significant difference between the average percentile for the cited industry and that which would be expected by chance (all Z scores > 3.27; $p < .001$, one-tailed test). On the mean return on sales indicator, there was a marginally significant ($Z = 1.52$; $p < .07$, one-tailed) difference between the average percentile for the cited industries and that expected by chance. The inferior performance of cited industries was also evidenced by the Kolmogorov-Smirnov test (Siegal, 1956, pp. 47-52) of the distribution of percentile scores. As shown in the table, the distribution of percentile scores for the cited industries differed significantly from the distribution which would be expected by chance.

Discussion

The data provided by this study offer support for the hypothesis that environmental munificence influences the commission of illegal acts. Comparisons of data in Table 1 indicate that cited companies performed less well than other firms in the *Fortune* 500 over the five years preceding a trade complaint. Although this difference in performance could have been due to factors either internal or external to the firm, the evidence weighs in favor of environmental factors. First, while cited firms performed below the average of all *Fortune* 500 firms, they performed no worse than other firms in their industries. In contrast, the industries in which cited firms operated displayed financial performance far below the average for all industries. Thus, it appears that the reason cited firms performed below the average for all *Fortune* 500 firms is not because of such internal organizational factors as poor management or internal structure, but because of factors common to the entire industry. The industries in which cited firms operated were low performing and may have been beset with industry-wide problems such as poor demand for a given class of products, shortages of raw materials, or widespread strikes. Although it is difficult to ascertain the exact problem facing each of these industries, it is clear that the industrial environments of the companies cited for illegal acts were less munificent than those of other companies in the *Fortune* 500.

It was broadly hypothesized that organizations with scarce environments would take actions to procure additional resources. It was also hypothesized that increased efforts to procure resources would increase the likelihood of committing illegal actions. The scope of such illegal behavior is beyond the purpose of this research, but environmental scarcity does appear to be related to a range of trade violations. Table 3 shows the mean difference in performance between cited industries and all firms, broken down by type of trade offense. As shown in the table, there is a good deal of consistency in the data across the trade offenses. With few exceptions, the cited industries performed below all firms in return on equity and return on sales.

It is interesting to note that many of the trade violations listed in Table 3 have been described by other authors (Cyert and March, 1963; Thompson, 1967; Pfeffer, 1972) as ways for an organization to reduce uncertainty. Actions such as price fixing, reciprocity, mergers, and acquisitions are modes by which the organization can control its market environment. These actions, however, are also ways by which an organization may extract additional resources from its environment. For the types of trade violations investigated in this research, the environment of the cited firms was generally shown to be less munificent than that of other *Fortune* 500 firms. Therefore, it seems conceptually more valid to consider these organizational actions as not just ways to reduce uncertainty but

Table 3. Mean Difference in Performance Between Cited Industries and All Firms
in Return on Equity and Return on Sales by Type of Offense[a]

Type of Trade Offense	Return on Equity	Return on Sales
Price fixing	−1.98 (N = 42)	−.92 (N = 42)
Reciprocity	−1.78 (N = 22)	−1.94 (N = 22)
Mergers and acquisitions	−1.36 (N = 17)	−1.39 (N = 17)
Refusal to deal	−1.55 (N = 10)	1.05 (N = 10)
Monopoly	−1.28 (N = 7)	−.49 (N = 7)
Tying arrangements	−.88 (N = 4)	−2.39 (N = 4)
Price discrimination	−1.49 (N = 4)	−1.43 (N = 4)
Allocation of markets	−1.52 (N = 2)	−1.98 (N = 2)
Other: foreclosure of entry, exclusive dealing, and conspiracy	−.07 (N = 5)	−1.94 (N = 5)

[a]The total number of complaints in the table exceeds the total number of cases of cited industries, since some trade complaints involved more than one type of offense.

as modes of resource procurement. Many actions which have previously been identified as evidence for the primacy of uncertainty reduction by organizations—for example, reciprocity agreements, joint ventures, mergers, and acquisitions—may also represent organizational attempts to glean additional resources from the environment.

Conclusion

Although the data of this research provide support for the hypothesis that scarcity-munificence of an organization's environment influences the commission of illegal acts, the present results do not unequivocally support a causal statement. Nonetheless, efforts were made in this research to measure the independent variable, environmental munificence, on time periods preceding the dependent variable, commission of illegal acts. This method provided an improvement over covariation measured within a single time frame, although further time-series data on both financial performance and trade violations would be necessary to fully substantiate a causal hypothesis.

An archival analysis of organizational phenomena such as that utilized in this study inherently has certain strengths and weaknesses. The primary advantages of archival analysis lie in the nonreactivity of measurement (Webb and others, 1966) and the relatively low cost of getting data from a wide number of organizations. The primary disadvantage of archival research lies in the rigidity of the data base. Archival data may not be available on critical variables, or data that are available may not be suitable for statistical analyses. Even with these liabilities, however, research in the organizational area has only barely touched the potential pool of useful archival data on the internal behavior of formal organizations and the actions of organizations in their environments.

This study suggests there is need for much additional research on the effects of the scarcity-munificence component of the environment. Little is known about the organization's reactions to environmental scarcity and how these differ from organizational actions within a munificent environment. For example, illegal actions may be only one means by which an organization attempts to procure resources from a scarce environment, and even this method of coping with the environment may be limited to powerful organizations or those operating within environments resembling an oligopolistic market structure (Stigler, 1964). Caution must therefore be exercised in generalizing from the relation between environmental munificence and illegal behavior on the part of large *Fortune* 500 firms to smaller and not-for-profit organizations. Instead of an increase in reciprocity, price fixing, and other restraint-of-trade activities, a scarce environment could lead to intense interfirm competition when the market consists of numerous small firms, as under perfect competition. Thus, when the organization initially lacks sufficient power over its environment or if the organization set (Evan, 1966) is too large or diverse to permit effective coordination of behavior, intensification of competition could be the organization's best way to procure additional resources. The scarcity-munificence component of the environment, then, may interact with organizational power or interorganizational relations in determining an organization's actions to procure environmental resources.

In addition to research on the influence of scarcity-munificence on organizational actions in the environment, further research should also be directed toward the effect of this environmental factor upon the internal dynamics of organizations. The intraorganizational consequences of environmental scarcity could, as noted by Hermann (1963), be related to those of other organizational crises. Environmental scarcity, for example, may lead to centralization of authority, restriction of communication channels (Hermann, 1963), as well as increases in intraorganizational conflict resulting from internal budgeting processes (Pondy, 1964, 1970). It is hoped that this study will stimulate further research on the intraorganizational consequences of a given level of environmental scarcity in addition to the influence of scarcity-munificence on organizational efforts to procure additional resources from the environment.

References

Aiken, M., and Hage, J. "Organizational Interdependence and Intraorganizational Structure." *American Sociological Review,* 1968, *33,* 912-920.

Bennis, W. G. *Changing Organizations.* New York: McGraw-Hill, 1966.

Burns, T., and Stalker, G. M. *The Management of Innovation.* New York: Quadrangle Books, 1961.

Cyert, R. M., and March, J. G. *A Behavioral Theory of the Firm.* Englewood Cliffs, N.J.: Prentice-Hall, 1963.

Duncan, R. B. "Characteristics of Organizational Environments and Perceived Environmental Uncertainty." *Administrative Science Quarterly,* 1972, *17,* 313-327.

Emery, F. E., and Trist, E. L. "The Causal Texture of Organizational Environments." *Human Relations,* 1965, *18,* 21-31.

Evan, W. M. "The Organization-Set." In J. D. Thompson (Ed.), *Approaches to Organizational Design.* Pittsburgh: University of Pittsburgh Press, 1966.

Galbraith, J. *Designing Complex Organizations.* Reading, Mass.: Addison-Wesley, 1973.

Haas, J. E., and Drabek, T. E. *Complex Organizations: A Sociological Perspective.* New York: Macmillan, 1973.

Hermann, C. F. "Some Consequences of Crises Which Limit the Viability of Organizations." *Administrative Science Quarterly,* 1963, *8,* 61-82.

Katz, D., and Kahn, R. L. *The Social Psychology of Organizations.* New York: Wiley, 1966.

Lawrence, P. R., and Lorsch, J. W. *Organization and Environment.* Boston: Graduate School of Business Administration, Harvard University, 1967.

Litwak, E., and Hylton, L. F. "Interorganizational Analysis: A Hypothesis on Co-ordinating Agencies." *Administrative Science Quarterly,* 1962, *7,* 395-420.

Lorsch, J. W., and Lawrence, P. R. *Studies in Organizational Design.* Homewood, Ill.: Irwin, 1970.

Macaulay, S. "Non-contractual Relations in Business: A Preliminary Study." *American Sociological Review,* 1963, *28,* 55-67.

March, J. G., and Simon, H. A. *Organizations.* New York: Wiley, 1958.

Perrow, C. *Organizational Analysis: A Sociological View.* Belmont, Calif.: Wadsworth, 1970.

Pfeffer, J. "Merger as a Response to Organizational Interdependence." *Administrative Science Quarterly,* 1972, *17,* 382-394.

Pondy, L. R. "Budgeting and Intergroup Conflict in Organizations." *Pittsburgh Business Review,* 1964, *34,* 1-3.

Pondy, L. R. "Toward a Theory of Internal Resource-Allocation." In M. N. Zald (Ed.), *Power in Organizations.* Nashville: Vanderbilt University Press, 1970.

Selznick, P. *TVA and the Grass Roots.* Berkeley: University of California Press, 1949.

Siegal, S. *Nonparametric Statistics for the Behavioral Sciences.* New York: McGraw-Hill, 1956.

Starbuck, W. H. "Organizational Growth and Development." In James G. March (Ed.), *Handbook of Organizations.* Chicago: Rand McNally, 1965.

Starbuck, W. H. "Organizations and Their Environments." In Marvin Dunnette (Ed.), *Handbook of Industrial and Organizational Psychology.* Chicago: Rand McNally, 1976.

Staw, B. M. "Attribution of the 'Causes' of Performance: A General Alternative Interpretation of Cross-Sectional Research on Organizations." *Organizational Behavior and Human Performance,* 1975, *13,* 414-432.

Stigler, G. J. "A Theory of Oligopoly." *Journal of Political Economy,* 1964, *72,* 44-61.

Terreberry, S. "The Evolution of Organizational Environments." *Administrative Science Quarterly,* 1968, *13,* 337-396.

Thompson, J. D. *Organizations in Action.* New York: McGraw-Hill, 1967.

Webb, E. J., and others. *Unobtrusive Measures: Nonreactive Research in the Social Sciences.* Chicago: Rand McNally, 1966.

Zald, M. N. "Urban Differentiation, Characteristics of Boards of Directors, and Organizational Effectiveness." *American Journal of Sociology,* 1967, *73,* 261-272.

PART II

Organizational Characteristics and Roles

Human social organizations are components of macroscopic ecological systems. They are a part of societies in which they serve distinctive and typical functions. In turn, organizations are comprised of subsystems, which consist of articulated roles performed by persons. Societies, organizations, subsystems, and roles, then, may be conceived in a hierarchy of nested systems—roles within subsystems, within organizations, within societies. Components are functionally linked at their own hierarchical system level and at lower and higher adjacent levels. The attributes of component systems and of the relationships (linkages) among them may be specified. Thus, the attributes of persons and roles, of interpersonal and interrole relationships, of organizations and interorganizational relations, and of societal and international relations may be investigated with respect to structure and process in a comprehensive systemic framework.

The concept of role in organizational theory embodies the requirements of an organization as a system and of its constituent members. As conceived by Kahn and associates (Kahn and others, 1964; Katz and Kahn, 1978), the behavioral specifications of a person's role are determined by the functional needs of the system, including relational requirements. The role requirements result from the expectations that members have of each other. *Pfeffer* and *Salancik* show how the behavior of fifty-three supervisors in the housing division of a large university was determined by the expectations of their superiors, subordinates, and peers. The role expectations of the supervisors' subordinates weighed more heavily than those of their bosses in influencing social behaviors, whereas the work-related behaviors of supervisors were more influenced by the expectations of their superiors than by those of subordinates. Different segments of a supervisor's role set were differentially influential with respect to different behaviors.

As open systems, organizations require the performance of activities that effectively link roles and subsystems and connect the organizations to their environments. Boundary roles, consisting of activities that functionally link organizations, are the focus of research by *Wall* and *Adams*. They demonstrate in a laboratory experiment that a sales manager's evaluations of a subordinate salesman instructed to negotiate purchases from a buyer were principally a function of the salesman's success and his obedience to instructions to bargain either cooperatively or competitively. Salesmen who made larger profits and were more obedient were evaluated more positively, granted more autonomy, and trusted more highly. The experiment points up the internal and external organizational linkage of roles and the feedback effects from one role to another. In this investigation role expectations, communicated as managerial sales instructions, resulted in compliance or noncompliance, which, in turn, induced the manager to grant salesmen more or less autonomy and trust.

In a field study of professional-level employees in nine government research and development organizations, *Miles* and *Perreault* examine the linkage between the objective role requirements of jobs, the consequent role-conflict perceptions, and various individual outcomes, such as tension, satisfaction, performance, and attitudes toward role senders. A number of objective role requirements sum additively to produce five characteristically different conflict orientations. For example, jobs that require *intra*organizational boundary spanning, as between departments within a laboratory, differ from *inter*organizational boundary-spanning roles. The former roles are more prone to intrasender conflict but less prone to conflicts of overload.

Different outcomes were associated with these differences in conflict orientation. To illustrate, a conflict orientation comprising moderate overload conflict and high levels of intrasender, intersender, and person-role conflict, which was typical of intraorganizational boundary spanners, was associated with very negative outcomes—the highest job tension, lowest job satisfaction, poorest attitudes toward role senders and lowest effectiveness. In contrast, an orientation consisting of very low levels of conflict of any type, which was characteristic of research scientists, was correlated with much more favorable outcomes—low tension, high satisfaction, good attitudes, and moderately high effectiveness. Although the causal linkage between role requirements, role conflict perceptions, and individual outcomes is not firmly established in this investigation because of its correlational nature, the study nevertheless provides a plausible model of role antecedents and consequences. It also offers a guide in the use of sophisticated analytic methods in the examination of complex organizational structures and processes.

Objective organizational characteristics that may significantly influence role behavior are organization type (Katz and Kahn, 1978) and functional division of labor. Dearborn and Simon (1958), for example, have shown that managers of different functional departments present distinct solutions to problems; these solutions are shaped by the orientation of the functional specialty, such as marketing and finance. In a provocative field experiment conducted in mental health institutions, *Rosenhan* gives convincing evidence that the function served by an organization in the larger society influences the role behavior of its members. As maintenance institutions charged with diagnosing and treating illness, professional staffs of hospitals would be predicted to err on the side of caution in their admission and discharge decisions and to exhibit a preference for type 2 over type 1 errors. It is more dangerous to misdiagnose illness than health. The prediction is borne out by Rosenhan's findings. Eight pseudopatients, unknown to hospital staffs, feigned hearing strange voices on arrival and were immediately admitted to twelve hospitals on the East and West coasts, in all but one case with a diagnosis of schizophrenia. Upon admission to the psychiatric ward, pseudopatients ceased the simulation of complaints and behaved as they did normally. Instead of being promptly discharged, they were hospitalized for an average of nineteen days—in one instance for fifty-two days. When they were discharged, it was with a diagnosis of "schizophrenia in remission." The ease of admission and the delayed, reluctant discharge of "sane" pseudopatients unmistakably testify to the powerful effect of institutional function on the role behavior of hospital staff.

Rosenhan's investigation reflects another clear organizational effect on staff role behavior. The pronouncement of mental illness has powerful derivative effects on the attitudes and behavior of staff toward "patients." As Rosenhan notes, "psychiatric diagnoses . . . carry with them personal, legal, and social stigmas." One might suppose that professionals in the mental health field would be free of such tendencies to stigmatize in their occupational roles. Quite the contrary was observed. In psychiatric hospitals, as compared to university campus and general medical center "control" organizations, professional staff distinctly avoided contacts initiated by pseudopatients. The rigor of data collection and of organizational comparisons in Rosenhan's field experiment leaves much to be desired. Nonetheless, unobtrusive participant observation procedures, such as those reported by Rosenhan, make available data that would otherwise be inaccessible.

A quite different type of formal organization than the hospital is the international organization, which serves as a vital linkage between nations. Such organizations cross the boundaries of nation-states and function as pipelines for the flow of information and commodities. In his study of multinational corporations and international professional associations, *Evan* observes positive rank-order correlations between the following: (1) the number of multinational corporations with parent companies in a given country and the gross national product per capita of the respective countries; (2) the nationality of the principal officials of international professional associations and the level of economic development of the nations of origin; and (3) the number of multinational firms in a nation-state and the number of principal officials of international associations from the same nations. Any other findings would have been astounding. Nevertheless, the line of inquiry may be productively pursued to unravel the texture of international interdependence, as is being done in the study of interorganizational structure and process dynamics. To this end, Evan offers a structural model of internation relationships.

As noted in the previous chapter, a dominant attribute of an organization is its technology, which imposes demands on management information processing and, consequently, on organizational structure. The nature of continuous-process technology requires rapid exchange and continual updating of technical information among technicians and decision makers responsible for the optimal usage and maintenance of costly capital machinery. As Galbraith (1973) has noted, this constant updating places a premium on decentralization and integration, or organic structure, so as to achieve high levels of organizational performance. *Keller* reexamines Woodward's (1965) finding that continuous-process industries perform more effectively with organic management systems. Using objective and subjective measures of the profitability and performance of four electric utilities and forty continuous-process manufacturers of a variety of products, he finds that deemphasis of impersonal hierarchy and of the use of rules in decision making is significantly related to higher profitability and performance. Separate analyses of relatively well-performing and poorly performing industries further show that the low-performing organizations were distinctly more mechanistic than the high-performing ones in their use of impersonal hierarchy and rules.

References

Dearborn, D. C., and Simon, H. A. "Selective Perception: A Note on the Departmental Identifications of Executives." *Sociometry,* 1958, *21,* 140-144.

Galbraith, J. *The Design of Complex Organizations.* Reading, Mass.: Addison-Wesley, 1973.

Kahn, R. L., and others. *Organizational Stress: Studies in Role Conflict and Ambiguity.* New York: Wiley, 1964.

Katz, D., and Kahn, R. L. *The Social Psychology of Organizations.* (Rev. ed.) New York: Wiley, 1978.

Woodward, J. *Industrial Organization: Theory and Practice.* London: Oxford University Press, 1965.

6

On Being Sane in Insane Places

David L. Rosenhan

If sanity and insanity exist, how shall we know them?

The question is neither capricious nor itself insane. However much we may be personally convinced that we can tell the normal from the abnormal, the evidence is simply not compelling. It is commonplace, for example, to read about murder trials wherein eminent psychiatrists for the defense are contradicted by equally eminent psychiatrists for the prosecution on the matter of the defendant's sanity. More generally, there are a great deal of conflicting data on the reliability, utility, and meaning of such terms as "sanity," "insanity," "mental illness," and "schizophrenia." Finally, as early as 1934, Benedict suggested that normality and abnormality are not universal. What is viewed as normal in one culture may be seen as quite aberrant in another. Thus, notions of normality and abnormality may not be quite as accurate as people believe they are.

To raise questions regarding normality and abnormality is in no way to question the fact that some behaviors are deviant or odd. Murder is deviant. So, too, are hallucinations. Nor does raising such questions deny the existence of the personal anguish that is often associated with "mental illness." Anxiety and depression exist. Psychological suffering exists. But normality and abnormality, sanity and insanity, and the diagnoses that flow from them may be less substantive than many believe them to be.

At its heart, the question of whether the sane can be distinguished from the insane (and whether degrees of insanity can be distinguished from each other) is a simple matter: do the salient characteristics that lead to diagnoses reside in the patients themselves or in the environments and contexts in which observers find them? From Bleuler, through Kretschmer, through the formulators of the recently revised *Diagnostic and Statistical Manual* of the American Psychiatric Association, the belief has been strong that patients present symptoms, that those symptoms can be categorized, and, implicitly, that the sane are distinguishable from the insane. More recently, however, this belief has been questioned. Based in part on theoretical and anthropological considerations, but also on philosophical, legal, and therapeutic ones, the view has grown that psychological categorization of mental illness is useless at best and downright harmful, misleading, and pejorative at worst. Psychiatric diagnoses, in this view, are in the minds of the observers and are not valid summaries of characteristics displayed by the observed.

Reprinted from *Science,* 1973 (Jan. 19), *179,* 250-258, with permission of the author and the American Association for the Advancement of Science. Copyright 1973 by the American Association for the Advancement of Science.

Gains can be made in deciding which of these is more nearly accurate by getting normal people (that is, people who do not have, and have never suffered, symptoms of serious psychiatric disorders) admitted to psychiatric hospitals and then determining whether they were discovered to be sane and, if so, how. If the sanity of such pseudopatients were always detected, there would be prima facie evidence that a sane individual can be distinguished from the insane context in which he is found. Normality (and presumably abnormality) is distinct enough that it can be recognized wherever it occurs, for it is carried within the person. If, on the other hand, the sanity of the pseudopatients were never discovered, serious difficulties would arise for those who support traditional modes of psychiatric diagnosis. Given that the hospital staff was not incompetent, that the pseudopatient had been behaving as sanely as he had been outside of the hospital, and that it had never been previously suggested that he belonged in a psychiatric hospital, such an unlikely outcome would support the view that psychiatric diagnosis betrays little about the patient but much about the environment in which an observer finds him.

This article describes such an experiment. Eight sane people gained secret admission to twelve different hospitals. Their diagnostic experiences constitute the data of the first part of this article; the remainder is devoted to a description of their experiences in psychiatric institutions. Too few psychiatrists and psychologists, even those who have worked in such hospitals, know what the experience is like. They rarely talk about it with former patients, perhaps because they distrust information coming from the previously insane. Those who have worked in psychiatric hospitals are likely to have adapted so thoroughly to the settings that they are insensitive to the impact of that experience. And while there have been occasional reports of researchers who submitted themselves to psychiatric hospitalization, these researchers have commonly remained in the hospitals for short periods of time, often with the knowledge of the hospital staff. It is difficult to know the extent to which they were treated like patients or like research colleagues. Nevertheless, their reports about the inside of the psychiatric hospital have been valuable. This article extends those efforts.

Pseudopatients and Their Settings

The eight pseudopatients were a varied group. One was a psychology graduate student in his 20s. The remaining seven were older and "established." Among them were three psychologists, a pediatrician, a psychiatrist, a painter, and a housewife. Three pseudopatients were women, five were men. All of them employed pseudonyms, lest their alleged diagnoses embarrass them later. Those who were in mental health professions alleged another occupation in order to avoid the special attentions that might be accorded by staff, as a matter of courtesy or caution, to ailing colleagues. With the exception of myself (I was the first pseudopatient and my presence was known to the hospital administrator and chief psychologist and, so far as I can tell, to them alone), the presence of pseudopatients and the nature of the research program were not known to the hospital staffs.

The settings were similarly varied. In order to generalize the findings, admission into a variety of hospitals was sought. The twelve hospitals in the sample were located in five different states on the East and West coasts. Some were old and shabby, some were quite new. Some were research-oriented, others not. Some had good staff-patient ratios, others were quite understaffed. Only one was a strictly private hospital. All of the others were supported by state or federal funds or, in one instance, by university funds.

After calling the hospital for an appointment, the pseudopatient arrived at the admissions office complaining that he had been hearing voices. Asked what the voices said, he replied that they were often unclear, but as far as he could tell they said "empty," "hollow," and "thud." The voices were unfamiliar and were of the same sex as the pseudopatient. The choice of these symptoms was occasioned by their apparent similarity to existential symptoms. Such symptoms are alleged to arise from painful concerns about the perceived meaninglessness of one's life. It is as if the hallucinating person were saying, "My life is empty and hollow." The choice of these symptoms was also determined by the *absence* of a single report of existential psychoses in the literature.

Beyond alleging the symptoms and falsifying name, vocation, and employment, no further alterations of person, history, or circumstances were made. The significant events of the pseudopatient's life history were presented as they had actually occurred. Relationships with parents and siblings, with spouse and children, with people at work and in school, consistent with the aforementioned exceptions, were described as they were or had been. Frustrations and upsets were described along with joys and satisfactions. These facts are important to remember. If anything, they strongly biased the subsequent results in favor of detecting sanity, since none of their histories or current behaviors were seriously pathological in any way.

Immediately upon admission to the psychiatric ward, the pseudopatient ceased simulating *any* symptoms of abnormality. In some cases, there was a brief period of mild nervousness and anxiety, since none of the pseudopatients really believed that they would be admitted so easily. Indeed, their shared fear was that they would be immediately exposed as frauds and greatly embarrassed. Moreover, many of them had never visited a psychiatric ward; even those who had, nevertheless had some genuine fears about what might happen to them. Their nervousness, then, was quite appropriate to the novelty of the hospital setting, and it abated rapidly.

Apart from that short-lived nervousness, the pseudopatient behaved on the ward as he "normally" behaved. The pseudopatient spoke to patients and staff as he might ordinarily. Because there is uncommonly little to do on a psychiatric ward, he attempted to engage others in conversation. When asked by staff how he was feeling, he indicated that he was fine, that he no longer experienced symptoms. He responded to instructions from attendants, to calls for medication (which was not swallowed), and to dining-hall instructions. Beyond such activities as were available to him on the admissions ward, he spent his time writing down his observations about the ward, its patients, and the staff. Initially these notes were written "secretly," but as it soon became clear that no one much cared, they were subsequently written on standard tablets of paper in such public places as the dayroom. No secret was made of these activities.

The pseudopatient, very much as a true psychiatric patient, entered a hospital with no foreknowledge of when he would be discharged. Each was told that he would have to get out by his own devices, essentially by convincing the staff that he was sane. The psychological stresses associated with hospitalization were considerable, and all but one of the pseudopatients desired to be discharged almost immediately after being admitted. They were, therefore, motivated not only to behave sanely but to be paragons of cooperation. That their behavior was in no way disruptive is confirmed by nursing reports, which have been obtained on most of the patients. These reports uniformly indicate that the patients were "friendly," "cooperative," and "exhibited no abnormal indications."

The Normal Are Not Detectably Sane

Despite their public "show" of sanity, the pseudopatients were never detected. Admitted, except in one case, with a diagnosis of schizophrenia, each was discharged with a diagnosis of schizophrenia "in remission." The label "in remission" should in no way be dismissed as a formality, for at no time during any hospitalization had any question been raised about any pseudopatient's simulation. Nor are there any indications in the hospital records that the pseudopatient's status was suspect. Rather, the evidence is strong that, once labeled schizophrenic, the pseudopatient was stuck with that label. If the pseudopatient was to be discharged, he must naturally be "in remission"; but he was not sane, nor, in the institution's view, had he ever been sane.

The uniform failure to recognize sanity cannot be attributed to the quality of the hospitals, for, although there were considerable variations among them, several are considered excellent. Nor can it be alleged that there was simply not enough time to observe the pseudopatients. Length of hospitalization ranged from seven to fifty-two days, with an average of nineteen days. The pseudopatients were not, in fact, carefully observed, but this failure clearly speaks more to traditions within psychiatric hospitals than to lack of opportunity.

Finally, it cannot be said that the failure to recognize the pseudopatients' sanity was due to the fact that they were not behaving sanely. While there was clearly some tension present in all of them, their daily visitors could detect no serious behavioral consequences—nor, indeed, could other patients. It was quite common for the patients to "detect" the pseudopatients' sanity. During the first three hospitalizations, when accurate counts were kept, 35 of a total of 118 patients on the admissions ward voiced their suspicions, some vigorously. "You're not crazy. You're a journalist or a professor [referring to the continual note taking]. You're checking up on the hospital." While most of the patients were reassured by the pseudopatient's insistence that he had been sick before he came in but was fine now, some continued to believe that the pseudopatient was sane throughout his hospitalization. The fact that the patients often recognized normality when staff did not raises important questions.

Failure to detect sanity during the course of hospitalization may be due to the fact that physicians operate with a strong bias toward what statisticians call the type 2 error (see Scheff, 1966). This is to say that physicians are more inclined to call a healthy person sick (a false positive, type 2) than a sick person healthy (a false negative, type 1). The reasons for this are not hard to find: it is clearly more dangerous to misdiagnose illness than health. Better to err on the side of caution, to suspect illness even among the healthy.

But what holds for medicine does not hold equally well for psychiatry. Medical illnesses, while unfortunate, are not commonly pejorative. Psychiatric diagnoses, on the contrary, carry with them personal, legal, and social stigmas. It was therefore important to see whether the tendency toward diagnosing the sane insane could be reversed. The following experiment was arranged at a research and teaching hospital whose staff had heard these findings but doubted that such an error could occur in their hospital. The staff was informed that, at some time during the following three months, one or more pseudopatients would attempt to be admitted into the psychiatric hospital. Each staff member was asked to rate each patient who presented himself at admissions or on the ward according to the likelihood that the patient was a pseudopatient. A ten-point scale was used, with a 1 and 2 reflecting high confidence that the patient was a pseudopatient.

Judgments were obtained on 193 patients who were admitted for psychiatric treatment. All staff who had had sustained contact with or primary responsibility for the patient—attendants, nurses, psychiatrists, physicians, and psychologists—were asked to make judgments. Forty-one patients were alleged, with high confidence, to be pseudopatients by at least one member of the staff. Twenty-three were considered suspect by at least one psychiatrist. Nineteen were suspected by one psychiatrist *and* one other staff member. Actually, no genuine pseudopatient (at least from my group) presented himself during this period.

The experiment is instructive. It indicates that the tendency to designate sane people as insane can be reversed when the stakes (in this case, prestige and diagnostic acumen) are high. But what can be said of the nineteen people who were suspected of being "sane" by one psychiatrist and another staff member? Were these people truly "sane," or was it rather the case that in the course of avoiding the type 2 error the staff tended to make more errors of the first sort—calling the crazy "sane"? There is no way of knowing. But one thing is certain: any diagnostic process that lends itself so readily to massive errors of this sort cannot be a very reliable one.

The Stickiness of Psychodiagnostic Labels

Beyond the tendency to call the healthy sick—a tendency that accounts better for diagnostic behavior on admission than it does for such behavior after a lengthy period of exposure—the data speak to the massive role of labeling in psychiatric assessment. Having once been labeled schizophrenic, there is nothing the pseudopatient can do to overcome the tag. The tag profoundly color others' perceptions of him and his behavior.

From one viewpoint, these data are hardly surprising, for it has long been known that elements are given meaning by the context in which they occur. Gestalt psychology made this point vigorously, and Asch (1946, 1952) demonstrated that there are "central" personality traits (such as "warm" versus "cold") which are so powerful that they markedly color the meaning of other information in forming an impression of a given personality. "Insane," "schizophrenic," "manic-depressive," and "crazy" are probably among the most powerful of such central traits. Once a person is designated abnormal, all of his other behaviors and characteristics are colored by that label. Indeed, that label is so powerful that many of the pseudopatients' normal behaviors were overlooked entirely or profoundly misinterpreted. Some examples may clarify this issue.

Earlier I indicated that there were no changes in the pseudopatient's personal history and current status beyond those of name, employment, and, where necessary, vocation. Otherwise, a veridical description of personal history and circumstances was offered. Those circumstances were not psychotic. How were they made consonant with the diagnosis of psychosis? Or were those diagnoses modified in such a way as to bring them into accord with the circumstances of the pseudopatient's life, as described by him?

As far as I can determine, diagnoses were in no way affected by the relative health of the circumstances of a pseudopatient's life. Rather, the reverse occurred: the perception of his circumstances was shaped entirely by the diagnosis. A clear example of such translation is found in the case of a pseudopatient who had had a close relationship with his mother but was rather remote from his father during his early childhood. During adolescence and beyond, however, his father became a close friend, while his relationship with his mother cooled. His present relationship with his wife was characteristically close and warm. Apart from occasional angry exchanges, friction was minimal. The children had rarely been spanked. Surely there is nothing especially pathological about such a history. Indeed, many readers may see a similar pattern in their own experiences, with no markedly deleterious consequences. Observe, however, how such a history was translated in the psychopathological context, this from the case summary prepared after the patient was discharged.

> This white 39-year-old male . . . manifests a long history of considerable ambivalence in close relationships, which begins in early childhood. A warm rela-

tionship with his mother cools during his adolescence. A distant relationship to his father is described as becoming very intense. Affective stability is absent. His attempts to control emotionality with his wife and children are punctuated by angry outbursts and, in the case of the children, spankings. And while he says that he has several good friends, one senses considerable ambivalence embedded in those relationships also.

The facts of the case were unintentionally distorted by the staff to achieve consistency with a popular theory of the dynamics of a schizophrenic reaction (Rosenthal and Jacobson, 1968). Nothing of an ambivalent nature had been described in relations with parents, spouse, or friends. To the extent that ambivalence could be inferred, it was probably not greater than is found in all human relationships. It is true the pseudopatient's relationships with his parents changed over time, but in the ordinary context that would hardly be remarkable—indeed, it might very well be expected. Clearly, the meaning ascribed to his verbalizations (that is, ambivalence, affective instability) was determined by the diagnosis: schizophrenia. An entirely different meaning would have been ascribed if it were known that the man was "normal."

All pseudopatients took extensive notes publicly. Under ordinary circumstances, such behavior would have raised questions in the minds of observers, as, in fact, it did among patients. Indeed, it seemed so certain that the notes would elicit suspicion that elaborate precautions were taken to remove them from the ward each day. But the precautions proved needless. The closest any staff member came to questioning these notes occurred when one pseudopatient asked his physician what kind of medication he was receiving and began to write down the response. "You needn't write it," he was told gently. "If you have trouble remembering, just ask me again."

If no questions were asked of the pseudopatients, how was their writing interpreted? Nursing records for three patients indicate that the writing was seen as an aspect of their pathological behavior. "Patient engages in writing behavior" was the daily nursing comment on one of the pseudopatients who was never questioned about his writing. Given that the patient is in the hospital, he must be psychologically disturbed. And given that he is disturbed, continuous writing must be a behavioral manifestation of that disturbance, perhaps a subset of the compulsive behaviors that are sometimes correlated with schizophrenia.

One tacit characteristic of psychiatric diagnosis is that it locates the sources of aberration within the individual and only rarely within the complex of stimuli that surrounds him. Consequently, behaviors that are stimulated by the environment are commonly misattributed to the patient's disorder. For example, one kindly nurse found a pseudopatient pacing the long hospital corridors. "Nervous, Mr. X?" she asked. "No, bored," he said.

The notes kept by pseudopatients are full of patient behaviors that were misinterpreted by well-intentioned staff. Often enough, a patient would go "berserk" because he had, wittingly or unwittingly, been mistreated by, say, an attendant. A nurse coming upon the scene would rarely inquire even cursorily into the environmental stimuli of the patient's behavior. Rather, she assumed that his upset derived from his pathology, not from his present interactions with other staff members. Occasionally, the staff might assume that the patient's family (especially when they had recently visited) or other patients had stimulated the outburst. But never were the staff found to assume that one of themselves or the structure of the hospital had anything to do with a patient's behavior. One psychiatrist pointed to a group of patients who were sitting outside the cafeteria entrance half an hour before lunchtime. To a group of young residents he indicated that such behavior was characteristic of the oral-acquisitive nature of the syndrome. It seemed not to occur to him that there were very few things to anticipate in a psychiatric hospital besides eating.

A psychiatric label has a life and an influence of its own. Once the impression has been formed that the patient is schizophrenic, the expectation is that he will continue to be schizophrenic. When a sufficient amount of time has passed, during which the patient has done nothing bizarre, he is considered to be in remission and available for discharge. But the label endures beyond discharge, with the unconfirmed expectation that he will behave as a schizophrenic again. Such labels, conferred by mental health professionals, are as influential on the patient as they are on his relatives and friends, and it should not surprise anyone that the diagnosis acts on all of them as a self-fulfilling prophecy (see Rosenthal and Jacobson, 1968). Eventually, the patient himself accepts the diagnosis, with all of its surplus meanings and expectations, and behaves accordingly.

The inferences to be made from these matters are quite simple. Much as Zigler and Phillips (1961) have demonstrated that there is enormous overlap in the symptoms presented by patients who have been variously diagnosed, so there is enormous overlap in the behaviors of the sane and the insane. The sane are not "sane" all of the time. We lose our tempers "for no good reason." We are occasionally depressed or anxious, again for no good reason. And we may find it difficult to get along with one or another person—again for no reason that we can specify. Similarly, the insane are not always insane. Indeed, it was the impression of the pseudopatients while living with them that they were sane for long periods of time—that the bizarre behaviors upon which their diagnoses were allegedly predicated constituted only a small fraction of their total behavior. If it makes no sense to label ourselves permanently depressed on the basis of an occasional depression, then it takes better evidence than is presently available to label all patients insane or schizophrenic on the basis of bizarre behaviors or cognitions. It seems more useful, as Mischel (1968) has pointed out, to limit our discussions to *behaviors,* the stimuli that provoke them, and their correlates.

It is not known why powerful impressions of personality traits, such as "crazy" or "insane," arise. Conceivably, when the origins of and stimuli that give rise to a behavior are remote or unknown, or when the behavior strikes us as immutable, trait labels regarding the *behaver* arise. When, on the other hand, the origins and stimuli are known and available, discourse is limited to the behavior itself. Thus, I may hallucinate because I am sleeping, or I may hallucinate because I have ingested a peculiar drug. These are termed sleep-induced hallucinations, or dreams, and drug-induced hallucinations, respectively. But when the stimuli to my hallucinations are unknown, that is called craziness, or schizophrenia—as if that inference were somehow as illuminating as the others.

The Experience of Psychiatric Hospitalization

The term *mental illness* is of recent origin. It was coined by people who were humane in their inclinations and who wanted very much to raise the station of (and the public's sympathies toward) the psychologically disturbed from that of witches and "crazies" to one that was akin to the physically ill. And they were at least partially successful, for the treatment of the mentally ill *has* improved considerably over the years. But while treatment has improved, it is doubtful that people really regard the mentally ill in the same way that they view the physically ill. A broken leg is something one recovers from, but mental illness allegedly endures forever. A broken leg does not threaten the observer, but a crazy schizophrenic? There is by now a host of evidence that attitudes toward the mentally ill are characterized by fear, hostility, aloofness, suspicion, and dread. The mentally ill are society's lepers.

That such attitudes infect the general population is perhaps not surprising, only upsetting. But that they affect the professionals—attendants, nurses, physicians, psychologists, and social workers—who treat and deal with the mentally ill is more disconcerting, both because such attitudes are self-evidently pernicious and because they are unwitting. Most mental health professionals would insist that they are sympathetic toward the mentally ill, that they are neither avoidant nor hostile. But it is more likely that an exquisite ambivalence characterizes their relations with psychiatric patients, such that their avowed impulses are only part of their entire attitude. Negative attitudes are there too and can easily be detected. Such attitudes should not surprise us. They are the natural offspring of the labels patients wear and the places in which they are found.

Consider the structure of the typical psychiatric hospital. Staff and patients are strictly segregated. Staff have their own living space, including their dining facilities, bathrooms, and assembly places. The glassed quarters that contain the professional staff, which the pseudopatients came to call "the cage," sit out on every dayroom. The staff emerge primarily for caretaking purposes—to give medication, to conduct a therapy or group meeting, to instruct or reprimand a patient. Otherwise, staff keep to themselves, almost as if the disorder that afflicts their charges is somehow catching.

So much is patient-staff segregation the rule that, for four public hospitals in which an attempt was made to measure the degree to which staff and patients mingle, it was necessary to use "time out of the staff cage" as the operational measure. While it was not the case that all time spent out of the cage was spent mingling with patients (attendants, for example, would occasionally emerge to watch television in the dayroom), it was the only way in which one could gather reliable data on time for measuring.

The average amount of time spent by attendants outside of the cage was 11.3 percent (range, 3 to 52 percent). This figure does not represent only time spent mingling with patients, but also includes time spent on such chores as folding laundry, supervising patients while they shave, directing ward cleanup, and sending patients to off-ward activities. It was the relatively rare attendant who spent time talking with patients or playing games with them. It proved impossible to obtain a "percent mingling time" for nurses, since the amount of time they spent out of the cage was too brief. Rather, we counted instances of emergence from the cage. On the average, daytime nurses emerged from the cage 11.5 times per shift, including instances when they left the ward entirely (range, 4 to 39 times). Late afternoon and night nurses were even less available, emerging on the average 9.4 times per shift (range, 4 to 41 times). Data on early morning nurses, who arrived usually after midnight and departed at 8 a.m., are not available because patients were asleep during most of this period.

Physicians, especially psychiatrists, were even less available. They were rarely seen on the wards. Quite commonly, they would be seen only when they arrived and departed, with the remaining time being spent in their offices or in the cage. On the average, physicians emerged on the ward 6.7 times per day (range, 1 to 17 times). It proved difficult to make an accurate estimate in this regard, since physicians often maintained hours that allowed them to come and go at different times.

The hierarchical organization of the psychiatric hospital has been commented on before (Stanton and Schwartz, 1954), but the latent meaning of that kind of organization is worth noting again. Those with the most power have least to do with patients, and those with the least power are most involved with them. Recall, however, that the acquisition of role-appropriate behaviors occurs mainly through the observation of others, with the most powerful having the most influence. Consequently, it is understandable that attendants not only spend more time with patients than do any other members of the staff—that is required by their station in the hierarchy—but also, insofar as they learn from their superiors' behavior, spend as little time with patients as they can. Attendants are seen mainly in the cage, which is where the models, the action, and the power are.

I turn now to a different set of studies, these dealing with staff response to patient-initiated contact. It has long been known that the amount of time a person spends with you can be an index of your significance to him. If he initiates and maintains eye contact, there is reason to believe that he is considering your requests and needs. If he pauses to chat or actually stops and talks, there is added reason to infer that he is individuating you. In four hospitals, the pseudopatient approached the staff member with a request which took the following form: "Pardon me, Mr. [or Dr. or Mrs.] X, could you tell me when I will be eligible for grounds privileges?" (or " . . . when I will be presented at the staff meeting?" or ". . . when I am likely to be discharged?"). While the content of the question varied according to the appropriateness of the target and the pseudopatient's (apparent) current needs, the form was always a courteous and relevant request for information. Care was taken never to approach a particular member of the staff more than once a day, lest the staff member become suspicious or irritated. In examining these data, remember that the behavior of the pseudopatients was neither bizarre nor disruptive. One could indeed engage in good conversation with them.

The data for these experiments are shown in Table 1, separately for physicians (column 1) and for nurses and attendants (column 2). Minor differences between these four institutions were overwhelmed by the degree to which staff avoided continuing contacts that patients had initiated. By far their most common response consisted of either a brief response to the question, offered while they were "on the move" and with head averted, or no response at all.

The encounter frequently took the following bizarre form: (pseudopatient) "Pardon me, Dr. X. Could you tell me when I am eligible for grounds privileges?" (physician) "Good morning, Dave. How are you today?" (Moves off without waiting for a response.)

It is instructive to compare these data with data recently obtained at Stanford University. It has been alleged that large and eminent universities are characterized by faculty who are so busy that they have no time for students. For this comparison, a young lady approached individual faculty members who seemed to be walking purposefully to some meeting or teaching engagement and asked them the following six questions:

1. "Pardon me, could you direct me to Encina Hall?" (at the medical school: ". . . to the Clinical Research Center?").
2. "Do you know where Fish Annex is?" [There is no Fish Annex at Stanford.]
3. "Do you teach here?"
4. "How does one apply for admission to the college?" (at the medical school: ". . . to the medical school?").
5. "Is it difficult to get in?"
6. "Is there financial aid?"

Without exception, as can be seen in Table 1 (column 3), all of the questions were answered. No matter how rushed they were, all respondents not only maintained eye contact but stopped to talk. Indeed, many of the respondents went out of their way to direct

Table 1. Self-Initiated Contact by Pseudopatients with Psychiatrists and Nurses and Attendants, Compared to Contact with Other Groups

Contact	Psychiatric Hospitals		University Campus (nonmedical)	University Medical Center Physicians		
	(1) Psychiatrists	(2) Nurses and Attendants	(3) Faculty	(4) "Looking for a psychiatrist"	(5) "Looking for an internist"	(6) No Additional Comment
Responses						
Moves on, head averted (%)	71	88	0	0	0	0
Makes eye contact (%)	23	10	0	11	0	0
Pauses and chats (%)	2	2	0	11	0	10
Stops and talks (%)	4	0.5	100	78	100	90
Mean number of questions answered (out of 6)	a	a	6	3.8	4.8	4.5
Respondents (No.)	13	47	14	18	15	10
Attempts (No.)	185	1,283	14	18	15	10

[a]Not applicable.

or take the questioner to the office she was seeking, to try to locate "Fish Annex," or to discuss with her the possibilities of being admitted to the university.

Similar data, also shown in Table 1 (columns 4, 5, and 6), were obtained in the hospital. Here, too, the young lady came prepared with six questions. After the first question, however, she remarked to eighteen of her respondents (column 4), "I'm looking for a psychiatrist," and to fifteen others (column 5). "I'm looking for an internist." Ten other respondents received no inserted comment (column 6). The general degree of cooperative responses is considerably higher for these university groups than it was for pseudopatients in psychiatric hospitals. Even so, differences are apparent within the medical school setting. Once having indicated that she was looking for a psychiatrist, the degree of cooperation elicited was less than when she sought an internist.

Powerlessness and Depersonalization

Eye contact and verbal contact reflect concern and individuation; their absence, avoidance and depersonalization. The data I have presented do not do justice to the rich daily encounters that grew up around matters of depersonalization and avoidance. I have records of patients who were beaten by staff for the sin of having initiated verbal contact. During my own experience, for example, one patient was beaten in the presence of other patients for having approached an attendant and told him, "I like you." Occasionally, punishment meted out to patients for misdemeanors seemed so excessive that it could not be justified by the most radical interpretations of psychiatric canon. Nevertheless, they appeared to go unquestioned. Tempers were often short. A patient who had not heard a call for medication would be roundly excoriated, and the morning attendants would often wake patients with "Come on, you m—f—s, out of bed!"

Neither anecdotal nor "hard" data can convey the overwhelming sense of powerlessness which invades the individual as he is continually exposed to the depersonalization of the psychiatric hospital. It hardly matters *which* psychiatric hospital—the excellent public ones and the very plush private hospital were better than the rural and shabby ones in this regard, but, again, the features that psychiatric hospitals had in common overwhelmed by far their apparent differences.

Powerlessness was evident everywhere. The patient is deprived of many of his legal rights by dint of his psychiatric commitment. He is shorn of credibility by virtue of his psychiatric label. His freedom of movement is restricted. He cannot initiate contact with the staff but may only respond to such overtures as they make. Personal privacy is minimal. Patient quarters and possessions can be entered and examined by any staff member, for whatever reason. His personal history and anguish is available to any staff member (often including the "grey lady" and "candy striper" volunteer) who chooses to read his folder, regardless of their therapeutic relationship to him. His personal hygiene and waste evacuation are often monitored. The water closets may have no doors.

At times, depersonalization reached such proportions that pseudopatients had the sense that they were invisible, or at least unworthy of account. Upon being admitted, I and other pseudopatients took the initial physical examinations in a semipublic room, where staff members went about their own business as if we were not there.

On the ward, attendants delivered verbal and occasionally serious physical abuse to patients in the presence of other observing patients, some of whom (the pseudopatients) were writing it all down. Abusive behavior, on the other hand, terminated quite abruptly when other staff members were known to be coming. Staff are credible witnesses. Patients are not.

A nurse unbuttoned her uniform to adjust her brassiere in the presence of an entire ward of viewing men. One did not have the sense that she was being seductive. Rather, she didn't notice us. A group of staff persons might point to a patient in the dayroom and discuss him animatedly, as if he were not there.

One illuminating instance of depersonalization and invisibility occurred with regard to medications. All told, the pseudopatients were administered nearly 2,100 pills, including Elavil, Stelazine, Compazine, and Thorazine, to name but a few. (That such a variety of medications should have been administered to patients presenting identical symptoms is itself worthy of note.) Only two were swallowed. The rest were either pocketed or deposited in the toilet. The pseudopatients were not alone in this. Although I have no precise records on how many patients rejected their medications, the pseudopatients frequently found the medications of other patients in the toilet before they deposited their own. As long as they were cooperative, their behavior and the pseudopatients' own in this matter, as in other important matters, went unnoticed throughout.

Reactions to such depersonalization among pseudopatients were intense. Although they had come to the hospital as participant observers and were fully aware that they did not "belong," they nevertheless found themselves caught up in and fighting the process of depersonalization. Some examples: a graduate student in psychology asked his wife to bring his textbooks to the hospital so he could "catch up on his homework"—this despite the elaborate precautions taken to conceal his professional association. The same student, who had trained for quite some time to get into the hospital and who had looked forward to the experience, "remembered" some drag races that he had wanted to see on the weekend and insisted that he be discharged by that time. Another pseudopatient attempted a romance with a nurse. Subsequently, he informed the staff that he was applying for admission to graduate school in psychology and was very likely to be admitted, since a graduate professor was one of his regular hospital visitors. The same person began to engage in psychotherapy with other patients—all of this as a way of becoming a person in an impersonal environment.

The Sources of Depersonalization

What are the origins of depersonalization? I have already mentioned two. First are attitudes held by all of us toward the mentally ill—including those who treat them—attitudes characterized by fear, distrust, and horrible expectations on the one hand, and benevolent intentions on the other. Our ambivalence leads, in this instance as in others, to avoidance.

Second, and not entirely separate, the hierarchical structure of the psychiatric hospital facilitates depersonalization. Those who are at the top have least to do with patients, and their behavior inspires the rest of the staff. Average daily contact with psychiatrists, psychologists, residents, and physicians combined ranged from 3.9 to 25.1 minutes, with an overall mean of 6.8 (six pseudopatients over a total of 129 days of hospitalization). Included in this average are time spent in the admissions interview, ward meetings in the presence of a senior staff member, group and individual psychotherapy contacts, case presentation conferences, and discharge meetings. Clearly, patients do not spend much time in interpersonal contact with doctoral staff. And doctoral staff serve as models for nurses and attendants.

There are probably other sources. Psychiatric installations are presently in serious financial straits. Staff shortages are pervasive, staff time at a premium. Something has to give, and that something is patient contact. Yet, while financial stresses are realities, too much can be made of them. I have the impression that the psychological forces that result in depersonalization are much stronger than the fiscal ones and that the addition of more staff would not correspondingly improve patient care in this regard. The incidence of staff meetings and the enormous amount of record keeping on patients, for example, have not been as substantially reduced as has patient contact. Priorities exist, even during hard times. Patient contact is not a significant priority in the traditional psychiatric hospital, and fiscal pressures do not account for this. Avoidance and depersonalization may.

Heavy reliance upon psychotropic medication tacitly contributes to depersonalization by convincing staff that treatment is indeed being conducted and that further patient contact may not be necessary. Even here, however, caution needs to be exercised in understanding the role of psychotropic drugs. If patients were powerful rather than powerless, if they were viewed as interesting individuals rather than diagnostic entities, if they were socially significant rather than social lepers, if their anguish truly and wholly compelled our sympathies and concerns, would we not *seek* contact with them, despite the availability of medications? Perhaps for the pleasure of it all?

The Consequences of Labeling and Depersonalization

Whenever the ratio of what is known to what needs to be known approaches zero, we tend to invent "knowledge" and assume that we understand more than we actually do. We seem unable to acknowledge that we simply don't know. The needs for diagnosis and remediation of behavioral and emotional problems are enormous. But rather than acknowledge that we are just embarking on understanding, we continue to label patients "schizophrenic," "manic-depressive," and "insane," as if in those words we had captured the essence of understanding. The facts of the matter are that we have known for a long time that diagnoses are often not useful or reliable, but we have nevertheless continued to use them. We now know that we cannot distinguish insanity from sanity. It is depressing to consider how that information will be used.

Not merely depressing, but frightening. How many people, one wonders, are sane but not recognized as such in our psychiatric institutions? How many have been needlessly stripped of their privileges of citizenship, from the right to vote and drive to that of handling their own accounts? How many have feigned insanity in order to avoid the criminal consequences of their behavior, and, conversely, how many would rather stand trial than live interminably in a psychiatric hospital—but are wrongly thought to be mentally ill? How many have been stigmatized by well-intentioned, but nevertheless erroneous, diagnoses? On the last point, recall again that a "type 2 error" in psychiatric diagnosis does not have the same consequences it does in medical diagnosis. A diagnosis of cancer that has been found to be in error is cause for celebration. But psychiatric diagnoses are rarely found to be in error. The label sticks, a mark of inadequacy forever.

Finally, how many patients might be "sane" outside the psychiatric hospital but seem insane in it—not because craziness resides in them, as it were, but because they are responding to a bizarre setting, one that may be unique to institutions which harbor nether people? Goffman (1961) calls the process of socialization to such institutions "mortification"—an apt metaphor that includes the processes of depersonalization that have been described here. And while it is impossible to know whether the pseudo-patients' responses to these processes are characteristic of all inmates—they were, after all, not real patients—it is difficult to believe that these processes of socialization to a psychiatric hospital provide useful attitudes or habits of response for living in the "real world."

Summary and Conclusions

It is clear that we cannot distinguish the sane from the insane in psychiatric hospitals. The hospital itself imposes a special environment in which the meanings of behavior can easily be misunderstood. The consequences to patients hospitalized in such an environment—the powerlessness, depersonalization, segregation, mortification, and self-labeling—seem undoubtedly countertherapeutic.

I do not, even now, understand this problem well enough to perceive solutions. But two matters seem to have some promise. The first concerns the proliferation of community mental health facilities, of crisis intervention centers, of the human potential movement, and of behavior therapies that, for all of their own problems, tend to avoid psychiatric labels, to focus on specific problems and behaviors, and to retain the individual in a relatively nonpejorative environment. Clearly, to the extent that we refrain from sending the distressed to insane places, our impressions of them are less likely to be distorted. (The risk of distorted perceptions, it seems to me, is always present, since we are much more sensitive to an individual's behaviors and verbalizations than we are to the subtle contextual stimuli that often promote them. At issue here is a matter of magnitude. And, as I have shown, the magnitude of distortion is exceedingly high in the extreme context that is a psychiatric hospital.)

The second matter that might prove promising speaks to the need to increase the sensitivity of mental health workers and researchers to the *Catch 22* position of psychiatric patients. Simply reading materials in this area will be of help to some such workers and researchers. For others, directly experiencing the impact of psychiatric hospitalization will be of enormous use. Clearly, further research into the social psychology of such total institutions will both facilitate treatment and deepen understanding.

I and the other pseudopatients in the psychiatric setting had distinctly negative reactions. We do not pretend to describe the subjective experiences of true patients. Theirs may be different from ours, particularly with the passage of time and the necessary process of adaptation to one's environment. But we can and do speak to the relatively more objective indices of treatment within the hospital. It could be a mistake, and a very unfortunate one, to consider that what happened to us derived from malice or stupidity on the part of the staff. Quite the contrary, our overwhelming impression of them was of people who really cared, who were committed, and who were uncommonly intelligent. Where they failed, as they sometimes did painfully, it would be more accurate to attribute those failures to the environment in which they, too, found themselves than to personal callousness. Their perceptions and behavior were controlled by the situation, rather than being motivated by a malicious disposition. In a more benign environment, one that was less attached to global diagnosis, their behaviors and judgments might have been more benign and effective.

References

Asch, S. E. "Forming Impressions of Personality." *Journal of Abnormal and Social Psychology,* 1946, *41,* 258-290.

Asch, S. E. *Social Psychology.* Englewood Cliffs, N.J.: Prentice-Hall, 1952.

Benedict, R. "Anthropology and the Abnormal." *Journal of General Psychology,* 1934, *10,* 59-80.

Goffman, E. *Asylums.* New York: Doubleday, 1961.

Mischel, W. *Personality and Assessment.* New York: Wiley, 1968.

Rosenthal, R., and Jacobson, L. *Pygmalion in the Classroom.* New York: Holt, Rinehart and Winston, 1968.

Scheff, T. J. *Being Mentally Ill: A Sociological Theory.* Chicago: Aldine, 1966.

Stanton, A. H., and Schwartz, M. S. *The Mental Hospital: A Study of Institutional Participation in Psychiatric Illness and Treatment.* New York: Basic Books, 1954.

Zigler, E., and Phillips, L. "Psychiatric Diagnosis and Symptomatology." *Journal of Abnormal and Social Psychology,* 1961, *63,* 69-75.

7

Multinational Corporations and International Professional Associations

William M. Evan

The sociology of organizations has for some years been preoccupied with problems of intraorganizational dynamics, principally in the context of industrial organizations. Only recently has a shift occurred in the angle of vision, with some researchers focusing on problems of interorganizational dynamics (Evan, 1972; Hirsch, 1972; Baty, Evan, and Rothermel, 1971; Turk, 1970; Litwak and Rothman, 1970; Aiken and Hage, 1968; Thompson, 1967; Evan, 1966; Emery and Trist, 1965). Another development, as yet embryonic, is a concern with cross-national comparative research in order to discover the effects of the sociocultural environment on organizational behavior (Boddewyn and Nath, 1970).

Under the circumstances, it is not surprising that scant research attention has been paid to organizations operating in what political scientists and others call the international system (Brams, 1969; Miles, 1968; Galtung, 1967). I refer to two categories of international or multinational organizations: one, a private, profit organization which in recent years has come to be designated as the "multinational corporation," and the other, an international professional association, a nonprofit, voluntary association often characterized as an international, nongovernmental organization and abbreviated as INGO (Skjelsbaek, 1971). Since World War II both types of organizations have undergone rapid growth (Skjelsbaek, 1971; Wells, 1971). Both organizations also involve participation of occupational elites—business executives and members of various professions—whose collective efforts could have far-reaching consequences, particularly for the state of the international system.

These two organizations pose intricate and challenging problems for the sociology of organizations. They raise questions not only of interorganizational dynamics but also of the interaction between organizations and their societal and intersocietal environment. In effect, such questions compel the researcher to shift his focus to a level of analysis more macroscopic than the boundaries of a formal organization (Evan, 1966, p. 188).

The purpose of this paper is to explore some features of multinational corporations and international professional associations as they bear on the degree of integration of the international system.

Reprinted from *Human Relations,* 1974, *27* (6), 587-625, in slightly abridged form, with the permission of the author and Plenum Publishing Corporation.

Alternative Models of Integration of the International System

It is indeed interesting that the term *international organization,* as used by most political scientists and other scholars in the field of international relations, refers to the interaction of nation-states (Haas, 1965; Luard, 1966). Haas, acknowledging the ambiguity of the term, states that "A loose definition of international organization . . . would say that it consists of intergovernmental institutions, members of which perceive each other to be basic units of the world polity" (1965, p. 505). The widespread assumption underlying this usage is that the international system is composed of various relationships among sovereign actors. In order to improve the prospects for peace between nations, it is necessary to generate normative integration—that is, a commitment to a common set of values and norms—through the mechanism of a universal intergovernmental organization. With the aid of multilateral agreements, a complex of intergovernmental organizations is created which builds commitment among nation-states to a body of international law designed to increase the forces for international order. With an increase in the level of normative integration, the international system evolves in the direction of a world community of peaceful sovereign states. In effect, the model implicit in this conception of the international system, diagramed in Figure 1, involves a direct linear process of normative

Figure 1. Direct Linear Model of Integration of the International System

integration increasing as a function of interaction of nation-states within the framework of intergovernmental organizations.

This model guided the formation of the League of Nations and, to some extent, that of the United Nations as well. The failure of the League of Nations to evoke compliance on the part of its sovereign members undermined its authority as well as its capability of generating normative integration. Without abridging national sovereignty, membership in an intergovernmental organization is neither a necessary nor a sufficient condition for the development of normative integration. Nor is normative integration a sufficient condition for significantly transforming the international system. Other modes of integration—notably economic, organizational, and occupational—which create new patterns of interdependence, are essential if the international system is to undergo a major transformation (Galtung, 1968).

The failure of the League of Nations was not lost on some of its former members in Western Europe. After World War II they began to explore problems of economic integration via regional organizations which would impose limitations on national sovereignty. The Economic and Steel Community, founded in 1952, was conceived as a supranational organization which paved the way for the more inclusive European Economic Community in 1958 (Haas, 1958; Schokking and Anderson, 1960). Among the Communist countries of Eastern Europe and the Soviet Union, a similar movement toward economic integration was initiated, which gave rise in 1949 to the Council on Mutual Economic Aid (CEMA or COMECON) (Grzybowski, 1964). Similar regional organizations have since emerged in Latin America (the Latin American Free Trade Area and the Central American Common Market), Africa, and elsewhere (Nye, 1970).

The UN Charter recognizes regional organizations and seeks to bring them into closer relations with the United Nations (Articles 32-54). And yet this has thus far not led to any structural changes in the UN to foster the growth of regional organizations, to encourage interactions among regional organizations, and to incorporate them within its structure, as has been proposed (Evan, 1962, pp. 396-398). In addition, of the 135 nation-states that are members of the UN, only a small proportion are actively involved in regional organizations. Thus, although the model underlying regionalism, as diagramed in Figure 2, shows much promise of generating economic and normative integration in the

Figure 2. Indirect Linear Model of Integration of the International System

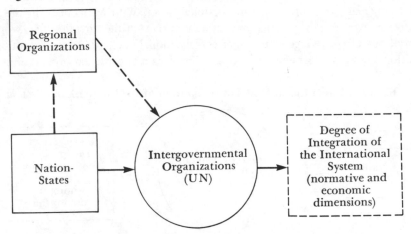

international system, it is probably premature to assess its effectiveness in this regard. However, it is doubtful whether, in the absence of an infrastructure of multinational, nongovernmental organizations of a profit and nonprofit variety, adequate system linkages can be forged among nation-states, regional organizations, and intergovernmental organizations. This conjecture about the potential role of multinational nongovernmental organizations suggests a complex, nonlinear model of integration of the international system, to which I now turn.

With few exceptions, social scientists engaged in the sociology of organizations, the sociology of occupations, and in the study of international relations have ignored the international, nongovernmental organization, in general, and the international professional association, in particular (White, 1951; Evan, 1962; Smoker, 1965; Galtung, 1967; Angell, 1968, pp. 240-243; Kriesberg, 1968). By contrast, researchers in international business and international economics have recently begun to speculate about and inquire into the multinational corporation (Robinson, 1967, 1969; Vernon, 1967; Fouraker and Stopford, 1968; Kindleberger, 1969; Behrman, 1969a, 1969b; Rolfe, 1969; Perlmutter, 1969a). Under the circumstances, it should come as no surprise that the functions of these organizations in the international system have not yet been systematically studied, much less clarified. Our basic assumption is that because these types of organizations are simultaneously subnational, cross-national, and multinational in character, they already provide or may provide in the future many significant linkages between nation-states, regional organizations, and intergovernmental organizations, thus contributing to the process of *normative, economic, organizational,* and *occupational* integration of the international system.

Instead of conceptualizing the international system with the aid of a direct or an indirect linear model of integration, as shown in Figures 1 and 2, a complex, nonlinear model with a variety of feedback loops is presented in Figure 3. Nation-states, particu-

Figure 3. Nonlinear Model of Integration of the International System

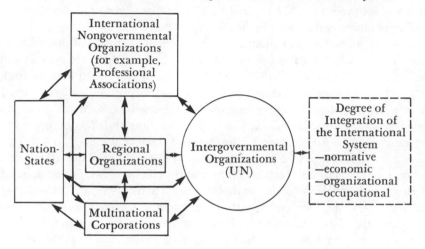

larly those that are highly industrialized, give rise to multinational corporations; that is, enterprises that develop production, research, and distribution facilities in various countries of the world. Nation-states also spawn a multitude of nongovernmental organizations —a high proportion of which consist of professional associations—which become federated at the international level. Some of these nongovernmental, nonprofit organizations are accorded official consultative status under the UN Charter (Article 71).

Each type of organization has mutual interactions with regional organizations; and although there are as yet few linkages between the multinational corporation and the international professional association, they are likely to develop in the future as these organizations discover their intersecting interests in common third parties such as nation-states, regional organizations, and various intergovernmental organizations. Occupations whose activities fall within multinational corporations and those that are organized into international occupational associations are growing in number and diversity. As these types of organizations proliferate, an increasing proportion of members within a growing population of occupations will perform part of their occupational roles in foreign contexts.

Collectively and cumulatively, multinational corporations, international nongovernmental organizations, and regional organizations interact with one another and with nation-states and intergovernmental organizations in such a manner as to increase the degree of integration of the international system along four dimensions: normative, economic, organizational, and occupational.

Growth and System Linkages

Multinational Corporations. Although the term *multinational corporation* has become current only in the past two decades, the phenomenon of international business operations is, of course, not new. "The first wave of foreign investment by manufacturing companies began in the closing decades of the nineteenth century and continued, gathering strength, up to 1914. Much of it was American, not only in Canada . . . but also in Europe. Between 1950 and 1967 the United States' capital stake in European manufacturing industry increased more than ten times, to a figure of $9,800,000,000 in the latter year" (Miles, 1969, p. 259). Other major industrial countries, such as Britain, France, West Germany, Canada, and Japan, have also participated in the burgeoning growth of the multinational corporation. And it is anticipated by some students of international business that the involvement of the Soviet Union and other Communist countries in multinational corporations will increase in the coming decade.

One of the factors that stimulated the exponential growth of multinational corporations in the past decade is the emergence of the European Economic Community (Rolfe, 1969, p. 11; Kaufmann, 1970, p. 103). It is now recognized that American corporations have taken more advantage of the economic opportunities created by this regional organization than European corporations themselves, so much so that it has prompted Servan-Schreiber to deplore this trend and exhort his fellow Europeans to ward off the invasion of the American enterprise (Servan-Schreiber, 1968).

For the first time in its history, the Union of International Associations included a section on multinational corporations in the twelfth edition of its *Yearbook on International Organizations* (Union of International Associations, 1969, pp. 1189-1214). In a preliminary survey, the *Yearbook* reports 7,045 parent companies in fourteen European countries and the United States with affiliates in one or more countries. Omitted from this survey are data on Japan, Canada, Communist countries, and others, presumably because they were unobtainable. A subset of these corporations with affiliates in ten or more countries, totaling 590, is listed by name, which suggested an analysis of the nationality of the corporate headquarters of these organizations. Of these relatively large multinational corporations, 46 percent are American, 26 percent are British, 7 percent are German, and 7 percent are French, with the remainder distributed among eight European countries. Underlying this uneven distribution of parent companies among countries is a differential in economic development. This is borne out by a statistically significant rank-order correlation coefficient of .39 (Kendall tau) between the number of multinational firms in a country and its GNP per capita.

Although no consensus has yet been reached as to the definition of a multinational corporation, it is evident from the foregoing discussion that we are dealing with a relatively large firm with extensive resources in many countries. "A multinational company does more than import and export from its . . . home plant. It may do research in Germany, engineering design in Japan, and then manufacture in Taiwan, Italy, and Mexico to supply a hundred national markets, including the . . . [home] market in which its headquarters may be located" (Rutenberg, 1970, p. B-337). To perform such highly complex operations in a multitude of differing environments, it is necessary to transfer products, capital, managers, and other technical personnel, as well as technology. The extensive transfer of the factors of production points to some of the effects—functional as well as dysfunctional—the multinational corporation is having on their host countries.

The most proximate effect is on the host countries in which affiliates are located. By employing nationals in various capacities, from unskilled laborers to professional and managerial personnel, the parent company creates many new employment and career opportunities in the host country. While no overall figure is available as regards the number of people employed in various countries by the 7,045 multinational corporations reported in the *Yearbook,* one estimate for approximately 3,000 American parent companies is 5,000,000 foreign employees, a staggering number which exceeds the size of the labor force of many countries. And for 1,000 Swedish companies operating in seventy countries, the estimate is 200,000 foreign employees (Kindleberger, 1969, p. 88). Invariably, employees in host countries are the recipients of new bodies of knowledge and skills essential to man the technology transferred by the parent company (Rolfe, 1969, pp. 48-60). As one researcher on the transfer of technology observes: "Repeatedly, multinational companies operate training programs for host country nationals on a scale which is equivalent to adding a large technical high school in the country. They train nationals as operators, functional executives, and eventually as top managers. Trained people who leave such companies often seed domestic organizations with competent personnel and so diffuse know-how elsewhere in the economy" (Quinn, 1969, p. 152).

Apart from such beneficial effects on a segment of the host country's labor force and, in turn, on the standard of living of employees, the inflow of foreign capital potentially stimulates economic development. On the other hand, the outflow of capital from the home country of the parent corporation may have dysfunctions for the labor force in question. Trade union officials in the United States point to a net loss of 400,000 jobs over five years due to capital and technology transfers by multinational firms (Adam, 1971; "Why Unions Fear the Multinationals," 1970). To counteract the threat posed by the internationalization of the corporation, trade unions are developing strategies for multinational union organization and collective bargaining (Casserini, 1972).

As for reciprocal effects—that is, from the host country on the parent company— several are noteworthy. First, it grants the company legal protection of incorporation. Secondly, it subjects the company to taxation which may be of economic as well as political importance to the host government. And thirdly, as a condition for admission in the first place, particularly in a developing country, the parent company may be required to enter into a joint venture with the host government as a partner.

Less proximate effects of the multinational firm may be discerned in the changing relations between nation-states. By virtue of the fact that these firms operate production facilities in various countries, they stimulate trade among nation-states. And to the extent that they have recourse to vertical integration, international trade includes the transfer of products among affiliates of multinational firms.

> Trade is no longer simply the result of national middlemen in one country interacting with importers in another. International firms have taken over, and there is every indication that international business is now the dominant factor in determining changes in the pattern of world exports as well as capital flows. . . . The movement of goods across national boundaries becomes foreign trade and exports even though the goods are only being transferred from one unit of the firm to another unit of the same firm to another unit of the same firm. . . . A large and growing share of world exports and changes in them are . . . accounted for by internal product movements of the international company [Robock and Simmonds, 1970, pp. 6, 7, 13].

Moreover, because such firms often have similar operations in more than one country, there is a tendency, over time, to standardize technology (Behrman, 1969b, pp. 74-75; Kindleberger, 1969, pp. 84-86). There is also a tendency to standardize various policies, including wage scales. At least one international economist has suggested that such companies are exerting an influence in the direction of wage equalization, thus in the long run contributing to a reduction of one source of income inequality between nations (Kindleberger, 1969, pp. 34-35, 188).

Yet another impact of these firms on the relationships between nation-states is the recent emergence of what Perlmutter has called the "transideological venture" (Perlmutter, 1969b). To modernize their industrial plant, Communist countries have encouraged their state-owned enterprises to enter into coproduction contracts with Western firms. Such contracts usually provide for the cooperative manufacture of finished industrial products. A Western firm, as a rule, contributes a technologically sophisticated component which an Eastern firm uses to produce a finished product salable in highly competitive markets (Herman, 1969).

Operating within and between sovereign states exposes the multinational firm to various hazards, chief of which, of course, is nationalization by a host country. Other hazards do not affect all multinational firms alike. If the home government, as in the case of the United States, restricts expansion of enterprises through horizontal integration, such firms can be subject to antitrust law violations. Another restriction on the operations of multinational firms occurs when a home government, in exercising its rights of extraterritoriality, intervenes in the operations of a subsidiary in a host country. A case in point is when the United States, committed to a policy of preventing the proliferation of nuclear weapons, prohibits IBM's subsidiary in France from selling the French government a particular type of computer needed for the production of nuclear bombs (Kindleberger, 1969, p. 43).

Such risks and restrictions, stemming from the fact that the multinational company is a citizen of several sovereign states, have prompted some scholars to speculate about a new legal status for this type of organization. Instead of being subject to various sovereignties, they advocate that it be chartered, taxed, and controlled by an international organization, perhaps some agency of the UN (Robinson, 1964b, p. 224; 1967, p. 154). If such a transformation in legal status were ever wrought, the UN and the international system obviously would be the primary beneficiaries. The UN would have a greatly expanded source of income from many thousands of companies to finance adequately its own activities as well as the urgent development programs of many poor member states, thus substantially strengthening the economic, organizational, and normative levels of integration of the international system.

An ongoing study, initiated in 1972 by the Economic and Social Council of the UN, is considering alternative mechanisms for international regulation of the multinational corporation (United Nations, Department of Economic and Social Affairs, 1973). Various proposals are being entertained, such as "a multilaterally negotiated charter and an international organization . . . to administer it" (p. 92); "a GATT type of agreement for multinational corporations" (p. 92); "some general agreement on a code of conduct for multinational corporations" (p. 93); "an international company law . . . administered by a body of the signatory countries" (p. 93).

In short, the multinationalization of the corporation has brought into being a new "transnational actor," which intentionally or unintentionally affects nation-states and relations among nation-states (Vernon, 1971; Wells, 1971).

At the level of home and host countries, multinational corporations have dysfunctional as well as functional effects. Issues have been raised in home countries concerning exploitation of cheap labor markets, tampering with national sovereignty, suppression of local entrepreneurial initiative, and promotion of "dependencia" or neo-colonialism; in host countries, the loss of jobs due to the outflow of capital has aroused protests from trade unions.

At the aggregate level of the international system, the multinational corporation may also have dysfunctional as well as functional effects. Attention has focused on "hot money" movements (United Nations, Department of Economic and Social Affairs, 1973, pp. 60-65), effects of intracorporation transactions on international trade, and taxation of the multinational corporations. Nonetheless, the unintended functional effects of the operations of multinational firms in fostering international integration merit equal attention: new patterns of economic interdependence among nation-states, new networks of relationships among enterprises, new roles for occupations, new patterns of transnational relationships among occupations, and new norms or incipient norms governing the transactions of multinational firms with nation-states, regional organizations, intergovernmental organizations, and international nongovernmental organizations.

International Professional Associations. Although it antedates the multinational corporation, the international professional association is also essentially a twentieth-century phenomenon. What is more, like the multinational corporation, its growth rate in the past two decades has been impressive (Skjelsbaek, 1971). It is by far the most numerous and probably the most influential type of organization in the class usually referred to as international, nongovernmental organizations or INGOs. In a study of INGOs, Smoker found that the rate of formation between 1870 and 1960 has increased exponentially, except for two slumps associated with World Wars I and II (Smoker, 1965, pp. 640-641). This finding very likely applies to international professional associations as well.

From the perspective of the sociology of occupations, we are dealing with a group of occupations which are either full-fledged professions or in the process of professionalization (Evan, 1969, pp. 100-101). In either case, professional associations are formed in order to contribute to the fund of technical and systematic knowledge underlying an occupation, to promote an orientation of service to society rather than self-interest, and to increase autonomy in professional practice. Some professions have ancient origins, such as medicine, law, the ministry, and teaching; others have come into being as a result of the emergence of industrialism and the rise of modern science and technology.

In the development of modern science, it is also possible to identify a sequence of stages of professionalization, which, however, differs in some respects from that of engineering. Already at the stage of the formation of local professional associations, there is an active interest in facilitating the dissemination of knowledge and the collaboration among scientists across national boundaries. With the advent of modern science, learned societies and academies were founded, such as the Royal Society of London in 1662, the Académie des Sciences in 1666, and, several decades later, the Berlin Academy of Sciences and the Academy of St. Petersburg. In an address commemorating the 300th anniversary of Isaac Newton, the renowned Russian physicist Kapitza refers to Newton's active role in the affairs of the Royal Society. He observes that the Royal Society, "in contrast to all academies, has still the character of a nonstate society. . . . Since the very beginning of its existence, the Royal Society has maintained contact with many foreign scientists. Sometimes foreigners were elected as Foreign Members of the Society, including our scientists Euler, Kruzenshtern, Struve, Chebyshev, Mechnikov, Pavlov, Timiryazev, Golitsyn. . . . Since Newton's times, the Royal Society has maintained a lively contact with scientific societies the world over" (Haar, 1967, p. 139).

Until the eighteenth century, the scientific community was relatively small, and communication was facilitated by the use of common languages—Latin and French—and a common core of knowledge, since there were still few fields of specialization. With the growth of the scientific community and the multiplication of specialties in the nineteenth century, national and international associations arose. One of the oldest international scientific organizations, the International Meteorological Committee, was founded in 1872. Numerous international associations were subsequently founded, so that by the end of World War I there was a felt need for a new association to coordinate the multitude of scientific organizations, thus giving rise in 1919 to a super-INGO called the International Council of Scientific Associations.

For a more precise assessment of the growth of different types of international professional associations, we turn again to the invaluable *Yearbook* of the Union of International Associations. Over the years this organization has struggled with the problem of classifying INGOs. In its twelfth edition, nineteen categories of organizations are presented, from which I have selected the following six that appear to include a great variety of professional associations: social sciences; law, administration; professions, employers; economics, finance; technology, science; health, medicine (Union of International Associations, 1969, p. 13). Examining various editions of the *Yearbook* yielded data on the number of associations reported in each of these six categories for a sixty-year period, from 1909 to 1969.

The first noteworthy finding is that as of 1969 there were 757 international professional associations, which constitute 50 percent of the population of 1,515 active INGOs for that year. In all likelihood, this percentage underestimates the total number of INGOs that are in fact engaged in professional activities. A reclassification of the population of associations in the *Yearbook* would probably yield a higher percentage. Secondly, over a sixty-year period these associations have increased about tenfold; and during the last twenty years they have increased about 169 percent. The average annual percentage increase in the past two decades is about 9 percent, a striking growth rate which approximates that of the multinational corporation.

How widely is nation-state participation dispersed geographically as well as ideologically? An examination of the nationality of principal officials of 757 associations in the Union of International Associations suggests a rather uneven distribution; France tops the list with 202 officials while four countries (Guatemala, Peru, Malaysia and UAR) have but one official each. The correlation between the number of multinational firms in a country and the number of principal officials of international professional associations is .69 (Kendall tau; significant at the .0005 level). It suggests that this dimension of participation in international professional associations is in part a function of economic development, since as the development of a country increases, so does the proportion of professionals in the labor force. Some evidence in support of this interpretation is provided by partialling out the effect of economic development (as reflected in GNP/capita) on the rank-order correlation. When this is done, the original Kendall tau of .69 is reduced to .55.

Given the number and growth rate of international professional associations, what effect are they having on the process of integration of the international system? In the absence of relevant systematic research, I shall approximate an answer to this question with the aid of the nonlinear model of integration of the international system, presented in Figure 3. This entails mapping the interaction patterns of these organizations with other components of the international system. To do this, we shall first consider some of the activities of these organizations.

The principal functions of these associations are to convene congresses and other special meetings, publish conference proceedings and research reports, facilitate an exchange of visits, stimulate collaborative research, and so forth. In organizing a congress, the international professional association depends upon the cooperation and assistance of its member organizations in various countries. Of the estimated 3,000-4,000 international congresses of INGOs held annually (Judge, 1969, p. 144), involving at least one million people, probably half are convened by international professional associations. It is, therefore, no wonder that the problems of planning and managing congresses have themselves become the subject of international congresses (Union of International Associations, 1961).

On the occasion of the Fifth World Congress of Sociology in 1962, Lazarsfeld and Leeds pointed out that congresses perform three important interrelated functions: they afford an opportunity for personal contacts, stimulate joint research projects, and sensitize participants to theoretical perspectives of members from different countries (Lazarsfeld and Leeds, 1962). That personal contacts, in turn, increase sensitivity to foreign perspectives was recently noted by Marshall, a former president of the International Sociological Association:

> When representatives of countries in which the Marxist-Leninist philosophy prevails began to attend international congresses and meetings in Western Europe, and when, under the auspices of UNESCO, similar meetings were held in one or other of the countries of Eastern Europe, there was naturally some tension in the air, and mutual suspicion, tempered by curiosity and a genuine desire to understand. Friendly debate took place in its early stages, more as an exchange of views between two sides than as the free intercourse of independent minds. But by the early 1960s things had changed; the experience of attending fully representative international meetings had become a familiar one, and many of the participants were now old friends. Ideological differences still make themselves felt, of course, and they are sometimes stimulating and sometimes frustrating, but a big step forward has been made toward finding a common ground of scientific discourse on which all can meet without distinction of national origin or political allegiance. It remains to be seen whether, or within what space of time, this idea can be fully realized [UNESCO, 1966, p. 11].

The various functions performed by international professional associations tend to increase the bonds between the parent international organization, as it were, and the affiliated national organizations; that is, the national professional associations in the various nation-states. And by eliciting participation of national professional associations from various nation-states, the international professional association unintentionally creates a network of relationships between nation-states. This is especially true for those associations that are relatively free of ideology. Thus, for example, Kriesberg found that in health and science INGOs, in which consensus is presumably high, participation of professional associations from the United States and the USSR is higher than in INGOs in which consensus is low, such as those dealing with international relations, art, and religion (Kriesberg, 1968, p. 471).

There are also other links with nation-states, one of which is of considerable moment to the international professional association. The nation-state is the source of incorporation of this type of association; and depending on how liberal its incorporation law is, it affects the legal status of the association and, more specifically, such rights as owning property, holding funds, entering into contracts, transferring funds from one country to another, and the freedom of its representatives to travel over the world (Rodgers, 1960). Another link with the nation-state, which is quite different, involves rendering expert professional guidance, as in the case of the International Statistical Institute, which has helped nations with their censuses to insure high professional standards and comparable classifications (Keyfitz, 1968, p. 235); and a variety of medical associations, such as the International Union Against Tuberculosis, have aided nation-states in the combating of diseases (White, 1951, p. 171).

Compared with the links between the international professional association and the nation-state, those with regional organizations are probably fewer. The European Economic Community has accorded consultative status to various INGOs, some of which would fall into the category of professional associations (Schokking and Anderson, 1960, pp. 392-395). In all likelihood, *regional* professional associations, such as the European Federation of National Associations of Engineers, develop closer ties with the European Economic Community than do *international* professional associations. This may also be true in other regional communities (for example, the Latin American Free Trade Area) and their corresponding professional associations (for example, the Pan-American Federation of Engineering Societies).

As regards the bonds between the international professional association and the multinational firm, they seem somewhat tenuous. Several international professional associations, such as the international arbitration tribunals of the International Chamber of Commerce and Inter-American Commercial Arbitration Commission, perform a direct service to multinational corporations by helping them resolve conflicts outside the framework of judiciaries of nation-states. (American Management Association, 1965, pp. 134-178). In view of the fact that there is a high overlap in membership of engineers and scientists in international professional associations and multinational firms and that both organizations struggle with the ambiguities of operating across national boundaries, one would expect a variety of types of interactions to develop among these organizations. It can reasonably be predicted that when each type of organization becomes fully cognizant of the others' existence—and the Union of International Associations already is, witness the addition of a section of multinational corporations in its *Yearbook*—new patterns of interaction will emerge which may significantly increase the level of organizational and possibly also normative integration of the international system.

By far the most highly developed interaction patterns are observable between international professional associations and intergovernmental organizations, or IGOs, as they are customarily abbreviated. This is to be expected, since some INGOs have for a long time sought to influence the decisions of IGOs. The fact that INGOs are accorded consultative status to the Economic and Social Council of the UN and to its many specialized agencies, such as the International Labor Organization, the World Health Organization, and UNESCO, has encouraged the growth of INGOs—so much so that it has been asserted that "Every IGO . . . has at least one counterpart in the INGO world" (Rodgers, 1960, p. 8). The reciprocal effects between these two types of organizations have been extensive. Some international professional associations have been instrumental in the formation of some IGOs, and, in turn, some IGOs have created some international professional associations.

The unique role of UNESCO in creating and reorganizing various international associations in the social sciences and in establishing two super-INGOs—namely, the International Social Science Council and the International Committee for Social Science Documentation—is well known (UNESCO, 1966). Less well known, and of considerable importance, is the fact that UNESCO provides subventions to various international professional associations to supplement their meager budgets.

In short, there is already in being an elaborate network of relationships between international professional associations and various components of the international system.

Some Hypotheses on the Integration of the International System

In our discussion of alternative models of the international system, we observed the operation of forces conducive to normative and economic integration. From our analysis of the growth and interaction patterns of multinational corporations and international professional associations, two additional forces appear to be developing; to wit, organizational and occupational integration. The many thousands of multinational firms have elaborate relationships with numerous other business organizations in different countries as well as with many host-government agencies and international governmental organizations. Similarly, the hundreds of international professional associations have developed, in the past few decades, an intricate network of relationships, as we have seen, with various components of the international system.

Each type of organization is generating, wittingly or unwittingly, loyalties—organizational, in the case of the multinational firm, and occupational, in the case of the international professional association—that cut across national boundaries. In effect, both types of organizations are socializing their members into the values of transnationalism; that is, identifying with the objectives of "an organization which transcends national borders, without comprising nations; it is subnational, yet international" (Galtung, 1967, p. 313). Thus, we hypothesize that these emergent loyalties are raising the level of integration of the international system. To test this general hypothesis would require operationalizing the nonlinear model of the international system presented in Figure 3 and gathering systematic data—a complex undertaking that would challenge the ingenuity of a team of social scientists. By way of illustrating the potential value of such an endeavor, I shall consider several more specific propositions applicable to both types of organizations.

It is frequently asserted that multiple affiliations breed multiple loyalties, and if the latter transcend national boundaries they can act as a brake on international conflict (LeVine, 1966, p. 68). Human networks "based on cross-cutting professional and other interests can contribute to the stability and integration of the international system by counteracting tendencies toward polarization along national lines. They create a vested interest in maintaining a pluralistic and peaceful international order" (Kelman, 1970, pp. 15-16). Assuming these are plausible, if not validated, propositions, do they have any implications for the organizational design and functioning of multinational corporations and international professional associations? In Table 1 I have identified several structural and motivational variables in terms of which comparative research on both types of organizations could be undertaken which would throw light on their actual or potential impact on the level of economic, organizational, occupational, and normative integration of the international system (Smoker, 1968, p. 501).

Hypothesis 1. Multinational ownership of corporations and multinational leadership of international professional associations, as contrasted with uninational ownership of corporations and uninational leadership of international professional associations, result in denser networks of interorganizational relationships and, in turn, contribute to a higher level of organizational and economic integration of the international system.

The second structural variable, authority, is frequently discussed in the literature on the multinational firm, but rarely, if ever, investigated. Arguments are advanced for the relative merits, in a particular industry, of a centralized versus a decentralized structure of authority (Oppenheim, 1967, p. 117). General Motors, Massey-Ferguson, and Krupp are cited as examples of highly centralized companies (Oppenheim, 1967; Rupert, 1967). On the other hand, Bata in discussing communication in his shoe-manufacturing company—eighty-four companies in eight countries—describes it as a decentralized firm (Bata, 1967). If a comparative study were undertaken of centralized versus decentralized firms, preferably in the same industry to control for type of products manufactured and technology employed, we could learn the consequences of contrasting authority structures for the network of interorganizational relationships.

A functionally equivalent variable of authority structure in the case of the inter-

Table 1. Within and Between Comparisons of Multinational Corporations
and International Professional Associations on Structural and
Motivational Dimensions

Dimension	Multinational Corporation	International Professional Association
A. *Structure*		
1. Nationality of stockholders and/or principal officers and HQ staff	One or few vs. many nations	One or few vs. many nations
2. Authority	Centralized vs. decentralized	Collective vs. individual membership
3. Interface functions of HQ staff	Low vs. high ratio of boundary/nonboundary personnel	Low vs. high ratio of boundary/nonboundary personnel
4. Movement of HQ staff between parent organization and affiliates	Low vs. high rate of rotation of managerial and technical personnel	Low vs. high rate of visits from HQ to member organization and vice versa
B. *Motivation*		
1. Local vs. cosmopolitan orientation	Loyalty to affiliate vs. loyalty to parent company or both	Loyalty to national association vs. international association or both
2. Attitude toward legal status of the organization	Preference for incorporation under nation-state vs. under UN or other international agency	Preference for incorporation under nation-state vs. under UN or other international agency

national professional association is whether the unit of membership is the individual professional or a collectivity, such as a national, regional, or international association. In most international professional associations—in fact, in most INGOs, in general—the unit of membership is the national association (White, 1951, p. 7). As it happens, the International Sociological Association has recently amended its statutes to provide for individual membership in the interests of democratizing and internationalizing the profession (as well as enlarging its sources of revenue). Clearly, there is sufficient variation among professional associations as regards unit of membership to warrant a study of its effects, for example, on loyalty to the association as well as loyalty to the profession.

Hypothesis 2. Decentralized authority in multinational corporations and individual membership in international professional associations, as contrasted with centralized authority and collective membership, result in a denser network of interorganizational relationships and in a higher degree of organizational and occupational loyalty, thus contributing to a higher level of organizational, occupational, and normative integration of the international system.

The third structural variable deals with a mechanism for handling the interface problems of an organization. Some members of the staffs of corporate and association headquarters specialize in functions pertaining to boundary relations of an organization whereas others specialize in internal functions. This suggests that a ratio of boundary/nonboundary personnel could be constructed for both types of organizations to inquire into, for example, whether there is a positive relationship between this ratio and the size of the organizational network of a given organization (Evan, 1966, 1969, 1972).

Hypothesis 3. The higher the ratio of boundary/nonboundary personnel in the headquarters of multinational corporations and international professional associations, the higher the level of coordination among affiliates and, in turn, the higher the level of organizational integration of the international system.

The last structural variable is concerned with the degree of movement of headquarters staff between a parent organization and its affiliates. Do firms with a high rate of rotation of managerial and technical personnel from headquarters to affiliates evidence greater internal coordination of functions and more effective patterns of interaction with other organizations than firms having a low rate of rotation of such personnel? A comparable question might be asked in the case of professional associations, but in view of the nonhierarchical relationship between member organizations and international headquarters, it would be important to establish the rate of visits from both directions.

Hypothesis 4. The higher the rate of movement of headquarters personnel from parent organization to affiliates, the greater the degree of coordination in multinational corporations and international professional associations and, in turn, the higher the level of organizational integration of the international system.

The four structural variables briefly reviewed above would in all likelihood be related to the type of motivational orientation of the members of an organization. A structural pattern partaking of transnationalism (that is, multinational ownership of the firm—principal association officers and staff drawn from many nations; decentralized authority structure of the firm—individual membership in the association; high ratio of boundary/nonboundary personnel in headquarters staff; high rate of movement between headquarters staff of parent organization and affiliates) would engender a motivational orientation of transnationalism.

A "cosmopolitan" as opposed to a "local" orientation in the firm would mean either greater loyalty to the parent company or a dual loyalty to the parent company as well as its affiliate; similarly, it would mean a greater loyalty to the international association than to the national association or a dual loyalty. As regards the second motivational variable, attitude toward the legal status of the organization, a preference for incorporation under the auspices of an international agency rather than a nation-state would reflect a transnational identification.

Hypothesis 5. The higher the level of transnational orientation of the members of multinational corporations and international professional associations, the higher the level of normative, organizational, and occupational integration of the international system.

Clearly, the four structural variables and the two motivational variables listed in Table 1 merely illustrate the range of organizational variables that could provide the basis for comparative research on the impact of these types of organizations on the level of economic, organizational, occupational, and normative integration of the international system. The hypotheses presented above indicate some of the relationships between the structural and motivational variables, on the one hand, and the integration variables on the other, that are in need of systematic empirical testing.

Conclusion

Two types of international organizations have thus far largely eluded the ken of awareness of researchers in the sociology of organizations. This oversight need not continue because the multinational corporation and the international professional association provide strategic sites for coming to grips with two frontier problems in the field: (a) the analysis of interorganizational relations; and (b) the cross-cultural comparison of organizations.

The field of international relations has likewise not done justice to these types of organizations. Many scholars in this field evidently assume that these types of organizations, though operating in the interstices of nation-states, have little consequence for the future development of the international system (Judge, 1969, p. 143). In subscribing to this view they may be overlooking the potential of these organizations for cumulatively and unanticipatedly transforming the international system. This conception of the international system is not unique to international relations specialists. Some futurologists, like Kahn and Wiener, in their broad-gauged analysis of various possible structural modifications of the international system within the next three decades, likewise ignore such non-governmental, international organizations as the multinational firm and the international professional association (Kahn and Wiener, 1967, pp. 359-385).

Yet the dynamism of the international system of the future may derive from a force for integration intimated in Durkheim's famous preface to the second edition of *The Division of Labor,* entitled "Some Notes on Occupational Groups."

> As advances are made in history, the organization which has territorial groups as its base steadily becomes effaced ... These geographical divisions are, for the most part, artificial and no longer awaken in us profound sentiments. The provincial spirit has disappeared never to return; the patriotism of the parish has become an archaism that cannot be restored at will ... the State is too remote from individuals; its relations with them too external and intermittent to penetrate deeply into individual consciences and socialize them within. Where the State is the only environment in which men can live communal lives, they inevitably lose contact, become detached. ... A nation can be maintained only if, between the State and the individual, there is intercalated a whole series of *secondary groups* near enough to the individuals to attract them strongly in their sphere of action and drag them, in this way, into the general torrent of social life. We have just shown how occupational groups are suited to fill this role, and that is their destiny [Durkheim, 1960, pp. 27-28].

Broadly conceived, the multinational corporation and the international professional association may be collectively performing the solidary functions at the international level which Durkheim envisioned for 'occupational groups' within the nation. To those social scientists who discern an intellectual challenge in the study of these organizations, the task that lies ahead is at least fourfold: (a) developing a model, akin to the nonlinear model of integration diagrammed in Figure 3, which copes with the complexity of the linkages among the components of the international system; (b) operationalizing various dimensions of integration of the international system, such as the four identified in the model presented in Figure 3; (c) designing an information system on various components of the international system—including multinational corporations and international professional associations—of the kind recently described and proposed by Judge (1971, pp. 47-64); and (d) providing for longitudinal data collection on the various system linkages—such as those postulated in our nonlinear model of integration—and the various dimensions of integration of the international system.

By studying the interaction patterns of these organizations to ascertain whether they are in fact creating networks of people transcending the nation-state and generating new levels of normative, economic, organizational and occupational integration, social scientists can discover whether Durkheim's anticipations are valid for the international system.

References

Adam, G. "New Trends in International Business: Worldwide Sourcing and Dedomiciling." Paper presented at International Conference on Multinational Corporations, May 1971, Queens University of Belfast.

Aiken, M., and Hage, J. "Organizational Interdependence and Intraorganizational Structure." *American Sociological Review,* 1968, *33,* 912-929.

American Management Association. *Resolving Business Disputes.* New York: American Management Association, 1965.

Angell, R. "The Growth of Transnational Participation." In L. Kriesberg (Ed.), *Social Processes in International Relations: A Reader.* New York: Wiley, 1968.

Bata, T. "Communicating in Growing International and Decentralized Organizations." In Conseil International pour l'Organisation Scientifique, *Management and Growth.* Rotterdam: Rotterdam University Press, 1967.

Baty, G. B., Evan, W. M., and Rothermel, T. W. "Personnel Flows as Interorganizational Relations." *Administrative Science Quarterly,* 1971, *16,* 430-443.

Behrman, J. N. "Multinational Corporations, Transnational Interest, and National Sovereignty." *Columbia Journal of World Business,* 1969a, *4,* 15-21.

Behrman, J. N. *Some Patterns in the Rise of the Multinational Enterprise.* Chapel Hill: Graduate School of Business Administration, University of North Carolina, 1969b.

Boddewyn, J., and Nath, R. "Comparative Management Studies: An Assessment." *Management International Review,* 1970, *10,* 9-11.

Brams, S. J. "The Search for Structural Order in the International System: Some Models and Preliminary Results." *International Studies Quarterly,* 1969, *13,* 254-280.

Casserini, K. "The Challenge of Multinational Corporations and Regional Economic Integration to the Trade Unions, Their Structure, and Their International Activities." In H. Gunter (Ed.), *Transnational Industrial Relations.* London: Macmillan, 1972.

Durkheim, E. *The Division of Labor in Society.* (G. Simpson, Trans.) New York: Free Press, 1960.

Emery, F. E., and Trist, E. L. "The Causal Texture of Organizational Environments." *Human Relations,* 1965, *18,* 21-32.

Evan, W. M. "Transnational Forums for Peace." In Q. Wright, W. M. Evan, and M. Deutsch (Eds.), *Preventing World War III: Some Proposals.* New York: Simon and Schuster, 1962.

Evan, W. M. "The Organization-Set: Toward a Theory of Interorganizational Relations." In J. D. Thompson (Ed.), *Approaches to Organizational Design.* Pittsburgh: University of Pittsburgh Press, 1966.

Evan, W. M. "The Engineering Profession: A Cross-Cultural Analysis." In R. Perrucci and J. E. Gerstl (Eds.), *The Engineers and the Social System.* New York: Wiley, 1969.

Evan, W. M. "An Organization-Set Model of Interorganizational Relations." In M. F. Tuite, M. Radnor, and R. K. Chisholm (Eds.), *Interorganizational Decision Making.* Chicago: Aldine, 1972.

Fouraker, L. E., and Stopford, J. M. "Organizational Structure and the Multinational Strategy." *Administrative Science Quarterly,* 1968, *13,* 47-64.

Galtung, J. "On the Future of the International System." *Journal of Peace Research,* 1967, *4,* 305-333.

Galtung, J. "A Structural Theory of Integration." *Journal of Peace Research,* 1968, *5,* 375-395.

Grzybowski, K. *The Socialist Commonwealth of Nations: Organizations and Institutions.* New Haven, Conn.: Yale University Press, 1964.

Haar, D. ter (Ed.). *Collected Papers of P. L. Kapitza.* Vol. 3. Elmsford, N.Y.: Pergamon Press, 1967.

Haas, E. B. *The Uniting of Europe.* Stanford, Calif.: Stanford University Press, 1958.

Haas, M. "A Functional Approach to International Organization." *Journal of Politics,* 1965, *27,* 498-517.

Herman, L. M. "COMECON Reform Depends on Trade with World Markets." *Columbia Journal of World Business,* 1969, *4,* 51-58.

Hirsch, P. M. "Processing Fads and Fashions: An Organization-Set Analysis of Cultural Industry Systems." *American Journal of Sociology,* 1972, *77,* 639-659.

Judge, A. J. N. "Evaluation of International Organizations." *International Associations,* 1969, *21,* 141-147.

Judge, A. J. N. "Information Systems and Interorganizational Space." *Annals of the American Academy of Political and Social Science,* 1971, *393,* 47-64.

Kahn, H., and Wiener, A. J. *The Year 2000.* New York: Macmillan, 1967.

Kaufmann, O. "Diverging Structural Patterns in the Development of American and European Firms." *Management International Review,* 1970, *10,* 101-107.

Kelman, H. C. "The Role of the Individual in International Relations: Some Conceptual and Methodological Considerations." *Journal of International Affairs,* 1970, *24,* 1-17.

Keohane, R. O., and Nye, J. S., Jr. (Eds.). *Transnational Relations and World Politics.* Cambridge, Mass.: Harvard University Press, 1971.

Keyfitz, N. "Government Statistics." In *International Encyclopedia of the Social Sciences.* Vol. 6. New York: Macmillan and Free Press, 1968.

Kindleberger, C. P. *American Business Abroad.* New Haven, Conn.: Yale University Press, 1969.

Kriesberg, L. "U.S. and U.S.S.R. Participation in International Non-governmental Organizations." In L. Kriesberg (Ed.), *Social Processes in International Relations: A Reader.* New York: Wiley, 1968.

Lazarsfeld, P. F., and Leeds, R. "International Sociology as a Sociological Problem." *American Sociological Review,* 1962, *27,* 732-741.

LeVine, R. A. "Socialization, Social Structure, and Intersocietal Images." In H. C. Kelman (Ed.), *International Behavior.* New York: Holt, Rinehart and Winston, 1966.

Litwak, E., and Rothman, J. "Toward the Theory and Practice of Coordination Between Formal Organizations." In W. R. Rosengren and M. Lefton (Eds.), *Organizations and Clients.* Columbus, Ohio: Merrill, 1970.

Luard, E. (Ed.). *The Evolution of International Organizations.* New York: Praeger, 1966.

Miles, C. M. "The International Corporation." *International Affairs,* 1969, *45,* 259-268.

Miles, E. "Organizations and Integration in International Systems." *International Studies Quarterly,* 1968, *12,* 196-224.

Nye, J. S. "Comparing Common Markets: A Revised Neo-functionalist Model." *International Organization,* 1970, *24,* 796-835.

Oppenheim, D. M. "Organizational Growth Through International Cooperation." In Conseil International pour l'Organisation Scientifique, *Management and Growth.* Rotterdam: Rotterdam University Press, 1967.

Perlmutter, H. V. "The Tortuous Evolution of the Multinational Corporation." *Columbia Journal of World Business,* 1969a, *4,* 9-18.

Perlmutter, H. V. "Emerging East-West Ventures: The Transideological Enterprise." *Columbia Journal of World Business,* 1969b, *4,* 39-50.

Quinn, J. B. "Technology Transfer by Multinational Companies." *Harvard Business Review,* 1969, *47,* 147-161.

Robinson, R. D. "Joint Ventures or Transnational Business?" *Industrial Management Review,* 1964a, *6,* 59-65.

Robinson, R. D. *International Business Policy.* New York: Holt, Rinehart and Winston, 1964b.

Robinson, R. D. *International Management.* New York: Holt, Rinehart and Winston, 1967.

Robinson, R. D. "Ownership Across National Frontiers." *Industrial Management Review,* 1969, *11,* 41-61.

Robock, S. H., and Simmonds, K. "International Business: How Big Is It—The Missing Measurements." *Columbia Journal of World Business,* 1970, *5,* 6-19.

Rodgers, R. S. *Facilitation Problems of International Associations.* Brussels: Union of International Associations, 1960.

Rolfe, S. E. *The International Corporation.* Paris: International Chamber of Commerce, 1969.

Rupert, A. A. "Communicating in a Growing International Organization." In Conseil International pour l'Organisation Scientifique, *Management and Growth.* Rotterdam: Rotterdam University Press, 1967.

Rutenberg, D. P. "Organizational Archetypes of a Multinational Company." *Management Science,* 1970, *16,* B-337-349.

Schokking, J. J., and Anderson, N. "Observations on the European Integration Process." *Journal of Conflict Resolution,* 1960, *4,* 385-410.

Servan-Schreiber, J. J. *The American Challenge.* New York: Atheneum, 1968.

Skjelsbaek, K. "The Growth of International Non-governmental Organizations in the Twentieth Century." In R. O. Keohane and J. S. Nye, Jr. (Eds.), *Transnational Relations and World Politics.* Cambridge, Mass.: Harvard University Press, 1971.

Smoker, P. "A Preliminary Empirical Study of an International Integrative Subsystem." *International Associations,* 1965, *17,* 638-646.

Smoker, P. "Nation-State Escalation and International Integration." In L. Kriesberg (Ed.), *Social Processes in International Relations: A Reader.* New York: Wiley, 1968.

Thompson, J. D. *Organizations in Action.* New York: McGraw-Hill, 1967.

Turk, H. "Interorganizational Networks in Urban Society: Initial Perspectives and Comparative Research." *American Sociological Review,* 1970, *35,* 1-19.

UNESCO. *International Organizations in the Social Sciences.* Paris: UNESCO, 1966.

Union of International Associations. *International Congress Organization: Theory and Practice.* Brussels: Union of International Associations, 1961.

Union of International Associations. *Yearbook of International Organizations.* Brussels: Union of International Associations, 1969.

United Nations, Department of Economic and Social Affairs. *Multinational Corporations in World Development.* New York: United Nations, 1973.

Vernon, R. "Multinational Enterprise and National Sovereignty." *Harvard Business Review,* 1967, *45,* 156-172.

Vernon, R. "Multinational Business and National Economic Goals." In R. O. Keohane and J. S. Nye, Jr. (Eds.), *Transnational Relations and World Politics.* Cambridge, Mass.: Harvard University Press, 1971.

Wells, L. T. "Multinational Business Enterprise: What Kind of International Organization?" In R. O. Keohane and J. S. Nye, Jr. (Eds.), *Transnational Relations and World Politics.* Cambridge, Mass.: Harvard University Press, 1971.

White, L. C. *International Non-governmental Organizations.* New Brunswick, N.J.: Rutgers University Press, 1951.

"Why Unions Fear the Multinationals." *Business Week,* Dec. 19, 1970, pp. 95-98.

Wilensky, H. L. "The Professionalization of Everyone?" *American Journal of Sociology,* 1964, *70,* 137-158.

8

✎ Dimensions of Management System and Performance in Continuous-Process Organizations

Robert T. Keller

Substantial interest has been shown in recent years in the relationships among type of management system, operations technology, and organizational performance. Empirical studies by Burns and Stalker (1961), Woodward (1965), Lawrence and Lorsch (1967), Harvey (1968), Zwerman (1970), Negandhi and Reimann (1973), Simonetti and Boseman (1975), and Osborn (1976) have found type of management system and locus of decision making to have important relationships with organizational performance. Generally, this body of research has shown that organizations which are managed in ways appropriate to their environmental and technological conditions are more effective. The purpose of this paper is to examine the relationships among dimensions of management system and the performance of manufacturing organizations which use continuous-process technologies. Such technologies have a continuous flow of a standardized product, as in an oil refinery or chemical plant. An understanding of the relationships among dimensions of management system and performance can have important implications for both organizational theory and practice.

Prior Research

A number of researchers have recognized that different environmental conditions require particular adaptations of management strategies in order to achieve success. A particular set of decision rules for the effective operation of an automobile assembly plant, for example, may not at all be appropriate for the operation of a chemical plant. A major question which has motivated these researchers is: What set of management practices is appropriate for which environmental conditions?

An initial study by Burns and Stalker (1961) conducted an in-depth investigation of twenty manufacturing firms in Great Britain from the electronics, engineering, and textile industries. Their method of data collection was to conduct in-depth interviews

Reprinted from *Human Relations,* 1978, *31* (1), 59-75, with permission of the author and Plenum Publishing Corporation.

with members of top management in each firm. Burns and Stalker determined that there were two basic types of management system utilized. The *mechanistic* management system emphasized a highly structured organization with a hierarchy of authority, specialized differentiation of functional tasks, and rules and regulations which specified roles and relationships. The *organic* management system, in contrast, emphasized a less formal organization with lateral rather than vertical relations, participation of lower members in decision making, and greater flexibility of roles and relationships. The basic findings of the Burns and Stalker research were that mechanistic systems were effective for those firms which faced relatively stable market and technological environments, while organic systems were best suited to firms which had to contend with relatively dynamic environments.

Lawrence and Lorsch (1967) conducted a field study of some of the same variables as did Burns and Stalker. The Lawrence and Lorsch research investigated United States firms in the plastics, consumer food, and standardized containers industries, and their data strongly supported the findings of Burns and Stalker. Basically, firms which faced dynamic market and technological environments were more economically successful with organic systems, while those firms in a relatively stable environment were more successful with mechanistic systems.

Technological conditions have also been shown to affect the relationship between management system and performance. For example, Woodward (1965) used structured interviews to study one hundred firms in South Essex, England, and found that firms which used mass-production and large-batch technologies were more economically successful with mechanistic systems. Firms which employed unit and small-batch technologies or continuous-process technologies were more successful if they utilized organic systems of management. Zwerman (1970) sought to replicate the Woodward study in the United States and used similar structured interviews with a sample of fifty-five firms from the Minneapolis area. He also found that the very successful firms in unit and small-batch technologies utilized organic systems, while firms which were very successful in mass-production and large-batch operations had mechanistic management systems. Unfortunately, Zwerman's sample contained too few firms which employed continuous-process technologies to draw meaningful inferences about type of management system and effectiveness.

A field study by Peterson (1975) of eighteen Norwegian firms supported the earlier work by Woodward (1965) and Zwerman (1970). Peterson used a mail questionnaire and found that professional, technical, and managerial employees of mass-assembly firms perceived a structured, mechanistic climate, while similar employees in small-batch and continuous-process technologies perceived an open, organic organizational climate.

An interesting extension in data analysis has recently been reported in this area by two different researchers, with rather comparable and consistent results. Reimann (1974) studied nineteen manufacturing organizations located in northeastern Ohio which were engaged in a number of technologies. The firms were rank-ordered on performance measures, and separated into high- and low-performance firms. Cluster analysis was then used to examine structural variables within the performance categories. The results showed much clearer clusters of structural variables for the high-performance firms, while only a "mixed" and unclear cluster resulted for the low-performance firms. Reimann concluded (1) that organizational structure is a multidimensional concept and (2) that high-performance organizations may have different relationships among structural variables than do low-performance organizations.

Khandwalla (1973, 1974) used a similar approach to data analysis on a separate sample of seventy-nine United States manufacturing firms with a mass-output orientation of their operations technology. Khandwalla studied three structural variables: decentralization in top-level decision making, vertical integration, and the use of sophisticated controls. A model which related these structural variables to one another and to technology was first constructed and then shown to be supported by the total sample. When the firms were separated into high- and low-profit subsamples that were otherwise comparable, it was found that the model was supported substantially more, via path analysis, by the high-profit subsample than by the low-profit subsample. Profit was measured by averaging the highest and lowest rates of before-tax profit on net worth during the previous five years. Khandwalla concluded that the impact of technological effects on organizational structure may be quite different for high-profit organizations than it is for low-profit organizations.

The present research sought to extend the examination of relationships among dimensions of management system and performance to organizations which utilize continuous-process technologies. This type of operations technology is in particular need of research because Zwerman (1970) did not have enough continuous-process firms to replicate the Woodward (1965) research. In addition, automation has moved certain large-batch technology industries, such as steel and paper manufacturing, toward continuous-process technologies, and continued technological change in this direction is predicted for the future. Specifically, the following two research questions were investigated: (1) Is the use of organic management systems related to relatively high performance among continuous-process organizations? (2) Among continuous-process organizations, do relatively high-performance organizations have more clearly defined clusters of management system dimensions than do low-performance organizations?

Method

Sample. Data were collected from forty-four plants located throughout Pennsylvania which utilized continuous-process production technologies. The products included chemicals (fourteen plants); paints, coatings, and adhesives (eight plants); pharmaceuticals (five plants); oil refinery products (four plants); electric power (four plants); synthetic fibers and films (four plants); and others, made up of paper, portland cement, and beverages (five plants). The median plant size was 176 total employees, and the median depreciated, total worth was $7 million.

Research Instruments. The methods of data collection included questionnaires and follow-up telephone interviews. The telephone interviews were used to validate and confirm the questionnaire data, and the interviews indicated that the questionnaire items were clearly understood and the information obtained was accurate. The first part of the questionnaire was completed by the chief executive and concerned information pertaining to the size, location, technology, products, and performance of the organization. The second part of the questionnaire consisted of a twenty-two-item Likert-type instrument which is contained in Table 1. This instrument was completed by the chief executive and two of his immediate subordinates and asked the respondent to describe the management system of the organization. The three top executives in each organization were chosen to provide a policy-level view of the type of management system in each organization and to enhance comparability across organizations. Kendall's coefficient of concordance was computed for the two levels of executives (chief executive officer and immediate subordinates) and was found to be significant beyond the .01 level for each factor score. Thus, substantial agreement was found among the highest two levels of the hierarchy on the management system dimensions.

The instrument was based upon prior work by Duncan (1971, 1973), Hall (1961,

Table 1. Management System Questionnaire Items[a]

1. People are encouraged to make suggestions when decisions are made.
2. People in this organization are not likely to express their feelings openly on important matters.
3. People in this organization are encouraged to speak their minds on important matters, even if it means disagreeing with their superiors.
4. If someone feels he has the right approach to carrying out his job in dealing with important matters, he can usually go ahead without checking with his superior.
5. People from different departments are often put together in a special group in order to solve important problems.
6. For many decisions the rules and regulations are developed as we go along.
7. It is always necessary to go through channels in dealing with important matters.
8. People in this organization always get orders from their superiors on important matters.
9. Talking to other people about the problems someone might have in making decisions is an important part of the process of decision making.
10. Getting along with other people is an important part of the decision-making process.
11. For special problems we usually set up a temporary task force until we meet our objectives.
12. The same rules and regulations are always followed in making most types of decisions.
13. Superiors in this organization usually make the decisions themselves.
14. In this organization most people do not have a voice in making decisions.
15. We have special groups for handling problems between different departments on important matters.
16. People in this organization do not share any influences with their superiors in making decisions.
17. People have to check with their superiors before doing almost anything on important matters.
18. Superiors often seek advice from their subordinates before decisions are made.
19. There are rules and regulations for handling any kind of problem which may arise in making most decisions.
20. Different individuals play important roles in making decisions.
21. Subordinates do not play an active role in making decisions.
22. In handling important problems between departments, we usually use a liaison group to work things out.

[a]The respondent was asked to circle one of five points on a scale ranging from "strongly agree" to "strongly disagree" for each of the items listed. One form each was completed by the chief executive and two of his immediate subordinates. Items 1, 2, 5, 7, 8, 11, 12, 15, 16, 17, 18, 19, and 22 were reverse-scored.

1963) and Galbraith (1970). Five basic dimensions of management system were expected a priori from the prior work: hierarchy of authority, impersonality, participation in decision making, rules and regulations, and groups and task forces. A varimax factor analysis routine was performed on the twenty-two items, since prior research on organization structure and climate has indicated that type of management system would be multidimensional, and the result was a three-factor solution. The factor loadings and communalities are reported in Table 2.

The first factor obtained consisted of eleven items and was labeled *impersonal hierarchy*. It explained 53 percent of the total variance, and the reliability (coefficient alpha) of the scale was .92. The second factor extracted had three items and was called *group decision making*. It explained 11 percent of the total variance, and the reliability was .58. The third factor, with four items, was named *rules for decision making*. This factor explained 8.4 percent of the total variance and had a reliability of .57. A composite scale called *organic management system* was also computed by the reverse scoring

Table 2. Rotated Factor Matrix and Loadings for Management System
Questionnaire[a]

Question	Factor I Impersonal Hierarchy	Factor II Group Decision Making	Factor III Rules for Decision Making	Communality
1	−.714	.211	−.322	.68
2	.680	.116	.208	.55
3	.751	−.120	.202	.66
4	.311	−.308	.393	.39
5	−.564	.389	−.072	.61
6	−.134	−.132	.382	.28
7	.281	.029	.629	.47
8	.213	.089	.577	.40
9	.162	−.350	−.036	.24
10	.235	−.246	.029	.31
11	−.443	.465	.190	.47
12	.115	.177	.447	.29
13	−.682	.064	−.044	.50
14	−.607	.019	−.150	.44
15	.029	.674	.021	.46
16	.663	−.215	.078	.55
17	.686	−.015	.322	.61
18	−.728	.279	−.040	.65
19	.291	.333	.390	.42
20	.775	−.219	.314	.76
21	−.827	.035	−.028	.67
22	−.080	.719	.013	.52

[a]Underlining indicates inclusion of an item in the above factor.

of the first and third scales and summing the scores on the three individual scales. The reliability of the organic scale, with eighteen items, was .93. This composite scale was developed so that the findings of the present study could be more easily compared to the prior research of Burns and Stalker (1961), Woodward (1965), and Lawrence and Lorsch (1967), who viewed management system in the unidimensional terms of the mechanistic-organic continuum. In addition, it was assumed that the composite scale would help to show the relative relationships of the separate dimensions to the mechanistic-organic continuum concept.

Performance was measured in two ways. First, the percentage change in the most recent five years of contribution to company profit for each plant was assessed. This profit measure in each year was determined by subtracting variable costs from the revenue realized by the plant's output. Fixed costs, such as depreciation or long-term debt payments, were not considered. Second, a measure similar to that used by Lawrence and Lorsch (1967) utilized a subjective assessment of total organizational performance by the chief executive of the respective organization. This measure asked for a percentage rating of the organization compared to ideal performance in the particular industry. The Spearman rank-order correlation between the two performance measures was .46 ($p < .01$), which indicates that a subjective assessment of performance is related to profitability, but that other factors do enter into a subjective performance assessment.

Results

The data were analyzed with Spearman rank-order correlations due to the ordinal nature of some of the data, and the necessity of splitting the sample in half, which resulted in an $N = 22$. Table 3 shows the correlational analysis of the six research variables for the total sample. These data basically show that the use of an organic management system is strongly related to high performance as measured by either profitability or subjective performance ratings. Most of this relationship is dependent upon the impersonal hierarchy factor, however, since the group-decision-making factor is not significantly related to performance, and the rules-for-decision-making factor is only related to the subjective rating measure. Since the impersonal-hierarchy factor explained the most variance after rotation, and was highest in reliability, these results were not too surprising.

Table 3. Spearman Correlational Analysis of Type of Management System and Organizational Performance for the Total Sample ($N = 44$)

	Organic System	Impersonal Hierarchy	Group Decision Making	Rules for Decision Making	Profitability	Performance Rating
Organic system		$-.92^c$	$.44^b$	$-.60^c$	$.53^c$	$.60^c$
Impersonal hierarchy			$-.30^a$	$.39^b$	$-.55^c$	$-.54^c$
Group decision making				$-.04$	$.14$	$.19$
Rules for decision making					$-.21$	$-.33^a$
Profitability						$.46^b$

[a] $p < .05$.
[b] $p < .01$.
[c] $p < .001$.

The results support an affirmative response to the first research question: The use of organic management systems is related to high performance among continuous-process organizations. This result also tends to support the prior work of Woodward (1965) and Peterson (1975) and may be explained by the needs for continuous-process organizations to adapt to a dynamic technological environment and to utilize large amounts of sophisticated knowledge.

To answer the second research question (Do the high-performance organizations have more clearly defined clusters of management system dimensions than the low-performance organizations?) the sample was rank-ordered on each of the two performance measures and split at the median into high- and low-performance subsamples. A correlational analysis was then performed on each of the subsamples, and these data are reported in Tables 4 and 5.

The data in Table 4 generally show the low-profitability organizations to have much higher intercorrelations among the dimensions of management system than do the high-profitability organizations. This pattern is especially true for the intercorrelations between impersonal hierarchy and the other dimensions of group decision making and rules for decision making. Table 5 reports the analysis for the high and low subsamples on the subjective performance rating. These data generally show a similar pattern, as did those for profitability, the intercorrelation between impersonal hierarchy and rules for decision making being much higher for the low-performance than for the high-performance subsample.

In order to more clearly analyze the pattern of interrelationships among the research variables, cluster analyses were conducted for the total sample and the high- and

Table 4. Spearman Correlational Analysis of Type of Management System and Organizational Performance for High- and Low-Profitability Subsamples (N = 22 each)

	Organic system		Impersonal hierarchy		Group decision making		Rules for decision making		Profitability		Performance rating	
	High	Low	High	Low	High	Low	High	Low	High	Low	High	Low
Organic system			-.77[c]	-.98[c]	.43[a]	.45[a]	-.38	-.73[c]	-.08	.26	.43[a]	.59[b]
Impersonal hierarchy					-.07	-.43[a]	-.03	.66[c]	-.12	-.31	-.18	-.58[b]
Group decision making							.02	.00	.10	-.10	.41	-.17
Rules for decision making									.29	-.14	-.06	-.56[b]
Profitability											-.09	.27

[a] $p < .05$.
[b] $p < .01$.
[c] $p < .001$.

Table 5. Spearman Correlational Analysis of Type of Management System and Organizational Performance for High- and Low-Performance Rating Subsample (N = 22 each)

	Organic system		Impersonal hierarchy		Group decision making		Rules for decision making		Profitability		Performance rating	
	High	Low	High	Low	High	Low	High	Low	High	Low	High	Low
Organic system			-.77[c]	-.98[c]	.53[b]	.30	-.45[a]	-.72[c]	.18	.40	.23	.08
Impersonal hierarchy					-.23	-.25	-.03	.67[c]	-.21	-.38	-.19	-.11
Group decision making							-.11	.13	.18	-.10	-.05	-.02
Rules for decision making									.22	-.30	-.24	.11
Profitability											-.01	.08

[a] $p < .05$.
[b] $p < .01$.
[c] $p < .001$.

low-performance subsamples. Cluster analysis, rather than factor analysis, is the appropriate technique for the categorical placement of variables into subsets which show the relationships of the variables to each other, as explained by Weiss (1976). In cluster analysis the variance of a variable is treated as a whole unit, and variables are grouped, or formed as subgroups, as whole variables. A hierarchical, average-linkage cluster analysis (Sneath and Sokal, 1973, chap. 5) via Biomedical Computer Program BMDP1M (Dixon, 1975) was performed on each of the correlation matrices in Tables 3, 4, and 5. A cluster tree is depicted for each cluster analysis. The trees are printed over correlation matrices, which are scaled from 0 to 100 (that is, values of 0-49 correspond to correlations of −1.0 to 0.0 and values of 50-100 correspond to correlations of 0.0 to +1.0). The trees indicate the extent to which the variables cluster together, and are reported in Tables 6 through 10.

Table 6. Cluster Tree Printed over Correlation Matrix (scaled 0-100) for the Total Sample (N = 44)[a]

Variable Name	Number					
Profitability	(1)	72	76	56	22	39
Performance rating	(2)	79	59	22	33	
Organic system	(6)	71	3	19		
Group decision making	(4)	34	47			
Impersonal hierarchy	(3)	69				
Rules for decision making	(5)					

[a]The following is an explanation of the variable clustering process shown in the tree printed above. The process begins with the cluster consisting of the performance rating variable (2), which is the second variable listed in the tree. This cluster is joined with the cluster below it, consisting of the organic system variable (6). The new cluster is indicated on the tree by the intersection of the line which begins above the performance rating variable (2) with the line starting next to the organic system variable (6). This cluster joins with the cluster above it, consisting of the profitability (1) variable. The new cluster is indicated on the tree by the intersection of the line which begins above the profitability variable (1) with the line which starts next to the organic system variable (6). The process is continued until each variable is joined to at least one other variable.

The tree for the total sample in Table 6 indicates a cluster composed of impersonal hierarchy and rules for decision making, as well as a cluster of organic system and performance rating. Other clusters may also be inferred. When the tree in Table 7 for the high-profitability subsample is examined, however, no clustering is found to occur. This lack of clustering is in contrast to the tree in Table 8 for the low-profitability subsample, where clustering which is stronger than that for the total sample is found. Here, impersonal hierarchy and rules for decision making form a strong cluster, and so do organic system and performance rating. The pattern of clustering is similar for the high- and low-subjective-performance subsamples presented in Tables 9 and 10 to that for the high- and low-profitability subsamples. No clustering occurs for the high-performance-rating subsample, but a strong cluster occurs between impersonal hierarchy and rules for decision making for the low-performance-rating subsample.

Table 7. Cluster Tree Printed over Correlation Matrix (scaled 0-100)
for the High-Profitability Subsample (N = 22)[a]

| Variable | | | | | | |
Name	Number					
Profitability	(1)	49	49	49	49	49
Organic system	(6)	49	49	49	49	
Rules for decision making	(5)	49	49	49		
Group decision making	(4)	49	49			
Impersonal hierarchy	(3)	49				
Performance rating	(2)					

[a]The cluster tree printed above shows no clustering of the variables, since a value of 49 is equal to a correlation of 0.00.

Table 8. Cluster Tree Printed over Correlation Matrix (scaled 9-100)
for the Low-Profitability Subsample (N = 22)[a]

| Variable | | | | | | |
Name	Number					
Profitability	(1)	63	62	44	34	42
Performance rating	(2)	79	41	20	21	
Organic system	(6)	72	0	13		
Group decision making	(4)	29	49			
Impersonal hierarchy	(3)	82				
Rules for decision making	(5)					

[a]The cluster tree printed above shows a strong clustering of the impersonal-hierarchy variable (3) with the rules-for-decision-making variable (5).

The answer to the second research question, then, is that high-performance organizations do not have more clearly defined clusters of management system dimensions than do low-performance organizations. To the contrary, the low-performance organizations are the ones with much more clearly defined clusters of management system dimensions. In fact, the high-performance organizations did not display any clustering at all, and all the clustering which occurred for the total sample appears to be due to the low-performance organizations.

Discussion

The results of this research imply support for Woodward (1965) and Peterson (1975) in that the use of organic management systems was positively related to the performance of continuous-process organizations as measured by both profitability and a

**Table 9. Cluster Tree Printed over Correlation Matrix (scaled 0-100)
for the High-Performance-Rating Subsample ($N = 22$)[a]**

Variable Name	Number					
Profitability	(1)	49	49	49	49	49
Organic system	(6)	49	49	49	49	
Rules for decision making	(5)	49	49	49		
Group decision making	(4)	49	49			
Impersonal hierarchy	(3)	49				
Performance rating	(2)					

[a]The cluster tree printed above shows no clustering of the variables, since a value of 49 is equal to a correlation of 0.00.

**Table 10. Cluster Tree Printed over Correlation Matrix (scaled 0-100)
for the Low-Performance-Rating Subsample ($N = 22$)[a]**

Variable Name	Number					
Profitability	(1)	69	44	53	30	34
Organic system	(6)	64	53	0	13	
Group decision making	(4)	48	37	56		
Performance rating	(2)	44	55			
Impersonal hierarchy	(3)	83				
Rules for decision making	(5)					

[a]The cluster tree printed above shows a strong clustering of the impersonal-hierarchy variable (3) with the rules-for-decision-making variable (5).

subjective performance assessment. Specifically, a deemphasis of both an impersonal hierarchy with a chain of command and the use of rules for decision making was significantly related to higher performance for this sample. Woodward's explanation would appear to apply also to the present study. That is, the effective operation of a continuous-process plant requires the rapid exchange and continual updating of technical information among engineers and others responsible for the operation of the large amount of capital equipment; furthermore, such information processing is best done with informal relationships rather than the use of a management hierarchy and prescribed rules and regulations.

The results of the cluster analyses in the present study stand in contrast to the results of Reimann (1974) and Khandwalla (1973, 1974). While these researchers found their high-performance organizations to have more clearly defined patterns among the variables studied, the present study found the low-performance organizations to have much more clearly defined clusters among the variables.

A possible explanation for these differences may be found in a comparison of the three samples. Reimann's sample (1973, 1974) consisted of nineteen manufacturing organizations located in northeastern Ohio. Of these nineteen organizations, only about four appear to be capable of using continuous-process technologies, to judge by the major product lines described by Reimann (1973, p. 463). Mass-production technologies appear to account for most of the organizations. Khandwalla (1973, 1974) described his sample as seventy-nine United States manufacturing firms which utilized a mass-output operations technology. The product lines listed for the sample indeed indicate that the firms employed mass-production technologies (Khandwalla, 1974, p. 81).

The sample in the present study, however, utilized continuous-process technologies for the manufacture of products. The present study, as well as Woodward (1965) and Peterson (1975), found the use of organic management systems best suited to continuous-process operations. The very nature of organic systems, it should be noted, is that they utilize a large number of mechanisms for decision making, communication, and implementation, including task forces and liaison groups, unstructured roles, mutual adjustment among subunits, knowledge-based authority, and informal communication networks. Mechanistic management systems, however, tend to have a more limited range of management alternatives. Here, a hierarchy of authority and communication, rules and regulations, and specialized roles characterize the organization.

In the present study, it may be that a mechanistic system is less appropriate for continuous-process organizations because of the need for the processing of sophisticated information, use of highly trained engineering and technical personnel, and coping with unpredictable and uncertain interruptions. The low-performance subsample, which tended to use mechanistic systems, would therefore have more clearly defined clusters among the management system variables due to the relatively limited range among alternatives for mechanistic designs. The high-performance subsample, with mostly organic systems, would not have as clearly defined patterns among the management system variables because of the greater range of alternatives available within the organic systems category. In essence, equifinality would appear to apply more to organic than to mechanistic management systems.

It would appear, then, that for the present study we know more about what *not* to do than what should be done with regard to normative implications for organizational design. A mechanistic system, with an emphasis on an impersonal hierarchy of authority and rules and regulations for decision making, is clearly inappropriate for continuous-process organizations. We cannot be as certain, however, about what particular form an organic system should take. Prior research suggests that a design for any particular organization would have to take into consideration a number of contextual factors, such as organizational size, information needs, relationships with suprasystems, and the orientations of personnel.

The present findings and those of Reimann (1974) and Khandwalla (1973, 1974) also have some important implications for future research on organizational dimensions. These studies all found that important differences emerged when the samples were separated into high- and low-performance subsamples. Recent reviews of research on organizational dimensions, however, indicate this approach to be the exception (James and Jones, 1976; Payne and Pugh, 1976). Most researchers either do not measure performance, or analyze performance for a total sample. We may find the comparison and contrast of high- and low-performance subsamples to be a potent method for understanding organizational dimensions, since the high-performance subsamples may tend to contain organizations which had better adapted to their environmental conditions, while the low-performance subsamples may tend to consist of inappropriately managed organizations.

Future research endeavors should attempt to measure organizational performance and to analyze high- and low-performance subsamples separately as well as in a total sample. These extra steps may result in considerable benefits for the understanding and management of organizations.

References

Burns, T., and Stalker, G. M. *The Management of Innovation.* London: Tavistock, 1961.

Dixon, W. J. (Ed.). *Biomedical Computer Programs.* Berkeley: University of California Press, 1975.

Duncan, R. B. "The Effects of Perceived Environmental Uncertainty on Organizational Decision Unit Structure." Unpublished doctoral dissertation, Yale University, 1971.

Duncan, R. B. "Multiple Decision-Making Structures in Adapting to Environmental Uncertainty: The Impact on Organizational Effectiveness." *Human Relations,* 1973, *26,* 273-291.

Galbraith, J. "Environmental and Technological Determinants of Organizational Design." In J. W. Lorsch and P. R. Lawrence (Eds.), *Studies in Organizational Design.* Homewood, Ill.: Irwin, 1970.

Hall, R. H. "An Empirical Study of Bureaucratic Dimensions and Their Relation to Other Organizational Characteristics." Unpublished doctoral dissertation, Ohio State University, 1961.

Hall, R. H. "The Concept of Bureaucracy: An Empirical Assessment." *American Journal of Sociology,* 1963, *69,* 32-40.

Harvey, E. "Technology and the Structure of Organizations." *American Sociological Review,* 1968, *33,* 247-259.

James, L. R., and Jones, A. P. "Organizational Structure: A Review of Structural Dimensions and Their Conceptual Relationships with Individual Attitudes and Behavior." *Organizational Behavior and Human Performance,* 1976, *16,* 74-113.

Khandwalla, P. N. "Viable and Effective Organizational Designs of Firms." *Academy of Management Journal,* 1973, *16,* 481-495.

Khandwalla, P. N. "Mass Output Orientation of Operations Technology and Organizational Structure." *Administrative Science Quarterly,* 1974, *19,* 74-97.

Lawrence, P. R., and Lorsch, J. W. *Organization and Environment.* Boston: Graduate School of Business Administration, Harvard University, 1967.

Negandhi, A. R., and Reimann, B. C. "Task Environment, Decentralization, and Organizational Effectiveness." *Human Relations,* 1973, *26,* 203-214.

Osborn, R. N. "The Search for Environmental Complexity." *Human Relations,* 1976, *29,* 179-191.

Payne, R., and Pugh, D. S. "Organizational Structure and Climate." In M. D. Dunnette (Ed.), *Handbook of Industrial and Organizational Psychology.* Chicago: Rand McNally, 1976.

Peterson, R. B. "The Interaction of Technological Process and Perceived Organizational Climate in Norwegian Firms." *Academy of Management Journal,* 1975, *18,* 288-299.

Reimann, B. C. "On the Dimensions of Bureaucratic Structure: An Empirical Reappraisal." *Administrative Science Quarterly,* 1973, *18,* 462-476.

Reimann, B. C. "Dimensions of Structure in Effective Organizations: Some Empirical Evidence." *Academy of Management Journal,* 1974, *17,* 693-708.

Simonetti, J. R., and Boseman, F. G. "The Impact of Market Competition on Organization Structure and Effectiveness: A Cross-Cultural Study." *Academy of Management Journal,* 1975, *18,* 631-638.

Sneath, P. H. A., and Sokal, R. R. *Numerical Taxonomy.* San Francisco: Freeman, 1973.

Weiss, D. J. "Multivariate Procedures." In M. D. Dunnette (Ed.), *Handbook of Industrial and Organizational Psychology.* Chicago: Rand McNally, 1976.

Woodward, J. *Industrial Organization: Theory and Practice.* London: Oxford University Press, 1965.

Zwerman, W. L. *New Perspectives on Organization Theory.* Westport, Conn.: Greenwood Press, 1970.

9

⟨⟩ Determinants of Supervisory Behavior: A Role-Set Analysis

Jeffrey Pfeffer
Gerald R. Salancik

In the organizational literature on leadership and supervision, leadership behavior or supervisory style has almost invariably been employed as the independent, or causal, variable in the analyses. Questions posed by this research have been focused on determining whether some styles of supervision are better than others in terms of employee satisfaction or productivity (Argyle, Gardner, and Cioffi, 1958; Day and Hamblin, 1964; Fleishman and Simmons, 1970; Fleishman and Harris, 1962; Patchen, 1962). While more refined conceptualizations have been employed, such as the notion that the most effective leadership behavior may be contingent on the psychological needs of the employees (Vroom, 1959) or on the favorableness of the leadership situation (Fiedler, 1967), the dominant concern of investigators has been with the *effects* of supervisory behavior.

In this paper, we explore some determinants of supervisory behavior in organizations. Heller and Yukl (1969, p. 229) noted that while there had been discussion in the literature of the constraints and demands placed on the leader, systematic investigation of the consequences of these constraints and demands has not been undertaken. When leader behavior has been viewed as a dependent variable, moreover, it has generally been only with respect to the dimension of subordinate participation in decision making. Heller and Yukl (1969) considered the extent to which the leader allowed subordinates to participate in decision making as a function of seven situational variables. Their results tended to support the idea that the amount of subordinate participation in decision making permitted by the leader was a function of situational factors. Subordinate participation in decision making has been related to the organizational technology by Mohr (1971).

The idea that variables of organizational technology, size, or context can affect managerial behavior has also been pursued by Pugh and associates (1969), Lawrence and Lorsch (1967), Burns and Stalker (1961), and Hage and Aiken (1969). These studies have typically not used as dependent measures concepts of leader or supervisory behavior that are comparable to those used in the examinations of the consequences of variations in

Reprinted from *Human Relations,* 1975, *28* (2), 139-154, with permission of the authors and Plenum Publishing Corporation.

supervisory style. Moreover, the variables utilized in these sociological analyses tended to be less directly related to the social processes which are potentially operating at the work-group level of analysis.

This paper explores supervisory behavior along the dimensions commonly used in studies of leadership behavior (see, for example, Fleishman and Harris, 1962), but explores the extent to which that behavior is determined by constraints deriving from the supervisor's set of organizational and social interactions.

The Role-Set Model

The basic concept we use to explain supervisory behavior is that of the role set. Kahn and associates (1964) defined role set as the set of other positions in the organization with which a given focal person interacts in the course of accomplishing his organizational role. The concept of the role set has also been employed by sociologists, including Merton (1957) and Evan (1966), who expanded its application to interorganizational analysis. Though Kahn's model was proposed a decade ago, it has not yet been used to analyze the behaviors of supervisors.

The interaction among the focal person and the members of his role set is likely to stabilize over time, as expectations and reciprocal behavior contingencies become known. Allport (1962) and Weick (1969) have described this process as the development of a collective structure of behavior. Elaborating on the "minimal social situation" explored by Kelley (Rabinowitz, Kelley, and Rosenblatt, 1966), Weick noted that a necessary part of an analysis of organizations is the consideration of the interlocking of individual behaviors. When individual behaviors interlock with one another, uncertainty is reduced as the behaviors of the interlocked individuals become more predictable to each. Within an organization, members of the role set have expectations and preferences regarding the focal person's behavior. These role expectations (Kahn and others, 1964) may be communicated to the focal person, at which time they may become role pressures which potentially structure his behavior.

The basic argument is straightforward. Organizations are composed of interdependent positions and interlocking behaviors. Occupants of these positions are exposed to the expectations and social pressures of other organizational members with whom they are interdependent. With experience, the expectations and demands become known, result in a collective structure of behavior, and stabilize to predictable patterns. In any given position, the occupant's behavior is influenced and constrained by the social pressures emanating from other persons in his role set.

Based on the argument that collective structures develop in organizations, we hypothesize that a supervisor's leadership behavior is influenced and constrained by the expectations of his subordinates, his boss, and his peers. Moreover, the amount of constraint provided by each of these members of his role set is a function of the extent to which their behaviors interlock. The supervisor, in this model, is not merely selecting that set of leadership behaviors that he prefers, or that he thinks will be the best for him to use, but selects his behaviors subject to the social influences coming from his subordinates, his boss, and his peers, and subject to their simultaneous selection of behaviors appropriate to interaction with him.

Hypotheses

Our basic argument that leadership behavior is partially a result of social influence processes leads to our first hypothesis:

Hypothesis 1: The behavior of the supervisor will be influenced by the expectations of his own boss, his subordinates, and his organizational peers.

By knowing the expectations of the supervisor's boss, subordinates, and peers, we should be able to account for a significant amount of the variance in supervisory leadership behavior.

While the supervisor attends to the demands of all members of his role set to some extent, it is likely that some members are more salient than others for various classes of behavior. As Weick (1969) has suggested, any particular interaction at any particular time will lead to only a partial inclusion of an individual in the collective structure, since only some of his behaviors will be included. The behaviors included in an interlocking relation with another are likely to be those behaviors which lead to mutually satisfying interaction. Thus, it is likely that supervisors will interlock their work-related behaviors with their bosses because the boss will define these behaviors as relevant for inclusion in his interaction with the supervisor. It is likely that the boss will define the supervisor's work-related behaviors as more important than the supervisor's behaviors toward his subordinates with regard to social interaction. On the other hand, supervisors should be more likely to interlock socially relevant behaviors with their subordinates, since mutually satisfying interactions are likely to be more obtainable for these behaviors than for work-related behaviors. Work-related behaviors, in the form of demands from the supervisor, are more likely to generate conflict with the subordinates and hence be less mutually satisfying than social interaction behaviors. Therefore, it is plausible to hypothesize:

Hypothesis 1a: The behavior of the supervisor toward his subordinates on work-related issues will be more influenced by the supervisor's own boss and less by his subordinates.

Hypothesis 1b: The behavior of the supervisor toward his subordinates on social interaction dimensions will be more influenced by the subordinates than by the supervisor's own boss.

If these latter two hypotheses are true, we would expect to find a higher correlation between the boss's expectations and supervisor behavior on work-related behaviors, and a higher correlation between the subordinates' expectations and the supervisor's behavior on social interaction-related behaviors.

It is likely that certain situational factors also affect the extent to which supervisory behaviors conform to the expectations of either bosses or subordinates. Frequency of interaction is one such possible mediating variable. Clearly, the more time spent with another, the more opportunity there is for the structure of interaction to include additional behaviors (Weick, 1969). Another such variable is the social similarity between the supervisor and those persons with whom he interacts. While frequency of interaction affects the opportunity for discovering additional potentially mutually satisfying interactions, social similarity affects the extent to which interactions are likely to lead to mutually satisfying outcomes. Relative social distance between the supervisor and his boss can produce less satisfactory interactions, as can differences in sex, education, or attitudes toward important issues. Below we present six hypotheses which posit that various situational constraints of frequency and similarity will mediate the extent to which the supervisor attends to the demands of his boss or his subordinates in work behaviors.

To the extent that the supervisor spends his time actually engaged in supervision, his activities are more likely to be like those of his own boss, and, consequently, he is more likely to be influenced by the expectations of his boss. On the other hand, to the extent that the supervisor spends his time engaged in more routine, task-related activities, he is more likely to be doing things that are more similar to his subordinates, and consequently will probably attend more to their expectations for his behavior. Thus, we hypothesize:

Hypothesis 2: The more the supervisor spends his time supervising, the more he will conform to the expectations of his boss; the more time the supervisor spends in routine task activities, the more he will conform to the expectations of his subordinates.

In Hypothesis 2, we argued that similarity in activities provides one indicator for predicting orientation to various sources of social pressure. It is likely that similarity in other characteristics is also related to orientation. The more similar the supervisor is to his boss, the more he will orient to him; the more similar he is to his subordinates, the more he will orient to them. One dimension of similarity which varied in the present research setting was sex. Some supervisors were male and others were female. But, invariably, the higher supervisory hierarchy was male. Then, we would predict:

Hypothesis 3: If the supervisor is male, he will attend more to the expectations of his own boss; if the supervisor is female, she will attend more to the expectations of the subordinates.

Similarity is a situational factor which should mediate the development of structures of interlocked behaviors in many interaction settings. In work settings, however, there is the unique characteristic that one party to the interaction may have more authority than another. This authority can be used to make the interaction more or less satisfying. Thus, the boss can made demands on the supervisor for specific actions, and can use his authority to make the cost of not complying relatively high. In the Kahn (1964) study, the authors found that persons tended to respond to felt pressures for role performance. In the present instance, it is likely that the greater the demands placed on the supervisor by his own boss to perform well, the more the supervisor will conform to the expectations of his boss. Thus, demands from a person within the role set for certain performance are likely to result in behaviors that are more congruent with the expectations of the role sender making those demands.

Hypothesis 4: The greater the demands made by the supervisor's boss for high performance, the more the supervisor will conform to the boss's expectations for his behavior.

Orientation to the demands of others is likely to be a function of the frequency of contact with those others. To the extent that the supervisor spends a great deal of time with a relatively few employees, he is likely to become more friendly and familiar with them and, consequently, is more likely to conform to their expectations for his behavior. Also, it might be argued that the greater the extent of social contact between the supervisor and his subordinates, the greater the influence of the subordinates on the supervisor's behavior, and, particularly, social behavior. Frequency of contact with specific others is likely to be decreased the larger the number of others in the set, so we hypothesize that:

Hypothesis 5: The greater the number of persons supervised, the less the contact with any one, and, consequently, the less the supervisor's behavior will be influenced by the expectations of his subordinates.

And, focusing on social contact, it is hypothesized:

Hypothesis 6: The more the social contact between the supervisor and his subordinates, the greater the influence subordinate expectations have on the supervisor's behaviors.

Finally, congruence with the demands of others is likely to be partially a function of the relative power and influence of the various individuals in the role set. To some extent, in any hierarchical organization it is necessarily true that the supervisor's boss has more power, and the supervisor's subordinates have less power, than the supervisor. However, it is also true that the locus of control does vary across organizations and across work groups within organizations. One possible indicator of power or influence is where the decisions relevant to the work-group task are made. To the extent that the subordinates make relatively more of the decisions, it holds that they have relatively more influence within the work setting. Therefore, we hypothesize that:

Hypothesis 7a: The greater the proportion of decisions made by the subordinates, the more the supervisor's behavior will conform to the expectations of the subordinates.

Hypothesis 7b: The greater the proportion of decisions made by the supervisor's own boss, the more the supervisor's behavior will conform to the expectations of his boss.

We have argued that, in general, leadership behavior is constrained by the demands of others in the leader's social setting. Further, we have argued that attention to the expectations of some members rather than others in the role set will be a function of frequency and intensity of interaction, relative power, similarity in task and in other characteristics, and the work demands the supervisor faces.

Method

The supervisors studied in this research were fifty-three first-level supervisors in the housing division of a large midwestern state university. The supervisors spent, on the average, 38.8 percent of their time engaged in supervisory tasks, and supervised, on the average, 7.5 persons. While all of the supervisors except one were white, 46.7 percent were female, and 53.3 percent were male. The work tasks involved were typically office and clerical, such as supervising secretaries, keypunchers, clerks, or accountants.

The data were collected over a three-day period. At the first session, supervisors indicated how frequently they engaged in fifteen behaviors with respect to their subordinates. The behaviors were taken from Stogdill and Coons' (1957) Leader Behavior Description Questionnaire and were selected to include both work and social behaviors:

1. Counseling subordinates on personal problems
2. Letting subordinates do their work the way they think best
3. Going to lunch with subordinates
4. Seeing to it that people under supervisor work up to limits
5. Expressing appreciation when person being supervised does a good job
6. Exchanging Christmas cards with subordinates

7. *Not* explaining actions to subordinates
8. Getting together socially with subordinates outside of work
9. Asking for sacrifices from subordinates for the good of the section
10. Being friendly and easily approached by subordinates
11. Insisting that subordinates be at work at 8:00
12. Insisting on being kept informed about decisions made by subordinates
13. Emphasizing the meeting of deadlines to subordinates
14. Being firm about having things done your own way by subordinates
15. Stressing the importance of high morale to subordinates

Frequency of behavior was assessed on a ten-point scale, from 0 for never do to 9 for always do.

At the second session, at least one day later, the supervisors were given a second questionnaire on which they indicated, for each of the fifteen behaviors, what they thought their boss, their peers, and their subordinates wanted them to do, using the same frequency scale. The questions were randomly rearranged in order to help mitigate any consistency effects. At the third session, again separated by at least one day, the supervisors were asked what they would do with respect to each of the fifteen behaviors in order to best accomplish their job. Also, on the third questionnaire, background data were gathered such as the number of persons supervised, the supervisor's race and sex, the demands made by their own bosses to produce, the proportion of their time spent in supervising, and the proportion of decisions involving their group work that are made by their boss, themselves, and their subordinates.

For each of the fifty-three supervisors, then, we have their own estimates of their behavior, and their assessment of the demands of their boss, peers, and subordinates. Because of the structure of the organization, most of the supervisors had few, if any, direct peers, and, consequently, the analyses will focus primarily on the expectations of their boss and their subordinates.

The behavior questions were grouped into conceptually meaningful subsets, based on both an a priori examination of the content and on examination of the intercorrelations among answers. Two subsets are of particular interest: one consisting of questions 4, 11, 12, 13, and 14, dealing with work or task behavior; and the second consisting of questions 3, 6, 8, and 10, dealing with the social interaction between the supervisor and the subordinates. In the analyses, then, it is these groupings of questions that are discussed.

Results

Our first and most general hypothesis was that supervisor's behavior could be accounted for by the expectations and demands of others in his role set. The report of the supervisor's own work-related behaviors was utilized as the dependent variable in a multiple regression equation, with boss, subordinate, and peer expectations as the independent variables. The results are indicated in Equation 1:

$$\text{WORK} = 13.95 + .45\,\text{BOSSWORK} + .094\,\text{SUBWORK} - .027\,\text{PEERWORK} \qquad (1)$$
$$\phantom{\text{WORK} = 13.95 + } (.13) \qquad\qquad (.115) \qquad\qquad (.084)$$
$$R = .49$$

where the numbers in parentheses are the standard errors of the respective regression coefficients, and BOSSWORK is the expectations of the boss with respect to work behaviors, SUBWORK is the expectations of the subordinates, and PEERWORK is the expectations of the peers. As seen in the equation, almost one-quarter of the variation in supervisory behavior can be accounted for by the formulation.

Also in Equation 1, we can see that the variable of the boss's expectations is the only one that is statistically significant. The simple correlations between work behaviors and the three sets of expectations are .48 for the boss, .22 for the subordinates, and .16 for the peers. Thus, as hypothesized in Hypothesis 1a, the boss has the most influence on the supervisor in terms of work-related behaviors. The difference in correlations with the boss's expectations and the subordinates' expectations is .26, which is statistically significant at less than the .05 level of probability.

In Equation 2, we present the results of a similar analysis for the supervisor's behaviors with respect to social interaction with subordinates:

$$\text{SOCIAL} = 10.35 + .15 \text{ BOSSSOC} + .402 \text{ SUBSOC} - .20 \text{ PEERSOC} \qquad (2)$$
$$\phantom{\text{SOCIAL} = 10.35 + } (.14) \qquad\qquad (.15) \qquad\qquad (.10)$$
$$R = .42$$

where BOSSSOC is the expectations of the supervisor's own boss with respect to social behaviors, SUBSOC is the expectations of the subordinates, and PEERSOC is the expectations of the supervisor's peers. Again, a significant amount of the variance in behavior is accounted for by the expectations of others in the supervisor's role set.

It is seen in Equation 2 that in this instance, as hypothesized, the subordinates' expectations account for more of the behavior than the demands of the boss. The simple correlations are .33 for the subordinates' expectations and .22 for the expectations of the boss. Though the difference in correlations is not statistically significant, in the multiple regression formulation the coefficient on the subordinate expectations variable is statistically significant while the coefficient for the boss's expectations variable is not.

To measure the difference in orientation of the supervisor's behavior to the expectations of the subordinates and the boss, three variables were constructed. DIFBOSSW represents the difference between the supervisor's behavior and the boss's expectations for work-related behaviors, and is computed by summing the squared differences between actual behavior and the boss's expectations for the work-related behaviors. DIFSUBW is the difference between the supervisor's actual behavior and the subordinates' expectations for work-related behavior, computed in a parallel fashion. Finally, we measured the relative orientation to either the subordinates or the boss for task behaviors. This latter measure represents the difference of the previously computed differences, or DIFBOSSW − DIFSUBW, and denotes whether the supervisor's actual behavior is more different from the boss's or the subordinates' expectations. The analysis of all of these differences in behavior would be expected to be less significant to the extent that a consistency effect in answering the question holds, so the estimates of the effects are generally conservative.

The percent of the time spent supervising is related, as expected, to the difference in work-related behavior from the expectations of the boss. The correlation is $-.34$ ($p < .01$), and means that the greater the time spent supervising, the greater the conformity between the supervisor's actual behavior and the supervisor's assessment of the boss's expectations for his behavior. The difference of the differences between the behavior and the demands of the boss and the subordinates is correlated $-.25$ ($p < .05$) with the percent of the time spent supervising, with the direction of the correlation again indicating greater orientation to the demands of the boss in work-related behaviors. There is not a significant correlation between the percent of the time spent supervising and differences from the subordinates' expectations for work-related behaviors.

Coding female as 1 and male as 2, the correlation between the supervisor's sex and DIFBOSSW was $-.32$ ($p < .05$), indicating that, as expected, male supervisors engaged in behaviors that were closer to the expectations of their boss. The correlation with DIFSUBW was .17 ($p < .15$), which is in the expected direction, indicating that female supervisors were less different in their work-related activities from the expectations of their subordinates. The correlation with the difference between the differences was $-.38$ ($p < .005$), indicating that male supervisors were more likely to conform to the expectations of their boss than were female supervisors.

The greater the demands made by the supervisor's boss for the supervisor to produce, the more the supervisor conformed in his work-related behaviors to the expectations of the boss ($r = -.35$, $p < .005$), but there was no relationship between the demands made and the difference from subordinates' expectations of task-related behaviors. The difference in orientation to the boss versus the subordinates was significantly related to the demands to produce ($r = -.32$, $p < .01$), with the direction of the correlation meaning that the greater the demands to produce, the more the supervisor conformed to the boss's expectations as compared with the expectations of the subordinates.

While there was not a significant correlation between the number of persons supervised and the difference from the boss's expectations for work behavior, there was a significant and positive correlation between the number supervised and the difference from the subordinates' expectations concerning work behavior ($r = .24$, $p < .05$). And, again, the correlation with differential orientation was significant, with the correlation of $-.30$ ($p < .05$) with the number supervised indicating that the more persons supervised, the more similar the supervisor was to the boss's expectations for the work behavior than to the subordinates'.

The hypothesized effects of social interaction were not generally found either with respect to work or social behaviors. The more the supervisor reported getting together with subordinates outside of work, the greater was the difference between his behaviors and the boss's expectations for this social behavior ($r = .19$, $p < .10$), but there was no relationship with the difference from subordinates' expectations for social behavior. It is possible that these social behaviors are of generally lower relevance, and hence do not respond to situational variations.

Finally, we can consider the differences in behavior from expectations as related to the locus of decision making with respect to the tasks of the work group. The larger the proportion of decisions made by the supervisor's own boss, the more the supervisor differed from the subordinates' expectations ($r = .24$, $p < .10$), while, conversely, the larger the proportion of decisions made by the subordinates, the less the supervisor differed from the work behavior expectations of the subordinates ($r = -.22$, $p < .10$). These decision variables were not related, however, to differences from the boss's expectations for behavior.

Discussion

The results of this study support the argument that supervisory behaviors can be partially explained by the constellation of social influences to which the supervisor is exposed. Work- or task-related supervisory activities in particular seem to be a function of the expectations of persons in the supervisor's role set. Furthermore, whether the supervisor attends more to the expectations of his boss or to those of his subordinates appears to be a function of (a) the demands to produce coming from his boss, (b) the percent of the time the supervisor actually engages in supervision rather than in routine task activities, (c) the number of persons supervised, (d) the sex of the supervisor, and (e) whether task decisions are made primarily by the supervisor, by his boss, or by his subordinates. Many of these factors can be parsimoniously summarized under the concept of social similarity and interaction. To the extent the supervisor supervises more and engages in routine tasks less, he is more like his boss. The sex variable is also a measure of similarity in this instance. The larger the number of persons supervised, the less likely it is that the supervisor will have extensive interaction with any one of them. The other two factors, the locus of decision making for the task and the task demands, relate to the locus of power for task accomplishment and the demands made on the supervisor, respectively.

One problem with the study is that the data were all collected from the same individual. Although the data collection was done over a three-day period and the ordering of the questions was altered, the fact that the same person provided the data on his own behaviors and the expectations of his subordinates, boss, and peers may have produced some consistency in the responses that would not otherwise have existed. However, it is not likely that such consistency could have produced the unique pattern of results which we have reported. Consistency would tend to diminish the reported differences between the subordinates' and the bosses' expectations and the supervisor's own behaviors as perceived by the supervisor. Hence, our analyses of these differences between behaviors and expectations are likely to be conservative estimates of the effects. More importantly, the supervisor's potential response consistency is unlikely to be complexly related to the situational variables that have been examined with reference to the differences between the supervisor's behaviors and the expectations of the bosses and subordinates.

Underlying much of the literature on the effects of different leadership styles is an implicit assumption that leadership behavior is a characteristic of the supervisor, to be either selected or trained to match the appropriate leadership style desired. One of the implications of this research is that leadership behavior is a characteristic of the social situation, constrained and influenced by the demands confronting the supervisor. As such, leadership behavior is itself a variable to be explained. Perhaps analyzing supervisory behavior in the context of the social setting in which it is embedded will assist in also developing better conceptualizations of the contingent consequences of varying leadership behaviors.

References

Allport, F. H. "A Structuronomic Conception of Behavior: Individual and Collective." *Journal of Abnormal and Social Psychology,* 1962, *64,* 3-30.

Argyle, M., Gardner, G., and Cioffi, F. "Supervisory Methods Related to Productivity, Absenteeism, and Labor Turnover." *Human Relations,* 1958, *11,* 23-40.

Burns, T., and Stalker, G. *The Management of Innovation.* London: Tavistock, 1961.

Day, R. C., and Hamblin, R. L. "Some Effects of Close and Punitive Styles of Supervision." *American Journal of Sociology,* 1964, *70,* 499-510.

Evan, W. M. "The Organization-Set: Toward a Theory of Inter-organizational Relations." In J. D. Thompson (Ed.), *Approaches to Organizational Design.* Pittsburgh: University of Pittsburgh Press, 1966.

Fiedler, F. E. *A Theory of Leadership Effectiveness.* New York: McGraw-Hill, 1967.

Fleishman, E. A., and Harris, E. F. "Patterns of Leadership Behavior Related to Employee Grievances and Turnover." *Personnel Psychology,* 1962, *15,* 43-56.

Fleishman, E. A., and Simmons, J. "Relationship Between Leadership Patterns and Effectiveness Ratings Among Israeli Foremen." *Personnel Psychology,* 1970, *23,* 169-172.

Hage, J., and Aiken, M. "Routine Technology, Social Structure, and Organizational Goals." *Administrative Science Quarterly,* 1969, *14,* 366-377.

Heller, F. A., and Yukl, G. "Participation, Managerial Decision-Making, and Situational Variables." *Organizational Behavior and Human Performance,* 1969, *4,* 227-241.

Kahn, R. L., and others. *Organizational Stress: Studies in Role Conflict and Ambiguity.* New York: Wiley, 1964.

Lawrence, P., and Lorsch, J. *Organization and Environment.* Boston: Graduate School of Business Administration, Harvard University, 1967.

Merton, R. K. *Social Theory and Social Structure.* (Rev. ed.) New York: Free Press, 1957.

Mohr, L. B. "Organizational Technology and Organizational Structure." *Administrative Science Quarterly,* 1971, *16,* 444-459.

Patchen, M. "Supervisory Methods and Group Performance Norms." *Administrative Science Quarterly,* 1962, *7,* 275-294.

Pugh, D. S., and others. "The Context of Organization Structures." *Administrative Science Quarterly,* 1969, *14,* 91-114.

Rabinowitz, L., Kelley, H. H., and Rosenblatt, R. M. "Effects of Different Types of Interdependence and Response Conditions in the Minimal Social Situation." *Journal of Experimental Social Psychology,* 1966, *2,* 169-197.

Stogdill, R. M., and Coons, A. E. *Leader Behavior: Its Description and Measurement.* Columbus: Bureau of Business Research, College of Commerce and Administration, Ohio State University, 1957.

Vroom, V. H. "Some Personality Determinants of the Effects of Participation." *Journal of Abnormal and Social Psychology,* 1959, *59,* 322-327.

Weick, K. E. *The Social Psychology of Organizing.* Reading, Mass.: Addison-Wesley, 1969.

10

Organizational Role Conflict: Its Antecedents and Consequences

Robert H. Miles
William D. Perreault, Jr.

Role conflict has recently received increased attention as a critical variable in organizational behavior. This general construct has been shown to be associated with unfavorable personal and job-involvement outcomes; yet the evidence reported in contemporary research suggests that the complex and simultaneous nature of relationships linking role conflict with its antecedents and consequences is not fully understood. For example, two individuals may experience the same degree of role conflict, in general, but the nature and sources of the conflict they experience may be quite different. These differences may explain variations in outcomes associated with role conflict. Only when we are able to comprehend the multivariate nature of role conflict, and the various antecedents and outcomes associated with these conflict types, will we be in a position to select with any degree of confidence the appropriate remedial strategy. The present investigation develops a comprehensive model of these interrelationships and reveals its underlying structure.

Previous Research

Recent evidence has demonstrated that the experience of role conflict is related to unfavorable personal and organizational outcomes and that objective antecedents residing in the organizational context and requirements of the role appear to predict the level of general role conflict experienced by the focal person. Evidence has been reported of direct relationships between the degree of role conflict a focal person experiences on the job and various work-related outcomes, including job-related tension and anxiety, job dissatisfaction, futility, propensity to leave, lack of confidence in the organization, inability to influence decision making, and unfavorable attitudes toward role senders (Kahn and others, 1964; House and Rizzo, 1972; Rizzo, House, and Lirtzman, 1970; Tosi, 1971).

Reprinted from *Organizational Behavior and Human Performance*, 1976, *17*, 19-44, with permission of the authors and Academic Press. Copyright © 1976 by Academic Press, Inc.

Thus, role conflict appears to be associated with a variety of undesirable individual outcomes which are generally regarded as dysfunctional for the organization.

In addition to this work on the general role-conflict variable, Kahn and associates (1964) have identified several components of role conflict, and House and Rizzo (1972) have developed operational measures of these components, but neither has reported results on the basis of these more specific conflict measures. It is possible, in fact likely, that two persons may experience the same degree of *general* role conflict, but the specific sources and the types or components of the general conflict they experience may be quite different. Consequently, for these two persons, the choice of strategies to effectively manage the level of role conflict should vary with its source and components. Thus, it becomes necessary to move beyond the general role-conflict construct if we are to comprehend the multivariate nature of conflict and the appropriateness of various strategies for successfully engaging role conflict and its consequences.

There is evidence to suggest that objective role requirements and organizational conditions may be useful in predicting the degree of experienced role conflict. Division and specialization have been regarded as a major source of conflict in organizations (Thompson, 1967; Argyris, 1964), and the delicate system of linkages across these specializations is viewed as a major source of strain and accommodation in complex organizations (Corwin, 1969). Therefore, role requirements which involve coordination responsibilities across organizational boundaries may be primary sources of role conflict. For example, integration and boundary-spanning activities are required to coordinate interdependent but differentiated individuals and subunits both within and across organizational boundaries. *Boundary relevance,* inferred from frequency of contacts with individuals outside a focal person's own organization, has been shown to be directly associated with degree of experienced role conflict (Kahn and others, 1964).

Relatively high levels of conflict have also been thought to characterize supervisory roles (Roethlisberger, 1945; Charters, 1952), and evidence concerning the inherent conflict in superior-subordinate relations in research organizations has been reported by Kaplan (1959) and Evan (1962). Thus, role conflict appears to be associated with organizational linking roles, whether they involve the integration of activities across intra- and interorganizational boundaries or up and down the chain of command. Furthermore, Kahn and associates have argued that role conflict is directly related to the degree of innovation required by the role; consequently, the degree of scientific research responsibilities assigned to focal persons in the present sample may be another objective source of experienced conflict. Finally, Kahn and associates have shown that the degree of formal authority and status of role senders relative to that of the focal person may be another source of conflict. High relative authority on the part of the role senders may make it easier for them to encourage compliance of the focal person to conflicting role demands. In addition to these plausible origins of conflict, there are those which are not role-specific. For example, House and Rizzo (1972) have found significant relationships between measures of leadership and organizational practices and degree of experienced role conflict. Thus, a host of conditions appear to be potential sources of experienced conflict. An important question, then, is: To what extent do simultaneous combinations of these objective conditions predict the degree and nature of role conflict experienced?

Theoretical Model

Figure 1 presents a theoretical model for this investigation. The model assumes a causal sequence beginning with objective sources of role-conflict perceptions and ending

Figure 1. Theoretical Role-Conflict Model

Objective Role Requirements	Role Perceptions	Individual Outcomes
Importance of selected job activities: —Integration and boundary-spanning activities —Personnel supervision —Scientific research Role-set characteristics —Organizational distance of role senders —Formal authority of role senders	Multivariate conflict orientations (based on the following subscales or types of role conflict) : —Person-role conflict —Intersender conflict —Intrasender conflict —Overload conflict	—Job-related tension —Job satisfaction —Perceived performance effectiveness —Attitudes toward role senders

with work-related consequences of these perceptions. The assumption that role conflict serves as an intervening variable in this sequence has been supported by House and Rizzo (1972). The rationale of the model and related research hypotheses are briefly discussed in this section. In a subsequent section the statistical structure and tests of the model are presented.

Role conflict has been defined as the degree of incongruity or incompatibility of expectations communicated to a focal person by his/her role senders. In the present investigation, role conflict is conceptualized as a multivariate perception consisting of the following four conflict types (after House and Rizzo, 1972):

(a) *Person-role conflict:* the extent to which role expectations are incongruent with the orientations or values of the role occupant.
(b) *Intersender conflict:* the extent to which two or more role expectations from one role sender oppose those from one or more other role senders.
(c) *Intrasender conflict:* the extent to which two or more role expectations from a single role sender are mutually incompatible.
(d) *Overload:* the extent to which the various role expectations communicated to a role occupant exceed the amount of time and resources available for their accomplishment.

The first phase of the investigation involved the empirical development of multivariate role-conflict profiles, subsequently referred to as *conflict orientations*. This phase enabled the researchers to move beyond general role conflict, revealing the multivariate nature of the conflict actually experienced by individuals in the performance of their assigned roles.

The second aspect of the model posits that these conflict orientations can be predicted on the basis of objective role requirements or job conditions imposed upon the individual. These objective sources of conflict were drawn from (a) the importance of major role requirements, including personnel supervision, integration and boundary-spanning activities, and scientific research, and (b) the characteristics of the focal person's role set, including the average organizational distance of important role senders (a measure of boundary relevance) and the degree of formal authority role senders as a group have relative to the focal person.

Finally, the relationships between conflict orientation of the individual and various work-related outcomes (that is, job-related tension, job satisfaction, attitudes toward role senders, and perceived effectiveness) are determined. Details on the development of these measures are included in a subsequent section of this paper.

While researchers have analyzed various aspects of the theoretical model, there has been no complete evaluation of the *simultaneous* relationships it suggests. These simultaneous relationships were translated into the following research hypotheses:

I. Individuals may be grouped on the basis of patterns of specific types of role conflict they experience, and these patterns will be significantly different between groups. (These groups are referred to as *conflict orientations.*)

II. Objective role requirements will systematically discriminate between conflict orientation of the individual. Objective conditions which are high in conflict potential (that is, heavy role requirements emphasizing supervisory activities, integration and boundary-spanning activities and scientific research activities, and/or role sets characterized by high-distance or superior-authority role senders) will be related to different and more intense conflict orientations.

III. Conflict orientation of the individual will be directly related to work outcomes, which include job-related tension, job dissatisfaction, unfavorability of attitudes toward role senders, and perceived ineffectiveness.

Method

Research Sample and Site

Professional-level personnel from nine governmental research and development organizations voluntarily completed a questionnaire administered in conference rooms located near their places of work. All personnel in the roles of division manager, group leader, and integrator (after Lawrence and Lorsch, 1967) were invited to participate. A roughly equivalent-sized, random sample of nonsupervisory scientists and engineers was also drawn. Of the 210 asked to participate, 202 completed questionnaires. After editing incomplete responses, 195 were usable in this investigation, resulting in an effective participation rate in excess of 92 percent.

Instruments

Role Perceptions. Role conflict was defined as the degree of incongruity or incompatibility of expectations associated with a role, and role ambiguity was defined as the lack of clarity regarding role expectations and performance evaluations. These definitions were consistent with previous research (see, for example, Kahn and others, 1964; Rizzo, House, and Lirtzman, 1970). The specific scales included in each of these measures were chosen because of their demonstrated factorial independence (Rizzo, House, and Lirtzman, 1970). In addition, subscale measures were obtained for various types of role conflict. These types of conflict were measured in the present study as subscales of the general role-conflict scale. A sample item for each conflict type follows:

(a) *Person-role conflict:* "I have to do things that should be done differently."
(b) *Intrasender conflict:* "I receive an assignment without the proper manpower to complete it."
(c) *Intersender conflict:* "I do things that are apt to be accepted by one person and not by others."
(d) *Role overload:* "I frequently have much more work to do than I can handle during the time available at work."

Intercorrelations between these role-conflict subscales were moderate and positive. For intersender conflict, correlations were .39 with intrasender conflict, .32 with person-role conflict, and .27 with role overload. Intrasender conflict was correlated .36 with person-role conflict and .38 with role overload. Person-role conflict was correlated .11 with role overload.

Work-Related Outcomes. The job-related tension scales developed by Rizzo and associates (1970) were employed. These scales included measures of work-related worry, "taking the job home," relief when leaving work, and items drawn from the Taylor Scale of Manifest Anxiety (Taylor, 1953).

The job satisfaction scale developed by Bullock (1952) was chosen on the basis of its published test-retest and split-half reliabilities, both in excess of .90.

The measure of perceived effectiveness was developed by Pym and Auld (1965) for use in ambiguous performance situations. This measure was shown to be related to actual job performance of industrial salesmen in a study reported by Pruden and Reece (1972).

Interpersonal relations was a measure of the favorability of attitudes of focal persons toward their role senders, and was developed by Kahn and associates (1964). It was composed of three attitudes, including trust, respect, and liking for each sender. To derive this measure, each focal person was asked to "map" his/her role set by listing those persons (up to a maximum of ten) who could significantly help or hinder his/her job performance. Focal persons then scored their attitudes toward each of their role senders, and these scores were combined into an unweighted role-set average, referred to as interpersonal relations.

Objective Conditions. The role-set mapping form provided two additional measures. Each focal person indicated how many distinct intra- and interorganizational boundaries separated him from each of his/her role senders. The role-set average on this dimension was a measure of the organizational distance of role senders. It was labeled the *average role-set distance* and was used to infer the boundary relevance of the role occupied by the focal person.

Focal persons also reported how much formal authority role senders had relative to their own. The role-set average on this dimension was a measure of discrepancy in formal authority between the focal person and members of his/her role set. This measure was labeled *average role-set authority.*

In addition to role-set measures of objective conditions, the extent of responsibility for performing various role requirements was assessed. Focal persons were asked to rate the importance of fifty job activities to the performance of their assigned roles. These activities were adapted from a longer list developed by Stogdill and Shartle (1955) and were scored in importance on a five-point scale, ranging from "definitely not a part of my job" to "a most significant part of my job." These ratings were factor-analyzed according to a principal components method using varimax rotation to reveal the major underlying role requirements for the sample of participants. Three factors accounted for approximately 46 percent of the common variance: personnel supervision activities (27.9 percent), integration and boundary-spanning activities (10.0 percent), and scientific research activities (8.5 percent).

These underlying role requirements were representative of the basic role differences for persons in this sample and were unambiguously anchored on the basis of organizational role. For example, integration and boundary-spanning activities were most important for integrators and least important for highly buffered, basic scientists; furthermore, the importance of these boundary-spanning activities increased monotonically through the roles from basic scientist, applied scientist and engineer, group leader, division manager, to integrator. Personnel supervision activities were rated as most important by division managers, followed by group leaders, and scientific research activities were most important to basic scientists. As shown in Table 1, the overall differences

Table 1. Differences Between Organizational Roles in Importance of
Major Role Requirements

Role-Requirement Factors	Integrator	Basic S & E	Applied S & E	Group Ldr	Div Mgr	F[a]	$p <$
Personnel supervision activities	1.64[b] (3)[c]	1.53 (5)	1.58 (4)	2.45 (2)	3.73 (1)	107.06	.001
Integration and boundary-spanning activities	3.45 (1)	2.15 (5)	2.38 (4)	2.95 (3)	3.37 (2)	21.28	.001
Scientific research activities	2.38 (5)	3.86 (1)	3.17 (4)	3.67 (2)	3.28 (3)	11.26	.001

[a]Comparisons of overall differences in role means on importance of role-requirement factors.

[b]*Importance* of major role requirement factors was the average rating, using a five-point response mode from "definitely not part of my job" to "a most significant part of my job," for all items in the role requirement factor.

[c]Rankings of role means on importance of role-requirement factor.

between roles on the importance their incumbents attached to each of these activities were significant: personnel supervision ($F = 107.06, p < .001$), integration and boundary-spanning activities ($F = 21.28, p < .001$), and scientific research ($F = 11.26, p < .001$). The estimates of the strength of statistical association (ω^2) between roles and role requirements are strong enough to support the practical significance of these differences. The percentage of variance in role requirements accounted for by organizational role was as follows: personnel supervision (68 percent), integration and boundary spanning (28 percent), and scientific research (17 percent). A complete listing of the items included in each of these role-requirement factors, along with their factor loadings, is included in the Appendix.

The reliabilities obtained for all of the multi-item measures described above exceeded generally accepted conventions for use in the analyses. The minimum Spearman-Brown reliability estimate for any scale was in excess of .80. The means, standard deviations, and reliabilities for all multi-item measures are shown in Table 2. A complete discussion of these scales is presented by Miles (1974).

Results

Multivariate Conflict Orientations

Each of the respondents may be characterized by a four-element conflict profile, consisting of measures on person-role, intersender, intrasender, and overload types of role conflict. Two persons may report the same degree of general role conflict, but the particular types of conflict they actually experience may be quite different. For example, one may be low on person-role conflict, medium on intersender conflict, and high on both intrasender conflict and role overload. The other may have a very dissimilar profile, while both may report the same level of role conflict in general. Our problem, therefore, was conceived as one of categorizing respondents who have similar multivariate conflict

Table 2. Scales, Items per Scale, Means, Standard Deviations,
and Reliabilities of the Measures

Measures	Number of Items	Mean[a]	SD	Spearman-Brown Reliabilities
Role perceptions				
Role-conflict types				
Intersender conflict	4	2.73	0.94	.81
Person-role conflict	3	2.64	0.91	.84
Intrasender conflict	2	2.98	1.19	.91
Overload	1	3.03	1.27	—
Role ambiguity	6	2.68	0.83	.92
Personal outcomes				
Job satisfaction	10	3.90	0.62	.91
Job-related tension	13	2.21	0.72	.89
Attitudes toward role senders	3	3.75	0.46	.81
Perceived effectiveness	1	3.83	0.81	—
Objective conditions				
Personnel supervision	12	2.21	1.04	.95
Integration and boundary-spanning activities	11	2.81	0.91	.91
Scientific research	5	3.29	1.02	.86
Average role-set distance	1	1.92	0.70	—
Average role-set authority	1	3.42	0.81	—

[a]All scales were scored using a five-point response mode.

profiles into the same group, while specifying groups which are differentiated in terms of conflict profiles.

Toward the objective of developing such an empirical classification system for conflict orientations, cluster analysis (numerical taxonomy) was used to determine groups of individuals with similar multivariate conflict profiles. Following such an approach, this study first determined existing groupings of individuals (based on *within*-group similarity of their conflict profiles), and then investigated differences *between* groups on the objective role-requirement measures and the job-outcome measures.

Cluster analytic procedures are well suited to this preclassification problem (Pinto and Pinder, 1972; Landy, 1972). In this research a simple and widely applied index of multivariate similarity was used. This index was a simple distance function, computed as the sum of squared distances between corresponding conflict scores and the multivariate profiles for each pair of individuals (Cronbach and Gleser, 1953). The clusters of similar profiles were formed in a hierarchical fashion (Ward, 1963) with the SUBGROUP program (Johnson, 1967).

The cluster analysis provided evidence of five distinct conflict patterns or orientations. The overall F test for discrimination between the conflict orientations on the conflict variables and each of the univariate F ratios for between-group differences are all significant at the .001 level. The differences were expected, since the orientations were formed in such a fashion as to be differentiated on these variables. Table 3 presents the average scores on the four conflict variables for individuals in each of the five conflict orientation groups. These average or "typical" response profiles provided a basis of comparison for the five conflict orientations. To facilitate comparison, these average response profiles are plotted in Figure 2. These averages have been labeled Orientations I to V, reflecting increasing levels of generalized conflict (see Table 3). It should be emphasized,

Table 3. Average Conflict Scores for Conflict Orientations

Conflict Orientation	Sample		Conflict Category Means				Summated General Role-Conflict Index[a]
	(N)	(%)	Over-load	Person-Role	Intra-sender	Inter-sender	
I	56	29	2.48 (0.99)	1.97 (0.49)	1.81 (0.64)	1.96 (0.59)	8.22
II	45	23	1.84 (0.64)	3.00 (0.92)	3.08 (0.96)	2.56 (0.98)	10.48
III	45	23	3.64 (0.61)	2.31 (0.51)	3.08 (0.87)	3.06 (0.67)	12.09
IV	18	9	3.05 (0.80)	3.89 (0.63)	4.22 (0.77)	3.81 (0.63)	14.97
V	31	16	4.97 (0.18)	3.14 (0.79)	4.16 (0.78)	3.28 (0.73)	15.55

[a]Summated general role-conflict index was calculated by giving each conflict category mean equal weight when summing them into an index.

however, that the conflict orientations are quite varied with respect to the *pattern* of the profile as well as on generalized conflict.

Low levels of conflict characterize the pattern for Orientation I. The profile pattern for this group is lower than any of the other orientations on person-role, intersender, and especially intrasender conflict. On overload, only Orientation II is lower. Orientation II is also a relatively low conflict group. It is characterized by the least overload, but its profile is relatively higher on person-role and intrasender. It is second lowest on intersender conflict. Orientation III is a higher conflict group in general and displays disproportionately high levels of overload. The individuals sharing this orientation report low person-role conflict. They are at about the organizational average for intrasender and intersender conflict. Orientation III, then, reflects an outlook to too much work, but not other forms of conflict.

Of all the conflict orientations, Orientation IV has the highest average profile on person-role, intrasender, and intersender conflict. In spite of these high levels, individuals

Figure 2. Conflict Orientation Profiles

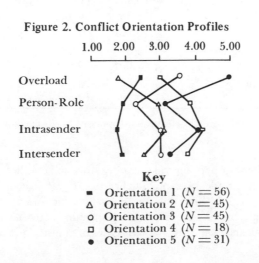

Key
- Orientation 1 (N = 56)
- Orientation 2 (N = 45)
- Orientation 3 (N = 45)
- Orientation 4 (N = 18)
- Orientation 5 (N = 31)

sharing this orientation score substantially lower on overload than other types of conflict. The mean of this group on overload is at the average of the whole organization. In total, this profile indicates a relatively high level of generalized conflict.

Orientation V, the highest group on generalized conflict, is lower than Orientation IV on person-role, intersender, and intrasender, but this group is extremely high on overload, which increases its level of generalized conflict. Almost without exception, individuals in this group chose the maximum point on the role-overload scale.

Several pattern similarities can be observed across the five conflict orientations. The multivariate conflict pattern of group III is almost identical to group V, except that the latter is substantially higher on each variable. Orientations II and IV are also characterized by a similar pattern, although that pattern differs from those found in the other groups. In each of these pairs, the patterns are the same within the pair, but they differ in absolute magnitude.

In summary, the cluster analysis uncovered five distinct conflict orientations. The orientations differ; they represent a hierarchy of different levels of generalized conflict and are based on very different patterns or profiles on the underlying types of conflict. The next section explores these differences on the basis of objective antecedents.

Objective Role Requirements as Predictors of Conflict Orientation

The conceptual model (Figure 1) of the structural hierarchy of effects suggests that various combinations of objective role requirements lead to different conflict orientations for the role occupant.

The means for each of the five conflict orientations on each of the five objective role requirements are presented in Table 4. Generally, the means tend to support the

Table 4. Objective Conditions by Conflict Orientation

Objective Conditions	Conflict Orientations				
	I	II	III	IV	V
Integration and boundary-spanning activities	2.52 (0.88)	2.68 (0.80)	2.77 (0.99)	3.00 (1.05)	3.34 (0.77)
Scientific research activities	3.28 (0.86)	3.09 (1.14)	3.19 (1.05)	3.21 (1.13)	3.67 (1.12)
Average role-set distance	1.79 (0.72)	1.86 (0.66)	1.93 (0.69)	1.73 (0.82)	2.23 (0.60)
Personnel supervision activities	2.03 (1.00)	2.04 (0.99)	2.25 (1.07)	2.19 (1.21)	2.68 (1.10)
Average role-set authority	3.46 (0.79)	3.52 (0.86)	3.28 (0.66)	3.39 (1.15)	3.25 (0.85)

Note: Tabular values are objective condition means, with standard deviations being reported in parentheses.

hypothesized relationship between role requirements and conflict orientation. For example, as the importance a focal person attaches to integration and boundary-spanning increases (from 2.521 to 3.340), so does the general conflict orientation he/she experiences from (I to V). Thus, the extent of boundary-spanning activities required in the performance of a role appears to stratify the five types of conflict orientations experienced by role incumbents. Scientific research activities, personnel supervision activities, and role-set distance also appear to do a reasonably good job of stratifying the conflict orientations. On the other hand, no clear pattern emerges for role-set authority. Multiple discriminant analysis was used to test these relationships and to further clarify differences among conflict orientations.

Multiple discriminant analysis (MDA) is a multivariate statistical procedure which produces a weighted combination of a set of predictor variables (in this case the objective role-requirement measures) to provide a function that maximally discriminates (in a least squares sense) between groups.

A summary of the MDA of objective role requirements on conflict orientation is presented in Table 5. The objective conditions provide a significant basis for discrimina-

Table 5. Summary of Multiple Discriminant Analysis: Conflict Orientations Predicted from Job Conditions

	F Ratio[a]	df $v_1;v_2$	Probability Less Than	Standardized Discriminant Function Coefficients	Discriminant Loadings[b]
Overall discrimination between conflict orientations	1.643	20;617	.039		
Contributions of predictors:					
Scientific research	1.519	4;190	.198	.495	.443
Distance of role senders	2.455	4;190	.047	.474	.591
Integration and boundary-spanning activities	4.461	4;190	.002	.401	.797
Personnel supervision	2.307	4;190	.060	.259	.601
Authority of role senders	0.773	4;190	.544	−.096	−.266

[a]The multivariate F ratio and its degrees of freedom are computed according to Wilks lambda criterion (1932). The univariate F ratios are based on the within-groups to between-groups mean square for each variable.

[b]These loadings are the correlations between the individual predictor variables and the discriminant function composite score (canonical variate); they are analogous to the loadings in a factor analysis.

tion between the conflict orientations, as evidenced by the Wilks (1932) lambda approximate multivariate F ratio (F (20, 617) = 1.643, $p < .05$) for the first discriminant function.

In Table 5, the individual role-requirement predictors of conflict orientation are listed in descending order of their relative contribution to the discriminant function, and thus prediction of conflict orientation. The univariate F ratios (based on standard ANOVA) are provided only to supplement the multivariate F ratio and the means in Table 5. The standardized discriminant function coefficients and loadings provide a better basis than the univariate F for evaluating the contribution of individual predictors to the multivariate function.

The standardized discriminant function coefficients are the "weights" for the predictor variables (that is, role-requirement measures) used to derive the best predictive equation for classifying individuals into an appropriate conflict orientation group. The discriminant function loadings are the simple correlations between the individual predictors and the overall discriminant function score. In this analysis one discriminant function is significant, providing one set of weights and one set of loadings.

The MDA summary statistics in Table 5 show that integration and boundary-spanning activities are highly correlated (.797) with the discriminant function score and are associated with a relatively large weight (.401) in the discriminant function. This is as expected from the works of previous researchers (see, for example, Kahn and others, 1964; Lawrence and Lorsch, 1967; Adams, 1976; Organ, 1971a) who have argued that conflict is a function of "boundary relevance" of a focal person's role.

The importance of scientific research to role incumbents demonstrates an issue important to this analysis. The ANOVA, testing scientific research independently from the other variables, resulted in an insignificant F; when its multivariate role is examined, however, this activity becomes the most heavily weighted variable (coefficient = .495) in the discriminant function. Both role-set distance and personnel supervision activities exhibit high positive loadings. Thus, support is obtained for our model, which hypothesizes that certain specified objective conditions may be used to predict the conflict orientation of an individual. There were differences on each of the role-requirement measures, with the exception of role-set authority, and the multivariate discriminant function was significant even though this authority condition was included.

The positive discriminant function weights and loadings suggest that the significant underlying dimension that discriminates between the groups is a generalized additive role-requirements continuum. The *additive* nature of this continuum means that individuals who score high are not simply reporting intense demands in one job condition, but two or more of these requirements simultaneously. A low score on the continuum would reflect a favorable condition or set of role requirements; a high score would reflect an unfavorable condition. It was expected that the favorable end (low scores) of this continuum would not be conducive to conflict, while the other extreme would be conducive to conflict. To test this hypothesis, a composite score was computed for each respondent by multiplying the function coefficients by the standardized predictor variables, and then summing them. Individuals were then grouped according to their respective conflict orientations, and an average composite score for each orientation was derived. The various orientations are plotted along the objective conditions continuum, according to this average score, in Figure 3.

Figure 3. Relative Position of Conflict Orientations on the Job Conditions Continuum

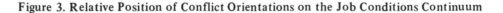
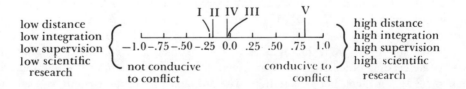

From Figure 3 it can be observed that the groups were stratified on the continuum in the fashion expected. Orientations I and II, both characterized by low levels of conflict, were closely positioned on the favorable end of the objective conditions continuum; individuals in these orientations would therefore have relatively low responsibilities for integration and boundary spanning, personnel supervision, and so forth. The mean scores in Table 4 support this pattern. The role-requirement predictors resulted in higher (less favorable) positions for groups III and IV on the continuum. The high-conflict group, Orientation V, was especially high on the continuum.

The predictive model seems to have some difficulty in discriminating between conflict Orientations I and II and Orientations III and IV on the basis of objective job conditions; on the other hand, discrimination is good between the three major groupings which emerge in Figure 3, especially with respect to group V. It could be that individual differences, as opposed to factors related to the job or to specific role requirements, account for the low discrimination between groups I and II and III and IV. It is compelling to speculate that individuals in these groups, who apparently operate under similar objective conditions, may differ in their predisposition or set toward potentially conflictful job conditions or they may vary in their choices of coping mechanisms under conditions of experienced conflict.

In summary, this portion of the analyses demonstrates the construct validity of the hypothesized relationships between objective conditions (role requirements) and the conflict orientations. All of the role-requirement measures, except degree of role sender formal authority, tend to contribute to the simultaneous discrimination among the conflict orientations. The next section reports the final stage in the analyses by revealing the extent to which differences in individuals' job outcomes may be explained by their conflict orientations.

Impact of Conflict Orientation on Job Outcomes

The evidence that objective role requirements of individuals affect their orientations toward conflict is important if, as suggested in Figure 1, conflict orientation influences various job outcomes (that is, tension, satisfaction, interpersonal relations, and effectiveness on the job). In this investigation the statistical model used to test the conceptual model was multivariate analysis of variance (MANOVA) with covariate control. Detailed discussions of the use of MANOVA in this type of research have been provided (see, for example, Jones, 1966; Bock and Haggard, 1968).

By way of review, like the more commonly used univariate analysis of variance, MANOVA focuses on systematic differences between groups of subjects. In the present investigation more than one dependent variable had to be considered. While it might be argued that univariate ANOVA could be performed on each outcome variable separately, this was not the most appropriate approach here (Bock and Haggard, 1968) because each of the variables was obtained from same subjects. Therefore, the measurements were correlated and separate F tests would not be independent. Because of this confounding, no exact univariate probability that at least one of the variables deviates from a specified null hypothesis can be computed. Furthermore, a single probability statement, applicable to all the outcome variables simultaneously (which, after all, is how they affect the individual), cannot be obtained from the separate F ratios. The sampling distributions for the multivariate tests, however, provide such exact probabilities and can account for the intercorrelations among the outcome measures. Thus, MANOVA was used to test departure from a null hypothesis of no differences in the outcome measures across the different conflict orientation groups.

The role-ambiguity measures developed by Rizzo, House, and Lirtzman (1970) were used as covariates in this analysis. In their study, these ambiguity measures were factorially independent from the role-conflict measures; however, in this study the ambiguity and conflict measures were weakly but significantly correlated. Therefore, role ambiguity was controlled using covariate analysis to eliminate the possibility that any relationship between the conflict orientations and the outcomes measures was confounded with individuals' differing levels of ambiguity. This covariance analysis was used to reduce error variability in the dependent measures and is analogous to the situation in correlational statistics where the relationship between conflict and job outcomes is examined after partialing out the influence of ambiguity.

The means for the job-outcome measures by conflict orientation are presented in Table 6, and the MANOVA results are found in Table 7. The multivariate F ratio asso-

Table 6. Job-Outcome Measures by Conflict Orientation[a]

Outcomes	Conflict Orientation				
	I (N = 56)	II (N = 45)	III (N = 45)	IV (N = 18)	V (N = 31)
Job-related tension[b]	2.564 (0.885)	2.929 (0.919)	2.803 (0.941)	3.240 (1.331)	2.935 (0.997)
Job satisfaction[c]	4.252 (1.390)	4.736 (2.989)	4.196 (1.483)	3.400 (0.535)	3.958 (0.555)
Interpersonal relations[c]	4.083 (1.090)	3.761 (0.752)	3.646 (0.431)	3.364 (0.996)	3.814 (0.405)
Perceived effectiveness[c]	3.768 (0.914)	3.756 (0.802)	3.978 (0.621)	3.722 (0.752)	3.903 (0.908)

[a]Tabled values are means, with standard deviations shown in parentheses.

[b]A high score depicts high tension (that is, a more unfavorable outcome).

[c]A high score depicts more satisfaction, better relations, or more effectiveness (that is, a more favorable outcome).

ciated with the first discriminant function is significant ($p < .05$) and indicates departure from a null hypothesis of no differences. Furthermore, the second discriminant function (which by construction is uncorrelated to the first) approaches significance ($p < .081$). These significant results are especially interesting in light of the univariate F tests. When treated separately, none of the outcomes appear to differ significantly across groups. The multivariate analysis, which is more consistent with the conceptualization of the model, uncovered true differences among the variables by examining them *simultaneously*.

While departure from the MANOVA null hypothesis was demonstrated, differences between the groups were not all in the same direction or magnitude for each variable (Table 6); therefore, one additional analysis was performed to characterize more clearly group differences. This final analysis was based on the fact that the formal equivalent of discriminant function analysis can be computed concomitant to MANOVA (Bock, 1963). While the MANOVA provided a test of significant departure from the null hypothesis, discriminant function analysis was used as an aid in interpreting these differences by showing the combination of the dependent variables that maximized departure from the null hypothesis.

The statistics for the discriminant function analyses are reported in Table 7. Just as the canonical representation of the discriminant analysis was plotted for a single function in the analysis of the role-requirements data, a visual representation using both discriminant function continua are useful here (see Figure 4). The coordinates used to position the groups in the two-dimensional space were the average group scores on the first and second discriminant functions, respectively. Inspection of the discriminant loadings

Table 7. Multivariate Analysis of Variance of Differences in Job Outcomes
Across Conflict Orientations[a]

	Tests of MANOVA		
	Ratio[b]	df v_1, v_2	Probability Less Than
Roots 1-4	1.716	16;554	.040
Roots 2-4	1.724	9;480	.081

Tests of ANOVA and Discriminant Function Estimates

Job Outcomes	F Ratio[c]	Mean Square	Prob. Less Than	Standardized Discriminant Function Coefficients		Loadings[d]	
				I	II	I	II
Tension	1.076	9.524	.370	−.315	−.247	−.285	−.288
Satisfaction	1.849	5.739	.121	−.051	.768	−.035	.738
Relations	1.869	1.051	.118	.754	.339	.690	.369
Effectiveness	1.955	1.021	.103	−.674	.481	−.576	.492

[a]This MANOVA was computed after the criterion variables (job outcomes) had been corrected for covariance with role ambiguity. The relationship between the covariate and the outcomes was significant ($p < .001$).

[b]Based on Wilks lambda criterion (1932); subsequent roots were not significant.

[c]The degrees of freedom for these F tests were 4 and 184.

[d]These loadings are the correlations between the individual outcomes and the canonical variable scores which are computed concomitantly with the MANOVA estimates.

in Table 7 provided a basis for labeling the underlying dimensions of group differences and for understanding the relative positions of the groups on those dimensions.

The vertical dimension (the second discriminant function) is treated first as it was more parsimonious. This dimension was highly correlated (.738) with job satisfaction, and positively related to both perceived effectiveness (.492) and attitudes toward role

Figure 4. Conflict Orientations in Outcomes Space

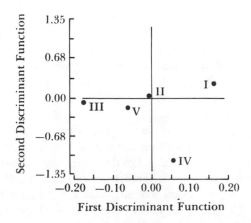

senders (.369); simultaneously, there was a negative loading on job-related tension (−.288). Therefore, this might be labeled an "overall attitude toward job" continuum, ranging from very favorable to very unfavorable. As shown in Figure 4, this continuum stratified the conflict orientation groups in the following ascending order: IV, V, III, II, I. Groups that are low on this function tend to dislike their job, and higher-scoring groups are more favorable toward their work. With the exception of the extreme position of Orientation IV on this continuum, the higher conflict groups are more unfavorable to their jobs.

The horizontal axis in Figure 4 represents the continuum of scores calculated for the groups on the first discriminant function. This function was more complex and provides insight into how the individuals in the various conflict orientation groups differed in work-related outcomes. As shown in Figure 4, this function distinguished between the groups following an ordering (from lower to higher scores) of III, V, II, IV, I. Once again, the discriminant function weights and loadings were helpful in understanding the differences. The loading for job satisfaction on this function was very close to zero (.035); job satisfaction therefore did not contribute to this function as a basis for discrimination. This was in sharp contrast to its role in the previously discussed second function. On the other hand, in this function there was a strong positive loading for attitudes toward role senders (.690) and a strong negative loading for perceived effectiveness (−.576). A negative correlation of only moderate strength was found for job-related tension (−.285). Low scores on this discriminant function appear to reflect a situation where individuals have unfavorable interpersonal relations but perceive themselves to be highly effective on the job; conversely, high scores on this function indicate individuals who enjoy favorable interpersonal relationships but do not perceive themselves to be particularly effective on the job.

The discriminant function may be labeled a "performance at the expense of interpersonal relations" continuum. One interpretation of the positioning observed by conflict orientation group on this continuum may be that groups III and V consist of individuals who derive much reinforcement intrinsically from task performance but who are not dependent upon, or are not responsive to, social demands of others. Orientation I was located at the other end of this continuum. While those sharing this orientation experience low levels of all four types of role conflict, they do not perceive themselves as strong performers on the job but do report very favorable relationships with their work associates.

Persons in groups III and V appear to exhibit a high need-for-achievement syndrome, with emphasis on performance effectiveness and unresponsiveness to social pressure; if so, it would not be surprising to find that (as shown in Figure 2) they are overloaded with work and receive conflicting demands from one dominant role sender (presumably their superior). Conversely, individuals in group I appear to be social creatures exhibiting characteristics of the need-for-affiliation syndrome. They report strong interpersonal relations with work associates but low effectiveness on the job. Perhaps the former characteristic of this group overrides the latter, since these individuals report the lowest level of generalized role conflict.

It should also be recalled that the patterns exhibited on the original conflict profiles (Figure 2) were very similar for Orientations III and V and for Orientations II and IV. The absolute levels of conflict seemed to differentiate these pairs of orientations, but not their overall patterns on the four conflict dimensions. This similarity reappeared in the stratification of these groups on the first discriminant function related to job outcomes. For example, the pair of orientations consisting of groups III and V are at the high-effectiveness end of the function. Orientation III, which is substantially lower than V on all conflict measures (especially role overload), was a higher effectiveness group. The higher level of conflict experienced by persons in Orientation V apparently inhibits job satisfaction and stimulates tension, but does not influence outcomes of perceived effectiveness or attitudes toward role senders (Table 6). Of course, taking this pair in general, an alternative explanation of their higher perceived effectiveness, relative to orientation groups I, II, and IV, may be the tendency of individuals to assume that hard work necessarily implies effective work; this may not be true when considered at the extremes.

Discussion

We have attempted to provide a comprehensive analysis of the linkages between role-conflict perceptions, their antecedents and their consequences. While selected aspects of the study replicate many findings reported in earlier research, the comprehensive approach brings to light new perspectives and issues which should be the subject of future research.

Many complex interrelationships complicate research on role conflict. While researchers frequently develop models which conceptualize these interrelationships (see, for example, Kahn and others, 1964; Pondy, 1967), all too frequently only a subset of the relationships of concern have been studied in a given organization. While such studies help identify critical variables and provide the building blocks of a theory of role stress, it is likely that richer understanding will accrue from more comprehensive studies. Several major findings in the present investigation may be used to support this view.

Implications of New Evidence

The first important finding is that individuals vary considerably in the *nature* of role conflict they experience. The empirical development of clusters of individuals revealed five conflict orientations which differed significantly in both the univariate sense and when all four conflict types were considered simultaneously. This means that the generalized role-conflict variable, frequently considered in recent research in organizational behavior, may serve to obscure the real nature of the conflict an individual experiences on the job. Thus, attempts to manage conflict, through organizational or role engineering or through selection, placement, and training of the individual, are likely to be unsuccessful when only generalized role conflict is considered. For example, person-role conflict may be more effectively managed through selection and placement of the role candidate, intrasender conflict may be reduced through leadership training, role overload may be alleviated by job redesign, and intersender conflict, through role sender recognition of and training in the vicissitudes of boundary-spanning activities.

Secondly, it is important to emphasize that while some role requirements do not, by themselves, lead to conflict, they assume much more importance when they are considered in conjunction with other major demands placed on a focal person. This combinatorial effect of multiple role requirements is best illustrated in this study for scientific research activities. When considered alone, these activities were not related to conflict (Table 5). Furthermore, persons in Orientation I, who rated only scientific research activities as an important part of their jobs, were characterized by low levels of conflict in all four categories (Table 3). On the basis of their objective role requirements (Table 4), Orientation I could be labeled as highly buffered scientists. On the other hand, scientific research activities had the highest loading on the discriminant function which considered simultaneously all five objective conditions as predictors of conflict orientation (Table 5). Thus, when an individual's scientific research role requirements are considered simultaneously with his other role requirements, they contribute to the prediction of his conflict orientation or profile. This generalization is illustrated by Orientation V.

Individuals in Orientation V reported high levels of integration, scientific research, and supervisory role requirements, and high role-set distance. These individuals could be characterized as manager-scientists who have integration responsibilities which require them to span interorganizational boundaries. As a group, they reported the highest level of generalized role conflict and the highest levels of all conflict categories except role overload.

It is also interesting to speculate about the kinds of individuals who are placed in these high-conflict roles. The boundary-spanning manager-scientist is probably one who has demonstrated expertise in a research specialty which is vital to the organization and has been chosen to develop and lead a subunit specializing in this area of research and to represent this part of the organization to relevant sectors of the environment (funding agencies, contractors, and so forth). The university analog is the person who is selected to chair a department, on the basis of demonstrated excellence as teacher and researcher, and to represent the department to outsiders on matters regarding funding, recruiting, and interdisciplinary research and training projects. Thus, as part of their strategy to put the best on top and out front, organizations may be exposing their most talented members to multiple role requirements involving chronic stress, for which there appear to be substantial health costs (see, for example, Selye, 1956; Caplan, 1971; Cobb, 1973; House, 1974) in addition to the direct work outcomes considered in this study. Furthermore, the lack of progress in developing and reinforcing a dual scientific-administrative ladder of advancement in research and other professional organizations is likely to exacerbate the propensity to encourage more effective individuals to rise to positions involving chronic role conflict.

A third interesting interpretation of the present findings is that *intra*organizational boundary spanners appear to have more unfavorable work-related outcomes as a result of conflict than *inter*organizational boundary spanners. For example, persons in Orientations IV and V report high levels of integration and boundary-spanning role requirements though they occupy the two extremes on role-set distance (Table 4). Orientation IV may therefore be characterized as *intra*organizational integrators, while the boundary-spanning activities of persons in Orientation V appear to be of the *inter*organizational variety. Both groups exhibit approximately the same degree of generalized role conflict, varying only in the levels of person-role and role overload categories.

Despite this general similarity in conflict orientation, intraorganizational integrators report substantially more unfavorable work-related outcomes than interorganizational boundary spanners; in fact, the former group scored the lowest of all five conflict orientations on the four outcome variables. Kahn and associates (1964) reported a slight difference in the degree of role conflict experienced by inter- and intraorganizational boundary spanners, but did not differentiate between these two groups on the basis of work-related outcomes. Organ (1971b), however, in a laboratory experiment found that persons occupying boundary roles experienced greater levels of tension if they believed that their behaviors were visible to their role senders. In light of these findings, one plausible interpretation of the present results is that interorganizational, in comparison to intraorganizational, boundary role persons may have more flexibility, given that their behaviors are more invisible to high-distance role senders.

Finally, it is interesting to note that the conflict orientations did not significantly distinguish the favorability of work-related outcomes in the univariate sense. However, conflict orientations were able to significantly distinguish the levels of outcomes when these outcomes were considered simultaneously, which obviously is the way they are experienced by the individual. Therefore, studies which do not consider these dependent variables simultaneously may overlook the dysfunctional consequences of role conflict.

Directions for Future Research

While these results contribute to an understanding of the structure of relationships linking conflict with plausible organizational antecedents and individual consequences, future research should focus on the determination of causality which was assumed in the linkages specified in the model. Additional work is also needed to be able to specify individual differences in sensitivity to role requirements which are high in conflict potential and in coping ability under conditions of role conflict. The effectiveness of various managerial strategies to reduce specific types of experienced conflict should be investigated. Those mentioned in this study are suggestive only. These research suggestions would appear to be critical because this study has shown that individuals with the greatest levels of conflict occupy roles which are crucial for organizational adaptation and survival. They include the intra- and interorganizational boundary spanner and the high-level manager, both of which assume greater significance in an era of increasing environmental turbulence.

Appendix. Results of Factor Analysis of Fifty Job Activity Items

Role-Requirement Factors and Items	Factor Loadings			% Var	Cum % Var
	I	II	III		
Factor I: *Personnel supervision activities*				27.9	27.9
1. Nominate personnel in the organization for promotion.	.89	.08	−.06		
2. Make decisions concerning the hiring and/or termination of employees.	.86	.09	−.05		
3. Counsel subordinates about their professional development.	.84	.12	.02		
4. Conduct regular staff meetings.	.84	.12	−.08		
5. Present awards to deserving employees.	.82	.15	.01		
6. Counsel subordinates about their personal problems.	.82	.12	.11		
7. Prepare personnel reports concerning subordinates.	.78	.23	.14		
8. Make assignments of jobs to subordinates.	.76	.15	.10		
9. Train new employees in performance of work.	.72	.16	.05		
10. Submit regular reports concerning accomplishments of groups of employees.	.67	.19	−.07		
11. Instruct subordinates in proper procedures.	.61	.04	.14		
12. Forecast the volume of work to be done in the near future.	.50	.34	−.17		

(continued on next page)

Appendix *(Continued)*

Role-Requirement Factors and Items	Factor Loadings			% Var	Cum % Var
	I	II	III		
Factor II: *Integration and boundary-spanning activities*				10.0	37.9
1. Represent your directorate/laboratory to outsiders.	.25	.74	.01		
2. Review plans with agencies outside the laboratory.	.27	.72	−.03		
3. Travel at least 30 days per year as a representative of your organization.	.09	.69	−.11		
4. Inspect or review projects under contract.	.17	.68	.19		
5. Integrate or coordinate interdependent activities of others.	.33	.58	−.06		
6. Prepare reports for governmental agencies outside the laboratory.	.27	.57	.34		
7. Request performance obligations from persons outside your immediate unit.	.18	.55	−.01		
8. Prepare and give several briefings per month.	.23	.51	.17		
9. Write or dictate at least 10 letters per week.	.31	.47	−.02		
10. Prepare contracts for approval by a superior.	.21	.46	−.02		
11. Act as liaison with other units of the organization.	.24	.41	−.18		
Factor III: *Scientific research activities*				8.5	46.4
1. Make contributions to a body of scientific knowledge.	.00	−.13	.84		
2. Write scientific/technical papers.	−.01	−.04	.74		
3. Personally conduct research.	−.09	−.23	.72		
4. Review manuscripts (technical).	.14	.31	.63		
5. Apply for patents and/or copyrights for work you have done.	.23	.00	.48		

References

Adams, J. S. "The Structure and Dynamics of Behavior in Organizational Boundary Roles." In M. D. Dunnette (Ed.), *Handbook of Industrial and Organizational Psychology*. Chicago: Rand McNally, 1976.

Argyris, C. *Integrating the Individual and the Organization*. New York: Wiley, 1964.

Bock, R. D. "Programming Univariate and Multivariate Analysis of Variance." *Technometrics*, 1963, *5*, 95-117.

Bock, R. D., and Haggard, E. A. "The Use of Multivariate Analysis of Variance in Behavioral Research." In D. K. Whitla (Ed.), *Handbook of Measurement and Assessment in Behavioral Science*. Reading, Mass.: Addison-Wesley, 1968.

Bullock, R. P. *Social Factors Related to Job Satisfaction: A Technique for the Measurement of Satisfaction*. Monograph No. 70. Columbus: Bureau of Business Research, Ohio State University, 1952.

Caplan, R. D. "Organizational Stress and Individual Strain: A Social-Psychological Study of Risk Factors in Coronary Heart Disease Among Administrators, Engineers and Scientists." Unpublished doctoral dissertation, University of Michigan, 1971.

Charters, W. W. "A Study of Role Conflict Among Foremen in a Heavy Industry." Unpublished doctoral dissertation, University of Michigan, 1952.

Cobb, S. "Role Responsibility: The Differentiation of a Concept." *Occupational Mental Health*, 1973, *3*.

Corwin, R. G. "Patterns of Organizational Conflict." *Administrative Science Quarterly*, 1969, *14*, 507-520.

Cramer, E. M. *The Revised MANOVA Program*. Chapel Hill: Psychometric Laboratory, University of North Carolina, 1967.

Cronbach, L. J., and Gleser, G. "Assessing Similarity Between Profiles." *Psychological Bulletin*, 1953, *50*, 456-473.

Evan, W. M. "Role Strain and the Norms of Reciprocity in Research Organizations." *American Journal of Sociology*, 1962, *68*, 346-354.

House, J. S. "Occupational Stress and Coronary Heart Disease: A Review and Theoretical Integration." *Journal of Health and Social Behavior*, 1974, *14*, 12-27.

House, R. J., and Rizzo, J. R. "Role Conflict and Ambiguity as Critical Variables in a Model of Organizational Behavior." *Organizational Behavior and Human Performance*, 1972, *7*, 467-505.

Johnson, S. C. "Hierarchical Clustering Schemes." *Psychometrika*, 1967, *32*, 241-254.

Jones, L. V. "Analysis of Variance in Its Multivariate Development." In R. B. Cattell (Ed.), *Handbook of Multivariate Experimental Psychology*. Chicago: Rand McNally, 1966.

Kahn, R. L., and others. *Organizational Stress: Studies in Role Conflict and Ambiguity*. New York: Wiley, 1964.

Kaplan, N. "The Role of the Research Administrator." *Administrative Science Quarterly*, 1959, *4*, 20-41.

Landy, F. T. "A Procedure for Occupational Clustering." *Organizational Behavior and Human Performance*, 1972, *8*, 108-117.

Lawrence, P. R., and Lorsch, J. W. *Organization and Environment*. Boston: Graduate School of Business Administration, Harvard University, 1967.

Miles, R. H. "Role Conflict and Ambiguity in Boundary and Internal Roles: A Field Study Using Role-Set Analysis and a Panel Design." Unpublished doctoral dissertation, University of North Carolina, Chapel Hill, 1974.

Organ, D. W. "Linking Pins Between Organizations and Environments." *Business Horizons*, 1971a, *14*, 73-80.

Organ, D. W. "Some Variables Affecting Boundary Role Behavior." *Sociometry*, 1971b, *34*, 524-537.

Overall, J. E., and Klett, C. J. *Applied Multivariate Analysis*. New York: McGraw-Hill, 1972.

Pinto, P. R., and Pinder, C. C. "A Cluster Analytic Approach to the Study of Organizations." *Organizational Behavior and Human Performance*, 1972, *8*, 408-422.

Pondy, L. R. "Organizational Conflict: Concepts and Models." *Administrative Science Quarterly*, 1967, *12*, 296-320.

Pruden, H. O., and Reece, R. M. "Interorganizational Role-Set Relations and the Performance and Satisfaction of Industrial Salesmen." *Administrative Science Quarterly*, 1972, *17*, 601-609.

Pym, D. L. A., and Auld, H. D. "The Self-Rating as a Measure of Employee Satisfaction." *Occupational Psychology,* 1965, *39,* 103-113.

Rizzo, J. R., House, R. J., and Lirtzman, S. E. "Role Conflict and Ambiguity in Complex Organizations." *Administrative Science Quarterly,* 1970, *15,* 150-163.

Roethlisberger, F. J. "The Foreman: Master and Victim of Double Talk." *Harvard Business Review,* 1945, *23,* 283-298.

Selye, H. *The Stress of Life.* New York: McGraw-Hill, 1956.

Stogdill, R. M., and Shartle, C. L. *Methods in the Study of Administrative Leadership.* Monograph No. 80. Columbus: Bureau of Business Research, Ohio State University, 1955.

Taylor, J. A. "A Personality Scale of Manifest Anxiety." *Journal of Abnormal and Social Psychology,* 1953, *48,* 285-290.

Thompson, J. D. *Organizations in Action.* New York: McGraw-Hill, 1967.

Tosi, H. W. "Organizational Stress as a Moderator of the Relationship Between Influence and Role Response." *Academy of Management Journal,* 1971, *14,* 7-20.

Ward, J. H., Jr. "Hierarchical Grouping to Minimize an Objective Function." *Journal of the American Statistical Association,* 1963, *58,* 236-244.

Wilks, S. S. "Certain Generalizations in the Analysis of Variance." *Biometrika,* 1932, *24,* 471-494.

11

Some Variables Affecting a Constituent's Evaluations of and Behavior Toward a Boundary Role Occupant

James A. Wall, Jr.
J. Stacy Adams

Kahn and associates (1964) define a *boundary position* as one in which some members of the role set are located in a different system—another unit within the same organization or another organization. An organization member who occupies such a position (BRP) finds himself in a structurally unique position. He is not only a member of his parent system and thereby subject to the expectations and influence attempts of internal members (constituents), but he is also a member of a boundary interaction system (Figure 1).

Figure 1. The BRP's Dual Membership

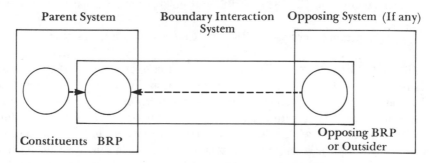

Consequently, a BRP is the target of potentially conflicting demands, some sent from his constituents and some from individuals outside his organization.

Recent work on boundary roles (Adams, 1969; Frey, 1971; Frey and Adams, 1972; Holmes, 1971; Organ, 1971) has focused on the conflicting influences exerted on a BRP

Reprinted from *Organizational Behavior and Human Performance*, 1974, *11*, 390-408, with permission of the authors and Academic Press. Copyright © 1974 by Academic Press, Inc.

by his constituents and outsiders. The constituent's evaluation of the BRP and his behavior toward him both have been shown to have a significant influence on the BRP's behavior (Frey and Adams, 1972; Organ, 1971). In a bargaining experiment in which the subjects were BRPs, Organ (1971) manipulated (a) the degree of constituent confidence in the BRP, (b) the degree of visibility of the BRP's activities to his constituent, and (c) the type of negotiating strategy demanded by the constituent. He found the degree of confidence transmitted to the subject by the constituent had slight effect upon how stringently the subject adhered to the constitutent's norm. However, when compared to subjects whose bargaining was not monitored, the subjects who believed their bargaining was visible to the constituent (a) displayed stronger adherence to the constituent's behavioral norm, (b) experienced a greater degree of tension, and (c) believed that their performance had a greater influence on the reward to be given by the constituent. Also, subjects whose constituent urged cooperative bargaining tactics made more cooperative responses in bargaining than subjects whose constituents urged exploitation of the opponent.

The aforementioned study by Frey and Adams manipulated the cooperative and exploitative internal and external demands to which the BRP was exposed. Trust of the BRP by the constituent also was manipulated. Distrusted subjects who faced a cooperative outsider were tougher bargainers than distrusted subjects who faced an exploitative outsider. Among the trusted subjects, there was no difference in the toughness of bargaining between those facing cooperative and exploitative opponents.

Investigations by Holmes (1971) and Frey (1971) similarly demonstrate the influence of constituents upon BRP bargaining behavior. Considering the findings of Lowin and Craig (1968) that managerial style (commonly studied as an independent variable) can be affected by subordinate productivity (commonly studied as a dependent variable), it seemed potentially fruitful to investigate some of the factors that might affect constituent evaluations of and behavior toward a BRP. The present study investigated the effect of three such factors: (a) the effectiveness of the BRP's organizational role—for example, outputting effectiveness, bargaining success; (b) reports concerning outsiders in the organization's environment; and (c) the BRP's obedience to the constituent's directives.

Factors Affecting Constituent's Evaluations and Behavior

Outputting Effectiveness. The constituent forms a set of expectations of his BRP; one of these is that the BRP fulfill his functional task. For example, a salesman is expected to sell the company product; a purchasing agent is expected to obtain necessary productive materials. The constituent expects the BRP to be functionally successful even though the outsiders with whom the BRP must deal may determine his success or failure (Kahn and others, 1964). When these expectations are met—in this case when outputting is successful—the constituent will evaluate the BRP's performance more positively than when the organization's outputting is not being conducted effectively. In addition, the BRP's functional success will induce the constituent to attribute its causality to the BRP. As Hastorf, Schneider, and Polefka (1970) point out, "nothing speaks louder than success, and, if anything, most people are inclined to overattribute ability based on success." Support for this remark is noted in the findings of Jones and DeCharms (1957) that persons who successfully complete assigned tasks are perceived to be more competent, dependable, and highly motivated than those who fail. In the BRP-constituent relationship, an additional factor inclines the constituent to overattribute causality to the BRP. The hedonic relevance of the BRP's activities to the constituent is quite high, and as a result he draws his inferences with a high degree of certainty (Jones and DeCharms, 1957; Jones and Davis, 1965). Therefore, it is predicted that effective outputting will lead the constituent to grant the BRP more autonomy in dealing with outsiders—specifically, by communicating fewer demands to him and accompanying these demands with weaker influence attempts—than will ineffective outputting. It will also lead him to evaluate his BRP more positively and place more trust in him.

Outsider Receptiveness. The constituent is cognizant of the fact that the BRP cannot always insure his success in dealing with outsiders. Consequently, he bases his initial expectations for the BRP's functional success partially upon reports and his observations concerning the relevant individuals in the environment. It is assumed that his expectations of outputting effectiveness will be higher when he has information that the outsiders are receptive than when he has no information. Also, his expectations will be higher when he has no information about the environment than when he receives information that the outsiders are unreceptive. When the results of the BRP's activities become known to the constituent, his evaluation of the BRP's performance will be based upon the extent of the BRP's fulfillment of the constituent's expectations. For a given level of outputting effectiveness, high expectations resulting from reports of outsider receptiveness will lead to a lower evaluation than will moderate expectations resulting from no information. Conversely, low expectations resulting from reports of outsider unreceptiveness will lead to a higher evaluation than will moderate expectations. Similarly, the amount of autonomy granted to the BRP will be based upon the BRP's fulfillment of the constituent's expectations, as will the personal evaluation of and trust placed in him.

BRP Obedience. The constituent possesses expectations not only about the organizational goals the BRP should fulfill but also about the manner in which these goals should be pursued. For example, a battalion commander expects his recruiting sergeant to fulfill his monthly quota of enlistees; however, he feels also that the sergeant in his recruiting should present an honest description of army life. Similarly, the president of General Electric might expect his negotiator to reach a favorable agreement with a union, but he also expects him to bargain via a Bouleware strategy. These expectations about the means employed and the resulting role pressures are important not only because they directly affect the BRP's behavior (Frey and Adams, 1972; Holmes, 1971; Organ, 1971) but also because they determine the extent to which the BRP is held responsible for his success or failure.

If he believes that the BRP conformed to his directives concerning the method for pursuing the organization's objectives, the constituent will not blame ineffective outputting totally on the BRP (Walton and McKersie, 1965). However, if the constituent has information that the BRP disobeyed his directives on how to behave, failure to output effectively will be attributed to him, with the consequence that his performance will be evaluated negatively, he will be given little autonomy, and will not be trusted.

If no information is available to the constituent about the BRP's compliance with directives, the blame for the outputting ineffectiveness will be ascribed to the BRP. This is based on the assumption that the constituent will use a simplistic, logical inference process in evaluating his BRP; his reasoning being, "If the BRP obeys my directive, outputting will be carried out successfully. If the outputting is not carried out successfully, the BRP must have not followed my directive on how to deal with the outsiders." That is, the constituent will assume that he has been disobeyed when outputting is ineffective and he lacks information about the BRP's behavior. As a result, the constituent's evaluations of the BRP and his performance, the autonomy granted to him, and the trust expressed in him will not differ significantly from conditions when outputting is ineffective and the BRP is known to have disobeyed.

The constituent is predicted to utilize the same inferential process when the outputting is reported to be effective. If he has no information concerning the BRP's obedience, he will believe that he has been obeyed. His evaluations of the BRP and his performance, autonomy given him, and trust in him, therefore, will be the same as when outputting is effective and the constituent knows the BRP has obeyed his directives. On the other hand, if the BRP disobeys, the constituent will evaluate the BRP and his performance more negatively, trust the BRP less, and grant him less autonomy than when he has no information on the BRP's obedience.

Hypotheses

In summary, the three factors—outputting effectiveness, outsider receptiveness, and BRP obedience—are hypothesized to have the following effects:

1. Outputting effectiveness: Compared to the constituent receiving a report of ineffective outputting, a constituent receiving a report of effective outputting (a) evaluates his BRP's performance more positively, (b) evaluates the BRP more positively, (c) grants him more autonomy, and (d) trusts him more.
2. Outsider receptiveness: Compared to the constituent receiving no report concerning outsider receptiveness, the constituent receiving a report that the outsider is unreceptive (a) evaluates his BRP's performance more positively, (b) evaluates the BRP more positively, (c) grants him more autonomy, and (d) trusts him more. Compared to the constituent receiving a report that the outsider is receptive, the constituent receiving no report concerning outsider receptiveness (e) evaluates his BRP's performance more positively, (f) evaluates the BRP more positively, (g) grants him more autonomy, and (h) trusts him more.
3. BRP obedience: Compared to the constituent receiving a report of BRP disobedience, the constituent receiving a report of BRP obedience (a) evaluates his BRP's performance more positively, (b) evaluates the BRP more positively, (c) grants him more autonomy, and (d) trusts him more.
4. Outputting-obedience interaction: Under the ineffective outputting condition, the constituent receiving no information concerning BRP obedience as compared to a constituent receiving a report of BRP obedience (a) evaluates his BRP's performance more negatively, (b) evaluates the BRP more negatively, (c) grants him less autonomy, and (d) trusts him less. However, his evaluations of the BRP and his behavior toward him do not differ from those of the constituent receiving a report of BRP disobedience.

Under the effective outputting condition, the constituent receiving no information concerning BRP obedience as compared to the constituent receiving a report of BRP disobedience (e) evaluates his BRP's performance more positively, (f) evaluates the BRP more positively, (g) grants him more autonomy, and (h) trusts him more. However, his evaluations of the BRP and his behavior toward him do not offer from those of the constituent receiving a report of BRP obedience.

Method

Subjects

One hundred and eighty male volunteers participated in the experiment. All were undergraduates enrolled in business administration courses at the University of North Carolina at Chapel Hill.

Procedure

Subjects were recruited to take part in an experiment allegedly to investigate the relationships between buyers and sales organizations. Three subjects met together at the beginning of each experimental session and were told that two would be assigned to play the role of members in a sales organization and that one would play the role of a buyer. One of the sales organization members was supposedly the sales director (constituent) and the other, the salesman (BRP). It was explained that the salesman and the buyer would interact in several sales sessions, in each of which the salesman would attempt to maximize his organization's profits by selling the most profitable amount of goods to the buyer. In turn, the buyer would attempt to maximize his profit by purchasing certain quantities from the salesman. Both the salesman and buyer were allegedly to be provided with a price-quantity schedule which showed their profits resulting from various quantities transacted at different prices per unit.

After the introduction, the subjects drew letters to determine which room they would occupy and, thereby, which role they would play. Regardless of the room he entered, each found a note stating he was the director of the sales organization.

As soon as the subject was informed of his role, he was asked to read his instructions. These were to familiarize him with the requirements of his role and the sequence of events in the experiment. He then answered a brief questionnaire designed to ascertain his understanding of the directions and to check on the manipulation of outsider receptiveness. Following this, he chose one of two directives to send to his salesman. One stated, "Try to be as reasonable as possible with the buyer. In your offers and counteroffers, search for an agreement that will benefit both parties, even though it may mean that we must sacrifice some team profit." The other read, "His loss is our gain and our loss, his gain. Therefore, determine what settlement is best for our team and then attempt to reach that settlement. The buyer will look after his interest; you look after ours." In addition to making the subject's role more realistic, allowing the subject to choose between the two directives enabled the experimenter to manipulate the salesman obedience variable. Having sent the directive, the subject awaited the results of the first sales session.

The report of the sales session consisted of (a) the profit or loss incurred by the team in the session (dependent upon the experimental condition) and (b) a report by the experimenter concerning the extent to which the salesman obeyed the subject's directive. At the end of one sales session, the subject completed a questionnaire in which he (a) evaluated the salesman and his performance, (b) expressed his trust in the salesman, and (c) expressed the extent of his desire to send a second directive to the salesman. He then sent again one of two directives on how the salesman should bargain, together with one of five scaled influence statements indicating how important it was for the salesman to obey the subject's directive. The strongest influence stated, "Follow this directive or you will not be paid," whereas the weakest read, "I don't care if you follow this directive or not." At this point the subject was still under the impression that more sales sessions would be conducted, though, in fact, the experiment had ended. He was told this and asked to reveal what his reactions had been during the experiment. Finally, the full purpose of the experiment was explained, and the subjects were asked not to discuss the experiment with their classmates.

Manipulations of Independent Variables

Outputting Effectiveness. Outputting effectiveness was manipulated by controlling the profit the salesman appeared to have made. In the effective outputting condition

(E), the transaction report sent to the subject (sales director) by the experimenter showed that the organization's funds increased from \$4,000 to \$5,500 during the first sales session. In the ineffective condition ($\bar{E}$) they were reported as having decreased from \$4,000 to \$2,500.

Outsider Receptiveness. In the unreceptive condition ($\bar{R}$) the subject was given a statement in his instructions that the buyer's profit schedule would make it unprofitable for him to purchase significant quantities of the salesman's products. In the receptive condition (R) the statement indicated that the buyer's profit schedule made it profitable for him to buy large quantities, which would also result in high profits for the selling team. In a third condition ($R/?$) no mention was made of the buyer's schedule, thus making his receptiveness unknown.

BRP Obedience. In the obedience and disobedience conditions, the subject was informed that the experimenter would observe the salesman's activities through the one-way mirror, listen to the bargaining session, and then inform the subject of his observations. In the obedience condition (O) the experimenter reported in the transaction report that the salesman behaved as the subject had directed. Conversely, in the disobedience condition ($\bar{O}$) he reported that the salesman did not obey the subject's directive. In a third condition, in which no information concerning the salesman's obedience was supplied ($O/?$), the subject's instructions stated that there was no way to determine whether or not the salesman had obeyed the directive.

Measures of Dependent Variables

The principal dependent variables consisted of the subject's evaluations of and responses to his salesman.

Performance Evaluation. Each subject was asked to evaluate his salesman's performance on four seven-point bipolar scales—good/bad, acceptable/unacceptable, farsighted/shortsighted, and effective/ineffective—which were combined into a measure designated "performance evaluation index."

Salesman Evaluation. Each subject was also asked to give his evaluation of his salesman by rating him on thirteen seven-point bipolar scales—for example, tough/soft, hard-working/lazy, loyal/disloyal. These ratings were combined into a single measure designated "salesman evaluation index."

Autonomy. The subject's willingness to grant autonomy to his salesman, or, conversely, his felt need to control him, was assessed by two means. First was the strength of the subject's desire to send a second directive to the salesman which was measured on a seven-point bipolar scale. Secondly, having sent a second directive, the subject indicated to his salesman how important it was to obey the directive by checking one of five statements previously scaled by the Thurstone equal-interval method.

Trust. Trust placed in the salesman was inferred from the subject's response on a seven-point scale to the question "If you had to choose an individual to carry out a critical confidential mission on your behalf, how likely would you be to choose your salesman to fill this role?"

Results

Manipulation Checks

The manipulation of system outputting effectiveness was checked by asking each subject to indicate how effective he felt his team had been in achieving profitable financial results. Those in the effective condition (*E*) indicated that their team was very effective, whereas those in the ineffective condition ($\bar{E}$) felt their team was not at all effective ($F(1, 158) = 2429.78, p < .001$).

To measure the perceived level of outsider receptiveness, each subject was asked what quantity of goods he believed the buyer would attempt to purchase from his salesman. The subjects in the unreceptive condition ($\bar{R}$) possessed the lowest quantity expectations; expectations of the subjects in the receptive condition (*R*) were the highest; and the expectations of the subjects receiving no information (*R*/?) were approximately midway between the former two ($F(2, 158) = 152.66, p < .001$).

The manipulation of the salesman's obedience was verified by asking each subject how well his salesman had obeyed his first directive. The differences in the responses were significant ($F(2, 158) = 119.26, p < .001$). Subjects in the obedience condition (*O*) indicated they had been obeyed, whereas those in the disobedience condition ($\bar{O}$) reported they had been disobeyed. Subjects given no information about salesman obedience (*O*/?) reported an intermediate level of obedience.

No significant interactions occurred in the manipulation checks.

Main Effects

Outputting Effectiveness. Outputting effectiveness affected all dependent variables as predicted (Hypothesis 1(a)-(c)). The performance of the salesmen in the $\bar{E}$ condition was considered to be significantly poorer than in the *E* condition ($F(1, 158) = 519.75, p < .001$) (Tables 1 and 2). Salesmen in the $\bar{E}$ condition were granted less autonomy in dealing with the buyer. Specifically, subjects expressed a stronger desire to send a second directive ($F(1, 158) = 9.83, p < .002$) and accompanied the directive with a stronger influence statement ($F(1, 158) = 12.67, p < .001$). Finally, salesmen in the $\bar{E}$ condition were evaluated more negatively ($F(1, 158) = 338.47, p < .001$) and trusted less ($F(1, 158) = 118.18, p < .001$).

Outsider Receptiveness. Hypothesis 2(a)-(g) received no support. This was surprising in view of the fact that outsider receptiveness, as assumed, did influence subjects' initial expectations for their salesmen's success, profit expectations being greater when the outsider was thought to be receptive ($F(2, 158) = 10.76, p < .001$). A plausible explanation may be found in whether the subject felt the salesman, the subject, or the buyer was responsible for his team's financial situation. In twelve of the eighteen experimental cells, the subjects held that their salesmen were most responsible for their team's financial situation, in four that they themselves were most responsible, and in only two that the buyer was responsible. It appears that subjects believed or came to believe that they and their salesmen were largely in control of their financial destiny. If the locus of causality were perceived as organizationally internal, no effect of environment receptiveness—an external variable—would be predicted. This, of course, leaves unanswered a key question: why was the locus of causality internal when it was explicitly stated and acknowledged that the outsider (buyer) could influence the performance of the organization?

The effect of environmental receptiveness upon the strength of the influence attempt ($F(2, 158) = 3.45, p < .03$) was not in the predicted direction. Subjects accompanied their directives with the weakest influence attempts when they had no information concerning the outsider (marginal means $R = 3.79$, R/? $= 3.63$, $\bar{R} = 3.95$). It was predicted that the weakest attempts would be sent in the $\bar{R}$ condition; however, the subjects in the *R*/? condition were the least inclined to demand a specific mode of action because they lacked environmental information.

BRP Obedience. As predicted, the favorableness of the evaluation of the sales-

Table 1. Analysis of Variance

Source[a]	df	Performance Evaluation		Desire to Send Second Directive		Strength of Influence Attempt		Salesman Evaluation		Trust	
		MS	F	MS	F	MS	F	MS	F	MS	F
E	1	7,005.61	519.75[b]	24.44	9.83[d]	5.77	12.67[b]	27,620.64	338.47[b]	222.64	118.18[b]
R	2	7.49	.56	2.87	1.15	1.57	3.45[c]	85.64	1.05	.87	.46
O	2	254.29	18.87[b]	17.76	7.14[b]	1.14	2.51	534.85	6.55[d]	40.77	21.64[b]
$E \times R$	2	7.71	.57	.62	.25	2.05	4.50[d]	62.13	.76	3.35	1.78
$E \times O$	2	48.55	3.60[c]	.61	.25	.01	.02	942.99	11.56[b]	9.71	5.15[d]
$R \times O$	4	6.14	.46	1.01	.41	.66	1.45	30.51	.37	4.03	2.14
$E \times R \times O$	4	12.88	.96	6.98	2.81[c]	1.21	2.65[c]	33.43	.41	1.45	.77
Error	158	13.48		2.49		.46		81.60		1.88	

[a] E—outputting effectiveness; R—outsider receptiveness; and O—salesman obedience.

[b] $p < .001$.

[c] $p < .05$.

[d] $p < .01$.

Table 2. Means and Marginal Means of Subjects' Evaluations of and Behavior Toward Their Salesmen

Performance Evaluation Index

	Obedience (O)			No Information on Obedience (O/?)			Disobedience (O̅)			Outputting Effectiveness Marginals
	R	R/?	R̄	R	R/?	R̄	R	R/?	R̄	
Effective outputting (E)	5.70	7.11	5.60	6.56	7.44	7.80	11.50	11.10	12.60	8.30
Ineffective outputting (E̅)	20.56	18.90	21.30	19.50	20.10	21.70	23.40	22.10	21.60	21.00
Obedience marginals		13.16			13.86			17.06		

Desire to Send Second Directive

	O			O/?			O̅			Marginals
	R	R/?	R̄	R	R/?	R̄	R	R/?	R̄	
E	4.00	2.78	2.30	2.89	3.33	4.00	2.20	3.10	2.30	3.01
E̅	2.11	2.70	2.30	3.30	3.20	2.00	1.70	1.60	1.40	2.26
Marginals		2.71			3.14			2.05		

Strength of Influence Attempt

	O			O/?			O̅			Marginals
	R	R/?	R̄	R	R/?	R̄	R	R/?	R̄	
E	3.57	3.50	3.48	3.70	3.50	3.48	3.66	3.84	3.75	3.60
E̅	4.11	3.64	3.84	3.39	3.75	4.58	4.30	3.54	4.57	3.97
Marginals		3.68			3.73			3.94		

(continued on next page)

Table 2 (*Continued*)

Salesman Evaluation Index

	O			*O/?*			*Ō*			*Marginals*
	R	*R/?*	*R̄*	*R*	*R/?*	*R̄*	*R*	*R/?*	*R̄*	
E	26.30	26.44	24.20	28.22	23.33	25.30	30.80	33.60	31.20	27.78
Ē	51.00	45.80	48.20	60.10	56.90	62.10	53.00	49.00	49.50	52.84
Marginals		36.94			42.81			41.18		

Trust

	O			*O/?*			*Ō*			*Marginals*
	R	*R/?*	*R̄*	*R*	*R/?*	*R̄*	*R*	*R/?*	*R̄*	
E	2.10	2.44	1.70	2.44	2.00	2.40	3.50	4.30	5.10	2.89
Ē	5.67	4.60	4.30	5.00	4.60	5.30	5.80	5.30	5.80	5.14
Marginals		3.45			3.63			4.97		

man's performance corresponded markedly to his obedience to the subject's first directive. Subjects receiving a report of salesman obedience evaluated their salesman's performance most positively, and those who felt they had been disobeyed evaluated the performance most negatively ($F(2, 158) = 18.87$, $p < .001$) (Hypothesis 3(a)). Obeyed subjects also placed the most trust in their salesmen, and the disobeyed, the least ($F(2, 158) = 21.64$, $p < .001$) (Hypothesis 3(d)). As predicted in Hypothesis 3(c), subjects expressed more need to send a second directive in the $\bar{O}$ condition than in the O; the least desire was expressed in the $O/?$ condition ($F(2, 158) = 7.14$, $p < .001$). The effect of obedience upon the strength of the influence attempt was not significant ($F(2, 158) = 2.51$, $p < .08$), but the strongest influence attempts were made in the $\bar{O}$ and the weakest in the O condition. Finally, obeyed subjects, as predicted in Hypothesis 3(b), did evaluate their salesmen more positively than did disobeyed subjects; however, the most negative evaluation was given in the no information ($O/?$) condition. The very negative evaluation in the $\bar{E}O/?$ condition, which is discussed below, accounted for this extremely negative evaluation.

Interactions

The interaction between salesman obedience and outputting effectiveness on the salesman evaluation ($F(2, 158) = 11.56$, $p < .001$) differed somewhat from the prediction. The relationships among the means of the evaluation index under the ineffective outputting conditions show that the salesmen were evaluated most *negatively* in the $O/?$ condition, whereas under the effective outputting conditions they were evaluated most *positively* in the $O/?$ condition (Table 3 and Figure 2). The relationships among the obedience

Table 3. Marginal Means for the Interaction of Outputting Effectiveness and Salesman Obedience on Salesman Evaluation, Performance Evaluation, and Trust

	Effectiveness Condition	Obedience Condition		
		O	$O/?$	$\bar{O}$
Salesman evaluation[a]	E	25.63	25.59	31.87
	$\bar{E}$	48.32	59.70	50.50
Performance evaluation[b]	E	6.13	7.26	11.73
	$\bar{E}$	20.25	20.43	22.37
Trust	E	2.08	2.28	4.30
	$\bar{E}$	4.85	4.97	5.63

[a]The smallest possible mean (best evaluation) is 7; the largest (worst evaluation) is 91.

[b]The smallest possible mean (best evaluation) is 7; the largest (worst evaluation) is 28.

means under the E condition were as predicted (Hypothesis 4(f)), the difference in the evaluations between the O and $O/?$ conditions being insignificant, with the evaluation in the $\bar{O}$ condition being significantly more negative. Under the $\bar{E}$ condition, however, no difference between the evaluations in the $O/?$ and $\bar{O}$ conditions was predicted. It was argued that in the absence of obedience information the subject would blame the salesman for the outputting ineffectiveness and would evaluate him the same as if he had been disobedient. Yet it appears that in the absence of information about how salesmen behaved, subjects were particularly apt to believe that their salesman had behaved in a highly *un*acceptable fashion if the sales session had resulted in a loss, and they based their

Figure 2. Interaction Between Outputting Effectiveness and Salesman Obedience
on Evaluations of the Salesman

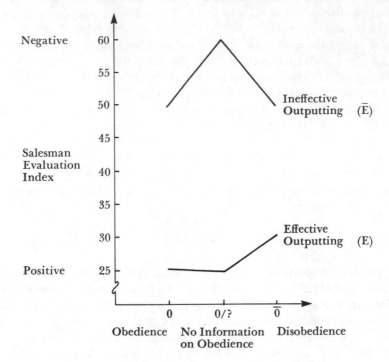

strong negative evaluations upon this assumption. This is consistent with the previously reported observation that subjects perceived the salesmen as largely responsible for the results of sales activities.

Under the effective outputting condition, subjects appeared to utilize similar inferential reasoning. When they had no information on salesman obedience, they appeared to assume that their salesman was conducting himself in an acceptable manner and based their positive evaluations upon this assumption.

An outputting-obedience interaction was also noted in the salesman's performance evaluation index ($F(2, 158) = 3.60, p < .03$) and in the trust scale ($F(2, 158) = 5.15, p < .007$). As can be noted in Table 3, obedience in the E condition had a more potent effect upon the subject's evaluation and trust than in the $\bar{E}$ condition. That is, the difference in the dependent variables between the $O/?$ and $\bar{O}$ conditions was much greater in the E condition. Again, the relationships among the obedience means were as predicted for only the E condition (Hypothesis 4(e) and (h)). Contrary to the prediction in Hypothesis 4(a) and (d), subjects under the $\bar{E}$ condition did perceive less disobedience under the $O/?$ as opposed to the $\bar{O}$ condition. As a consequence, they evaluated the salesman's performance more positively and trusted him more under the $O/?$ condition.

It seems plausible that differing levels of subject confidence in his directive account for the unpredicted ER interaction upon the strength of the influence attempts ($F(2, 158) = 4.50, p < .03$). As can be noted in Table 4, the difference between the toughness of the influence attempt in the E and $\bar{E}$ conditions is greatest when the salesman is known to be facing an unreceptive environment. When the subjects encountered a loss and knew the buyer to be unreceptive, they were probably rather certain

Table 4. Marginal Means for the Interaction of Outputting Effectiveness
and Outsider Receptiveness on Strength of Influence Attempt

	Effectiveness Condition	Receptiveness Condition		
		R	$R/?$	$\overline{R}$
Strength of influence attempt	E	3.64	3.61	3.57
	$\overline{E}$	3.70	3.64	4.33

about the proper strategy for dealing with him. However, the effective outputting to an unreceptive buyer (the $\overline{ER}$ condition) probably generated some uncertainty (but no displeasure) for the subjects. Therefore, they did not strongly support their directives.

Discussion

To summarize, these are the principal findings of the study: (a) ineffective outputting resulted in lower performance and personal evaluations of the salesman, less trust of him, and a greater felt need to control him or to reduce his autonomy; (b) environmental receptiveness did not have the predicted effects on the variables, and there was a clear tendency by subjects to perceive the salesman as responsible for the financial results of his encounter with the buyer; (c) the salesman's disobedience to directives resulted in lower evaluations of the salesman and his performance, less trust in him, and a greater felt need to control him; and (d) BRP obedience interacted with outputting effectiveness to affect the performance evaluation as well as the evaluation of and trust in the salesman.

These results indicate that two of the independent variables—outputting effectiveness and BRP obedience—strongly affect the constituent's evaluations of and behavior toward a BRP. When taken in the context of previous work by Frey (1971), Frey and Adams (1972), Holmes (1971), Organ (1971), and Walton and McKersie (1965), these results suggest that the constituent-BRP-outsider interaction would best be studied as a deviation-amplifying mutual causal process (Adams, 1976; Maruyama, 1963). Such a process is illustrated in Figure 3. As seen in the present study, both ineffective outputting and disobedience by the BRP lead to low evaluations of the BRP by his constituents

Figure 3. Dynamic Processes Involving Organization, Constituent, and BRP Variables

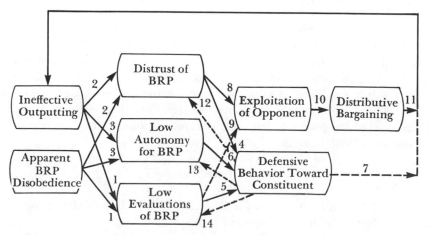

(arrows 1). They result also in distrust of the BRP (arrows 2) and in giving him little autonomy (arrows 3). Low evaluations and distrust of the BRP lead to defensive behavior toward the constituents on his part (arrows 4 and 5), as does his being granted little autonomy in bargaining (arrow 6). Facework of various kinds, reduced or biased communication with constituents, misrepresentation, and other task-irrelevant activities aimed at increasing trust, improving evaluations, and obtaining autonomy serve principally to defend the BRP or his status as a person (Walton and McKersie, 1965) and may be assumed, then, to increase further the outputting ineffectiveness (arrow 7) because energies are diverted from task functions and because insufficient or spurious information is fed into the organization system.

Distrust of the BRP by constituents has been shown by Frey (1971) and Frey and Adams (1972) to increase exploitation of the opponent by the BRP (arrow 8). Despite the evidence on the point, low constituent evaluations of the BRP probably induce similar behavior (broken arrow 9). Such behavior by the BRP increases the likelihood of tough distributive bargaining (Holmes, 1971; arrow 10), which leads ultimately to reduce further the outputting effectiveness (arrow 11).

Under the conditions described, both ineffective organization outputting and apparent BRP disobedience result in progressive deterioration of outputting effectiveness. In the case of ineffective outputting alone, the effects traced through in Figure 3 are self-amplifying (Maruyama, 1963). Organizations obviously often output ineffectively and, equally obviously, do not usually become totally ineffective, as would be demanded if only self-amplifying processes of the type described were operative.

The fact that most organizations and their outputting functions typically survive has multiple explanations. First, increments in outputting effectiveness also are self-amplifying. In the chain of variables discussed, an increase in effectiveness would reduce distrust of the BRP (though he might have no responsibility for the increase), reduce his tendency to exploit the opponent, which would shift bargaining toward an integrative style, and, thus, further enhance effectiveness.

Secondly, counteracting processes may occur. An example may be derived from Figure 3. Assume that the BRP engages in successful facework upon his constituent to "prove" his trustworthiness and thereby influences him to trust the BRP more (arrow 12). Trust induces more cooperative behavior toward the opponent (Frey, 1971; Frey and Adams, 1972), which, in turn, promotes more integrative bargaining, which should induce greater organization functional effectiveness. Similar counteracting processes may result if BRP defensive behavior improves constituent evaluations (arrow 14) or influences the constituent to give the BRP greater autonomy (arrow 13).

The "mutual causal processes" (Adams, 1976; Maruyama, 1963) described, even if hypothetical in part, link important variables in organization boundary interaction systems. The suggested relationships among these variables are such that changes in some variables result in amplification or counteraction of the changes. Clearly, much more research is required to uncover other relevant variables and their complex, systemic interrelationships, but the processes described here, limited though they are, provide a model for the pursuit of such research.

References

Adams, J. S. "Behavior in Organization Boundary Roles." Unpublished manuscript, University of North Carolina at Chapel Hill, 1969.

Adams, J. S. "The Structure and Dynamics of Behavior in Organization Boundary Roles."

In M. D. Dunnette (Ed.), *Handbook of Industrial and Organizational Psychology.* Chicago: Rand McNally, 1976.

Frey, R. L., Jr. "The Interlocking Effects of Intergroup and Intragroup Conflict on the Bargaining Behavior of Representatives." Unpublished doctoral dissertation, University of North Carolina at Chapel Hill, 1971.

Frey, R. L., Jr., and Adams, J. S. "The Negotiator's Dilemma: Simultaneous In-Group and Out-Group Conflict." *Journal of Experimental Social Psychology,* 1972, *4,* 331-346.

Hastorf, A. H., Schneider, D. J., and Polefka, J. *Person Perception.* Reading, Mass.: Addison-Wesley, 1970.

Holmes, J. G. "The Effects of the Structure of Intragroup and Intergroup Conflict on the Behavior of Representatives." Unpublished doctoral dissertation, University of North Carolina at Chapel Hill, 1971.

Jones, E. E., and Davis, K. E. "From Acts to Disposition: The Attribution Process in Person Perception." In L. Berkowitz (Ed.), *Advances in Experimental Social Psychology.* Vol. 2. New York: Academic Press, 1965.

Jones, E. E., and DeCharms, R. "Changes in Social Perception as a Function of the Personal Relevance of Behavior." *Sociometry,* 1957, *20,* 75-85.

Kahn, R. L., and others. *Organizational Stress.* New York: Wiley, 1964.

Lowin, A., and Craig, J. R. "The Influence of Level of Performance on Managerial Style: An Experimental Object-Lesson in the Ambiguity of Correlational Data." *Organizational Behavior and Human Performance,* 1968, *3,* 440-458.

Maruyama, M. "The Second Cybernetics: Deviation-Amplifying Mutual Causal Processes." *American Scientist,* 1963, *51,* 164-179.

Organ, D. W. "Some Variables Affecting Boundary Role Behavior." *Sociometry,* 1971, *34,* 524-537.

Walton, R. E., and McKersie, R. B. *A Behavior Theory of Labor Negotiations.* New York: McGraw-Hill, 1965.

PART III

Effectiveness and Performance

If the bottom line for individual psychology is behavior, then the bottom line for organizational psychology is effective performance. From a practical point of view, effectiveness is often equated with profitability, and the assumption is made that an effective (profit-making) organization is also an efficiently operated organization. Effectiveness and efficiency are not the same, however, since efficiency refers to the use of inputs to obtain a maximum return, whereas effectiveness refers to the exploitation of the environment (Yuchtman and Seashore, 1967). Thus, a plant may be profitable and effective, not because of the efficiency of its internal operations but because of its accessibility to raw materials, the availability of a skilled labor force, or a quasi-monopolistic position in the marketplace. Moreover, profitability needs to be viewed in a long-term frame of reference, since this year's gains may be offset by losses in the years ahead. Then, too, many organizations are not profit making and do not depend for survival on their competitive performance in the market. Therefore, in evaluating effectiveness we must seek other indicators of performance than profit margins. Common criteria in such an evaluation are growth and decline, survival, adaptability, productivity, turnover, absenteeism, member satisfaction, and client satisfaction.

The inadequacy of profit margins as the sole measure of organizational effectiveness is dramatically demonstrated by *Hirsch*'s comparison of pharmaceutical manufacturing plants and phonograph record companies. The best-performing record concerns "exceeded the worst-performing drug manufacturer's rate of return by less than 1 percent." Differential profitability, then, is more a function of the industry than of the individual company. The industries differ in their ability to control three aspects of their environment: pricing and distribution, patent and copyright law, and external opinion leaders. A major institutional difference is that copyrights do not give royalties for radio performance, whereas a patented drug is the exclusive possession of a company. *Hirsch*'s report is a descriptive rather than an experimental study. He interviewed executives in the least and most successful companies, attended trade meetings, and consulted thirty volumes of congressional hearings. Although more a case study than a quantitative research article, this type of penetrating account of the social realities affecting organizational functioning enriches our knowledge. The substantive contribution here is the finding that the institutional environment of the entire industry affects the performance of the single organization.

Standardized nationwide tests of achievement have furnished an effectiveness criterion for school systems. In their famous study of equality of educational opportunity, James Coleman and his colleagues (1966) reported that extra-school factors are more responsible for academic achievement than the school itself. But *Bidwell* and *Kasarda* have challenged the design of the Coleman study—specifically, its lack of consideration of organizational variables (such as structure, curricular differentiation, and variation in resource allocation) and its use of the school, rather than the school district, as the unit of analysis. *Bidwell* and *Kasarda* accordingly studied 90 percent of the school districts in the state of Colorado and found that organizational variables did have significant effects on achievement scores. Districts that put their resources into teachers rather than administrative personnel showed higher achievement levels. Districts with better-qualified front-line staffs (teachers and professional specialists) had higher-performing pupils. Increasing the ratio of students to teachers decreased performance. In other words, the much-publicized findings of the Coleman study are called into question by an investigation based on a consideration of organizational variables and units.

Absenteeism has long been used as a measure of effectiveness because of its face validity and because of its ready quantifiability. Its weaknesses are twofold: justifiable absences due to illness are not easy to establish, and, under some conditions, there is little variation in the measure. Nonetheless, attendance records do furnish one of the few sources of hard data and, with the decline in the Protestant ethic, may be a source of significant variation among organizational members. *Baum* carried out a field experiment with pre and post measures on experimental and control groups, in which legal compliance was emphasized for the experimental group. In the experimental group, among other procedures, workers were informed that detailed records would be kept by their supervisors and that management would personally counsel all workers with unauthorized absences. The program had a marked effect on chronic absentees but did not influence those who were already in conformance with the organization's attendance norms. This result was to be expected theoretically, in that emphasis on legal compliance produces conformity to standards but does not provide incentives to exceed minimum behavior. *Baum*'s study is one of the few field experiments that justify that designation, since it not only employed before and after measurements but also applied these measurements to the experimental and the control groups. Without a control group, it is difficult to tell how much of the change comes from the experimental variables and how much from other changes occurring over time. Unfortunately, it was not possible to assign subjects to the two groups randomly, but there were no significant differences on a host of variables between the two groups.

Another study using absenteeism as a criterion is *Smith*'s account of attendance on a particular day following a crippling snow storm in Chicago. Managerial employees, for whom job-satisfaction scores were available, constituted the primary sample, and their attendance was checked for the critical day. Sizable correlations were found between six attitude measures and attendance levels. In New York, where no storm occurred, there were no significant correlations with attendance, which is the more general finding. *Smith* interprets his results as showing that work attitudes predict to work-related behavior when the behavior is under the control of the subject. In the New York office, under normal conditions, managerial employees were under constraints to come to work. This interpretation can be generalized to the relationship between work attitudes and productivity, and Likert (1967) has theorized that there is little margin for the worker to affect production when the speed of the assembly line is already determined. The *Smith* study also demonstrates the payoff for an investigator's alertness in taking advantage of naturally occurring events.

Figures on absenteeism, turnover, and productivity are regarded as hard data, in contrast to the soft data of attitude and satisfaction measures. But if psychological indicators in employee surveys do predict to behavioral outcomes, they can be used when it is difficult, costly, or impossible to get measures of productivity. *Mirvis* and *Lawler* attack this problem boldly and attach a dollar-and-cents value to employee attitudes, based on a study of 160 tellers in a midwestern bank. They examined the costs of turnover, absenteeism, and error and, after an analysis of the relationship of attitudes to these behaviors, arrived at an estimate of the financial impact of attitudes. Though overgeneralization to all conditions is to be avoided, this study demonstrates that soft data can be put on a dollar scale with some reasonable rationale. The challenge here is for the research of the future to specify the types of organizations and conditions under which attitudes predict to work-related behavior.

References

Coleman, J. S., and others. *Equality of Educational Opportunity.* Washington, D.C.: U.S. Government Printing Office, 1966.

Likert, R. *The Human Organization.* New York: McGraw-Hill, 1967.

Yuchtman, E., and Seashore, S. "A System Resource Approach to Organizational Effectiveness." *American Sociological Review,* 1967, *32,* 891-903.

12

~~~ Organizational Effectiveness and the Institutional Environment

Paul M. Hirsch

One of the most widely discussed and least studied concepts in the field of organizational analysis is the institutional environment. As originally conceived by Parsons (1956a, 1956b) and elaborated by others (Dill, 1958; Thompson, 1967; Evan, 1966, 1972), organizations interact with elements in their institutional environment whenever decisions must be made about issues concerning both the organization and the community of which it is a part.

Review of Literature

A major task for high-level administrators is to reduce or neutralize threats to organizational stability resulting from dependence on the environment (Aldrich and Pfeffer, 1975), and an important aim of trade associations is to enable members to collectively manage and negotiate the outcome of such dependency. Katz and Kahn (1966) described these efforts as political and linked organizational effectiveness explicitly to an external referent, and efficiency to internal activities more easily controlled by the organization. Zald (1970), in his political-economy framework for organizational analysis, further divided each of these internal and external dimensions of organizational behavior into political and economic components.

It follows that a fruitful way to study how the external political and economic environments of organizations engaged in similar activities affect their performance is to examine the interaction of sets of organizations with agencies in their institutional environments (Evan, 1972). The unit of analysis would be an entire industry (or its nonprofit analog), whereas the study of efficiency would focus on the analysis of individual organizations.

A few studies have tried to specify components of the institutional environment and follow their interaction with a class of organizations (Ridgeway, 1957; Pfeffer and Leblebici, 1973; Epstein, 1973a, 1973b, 1969; Wilson, 1973; Allen, 1974; Benson, 1975; Wamsley and Zald, 1973). The finding of Lieberson and O'Connor (1972) that leadership

Reprinted from *Administrative Science Quarterly*, 1975, *20* (1), 327-344, by permission of the author and the publisher. Copyright © 1975 Cornell University.

succession in large corporations bore only a limited relation to the performance of large corporations further suggests that much of the unexplained variance in present research on organizational success may be due to the complex web of institutional processes still largely unexplored by students of organizations. For example, a useful extension of the study by Lawrence and Lorsch (1967) would be to examine more closely the institutional environment in which each of the three industries studied had been operating over the last twenty years. If it were found that the rate of return to the worst-performing container manufacturer sampled was higher than that of the best-performing plastics manufacturer, then it might not be simply that the internal organization of the container manufacturer was inappropriate (relative to better-performing organizations in the same industry), but also that the institutional environment of these two industries was so different that the best-performing plastics manufacturer could not overcome external constraints placed upon the entire plastics industry. Yet the relative performance of the industries from which samples are drawn is not examined in most studies of organizational effectiveness, largely because their environments are often defined as beyond the scope of measures used to assess the major components of each organization's task environment (Hirsch, 1975).

This paper compares the organizational effectiveness of the phonograph record industry and the ethical pharmaceutical industry (that is, requiring a doctor's prescription, about 60 percent of all drug sales) to explore the collective interaction of organizations in each industry with their institutional environment. Special note is taken of specific institutional mechanisms that influence the context for industry profitability (that is, the upper and lower limits on profit for individual organizations in any given industry) and of specific rules and procedures negotiated between government agencies and industry trade associations for their members. Finally, a study is made of how events at the institutional level influence decisions within industries and organizations about which types of new products to sponsor and promote, decisions that often result in further interaction and negotiation with the institutional environment.

Operation and Criteria for Comparison

Phonograph record and ethical pharmaceutical manufacturing are both process-production industries (Woodward, 1965, p. 152). Both employ highly mechanized and relatively simple batch production technologies, which come at the end of the manufacturing cycle: record manufacturing entails stamping vinyl from sounds; pharmaceutical manufacturing involves tableting drugs according to standardized procedures.

Both industries are strikingly similar in other ways. Both are dependent on external gatekeepers (physicians and radio station personnel) to introduce their products to consumers. They also derive the greatest percentage of profits from the sale of new products and, therefore, place a high premium on product innovation, for new products become rapidly obsolescent and experience unstable consumption patterns. Both have been stimulated by important technological inventions since World War II, and experienced growth and expansion well above average for most manufacturing industries. Both also exist in legal environments predicated upon patents, trademarks, and/or copyrights and their administration by the United States Patent Office. Both industries entail a long chain of organizational stages at which decisions on new products must be made. Finally, both actively project an image of high risk and attendant uncertainties about profits.

Particular care was taken to hold constant the effect of production technology on organization structure and performance. Marketing, described by Woodward (1965) as the critical function for pharmaceutical manufacturers, is also the most uncertain task faced by record manufacturers; in general, most of the uncertainty occurs on their research and marketing, and regulatory boundaries. For example, both, in addition to requiring capital and raw materials, depend on independent organizations and individuals in the technical subsystems of their industries for many of their product innovations. Both use boundary-spanning representatives to direct a flow of new product ideas to their employers for possible sponsorship: in record manufacturing, seeking and signing new musical groups to exclusive recording contracts with their organizations; in pharmaceutical manufacturing, doing research on in-house projects, sponsoring basic research by outside investigators. Pharmaceutical manufacturers are also on the alert for exclusive patent rights or licenses to develop and manufacture newly discovered drugs—for instance, the Salk vaccine.

Although new products may be discovered by smaller organizations, marketing them on a large scale generally falls to the leaders of each industry. The stratification of organizations in such distribution industries is often based on the ability of each organization to market items (within product categories) that are essentially indistinguishable to consumers. At the output boundary of these organizations, massive advertising campaigns narrow the distance between manufacturers and consumers. For the industries studied, most advertising must be directed to doctors and disk jockeys, the gatekeepers and opinion leaders for mass constituencies. Hollander (1970) has suggested that, as societal complexity increases, the roles of professional opinion leader and purchasing agent may merge in a wide variety of consumer-oriented industries. Here, such institutional regulators of innovation are required by law (the Food and Drug Administration and the Federal Communications Commission) to be independent of the producer organizations at the technical and managerial levels of the industry, so that the success of new drugs and records depends primarily on the reception of each product innovation by doctors and disk jockeys, who may choose among the wide selection released by many organizations. Where direct advertising is prohibited (prescription drugs) or economically unfeasible (records), only a few new products will become known or available to the general public. Therefore, these two industries require contact men to coopt the opinion leaders whose allegiance cannot be purchased legally and who are delegated the task of screening out inferior candidates: record companies use regional promoters; pharmaceutical houses detail the physician. The power of role occupants in the system (such as talent scouts, disk jockeys, record-reviewing wholesale buyers, doctors, hospital pharmacy committees, and government regulatory agencies) to influence the success or failure of a given product innovation increases largely as a function of their temporal position in the processing sequence outlined. The resulting power differential, in turn, has produced a variety of strategies and tactics by manufacturing organizations to influence or coopt doctors and disk jockeys and thereby reduce their level of marketing uncertainty (Hirsch, 1972).

Retail outlets and ultimate consumers comprise the societal subsystem that rewards the preceding subsystems through purchase and other positive feedback (legitimation), and also regulates their activities by supporting legislation designed to prohibit the marketing of goods and other practices judged harmful by public representatives.

The focal organization in each system, at the managerial level of organization, is the manufacturing organization engaged in locating, developing, producing, promoting, and distributing new drugs and recordings.

Differential Profitability

Between 1950 and 1965, pharmaceutical manufacturing was one of the most profitable of all industries in the United States, and phonograph record manufacturing one of the least. Reported mean annual rates of return on investment for all pharmaceutical manufacturers between 1956 and 1966 ranged from 16.7 to 20.3 percent (Mueller, 1969). For twenty-nine publicly held organizations between 1950 and 1966, Conrad and Plotkin (1967) found an average rate of return of 17.5 percent, with a standard deviation of 8.6. Using this estimate, it appears that, for the industry as a whole, roughly two thirds of all pharmaceutical manufacturers realized rates of return from 8.9 to 26.1 percent, assuming a normal distribution. In contrast, the record industry's reported rate of return between 1955 and 1964 was about 7 percent, with a standard deviation of 2.5 (Glover and Hawkins, 1965); roughly two thirds of the organizations in this industry had rates of return ranging from 4.5 to 9.5 percent. As shown in Figure 1, the

Figure 1. Reported Rates of Return in the Pharmaceutical[a] and Recording Industries

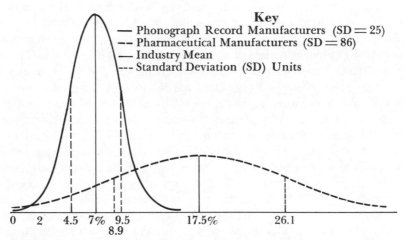

Key
— Phonograph Record Manufacturers (SD = 25)
-- Pharmaceutical Manufacturers (SD = 86)
— Industry Mean
--- Standard Deviation (SD) Units

[a]This study follows the practice of the U.S. Census of Manufactures in combining data from both ethical and over-the-counter drug manufacturers. If this has any biasing effect, it is likely to understate the profitability of the ethical pharmaceutical industry.

Sources: Conrad and Plotkin, 1967; Glover and Hawkins, 1965.

best-performing record company, within one standard deviation of the average, therefore, exceeded the worst-performing drug manufacturer's rate of return by less than 1 percent. Although industry concentration seldom is associated with low profitability, concentration ratios reported in the United States *Census of Manufactures* (U.S. Bureau of the Census, 1971) showed that, in 1967, the four-firm concentration ratio was higher (58 percent) for record manufacturers than for drug companies (24 percent, combining ethical and over-the-counter manufacturers). How can one best account for the differential performance of the two industries?

Differences between Industries

These industries differ in (1) demand elasticity, (2) the absolute dollar amount of sales, (3) scale of capital investment (in absolute dollars), (4) the percentage of sales invested in research and development, and (5) relative prestige. Pharmaceutical manufacturers are favored by more stable demand patterns and repeat sales than are recording manufacturers. Although both industries rely upon a few best sellers to offset losses on product failures or those with small volume, once a pharmaceutical manufacturer succeeds in promoting a successful new drug or trademark, the product will, in turn, contribute to the firm's profitability for a longer period than the hit record or popular recording artist of a record manufacturer. The likelihood of a positive serial correlation between individual firms' rates of return in the drug industry, and a negative serial correlation in the record industry, would account in part for the smaller variance in record industry profits, once these are averaged over time.

The record industry is also substantially smaller than the pharmaceutical industry: in 1969 retail sales at list prices were slightly over $3 billion for ethical pharmaceutical manufacturers and under $1 billion for record manufacturers, and with the latter and their retailers engaged in far more price discounting. Although in percentage each industry invests approximately the same proportion of its sales on capital expenditures, the amounts spent by pharmaceutical manufacturers are higher in absolute dollars. Large pharmaceutical manufacturers also invest substantially in research and development, while in the recording industry many analogous expenditures of this type are borne by the musical groups themselves, and not by the manufacturer. Finally, the social value of pharmaceuticals to society in prestige and functional importance tends to be substantially higher than that of records; for example, in a national survey Siegel (1970) found that pharmaceutical manufacturers ranked third in twenty-three industries (which did not include the record industry, however). While such a prestige differential might lead to the speculation that a corresponding difference in rewards (profitability) should be expected (Davis and Moore, 1945), the primary aim of this study is to find out how and which institutional mechanisms worked in favor of one industry and against the other.

These differences between the two industries should be borne in mind, for they are difficult to control and are not factored into the analysis. One can fairly assume, however, that more detailed study of differences in internal efficiency in manufacturing and administrative operations, among the organizations in the two industries, would add little light on the overall discrepancy in profitability between the industries. For example, manufacturing costs in both industries have declined since World War II, and in the pharmaceutical industry the economic performance of individual manufacturers has not been associated with the use of project or disciplinary teams in research, nor with the role accorded manufacturing departments in new product development (Hirsch, 1973, pp. 217-220; 1976). At the industry level of analysis, organizational effectiveness encompasses the relative success of each industry in handling (1) uncertainties inherent in market mechanisms, (2) the selection of new products by external gatekeepers, and (3) the persuasion of government agencies that the public interest is best served by special concessions in the development and interpretation of statutes relating directly to industry profitability.

Method

Personal interviews were conducted between 1969 and 1972 with fifty-three executives and managers, consisting of twenty-three from the pharmaceutical industry, twenty-one from the recording industry, and nine in radio broadcasting. Respondents from the most and least successful organizations in each industry were included. Fieldwork also included attendance at six trade meetings, such as the National Association of Broadcasters, American Medical Association, and Pharmaceutical Advertising Club. Over thirty volumes of congressional hearings on the pharmaceutical industry were also consulted, as were published industry biographies and other secondary material.

Institutional Mechanisms Affecting Industry Profitability

Profitability of both the pharmaceutical and record industries has also been strongly affected by three aspects of their institutional environment: (1) degree of control over the distribution and wholesale price of their products, (2) patent and copyright statutes and their administration, and (3) predictability of adoption behavior by independent gatekeepers and opinion leaders.

Control over Distribution and Prices

For consumer goods, wholesale and retail distribution is often a difficult and complex boundary contingency. Classes of new products must be presold to the salesmen of the organization, enthusiasm and/or financial incentives offered to national or regional distributors, and requests for shelf space from the retailer must be justified by the promise of consumer demand. For new products, especially, the manufacturer tries to retain autonomy over decisions about both channels of distribution and prices charged. The pharmaceutical and record industries are typical in this regard.

Shortly after World War II, both industries were engaged in the development and marketing of highly innovative products: antibiotics and other "wonder drugs," and unbreakable long-playing and 45-rpm records. Because prescription drugs are so central to health and had to be sold through licensed pharmacists, the pharmaceutical industry had little likelihood of its products being sold at retail through alternative channels. However, competition was increasing among manufacturers as a growing number of national, regional, and local organizations began to market more chemically equivalent ("generic") drugs. Such interchangeable products did pose a threat to many of the larger manufacturers, whose pricing policies and market shares could be affected, and in 1954 they formed a trade association, the National Pharmaceutical Council (NPC). Its major achievement was a successful campaign before state boards of pharmacy, to redefine the meaning of substitution at the retail level. Whereas the traditional definition of the term had been the provision of a different *type* of drug from that prescribed by the physician, the proposed redefinition prohibited the druggist's substitution of one manufacturer's *brand* of a specific drug for another's (U.S. Congress, Senate, 1961). For example, if buffered aspirin were a prescription drug, the Rexall or Norwich brands of buffered aspirin could not be substituted for Bufferin if the prescription read Bufferin.

Within eight years, at least thirty-eight state boards of pharmacy had adopted the proposed redefinition of substitution at the retail level, and hospitals, whose pharmacies routinely practice substitution, had to devise legal arguments to protect their formulary procedures. While any medical judgment on the merits of this change is beyond the scope of this article, it is important to note that major manufacturers collectively moved rapidly and effectively to protect themselves through the formation of a trade association and succeeded in stabilizing this aspect of their market by altering their institutional environment. Quite likely one reason for the absence of organized opposition by retail pharmacists to the resultant change was that prescriptions were filled on the basis of markups, not fee-for-service. Consequently, if this definition increased the cost of retail prescriptions, the druggist's income would increase correspondingly.

Upon the invention of the long-playing (33-rpm) record by the Columbia

Broadcasting System, RCA launched a competing (45-rpm) record. Apparently as an inducement to manufacturers of record players to produce machines that could play these recordings, both firms freely licensed patents to these inventions to all competitors, including new entrants, so that the new speeds would become standard throughout the industry (Gelatt, 1965). Since United States copyright law already required the compulsory licensing of all songs (by their owners) to all manufacturers wishing to record them—in direct contrast to the awarding of exclusive patents in the pharmaceutical industry—conditions were ripe for record manufacturers to find it increasingly difficult to differentiate their records from those of other companies (Peterson and Berger, 1975).

With the adoption of the long-playing record during the 1950s, the industry experienced unanticipated challenges in distribution, since the new type of unbreakable record proved highly attractive to mail-order businesses (such as the Book-of-the-Month Club) and to mass merchandisers with central purchasing offices, ranging from department stores to supermarkets. High-volume purchasers obtained quantity discounts from new entrants into manufacturing (having free access to its technology), and also circumvented local full-line distributors in favor of direct purchase of specific ("hit") records from their producers (Gelatt, 1965). Within a short time, the efforts of major manufacturers to continue selling only to authorized dealers through franchised distributors failed: their autonomy over both the price of the product and its distribution was greatly diminished. As sales rose, margins and profits fell, and industry leaders soon spoke of experiencing a "profitless prosperity," as illustrated in the questions addressed to a spokesman for the industry by a member of the House subcommittee holding hearings on copyright-law revision (U.S. Congress, House, 1965, part 2, p. 898):

> Q. At the top of the chart, with the heading "typical margins on a $3.98 list price monaural long-playing record," do I understand correctly that the margin for the independent distributor, which you have listed at 15 percent, would be 60 cents on that record?
> A. No sir. . . . The average price here is . . . about $2.83.
> Q. Well, the chart says $3.98.
> A. This is what it is called, sir. It is called a $3.98 record, but nobody pays it.
> Q. Is the independent distributor's margin calculated on the $3.98 selling price?
> A. No, sir; it is calculated on the $2.83.
> Q. Well, what does $2.83 represent?
> A. His actual selling price.
> Q. Is $3.98 the consumer price?
> A. No.
> Q. Is it the consumer listed price?
> A. Yes.
> Q. It is the consumer listed price. Now, what is the selling price from the record company or the wholesaler, and will you describe the term and fit it to that chart, so that we can understand it?
> A. . . . To answer Mr. Tenzer's question, . . . on this so-called $3.98 record. This is very misleading, because . . . scarcely ever does anyone now pay $3.98. . . . There are all kinds of prices for the so-called $3.98 record.

During this time period, major manufacturers took little or no concerted action, partly because there was no legal basis for restricting competition or sales to qualified retailers, and collective measures to do so may well have violated United States antitrust laws. The movement of Columbia Records and other manufacturers into direct mail-order sales, and, later, into the retail field through wholly owned chain record stores, illustrates two adaptations to these changes in their marketing environment. To further recapture control over the distribution and price of their records, large manufacturers have also belatedly followed the example of drug manufacturers by setting up wholly owned distribution operations and adhering more closely to posted wholesale prices.

Patent and Copyright Protection

Pharmaceutical Manufacturers. Patent, trademark, and copyright legislation makes up an important aspect of the legal and economic environment of many American industries. The individual or company awarded the patent may legally enforce a monopoly right to be the sole producer of the invention registered with the United States Patent Office. Prior to World War II, no "naturally occurring" substances (for instance, most antibiotics) were patentable, according to the Patent Office. Beginning with the discovery of penicillin (unpatented), the pharmaceutical industry became more seriously involved in research and development. Ease of entry into antibiotic production, encouraged by government tax incentives and the potential for further therapeutic advances, led to many sellers with excess capacity and severe price cutting by manufacturers of the new drug. Between 1945 and 1955, bulk prices per billion units fell from $6,000 to $35, and in seven years the wholesale cost of a single vial of procaine penicillin had dropped to less than 6 percent of its original price. By 1950 manufacturers referred to unpatented antibiotics as "distress merchandise" and a Pfizer Company executive stated (U.S. Federal Trade Commission, 1958): "If you want to lose your shirt, start making penicillin or streptomycin."

Contending that an extension of patent protection to all new drug discoveries was necessary to stimulate further investments in research, industry representatives pressed successfully in the late 1940s for a relaxation of the traditional interpretation (U.S. Task Force on Prescription Drugs, 1968), and the industry did subsequently step up research for patentable new drugs. The industry was substantially restructured as manufacturers integrated forward and backward to reap the benefits which would accrue to those organizations successful in the ensuing competition to discover effective new drugs. For example, by 1956 four patented broad-spectrum antibiotics accounted for 50 percent of all antibiotic sales in dollars, but only 24 percent of all antibiotics prescribed; although three of the newer drugs were manufactured by the same process utilized in penicillin production, the price differential between patented and unpatented antibiotics produced by the same firms yielded a gross profit of 75 percent or more on patented products, but only 20 percent on the others (U.S. Federal Trade Commission, 1958). Thus, an important change in the industry's context for profitability—at least for the short run—was effected by a change in policy followed by an organization in its institutional environment; that is, the Patent Office. By 1950 it was clear that unpatented products were poor investments, but that patents on new drugs and on minor variations or combinations of existing drugs could be obtained if adequate resources for research, advertising, promotion, and possible lawsuits by competitors were available. To minimize litigation, a long-standing and occasionally controversial practice of the Patent Office has been to promote a private settlement, in which those competing for the same patent decide among themselves which one will become the sole applicant. Typically a winning pharmaceutical manufacturer would then grant exclusive production or marketing licenses to the "losers," whose applications would be withdrawn, and reject applications from all other organizations for the same privileges. Between 1950 and 1958, nearly 2,000 patents on antibiotics produced by new molds had been awarded, though many would not be produced commercially by the owners of the patents, and an unprecedented total of 6,107 new prescription drug products had been introduced by American pharmaceutical manufacturers.

Trademarks are awarded for a period of forty years; patents for seventeen years. Since 1948 most pharmaceutical products have been identified by both an official chemical ("generic") name, which includes a description of the drug's active chemical ingredient, and by one or more brand names (trademarks), which are registered with the Patent Office by the manufacturer(s). In the advertising and promotion of most drugs to the medical profession, the brand name is more prominently featured. Since the manufacturer is usually accorded the right to provide both of the names for each new drug, brand names are nearly always shorter and simpler than their generic equivalents, an outcome often discussed in the course of congressional hearings. For example (U.S. Congress, Senate, 1967, part 2, p. 764):

> Senator Nelson: "You did not happen to bring along a list of generic names supplied by the brand name companies that are shorter than the brand names they created for themselves, did you?"
> Commissioner of Food and Drug Administration (Goddard): "That would be a very short list, Senator."

During the early 1950s, pharmaceutical promotion shifted from using the manufacturer's trade name in association with the generic name of a drug (for example, Bayer Aspirin) toward using a brand name, which referred neither to the generic or chemical contents nor to its manufacturer (for example, Excedrin, Miltown). This strategy, employed by many of the largest firms in the industry, would increase in effectiveness once physicians could be persuaded to remain loyal to brands and once antisubstitution laws were modified to prevent the pharmacist from treating generically equivalent drugs as identical.

The increased access to patents and the new reliance on brand names and new laws against substitution comprise two aspects of the pharmaceutical industry's institutional environment which were effectively combined to prestructure a more favorable context for high profitability.

Phonograph Record Manufacturers. Record manufacturers are similarly affected by laws on copyright protection. All musical compositions less than 100 years old are subject to copyright protection, and manufacturers must pay a fixed royalty to the copyright holder on every recorded version of the selection sold. The United States Copyright Act of 1909, however, requires the publisher of a song to grant all manufacturers the right to record any composition on equal terms, once it has been licensed to a single organization. This foreclosed the possibility that a single manufacturer might obtain an exclusive license to record and promote a particular song for a period of time—in contrast to the pharmaceutical industry, where it is precisely the possession of exclusive licenses or patents which came to differentiate the major organizations from each other and from all others. Corry (1965, pp. 250-251) has assessed the impact of the copyright act on the record industry as follows:

> A . . . major determinant of conditions in the record industry . . . is the statutory requirement of compulsory licensing. The availability of musical compositions for recording to all who pay the mechanical royalties has affected the

record industry since its inception. . . . It has largely eliminated competition for composition recording rights, since they are openly available. Competition in the record industry has instead focused on such other elements as the recording artist, promotion, and pricing. . . . Entry into the industry is easier, since even the newest, smallest firm has access to copyrighted compositions. Conversely, large companies with extensive artist rosters and financial resources may release recordings of compositions popularized by small firms. Although there are some differences in the mechanical royalties paid, authors and composers generally receive a set royalty rather than one established by market conditions. Both the relative bargaining strength of the music publisher and the record company and the interownership now prevalent in the industry would be more significant if there were no compulsory licensing.

General. Relations among organizations in both industries have been substantially altered and determined over time by the changing language and administration of American patent and copyright law. In this respect, and in terms of the broader class of institutional arrangements encompassing statutes and administrative law on taxes, tariffs, and labor relations as well, they are hardly unique. In each of these arenas, industries have been differentially successful in negotiating favorable institutional arrangements, which, in turn, feed back onto the range of potential profits to be realized by their member firms (Hirsch, 1975). For both industries studied, patents and copyrights, as aspects of their legal environment, seem crucial to an evaluation of organizational performance and to an understanding of the choices made by manufacturers in selecting product innovations. If, for example, proposals in Congress to require compulsory licensing of patents and the abolition of brand names after a specified time period in the pharmaceutical industry are enacted, the broadened access to new chemical compounds would be roughly equivalent to the compulsory licensing of musical compositions mandated by the copyright act. Most economic analyses of the pharmaceutical industry agree that this would alter the structure of the industry, lower profitability, and affect product innovation (Walker, 1971), so one can expect that such an institutional change would also affect the day-today operations and performance of individual manufacturers.

In general, patent arrangements have influenced the structure and profitability of industries in which technological change or product innovations are important factors, ranging from refining gasoline, manufacturing automobile and aircraft parts, and photographic, telephone, and electrical equipment, to manufacturing eyeglass frames, bathtubs, dry ice, and fire alarms (Vaughn, 1956; Bowman, 1973; Stocking and Watkins, 1968). Copyright law and its administration, while affecting a smaller number of industries, is especially important to organizations and individuals engaged in the production, processing, or dissemination of information, ranging from writers and publishers, computer programmers, and copy machine makers, to movie production companies, cable television operators, and broadcasting organizations. Many American industries are similarly built around the fragile structure of these and other negotiated institutional mechanisms and arrangements (Scherer, 1970; Stigler, 1968; Kahn, 1971; U.S. Congress, House, 1965).

In the record industry, since neither performers nor manufacturers were afforded protection for their products by the early legislation, both subsequently lobbied unsuccessfully for an extension of the coverage of the copyright law. Historically, both argued that the law did not envision the development of radio and the jukebox, and that they were entitled to a performance fee or royalty for the public performance of their product by other profit seeking organizations. The radio medium is an especially important aspect of the environment, for it is the most important means by which consumers hear new records (Hirsch, 1969, 1972). Since managers of radio stations have no vested interest in promoting or selling records, however, executives of the record industry argue that they have to adapt their productions to whatever will be played on radio stations directed to teenagers, who account for the majority of record purchasers. While it is difficult to assess the following claims in economic terms, it is especially interesting that some major spokesmen for this industry have attributed both its major emphasis on rock music and recurrent profit squeezes to the absence of copyright protection. For example, an executive of Capitol Records has argued (U.S. Congress, House, 1965, pp. 951-956):

> A radio station takes our product, and performs it on the air, and sells the time to reach an audience with that performance, but does not have to pay for that performance. They are reusing the product as a business . . . without our being able to control it. . . . [Radio] has a wide listening audience who do not buy records. Why should they? It is cheaper and easier to turn on the radio and get it for nothing. . . . In spite of an extensive catalog of standard recordings in all fields built up over a period of twenty-five years . . . 70 percent of [our] sales are on new records released in the last three months. . . . If performance fees were to go to the record company and the performer, the frantic concentration on teenage rock and roll in the search for fast and large sales and quick returns would stop. Sales are the only means of profit for the performer and record company right now, so all music must be designed . . . to get records played . . . on that one radio station in each market that plays the so-called top forty records. . . . Let us be compensated for the use of our records on [all radio stations] and we can record for the benefit of the vast listening audience who want good music, but do not necessarily buy records.

One can see that, in the control over distribution and access to increased patent or copyright protection, the record industry has been much less successful than the pharmaceutical industry. Both outcomes, however, stem from a set of similar strategic problems and negotiation processes, with each industry seeking gains through use of the same mechanisms. The comparative effectiveness of the pharmaceutical manufacturers vis-à-vis these aspects of their institutional environment helps to account for the wide profit differential between the comparable manufacturers in the two industries.

Cooptation of Institutional Gatekeepers

The final component of the institutional environment studied was the degree of success in reducing uncertainty about new product selection by powerful gatekeepers and opinion leaders on each industry's marketing boundary. Before 1950 the American Medical Association (AMA) was the major organizational gatekeeper mediating between the pharmaceutical manufacturer and the consumer. No drug could be advertised to doctors in any of the Association's twelve journals unless it had been evaluated and approved as safe and effective by the AMA's own Council on Drugs. When a new drug was accepted, only its originator was permitted to advertise the product by a brand name; all other versions could be advertised by their generic name only, accompanied by the trade name of the manufacturer. The association also published an annual volume, *Useful Drugs,* with a critical evaluation of pharmaceutical products. The *Journal of the American Medical Association,* during the late 1940s, also rebuked the industry (in editorials such as "Silly Names for Penicillin") for confusing physicians by its adoption of brand names as a promotional device, and discouraged their inclusion in its advertisements (U.S. Federal Trade

Commission, 1958). During the early 1950s, relations between the organized profession and the industry underwent a dramatic change. The AMA adopted policy changes permitting advertisements by brand name for any drug certified as safe by the United States Food and Drug Administration; it transferred authority to screen advertisements to a new committee with more lenient standards than the Council on Drugs. It also halted the publication of *Useful Drugs,* creating a vacuum filled by *Physician's Desk Reference,* an industry-produced volume comprised of copy submitted by manufacturers. Between 1953 and 1960, the income of the AMA from advertisements tripled while revenues from membership dues and subscriptions increased 20 percent; as a proportion of total revenues, income from advertising rose from less than one-third to approximately one-half. For the pharmaceutical industry, this represented an eightfold increase in advertisements solely in AMA journals, from $11.5 to $88.5 million by 1966, by which time the number of pages of advertising in the *Journal of the American Medical Association* alone exceeded both *Time* and *Life* (Mintz, 1967). These policy changes were also accompanied by an unusual degree of job mobility between the AMA and the Pharmaceutical Manufacturers Association, a trade group formed in 1958. About this time, the AMA also began lobbying against federal legislation to require proof of a new drug's effectiveness for pre-market clearance from the Food and Drug Administration. In effect, passage of the 1962 Kefauver-Harris Amendments to the Pure Food and Drug Act transferred to the government the regulatory function which the Council on Drugs of the AMA had performed prior to the Association's internal policy changes.

In organizational terms, it is clear that the medical profession was effectively coopted by the drug industry. Barriers to the promotion of new and duplicative or combination drugs were removed, and much of the subsequent political controversy over increased government regulation of the industry can be traced back to the deregulation in the private sector. James Burrow (1971) suggests that, during the early 1950s, the priorities of the AMA were primarily the defeat of a growing number of proposals to establish national compulsory health insurance, and any incursion of the federal government into the health care field. Among the objectives he reported, the evaluation of new drugs received no mention; the Council on Drugs was only one of a multitude of committees, councils, and bureaus comprising the AMA's organizational structure. When a management consultant was asked to suggest new sources of revenue from advertising, an obvious answer lay in displacing the Council's goals and tapping the potential revenue from advertisements promoting more trademarked products (Burack, 1967). A reasonable inference is that the Association altered its standards on drug advertising in order to realize higher-priority goals. Although the industry's strategy of brand names preceded its unrestricted access to physicians through the Association's journals, the combination of increased access with the cessation of routine and well-publicized evaluation of new drugs further increased the economic incentives and rewards to manufacturers for releasing a multitude of new products and dosage forms. While these were promoted as medical advances, many were also publicly criticized as of undetermined therapeutic value by independent authorities, whose disapproval was one of the stimuli for the series of governmental inquiries initiated shortly thereafter.

In sum, much of the organizational effectiveness of the pharmaceutical industry, as measured by the economic success among its member organizations from 1950 to 1965, has been attributed to (1) increased access to patents, (2) its brand name strategy, and (3) a dramatic reversal of policy by the American Medical Association toward the regulation and promotion of new drugs. Each instance highlights changes in the institutional environment of the industry, which provided the context in which many of its member organizations were able to achieve higher profits than their counterparts in the recording industry.

In the record industry's attempt to coopt professional gatekeepers, nearly an opposite set of events occurred. Traditional patterns of promotion were disrupted by radio's loss of audience to the emerging television industry. Between 1949 and 1959, for example, advertising revenues realized by four national radio networks declined from $128 to $35 million. Radio station managements undertook a major search to locate new audiences, markets, and advertisers; they also looked to record companies to produce records to attract new listeners. For a short time, access to having records played by radio (a functional equivalent to free advertising) became far easier for all record producers: many new manufacturers entered the industry, and gradually the market share of the eight largest firms dropped from 87 percent in 1947 to 67 percent in 1967 (U.S. Bureau of the Census, 1971). By 1963, however, fewer than 25 percent of all singles records released were played by radio stations in any American city (Shemel and Krasilovsky, 1964). As competition increased and the new radio formats stabilized, organizations wanting to have their records played by radio resorted to outright bribes on an unprecedented scale. In organizational terms, they became both more dependent and less effective vis-à-vis this aspect of their marketing environment. Efforts to coopt mass-media opinion leaders did not succeed.

Three significant aspects of the record industry's external environment help to explain its organizational ineffectiveness as measured by its characteristically low rate of return during the time period covered in this article: (1) the loss of control over price and the channels through which records are distributed, (2) the decrease in the predictability of decisions taken by programmers of radio stations, and (3) the failure to effect legislation granting full copyright protection to recordings. Each instance highlights elements in the institutional environment which provided the context in which major firms lost a significant share of the market and experienced declining rates of profit, in contrast to pharmaceutical manufacturers, whose efforts to control analogous aspects of their environment were far more successful.

Discussion

In this article, we have explored the interface between constraints imposed by the environment of two industries and the comparative effectiveness of the industries in shaping and reaching accommodations with market mechanisms controlled by institutional agencies. The analysis provided an illustrative example of the utility of taking whole industries as units of analysis to better specify concrete institutional mechanisms and their relation to organizational performance. While no claim of proof is offered regarding these specific instances, the comparison also suggests that the examination of industry biographies can uncover institutional arrangements that significantly influence the collective performance of organizations engaged in similar activities.

The question remains as to why the pharmaceutical industry was the more successful at influencing the operation of these institutional mechanisms. Functional theory would stress prestige and societal importance. Conflict theory suggests that its greater profitability could follow from its larger size, which should enable an industry to better marshall the resources needed to recruit better lawyers, lobbyists, and other skilled professionals to manage contingencies posed by regulatory agents in its environment; furthermore, that an industry's degree of prestige in society is itself another institutional-level variable—the outcome of a negotiated process, subject to revision, and often entailing advertising and related campaigns to raise or maintain existing levels of legitimacy.

While these competing causal explanations may be empirically testable over a large sample of industries, neither interpretation is sufficiently persuasive in this instance to warrant the rejection of its alternative. For example, although the recording industry is smaller than the pharmaceutical, many of its major organizations are subsidiaries of large entertainment or broadcasting conglomerates well versed in the skills of collective action in other fields where their interests are at stake (such as obtaining passage of legislation to extend the duration of broadcasters' licenses from the FCC). Similarly, the functionalist interpretation is weakened by the observation that, since 1960, the pharmaceutical industry has come under considerable political pressure to reduce or better justify its high profitability. It has been forced to struggle hard to retain the legitimacy and prestige which, the theory would argue, once established would easily be retained. Concerning prestige and profitability differentials more generally, the broad functional interpretation may serve as a good point of departure from which to explore (1) the strategies and tactics employed by industries to ensure or overcome the mean rates of return that functionalist theory would roughly project for them; (2) the processes and institutional mechanisms involved in negotiations over industry-wide profitability contexts, often entailing hard-fought battles among competing sets of organizations; and (3) the economic and sociological bases of differences between observed and expected rates of return among industries, given some initial ranking of their respective prestige scores and contribution to society. For example, while the prestige of pharmaceutical manufacturers has probably risen along with earnings since the advent of "wonder drugs," this correlation in itself would be an unlikely (and at best insufficient) explanation for the comparatively higher returns reported by some ultimate consumer-oriented industries (such as soft drinks, confectionary, and cosmetics), relative to others (such as textile manufacturing and food products).

Changes in the internal organization of each industry's typical firm have not been reported here, nor have variations in the structure and performance of individual companies. That events at the institutional level have influenced their operations, however, is evidenced in the pharmaceutical industry (1) by a substantial increase in funds allocated to research and development after the liberalization of patent restrictions; (2) by a steep increase in the cost of clinically testing new drugs in order to conform to new FDA standards mandated by passage of the Kefauver-Harris Amendments to the United States Pure Food and Drug Act; and (3) by the growth in size and stature of the Office of Legal Counsel, as the enforcement of government regulations has become stricter. In the record industry, (1) the organization of (artistic) production became debureaucratized (Peterson and Berger, 1971), (2) contracts with musicians and independent producers came to delegate to them an unusual degree of artistic control over the final product, and (3) promotion and distribution became centralized functions (Hirsch, 1972). Each of these changes constitutes an adaptation to new conditions imposed on the typical firm by the dependence of the industry on radio and the inability to effect changes in wholesale distribution. Since 1960 the record industry has been the object of new investigations into bribery; and recent reported rates of return (where available) suggest that it also continues to be more volatile and less profitable than average for American manufacturing industries. Government inquiries into pharmaceutical industry profitability have continued to focus on its success in dealing with the institutional mechanisms we have discussed (Silverman and Lee, 1974). Although profit rates have not declined, the expiration of key patents, a government ruling that reimbursements to Medicare patients for prescriptions be limited to generic drugs wherever possible, and repeal of antisubstitution laws in at least one state, contribute to what *Business Week* recently called the "clouded future" of the pharmaceutical industry ("The Drug Industry's Clouded Future," 1974).

Of course, among the set of companies within an industry, there is a clear range of variation in performance, and a detailed analysis of such differences often does yield insights and findings that distinguish the high and low performers in terms of their internal organization and management styles. We have not dealt with these questions here. Rather, emphasis has been placed on the stratification of whole industries interacting with their institutional environment, utilizing readily available data, accessible and highly relevant to many current propositions and hypotheses of organization theorists.

Chandler (1962, p. 492) has addressed the divorcement of environmental issues from organizational analysis and noted an important consequence of this problem: "That the expansion and government of industrial enterprises in a market economy should be closely related to the changing nature of the market seems obvious enough. Yet many writers dealing with business administration often discuss leadership, communication, and structure with only passing reference to the market. On the other hand, economists, antitrust lawyers, and other experts on market behavior have said little about the impact of the market on corporate administration."

In this context, the boundaries of research and theory on organizations and administrative science might well be expanded to account better for organizational effectiveness and to integrate processes at the institutional level of organization.

References

Aldrich, H., and Pfeffer, J. "Organizations and Environments." Unpublished paper, New York State School of Industrial and Labor Relations, Cornell University, 1975.

Allen, M. P. "The Structure of Interorganizational Elite Cooperation: Interlocking Corporate Directorates." *American Sociological Review,* 1974, *39,* 393-406.

Benson, J. K. "The Interorganizational Network as a Political Economy." *Administrative Science Quarterly,* 1975, *20,* 229-249.

Bowman, W. S. *Patent and Antitrust Law.* Chicago: University of Chicago Press, 1973.

Burack, R. *The Handbook of Prescription Drugs.* New York: Pantheon, 1967.

Burrow, J. A. *AMA: Voice of American Medicine.* Baltimore: Johns Hopkins University Press, 1971.

Chandler, A. D. *Strategy and Structure: Chapters in the History of the American Industrial Enterprise.* Cambridge, Mass.: M.I.T. Press, 1962.

Conrad, G. R., and Plotkin, I. H. *Risk and Return in American Industry: An Econometric Analysis.* Cambridge, Mass.: Arthur Little, 1967.

Corry, C. S. *The Phonograph Record Industry: An Economic Study.* Washington, D.C.: Library of Congress Legislative Reference Service, 1965.

Davis, K., and Moore, W. E. "Some Principles of Stratification." *American Sociological Review,* 1945, *10,* 242-249.

Dill, W. "Environment as an Influence on Managerial Autonomy." *Administrative Science Quarterly,* 1958, *2,* 409-443.

"The Drug Industry's Clouded Future." *Business Week,* Nov. 23, 1974, pp. 64-73.

Epstein, E. M. *The Corporation in American Politics.* Englewood Cliffs, N.J.: Prentice-Hall, 1969.

Epstein, E. M. "Dimensions of Corporate Power—I." *California Management Review,* 1973a, *16,* 9-23.

Epstein, E. M. "Dimensions of Corporate Power—II." *California Management Review,* 1973b, *16,* 32-47.

Evan, W. "The Organization-Set: Toward a Theory of Inter-organizational Relations." In J. D. Thompson (Ed.), *Approaches to Organizational Design.* Pittsburgh: University of Pittsburgh Press, 1966.

Evan, W. "An Organization-Set Model of Interorganizational Relations." In M. Tuite, M. Radnor, and R. Chisholm (Eds.), *Interorganizational Decision Making.* Chicago: Aldine, 1972.

Gelatt, R. *The Fabulous Phonograph: From Edison to Stereo.* (Rev. ed.) New York: Appleton-Century-Crofts, 1965.

Glover, J. D., and Hawkins, D. *Economic Analysis of the Proposal to Increase Copyright License Fee for Phonograph Records.* Hearings Before Subcommittee No. 3 on H.R. 4347, H.R. 5680, H.R. 6831, and H.R. 6835:771-888. 89th Congress, First Session. Washington, D.C.: U.S. Government Printing Office, 1965.

Hall, M. "A View of the Copyright Copout—Stall, Separatism, and Standoff." *Billboard,* Jan. 16, 1971, pp. 3-90.

Hall, M. "Lawmakers in for Hectic 12 Months." *Billboard,* Jan. 8, 1972, pp. 1-5.

Hirsch, P. M. *The Structure of the Popular Music Industry: An Examination of the Filtering Process by Which Records Are Pre-Selected for Public Consumption.* Ann Arbor: Survey Research Center, University of Michigan, 1969.

Hirsch, P. M. "Processing Fads and Fashions by Cultural Industry Systems: An Organization-Set Analysis." *American Journal of Sociology,* 1972, *77,* 639-659.

Hirsch, P. M. "The Organization of Consumption." Unpublished doctoral dissertation, University of Michigan, 1973.

Hirsch, P. M. "Organizational Analysis and Industrial Sociology: An Instance of Cultural Lag." *American Sociologist,* 1975, *10,* 3-12.

Hirsch, P. M. *Organizational Effectiveness and the Institutional Environment: A Sociological Comparison of the Pharmaceutical and Recording Industries.* Beverly Hills, Calif.: Sage, 1976.

Hollander, S. "She 'Shops for You or with You': Some Notes on the Theory of the Consumer Purchasing Surrogate." In G. Fisk (Ed.), *Essays in Marketing Theory.* Boston: Allyn and Bacon, 1970.

Kahn, A. E. *The Economics of Regulation: Principles and Institutions.* Vol. 2. New York: Wiley, 1971.

Katz, D., and Kahn, R. L. *The Social Psychology of Organizations.* New York: Wiley, 1966.

Lawrence, P., and Lorsch, J. *Organization and Environment.* Boston: Graduate School of Business Administration, Harvard University, 1967.

Lieberson, S., and O'Connor, J. "Leadership and Organizational Performance: A Study of Large Corporations." *American Sociological Review,* 1972, *37,* 117-130.

McCaghy, C., and Denisoff, R. S. "Pirates and Politics: An Analysis of Intergroup Conflict." In R. S. Denisoff and C. McCaghy (Eds.), *Deviance, Conflict, and Criminality.* Chicago: Rand McNally, 1974.

Mintz, M. *By Prescription Only.* (2nd ed.) Boston: Houghton Mifflin, 1967.

Moller, W., Jr., and Wilemon, D. (Eds.). *Marketing Channels: A Systems Viewpoint.* Homewood, Ill.: Irwin, 1971.

Mueller, W. F. "Profitability in the Drug Industry: A Result of a Monopoly or a Payment for Risk?" In U.S. Federal Trade Commission, *Economic Papers by the Staff of the Bureau of Economics, 1966-1969.* Washington, D.C.: U.S. Government Printing Office, 1969.

Parsons, T. "Suggestions for a Sociological Approach to the Theory of Organization—I." *Administrative Science Quarterly,* 1956a, *1,* 63-85.

Parsons, T. "Suggestions for a Sociological Approach to the Theory of Organizations—II." *Administrative Science Quarterly,* 1956b, *1,* 225-239.

Peterson, R. A., and Berger, D. G. "Entrepreneurship in Organizations: Evidence from Popular Music Industry." *Administrative Science Quarterly,* 1971, *16,* 97-106.

Peterson, R. A., and Berger, D. G. "Cycles in Symbol Production: The Case of Popular Music." *American Sociological Review,* 1975, *40,* 158-173.

Pfeffer, J., and Leblebici, H. "Executive Recruitment and the Development of Interfirm Organizations." *Administrative Science Quarterly,* 1973, *18,* 449-461.

Ridgeway, V. P. "Administration of Manufacturer-Dealer Systems." *Administrative Science Quarterly,* 1957, *1,* 464-483.

Scherer, F. *Industrial Market Structure and Economic Performance.* Chicago: Rand McNally, 1970.

Shemel, S., and Krasilovsky, M. W. *This Business of Music.* New York: Billboard Publishing Co., 1964.

Siegel, P. M. "Prestige in the American Occupational Structure." Unpublished doctoral dissertation, University of Chicago, 1970.

Silverman, M., and Lee, P. R. *Pills, Profits, and Politics.* Berkeley: University of California Press, 1974.

Stigler, G. *The Organization of Industry.* Homewood, Ill.: Irwin, 1968.

Stocking, G. W., and Watkins, M. *Monopoly and Free Enterprise.* Westport, Conn.: Greenwood Press, 1968. (Reprint of 1961 Report of the Twentieth Century Fund.)

Telser, L. "The Supply Response to Shifting Demand in the Ethical Pharmaceutical Industry." Paper presented at Conference on Drug Development and Marketing, American Enterprise Institute, Washington, D.C., 1974.

Thompson, J. D. *Organizations in Action.* New York: McGraw-Hill, 1967.

U.S. Bureau of the Census. *1967 Census of Manufactures: Industry Statistics.* Vols. 1 and 2. Washington, D.C.: U.S. Government Printing Office, 1971.

U.S. Congress, House, Committee on the Judiciary. *Copyright Law Revision.* Parts 1-3. Hearings Before Subcommittee No. 3 on H.R. 4347, H.R. 5680, H.R. 6831, H.R. 6835, 1965.

U.S. Congress, Senate, Committee on the Judiciary. *Administered Prices: Drugs.* Report of the Subcommittee on Antitrust and Monopoly. 87th Congress, First Session, 1961.

U.S. Congress, Senate, Select Committee on Small Business. *Competitive Problems in the Drug Industry.* Parts 1-20. Hearings Before the Subcommittee on Monopoly. 90th Congress, First and Second Sessions, 91st Congress, First and Second Sessions, 92nd Congress, Second Session, 1967-71.

U.S. Federal Trade Commission. *Economic Report on Antibiotics Manufacture.* Washington, D.C.: U.S. Government Printing Office, 1958.

U.S. Task Force on Prescription Drugs. *The Drug Makers and the Drug Distributors.* Washington, D.C.: U.S. Government Printing Office, 1968.

Vaughn, F. L. *The United States Patent System.* Norman: University of Oklahoma Press, 1956.

Walker, H. D. *Market Power and Price Levels in the Ethical Drug Industry: A Critical Analysis.* Bloomington: Indiana University Press, 1971.

Wamsley, G., and Zald, M. N. *The Political Economy of Public Organizations.* Lexington, Mass.: Lexington Books, 1973.

Wilson, J. Q. *Political Organizations.* New York: Basic Books, 1973.

Woodward, J. *Industrial Organization: Theory and Practice.* London: Oxford University Press, 1965.

Zald, M. N. "Political Economy: A Framework for Analysis." In M. N. Zald (Ed.), *Power in Organizations.* Nashville: Vanderbilt University Press, 1970.

13

⧼⧽ School District Organization and Student Achievement

Charles E. Bidwell
John D. Kasarda

What makes an organization effective? The literature is conceptually scattered, the pertinent research uneven. (Price, 1968, offers a useful attempt at synthesis.) Of greatest theoretical interest are the works on the adaptiveness of organizations (see, for example, Burns and Stalker, 1961; Chandler, 1962; Lawrence and Lorsch, 1967; Thompson, 1967; Woodward, 1965). With its open-system perspective, this portion of the literature has an implicit social-ecological approach; that is, it treats organizational effectiveness as the result of a transformation of environmental inputs by social-organizational means. But this approach has not been well developed.

Woodward (1965) and Lawrence and Lorsch (1967) have advanced the idea that there is an equilibrium point for any organization at which its structure somehow matches such attributes of products and markets as predictability and divisibility and such attributes of work process as interdependence. Unfortunately, they do not specify the processes that transform input into output or the conditions under which these processes foster or retard effectiveness. Thompson's (1967) propositional essay marks the greatest advance so far, but Thompson has been faulted for a restricted view of organizations' environments (Hirsch, 1975). We badly need empirical studies, conducted in a variety of organizational settings, that use well-defined models of the links between input and output.

The school district is one such setting, and since *Equality of Educational Opportunity* (Coleman and others, 1966) there has been a good deal of attention to the outputs (especially the academic outputs) of schools. This work, however, has not been conducted from the standpoint of organization analysis. Our study takes this standpoint, using the social-ecological approach to ask whether and how attributes of school district organization affect the transformation of environmental inputs into students' aggregate levels of academic achievement.

The existing findings on school-specific antecedents of students' achievement are

Reprinted from *American Sociological Review*, 1975, *40*, 55-70, with permission from the authors and the American Sociological Association.

almost entirely negative. The central study, *Equality of Educational Opportunity,* reports little effect of the social composition of a school's student body, the richness of its resources and facilities, or the training and language skill of its teachers on students' attainments, whether in the elementary or the high school grades. Discovering substantially more variance in attainment within than between the schools in their sample, Coleman and his associates attributed this within-school variance primarily to extra-school factors.

Though the Coleman work has been the object of a good deal of methodological criticism, reanalysis of the *EEO* data using more sophisticated techniques does not alter the principal findings (Mosteller and Moynihan, 1972). Indeed, there is evidence to suggest that the original Coleman findings overestimate the effects of school attributes on achievement (Smith, 1972).

Despite the reanalyses reported in the Mosteller-Moynihan volume, there are good reasons to suspend judgment about the negative conclusions of *EEO.* Some of these are technical and center largely on errors of measurement (Jencks, 1972). Others are substantive and have to do with the failure of *EEO* to take school and school district structure into account. It is likely that a part of the within-school variance in pupil achievement that Coleman and his associates observed was the result not of extra-school influences but, at least in the high schools, of curricular differentiation and variation in resource allocation to the several curricular "tracks." Indeed, another reanalysis of the *EEO* data suggests the possibility of such within-school organizational variability (Heyns, 1974).

Nor did Coleman and his associates investigate very deeply organization structures or practices in their sample of schools and so could say relatively little about covariation of organization variables and pupils' achievement. They did not consider how between-school differences in such organization attributes as the division of labor, formalization of teaching activities, supervision of teaching, or the morphology of control might have mediated or otherwise affected relationships between inputs to schools and pupil achievement.

Note also that the *school* was the unit of analysis in the *EEO* study. It is entirely possible, however, that the school is not the most appropriate unit for discovering effects of schooling on pupils' achievement (or other outcomes), especially if organization attributes are to be the independent variables. On the one hand, within-school variation in resource allocation, classroom-group composition and norms, and similar characteristics of pupils' proximal school environments may have greater salience for the activities of both teachers and students than such attributes when measured at the school level.

On the other hand, if we view organizational phenomena as means for transforming environmental inputs into outputs, then one principal locus of these phenomena may be the school district rather than the individual school. There is little variation between schools in the centralization of administrative control, more between school districts. Budget making, which affects such things as the differential allocation of resources between functions (for example, teaching versus nonacademic services) or between schools, is a central-office and school board responsibility. The supervision of teaching and the work of such specialists as counselors or therapists often are conducted district-wide. One important component of the specialization of instruction, the specialization of schools (for example, the relative number of vocational or other subject-specialized high schools), pertains to the district. Such attributes of school districts may vary sufficiently from one district to another to interpret observed zero-order associations between such environmental phenomena as resources or population characteristics and levels of student achievement.

In addition, preoccupation with the school may have resulted in the inattention to dependencies among environmental and organizational variables characteristic of the earlier research on "school effects." So, for example, the fact that fiscal resources are initially received and allocated at the school district level may have led investigators to ignore imparities in the allocation of resources across schools within a district and ways in which a school's budgeted funds possibly affect the staffing, structure, and activities of the school. Thus, the *EEO* study measured expenditures at the school district level, despite the fact that the school was the unit of analysis.

Nevertheless, the more important shortcoming of the earlier work is the failure to explore ways in which the organization of education may intervene between inputs to schooling and its outcomes. Specific models of this organizational mediation are required, whether the level of analysis is the school district or the individual school (or, indeed, still higher levels of aggregation, such as national systems of education). There is some irony in the fact that one of the early studies of the relation between organization size and administrative morphology was conducted in schools (Terrien and Mills, 1955), while the bearing of such phenomena on school and school district effectiveness has been ignored.

The present study not only will broaden the basic findings about organization structure and effectiveness, but also may cause us to question whether schools (or, perhaps better, school districts) are so little able to affect observed variation in student achievement. Moreover, from the standpoint of policy, aspects of organization structure and staff composition, compared with such phenomena as pupil composition or classroom-group norms, are relatively manipulable variables.

The analysis will be presented on two levels. First, we shall examine relationships among certain environmental, structural, and staff-compositional attributes of school districts. We then shall ask whether these attributes, as they vary together, significantly influence aggregate levels of academic achievement. Ours is a preliminary study. We shall indicate certain variables that should have been included but do not appear in our analysis because of limited data. Data limitations also presented certain problems of measurement and epistemic correlation that we shall note. Our primary purpose, however, is to lay out a framework of analysis and a way of thinking about organization effectiveness generally and school effects specifically and to report findings that suggest the fruitfulness of our approach.

Preliminary Considerations

There are many ways to define organizational effectiveness—among them survival, sheer adaptation to input, and goal attainment. We chose to regard effectiveness as goal attainment. We asked what influences the ability of a school district to produce what it sets out to produce in a volume appropriate to the demand. While the goals of schooling are many and vague, the academic attainment of students is clearly among them. Moreover, it is the only output of schools and school districts that is widely and publicly measured.

We have limited our focus to the short-run effectiveness of school districts. In the short run, an organization faces environmental conditions that it can do little to control. For school districts, these include, among others, instructional technology, the size and composition of the school-age population, the level of fiscal input, community and parental preferences about schooling, and laws and public policies concerning education.

The short-run problem for school districts is to transform such inputs as students, resources, staff, technology, and community preferences into such outputs as student achievement, operating within limits set by law and public policy. School districts, of course, may try to control or influence these inputs; but such efforts raise problems that are conceptually different from those that we have addressed in our study and usually involve relatively long-run activities.

Our working hypothesis is that the environmental conditions that confront a school district will affect levels of student achievement primarily through their effects on the structure and staff composition of these districts. The propositions that specify this working hypothesis follow from certain characteristics of instructional technology, the goals of schooling, and the legal and policy framework of public education in the United States.

At a given level of school district income, student input—both the numbers of students to be taught and their ability and motivation—sets the immediate conditions for the district's academic effectiveness. But these conditions take shape within the limits of instructional technology. Thompson (1967, p. 17) would characterize this technology as "intensive"; that is, as involving "a variety of techniques drawn on in order to achieve change in some specific object; [with] the selection, combination, and order of application . . . determined by feedback from the object itself." More, however, must be said.

The technology of instruction is primitive, uncodified, and labor intensive, with the classroom teacher at the focal point of the work process. Whatever the variation in the size or quality of student input to a school district, there are few "nonhuman" substitutes for, or supplements to, the interaction of teacher and students. Nor is there a very wide array of existing alternatives to the typical one-teacher—one-classroom division of instructional labor. The absence of codified procedures means that the teacher, working alone in a classroom, must use his own judgment and fund of experience to evaluate and respond to feedback from students.

There is little variation in instructional technology, then, that might induce structural variation across school districts. One exception is the provision of professional staff support to the teaching function. Some support staff primarily provide information to teachers (for example, achievement testing or the diagnosis of learning difficulties); others work more directly with students (for example, counseling or speech therapy). Although a high proportion of such specialists in a school district may in part reflect efforts to "professionalize" its staff, it is likely also to reflect both characteristics of the student body (for example, a high incidence of learning difficulties or of college attendance) and community and parental preferences.

Law and public policy are pertinent in two ways to a school district's adaptation to student input. First, they require school districts to enroll all students who present themselves in any year. Consequently, in Thompson's (1967) terms, school districts can do little to level either the sheer size of enrollment or the ability and motivation of entering students. Second, the primary inputs of operating income to school districts are from local property taxes and state aid. Since the allocation of these revenues to school districts is fixed by law and government policy, there is little that school districts can do in the short run to alter available income.

Therefore, the primary means available to school districts for adapting to student input are, again following Thompson (1967), input buffering and rationing. A district may attempt to buffer instructional activities by hiring more teachers as its enrollment grows, or better-qualified teachers when the quality of student input appears problematic (for example, substantial proportions of students of either high or low ability).

But because in the short run fiscal resources are relatively fixed (and usually not easily reallocated in a public bureaucracy), unless they are very affluent, school districts faced with rising enrollments will be constrained fairly quickly to ration teachers as enrollment outruns income. Indeed, at any level of school district income, there should be an observable effect of rationing in the form of covarying pupil-teacher ratios and enrollments.

We have noted the vagueness of educational goals; usually they are subject to a good deal of disagreement within a school district's community. Moreover, there is no clear or widely accepted evidence of relationships between various curricula or teaching methods and student outcomes. As a result, even when information about levels of student attainment in a school district is public, such district attributes as teacher qualifications, the availability of student services, and curricular "innovation" usually serve for both school personnel and community members as presumptive evidence of the district's effectiveness. The inchoate character of educational goals and of the link between instruction and outcome means that school districts are highly vulnerable to such parental and community preferences. It also means that, as school district income grows, it is likely to be invested relatively heavily in such things as numerous, well-trained teachers or support specialists, independently of the size or quality of pupil input.

Propositions and Methods

With these characteristics of schooling and school districts in mind, we can now turn to the data available for the present study and to the specific propositions that these data allowed us to test. The study required a sample of school districts for which there was a substantial range of size and fiscal resources and a determinable division of labor among instructional, administrative, and supporting professional staff. Furthermore, data were required on the professional qualifications of key school district personnel, the socioeconomic characteristics of the school district population, and the academic achievement of the district's students. In the school year 1969-70, 104 of the 178 K-12 public school districts in the state of Colorado met these conditions. These 104 districts enrolled over 90 percent of the public school students in Colorado in 1969-70.

The 1969-70 annual report of the superintendent of each Colorado school district lists personnel employed, along with the functions that they performed. From these lists the numbers of persons in each district in each of three employee categories were calculated: administrative personnel (including superintendents, assistant superintendents, principals, assistant principals, directors, assistant directors, administrative assistants, business managers, coordinators, and supervisors), professional support staff (including guidance counselors, librarians, psychologists, social workers, speech therapists, and school nurses), and instructional staff (including all classroom teachers employed by the school district).

A summary report on the Colorado school districts (Colorado Department of Education, 1971) was used to obtain measures of fiscal resources, size, the professional qualifications of the certificated personnel, and standardized verbal and mathematics group achievement levels of secondary school students. In addition, 1970 Census of Population data were employed to measure socioeconomic characteristics of the population which the school district served. The census data were reconstructed to be coterminous with the geographic boundaries of each school district.

The variables and their operationalization are as follows:

Environmental Conditions (Exogenous Variables)

School District Size—Average daily student attendance. This variable was transformed via logarithms ($\log_{10}$) to correct for the skewed distribution caused by a few very large school districts (SIZE).

Fiscal Resources—The sum of all local, state, and federal revenue received by the school district, divided by pupils in average daily attendance to standardize for size (RESOURCES).

Disadvantaged Students—The percent of all school-age children residing in the school district who came from families with incomes below the nationally defined poverty level (DISAD).

Education (parent risk population)—The percent of males 20-49 years old and females 15-44 years old residing in the school district who had completed at least four years of high school education (EDUC).

Percent Nonwhite—The percent of the population residing in the school district who were classified by census definition as nonwhite (PNONW).

Organizational Attributes (Intervening Variables)

Pupil-Teacher Ratio—The number of pupils in average daily attendance divided by the number of classroom teachers, converted to full-time equivalents (PTRATIO).

Administrative Intensity—The ratio of administrators to classroom teachers (ADMIN).

Professional Support Component—The ratio of professional support staff to classroom teachers (PROF).

Certificated Staff Qualifications—The percent of the total certificated staff who held at least the master's degree (QUALIF).

Achievement (Dependent Variables)

Reading Achievement—Median grade-standardized reading achievement level (nationally normed percentile) for high school students (RACH).

Mathematics Achievement—Median grade-standardized mathematics achievement level (nationally normed percentile) for high school students (MACH).

The exogenous variables, then, measure certain environmental conditions under which a school district in the short run must operate. Intervening between these variables and output (aggregate levels of student achievement) is a set of organizational attributes involving key district functions: classroom teaching, professional support, and administration. (See Figure 1.)

Given the limits of our data, we have measured proportional relations between numbers of persons to provide indicators of the structure and staff composition of the Colorado school districts. Two of these measures pertain to teaching: the pupil-teacher ratio and the proportion of all certificated personnel with at least the master's degree. The first of these variables is an indicator of the availability of teachers in relation to the

Figure 1. A Model of School District Organization and Student Achievement

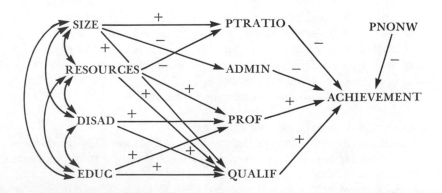

number of pupils to be taught. The second is a rough measure of the aggregate professional qualifications of the teaching staff.

We did not have information on qualifications by subgroups of the certificated staff, which includes administrators and nonteaching professional specialists as well as teachers. But in all school districts the great majority of certificated personnel are teachers. We used the percentage measure, which will be affected minimally by a concentration of higher degrees outside the teaching force. So we feel justified in using the percent of the certificated staff holding the master's degree or better as an indicator of the qualifications of a district's teachers.

Our model includes two measures of proportional relations between functions. One of these, the ratio of supporting professional staff to classroom teachers, can be regarded as an approximate indicator of professional support for the instructional activities of a district. The other, the ratio of the number of administrators to the number of classroom teachers, is a measure of the dominance of administration in relation to instruction (administrative intensity). Note that the number of administrators was limited to managers. Thus, it excludes clerical personnel in administrative offices.

Turning to our environmental variables, the level of fiscal resources should be related negatively to pupil-teacher ratio and positively to professional support and staff qualifications. Such relationships are, in point of fact, to be expected generally of publicly sponsored organizations, which are under less pressure than private ones to accumulate capital reserves. For school districts this proposition follows especially from the consequences of vague goals and unclear links between technical means and goal attainment.

Our chief measure of pupil input and, for the purposes of this study, of school district size is the district's average enrollment. Other pertinent aspects of pupil input (most notably, aggregate academic ability) could not be measured with the data available to us. This gap in our data will make us cautious about our conclusions. Nevertheless, enrollment in itself should affect a district's structure in several ways. Here we discuss only those that our model can reveal.

First, given the high probability of rationing as a response to growth in enrollment and to large enrollments given fixed resources, per-pupil shares of teachers should decline across districts as enrollment increases. Second, in view of the simple organization of teaching in most school districts (the enclosed classroom and school), there is low interdependence between a district's main subunits. Therefore, a school district should be able to accommodate increasing enrollment without a notable increase in coordinative problems. Moreover, this simple structure may make it possible for districts to lower the intensity of instructional supervision without immediately apparent results. Consequently, we should find among the Colorado districts a negative effect of size (number of pupils) on administrative intensity.

Third, since enrollment is usually a correlate of community size, number of pupils should have a positive direct effect on teachers' qualifications. Larger places are likely to have larger pools of well-qualified teachers to draw from, to provide attractive employment for the spouses of married teachers, and to afford more of the amenities of life that attract and hold competent teachers.

The remaining environmental conditions in Figure 1 are three measures of certain nonfiscal inputs from a school district's community: the aggregate educational level of the parental risk population, the percentage of students from below the census definition of the "poverty line," and the percent of the total population nonwhite.

Education of the parental risk population and the proportion of disadvantaged students in a district's population should be correlated with the content and force of community expectations for the instructional program of the district. In addition, children of well-educated parents in general are more highly motivated and more able than others, and, given their (and their parents') educational and occupational aspirations, they may require more advanced curricula and therefore better-qualified teachers. They may also require certain special student services, such as college counseling. Students from so-called disadvantaged families tend to be less motivated and less able. If a district seeks a more-than-minimal standard of achievement for all of its pupils, the presence of high proportions of such students may require a district to provide competent teachers and such professional services as remedial reading programs. Thus, these two variables serve in our study as rough measures of both community and parental preferences and certain qualitative attributes of the districts' student inputs. If our argument about these inputs is correct, then, net of district size and resources we should find positive direct effects on staff qualifications and professional support from both the level of parental education and the proportion of students from disadvantaged families.

The percent nonwhite, net of other environmental variables, should not affect either the structure or the staff composition of school districts. But this variable has been found to have a negative effect on achievement (though most of the pertinent literature examines this relationship at a level of aggregation lower than the district; see, for example, Armor, 1972; Coleman and others, 1966; Crain, 1971; St. John and Smith, 1969). Therefore, we wished to control for percent nonwhite as a disturbance term, when estimating the effects of the other independent variables on achievement levels.

What, finally, should be the effects of each of the variables in our model on district levels of students' academic achievement? If our working hypothesis is correct, none of the environmental conditions will have a direct effect on achievement, except for percent nonwhite. So far as the measures of district structure and staff composition are concerned, whether any of them is consequential for the academic effectiveness of school districts is moot. But if there are any school district effects at all on aggregate student attainment, then attainment should be influenced by student-teacher ratios, teacher qualifications, administrative intensity, and the relative size of the professional support staff—more heavily by the first three than by the fourth.

This prediction derives from our view of instruction: that it is teacher intensive, that it involves at its center teacher response to feedback from students, and that it generates a low level of interdependence between the subunits of school districts.

Teacher Qualifications. Our argument with respect to this variable is straightforward. If we are willing to entertain the possibility that teachers' qualifications are in fact related to teaching skill, then the teacher-intensive character of instruction implies that the greater the proportion of well-qualified teachers in a school district, the higher the district's level of student attainment.

Pupil-Teacher Ratio. The more students a teacher must handle during a class session, the less refined (that is, the less adaptive to specific performances and characteristics) his response to them is likely to be. In other words, the greater the teacher's classroom "span of control," the poorer his daily decisions in teaching. Per pupil, there is less information to attend to and less time to evaluate it. Moreover, in the usual classroom pupil-teacher interaction is heavily dyadic. If we assume that student achievement is some positive function of the rates of such interaction, then the more pupils per teacher, the lower the aggregate level of achievement.

In addition, just as school districts are likely to ration teachers in the face of large student enrollments, so teachers themselves may ration their time in the classroom. This rationing is especially likely to take the form of differential treatment of students (for example, disproportionate amounts of time devoted to discipline for low-performing students). Such rationing by the teacher presumably is a function of classroom size; for this reason also, higher pupil-teacher ratios in a district should be associated with lower levels of student attainment.

Relative Size of Professional Support Staff. To the extent that these staff members provide information directly to teachers, a high proportion of support staff should make a very small contribution to a district's effectiveness net of staff qualifications and pupil-teacher ratios. If these staff specialists work directly with pupils, their efforts are likely to be concentrated on relatively small proportions of students (for example, those with severe learning problems) or to be directed toward matters that do not pertain directly to academic achievement (for example, vocational or college counseling). On balance, then, the proportionate size of the professional support staff of a school district should have only a small direct effect on levels of student achievement.

Administrative Intensity. From the low interdependence among subunits of a school district, it follows that any contribution of administration to school district effectiveness will occur primarily in nonacademic areas, with the possible (and in the present study untestable) exception of instructional supervision. Even if the work of professional support staff requires and receives effective coordination, the expected low contribution of professional support to student achievement should weaken this indirect effect of administrative intensity on achievement levels. Therefore, given the short-run inelasticity of school district resources, as the relative size of the administrative component of a district grows, it should divert human resources from instruction at a rate not overcome by the contribution of administration to instructional effectiveness. Consequently we would expect levels of student achievement to be affected negatively by administrative intensity.

Since all variables in the model form interval scales, conventional regression analysis will be our primary statistical method. The main thrust of our analysis, however, is not based on a search for multivariate findings to maximize aggregate explanatory power. Rather, the strategy is to assess the merit of our model linking environmental conditions, organizational attributes, and district levels of pupil achievement. Therefore, we shall use the Simon-Blalock method to evaluate the accuracy of the model and techniques of path analysis to decompose zero-order relationships between pertinent variables into direct, indirect, and joint effects.

It is important to reiterate that all measured relationships are at the level of the school district. None pertains to individuals, schools or other subunits of the district. The reader should keep in mind especially that we are not analyzing antecedents of the academic achievement of individual students, rather the overall effectiveness of a school district as measured by the aggregate achievement level for all its students at a given grade. Introducing multiple levels of analysis into the same model brings difficulties of estimation and interpretation (for example, the "ecological fallacy") that we wish to avoid.

Results

Table 1 presents the zero-order correlation matrix for all variables in the study, while Table 2 provides regression estimates (in standard form) of the effect parameters that show dependencies between the environmental and organizational variables and among the organizational variables themselves.

The results shown in Table 2 are largely consistent with our predictions. As we anticipated, administrative intensity was affected at a statistically significant level only by

Table 1. Correlation Matrix, Means, and Standard Deviations of Variables in the Model

	X_1	X_2	X_3	X_4	X_5	X_6	X_7	X_8	X_9	X_{10}	X_{11}
X_1 RACH											
X_2 MACH	.722										
X_3 QUALIF	.269	.121									
X_4 PTRATIO	-.177	-.227	.262								
X_5 PROF	.172	.105	.206	.064							
X_6 ADMIN	-.217	-.213	-.143	-.136	-.014						
X_7 SIZE	.031	-.053	.461	.583	.225	-.389					
X_8 RESOURCES	.301	.268	.115	.671	.203	.002	-.228				
X_9 DISAD	-.137	-.165	-.203	-.147	-.155	.286	-.340	-.221			
X_{10} PNONW	-.179	-.231	.010	.046	-.104	-.140	.077	-.070	.055		
X_{11} EDUC	.272	.280	.516	.143	.232	-.319	.409	.275	-.555	-.084	
Mean	52.1	53.8	29.5	21.2	.0567	.0912	3.18	875.8	17.7	2.23	64.0
SD	11.2	13.0	9.5	2.8	.0264	.0295	0.55	174.1	11.2	3.44	10.0

$N = 104$

Table 2. Standardized Partial Regression Coefficients from Regression of
Each Organizational Attribute of School Districts on Environmental Conditions
and Other Organizational Attributes

Independent Variables	Dependent Variables			
	ADMIN	PROF	PTRATIO	QUALIF
SIZE	−.400[b]	.225	.300[b]	.307[a]
RESOURCES	.056	.380[a]	−.681[b]	.293[a]
EDUC	−.228	.063	.063	.420[b]
DISAD	.104	.038	−.140	.211[a]
PNONW	−.137	.004	−.004	.031
QUALIF	.114	−.005	.136	−
PTRATIO	.153	.200	−	.262
PROF	.100	−	.073	−.003
ADMIN	−	.108	.062	.089
Multiple R	.489	.385	.832	.637

[a]Coefficient is twice its standard error.

[b]Coefficient is three times its standard error.

district size, declining across districts as size increased. Large district size did seem to foster wider spans of administrative control and concomitant economies of scale in administration.

Fiscal resources alone among the environmental measures had a significant direct effect on the relative numbers of professional support staff. School districts with more resources employed larger proportions of professional staff specialists. Contrary to our expectations, there is a negligible relationship between each of the two indicators of aggregate parental socioeconomic status and professional staff support. Nonfiscal inputs to the Colorado districts had little effect on the balance between support staff and teachers. Note also that larger student enrollment did not generate disproportionately large numbers of professional staff specialists. Other things being equal, with larger enrollment, teachers and supporting professionals joined the districts at approximately equal rates.

Table 2 also supports our prediction that pupil-teacher ratio would be responsive primarily to district size and fiscal resources. As enrollment increased, so did the average number of students per teacher. Even more important is the strong negative impact of fiscal resources on number of pupils per teacher. Wealthier school districts were able to provide not only higher proportions of professional staff support to aid in the instructional process, but more teachers per pupil as well.

The qualifications of certificated personnel employed by the school districts were significantly affected by all of the environmental conditions except percent nonwhite. Across school districts, increases in both district size and fiscal resources are associated with better-trained personnel. Where the average educational level of the school district's parental risk population was high, the qualifications of the certificated staff also tended to be high. Staff qualifications also are positively associated with a district's percentage of school-age children from disadvantaged families, consistent with our argument that staff qualifications are in part responsive to the difficulty of instruction in a school district.

To sum up, while socioeconomic characteristics of a school district's population influence staff qualifications, they have no significant direct effects on the formal structure of school districts. Structure is responsive only to the size of the school district and the available fiscal resources. It is also important to note that, as we had expected, percent nonwhite influences neither the structure nor the staff qualifications of school districts. Indeed, it is not even moderately correlated with the other environmental conditions in our Colorado sample (see Table 1).

Now, what are the effects of each independent variable—environmental conditions, school district structure, and staff qualifications—on levels of student achievement? We shall first assess the relative effects of all variables proposed to have a direct effect on achievement. Table 3 presents the standardized partial regression coefficients for the equation:

$$X_1 = p_{12}X_2 + p_{13}X_3 + p_{14}X_4 + p_{15}X_5 + p_{16}X_6 + p_{1r}X_r$$

where X_1 is median reading or mathematics achievement, X_2 through X_5 are the four measures of the organizational attributes of the school districts, X_6 is percent nonwhite, and X_r is the residual term.

Table 3. Standardized Partial Regression Coefficients for Variables
Expected to Affect Achievement Directly

Independent Variables	Reading Achievement	Math Achievement
PTRATIO	−.284[b]	−.296[b]
ADMIN	−.242[a]	−.268[a]
QUALIF	.286[b]	.145
PROF	.125	.087
PNONW	−.201[a]	−.255[a]
Multiple R	.487	.458

[a]Regression coefficient is twice its standard error.

[b]Regression coefficient is three times its standard error.

With certain exceptions, the regression coefficients support our predictions. Several of these coefficients show the importance of a district's relative investment in teachers for its aggregate levels of student achievement. As pupil-teacher ratios declined across districts, the two median achievement scores rose. As administrative intensity rose, the achievement scores declined. Recall our argument that, so far as student achievement is concerned, administrative overhead mainly diverts human resources from teaching and from other staff functions related to instruction. Table 3 also shows that the better qualified the certificated staff, the higher the levels of reading and mathematics achievement. Contrary to our expectations, however, the relationship between staff qualifications and mathematics achievement is not statistically significant. Although the lack of statistical significance may have resulted from measurement error, perhaps the development of mathematical skills is not as responsive to the aggregate qualifications of teachers and other key personnel as are reading skills.

The effects of professional staff support on district levels of achievement were even weaker than we had predicted. The effect of this variable on mathematics achievement was slight, on reading achievement positive but not statistically significant. Our measure perhaps was too flawed an indicator of a school district's relative investment in those professional support staff whose work does affect achievement. Perhaps, though, as we have argued, support staff provide too little information to teachers that is consistently used, tend not to work directly with students, or center their efforts at the extremes of the pertinent student distributions (for example, the most or least able). They may, in point of fact, lack effective techniques to foster the academic work of either students or teachers. We should test these possibilities with better measures of professional staff components.

As do findings from earlier studies of achievement using disaggregated data, our results indicate that percent nonwhite has a depressing effect on median levels of student achievement. But what about the other environmental conditions? Our model stipulates that only insofar as school district size, fiscal resources, and the educational and income characteristics of the parent risk population influence the internal structure and staff composition of school districts should they affect achievement.

To evaluate this causal chain, we regressed reading and mathematics achievement levels on each of the measures of environmental input, controlling for the intervening structural variables and staff qualifications. If there were no measurement error, and if the environmental conditions affected achievement only through their influence on district structure and staff qualifications, then the partial regression coefficients should be zero. Because of measurement error, we will not in fact observe partial coefficients of zero; but if our model is correct, none of these partial relationships should be statistically significant.

Table 4 presents the partial regression coefficient (in standard form) for each relationship between the environmental variables in our model and achievement, controlling

Table 4. Standardized Partial Regression Coefficients Between Four Environmental Conditions and Achievement, Controlling for Organizational Attributes and Percent Nonwhite

Environmental Conditions	Reading Achievement	Math Achievement
SIZE	−.091	−.110
RESOURCES	.092	.043
DISAD	−.025	−.087
EDUC	.065	.188

for the organizational attributes and percent nonwhite. Since none of the coefficients in Table 4 is statistically significant and all coefficients except that for the relationship between education of the parental risk population and mathematics achievement approach zero, the posited causal chain is supported.

As a final step, we computed the effect parameters and decomposed the pertinent correlations into direct and indirect causal effects and joint associations on the basis of a full model, which included all possible causal paths. By using this full model, we can show more clearly how each of the independent variables may have influenced district levels of student achievement. Thus, we regressed median reading and mathematics achievement scores on all nine independent variables simultaneously. The correlation between each independent variable and achievement score (Table 1) will be equivalent to the standardized partial regression coefficient (direct effect) plus the product of the regression coefficients along each causal transverse tracing forward only (indirect effect) and an unspecified (possibly spurious) joint association due to the independent variable's association with other antecedent variables that influence achievement.

Table 5 presents the direct and indirect effects and joint associations computed on

Table 5. Decomposition of Zero-Order Correlations Between Independent Variables and Average Achievement Levels

	Reading Achievement				Mathematics Achievement			
	Total Effect	Direct Effect	Indirect Effect	Joint Assoc.	Total Effect	Direct Effect	Indirect Effect	Joint Assoc.
RESOURCES	.301	.074	.221	.006	.268	-.053	.229	.092
SIZE	.031	-.105	.155	-.019	-.053	-.152	.073	.026
DISAD	-.137	.006	.059	-.202	-.165	-.037	.037	-.165
EDUC	.272	.059	.166	.047	.280	.201	.087	-.008
PNONW	-.179	-.189	—	.010	-.231	-.227	—	-.004
ADMIN	-.217	-.250	—	.033	-.214	-.250	—	.036
PROF	.172	.117	—	.055	.105	.087	—	.018
PTRATIO	-.177	-.178	—	.001	-.227	-.265	—	.038
QUALIF	.269	.268	—	.001	.121	.104	—	.017

Multiple R = .497   Multiple R = .494

Decomposition of Indirect (Causal) Effects

	Reading Achievement				Mathematics Achievement			
	Via QUALIF	Via PTRATIO	Via PROF	Via ADMIN	Via QUALIF	Via PTRATIO	Via PROF	Via ADMIN
RESOURCES	.070	.121	.044	-.014	.030	.180	.033	-.014
SIZE	.082	-.053	.026	.100	.032	-.079	.020	.100
DISAD	.056	.025	.004	-.026	.021	.037	.005	-.026
EDUC	.113	-.011	.007	.057	.044	-.017	.003	.057

the basis of the full model. This table reveals the strong indirect influence of fiscal resources on achievement levels. While attention only to the direct effects would lead one
to infer that resources had little impact on achievement, the indirect effects show that, by
influencing the structure and staff qualifications of the school districts, resources did have
a substantial impact. The indirect effect of this variable results primarily because it lowered the number of pupils per teacher and raised staff qualifications.

School district size, on the other hand, has virtually no net effect on reading or
mathematics achievement levels. Not only are its direct effects fairly small, but size has
opposing indirect effects on achievement. While it improved achievement especially by
decreasing administrative intensity and raising staff qualifications, large size lowered
achievement levels by increasing pupil-teacher ratios.

Median school district scores for neither reading achievement nor mathematics
achievement were independently influenced by the proportion of students from economically disadvantaged families. Note that both the direct and indirect effects of this variable
are negligible. The negative zero-order correlations between the proportion of disadvantaged students and reading and mathematics achievement resulted primarily from the
association of this variable with other environmental conditions that influenced achievement.

While the total effects of the educational attainment of the parent risk population
on reading and mathematics achievement are of similar magnitude, the causal patterns
differ. This variable had only a slight direct effect on reading achievement but a much
stronger direct effect on mathematics achievement. Conversely, parental education affected reading achievement positively through its influence on staff qualifications, while
this indirect effect was negligible for mathematics achievement.

Education of the parental risk population is very likely a proxy for a variety of
family and community attributes that influence academic achievement (for example, the
proportion of families providing high levels of cognitive stimulation to children or the
availability of books in public libraries). That this variable had only a slight direct effect
on reading achievement, therefore, is unusually strong evidence of the association between the staff qualifications and the academic output of the Colorado school districts—
the more so since the level of qualifications of the certificated staff is no more than an
approximate indicator of teachers' competence. The findings for mathematics achievement are more what one might realistically expect—a relatively strong direct effect of
education of parents and a modest direct effect of staff qualifications.

Decomposition of the correlation coefficients supports our prediction that percent nonwhite should affect achievement levels independently of other variables in the
model. Controlling for the other eight independent variables, the standardized partial regression coefficients between percent nonwhite and median reading and mathematics
achievement scores are of essentially the same magnitude as the zero-order correlations.

In brief, decomposition of the pertinent zero-order correlations strongly supports
our district-level model when the dependent variable is reading achievement and moderately supports this model when the dependent variable is mathematics achievement. The
coefficients of multiple determination show that we have accounted for approximately
25 percent of the variance in median reading achievement scores and 24 percent of the
variance in median mathematics achievement scores.

Conclusions and Policy Implications

Our study provides substantial evidence of the significance of organizational structure and staffing for school district effectiveness. This evidence is especially striking since

earlier research on schools suggests that student achievement is largely impervious to variation in the attributes of educational organizations. We have seen certain ways in which the structure and staffing of school districts appear to transform inputs to school districts into outputs of student achievement. These inputs included students, funds, and certain postulated correlates of community and parental population characteristics. Further study of this transformation process, in many varieties of organization settings, is clearly warranted.

The findings concerning the consequences of administrative intensity point up the value of analysis at the school district level, since the primary contribution to administrative overhead occurs at administrative levels above the individual school. It is not immediately clear why we have found for the Colorado *districts* effects of staff qualifications on pupil achievement while similar effects have not appeared in earlier studies of *schools*. But our results for pupil-teacher ratios suggest the need for further attention to the per-pupil availability of teachers and to the ways in which teachers and teachers' time are allocated among students, in studies at the school as well as the district level.

Two of our findings are especially noteworthy. First, most studies of organizational structure have stressed the centrality of size as a "prime mover" of variation in the morphology of organizations. We have observed also among the Colorado school districts the centrality of size to morphology. But size had, overall, a very slight effect on output, whether reading or mathematics achievement. The total effects of size were slight because its consequences for output, transmitted mainly by the structural and staff qualifications variables, were of roughly equal strength in a positive and in a negative direction. At least for the Colorado districts, increasing size created an organizational dilemma. It was associated with well-qualified staff and low administrative intensity (and therefore, we have argued, with minimal diversion of human resources away from front-line tasks). But large size also meant more students to teach and thus higher ratios of students to teachers.

Second, by contrast with size, fiscal resources had significant total effects on output (both reading and mathematics achievement), even though their direct effects were very small. Most studies of schooling and pupil achievement have concluded that variation in resources has little to do with variation in achievement. This conclusion reflects a failure to examine dependencies among environmental and organizational properties of school districts and the consequences for student achievement of these dependencies.

Our Colorado findings give clear evidence of the simple but important fact that, as school districts command more income, they buy more and better-qualified front-line staff, investing in both teachers and supporting professional specialists. Therefore, at the district level, at least so far as investment in teachers is concerned, the availability of revenues has important consequences for student achievement.

A word, finally, about some of the implications of our Colorado findings for educational policy. Our comments are tentative, since the coefficients that we have reported are modest, and we could not control for several pertinent student inputs (especially levels of academic ability). Nevertheless, to argue that little can be done through the formal organization of schooling to affect students' academic attainment is, in the light of our study, premature. If our findings are sustained by further work, three of them will have direct bearing on steps at the school district level (whatever may or may not prove possible in individual schools or classrooms) to maximize aggregate levels of students' academic achievement.

First, well-qualified teachers in large relative numbers will stand as a potent resource for schooling. This statement may be a truism, but it is often forgotten.

Second, school district revenue will have been reaffirmed as a major influence on attainment, especially as it affects the rates and quality levels at which teachers are hired and retained. The long-standing effort in the United States to increase and equalize the revenues of school districts will not then have been misplaced. A concern for distributive justice, at least among school districts, necessarily will involve a concern for the allocation of funds between districts.

Third, the mixed blessings of large school districts will have been demonstrated. The received wisdom in this country is that larger school districts do a better job of instruction because of the amount and diversity of resources for instruction (see Conant, 1967). Our findings are consistent with this notion so far as administrative intensity and teacher qualifications are concerned. But in Colorado, as district size increased, the number of students outran the number of teachers provided. If this finding holds true, unless a school district has a large absolute amount of disposable funds to invest in teachers, increases in size should have at least partially self-defeating consequences for students' achievement. There may be alternatives to the traditional organization of instruction into classroom segments and alternative curricular arrangements that would permit school districts to benefit from the gains of increased size without incurring these presumed losses from unfavorable pupil-teacher ratios. To devise and evaluate such alternatives may be among the more important avenues for applied social science research.

References

Armor, D. J. "School and Family Effects on Black and White Achievement." In F. Mosteller and D. P. Moynihan (Eds.), *On Equality of Educational Opportunity*. New York: Vintage Books, 1972.

Boulding, K. "Toward a General Theory of Growth." *Canadian Journal of Economics and Political Science,* 1953, *19,* 326-340.

Burns, T., and Stalker, G. M. *The Management of Innovation.* London: Tavistock, 1961.

Chandler, A. D., Jr. *Strategy and Structure.* Cambridge, Mass.: M.I.T. Press, 1962.

Coleman, J. S., and others. *Equality of Educational Opportunity.* Washington, D.C.: U.S. Government Printing Office, 1966.

Colorado Department of Education. *Consolidated Report on Elementary and Secondary Education in Colorado.* Denver: Colorado Department of Education, 1971.

Conant, J. B. *The Comprehensive High School: A Second Report to Interested Citizens.* New York: McGraw-Hill, 1967.

Crain, R. L. "School Integration and the Academic Achievement of Negroes." *Sociology of Education,* 1971, *44,* 1-26.

Freeman, J. H., and Kronenfeld, J. E. "Problems of Definitional Dependency: The Case of Administrative Intensity." *Social Forces,* 1973, *52,* 108-121.

Fuguitt, G. V., and Lieberson, S. "Correlation of Ratios or Difference Scores Having Common Terms." In H. L. Costner (Ed.), *Sociological Methodology, 1973-1974.* San Francisco: Jossey-Bass, 1974.

Haire, M. "Biological Models and Empirical Histories of the Growth of Organizations." In M. Haire (Ed.), *Modern Organization Theory.* New York: Wiley, 1959.

Heyns, B. "Social Selection and Stratification Within Schools." *American Journal of Sociology,* 1974, *79.*

Hirsch, P. M. "Organizational Analysis and Industrial Sociology: An Instance of Cultural Lag." *American Sociologist,* 1975, *10,* 3-12.

Jencks, C. S. "The Quality of the Data Collected by the Equality of Educational Opportunity Survey." In F. Mosteller and D. P. Moynihan (Eds.), *On Equality of Educational Opportunity*. New York: Vintage Books, 1972.

Kasarda, J. D. "The Structural Implications of Social System Size: A Three-Level Analysis." *American Sociological Review*, 1974, *39*, 19-28.

Lawrence, P. R., and Lorsch, J. W. *Organization and Environment*. Boston: Graduate School of Business Administration, Harvard University, 1967.

Mosteller, F., and Moynihan, D. P. (Eds.). *On Equality of Educational Opportunity*. New York: Vintage Books, 1972.

Price, J. L. *Organizational Effectiveness*. Homewood, Ill.: Irwin, 1968.

Schuessler, K. "Analysis of Ratio Variables: Opportunities and Pitfalls." *American Journal of Sociology*, 1974, *80*, 379-396.

Smith, M. S. "Equality of Educational Opportunity: The Basic Findings Reconsidered." In F. Mosteller and D. P. Moynihan (Eds.), *On Equality of Educational Opportunity*. New York: Vintage Books, 1972.

St. John, N. H., and Smith, M. S. *School Racial Composition, Achievement and Aspiration*. Cambridge, Mass.: Center for Educational Policy Research, Harvard University, 1969.

Terrien, F. W., and Mills, D. L. "The Effect of Changing Size upon the Internal Structure of Organizations." *American Sociological Review*, 1955, *20*, 11-13.

Thompson, J. D. *Organizations in Action*. New York: McGraw-Hill, 1967.

Woodward, J. *Industrial Organization: Theory and Practice*. London: Oxford University Press, 1965.

14

Effectiveness of an Attendance Control Policy in Reducing Chronic Absenteeism

John F. Baum

What can organizations do to counteract the tendency of some workers to absent themselves excessively from the workplace? In response to an apparent secular trend of increasing absenteeism in important segments of the work force (Bureau of National Affairs, 1974; Hedges, 1973), managers have become increasingly interested in attendance control policies that will lead to a meaningful reduction in unauthorized absenteeism. Managerial concern is well illustrated in a national survey of some 200 organizations conducted by the Bureau of National Affairs (1973), in which the vast majority (79 percent) of the respondents indicated that absenteeism was their most serious disciplinary problem. Moreover, 25 percent of the respondents stated that disciplinary problems were more serious at the time the survey was conducted (1973) than was the case five years previously.

Despite the fact that the available literature on the causes of absenteeism (Porter and Steers, 1973) stresses the importance of job redesign, improvements in the work environment, more effective reward systems, and other long-term policies designed to enhance job satisfaction and intrinsic motivation, many organizations continue to place heavy reliance on management sanctions when workers violate the attendance norms (Bureau of National Affairs, 1974). In view of the widespread use of sanctions, such as progressive discipline for repeated violations, it is surprising how little actual research has been reported on the effectiveness of sanctions in deterring counterproductive behaviors such as absenteeism. Moreover, the available literature is characterized by divided opinions and conflicting findings concerning the efficacy of sanctions in reducing absenteeism. In an attempt to speak to this controversy, this paper reports the results of an empirical assessment of the effectiveness of an attendance control policy, based on the imposition of legitimate management sanctions, in reducing the absence rates of workers in a large industrial organization.

Much of the opposition to the use of sanctions is based on two grounds: (1) be-

Reprinted from *Personnel Psychology*, 1978, *31*, 71-81, with permission of the author and the publisher.

havior modification techniques based on positive reinforcement of desired behaviors (coming to work regularly) are more suitable and effective in dealing with absenteeism; (2) sanctions based on the use of disciplinary procedures (punishments) tend to produce undesirable side effects that are as objectionable as the behavior of primary interest. Nord (1969) and Porter (1973) have reviewed the conceptual arguments favoring the use of behavior modification based on positive reinforcements and concluded that marginal workers would attend work more regularly if the organizational reward system was made more applicable to the basic sociopsychological needs of workers. Recent empirical evidence provides some support for the effectiveness of behavior modification approaches. Pedalino and Gamboa (1974) found that a lottery incentive system led to a meaningful increase in attendance among blue-collar workers in a manufacturing distribution center. Although not using an explicit operant paradigm, Nord and Costigan (1973) reported significant improvements in attendance resulting from the implementation of a four-day workweek. Likewise, Lawler and Hackman (1969) demonstrated that part-time custodial workers improved their attendance when they were allowed to participate in the development of a pay incentive plan.

The issue of undesirable side effects resulting from the use of sanctions in absenteeism control has been examined by Nicholson (1976). Using a pre-post design, Nicholson found that the sudden imposition of management sanctions, based on the existing system of progressive discipline, caused the workers in his sample to alter the form rather than the level of absences. Specifically, the "clamp-down" on absenteeism led to the substitution of longer for shorter absences and, perhaps more importantly, the substitution of certified for uncertified absences. Workers were thereby able to circumvent the sanctioning system without reducing appreciably the overall level of absenteeism. Based on this finding, Nicholson (1976) argued that rigorously enforced sanctions were likely to cause workers to resort to longer, medically related absences to escape the consequences of the disciplinary system.

Despite the widespread use of management sanctions in business organizations (Bureau of National Affairs, 1973, 1974), the evidence supporting their effectiveness in attendance control is limited largely to anecdotal case studies. For example, Seatter (1961) discussed an attendance control program based on relatively strict disciplinary measures implemented over a five-year period. While Seatter reported a major (and sustained) reduction in absence rates during the time period, it was impossible to separate the program's effects from the multitude of exogenous variables that could have accounted for the improvement in attendance.

In a recent paper, Baum and Youngblood (1975) reported the results of an experimental study of the impact of an organizational control policy on absenteeism, performance, and satisfaction among students in an educational setting. In general, it was found that a control policy based on the Katz and Kahn (1966) motivational pattern of *legal compliance* with established organizational norms led to significant improvements in attendance and performance without adversely affecting levels of satisfaction. These results were interpreted as providing support for the potential effectiveness of control policies based on the relatively simple notion of mandating certain behaviors (regular attendance) as a condition for continued participation in the organizational unit.

The present study attempts to extend the Baum and Youngblood (1975) findings by assessing the effectiveness of an attendance control policy based on the imposition of legitimate management sanctions in those instances in which workers violate the attendance norms by engaging in excessive absenteeism. The attendance control policy is based on the motivational pattern of legal compliance proposed by Katz and Kahn (1966).

Legal compliance as a means of organizational control relies heavily on punishment for rule violations and is activated by objective conditions such as the use of appropriate symbols of authority, clarity of legal norms, use of specific penalties, and expulsion of nonconformers. As long as these conditions are correctly perceived by organization members—that is, workers recognize and accept the legitimacy of the control policy and desire to remain in the organization—then Katz and Kahn predict that policies based on legal compliance will lead to improved attendance.

Control policies based on legal compliance are accompanied by certain consequences that make them more appropriate in some organizational settings than others. For example, Katz and Kahn point out that heavy reliance on formal rules may not only inhibit spontaneous and innovative behavior but also limit worker performance to minimally acceptable levels. Like many large industrial organizations, the present company has developed a highly bureaucratic structure with well-defined rules to cover most work-related contingencies. Production standards govern most jobs, and workers are provided with few, if any, incentives to exceed the minimum levels of output. Most of the production jobs are relatively routine in nature, with heavy reliance being placed on dependable rather than innovative role performance. Hence, the potential negative consequences of legal compliance do not appear to be prohibitive in the present case.

A control policy that attempts to enforce minimally acceptable levels of attendance will have no effect on the majority of the work force, since most workers are willing to conform voluntarily to such guidelines as a condition for continued participation in the organization. The worker who systematically exceeds the attendance norms is most likely to be affected by an attendance control policy. Chronically absent workers are, by definition, those who have failed to respond to normal incentives to attend regularly (wages, supervisory or peer pressures, and intrinsic rewards from role performance). Hence, a legalistic control policy would appear to have the greatest impact on workers who are considered by the organization to be chronic offenders.

The following basic hypothesis was tested in the present study: Chronically absent workers who experience an attendance control policy based on legitimate management sanctions will exhibit more regular attendance (less absenteeism) than comparable subjects who do not experience the control policy.

Method

Subjects and Design. Subjects were 336 workers selected randomly from three departments of a large midwestern components-manufacturing division of one of the big three automobile companies. The sample was composed of mature (median age was 39 years) males with approximately eleven years of seniority with the company. Two-thirds of the subjects were white, 22 percent were black, and 11 percent were Spanish surnamed. The median level of schooling completed by the sample was the tenth grade, and just under one-half (47 percent) of the subjects had prior military service. The vast majority (90 percent) were married with an average of three dependents. Finally, the median distance from home to work was just under 17 miles.

All subjects were employed on a full-time basis during the two-year period studied, and all held membership in a well-known international union. The jobs in question were blue-collar production and maintenance jobs at the same hierarchical level within the company but paying considerably above the median wage for the geographic region.

The study employed a nonequivalent control group design (Campbell and Stanley,

1963), since it was not possible to randomly assign subjects to the treatment (one department) and control (two departments) groups. While the lack of randomization of subjects was less than optimal from a research design viewpoint, preliminary analyses revealed that the demographic profiles of the treatment and comparison departments were very similar (one-way analyses of variance produced no significant differences on race, age, seniority, education, military service, marital status, number of dependents, and distance from home to work). Thus, for purposes of analysis, treatment and comparison subjects were assumed to be drawn from the same population.

Procedure and Variables. Prior to the implementation of the attendance control policy, absenteeism data were collected on all subjects for a base period of one year. The attendance control policy was introduced into one of the three departments at the beginning of the following year. In order to meet the assumptions of the Katz and Kahn (1966) motivational pattern of legal compliance, workers in the treatment department (N = 120) were informed that the following six-step procedure would be followed by management in all cases of unauthorized absenteeism: (1) detailed attendance records would be kept by the worker's supervisor, (2) written excuses from legitimate outside sources would be required for unauthorized absences, (3) questionable excuses would be independently investigated, (4) management would personally counsel all workers with unauthorized absences, (5) the existing progressive discipline system would be used to penalize excessive absenteeism, and (6) updated discipline and attendance records would be maintained on all workers.

The managers in the two comparison departments (N = 216) continued with the existing attendance policy that delegated the responsibility for attendance control to the immediate supervisor. Under that policy, supervisors were given considerable latitude in dealing with absentees; that is, each supervisor made the initial decision as to what formal action (if any) would be taken when his or her workers were absent. This policy is thought to be representative of the way in which many large industrial organizations deal with worker absenteeism.

Absenteeism was defined as the number of days the worker failed to report to the job when work was scheduled. The company maintained an internal classification system that made it possible to categorize absenteeism as follows: (1) casual absenteeism (absences of short duration that were primarily discretionary in nature), (2) long-term illness absenteeism (medically related absences of more than five continuous days), and (3) contractual absenteeism (paid vacations and holidays, leaves of absence, jury duty, and so forth, that were guaranteed in the union contract). Since the company's management was primarily concerned with casual absenteeism, the analyses reported below were based on this measure. It seemed unlikely that the attendance control policy would affect contractual absences, since the provisions governing their use were spelled out in detail in the labor-management agreement.

The first factor in the design was the attendance control policy. A second factor, absence groups, was included in the design, since it was hypothesized that the control policy would have the greatest impact on workers who had a history of chronic absenteeism prior to the implementation of the policy. The workers in the treatment and comparison departments were divided into three groups, based on the total number of casual absences during the pretreatment year. The *high* absence (chronic) group consisted of all subjects who had missed thirty or more days during the year (M = 47.5). The casual absence rate for this group was 21.1 percent for the year. There was unanimous agreement among the company's management that these workers had a serious attendance problem and could be considered chronic absentees. The *average* absence group consisted of workers who had missed from seven to twenty-nine days during the pretreatment year (M = 17.6), with a casual absence rate of 7.3 percent for the year. While a portion of these workers exceeded the company's implicit attendance norm, management was willing to acknowledge that on average the group could not be considered chronic offenders in light of previous experience. The *low* absence group consisted of workers who missed six or less days during the year (M = 2.6). With a casual absence rate of only 1.1 percent, these workers were committed to the importance of regular attendance and missed work infrequently.

The design can be summarized as a 2 × 3 factorial consisting of two levels of the attendance control policy (a formal policy based on the Katz and Kahn motivational pattern of legal compliance and a more informal policy based on individual supervisory discretion) and three levels of absence groups (high, average, and low) based on the pretreatment absence measure. The criterion, absenteeism, was converted into a change score (pre year minus post year); a square root transformation of the change scores met the homogeneity of variance assumptions of the model. Kenny's (1975) analysis of nonequivalent control group designs suggests that change score analysis is appropriate when the groups selected for investigation are stable; that is, variances are stationary from pretest to posttest. In this design, a treatment by absence groups interaction is predicted, since the attendance control policy is hypothesized to have the greatest influence on the high-absence group. Therefore, the absence groups factor was built into the design to test for the hypothesized interaction.

Results

Table 1 presents the means and standard deviations of absenteeism for the treatment and comparison groups during the pre- and posttreatment years. An analysis of vari-

Table 1. Means and Standard Deviations of Absenteeism

Depts./Absence Groups	Pre Year		Post Year	
	M	SD	M	SD
Treatment dept.				
Low absence	2.9	2.2	3.9	4.6
Average absence	17.3	6.5	14.4	10.5
High absence	49.1	15.3	26.1	15.5
Comparison depts.				
Low absence	2.5	1.8	2.7	9.0
Average absence	17.7	6.7	12.7	9.8
High absence	46.6	13.2	30.5	15.4

ance with the transformed change scores (absenteeism) as the criterion produced a significant main effect for absence groups, $F (2, 335) = 129.53$, $p < .001$, and, as expected, a significant control policy by absence groups interaction, $F (2, 335) = 2.01, p < .05$. Since it was hypothesized that the control policy would be most effective with the high absence (chronic) group, planned comparisons were performed on the high, average, and low absence groups to investigate the nature of the interaction effect. These analyses revealed that the control policy was not effective in reducing the absenteeism of workers in the average and low absence groups, although there was a small overall reduction in the absenteeism of all workers in the average absence group. As predicted, the decline in absenteeism among high absence workers who were exposed to the control policy ($M = -23.0$ days) was significantly greater than their counterparts in the comparison groups ($M = -16.1$ days), $F(1, 81) = 3.95$, $p < .05$. These results suggest that an attendance control policy based on legal compliance can lead to a significant reduction in absenteeism among workers who have a history of chronic absenteeism.

Since the high absence treatment group was composed of workers who were extreme in their pretreatment absence behavior, the existence of a homogeneous comparison group was a must to control for statistical regression. A significant pre to post reduction in the average number of days absent occurred for the treatment and comparison groups combined ($M = -6.4$ days), and an even more dramatic reduction occurred among the high absence groups ($M = -18.5$ days). The overall reduction in absenteeism was due possibly to a general worsening of the economic environment faced by the company during the period under study. Workers were made more aware of the worsening environment by layoffs in other divisions of the company, a decline in the number of overtime opportunities, and supervisory exhortations for greater efficiency in the production process. Despite the exogenous pressures for more regular attendance, the chronically absent workers who were subject to the attendance control policy improved their attendance an average of seven days over the comparison group. Given the similar sociodemographic profiles of the treatment and comparison groups, the assumption of uniform regression seems tenable, and the attendance control policy appeared to provide a meaningful incentive for chronic absentees to attend work on a more regular basis.

In view of Nicholson's (1976) finding that the imposition of management sanctions caused workers to substitute certified for uncertified absences to avoid the negative consequences of the sanctions, additional analyses of variance were performed, with the criteria being long-term illness absenteeism and contractual absenteeism. The results indicated that the attendance control policy had no discernible effect on either long-term illnesses or contractual absences. Interestingly, the chronic absentees who were exposed to the attendance control policy took fewer days ($M = 4.2$ days) of long-term illness absenteeism in the posttreatment year than in the pretreatment year. In contrast to the workers in Nicholson's (1976) study, there is no evidence to suggest that these workers attempted to thwart the control policy by taking a greater number of certified (illness) absences.

Data limitations made it impossible to rigorously investigate whether other undesirable side effects resulted from the use of the attendance control policy. It is conceivable that workers could have responded to the control policy by lowering productivity, filing excessive grievances, engaging in minor sabotage of equipment, and other forms of protest designed to express their disapproval of the policy. Interviews with line managers indicated that they were unaware of any increased incidence of protest behaviors on the part of the work force. While it is still open to question, the available evidence does not support the generalization that management sanctions will be accompanied by undesirable side effects.

Discussion

The results of the present study have important implications for organizations that are attempting to deal with the problem of chronic absenteeism by implementing attendance control policies. While generalizations must be made with considerable care, the study supports one of the major findings of Baum and Youngblood (1975), that absentecism can be reduced meaningfully by mandating more regular attendance as a condition of continued participation in an organization. It is important to note, however, that in this study the effectiveness of the attendance control policy was limited to chronic absentees. The policy had no discernible effect on the workers who were already in conformance with the organization's attendance norms. This was expected, since a policy based on legal compliance, by itself, provides no incentive to exceed minimum standards of behavior. The fact that the experimental effect was limited to chronic absentees does not detract from the usefulness of the attendance control policy in the present organization, since this group of workers (25 percent of the sample) accounted for a disproportionately large amount (56.5 percent) of the total days lost. By concentrating on a relatively small percentage of the total work force that was habitually absent, the organization was able to effect a sizable reduction in the overall absence rate.

Can the results of this study be synthesized with the promising body of research in which control policies based on positive reinforcements have been effective in reducing absenteeism? A possible synthesis appears to revolve around the nature of the attendance patterns of workers in the organization. It seems unrealistic for managers to assume that a given control policy will be perceived in the same way by the best and worst attenders in the work force. Workers who are absent infrequently have demonstrated a basic commitment to the managerial ethic that good attendance is a prerequisite to successful performance. The organizational reward system (pay, promotion opportunities, supervisory praise, and so forth) has been internalized to the point that these workers perceive that it is in their best interest to attend regularly. The use of sanctions to encourage marginal improvements in attendance would appear to be dysfunctional in the case of regular attenders. If improvements in attendance are desired among these workers, then positive reinforcements to attend more regularly have considerable potential.

Chronic absentees, however, have already exhibited a pattern of behavior suggesting that the organizational reward system is not particularly salient to their basic needs. They have been willing to forgo higher pay and other rewards associated with regular attendance for more time away from the job. It seems highly unlikely that a control policy based on positive reinforcements similar to the lottery incentive system of Pedalino and Gamboa (1974) will be sufficiently attractive to cause chronic absentees to alter their previous patterns of behavior. In the context of the present study, the workers who were absent thirty or more days in the previous year, with the concomitant loss of pay and other rewards, were not likely to be enticed to attend regularly over a relatively long period of time in order to qualify for a small monetary prize. While it is still open to question, the results of this study suggest that rigorously enforced sanctions are effective in reducing the absence rates of chronic absentees.

It would seem, then, that managers should consider the possibility of designing multifaceted control policies that rely simultaneously on positive reinforcements, such as those reviewed by Porter (1973), and sanctions based on the motivational pattern of legal compliance. Once it is recognized that all workers in an organization are not likely to respond to a control policy in the same way, there is no obvious reason why managers cannot tailor the control policy to these differing responses. For those who would argue that the presence of management sanctions would defeat the intent of a system of positive reinforcements, it is important to note that the sanctions become operational only after the worker has failed to respond to the reinforcements (and other incentives to attend regularly, such as pay). Hence, the vast majority of workers who have the highest probability of responding to positive reinforcements would not be adversely affected by the presence of sanctions that apply to the chronic absentee. It is hoped that future researchers will examine the efficacy of this approach.

References

Baum, J. F., and Youngblood, S. A. "Impact of an Organizational Control Policy on Absenteeism, Performance, and Satisfaction." *Journal of Applied Psychology,* 1975, *60,* 688-694.

Bureau of National Affairs. "Employee Conduct and Discipline." In *Personnel Policies Forum.* Washington, D.C.: Bureau of National Affairs, 1973.

Bureau of National Affairs. "Employee Absenteeism and Turnover." In *Personnel Policies Forum.* Washington, D.C.: Bureau of National Affairs, 1974.

Campbell, D. T., and Stanley, J. C. *Experimental and Quasi-experimental Designs for Research.* Chicago: Rand McNally, 1963.

Hedges, J. N. "Absence from Work—A Look at Some National Data." *Monthly Labor Review,* 1973, *96,* 24-30.

Katz, D., and Kahn, R. L. *The Social Psychology of Organizations.* New York: Wiley, 1966.

Kenny, D. A. "A Quasi-experimental Approach to Assessing Treatment Effects in the Nonequivalent Control Group Design." *Psychological Bulletin,* 1975, *82,* 345-362.

Lawler, E. E., III, and Hackman, R. J. "Impact of Employee Participation in the Development of Pay Incentive Plans: A Field Experiment." *Journal of Applied Psychology,* 1969, *53,* 467-471.

Nicholson, N. "Management Sanctions and Absence Control." *Human Relations,* 1976, *29,* 139-150.

Nord, W. R. "Beyond the Teaching Machine: The Neglected Area of Operant Conditioning in the Theory and Practice of Management." *Organizational Behavior and Human Performance,* 1969, *4,* 375-401.

Nord, W. R., and Costigan, R. "Work Adjustment to the Four-Day Week: A Longitudinal Study." *Journal of Applied Psychology,* 1973, *58,* 60-66.

Pedalino, E., and Gamboa, V. U. "Behavior Modification and Absenteeism: Intervention in One Industrial Setting." *Journal of Applied Psychology,* 1974, *59,* 694-698.

Porter, L. W. "Turning Work into Nonwork: The Rewarding Environment." In M. D. Dunnette (Ed.), *Work and Nonwork in the Year 2001.* Monterey, Calif.: Brooks/Cole, 1973.

Porter, L. W., and Steers, R. M. "Organizational, Work, and Personal Factors in Employee Turnover and Absenteeism." *Psychological Bulletin,* 1973, *80,* 151-176.

Seatter, W. C. "More Effective Control of Absenteeism." *Personnel,* 1961, *38,* 16-29.

U.S. Department of Labor. *Suggestions for Control of Turnover and Absenteeism.* Washington, D.C.: U.S. Government Printing Office, 1972.

15

Work Attitudes as Predictors of Attendance on a Specific Day

Frank J. Smith

Past reviews of literature dealing with the relationship between job satisfaction and such work-related behavior as job performance, turnover, and absenteeism have noted the extreme variation in findings, but have tended to conclude that job satisfaction and job withdrawal behavior are inversely related, while performance has a low and inconsistent relationship to satisfaction (Brayfield and Crockett, 1955; Herzberg and others, 1957; Katzell, 1957; Porter and Steers, 1973).

The seemingly inconsistent nature of many of the results has been treated differently by different investigators. The most frequent approach involves the attempt to identify variables that might moderate the performance-satisfaction relationship and help explain the previous findings. Examples can be seen in review by Schwab and Cummings (1970). Still others have taken a view that performance and job withdrawal behavior are different phenomena and that the job satisfaction/job performance relationship is quite different than that between job satisfaction and job withdrawal. Lawler and Porter (1967), for example, argue that, while job satisfaction has the power to influence both absenteeism and turnover, it can best be seen as being caused by job performance rather than being the cause of it.

Herman (1973), on the other hand, contends that work attitudes can be seen as predictive of either type of work-related behavior as long as such behavior is under the control of individual workers. She also points out that many of the studies relating satisfaction and performance were carried out under situational constraints that may have so limited performance variance as to insure low correlational results.

The present study is in line with Herman's (1973) reasoning, though it deals with only one aspect of the discussion; namely, attendance (the converse of absenteeism). While this work-related behavior is usually the result of an individual's decision that is often under his or her control, it should be noted that even in this instance a number of conditions exist that often confound the actual relationship of attendance to work-related attitudes. For example, the availability of alternatives to work attendance, the financial or social penalties associated with absenteeism, and simply the effort required in

Reprinted from *Journal of Applied Psychology*, 1977, *62* (1), 16-19. Copyright 1977 by the American Psychological Association. Reprinted by permission.

attending work may all influence the attendance decision but may be relatively unrelated to attitudes toward work. Because almost all of the studies reported have been carried out among hourly paid employees, the influence of financial penalty for absenteeism has been present, yet rarely accounted for or even acknowledged. As Porter and Steers (1973) have noted, only in the case of permissive illness pay programs would this penalizing factor be insignificant. It should also be noted that absenteeism over any given period is often relatively slight and is so widely distributed among employees as to be insignificant.

The present study takes advantage of a naturally occurring situation, which is particularly free of some of the confounding conditions mentioned. It also involves behavior requiring considerable effort. While it examines the relationship between attitudes and attendance within narrow time periods, it does so in a situation in which the extent of the behavior within and its variance across the groups studied were of sufficient magnitude to be organizationally significant.

Specifically, the study investigates the relationship between attitudes and attendance on a particular day among groups of managerial personnel, all of whom were located in a single headquarters building of a large merchandising corporation. The observation of attendance occurred on the day following an unexpected and severe snowstorm that greatly hampered the city's transportation system. Because the storm happened to occur shortly after a complete organizational survey of the entire managerial group, it was possible to relate the work attitudes surveyed to attendance.

Since occasional absenteeism by managerial people is not subject to financial penalty and is relatively free of social and work-group pressure, it can be viewed as being under the general control of the individual. Moreover, attendance following a crippling snowstorm is unique in that the decision to attend is not only under individual control but requires considerable personal effort.

It would be predicted, following Herman (1973), that job satisfaction and job attendance would be positively correlated on the day following the snowstorm but that on any randomly chosen day the correlation would be low or zero.

Method

The attitude measures used were part of a larger organizational survey carried out among all members of the company's headquarters staff. The development of these scales and their validity is described by Smith (1962), and additional validity data are presented by Hulin (1966), Dunham (1975), and Dunham and Smith (in press). Multiple-response items that were designed to meet the Guttman criteria and that assess attitudes toward six work-related areas were measured by the following scales: Supervision, Kind of Work, Amount of Work, Career Future and Security, Financial Rewards, and Company Identification.

Sample. The primary sample consisted of 3,010 salaried employees in the company's Chicago headquarters building. Employees performed a mixture of administrative, professional, and technical functions. All job levels below that of the president were involved in the study.

A comparison sample consisted of the 340 salaried members of the company's New York headquarters office, where no storm had occurred. Though the sample is much smaller in number, the job functions and levels included in it are practically identical with those in Chicago.

Procedure. The attitudinal data were collected in November and December of 1974. Since the survey was administered anonymously, subjects were identified only in terms of large functionally related groupings. (The Men's Store, for example, consisted of a large group of men and women working in related merchandise departments.) A total of twenty-seven functional groupings in Chicago and thirteen in New York were used in this study. The sample sizes within each unit ranged from 59 to 228 in Chicago and from 28 to 48 in New York.

The attendance data were collected by personnel department representatives, who were not aware of the study's design or intent. Since attendance data are not systematically collected for salaried people, a special effort was made to determine the extent of, and the specific reasons for, nonattendance. Moreover, nonattendance was carefully defined to reflect voluntary absence on only the day studied. Thus, subjects who were absent because of out-of-town travel, were on vacation, or were ill prior to the storm were not counted. Group-attendance percentages were computed by dividing the number of people attending by those who reasonably could have attended on the days in question. Thus, the measure obtained here was considerably refined.

For each departmental grouping in Chicago and New York, the percentage of attendance, as defined, was computed. The Chicago distribution, the primary research sample, was unimodal and appeared free of noticeable skew. The average score for each department grouping on each of the six attitude scales was also computed, and Pearson product-moment correlation coefficients were then computed between these two sets of data.

The satisfaction and attendance data collected on the New York sample were for comparison purposes only. They allow for a comparison prediction of attendance on what amounts to a random day. Since no storms had occurred in New York on the day studied, no greater effort was required in attending work than on any other day, and pressures to attend represented the situation normally encountered.

Results

On April 3, 1975, the day after the storm, attendance ranged from 97 percent to 39 percent in Chicago (median = 70 percent). In New York, where no storm occurred, attendance was much higher, ranging from 100 percent to 89 percent (median = 96 percent).

Table 1 presents the correlational data for both locations. As can be seen, the

Table 1. Correlations Between Job-Satisfaction Levels and Attendance Levels on Individual Days for the Chicago and New York Groups

Scale	Chicago[a] (N = 27)	New York[b] (N = 13)
Supervision	.54[d]	.12
Amount of Work	.36[c]	.01
Kind of Work	.37[c]	.06
Financial Rewards	.46[d]	.11
Career Future	.60[d]	.14
Company Identification	.42[c]	.02

[a]Group following storm, April 1975.

[b]Group, April 1975.

[c]$p < .05$, one-tailed test.

[d]$p < .01$, one-tailed test.

storm-related attendance in Chicago is significantly correlated with all six attitude measures and, in the case of three scales, is highly significant. It should be noted, however, that only the extreme differences among these correlations are significant. Thus, the correlation between attendance and the Career Future scale was significantly higher than was that between attendance and either the Kind of Work or the Amount of Work scale, $t(24)$ = 2.02, $p < .05$ (one-tailed); $t(24) = 1.73$, $p < .05$ (one-tailed).

While the comparison analysis in the New York sample is limited by the small sample (thirteen department groupings) and the extreme restriction in range of the attendance rates, the small variance in attendance does represent a typical attendance pattern for managers in these functional units. None of the correlations is significant. There appears to be no relationship, on a specific day, between attitudes and attendance.

Discussion

While the situation studied was fortuitous in nature, it did present an opportunity to study behavior that was free of several situational constraints. Within the limitations of the setting, it does appear that job-related attitudes measures can predict job behavior when that behavior is substantially under the control of the employee. This finding is consistent with the point of view expressed by Herman (1973).

The present results also suggest that the behavior predicted should involve considerable effort and should be of sufficient magnitude to be worthy of study. Thus, in the present study, the extent of variation in attendance behavior (ranging from 39 percent to 97 percent) and the effort it involved were of considerable magnitude for the Chicago group. For the New York group, these conditions were lacking, and the attempt to predict attendance in such a case seems almost frivolous but was necessary to provide a baseline.

The findings also indicated that attitudes toward certain work aspects are significantly more highly correlated with attendance than others. This emphasizes the importance of looking at these scales separately. When viewed this way, they provide the basis for some insight into the possible specific precursors of absenteeism.

While the present study is of a one-shot nature, with only a modest chance of realistic replication, it does point to the value of taking advantage of naturally occurring events that offer a glimpse of behavior in which several obscuring influences have been removed, a condition ordinarily achieved only in laboratory settings.

References

Brayfield, A. H., and Crockett, W. H. "Employee Attitudes and Employee Performance." *Psychological Bulletin,* 1955, *52,* 396-424.

Dunham, R. B. "Affective Responses to Task Characteristics: The Role of Organizational Function." Unpublished doctoral dissertation, University of Illinois, 1975.

Dunham, R. B., and Smith, F. J. "Validation of the Index of Organizational Reactions with the Job Description Index, the Minnesota Satisfaction Questionnaire, and Faces Scales." *Academy of Management Journal,* in press.

Herman, J. B. "Are Situational Contingencies Limiting Job Attitude-Job Performance Relationships?" *Organizational Behavior and Human Performance,* 1973, *10,* 208-224.

Herzberg, F., and others. *Job Attitudes: Review of Research and Opinion.* Pittsburgh: Psychological Service of Pittsburgh, 1957.

Hulin, C. L. "The Effects of Community Characteristics on Measures of Job Satisfaction." *Journal of Applied Psychology,* 1966, *50,* 185-192.

Katzell, R. A. "Industrial Psychology." *Annual Review of Psychology,* 1957, *8,* 237-268.

Lawler, E. E., III, and Porter, L. W. "The Effect of Performance on Job Satisfaction." *Industrial Relations,* 1967, *7,* 20-28.

Porter, L. W., and Steers, R. M. "Organizational, Work, and Personal Factors in Employee Turnover and Absenteeism." *Psychological Bulletin,* 1973, *80,* 151-176.

Schwab, D. P., and Cummings, L. L. "Theories of Performance and Satisfaction: A Review." *Industrial Relations,* 1970, *9,* 408-430.

Smith, F. J. "Problems and Trends in the Operational Use of Employee Attitude Measurements." Paper presented at 70th Annual Convention of the American Psychological Association, St. Louis, August 1962.

16

Measuring the Financial Impact of Employee Attitudes

Philip H. Mirvis
Edward E. Lawler III

The literature contains a large number of job studies of the relationship between attitudes and absenteeism, turnover, tardiness, job performance, strikes, and grievances (see, for example, Porter and Steers, 1973; Vroom, 1964). Further, there is experimental evidence suggesting that improved job satisfaction can reduce absenteeism, turnover, tardiness, and grievances in organizations (Hill and Trist, 1962; Marrow, Bowers, and Seashore, 1967). No study in the literature, however, has measured the costs associated with different levels of job satisfaction and motivation. Thus, psychologists are still unable to talk in dollars-and-cents terms when they argue for measuring employee attitudes and for improving job satisfaction.

The need for economic criterion measures was suggested in a classic article by Brogden and Taylor (1950). Yet, historically, accountants and organizational researchers have largely ignored the financial impact of the behavioral outcomes associated with job attitudes. Interest in this area has increased, however, since the original work on human-resource accounting (Brummet, Flamholtz, and Pyle, 1968). Several accounting models have recently been proposed that attach financial costs to such nonproductive behaviors as absenteeism, turnover, and the like (Alexander, 1971; Flamholtz, 1974; Herrick, 1975; Macy and Mirvis, 1976). Admittedly, these models suffer from some conceptual and methodological inadequacies (Lawler and Rhode, 1976; Mirvis and Macy, 1976b; Rhode and Lawler, 1973), but they have reached a point where approximate dollar costs can be assigned to such events as employee turnover and absenteeism. Thus, the possibility exists for attaching a dollar figure to different levels of job satisfaction and motivation. Indeed, two studies have proposed methods for undertaking such calculations. An examination of the limitations of each approach will serve to highlight the complexity of the problem and point the way to a better alternative.

The work of Myers and Flowers (1974) takes a traditional human-asset valuation approach: it assigns a value to individuals rather than to their behavior. It does this by multiplying salary dollars times a weighted attitude score to measure the potential dollar

Reprinted from the *Journal of Applied Psychology*, 1977, *62*, 1-8. Copyright 1977 by the American Psychological Association. Reprinted by permission.

value increases that would be associated with improved employee attitudes. Essentially, this approach starts by equating employees' salaries with their value to the organization. By multiplying this figure by an attitude score, it suggests that attitudinal improvements can somehow make the employee more valuable to the organization. Whether this means the employees will be more productive, less absent, or less likely to turnover as a result of attitude improvements is not stated. Further, whether the actual cost savings associated with any behavioral changes will equal their estimated value improvement is ignored by this approach. Finally, Myers and Flowers present no data on the relationship between the attitudes they measure and the individual's behaviors. At best, the Myers and Flowers effort provides a way for organizations to judge the impact of organizational investment on employee morale. They provide no clues to the direct financial impact of job satisfaction and motivation.

The second method for assigning values to attitudes was developed by Likert (1973) and Likert and Bowers (1973). Rather than trying to assign a value to the overall worth of an employee to an organization, this method is concerned with determining the short-term costs of employee behavior. It does this by correlating standardized attitude scores with unit cost. It then predicts changes in unit cost from anticipated changes in attitudes and argues that the cost change represents the economic impact of the attitudes.

The Likert and Bowers (1973) approach is complicated by four factors. First, their choice of criterion measure is problematic, as cost per unit includes both fixed costs (those that are incurred regardless of the number of units or level of service produced) and variable costs (those that are directly related to the level of activity). Only variable costs can be immediately influenced by such employee behaviors as increased productivity and reduced absenteeism and turnover. Furthermore, both cost components are influenced by inflationary trends. If fixed costs and inflationary factors are in the criterion measure, there is necessarily a significant amount of nonattitudinally related variance. Second, past research suggests that improvements in job satisfaction should reduce levels of absenteeism and turnover, which in turn should result in lower unit cost. Simply relating attitudes to unit cost ignores this sequential effect, and the resulting relationship and financial consequences might well be over- or understated. Third, this model assumes a constant attitude-behavior relationship over time. Improvement in attitude scores, however, could be accompanied by stronger or weaker predictive relationships to behavior. Predicted savings based upon this constant relationship would understate the resulting benefits if the relationship was stronger. Fourth, the model relies on analysis at the workgroup level, while much of the behavior change represents individual-level phenomena. Unless organizations are extremely large, the derived relationships at the group level may be unnecessarily unstable (see Robinson, 1950).

The present paper proposes a new methodology to assess the costs associated with job attitudes in a work setting. The methodology treats attitudinal measures as indicators of subsequent employee behavior, which in turn has economic implications for the organizations that can be assessed using cost-accounting procedures. Attitudes (satisfaction and performance-outcome beliefs) and behaviors (absenteeism, turnover, and performance), which have been the subject of a great deal of past theorizing and research, are utilized (Lawler, 1973; Vroom, 1964). The cost figures used in the calculations reflect only the short-term direct costs associated with the behaviors.

Method

Site. The research site selected for demonstration purposes was the branch system of a midwestern banking organization. Respondents included 160 tellers from twenty branches. The tellers, who served as cashiers handling customer deposits, withdrawals, and other transactions, were primarily (94 percent) female. Over 98 percent had a high school degree, while 41 percent had attended some college. The average age of tellers in the bank was 30. The branches serviced urban, suburban, and semirural areas, and tellers generally lived near their branches.

Attitude Measures. In the conceptual framework underlying this approach, employee attitudes were treated as predictors of subsequent employee behavior. This idea stems from expectancy theory, which emphasizes that employees' behavior at work is the result of choices about whether or not to appear at the workplace ("participation-membership," March and Simon, 1958) and of choices about how to behave at work ("work strategies," Lawler, 1973). This framework assumes that employees will be more likely to come to work than be absent or quit if they obtain satisfaction from their jobs. They are likely to give more effort and choose more effective performance strategies if they expect to be rewarded either intrinsically or extrinsically for their efforts (Vroom, 1964). Thus, attitudinal indexes of employee satisfaction and job involvement were expected to be the best predictors of participation-membership, since they reflect perceptions of the rewards associated with being at work (Lawler, 1973). Employee intrinsic motivation was expected to be the best predictor of performance, since it reflects some of the performance outcomes contingent on doing a good job. Attitude measures reported here were taken from the Michigan Assessment of Organizations (Survey Research Center, 1975). Items contained seven-point response anchors and were empirically grouped into scales reporting intrinsic satisfaction (six items), organizational involvement (two items), and intrinsic motivation (three items). Sample items included the following:

> *Intrinsic satisfaction.* Please indicate how satisfied you are with the following aspects of your job: (a) the chances you have to do the things you do best; (b) the chances you have to learn new things; (c) the opportunity to develop your skills and abilities.
> *Organizational involvement.* What happens in this branch is really important to me.
> *Intrinsic motivation.* When I do my job well, I feel I've done something worthwhile. I get a feeling of personal satisfaction from doing my job well.

The questionnaire items of interest were part of a larger instrument designed to gather baseline data precursor to the introduction of an experimental employee feedback system in the branches (Nadler, Mirvis, and Cammann, 1976). Tellers were asked to complete their questionnaires during breaks, lunch periods, or at home. The response rate was 95 percent.

Behavioral Measures. Measures of participation-membership behavior and work performance were collected monthly after administration of the attitude questionnaire. Behavioral data had been routinely collected in the firm, and the research measures were constructed from existing attendance and performance information. The researchers began with a set of standardized definitions and measures of behavioral outcomes (Macy and Mirvis, 1976) and adapted the site's data to fit those specifications. The relevant set of individual performance and participation-membership measures were defined as follows:

> *Short-term absence or illness.* Unauthorized absences of less than three consecutive days, including short-term illness and absence for personal reasons.
> *Voluntary turnover.* Voluntary employee departure from the bank, excluding terminations, maternity leaves or turnovers, and transfers.

Teller balancing shortages. The number of teller shortages or overpayments to customers.

Results

Table 1 reports the means and standard deviations for the April attitude measures and for the behavioral measures for the subsequent three months. It also reports the

Table 1. Means and Standard Deviations for Attitudes and Behaviors

Variable	M	SD
Employee Attitudes		
Intrinsic satisfaction	4.83	1.35
Job involvement	5.81	.75
Intrinsic motivation	6.11	.96
Employee Behaviors[a]		
Absenteeism		
1 month	.22	.23
2 months	.26	.38
3 months	.23	.44
Overall	.24	.33
Turnover		
1 month	.06	.24
2 months	.04	.20
3 months	.07	.25
Overall	.06	.23
Shortages		
1 month	3.10	2.17
2 months	2.82	2.03
3 months	2.75	2.04
Overall	3.07	1.74

Note: Overall mean number of absent days = 37.76 days per month. Overall mean turnover rate = 9.28 persons (computed in table as turnover = 1; no turnover = 0).

[a]Measures were taken one month, two months, or three months after administration of the attitude questionnaire.

overall means and standard deviations for the behaviors. Stability coefficients (*ss*) were computed for the behaviors (Heise, 1969). There are no stability coefficients for turnover as employees left the data-recording system. The absenteeism measure reflected some stability ($s_{12} = .61$, $s_{23} = .71$, $s_{13} = .52$). However, no one who was absent in the first month was absent in the next two months. Thus, absenteeism was negatively correlated over the period, and those individuals who were absent varied from month to month. In contrast, the number of teller balancing shortages was more stable ($s_{12} = .82$, $s_{23} = .71$, $s_{13} = .59$). There were few significant correlations between turnover and shortages (median $r = .15$) and no significant correlations between turnover and shortages (median $r = -.06$). Surprisingly, there was no correlation between absenteeism and turnover during the period.

Each behavior has a cost to the organization. Teller shortages represent a direct cost and were estimated to be $8.23 per shortage. This figure includes the cash outlay minus recoveries and is reported in constant dollar terms. The other behavioral outcomes have direct and indirect financial implications for the organization, too. When a teller is absent, for example, the supervisor must find a suitable replacement or extend the existing staff. Besides the variable salary costs associated with replacing a missing teller, there are additional fixed costs, including the employee's fringe benefits, the supervisor's time spent in arranging for a replacement, and the underabsorbed overhead rate. This final cost component includes the expense of lights, rent, staff functions, and so on, which was allocated to budgeted staffing levels. The acquisition, replacement, and unabsorbed overhead costs are magnified in the case of a turnover. All of these costs were measured using an approach that has been outlined elsewhere (Macy and Mirvis, 1976). Table 2 displays

Table 2. Cost per Incident of Absenteeism and Turnover

Variable	Cost (in dollars)
Absenteeism	
Absent employee	
Salary	23.04
Benefits	6.40
Replacement employee	
Training and staff time	2.13
Unabsorbed burden	15.71
Lost profit contribution	19.17
Total variable cost	23.04
Total cost	66.45
Turnover	
Replacement acquisition	
Direct hiring costs	293.95
Other hiring costs	185.55
Replacement training	
Preassignment	758.84
Learning curve	212.98
Unabsorbed burden	682.44
Lost profit contribution	388.27
Total variable cost	293.95
Total cost	2,522.03

both the variable and total costs per incident of teller absenteeism and turnover at the bank. The distinction between variable and total costs is important, for a reduction in turnover and absenteeism will result in variable-cost savings only. A reduction in fixed costs or realization of opportunity costs is predicated on subsequent reallocation of fixed costs or staff work loads. Thus, fixed and opportunity costs are not included in the financial estimates.

Table 3 reports the relationship between teller attitudes and absenteeism, turnover, and balancing shortages three months later. The correlations between employee attitudes and turnover are relatively low, yet consistent with those found in past research (Vroom, 1964). The findings also indicate that teller's intrinsic motivation correlates positively with shortages three months later. The negative correlation between satisfaction and absenteeism is quite high but should be regarded with caution. July is a primary vacation month for the tellers, and some took additional, unauthorized days off, both before and after their paid vacation periods. The findings suggest that the most dissatisfied employees took this extra time off. Further, individual absences varied over time, and the correlations between the attitude measures and absenteeism fluctuated over the three

Table 3. Relationship Between Attitudes and Behavior
(Lagged Three Months)

Attitudes (measured in April)	Behaviors (measured in July)		
	Absenteeism	Turnover	Shortages
Intrinsic satisfaction	−.81[b]	−.20[a]	.10
Job involvement	.08	−.29[b]	−.12
Intrinsic motivation	−.26[b]	−.16[a]	−.23[b]

[a]$p < .05.$
[b]$p < .01.$

reporting periods. Accordingly, the cost savings associated with reduced absenteeism may be particular to the measurement period.

Tables 1, 2, and 3 provide the information necessary for relating the attitudinal measures to financial results and for estimating the potential benefits accruing from attitudinal improvements. Likert (1973) proposes the statistical approach for accomplishing this. Figure 1 reflects the relationship between two illustrative variables: tellers' intrinsic motivation ($M = 6.11$, $SD = .96$) and the average balancing shortages ($M = 3.07$, $SD =$

Figure 1. Behavioral Change ($y_1 = 3.07$; $y_2 = 2.87$) Associated with
Attitude Improvement ($x_1 = 6.11$; $x_2 = 6.59$)

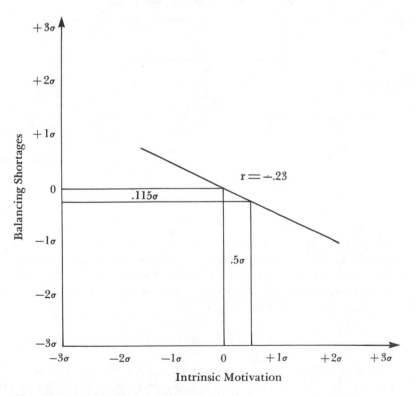

Note: Sigma (σ) signifies sample standard deviation.

1.74). To estimate the potential savings from improved motivation, the steps are as follows:

1. Present cost level   = 3.07 × (cost per incident)
        = 3.07 × \$8.23
        = \$25.27 per employee, per month

2. Planned attitudinal improvement   = .5 *SD*

3. Estimated behavioral improvement = (.5) (*SD* of behavior) × $r_{att, beh}$
        = (.5) (1.74) × (−.23)
        = −.20

4. New behavioral rate   = 3.07 present rate
        <u>−.20</u> improvement
        = 2.87 per employee, per month

5. New cost level   = 2.87 × (cost per incident)
        = 2.87 × \$8.23
        = \$23.62 per employee, per month

Figure 1 graphically depicts the estimated relationship between teller shortages and intrinsic motivation. A similar procedure was used to estimate the cost levels associated with the other attitudes that were measured. Table 4 illustrates the costs associated

Table 4. Costs per Month, per Teller

Attitude	Change	Cost (in dollars)			
		Absenteeism	Turnover	Shortage	Total
Intrinsic satisfaction	+.5 SD	2.40	10.17	25.98	38.55
	0	5.44	17.04	25.27	47.75
	−.5 SD	8.48	23.93	24.55	56.96
Job involvement	+.5 SD	5.74	7.08	23.62	36.44
	0	5.44	17.04	25.27	47.75
	−.5 SD	5.14	27.01	26.91	59.06
Intrinsic motivation	+.5 SD	4.45	11.55	24.41	40.41
	0	5.44	17.04	25.27	47.75
	−.5 SD	6.43	22.54	26.13	55.10

with different levels of teller satisfaction, involvement, and motivation. For most measures, more positive attitudinal levels are shown to be associated with lower costs. The cost figures reflect only the variable costs per teller for one month. Taking the bank tellers as a whole ($N = 160$) for a one-year period, an improvement in teller satisfaction of .5 standard deviations would be estimated to result in direct savings of \$17,664. The potential total cost savings would be \$125,160.

Discussion

There are a number of obvious advantages to the method used in the present paper to estimate the financial impact of employee attitudes. It provides a practical approach to the problem of relating attitudes to costs, which can be used in a wide variety of organizations, and it has the potential to significantly increase the impact and usefulness of attitudinal data. An attitude report to managers containing this information could serve to focus attention on the whole concept of employee satisfaction and motivation; and it could also stimulate them to introduce changes that would improve satisfaction and motivation. One useful feature of the model used in this paper is that it relates attitudes to future costs. Thus, organizations could use it as a way of diagnosing future costs and could initiate programs designed to reduce those costs. For example, this system enables the firm to estimate future levels of turnover, absenteeism, and performance and to better plan staffing and allocations of fixed costs in hiring, training, staffing, and quality-control functions. Further, by utilizing the relationship between attitudes and behavior, managers can estimate the cost savings and potential benefits associated with improved morale and unit functioning. Ultimately, the method could be used for undertaking a cost-benefit analysis of programs designed to improve employee satisfaction, motivation, group functioning, or supervision (Mirvis and Macy, 1976a).

Notwithstanding the promises, there are a number of difficulties with this approach. A primary concern is the validation of the predicted cost savings that are based on correlational data like those in the present study. This can only be done by observing what happens when attitude changes actually take place. In order to test the validity of the cost figures given in the present study, data were collected one year later. They showed that the tellers' personal motivation had increased to 6.25, or .145 standard deviations. The actual average teller shortages had decreased to $21.71 per month, somewhat below the anticipated level but in the predicted direction. Such evidence is suggestive of an attitude-behavior causal relationship, yet correlational analyses do not preclude an alternative causal explanation. Further, there are a number of factors that must be considered when estimating behavior change and cost savings from attitude improvements.

Two of the most difficult problems in predicting behavioral rate changes and costs from attitudinal data center on the nature of the attitude-behavior relationship. The first has to do with the appropriateness of the time lag. The present study used a three-month lag but also examined one- and two-month lags. In all cases, relationships between attitudes and behavior were found, but the relationships were stronger in the three-month lag. The organizational literature has suggested that a variety of time lags produce significant effects (Hulin, 1966; Taylor and Bowers, 1972), but the economic literature tends to support a three-month effect (Katona, 1975). At this point, there is no rule of thumb on the proper time perspective. This suggests that as organizations collect time-series data on attitudes and behavior, they should empirically distinguish the interval yielding the most stable and representative relationship.

This raises a second problem concerning the stability of attitude-behavior relationships. Both the magnitude and linearity of the relationship between these variables can change over time. In the present study, for example, secondary analyses revealed that monthly time-series relationships between a single item measure of intrinsic satisfaction and teller shortages ranged from −.67 to −.06 over a four-month period. Changes in this relationship invalidate the predicted financial changes. Consequently, these relationships must be monitored over time, with periodic corrections in the predicted savings based on the new relationships.

Part of the fluctuation in the relationship may be due to nonemployee-controlled variation and environmental events. For example, the relationship between satisfaction and turnover may be higher in a full-employment economy than it is in a period of high unemployment. This, too, must be considered in interpreting the financial estimates.

Attention must also be given to avoiding over- or understating the cost savings.

Job-enrichment programs, participative management styles, and better employee-selection procedures could improve both job satisfaction and involvement. Since these attitudes are often correlated, to separately estimate the cost savings associated with each would overstate the resulting benefits. In the present study, for example, the multiple correlation of job involvement and intrinsic satisfaction with voluntary turnover was .39. This argues for relating the monthly behavior measures to configurations of relevant attitude measures, which can be weighted through regression techniques. The result would be better estimate of the attitude-behavior relationships and the eventual financial benefits.

Financial benefits might also be overstated if there is substantial covariance between the rates or costs of absenteeism, turnover, and performance. It would seem appropriate to parcel out absenteeism and turnover from performance in estimating behavioral change and financial benefits. While this had little impact when it was tried in the present data, it may have a decided effect in other circumstances. Ideally, performance measures can be reflected in units of production. Estimates of the cost or benefits, including inflation factors, are then assigned on a cost-per-unit basis. Alternatively, if performance is reported in financial terms, the use of constant dollars should stabilize resulting attitude-costs relationships by controlling for inflation.

It is also important to note that the costs that were estimated in the present study are probably not generalizable to other organizations. The cost of absenteeism, turnover, and tardiness varies widely from one organization to another. Thus, it is unlikely that these costs would be applicable elsewhere. If anything, they are probably higher in most other organizations, since the teller's job does not require substantial individual training and the recruitment costs are minimal. The rate of turnover that exists in the present study may also be unusually low because of the high unemployment rate that existed at the time of the study. The effect of this was probably to lower the costs that are associated with each attitudinal level.

Finally, the behavioral cost-accounting approach yields the financial measure most related to employee attitudes. Human-resource accounting has typically valued employee's service at gross book value (the original investment expense), net book value (the original investment minus depreciation), and economic value (the anticipated financial return of the investment). In contrast, behavioral accounting shifts the emphasis from assigning a value to employees to assessing the economic consequences of their behavior. Conceptually, behavioral cost measures should be most sensitive to changes in employee satisfaction and motivation (see Lawler and Rhode, 1976; Mirvis and Macy, 1976b). The attitude-costs model presented in this paper can be used to empirically verify that contention.

In summary, there are clearly a number of problems in relating attitudes to costs, and refinements may be needed in the approach taken in the present study. These refinements could make the calculations more complex. Still, the promise of the approach for stimulating interest in employee attitudes and for guiding personnel and financial planning is great and would seem to justify the effort.

References

Alexander, M. "Investments in People." *Canadian Chartered Accountant,* 1971, *98,* 1-8.

Brogden, H., and Taylor, E. "The Dollar Criterion—Applying the Cost Accounting Concept to Criterion Construction." *Personnel Psychology,* 1950, *3,* 133-154.

Brummet, R., Flamholtz, E., and Pyle, W. "Human Resource Accounting—A Challenge for Accountants." *Account Review,* 1968, *43,* 217-224.

Flamholtz, E. *Human Resource Accounting.* Encino, Calif.: Dickenson, 1974.

Heise, D. R. "Separating Reliability and Stability in Test-Retest Correlation." *American Sociological Review,* 1969, *34,* 93-101.

Herrick, N. *The Quality of Work and Its Outcomes.* Columbus, Ohio: Academy for Contemporary Problems, 1975.

Hill, J., and Trist, E. *Industrial Accidents, Sickness, and Other Absences.* London: Tavistock, 1962.

Hulin, C. L. "Job Satisfaction and Turnover in a Female Clerical Population." *Journal of Applied Psychology,* 1966, *50,* 280-285.

Katona, G. *Psychological Economics.* New York: American Elsevier, 1975.

Lawler, E. E. *Motivation in Work Organizations.* Monterey, Calif.: Brooks/Cole, 1973.

Lawler, E. E., III, and Rhode, J. G. *Information and Control in Organizations.* Pacific Palisades, Calif.: Goodyear, 1976.

Likert, R. "Human Resource Accounting: Building and Assessing Productive Organizations." *Personnel,* 1973, *50,* 8-24.

Likert, R., and Bowers, D. G. "Improving the Accuracy of P/L Reports by Estimating the Change in Dollar Value of the Human Organization." *Michigan Business Review,* 1973, *25,* 15-24.

Macy, B. A., and Mirvis, P. H. "Measuring Quality of Work and Organizational Effectiveness in Behavioral-Economic Terms." *Administrative Science Quarterly,* 1976, *21,* 212-226.

March, J., and Simon, H. *Organizations.* New York: Wiley, 1958.

Marrow, A. J., Bowers, D. G., and Seashore, S. E. *Management by Participation.* New York: Harper & Row, 1967.

Mirvis, P. H., and Macy, B. A. "Accounting for the Costs and Benefits of Human Resource Development Programs: An Interdisciplinary Approach." *Accounting, Organization and Society,* 1976a, *1,* 179-194.

Mirvis, P. H., and Macy, B. A. "Human Resource Accounting: A Measurement Perspective." *Academy of Management Review,* 1976b, *1,* 74-83.

Myers, M. S., and Flowers, V. S. "A Framework for Measuring Human Assets." *California Management Review,* 1974, *16* (4), 5-16.

Nadler, D. A., Mirvis, P. H., and Cammann, C. "The Ongoing Feedback System: Experimenting with a New Managerial Tool." *Organizational Dynamics,* 1976, *4,* 63-80.

Porter, L. W., and Steers, R. M. "Organizational, Work, and Personal Factors in Employee Turnover and Absenteeism." *Psychological Bulletin,* 1973, *80,* 151-176.

Rhode, J., and Lawler, E. E. "Auditing Change: Human Resource Accounting." In M. D. Dunnette (Ed.), *Work and Nonwork in the Year 2001.* Monterey, Calif.: Brooks/Cole, 1973.

Robinson, W. S. "Ecological Correlations and the Behavior of Individuals." *American Sociological Review,* 1950, *15,* 351-357.

Survey Research Center. *Michigan Organizational Assessment Package.* Ann Arbor: Institute for Social Research, University of Michigan, 1975.

Taylor, J., and Bowers, D. *Survey of Organizations.* Ann Arbor: Institute for Social Research, University of Michigan, 1972.

Vroom, V. H. *Work and Motivation.* New York: Wiley, 1964.

PART IV

❦ Motivation

Punishment and reward have been the twin tools of motivational theory and of practice for centuries. With the development of the modern reinforcement theory of Skinner, the emphasis has shifted from punishment to reward: responses that are positively reinforced will persist, whereas responses that are punished may or may not be extinguished. Another important approach to motivational problems centers attention not on external incentives and sanctions but on the individual's personal needs. Thus, a person can be a productive worker not because of pay but because he finds ego satisfaction in his work. Because monistic conceptions of the universe are popular, many writers have developed either a punishment model, a reward model, or an ego model. The complexities of human behavior are such, however, that all three sources of motivation need to be considered. People want good-paying jobs, they do not want tasks hazardous to health, and they also want work that is interesting and that gives them a chance to show what they are worth. Our selection of research studies, therefore, covers articles that deal with external forms of control, both positive and negative, as well as with internalized motivation.

Recent research has been directed more at rewards and internal motives than at penalties. The study by Smith (1977) (Chapter Fifteen in this volume), on reducing absenteeism through inducing legal compliance, is one of few to face the issue of aversive stimuli. Penalties in organizations are tied to legal sanctions and are enforced more by norms of conformity than by the imposition of specific punishments, such as fines or demotion. Hence, the punishment model must take into account not only the actual sanctions employed but also the perceptions of organizational members about the probability of their being invoked, and even about the acceptance of such sanctions as legitimate. Thus, the punishment model starts with the use of penalties and then becomes a model of power and authority. Control rather than punishment becomes the central concept, and there is the tacit assumption that the organization has the power to control or secure legal compliance. Research has moved to explore the mechanisms of control and the relationship of these mechanisms to effectiveness and other organizational variables.

How control is actually exercised in organizations is difficult to measure. Tannenbaum (1968) has led the way in the development of measurements by using the perception of members at various levels in the hierarchy. His method requires organizational members to assess the influence of all major levels in the system including their own. Control graphs are constructed to summarize these perceptions, and the steepness or flatness of the curve indicates the extent to which a hierarchical pattern characterizes the system.

In their review of the literature on control graphs, McMahon and Ivancevich (1976) report many findings that participation in the influence process is positively related to member satisfaction and effectiveness. Their own study, however, fails to confirm these results and raises questions about the conditions under which participatory practices are effective. They report that neither total control nor flatness of the control curve is consistently related to performance or to member satisfaction, but agreement about control patterns does go with positive outcomes. In other words, clarity of structure in the power picture, rather than the distribution of control, predicted to satisfaction and performance. *Agreement* about who was in charge was more important than the perception of who was in charge. The authors suggest that diffusion of power could be dysfunctional for the mass-production industry they studied. A methodological difference in their approach, compared to that of earlier studies, should be noted. Their measures for the control graphs came from three levels of managerial personnel, and their measures of satisfaction and performance came from nonmanagerial workers. These separate sources of data guard against the contamination of halo effects when all measures come from the same respondents. In general, research does not seek data from independent sources but the McMahon-Ivancevich study is a welcome exception. An addition to their procedure, however, could have added comparability to their investigation if, at another point in time, they had extended their control perceptions to the nonsupervisory personnel. This would have made possible a comparison with studies which have not excluded workers from the control curves.

The bulk of the research evidence, McMahon and Ivancevich to the contrary notwithstanding, does support the Tannenbaum thesis that the most hierarchical system is not the most effective or the most productive of member satisfaction. The relationship may vary according to type of organization, type of task, or type of environment, and hence we need to take more variables into account than hierarchy and effectiveness. The inclusion of more organizational variables means that investigators need to look at more organizations. The N of organizations becomes a paramount consideration.

The mechanisms of control are studied by *Ouchi,* who distinguishes between behavior control and outcome control. A supervisor attempts to control those under him by monitoring what they do or by counting their products. The problem that *Ouchi* addressed himself to was the loss of control of either type on transmission down the hierarchy. Questionnaires from two department stores, from three levels, from department manager downward, furnished the data on the basis of self-reports of procedures for supervising and checking performance. From one supervisory level to another, output controls were accurately transmitted, but behavior control was not. This imaginative study raises a number of organizational problems. How can large organizations decrease a long chain of command in which there will be loss of behavior controls? Will output controls, which can be readily measured, not assume dominant attention from the organization at the risk of missing out on other aspects of performance? How much control loss can be tolerated by the organization? *Ouchi* views all control as downward influence. If one takes the Tannenbaum approach, there can be mutual influencing with some movement laterally or upward. Hence, what appears in *Ouchi*'s study as control loss could really be control gain. Finally, a methodological issue concerns the need for supplementing the questionnaire findings with some observational procedure.

In an investigation of downward influence, Franklin (1975) investigated four factors and their correspondence from level to level in organizational hierarchies, specifically —group process, organizational climates, managerial leadership, and peer leadership. He found that group process was uniquely important. Not only did group process at one level predict to group process at the next lower level but it also had positive effects on the transmission of organizational climate, managerial leadership, and peer leadership.

One of the perplexing outcomes of early industrial research was the lack of consistency in the relationship between job satisfaction and performance. Many explanations were offered: (1) many nonrelevant factors were considered in the measurement of job satisfaction, (2) high-performing workers might have higher standards for themselves than low-performing workers, and (3) measures of satisfaction are not measures of motivation. *Cherrington, Reitz,* and *Scott* present an elaboration of the last explanation and theorize that the nature of the performance-contingent conditions determines the relationship. Specifically, if rewards are distributed randomly, independent of performance, there will be no relation between satisfaction and performance; if rewards are distributed on the basis of performance, there will be a positive relationship between performance and satisfaction; and, finally, if rewards are distributed in inverse relationship to performance, the correlation will be negative. Subjects were undergraduates in a business course and were assigned tasks under various conditions of contingent rewards. The theory was supported by the experimental outcomes; and the authors conclude, as do other writers in the organizational field, that applications of motivational theory to satisfaction and behavior must be specified with respect to contingent conditions. This study demonstrates neatly how a well-conceived experiment, even in a nonorganizational setting, can cut through the complexities to get at the significant variables. Of course, not all problems can be as readily solved within the laboratory, but the thoughtful researcher can do a great deal with the power of the laboratory to advance the field.

The tendency for practitioners is to use a number of motivational devices to increase performance. If a given method seems to work, they combine it with other methods that also seem to be effective—for example, motivating the worker by giving him a supervisor trained in human relations, making his pay as good as or better than in other companies, giving him recognition and interesting work. The question raised is whether these motives are additive, whether what is appropriate for arousing one motive will be appropriate for arousing another. Emphasis on sanctions may increase compliance with reduced absenteeism but may not increase performance. The whole field of appropriate conditions for arousing given motives and for their possible differential outcomes is wide open for the research-oriented industrial psychologist. Experimentation has already begun in the work of Deci (1971) on whether extrinsic reward increases intrinsic motivation. From his laboratory study, Deci concluded that noncontingent pay has no effect on intrinsic motivation but that contingent pay adversely affects intrinsic motivation. Deci advanced a cognitive evaluation theory to account for these findings. According to this theory, when a person is paid for doing interesting work, the perceived locus of causality shifts from the person himself to the environment. But Hamner and Foster (1975), in a detailed follow-up of the Deci work, found that intrinsic and extrinsic rewards do summate in increasing task motivation. These investigators used a boring and a nonboring task in their laboratory experiment and found that contingent monetary payments that were not delayed had an additive effect. The conflicting findings can be explained in part by the delay in payment, but in part we are dealing with a large number of variables that can affect the outcome. We need more independent measures of the methods of motivating people, of the motivational states produced, and of differential behavioral outcomes.

The complexity of motivational problems is recognized in the work of *Folger, Rosenfield,* and *Hays,* who deal with the role of choice as it affects performance under varying amounts of pay. Choice refers to the individual's freedom to refuse to engage in a given activity. Dissonance theory, as formulated by Brehm and Cohen (1962), states that unpleasant tasks engaged in voluntarily will create greater dissonance than tasks entered into with little choice. The equity theory of Adams (1965) predicts that people will experience dissonance when they see the ratio of their inputs to their outputs as not equivalent to those of their fellows. When relatively underpaid, they will do inferior work; when overpaid, they will do superior work. Pay and productivity are thus directly related. *Folger* and his colleagues hypothesized, however, that the positive relationship between pay and productivity will hold under conditions of low choice. Under high choice, productivity will fall with high pay. A laboratory experiment confirmed these hypotheses. When people choose an activity for themselves, intrinsic motivation is at work. Adding external incentives actually decreases performance. These findings support the Deci thesis about the nonadditive character of intrinsic and extrinsic rewards and are not consistent with the findings of Hamner and Foster. The definitive experiments in this area remain to be done.

Attempts to relate job satisfaction to productivity, wages, and supervisory practices have often foundered because global measures of job satisfaction were employed (like "taking your job as a whole") or sometimes a miscellany of specific questions were aggregated to give a single score. Some questions may relate to satisfaction with extrinsic factors, such as pay, and other questions may relate to intrinsic satisfaction, such as job challenge; even when both are positive, they still may not be additive as Deci maintains. But often one aspect of a job may be positive and another negative (people may like the pay but dislike the work), so it is important to examine the independent job factors at work and then determine which ones are related to performance or supervision. The first step in this process has been taken by *Quinn* and *Cobb*, who factor-analyzed worker ratings of twenty-five facets of work in terms of their importance. Five factors emerged, including challenge, financial rewards, and relations with co-workers. The factor structure was consistent with previous but more limited studies. The same structure appeared for two random half-samples of workers. When the question wording was shifted from importance to satisfaction, with the twenty-five facets the same, five factors appeared, but in addition a sixth factor emerged (satisfaction with supervision). The data come from a national probability sample of American workers, and the study is the most definitive work to date of the dimensions of job satisfaction. The sample is representative of the nation, the job facets are sufficiently numerous, two forms of questioning were employed, and the factorial structure was replicated in the sample. We now have standard questions for dealing with the various dimensions of responses to jobs. It remains for investigators to relate these dimensions either to individual variables or to organizational variables—such as pay, industry, occupation, status, productivity, hierarchical character, supervising, and communication patterns.

Motivation on the job is viewed by *Gardell* in a broader system context than in most studies of job satisfaction. He examines job design in relation to organization design and predicts to outcomes such as aspirations about direct democracy and representative democracy. His study starts with an examination of the nature of the job (discretion and skill level), and predicts to the desire to increase one's decision-making influence both at the team and departmental level and at the plant level. In the two industries studied, pulp and paper and engineering, there was a greater desire for exerting influence for team-departmental matters than for plant matters. In the paper and pulp mills, but not the engineering industry, the more skilled the job, the higher the aspirations for participating in local and plant decisions. The positive findings in the paper and pulp mills may be due to the more integrated character as against the more individually contained character of the engineering industry. Subjective job involvement was not as critical as actual level of skill and discretion, and the overall results suggest the importance of redesign affecting more than the single job. *Gardell* addresses the implications of increasing job autonomy. If, as his results suggest, increasing job autonomy raises aspirations for decision making both at the local and plant levels, is there also a carry over to employees wanting more control in larger groupings such as province or nation? And if this aspiration is exercised through representative democracy, what will be the effects on direct democracy in the plant or community? Once the process starts, where does it stop and what forms does it take? Though this one study cannot answer all these questions, it points the way methodologically for finding such answers. It is suggestive, moreover, in finding no direct contradictions between desires for direct and representative democracy.

Though *Gardell* found involvement in work problems and high aspirations for democratic participation among industrial workers, the older findings based on mass production emphasized the alienative character of assembly-line technology. In an early study of the auto assembly line, Walker and Guest (1952) reported dissatisfaction with repetitive work and with reduced social interaction and, in general, a sense of depersonalization. Other investigations in mass industries support these conclusions and in general show little identification with the company and commitment to its goals. Osako (1977) points out the culture-bound character of the thesis that a robot-like role produces anomie and alienation. She studied a Japanese automobile factory and found the same dissatisfaction with the work itself, but attitudes toward the company and toward management were positive rather than negative. Feelings about the work did not rub off on commitment to the organization. She attributes this to the social pattern of the Japanese factory, in which the worker has tenure and membership in various social groups. Thus, he has two roles: one as an assembly-line worker and the other as a member of the factory community. The comparison of Japanese and American workers leaves something to be desired because of the twenty-year interval between the two studies. Nonetheless, the issue raised by Osako is an important one in that we have assumed in the past that job design or technology is critical in worker motivation. The Japanese study suggests, however, that the social structure can be central in worker involvement. In other words, the social part of a sociotechnical system can have effects in its own right and may counteract the effect of the technical system.

References

Adams, J. S. "Inequity in Social Exchange." In L. Berkowitz (Ed.), *Advances in Experimental Social Psychology*. Vol. 1. New York: Academic Press, 1965.

Brehm, J. W., and Cohen, A. R. *Explorations in Cognitive Dissonance*. New York: Wiley, 1962.

Deci, E. L. "Effects of Externally Mediated Rewards on Intrinsic Motivation." *Journal of Personality and Social Psychology*, 1971, *18*, 105-115.

Franklin, J. "Down the Organization: Influence Processes Across Levels of Hierarchy." *Administrative Science Quarterly*, 1975, *20*, 153-164.

Hamner, W. C., and Foster, L. W. "Are Intrinsic and Extrinsic Rewards Additive: A Test of Deci's Cognitive Evaluation Theory of Task Motivation." *Organizational Behavior and Human Performance*, 1975, *14*, 398-415.

McMahon, T. J., and Ivancevich, J. M. "A Study of Control in a Manufacturing Organization: Managers and Nonmanagers." *Administrative Science Quarterly*, 1976, *21*, 66-83.

Osako, M. "Technology and Structure in a Japanese Automobile Factory." *Sociology of Work and Occupations*, 1977, *4*, 397-426.

Smith, F. J. "Work Attitudes as Predictors of Attendance on a Specific Day." *Journal of Applied Psychology,* 1977, *62* (1), 16-19.

Tannenbaum, A. S. *Control in Organizations.* New York: McGraw-Hill, 1968.

Walker, C. R., and Guest, H. *The Man on the Assembly Line.* Cambridge, Mass.: Harvard University Press, 1952.

17

The Transmission of Control Through Organizational Hierarchy

William G. Ouchi

The transmission of control is a central problem in the study of hierarchical organizations because the opportunities for miscommunication and distortion are so rich. A number of authors have noted the errors, both unintentional and intentional, which occur between superior and subordinate in a hierarchy (Downs, 1956; Parsons, 1960; Patchen, 1963; Tullock, 1965; Williamson, 1971; Hopwood, 1972; Evans, 1975). In hierarchical organizations, policies and objectives are typically set or at least ratified by occupants of higher-level positions and are then communicated to lower participants, who are charged with the responsibility to carry out the necessary actions. It is up to the higher-level managers to determine whether or not the objectives have been met and, if not, to take appropriate steps. This is the process of control.

It has been noted by Williamson (1975) that hierarchy aids the process of communication because occupants of high-status positions have legitimacy ascribed to their directives, so that lower participants can tell which orders ought to be followed. Williamson also notes, however, that it is often difficult for superiors to determine whether or not subordinates have actually responded to the understood requests. Evans (1975) suggests that the problem of control loss, which is compounded at each level of the organization, becomes overwhelming in an organization of more than three levels.

The process of control can be summarized as a process of monitoring, evaluating, and providing feedback (Dornbusch and Scott, 1975). In a hierarchical organization, the top-level managers must not only arrange a mechanism for controlling their immediate subordinates; they must also arrange a mechanism whereby their subordinates are sure to maintain control over the level below them, and so on to successively lower levels. In a multitier hierarchy, the top level of managers can also be expected to desire some consistency in the process of control at various levels in the organization if for no other reason than to render manageable the task of remembering how to interpret reports from various levels. Yet Franklin (1975) shows that leadership styles maintain virtually no consistency between levels of organization.

However, all forms of control may not be equally susceptible to hierarchical loss.

Reprinted from *Academy of Management Journal,* 1978, *21* (2), 173-192, with permission of the author and the Academy of Management.

Since it is demonstrably true that organizations achieve five and more levels of hierarchy, there must be some forms of control which can operate through multiple levels. That is the point to be argued in this paper, that control based on outputs is relatively less susceptible to hierarchical attenuation than is control based on behavior.

Behavior Control and Output Control

If we accept the rather simple notion that control in organizations can be described as a process of monitoring, evaluating, and providing feedback, then we can ask what it is that is monitored and evaluated. In organizational evaluation, there are only two kinds of phenomena which can be monitored or counted; these are behavior and outputs which result from behavior. (This distinction is made by March and Simon, 1958, pp. 136-171.)

No one would disagree with the assertion that it is possible for a manager to observe his or her subordinates and count the number of times that they engage in any particular behavior. Alternatively, the supervisor in some cases may be able to measure performance less obtrusively by monitoring the aftereffects of behavior, which are the outputs of the productive process. Some managers may choose instead to measure inputs, but we will regard that common practice as falling outside the domain of control, since there is no necessary relationship between inputs and goal achievement except at the extreme, where zero inputs will ordinarily guarantee lack of goal attainment.

Now, given that the supervisor is able to monitor either behavior or the aftereffects of behavior, we can ask whether evaluation is possible. Briefly, the measures of behavior may be used for evaluation only if the technology is sufficiently well understood that "proper" or "good" behavior is recognizable. If the appropriate behavior is unknown, then the observations of actual behavior are of no use for control purposes. As for the leavings of behavior, these can be evaluated only if they are valid representations of goal attainment. If these observable outputs are representative of the desired objectives, then output control is possible (Ouchi, 1977).

Thus, conditional on the state of the organization's technology and its ability to measure desired end-states, we can speak of behavior control and output control as the two alternative methods. Ordinarily, behavior control will be more subtle, more flexible, and richer. It will be able to capture a larger range of desired activities and do so with the flexibility to take account of local differences. Because of this very flexibility, however, and because of the subjective quality of the assessments, behavior control will have poor transmittal qualities through organizational levels. We cannot expect the president to be aware of the subtleties of behavior which are valued in each organizational subunit, with the result that behavior control will serve very well as a local control mechanism but very poorly as an organization-wide control mechanism (Ouchi and Maguire, 1975).

Output control is typically quantifiable and therefore at least apparently comparable across levels and across functions. However, it will ordinarily be impossible to capture all of the complexity of what a department should be doing in one or a few such measures. As a result, output control will be relatively successful at satisfying the organizational need for some commensurable measures of performance, imprecise though they may be, but it will be poor at satisfying local needs for detailed performance information.

Let us note that, whether the control process is based on behavior or on output, it is always behavior that is the ultimate object of feedback and of change. Hopwood (1972) notes that accounting data, which are ordinarily measures of output, have a profound effect on the behavior of managers when these data are knowingly used for performance evaluation. In a sense, then, all control is behavior control. In the language of Thibaut and Kelley (1959), unless fate control can be converted to behavior control, no change will occur.

Returning to the problem of control loss in hierarchies, we can now ask whether behavior control and output control ought to be equally susceptible to attenuation. If a manager wishes to emphasize output control as the dominant mode, with what accuracy does he transmit that wish to subordinates who are also managers and, through them, to their subordinates? If, on the other hand, the manager wishes to emphasize the monitoring of behavior as the dominant mode of control, will transmission of that wish be accomplished more or less accurately through the tiers than transmission of an output control mechanism? If it is true, as expected, that output control is transmitted with greater consistency or accuracy through the levels of a hierarchy than is behavior control, then we can expect that multilevel organizations will rely relatively more heavily on output control for coordinative purposes, at the cost of sometimes misrepresenting true subunit performance or even causing subunits to respond in a manner which will yield favorable performance measures but unfavorable outcomes for the organization (for an example, see Hopwood, 1972).

The Study

This study draws on a set of data collected through questionnaires during 1972. Two department store companies in the midwestern United States provided a total of five sites, including the central administrative offices and branch stores. From these, a sample of 215 departments was drawn, representing both sales and sales support functions. Questionnaires were administered to each employee in every department in the sample, yielding 2,363 usable questionnaires, a response rate of 83 percent. These were then aggregated into the original 215 departments, so that each case includes data from the department manager; the mean of scores of assistant department managers, if any; and the mean of scores from first-line employees. Data on employees above the level of department manager are not reported in this paper.

Retail department stores differ from other organizations in many ways. One major difference is that measures of output are easily obtainable for their sales function. These measures usually consist of a gross measure of sales volume, and they sometimes also are adjusted for returns and exchanges. Even this more complex output measure, however, fails to reflect many of the other areas in which performance is considered important, such as stock work, training new salespeople (a large task, since turnover is high in most retail stores), and coordinating delivery dates.

Even in nonsales departments, output measures are commonly used. Some stores, for example, keep records of the number and dimensions of parcels processed through the wrapping and packing department. Others measure the performance of the receiving and marking function by keeping track of the number of hours from the time that a shipping container is received at the warehouse until the goods are on the shelves and racks in the stores. In general, however, the use of output measures in sales support areas is less common than in sales departments.

While output control is perhaps more common in department stores than in other kinds of organizations, behavior control is also widely used. The study reported by Ouchi and Maguire (1975) used a modified Echo Technique to identify eleven principal performance goals which most department stores apply to sales personnel. Of these, only one or two are represented in the sales volume measure. The others must be evaluated through the supervisory skills of the department manager applying behavior control as he or she watches, corrects, and guides the first-level employees. Thus, both forms of control are commonly used in retail department stores, whereas other kinds of organizations may tend to rely more heavily on behavior control alone.

The hypothesis to be tested is simply that output control will be transmitted more accurately through the hierarchy than will behavior control. The test is a weak one, because it does not measure agreement between levels on the substance of the goals and the exact levels of performance which are considered satisfactory and unsatisfactory. Instead, the measures used here reflect the agreement between levels on how much emphasis is placed on output and how much emphasis is placed on behavior.

The principal measures are of "behavior control given," "behavior control received," "output control given," and "output control received." For department managers and assistant department managers, all four measures were obtained. For first-level employees, who have no subordinates to whom control can be given, only the measures of behavior control received and output control received were obtained.

These four measures were obtained from the following questionnaire items:

1. *Output Control Given.* An index coded into values 1, 2, 3 from the following item: "When you are evaluating the people who report directly to you for raises or promotions, how much weight do you give to their output records?" (1 = output records are not considered at all in the decision; 7 = decision is based entirely on output records.) More than one-half of the department managers and assistant department managers reported having no records of output. Those were coded as 1, original values of 2-4 were coded as 2, and 5-7 were coded as 3. A comparison of correlations between the original and recorded variables is presented in Table 1. The path analysis reported below was also run with both sets of variables; the findings in each case were the same.

Table 1. Output Control Correlations: Original and Recoded Scales

Output Control Given by Department Manager with:	*Original Scale*[a]		*Recoded Scale*[a]	
Output control received by department manager	.70[c]	(51)	.34[b]	(215)
Output control received by others	.23	(48)	.36[c]	(215)
Behavior control given by department manager	.10	(79)	−.02	(208)
Behavior control received by others	.14	(78)	.10	(214)

[a]Number of cases (N) in parentheses.

[b]$p < .01$.

[c]$p < .001$.

2. *Behavior Control Given.* "How often do you see each of the people who report directly to you?" (1 = I see each person less than once a week; 7 = they are almost never out of my sight.)

3. *Output Control Received.* An index coded into values 1, 2, 3 from the following item: "In some departments, records are kept for each employee which show his or her output—for example, sales volume, selling cost, number of parcels handled, etc. Does your immediate superior keep such records of your individual output? If yes, then: "When you are being evaluated for a raise or promotion, how much weight does your supervisor give to the records of your output?" (1 = output records are not considered at all in the decision; 7 = decision is based entirely on output records.)

4. *Behavior Control Received.* "How often does your immediate supervisor check to see what you are doing on the job?" (1 = checks once a week or less; 8 = can see me almost all the time.) "Behavior control given" refers to how often you "see" your subordinates, while "behavior control received" asks how often your supervisor "checks" on you. These different wordings were used for the following reason: The most direct measure of the underlying construct is represented by asking how often your supervisor "checks" on you, and that form was used for control received. A pre-test of the item suggested, however, that the word "checking" on someone carried negative connotations when applied to the giving of control and that supervisors were underreporting their behavior. For that reason, the less threatening form, asking how often you "see" your subordinates, was substituted for measuring control given.

The other operational measures are reported in Table 2 along with their means and standard deviations. The matrix of zero-order correlation coefficients is reported in Table 3.

Table 2. Operational Measures

1. *Output Control Given:* Description of this variable is in the text.

Sample	Mean	SD	N
Department managers	1.61	.86	215
Assistant department managers	1.68	.95	36

2. *Behavior control given:* Description of this variable is in the text.

Sample	Mean	SD	N
Department managers	4.53	2.47	208
Assistant department managers	4.57	1.21	36

3. *Output control received:* Description of this variable is in the text.

Sample	Mean	SD	N
Department managers	1.76	.91	215
Assistant department managers	1.39	.77	36
Others (first-level)	1.68	.96	215

4. *Behavior control received:* Description of this variable is in the text.

Sample	Mean	SD	N
Department managers	2.39	2.47	214
Assistant department managers	3.97	2.80	36
Others (first-level)	4.50	1.82	214

5. *Information from Observing:* "How much can you tell by watching the people who report directly to you while they are working?" (1 = I can't tell anything about how well they are doing their job by watching them; 4 = I can tell exactly whether they are doing their jobs properly or not.) For department managers only in this study (*mean* = 2.40, *SD* = .59, *N* = 209).

6. *Percent routine:* "What percentage of your time on the job do you spend carrying out routine tasks?" (0-100 percent, in steps of 20 percent.)

Sample	Mean	SD	N
Department managers	.44	.24	214
Assistant department managers	.52	.24	36
Others (first-level)	.54	.18	214

7. *Manager's expertise:* Ability of the department manager, as rated by his first-level subordinates (others). "Regardless of whether or not your supervisor checks often, how

Table 2 *(Continued)*

familiar is your supervisor with your on-the-job performance?" Asked of others only, for this study (1 = not familiar at all, 5 = very familiar; *mean* = 3.51, *SD* = .54, *N* = 215).

8. *Autonomy:* "How often are you given a chance to try out your own ideas on the job?" (1 = never; 5 = always.) For department managers only in this study (*mean* = 3.13, *SD* = .74, *N* = 214).

9. *Interdependence:* "To what extent does your performance depend upon how well others do their job?" (1 = almost none; 5 = a very great deal.) For department managers only in this study (*mean* = 3.43, *SD* = .59, *N* = 214).

10. *Company:* A dummy variable representing membership in either company 1 or company 2. Both were full-line, nondiscount, retail department stores in the midwestern United States. Company 1 had a main store and five branches; departments were drawn from the main store and from one branch. Company 2 was approximately six times the size of company 1 in sales volume and in number of employees. Departments were drawn from the main store and from two branches (*mean* = 1.73, *SD* = .45, *N* = 215).

11. *Departmental performance:* "In terms of overall performance, how would you rate your department?" (1 = one of the very best; 5 = below average.) For department managers only (*mean* = 1.88, *SD* = .81, *N* = 215).

Of the 215 departments, only 36 had one or more assistant department managers; the others had no one in this position, thus having only two levels of hierarchy. A person who identified himself as an assistant manager in rank but who had no superior within the department was treated as the manager of that department. All departments had at least one subordinate and had only one department manager. Data for the 36 departments with three levels of hierarchy will be reported separately from data for all 215 departments.

Results

The amounts of each form of control given and received at each of the three levels are reported in Table 4. These figures, which are the means of the mean scores for each department rather than the mean of individual scores, support the same conclusions reported in Ouchi and Maguire (1975). While department managers and assistant department managers do not differ in the amounts of behavior control and output control which they give, all three levels differ in the predicted direction in the amount of control which they receive. As one rises in the hierarchy, the amount of behavior control received decreases, while the amount of output control received increases.

The transmission hypothesis was tested by comparing two sets of correlations for each form of control. The first was to test for emulation effects; that is, to inspect the correlation between behavior control received and behavior control given and the correlation between output control received and output control given, within each of the two supervisory ranks. The hypothesis was that these correlations would be greater for output control than for behavior control, suggesting that subordinates more closely copy their superiors in output control than in behavior control.

The second set of correlations, to test for interlevel transmission, is between behavior control given by a higher level and behavior control received by a lower level and

Table 3. Matrix of Zero-Order Correlation Coefficients[a]

	1	2	3	4	5	6
1. Output control given—DM[b]		−.02	.34[d]	−.04	.68[e]	−.06
2. Behavior control given—DM	208		.02	.09	−.08	.34[c]
3. Output control received—DM	215	208		.04	.33[c]	−.05
4. Behavior control received—DM	214	208	214		.08	.05
5. Output control given—ADM	36	35	36	36		.05
6. Behavior control given—ADM	36	35	36	36	36	
7. Output control received—ADM	36	35	36	36	36	36
8. Behavior control received—ADM	36	35	36	36	36	36
9. Output control received—Others	215	208	215	214	36	36
10. Behavior control received—Others	214	207	214	213	36	36
11. Information from observing—DM	209	207	209	208	36	36
12. Percent routine—DM	214	207	214	213	36	36
13. Percent routine—ADM	36	35	36	36	36	36
14. Percent routine—Others	214	207	214	213	36	36
15. Manager's expertise—Others	215	208	215	214	36	36
16. Autonomy—DM	214	208	214	214	36	36
17. Interdependence—DM	214	207	214	213	36	36
18. Company (dummy variable)	215	208	215	214	36	36

[a]Correlation coefficients in upper-right triangle, sample size in lower-left triangle.

[b]DM = department manager; ADM = assistant department manager.

[c]$p < .05.$

[d]$p < .01.$

[e]$p < .001.$

between output control given by a higher level and output control received by a lower level. The prediction was that these correlations would be higher for output control than for behavior control. This suggests that output control is transmitted between levels more accurately than is behavior control. The results are combined in Figure 1, which demonstrates the striking difference in transmission between the two forms of control.

In Figure 1, it seems as though everything is correlated with everything else within the set of output measures, while few significant correlations appear within the set of behavior control measures. This pattern is true of both the three-level and the two-level departments. The initial explanation that suggests itself is that output control is either emphasized or deemphasized as a matter of company policy, while behavior control is arrived at through local decisions by department managers. The data fail to support that

Table 4. Hierarchical Position and Control: Mean Values

Level of Hierarchy	Control Type			
	Output Control Given (1)	Behavior Control Given (2)	Output Control Received (3)	Behavior Control Received (4)
Department manager	1.61 (215)[a]	4.53 (208)	1.76 (215)	2.39 (214)
Assistant department manager	1.68 (36)	4.57 (36)	1.39 (36)	3.97 (36)
Others	na	na	1.68 (215)	4.50 (214)

[a]Numbers in parentheses are the number of departments.

7	8	9	10	11	12	13	14	15	16	17	18
.55^e	.09	.36^e	.10	−.001	.01	.07	−.03	.06	.11	.13^c	.06
.02	.25	.04	.12^c	.28^e	.19^d	.08	.12	.22^e	.13^c	.17^d	.29^e
.31^c	.21	.26^e	.08	.08	−.01	−.01	−.05	.08	.04	−.02	.08
.18	.05	−.08	.09	.06	.15	.19	.03	−.01	−.09	.04	.21^e
.49^e	.14	.29^c	.20	−.25	.31^c	−.20	−.01	.23	.11	−.04	.29^c
−.21	.37^c	−.07	.33^c	−.07	.32^c	.30^c	.41^d	−.20	.04	−.05	.36^c
	.16	.45^d	.08	.13	.09	−.02	−.13	.15	.15	.03	.16
36		.24	.27	.13	.26	.02	.14	.01	−.08	−.04	.23
36	36		.10	.04	.10	−.14	−.10	−.07	.01	−.08	.16^d
36	36	214		.29^e	.06	.12	.07	.30^e	.10	−.004	.33^e
36	36	209	208		.11	.14	−.05	.25^e	.12^c	.17^d	.19^d
36	36	214	213	209		−.04	.08	.01	−.03	.06	.14^c
36	36	36	36	36	36		.58^e	.01	.10	−.05	.20
36	36	214	213	208	213	36		−.14^c	.09	.05	.09
36	36	215	214	209	214	36	214		.08	−.03	.28^e
36	36	214	213	208	213	36	213	214		.21^e	.08
36	36	214	213	209	214	36	213	214	213		.05
36	36	215	214	209	214	36	214	215	214	214	

hypothesis, however, with the correlations between the dummy variable for "company" and the measures of output control ranging from $r = .06$ to $r = .29$ (see Table 3). In fact, the average correlations between the company variable and the measures of behavior control are much larger. A further breakdown of the data into organizational subunits within companies also failed to produce any difference in the relationships.

This led to a path analysis, the results of which are presented in Figures 2 and 3. Figure 2 shows all significant paths for the output control variables. None of the paths between behavior control variables reached that level, so the same paths are shown for purposes of comparison. In Figure 3, the complete path diagrams are shown for both forms of control and for two- and three-level departments.

Figure 2 shows that the expected effects take place. That is, output control is accurately emulated within each supervisory level and is accurately transmitted between levels, while there is little emulation or transmission of behavior control. There is no evidence here that a general policy orientation accounts for the transmission of output control, for such an orientation would yield significant path coefficients between the three measures of control received and between the two measures of control given. Rather, the zero-order association between the receipt of output control by managers and by assistant managers is accounted for by the fact that managers transmit their control style to their assistant managers. After that transmission effect is accounted for, there is no remaining significant similarity between output control received by the two levels of managers.

In the case of output control given, however, there is some remaining similarity (although not significant) between the supervisory ranks even after the transmission effect is removed ($b = .29$, Figure 3). This similarity may be accounted for by the fact

Figure 1. The Transmission of Control: Zero-Order Effects
(Zero-Order Correlation Coefficients)

Departments with Three Levels (N = 36)[a]

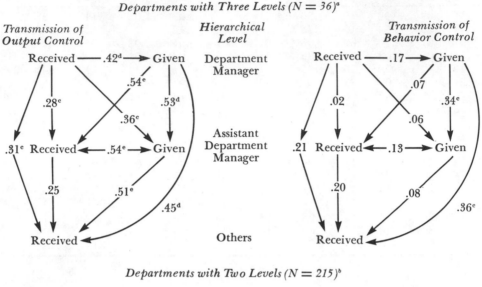

Departments with Two Levels (N = 215)[b]

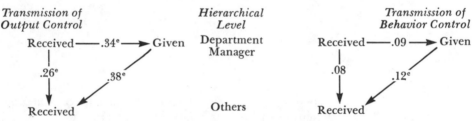

[a]Of these 36 departments, 21 are from Company A and 15 from Company B.
[b]These data include departments which have three levels, with the middle level excluded from this
  particular analysis. Results for only those departments which do not have assistant managers
  (N = 179) do not differ from these.
[c]$p < .05$.
[d]$p < .01$.
[e]$p < .001$.

that assistant department managers, on the whole, are upwardly mobile and feel that they
are "in training" to become department managers. They are thus subject to anticipatory
socialization, and these data suggest that there is a general policy orientation which is
shared by both department managers and their assistants. Even with the transmission
effect removed, therefore, there is some remaining similarity between the output control
orientation held by the two levels of managers.

It is also interesting that there is some antitransmission of behavior control. The
more behavior control assistant managers receive, the less they will pass on to their subordinates. This may be due to the assistant managers' following the "golden rule" and
doing unto their subordinates as they wish their superior would do unto them. Those
whose superiors exercise very close behavior control may be highly sensitive to that form
of control, dislike it, and take care not to use that form of control on their subordinates.
Conversely, those whose supervisors exert very little behavior control may feel neglected
and respond by watching more closely over their own subordinates.

Figure 2. Transmission of Control: Path Coefficients

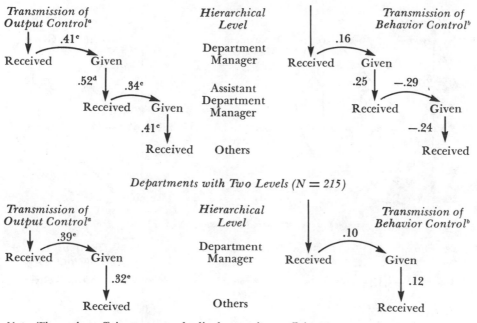

Departments with Three Levels (N = 36)

Departments with Two Levels (N = 215)

Note: The path coefficients are standardized regression coefficients.
[a] These path diagrams show only paths which are at least two times their standard error.
[b] In these path diagrams, none of the paths are at least two times their standard error, so the predicted paths are shown to provide a comparison with the other diagrams.
[c] $p < .05$.
[d] $p < .01$.
[e] $p < .001$.

The much larger number of cases in the analysis of two-level departments, 215 departments versus only 36 departments with three levels, produces the same findings. Here it is clear that both emulation and transmission take place with respect to output control, but neither effect exists for behavior control.

A number of further investigations were conducted, the most important of which are reported here. First, a discriminant validation was performed by combining output control given with behavior control received and behavior control given with output control received. The test should demonstrate no difference between these two mixed transmission processes. The results revealed no difference between the mixed processes in either two-level or three-level departments. None of the correlations in this test reached significance.

The next test was to examine more closely the meaning of the operational measure of behavior control given. The questionnaire item asks, "How often do you see each of the people who reports directly to you?" It is entirely possible that this question was interpreted by supervisors as referring to the frequency with which they could physically see subordinates, rather than to the frequency of checking on or otherwise controlling them. In that case, the lack of correlation between that variable and the measure of behavior control received, which refers more directly to frequency of checking to see how you are doing on the job, would not be surprising, since the two would be measuring quite different things.

Figure 3. Transmission of Control: Path Coefficients

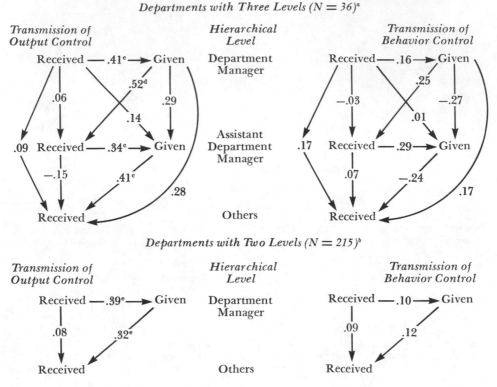

Departments with Three Levels (N = 36)[a]

Departments with Two Levels (N = 215)[b]

[a]Of these 36 departments, 21 are from Company A and 15 from Company B.
[b]These data include departments which have three levels, with the middle level excluded from this
 particular analysis. Results for only those departments which do not have assistant managers
 (N = 179) do not differ from these.
[c]$p < .05$.
[d]$p < .01$.
[e]$p < .001$.

In order to check, an additional variable, "information from observing," was introduced. This variable (see Table 2) measures the supervisor's perception of how much intelligence he can gain from watching his subordinates. Clearly, if he feels that observation is of no use, then he cannot rationally apply behavior control. If this variable, when substituted for "behavior control given" in Figure 2, produced results similar to those for output control in that table, then the original results must be discarded. Information from observing is correlated with behavior control given, $r = .28$ ($p < .001$) for department managers and $r = .35$ ($p < .05$) for assistant managers. However, making the substitution produced a transmission pattern that is indistinguishable from the pattern for behavior control in Figure 2. This third test also fails to invalidate the results of Figure 2.

If the results in Figure 2 can be generally accepted as valid, then a number of other interesting questions arise. First is the question whether the transmission of control pattern differs between the two companies, between the sales and sales support departments, or between high- and low-performing departments.

Between the two companies in the sample, there is no difference in the patterns of transmission. Both companies display a relatively consistent transmission of output control, and both show virtually no transmission of behavior control. Between the sales and the sales support departments there are some consistent differences in the direction first suggested by Ouchi and Maguire (1975). The transmission is somewhat more accurate (the correlations are higher by about .10) for both output control and for behavior control in the sales support departments. While the interpretation of this finding must be speculative, it suggests that in sales departments, where a hard measure of performance is ordinarily used, subordinates pay less attention to the control schemes of supervisors. They are less likely to accurately receive what their supervisor is sending, and they are less likely to emulate their supervisor in their own control attempts. That may be the freedom which accompanies a relatively unambiguous measure of performance. The professor in a research university is in a similar position. If he knows that the volume of his publications and the frequency with which they are cited determine his standing, then he will pay little or no attention to other control devices which the administration may be attempting to employ.

Perhaps more interesting is the similarity in transmission patterns between high-performing departments and low-performing departments. The results of this analysis are in Figure 4.

The departments were separated into high- or low-performing categories according to a self-reported measure of departmental performance (see Table 2). The rating used

Figure 4. Transmission of Control in High- Versus Low-Performing Departments[a]
(Zero-Order Correlation Coefficients)

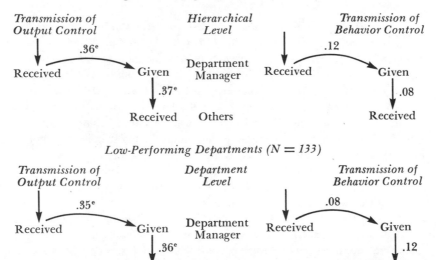

Departments with Two Levels (N = 215)[b]

High-Performing Departments (N = 82)

Low-Performing Departments (N = 133)

[a]Departments were separated into high- or low-performance categories according to a self-reported measure of departmental performance. The rating used here was the department manager's rating, which is significantly correlated with the ratings of assistant managers and of others. Like other self-report measures, this one is associated with job satisfaction ($r = 17$, $p < .001$).
[b]These data include the departments which have three levels, although the middle level was excluded from this particular analysis. Results for only those departments which do not have assistant managers ($N = 179$) do not differ from these.
[c]$p < .05$.
[d]$p < .01$.
[e]$p < .001$.

here was the department manager's rating of departmental performance, which is highly correlated with the assistant managers' rating ($r = .66, p < .001$) and less highly correlated with the ranking given by others ($r = .23, p < .001$). This measure of performance, like all self-report performance measures, is associated with job satisfaction ($r = .17, p < .01$), but the correlation is not close to unity.

The lack of difference in transmission patterns between high- and low-performing departments is surprising, since common sense suggests that high-performing departments should have better consistency of control than low performers. The only observation that can be made in addition to that is that the significant interlevel effect for behavior control in Figure 1 seems to be due mostly to the low-performing departments. That observation is at least not refuted by the skimpy data on the three-level departments. After division on level of performance, there are only thirteen such high-performing departments and twenty-two low performers with three levels.

The data on the three-level departments suggest that behavior control is transmitted with significantly greater consistency in low-performing departments than in high performers. The implications are tantalizing, but the data are insufficient to warrant further investigation or speculation.

Thus, we are left with two questions. First, if behavior control is not determined by transmission through levels of a hierarchy, what does influence it? Can we identify some factors which will reveal the sources of behavior control and suggest why it is that interlevel transmission is so weak? Second, how can it be that high- and low-performing departments do not differ in control? In particular, how can high-performing departments have the same lack of transmission of behavior control which characterizes the low performers? Or is it that interlevel transmission of behavior control is not necessarily desirable?

In order to get at these questions, behavior control given by department managers was regressed on a set of variables which are of two kinds. First are variables which reflect the possibility that behavior control given is tailored to the specific control needs of a department—for example, the usefulness of observational monitoring ("information from observing"); the familiarity of the manager with the particular techniques used by his or her subordinates ("manager's expertise"); and the level of interdependence with other departments ("interdependence"), which might call for closer behavior control. Second were variables which reflect the freedom or autonomy of the manager to apply as much or as little behavior control as he or she wants to—for example, routineness of the manager's job ("percent routine"), which leaves more time for close monitoring; the manager's general freedom to try out innovations ("autonomy"); evidence of emulation ("behavior control received"); and a dummy variable to reflect possible company-wide common practice ("company"). It was hoped that this investigation would clarify the reason that behavior control is not transmitted through hierarchy and also suggest why it is that accurate transmission of behavior control does not seem to be associated with departmental performance. The results of this analysis are presented in Table 5.

The variables in Table 5 are essentially those discussed in Ouchi and Maguire (1975), except that two are renamed, one has been excluded, and one has been added. "Information from observing" was called "technical knowledge" in the earlier study, and "manager's expertise" was called "supervisor's expertise." "Hierarchical level" has been excluded, since this analysis occurs only at one level of the hierarchy, the department manager, and "autonomy" has been added. Descriptions of the variables are in Table 2.

The findings are consistent with the unaggregated data reported in the earlier study. Department managers place greater emphasis on behavior control when they feel

Table 5. Regression on Behavior Control Given by Department Managers

Standardized Regression Coefficients	Sample		
	All Departments (N = 207)	*High-Performing Departments (N = 80)*	*Low-Performing Departments (N = 127)*
Information from observing	.16[b]	.18[a]	.15[a]
Percent routine	.14[b]	.06	.17[a]
Manager's expertise	.14[b]	.17[a]	.12
Behavior control received	.01	.07	−.02
Autonomy	.12[a]	−.05	.22[b]
Interdependence	.11[a]	.21[a]	.05
Company	.22[b]	.27[b]	.20[b]
Multiple R^2	.21	.26	.21

[a] At least one and a half times its standard error.

[b] At least two times its standard error.

that it yields more information about performance, when their own task is more routine and therefore gives them more time for surveillance, when they are more knowledgeable about their subordinates' tasks (as reported by others), when they enjoy greater autonomy in initiating, when their tasks are more interdependent, and when they are in Company A as opposed to Company B. As expected, behavior control received has no effect on behavior control given.

High-performing departments differ from low-performing departments in what determines the use of behavior control by managers. In particular, in high-performing departments only, task interdependence and manager's expertise influence the giving of behavior control. In both high- and low-performing departments, the information from observing and company membership influence the giving of behavior control.

Thus, high performers are distinguished by the fact that the use of behavior control is influenced by task interdependence, which can be reasonably assumed to affect the need for control, and it is influenced by the expertise of the manager, with more knowledgeable managers applying more behavior control while less knowledgeable managers apparently leave well enough alone and apply little behavior control. In low-performing departments, however, those considerations are unimportant, and the use of behavior control is tied to the manager's free time and his freedom from control from above. In such low performers, the manager with more time on his hands and greater autonomy will apply more behavior control, a condition which suggests the creation of feudal despots within the organization.

These factors together account for one-fifth to one-fourth of the variance in behavior control given by department managers. That is clearly not the majority of the variance, but the character of the variables is important to this argument. The factors which influence the giving of behavior control are closely tied to the characteristics of the tasks of superior and of subordinate. Inasmuch as tasks differ across levels of hierarchy, it would be difficult for a top manager to create behavior control procedures from his experience which could be applied down through the organization. In addition, there is a strong "company effect," which suggests an effect of company size (see Table 2, item 10), as well as a norm of great or little behavior control in each firm. This effect is not transmitted through the hierarchy, except insofar as anticipatory socialization may be a hierarchical effect.

Regressions were also run with behavior control received as the dependent variable. These were run for all three levels of the hierarchy and by store, by sales/sales support, and by high-/low-performing departments. The results are similar to those for behavior control given, except that only one-half as much of the variance in the dependent variable is explained. In every case, company membership has a large effect, although it is most pronounced for others (beta = .25), then for department managers (beta = .20), with the least effect on assistant managers (beta = .10).

High- and low-performing departments are distinguished mostly by the fact that "manager's expertise" has a significant effect in high-performing departments and no effect in the low performers. Conversely, "percent routine" has a significant effect on behavior control received in low-performing departments but no effect in the high performers.

Thus, it appears that because behavior control is tailored to the task needs and the personal abilities of each department, it is not easily transmitted through an organizational hierarchy. A high emphasis on behavior control may be appropriate for one level but inappropriate for the level below. Thus, it is not surprising that high- and low-performing departments do not differ in the transmission of behavior control, although they do differ in the pattern of variables which determines the emphasis on behavior control.

Control loss in hierarchies is a many-faceted phenomenon, one which we have only begun to probe. That control which is passed only from one level to another rather than from a central point to all levels will suffer a great deal of loss is unquestionably true. Those who have advanced the arguments surrounding control loss in hierarchies pose a problem which organizations have obviously solved, however, since they often have as many as five or six levels. The dual hierarchy proposed by Evans (1975) is certainly one mechanism for minimizing control loss, but it is a sufficient protection only if one assumes levels of interlevel control which reach .9. As Franklin (1975) has suggested, such high levels of consistency in climate or managerial style between levels are unrealistic. On the other hand, if Franklin's more modest interlevel correlations are common, then we are back to the problem of an intolerable control loss which large organizations manage to tolerate.

A partial answer to this puzzle is that our view of the process of control must be sharpened and refined. When control is viewed in the terms presented here, it becomes apparent that control loss will not apply equally to all forms of control. Behavior control is tailored to the needs of each department; it is perhaps closest to the notions of control expressed by Williamson (1971). Output control, however, can be maintained by a central office which communicates directly with each organizational subunit, so that each level receives and gives similar forms of control, as with the high correlations between the supervisory levels on control received or on control given. Output control is perhaps also more readily communicated and perceived accurately between levels because it is less subjective, and it is more readily emulated for similar reasons.

On the other hand, output control is far from being a complete means for assessment of performance, at least in department stores. It fails to capture the important but evasive dimensions of performance which cannot be measured in terms of output or perhaps can only be measured in terms of output in the distant future. Behavior control continues to play an important role in most organizations.

It must also be remembered that the forms of control dealt with in this paper represent only a small part of the total process of control within organizations. Both behavior control and output control are relatively obvious, explicit forms. Before they are ever exerted, organizational members have been selected into the organization, and a major form of control has already taken place. Most organizations are able to select from a large pool those individuals who already possess the skills and attitudes which the organization values. Those individuals then pass through a period of socialization which further homogenizes them, and they become members of groups which may be able to exert significant peer pressure on them to conform still further to the organization's norms. It is only after most of the variance in the population of potential employees has been reduced through these processes of selection, socialization, and peer pressure that the explicit forms of control discussed here take place.

It would not be at all unreasonable to suggest that many organizations operate quite successfully without any transmission at all of behavior or output control. In a mature organization, one which has a stable and homogeneous culture, we would expect to find no transmission at all between levels of a hierarchy. That is not to say that the emphasis on behavior or output control would be randomly distributed through the organization; quite the opposite, we would expect to find a great deal of similarity on control received between levels, on control given between levels, and therefore between control given at a higher level and control received at a lower level. However, all of this similarity would be due, in this case, to the dominance of a culture which embraces all organizational members. Within any one organization, we would find no variance on these dimensions.

Perhaps the most central point developed here is that control in organizations is a process that depends upon the gathering and dissemination of reliable and valid information. As in many organizational problems, information is at the very heart of the control issue. Good information is difficult and expensive to come by (Williamson, 1975, provides a brilliant discussion), and, in this case, performance information is specialized by function—local management *versus* interunit coordination. In this context, we can now see that it is possible to consider the role of technology in organizations as being important insofar as different technologies impose different informational needs on the organization, including needs for control purposes. We can see that organizational size is an important determinant of structure and control, in large part because big organizations have needs for performance information which differ from the informational needs of small organizations. The view of organizational control as a problem of information leads to a large number of new possibilities for understanding organizations.

References

Dornbusch, S. M., and Scott, W. R. *Evaluation and the Exercise of Authority: A Theory of Control Applied to Diverse Organizations.* San Francisco: Jossey-Bass, 1975.

Downs, A. *Inside Bureaucracy.* Boston: Little, Brown, 1956.

Evans, P. B. "Multiple Hierarchies and Organizational Control." *Administrative Science Quarterly,* 1975, *20,* 250-259.

Franklin, J. L. "Down the Organization: Influence Processes Across Levels of Hierarchy." *Administrative Science Quarterly,* 1975, *20,* 153-164.

Hopwood, A. G. "An Empirical Study of the Role of Accounting Data in Performance Evaluation." *Empirical Research in Accounting: Selected Studies, Supplement to the Journal of Accounting Research,* 1972, *10,* 156-182.

March, J. G., and Simon, H. A. *Organizations.* New York: Wiley, 1958.

Ouchi, W. G. "The Relationship Between Organizational Structure and Organizational Control." *Administrative Science Quarterly,* 1977, *22,* 95-113.

Ouchi, W. G., and Maguire, M. A. "Organizational Control: Two Functions." *Administrative Science Quarterly,* 1975, *20,* 559-569.

Parsons, T. *Structure and Process in Modern Societies.* New York: Free Press, 1960.

Patchen, M. "Alternative Questionnaire Approaches to the Measurement of Influence in Organizations." *American Journal of Sociology,* 1963, *69* (1), 41-52.

Tannenbaum, A. S. *Control in Organizations.* New York: McGraw-Hill, 1968.

Thibaut, J. W., and Kelley, H. H. *The Social Psychology of Groups.* New York: Wiley, 1959.

Tullock, G. *The Politics of Bureaucracy.* Washington, D.C.: Public Affairs, 1965.

Williamson, O. E. *Corporate Control and Business Behavior.* Englewood Cliffs, N.J.: Prentice-Hall, 1971.

Williamson, O. E. *Markets and Hierarchies: Analysis and Antitrust Implications.* New York: Free Press, 1975.

18

✥ Effects of Contingent and Noncontingent Reward on the Relationship Between Satisfaction and Task Performance

David J. Cherrington
H. Joseph Reitz
William E. Scott, Jr.

Many current speculations on the relationship between worker satisfaction and task performance, as reviewed by Schwab and Cummings (1970), still imply that performance and satisfaction are causally related in one direction or the other. Some theorists have now added moderating variables to their behavioral formulas in hopes of facilitating the prediction of one variable from the other.

In contrast, the present authors postulate not only that (1) there is no inherent relationship between satisfaction and performance but also that (2) one can produce about any empirical relationship between task performance and self-reports of satisfaction that one wishes. The first proposition is consistent with the conclusions of empirical reviews such as Brayfield and Crockett (1955) and with theoretical positions such as those of Porter and Lawler (1968). The second proposition was derived from operational proposals by Skinner (1969) and Bandura (1969) and from speculations by a variety of reinforcement theorists (see, for example, Berlyne, 1967; Bindra, 1968; Rescorla and Solomon, 1967; Weiskrantz, 1968).

Skinner (1969), for instance, insists that feelings are, at best, accompaniments rather than causes of behavior and that both are the products of common environmental variables. Bandura (1969, p. 598) pointedly suggests that we might better treat self-reports of satisfaction simply as another class of behavior rather than as indexes of an underlying state endowed with special causal powers. From this point of view, there exists no inherent relationship between performance and self-reports of satisfaction, and the empirical problem becomes that of examining the conditions under which the different response systems are correlated *or* independent.

We suggest that the type of reward system under which workers perform might strongly influence the satisfaction-performance relationship. One should be able to directly influence satisfaction by proffering or withdrawing rewards. To significantly influence performance, however, one must use *performance-contingent* rewards. Theoretically, then, by manipulating the contingencies of a reward system, one should be able to create conditions under which satisfaction and performance can be, empirically, either independent, or positively related, or negatively related.

To test these propositions, let us define three types of performance-reward systems:

1. *Random rewards.* Rewards are distributed on bases independent of performance. The percentage of high performers receiving rewards does not differ from the percentage of low performers receiving rewards. Under this system we hypothesize that correlations between satisfaction and performance would not significantly differ from zero.
2. *Positively contingent rewards.* Rewards are based directly on performance. All high performers are rewarded; all low performers are not rewarded. Under this system we hypothesize a positive correlation between satisfaction and performance.
3. *Negatively contingent rewards.* Rewards are based on factors inversely related to performance. Low performers are rewarded; high performers are not rewarded. Under this system we hypothesize a negative correlation between satisfaction and performance.

Method

Subjects. The Ss were ninety undergraduate students, both male and female, enrolled in a junior-level business course. Students were enlisted as volunteers to score Closure Flexibility Tests, for which they would be paid at least $1 per hour.

Procedure and Task. The Ss reported to the laboratory in groups that varied from seven to nine individuals and were met by E, who introduced himself as a graduate student who would be their supervisor.

When all Ss had arrived and had familiarized themselves with the Closure Flexibility Test booklet, each was told that his task would be to score the tests at his work station. The Ss were also told that the tests had been completed by employees in a paper mill. All of the Closure Flexibility Test booklets had in fact been marked according to twenty-four patterns of response. Therefore, the difficulty of the task was controlled, and the correct responses were known in advance.

The Ss were told that they would be paid a minimum of $1 per hour but that the best performers in terms of quality and quantity would receive an additional $1 bonus. The Ss were told that each had a 50-50 chance of receiving the bonus. The task of scoring the test booklets was explained to Ss, aided by diagrams showing a partially marked answer sheet.

After Ss began the task, E returned every ten minutes to bring additional booklets and collect the booklets and answer sheets that had been completed. At the end of one hour, E stopped Ss and asked them to indicate on four seven-point scales an estimate of their quantity, quality, and overall performance and probability of receiving a reward. The experimental manipulations of financial reward were then performed, which consisted of the following statements and payments.

I have collected the tests as you have scored them and selected a sample from each of you to check your work. I've used a rather complicated index, which combines quantity and quality of performance into one index. Based upon this index, four of you will receive $2 for the last hour's work. The other four will get $1. The four winners are _____ and the four losers are _____ .

In fact, the monetary bonus was randomly distributed to half of the high-performing and half of the low-performing Ss.

The performance score for each S was the total number of rows of figures in the Closure Flexibility Test booklets that S scored correctly. This was determined by subtracting the number of errors from the total number of rows scored. Thus, performance scores were a measure of both quality and quantity.

The Ss were then asked to complete a self-report measure of satisfaction developed by Scott and his colleagues (Scott, 1967; Scott and Rowland, 1970). The format of the self-report measure was a semantic differential questionnaire as shown below.

Me at This Task

	Extreme-ly	Quite	Slight-ly	Neither one nor the other	Slight-ly	Quite	Extreme-ly	
Appreciated	____	____	____	____	____	____	____	Unappreciated
Bored	____	____	____	____	____	____	____	Interested
Efficient	____	____	____	____	____	____	____	Inefficient

Bipolar adjective pairs were set against four concepts: me at this task, my pay, my fellow workers, and the task. The response to each scale was scored from 1 to 7, with 7 assigned to that response which appeared to indicate the most preferred condition. A factor score was computed for each S by averaging S's responses to each of the scales previously found to comprise that factor.

Eight factor scores were computed for each S. General affective tone score was obtained by averaging S's responses to the following bipolar scales set against the concept "me at this task": appreciated-unappreciated, rewarded-penalized, satisfied-dissatisfied, and encouraged-discouraged. The remaining self-report measures and the semantic scales defining each factor were as follows: general arousal (me at this task): interested-bored, spirited-lifeless, and alert-listless; personal competence (me at this task): efficient-inefficient, productive-unproductive, reliable-unreliable, and effective-ineffective; general satisfaction with pay (my pay): pleasing-annoying, reasonable-unreasonable, superior-inferior, and rewarding-penalizing; equitableness of pay (my pay in comparison with what others in my group received): fair-unfair, high-low, and reasonable-unreasonable; adequacy of pay (my pay in comparison with what others get for similar work on the campus): superior-inferior, high-low, and reasonable-unreasonable; interpersonal attractiveness (my fellow workers): sociable-unsociable, helpful-obstructive, pleasant-unpleasant, unselfish-selfish, and cooperative-uncooperative; task attractiveness (the task): attractive-repulsive, exciting-dull, good-bad, interesting-boring, superior-inferior, and wholesome-unwholesome.

After completing the semantic differential scales, Ss took a five-minute break, after which they were given more test booklets and asked to continue scoring them for another hour. The procedure at the end of the second hour was identical to that at the end of the first hour. First, Ss were asked to estimate their perceived performance and probability of reward on the four scales. Then they were paid and asked to fill out the semantic differential questionnaire. The monetary bonus was distributed to the same Ss who received it at the end of the first hour.

After the questionnaires were filled out for the second time, Ss were debriefed. They were told that all rewards were given at random, and since it was only by chance someone received more than the others, the winners were asked to share their rewards with the losers, although E did not insist that they do so.

Results

We have hypothesized that there is no inherent relationship between satisfaction and performance but that there is a direct relationship between the rewards and self-reports of satisfaction. Whatever covariation one does observe between satisfaction and performance, then, may depend upon other environmental conditions, particularly the kind of performance-reward contingency that has been arranged or has evolved.

The results summarized in Table 1 demonstrate the differential effects of rewards on performance and satisfaction. Performance scores of rewarded Ss did not differ from those of nonrewarded Ss.

Table 1. Comparison of Mean Performance and Satisfaction Scores of Rewarded Versus Nonrewarded Subjects

| | $\bar{X}$ Scores | | |
Item	Rewarded Ss	Nonrewarded Ss	D_m
Performance			
First hour	285.6	286.6	−1.0
Second hour	403.8	411.2	−7.4
Satisfaction indexes			
General affective tone	5.16	3.83	1.33[c]
General arousal	4.98	4.44	.54[b]
Personal competence	5.82	5.01	.81[c]
General satisfaction with pay	5.61	3.69	1.92[c]
Equity of pay	5.24	3.74	1.50[c]
Adequacy of pay	4.76	3.40	1.36[c]
Attractiveness of fellow workers	4.96	4.63	.33[a]
Attractiveness of task	3.80	3.19	.61[c]

Note: Abbreviation D_m = Difference of means.

[a] $p < .01$.

[b] $p < .005$.

[c] $p < .001$.

Mean satisfaction scores of rewarded Ss, however, were significantly greater than mean scores of nonrewarded Ss on each of the eight satisfaction indexes. Thus, self-report measures of satisfaction can be highly dependent on the occurrence or nonoccurrence of monetary reward, but if that reward is delivered independent of performance, it fails to have incremental effects on subsequent performance.

To test the effects of variations in performance-reinforcement contingency, Ss were classified on the basis of first-hour performance. The forty-two Ss whose performance scores were above the median of their group are referred to as high performers, and the forty-two Ss below the median as low performers. Six Ss who performed at the median were excluded from further analysis. Rewards at the end of the first hour were distributed randomly among high and among low performers, so that half the Ss in each performance classification were rewarded. The appropriateness of each S's reinforcement was then defined by the performance-reward contingency that happened to occur for that S. The twenty-one rewarded high performers and the twenty-one nonrewarded low performers were classified as appropriately reinforced. The twenty-one rewarded low performers and the twenty-one nonrewarded high performers were classified as inappropriately reinforced.

The results shown in Table 2 reveal, first, that the average second-hour (postreinforcement) performance of appropriately reinforced Ss was significantly higher than that

Table 2. Comparison of Mean Performance and Satisfaction Scores of
Appropriately Versus Inappropriately Reinforced Subjects

| Item | $\bar{X}$ Scores | | |
	Appropriately Reinforced Ss	Inappropriately Reinforced Ss	D_m
Performance			
First hour	291.6	280.9	10.7
Second hour	428.4	385.9	42.5[b]
Satisfaction			
General affective tone	4.26	4.11	.15
General arousal	4.12	4.02	.10
Personal competence	5.30	5.07	.23
General satisfaction with pay	4.56	4.11	.45
Equity of pay	4.40	4.18	.22
Adequacy of pay	4.18	3.64	.54[a]
Attractiveness of fellow workers	4.85	4.78	.07
Attractiveness of task	3.31	3.27	.04

Note: Abbreviation D_m = Difference of means.

[a] $p < .05$.

[b] $p < .01$.

of inappropriately reinforced Ss, whereas the first-hour (prereinforcement) performance of the two classes did not differ significantly. Comparisons between the two classes on self-reports of satisfaction, however, revealed a significant difference on only one of the eight satisfaction indexes, adequacy of pay. The tests summarized in Tables 1 and 2 thus establish that, as hypothesized, it is the contingency of a reward on performance that enables it to bring about increments in performance. That contingency characteristic, however, has little or no effect on satisfaction.

Two different relationships between satisfaction and performance were investigated: (1) the relationship between self-reports of satisfaction and subsequent performance, and (2) the relationship between performance and subsequent self-reports of satisfaction.

Table 3 presents the results of correlational analyses performed between the eight satisfaction indexes recorded at the end of the first hour and subsequent performance during the second hour. The data for all Ss, among whom as many low performers as high performers were rewarded, revealed only one significant correlation between satisfaction and subsequent performance. However, when the data were separated according to Ss'

Table 3. Correlations Between Satisfaction at End of First Hour and
Subsequent Performance During Second Hour

Satisfaction Indexes	All Ss (N = 90)	Appropriately Reinforced Ss (N = 42)	Inappropriately Reinforced Ss (N = 42)
General affective tone	.00	.56[c]	−.32[a]
General arousal	.10	.42[b]	−.15
Personal competence	.21	.54[c]	−.01
General satisfaction with pay	.04	.46[b]	−.29
Equity of pay	−.17	.15	−.44[b]
Adequacy of pay	.04	.39[b]	−.31[a]
Attractiveness of fellow workers	.22[a]	.33[a]	.13
Attractiveness of task	.04	.21	−.08

[a] $p < .05$.
[b] $p < .01$.
[c] $p < .001$.

performance-reward contingencies, distinct differences in the satisfaction-performance relationships were observed. For the forty-two *appropriately* reinforced Ss, significant *positive* correlations were found between six of the eight satisfaction indexes and subsequent performance. But for the forty-two *inappropriately* reinforced Ss, *negative* correlations were found between seven of the eight satisfaction indexes and subsequent performance, of which three correlations were statistically significant, and one closely approached significance at the .05 level.

Table 4 presents the results of correlational analyses performed between performance during the second hour and the eight satisfaction indexes subsequently recorded at the end of the second hour. The similarities between Tables 3 and 4 are striking. The data for all Ss revealed no significant correlations between performance and subsequent satisfaction. However, when distinctions were made between appropriately and inappropriately reinforced Ss, where the performance classifications were based on the second hour's productivity scores, widely disparate performance-satisfaction relationships were

Table 4. Correlations Between Performance During Second Hour and
Satisfaction at End of Second Hour

Satisfaction Indexes	All Ss (N = 90)	Appropriately Reinforced Ss (N = 42)	Inappropriately Reinforced Ss (N = 42)
General affective tone	−.03	.55[c]	−.51[c]
General arousal	.02	.42[b]	−.26
Personal competence	.13	.48[b]	−.16
General satisfaction with pay	.03	.67[c]	−.56[c]
Equity of pay	−.09	.45[b]	−.51[c]
Adequacy of pay	−.03	.59[c]	−.57[c]
Attractiveness of fellow workers	.20	.44[b]	.04
Attractiveness of task	−.06	.32[a]	−.16

[a] $p < .05$.
[b] $p < .01$.
[c] $p < .001$.

observed. For the appropriately reinforced Ss, significant positive correlations were obtained between performance and each of the eight satisfaction indexes. For the inappropriately reinforced Ss, negative correlations were obtained between performance and seven of the eight satisfaction indexes, with four of the correlations being highly significant.

Discussion

The results of this study support the hypothesis that the nature and magnitude of the relationship between satisfaction and performance depend heavily upon the performance-reward contingencies that have been arranged. The findings are consistent with the predictions of the Porter and Lawler (1968) model, although the theoretical bases for our hypothesis differ from that model. For instance, Porter and Lawler's model implies that, under contingent reward conditions, performance causes satisfaction because performance leads to rewards, which, in turn, cause satisfaction. Our theory implies no cause-effect relationship between performance and satisfaction; instead, it stresses the performance-reinforcing as well as the satisfaction-increasing potential of contingent reinforcers.

The random reward system described here has as its organizational counterpart companies in which rewards such as pay increases and promotion are alleged to be performance-contingent but, in fact, are contingent upon factors independent of performance, such as age, seniority, or upward influence of one's supervisor. In such an organization we would expect satisfaction and performance to be unrelated.

The negatively contingent reward system is analogous to an organization in which rewards are based on factors that happen to be inversely related to performance. Such systems are not, unfortunately, as rare as one might think. One of the authors recently encountered a company in which pay increases were based on supervisor ratings, until it was discovered that the supervisors' ratings were negatively related to performance. In such an organization we would expect to find satisfaction and productivity negatively related. High performers are dissatisfied because they feel cheated; low performers are more than satisfied with their relative increases in pay.

So the importance of taking into account the contingencies between performance and rewards is again emphasized for those who seek to affect employee attitudes and/or behavior through various reward systems. If rewards are not positively contingent, then the administration of rewards will not only fail to encourage performance increments, it may also increase dissatisfaction and, ultimately, absenteeism and resignations among the highest-producing employees.

References

Bandura, A. *Principles of Behavior Modification.* New York: Holt, Rinehart & Winston, 1969.

Berlyne, D. E. "Arousal and Reinforcement." In D. Levine (Ed.), *Nebraska Symposium on Motivation.* Lincoln: University of Nebraska Press, 1967.

Bindra, D. "Neuropsychological Interpretation of the Effects of Drive and Incentive-Motivation on General Activity and Instrumental Behavior." *Psychological Review,* 1968, *75,* 1-22.

Brayfield, A. H., and Crockett, W. H. "Employee Attitudes and Employee Performance." *Psychological Bulletin,* 1955, *52,* 396-424.

Porter, L. W., and Lawler, E. E., III. *Managerial Attitudes and Performance.* Homewood, Ill.: Dorsey Press, 1968.

Rescorla, R. A., and Solomon, R. L. "Two-Process Learning Theory: Relationships Between Pavlovian Conditioning and Instrumental Learning." *Psychological Review,* 1967, *74,* 151-182.

Schwab, D. P., and Cummings, L. L. "Theories of Performance and Satisfaction: A Review." *Industrial Relations,* 1970, *9,* 408-430.

Scott, W. E., Jr. "The Development of Semantic Differential Scales as Measures of 'Morale.'" *Personnel Psychology,* 1967, *20,* 179-198.

Scott, W. E., Jr., and Rowland, K. M. "The Generality and Significance of Semantic Differential Scales as Measures of 'Morale.'" *Organizational Behavior and Human Performance,* 1970, *5,* 576-591.

Skinner, B. F. *Contingencies of Reinforcement: A Theoretical Analysis.* New York: Appleton-Century-Crofts, 1969.

Weiskrantz, L. "Emotion." In L. Weiskrantz (Ed.), *Analysis of Behavioral Change.* New York: Harper & Row, 1968.

19

∾ Equity and Intrinsic Motivation:
The Role of Choice

Robert Folger
David Rosenfield
Robert P. Hays, Jr.

There can be little doubt that the level of reward given for engaging in an activity can affect the orientation toward that activity. It is also likely that variations in the *process* whereby rewards are administered can affect task-related attitudes and behaviors (see the recent distinction between *distributive justice* and *procedural justice* made by Folger, 1977; Leventhal, 1976; Thibaut and Walker, 1975). The present research focuses on one such procedural variation, the degree of choice an individual is given prior to undertaking a task for a given wage. We suggest that the choice variable can serve to resolve some apparent discrepancies in past research. These seemingly contradictory results have emerged from the empirical traditions established by equity theory, on the one hand, and by research on "insufficient justification," on the other. After describing the typical equity and insufficient justification findings, we will briefly review pilot data that reconcile the apparent contradictions about the relationship of pay and productivity, and then we will describe an experiment that extends the predictions to research on intrinsic motivation.

Research on Pay and Productivity

Equity theory (Adams, 1965; Walster, Berscheid, and Walster, 1973) suggests that individuals attempt to make their ratios of outcomes to inputs equivalent with the corresponding ratios of other people. One way of resolving an inequity is to vary inputs by adjusting one's level of performance accordingly. When feeling overpaid, for example, a person can reduce the inequity by doing a better than average job, whereas inadequate compensation can be offset by doing inferior work. The equity literature thus predicts

Reprinted from *Journal of Personality and Social Psychology*, 1978, *36* (5), 557-564. Copyright 1978 by the American Psychological Association. Reprinted by permission.

and typically finds a direct relationship between pay and productivity (see, for example, Andrews, 1967; Lawler and O'Gara, 1967).

A different line of investigation, yielding results at odds with the equity findings, has evolved from research on insufficient justification. Several studies have shown that dissonance reduction can have behavioral implications that are the opposite of those suggested by the equity results. Weick (1964) demonstrated that those choosing to perform a task in spite of low compensation responded by enhancing their performance relative to those who were adequately compensated. A field study by Staw (1974) yielded similar findings. Other studies have shown that nonrewarded subjects do work that is superior to that done by rewarded subjects (Kruglanski, Freedman, and Zeevi, 1971; Lepper, Greene, and Nisbett, 1973). Thus, this tradition seems to imply that there should be an inverse relationship between pay and productivity.

Deci and Landy (Deci, 1975; see also Deci and others, 1977) have recently proposed a framework to reconcile the apparently conflicting predictions of equity and insufficient justification. They suggest that one reason the positive relationship between pay and productivity occurs in equity research is that the subjects "go to a job committed to doing the job but unaware of the amount of compensation" (Deci, 1975, p. 206). Subsequent knowledge of wages thus represents a low choice or fait accompli situation, conditions in which dissonance theory does *not* predict an inverse relationship between incentive level and task orientation (Cooper and Brehm, 1971). An inverse relationship will be obtained under conditions of high choice, however, as suggested by the results of forced-compliance experiments (see, for example, Calder, Ross, and Insko, 1973; Collins and Hoyt, 1972; Linder, Cooper, and Jones, 1967).

Pilot Study

We conducted a pilot study to verify this prediction of an interaction between degree of choice and level of incentive (that is, a positive relationship between pay and productivity under low choice and an inverse relationship under high choice). Subjects first completed a bogus experiment and then were enlisted to help an accomplice of the experimenter, who supposedly needed assistance setting up a project. The experimenter either told the subject to begin working on the project (low choice) or explicitly gave the subject the option of refusing to work on it (high choice); subjects were also told that their extra efforts would entitle them either to no additional credit (underpay), to twice the normal credit (overpay), or to the standard experimental compensation (equity). The results from the performance measure lent support for our hypothesis: Under high choice, lower pay led to greater productivity (the insufficient justification finding), while under low choice, lower pay led to reduced productivity (the standard equity finding).

Extension to Intrinsic Motivation

While these results show that pay and choice interact in affecting productivity, an interesting question remains: What happens when other constraints suppress performance differences? It is reasonable to assume that in many work situations productivity is maintained at a reasonably high level despite negative feelings about a task (for example, such constraints as close surveillance or fear of being fired could induce uniformly high effort on even aversive tasks). Similar pressures are also likely to be present in many laboratory experiments, since demand characteristics (Orne, 1962) and evaluation apprehension

(Rosenberg, 1965) can encourage high performance from all subjects participating in an experiment. (Note that our pilot study was designed to maximize productivity differences; hence, when subjects engaged in the target activity, they were led to believe that they were not in an experiment.) In experimental situations, then, it is necessary to look for differences on measures other than performance, such as unobtrusive measures of a person's intrinsic motivation to engage in the task.

Research on intrinsic motivation (see, for example, Deci, 1971; Lepper, Greene, and Nisbett, 1973) has shown that "oversufficient justification" can create a negative orientation toward a task (that is, substantial rewards cause reduced interest). Because our pilot study and the dissonance literature suggest that choice should be a variable mediating this effect, we designed an experiment in which both choice (high versus low) and reward (high versus low) were manipulated, and dependent measures of intrinsic motivation were assessed. We predicted that, under high choice, the more reward offered, the less likely a subject would be to infer that the task was undertaken because of its intrinsic interest. This prediction is consistent with the typical results of the intrinsic motivation studies, although it is impossible to know whether subjects in these studies felt that they had been given a choice, since choice was not explicitly manipulated. Predictions about intrinsic motivation under low choice are more problematic; we discuss the low-choice/low-pay versus low-choice/high-pay cases separately below.

People who are forced to work on a task for *inadequate compensation* (or no reward at all) should experience reduced interest in the task. When external pressures are salient ("I did it because I had to"), the causal importance of intrinsic interest in the task is likely to be discounted. Although intrinsic motivation has not been assessed previously under explicit low-choice/low-pay conditions, this reasoning seems to be consistent with Nisbett and Valins' (1971) arguments: "Lack of perceived volition or choice means causal attribution to some compelling extra-stimulus feature of the situation [hence, reduced attribution to the stimulus, the task]. This [compelling feature] may be the experimenter's demand, as in the "low-choice" control condition of a host of dissonance studies, or a large monetary inducement, as in the Festinger and Carlsmith experiment" (p. 67).

When an individual is forced to do something and is given a *large reward,* on the other hand, the attributional situation is somewhat ambiguous: Does the person experience greater or lesser external pressure than a subject in low-choice/low-pay conditions? Nisbett and Valins' remarks seem to imply that low choice and high pay can both operate to create the impression of being coerced. According to this interpretation, either factor should reduce subjects' attributions of their intrinsic motivation; hence, both factors operating in concert might combine additively to magnify perceptions of coercion, thereby further decreasing perceived interest in the task.

There is an alternative way of construing the low-choice/high pay subjects' attributions. When a person is not given the option of refusing a task assignment, high pay may not be perceived as any more coercive than low pay; the amount of pay becomes irrelevant to the perception of choice, because at either level the person is still being forced to work on the task. Forced-compliance research, however, has pointed out a way that the level of pay does have an impact: Under precisely the kinds of low-choice conditions that we are using, it has been found that positive affect from the reward can generalize to the task itself (see Insko and others, 1975). Thus, we predict that, rather than low-choice and high-pay combining additively as external constraints to reduce intrinsic motivation, low-choice/high-pay subjects should actually show greater intrinsic motivation than low-choice/low-pay subjects.

Method

Subjects and Design. Pay (low versus high) and choice (low versus high) were manipulated in a 2 × 2 between-subjects factorial design. The subjects were fifty female undergraduates (gender restricted for convenience) enrolled in introductory psychology classes, who signed up to participate in an experiment listed as taking half an hour. Each half hour of experimental participation (any amount of time up to thirty minutes) entitled students to one unit of credit, and these units were converted into points that were added to their final course grades. Of the students who participated, two subjects declined to continue when they were informed that the experiment would take longer than thirty minutes. The remaining forty-eight students were randomly assigned to conditions (N = twelve per cell), and only a single student participated in each experimental session. Debriefing revealed that no students entertained any suspicions about the experiment.

Procedure. The experimenter, one of two males, explained to arriving students that the study was part of a project designed to investigate new procedures for improving vocabulary skills. The students were told that their experimental task had been chosen because it showed promise as a technique for decreasing the drudgery associated with vocabulary work. The experimenter then described the task, which involved a modification of the crossword game "Ad Lib" (Milton Bradley Company). The students were given a stack of index cards, each card having thirteen letters written on it. They were to search through a group of twenty-six dice, each having a letter on every face, to select thirteen dice with letters that matched those on the index card. Then they were to combine those letters in a crossword fashion, using as many letters as possible and writing down their final crossword pattern on paper. They were instructed to go through as many of these index cards as they could in the time allotted.

After learning about the task, students were given six minutes of practice time. This practice time allowed premanipulation observation through a one-way mirror, which was covered by a screen so that students were unaware of its presence. These observations were made by an accomplice who was blind to the experimental condition. This observer recorded how much time the student took setting up the dice between trials. This record was used as one unobtrusive measure of effort exerted on the task, since students exerting less effort should take longer to set up the dice for the next thirteen-letter combination. In addition to this set-up time measure, a record of practice performance (how many total letters they used in forming their crosswords) was available from the paper on which the students wrote down the crosswords they had formed. These practice session data served as covariates for the corresponding measures from the test phase of the experiment (see *Dependent Measures* below).

The experimenter, who during the practice session had been out of the room determining the experimental condition, returned and introduced the manipulations as follows: "Listen, I know you only signed up for half an hour, but it turns out that, with the practice session, this experiment actually takes forty-five minutes. So you won't be through until _____" (fifteen minutes past the time to which the subjects had originally committed themselves). At this point the pay manipulation was delivered. *Low-pay* subjects were told, "Now, even though you'll be working fifteen minutes overtime, I can still only give you the thirty minutes' worth of credit that you signed up for—so you'll get *one* unit." *High-pay* subjects were told, "Now, even though you'll only be working fifteen minutes overtime, I'm going to go ahead and give you two extra units of credit—so you'll get *three* units in all."

Immediately following the manipulation of pay, the choice manipulation was given. In *low-choice* conditions the experimenter said, "Well, anyway, here's what you have to do." In *high-choice* conditions the experimenter said, "Of course, I want to emphasize that you don't have to participate if you don't want to. It's entirely up to you."

The student then worked with the Ad Lib game while the experimenter was absent from the room. During this test phase, the observer again recorded set-up times. When fifteen minutes had elapsed, the experimenter returned to the subject's room and said, "Go ahead and take a break for just a second, long enough to fill out this questionnaire about what you've done so far," implying that the student should stop only long enough to complete the questionnaire and then return to work. The experimenter handed the student a "Task Evaluation Questionnaire" and then stepped out of the room, returning a few moments after the observer, who had recorded how long the student took to complete the questionnaire, signaled that the subject was through.

After picking up the questionnaire, the experimenter announced that there would not be enough time for any more work on the task. The experimenter then said that he would fill out the student's record of participation for experimental credit. Claiming that he had forgotten to get the appropriate form, the experimenter said that he would have to go upstairs to the Psychology Department office. While the experimenter was gone, the observer recorded the amount of time that the student spent playing with the game during this "free-time" period. When the experimenter returned (after three minutes), he filled out the credit form and then directed the student to an office where she was to turn in her record of participation. The observer, who had exited unnoticed through a back door, greeted the student at the office and took the credit form. At this point, the observer mentioned that the Psychology Department was conducting a brief survey of students who had participated in experiments, and the subject was given a "Ratings of Experiment Form." This questionnaire contained several filler items as well as two questions that served as manipulation checks.

After finishing the Ratings of Experiment Form, the student left the office and was greeted by the experimenter, who said that he had forgotten to ask her a few questions. The subsequent conversation allowed the experimenter to check for any suspicions that the student might have had about the experiment. Each student was then debriefed and sworn to secrecy, and all students were given three units of credit for their participation.

Dependent Measures. The time that a student took to complete the Task Evaluation Questionnaire constituted an unobtrusive measure of intrinsic motivation. Because this questionnaire time was described to the student as a "break" from working on the task, the faster a student finished answering the questions, the more she indicated an eagerness to return to work on the task activity. The time that a student spent playing with the Ad Lib game during the free-time period (while the experimenter was allegedly away getting the credit form) was another behavioral indicator of intrinsic interest in the task. It was assumed that the more time engaged in the target activity, the greater the intrinsic motivation (see Deci, 1975; Lepper, Greene, and Nisbett, 1973).

Two other behavioral measures were designed to assess test-phase productivity, using the corresponding practice measures as covariates. These performance measures were the total number of letters formed into crossword patterns and the time spent setting up correct letters on the dice.

The Task Evaluation Questionnaire included self-report measures of liking for the task. Subjects were asked to indicate "your feelings about the task" on fifteen-point semantic differential-type scales anchored by the following bipolar adjective pairs: unpleasant-pleasant, boring-interesting, not at all entertaining-entertaining, dull-exciting, unenjoyable-enjoyable, and bad-good. The ratings on these six scales were summed to form a composite liking index. In addition, a statement on this questionnaire informed subjects that further studies using the same task were being conducted, for which volunteers would be paid $1.75 per hour. To indicate their interest in participating at a later time, students responded on a fifteen-point scale ranging from "Not at all willing" to "Very willing." These two measures, the liking index and the willingness item, were included as questionnaire supplements to the behavioral indicators of intrinsic motivation.

The Ratings of Experiment Form, which students completed in the accomplice's office, contained two questions used to validate the choice and pay manipulations. The choice manipulation check ("How much choice were you given to refuse to participate in this experiment?") ranged from "Not at all given choice" (1) to "Very explicitly given choice" (15). The pay manipulation check ("How fair was the amount of credit you received for your participation in the experiment?") ranged from "Too little credit given" (1) to "Too much credit given" (15).

Results

Manipulation Checks. Two items on the Ratings of Experiment Form assessed the extent to which the pay and choice manipulations were successful. The data from the manipulation checks were analyzed using a 2×2 univariate analysis of variance. On the manipulation check of the pay factor, a significant main effect for pay was obtained, $F(1, 44) = 39.34$, $p < .001$. High-pay subjects ($M = 10.5$) rated their compensation higher than did the low-pay subjects ($M = 6.46$). The manipulation check of perceived choice yielded a significant choice main effect, $F(1, 44) = 6.13$, $p < .02$. High-choice subjects ($M = 12.96$) perceived themselves to have had greater freedom to refuse participation than did the low-choice subjects ($M = 10.13$). No other effects were significant for either of these measures ($p > .10$ in all cases).

Multivariate Analysis. A 2×2 multivariate analysis of variance was performed on the data from the six dependent measures: total number of letters used in crossword patterns, average amount of time setting up dice, time spent answering questionnaire, liking index, willingness questionnaire item, and free time spent on target activity (log transformation). The only significant effect revealed by this analysis was the Pay × Choice interaction, $F(6, 39) = 2.49$, $p < .04$ (all other Fs < 1). Because the multivariate F is significant, we can now examine the univariate analyses to yield further insight into which of the individual variables were also significant.

Behavioral Measures. The behavioral indicators of intrinsic motivation provided strong support for our predictions: A significant Pay × Choice interaction was obtained on both the questionnaire-time and free-time measures, $F(1, 44) = 8.75$, $p < .005$, and $F(1, 44) = 5.10$, $p < .03$, respectively. Under low choice, high-pay subjects took less time to complete the questionnaire and spent more free time on the target activity than low-pay subjects. The high-choice conditions produced the opposite trend, with high-pay subjects being slower in finishing the questionnaire and having lower free-time scores than low-pay subjects (see Figure 1 and Table 1).

The other behavioral measures in this study (the number of letters formed into crossword patterns and the time spent setting up correct letters on the dice) were directly related to productivity, and these performance measures yielded nonsignificant effects ($p > .10$) for both analyses of variance and covariance (using the practice-session measures as covariates).

Questionnaire Items. The liking index, composed of task ratings on six semantic

Figure 1. Effect of Choice and Pay on Free Time

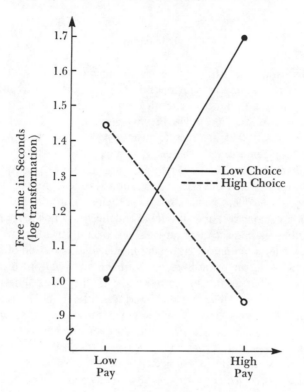

differential-type scales, and the willingness item, designed as a behavioroid assessment of intrinsic motivation, both produced results that were consistent with the results on the questionnaire-time and free-time measures (Table 1). That is, high pay tended to lead to lower liking and less willingness to work on the task in the future in the high-choice conditions, but to greater liking and more willingness to work on the task in the future in the low-choice conditions. However, neither of these Pay × Choice interactions reached signifi-

Table 1. Treatment Means for Questionnaire Time, Free Time, Liking Index, and Willingness Item

Measure	Low Choice		High Choice	
	Low Pay	High Pay	Low Pay	High Pay
Questionnaire time[a]	97.75	71.17	62.83	96.50
Free time[b]	1.00	1.69	1.44	.94
Liking index[c]	68.42	78.92	72.83	70.92
Willingness item[d]	8.33	10.33	11.92	10.25

[a]Time in seconds, higher numbers indicating more time taken to complete questionnaire.

[b]Logarithmic transformation of time in seconds, higher numbers indicating more time spent playing with Ad Lib game.

[c]Composite formed by summing six 15-point scales, higher numbers indicating greater liking for the task.

[d]Higher numbers indicate greater willingness to participate in future: 15-point scale.

cance: $F(1, 44) = 2.75$, $p < .11$, for the liking index, and $F(1, 44) = 1.84$, $p < .19$, for willingness.

Discussion

Before discussing these findings, let us consider them in light of the paradox facing someone in charge of administering rewards. Suppose that this hypothetical allocator, cognizant of the literature on intrinsic motivation, is worried about the potentially deleterious consequences of large incentives. Previous insufficient and oversufficient justification experiments suggest that in order to sustain greater involvement in the rewarded activity, the less compensation the better. A familiarity with equity research, however, would caution that people are apt to respond unfavorably to inadequate levels of payment. Caught on the horns of this dilemma, administrators might well decide to disregard the confusing empirical evidence and fall back on their own intuitions.

Our results demonstrate that it is more fruitful to acknowledge the importance of choice in mediating the impact of rewards on intrinsic motivation. When students were informed about the level of compensation and then given the option of refusing to engage in the target activity, larger rewards reduced intrinsic motivation: high-choice/high-pay subjects were less eager to return to the task (that is, they took longer to complete the questionnaire during their "break") and showed less interest in the activity during their "free time" than high-choice/low-pay subjects. On the other hand, when subjects were not given any choice about their assignment, the pay variable had the opposite effect: questionnaire-time scores were faster and free-time scores higher for low-choice/high-pay subjects than for low-choice/low-pay subjects.

Qualification of Overjustification Effect. Thus, the interaction obtained on the intrinsic motivation measures serves to qualify what has been termed the "overjustification hypothesis" (that substantial extrinsic rewards reduce intrinsic motivation), since an overjustification effect was found only under high choice. Previous investigators (Calder and Staw, 1975; Deci, 1975; Kruglanski, Freedman, and Zeevi, 1971; Lepper, Greene, and Nisbett, 1973; Ross, 1977; Staw, 1976) have stated that extrinsic rewards must be expected, salient, and perceived as means to an end in order to undermine subsequent interest in the rewarded activity. The last of these conditions, the perceived instrumental character of rewards, is more likely to be met when individuals make a conscious decision whether to accept or reject the offer of rewards, because it is only in these high-choice situations that rewards assume the role of inducements or incentives. The person proffering rewards prior to choice is in effect saying, "If you do x, I will pay you y"; hence, the rewards can be seen as instrumental in determining whether to undertake the task. When they are seen primarily as inducements to perform the task, large rewards (and not intrinsic interest in the task) are likely to be perceived as the reason for performing the task.

This interpretation explains why the inverse relationship between level of payment and degree of interest did not hold under low-choice conditions. In such situations, the rewards are *not* offered as inducements for undertaking a task; rather, the task is an assignment that must be carried out, and the rewards are simply compensation associated with a job. Thus, in the low-choice situations, choice and pay did not combine additively to doubly increase the perceived pressure to work on the task and to thereby further decrease intrinsic motivation. Instead, higher pay in the low-choice situation tended to increase intrinsic motivation.

Implications. Let us return now to our hypothetical allocator, locked in the throes of a conflict over what level of rewards to administer. Based on our arguments, it is likely that providing minimal compensation will be advantageous for maintaining intrinsic motivation only when the statement of wages is an offer that a person feels free to accept or reject. This freedom might exist during initial contract negotiations with a new employee, for example. But allocators must realize that often people feel constrained to undertake a task regardless of the pay. Many employees are reluctant to quit their jobs because of the favorable location, the nature of the work, the unavailability of viable alternatives, or the cost involved in pursuing other options. Such external constraints can induce a sense of low freedom of choice. When a person experiences little choice in undertaking or continuing in an activity, the allocator who gives that person inadequate compensation is following a potentially disastrous policy: those who feel unfairly underpaid will respond negatively, whereas higher levels of reward not only fail to reduce interest but may actually be necessary to sustain it.

In summary, the distinction between low-choice and high-choice situations implies that investigators should also distinguish between two types of rewards: rewards as compensation for an activity to which a person already feels constrained versus rewards as incentives offered to induce a person to engage in the activity. Our research suggests that equity effects predominate when rewards are of the former type, whereas insufficient/oversufficient justification effects predominate when the latter aspect of rewards is most salient. This distinction points out the need for further investigations to clarify the nature of rewards, and our research suggests that future studies should attend to those aspects of allocation procedures that give different connotations to rewards.

References

Adams, J. S. "Inequity in Social Exchange." In L. Berkowitz (Ed.), *Advances in Experimental Social Psychology*. Vol. 2. New York: Academic Press, 1965.

Andrews, I. R. "Wage Inequity and Job Performance: An Experimental Study." *Journal of Applied Psychology,* 1967, *51,* 39-45.

Calder, B. J., Ross, M., and Insko, C. A. "Attitude Change and Attitude Attribution: Effects of Incentive, Choice, and Consequences." *Journal of Personality and Social Psychology,* 1973, *25,* 84-99.

Calder, B. J., and Staw, B. M. "Interaction of Intrinsic and Extrinsic Motivation: Some Methodological Notes." *Journal of Personality and Social Psychology,* 1975, *31,* 76-80.

Collins, B. E., and Hoyt, M. F. "Personal Responsibility for Consequences: An Integration of the 'Forced Compliance' Literature." *Journal of Experimental Social Psychology,* 1972, *8,* 558-593.

Cooper, J., and Brehm, J. W. "Prechoice Awareness of Relative Deprivation as a Determinant of Cognitive Dissonance." *Journal of Experimental Social Psychology,* 1971, *7,* 571-581.

Deci, E. L. "Effects of Externally Mediated Rewards on Intrinsic Motivation." *Journal of Personality and Social Psychology,* 1971, *18,* 105-115.

Deci, E. L. *Intrinsic Motivation.* New York: Plenum, 1975.

Deci, E. L., and others. "Toward Reconciling Equity Theory and Insufficient Justification." *Personality and Social Psychology Bulletin,* 1977, *3,* 224-227.

Folger, R. "Distributive and Procedural Justice: Combined Impact of 'Voice' and Improvement on Experienced Inequity." *Journal of Personality and Social Psychology,* 1977, *35,* 108-119.

Insko, C. A., and others. "A Balance Theory Interpretation of Dissonance." *Psychological Review,* 1975, *82,* 169-183.

Kruglanski, A. W., Freedman, I., and Zeevi, G. "The Effects of Extrinsic Incentive on Some Qualitative Aspects of Task Performance." *Journal of Personality,* 1971, *39,* 606-617.

Lawler, E. E., III, and O'Gara, P. W. "Effects of Inequity Produced by Underpayment on Work Output, Work Quality, and Attitudes Toward Work." *Journal of Applied Psychology,* 1967, *51,* 403-410.

Lepper, M. R., Greene, D., and Nisbett, R. E. "Undermining Children's Intrinsic Interest with Extrinsic Reward: A Test of the 'Oversufficient Justification' Hypothesis." *Journal of Personality and Social Psychology,* 1973, *28,* 129-137.

Leventhal, G. W. *Fairness in Social Relationships.* Morristown, N.J.: General Learning Press, 1976.

Linder, D. E., Cooper, J., and Jones, E. E. "Decision Freedom as a Determinant of the Role of Incentive Magnitude in Attitude Change." *Journal of Personality and Social Psychology,* 1967, *6,* 245-254.

Nisbett, R. E., and Valins, S. *Perceiving the Causes of One's Own Behavior.* Morristown, N.J.: General Learning Press, 1971.

Nisbett, R. E., and Wilson, T. D. "Telling More Than We Can Know: Verbal Reports on Mental Processes." *Psychological Review,* 1977, *84,* 231-259.

Orne, M. T. "On the Social Psychology of the Psychological Experiment: With Particular Reference to Demand Characteristics and Their Implications." *American Psychologist,* 1962, *17,* 776-783.

Rosenberg, M. J. "When Dissonance Fails: On Eliminating Evaluation Apprehension from Attitude Measurement." *Journal of Personality and Social Psychology,* 1965, *1,* 28-42.

Ross, M. "The Self-Perception of Intrinsic Motivation." In J. H. Harvey, W. J. Ickes, and R. F. Kidd (Eds.), *New Directions in Attribution Research.* Vol. 1. Hillsdale, N.J.: Erlbaum, 1977.

Staw, B. M. "Attitudinal and Behavioral Consequences of Changing a Major Organizational Reward: A Natural Field Experiment." *Journal of Personality and Social Psychology,* 1974, *29,* 742-751.

Staw, B. M. *Intrinsic and Extrinsic Motivation.* Morristown, N.J.: General Learning Press, 1976.

Thibaut, J., and Walker, L. *Procedural Justice: A Psychological Analysis.* Hillsdale, N.J.: Erlbaum, 1975.

Walster, E., Berscheid, E., and Walster, G. W. "New Directions in Equity Research." *Journal of Personality and Social Psychology,* 1973, *25,* 151-176.

Weick, K. E. "Reduction of Cognitive Dissonance Through Task Enhancement and Effort Expenditure." *Journal of Abnormal and Social Psychology,* 1964, *68,* 533-539.

20

What Workers Want: Factor Analyses of Important Ratings of Job Facets

Robert P. Quinn
William Cobb, Jr.

The question of what American workers want out of their jobs has been answered largely in terms of generalities. It has been asserted, for example, that women are less "intrinsically" oriented toward their jobs than men and are more concerned than men with relations with their co-workers. Blacks, or at least underprivileged blacks, have been described as being more "financially oriented" to their jobs than whites and less concerned with the "content" of their jobs. For years the issue has existed about the extent to which the typical American worker is motivated by economic, as opposed to noneconomic, considerations, and the classic debate as to whether the typical worker better conforms to the abstract model of "the economic man" rather than "the self-actualizing man" persists.

Such generalities as these presuppose that the motivational orientations of workers toward their jobs can be adequately described by a limited number of terms like "intrinsic orientation," "concern with relations with co-workers," "financially oriented," "concerned with job content," "economically oriented," "noneconomically oriented," and so on. Some of these terms, as well as many others not cited, have clear theoretical linkages and by virtue of this attain respectability; others are merely shorthand phrases intended to describe an ill-defined set of matters in which workers may be interested.

All these terms represent attempts to impose some sort of conceptual order upon an otherwise vast and exquisitely localized array of matters that may be of concern to workers. Unless such basic dimensions are adequately identified, any analysis that attempts to estimate what workers want from their jobs will be mired in miscellany. For lack of any empirical or theoretical justification for combining importance ratings of job facets, no measures of individual differences can be constructed that can represent reliably the more general aspects of workers' orientations toward their jobs. That a worker

Reprinted in abridged form from *The 1972-73 Quality of Employment Survey: Continuing Chronicles of an Unfinished Enterprise* (Ann Arbor: Institute for Social Research, 1974), pp. 27-84, with permission of the authors and the Institute for Social Research.

assigns a high importance to good fringe benefits, for example, could conceivably be interpreted as indicating that he is extrinsically or financially oriented toward his job. But combining his importance ratings of fringe benefits with his importance ratings of his basic pay will produce a more reliable indicator of his concern with the financial aspects of his job only if the two importance ratings are positively correlated. Are they? And to what extent should his ratings of the importance to him of job security be regarded as also indicating his concern with financial matters? Can any empirical justification be offered for constructing for a worker an index score which summarizes the overall level of importance he assigns to economic matters? Or his concern with the intrinsic aspects of his job? Or his concern with his relations with co-workers? Or, for that matter, any other presumably "basic" dimension of job-related motivation that one may name?

These questions obviously invite factor analytic answers that not only may identify basic dimensions of workers' importance ratings of job facets but may suggest as well an appropriate conceptual language for describing what workers want. Although many previous factor analytic studies have indeed suggested such dimensions, the identification of these dimensions has been based exclusively upon factor analyses of workers' ratings of their *satisfaction* with various facets of their jobs. There is little a priori reason to think that the dimensions identified in such analyses should be equally qualified to organize workers' ratings of the *importance* to them of these same facets.

One of the ultimate aims of the present study was to identify those facets of work that were most important to a national probability sample of American workers. Ideally, workers' importance ratings of facets of their jobs would have been summarized, interpreted, and reported in terms of those dimensions that had already been reliably identified in previous investigations. Unfortunately, there were no such previous investigations. Lacking any empirically justified means of consolidating workers' importance ratings, a possible basis of organizing workers' importance ratings was sought instead in previous factor analytic studies of workers' job-satisfaction ratings.

Even these factor analytic studies failed to provide consistent information with regard to what may be the basic dimensions of job satisfaction. Herzberg and associates (1957) identified six factors as having emerged in several previous factor analytic studies of job satisfaction: general satisfaction and morale, attitudes toward the company and its policies, satisfaction with intrinsic aspects of the job, attitudes toward immediate supervision, attitudes toward satisfaction of aspirations, and satisfaction with conditions of present job. Vroom's (1964) review suggested that seven factors of job satisfaction might exist: attitudes toward the company and company management, attitudes toward promotional opportunities, attitudes toward job content, attitudes toward supervision, attitudes toward financial rewards, attitudes toward working conditions, and attitudes toward co-workers. In a more critical review of the previous factor analytic work on job satisfaction prior to their development of a new job-satisfaction measure, Smith, Kendall, and Hulin (1969) concluded that "the factors which seem to emerge most consistently are a general factor, a pay and material-rewards factor, a factor dealing with the work itself, a supervision factor, and a factor related to the other workers on the job. Subsequent literature has not greatly changed this picture.... We originally planned to investigate only four areas of satisfaction. These were work, pay and promotions (as a combined area), supervision, and co-workers. Our preliminary analyses, however, indicated quite clearly that the pay-and-promotions factor was breaking down into two clearly discriminable although correlated subfactors, one dealing specifically with pay, and one dealing with promotional opportunities. Therefore, our analyses and our final scales have been designed around five areas of job satisfaction: work, pay, promotions, supervision, and co-workers" (p. 30).

The three reviews of factor analytic studies of job satisfaction just cited, plus the even more discouraging review by Robinson, Athanasiou, and Head (1969), indicated that there was not a great deal of empirical agreement as to what are the basic dimensions of job satisfaction. Thus, faced both with an absence of reliable factor analytic studies of workers' importance ratings and with a large yet inconclusive and often contradictory array of factor analytic studies of job-satisfaction ratings, the present study was compelled to fall back upon its own factor analysis of workers' importance ratings.

The results of these factor analyses are described below and are intended to answer several questions concerning what American workers regard as important to them in their jobs. First, what are the basic dimensions underlying workers' importance ratings of job facets? This question will be answered through a factor analysis performed upon data obtained from a random half-sample of workers selected from the study's full sample. Second, how reliable are the results of this factor analysis? This will be answered through an attempted replication of the factor structure on a second random half-sample of workers.

Method

Sample. Personal interviews were conducted with a national probability sample of 1,533 persons who were living in households, were 16 years old or older, and were working for pay for twenty hours a week or more. Since interviews were obtained from all eligible workers in a household, each worker had an equal probability of being selected; as a result, the sample was self-weighting. Additional details concerning sampling and other aspects of the survey that provided data for the present analysis are provided by Quinn and associates (1971).

Measures. The analysis was performed on workers' ratings of twenty-five facets of jobs in terms of how important each facet was to the worker in his job. Each facet was represented by a descriptive statement (for example, "the pay is good") printed on an IBM card. At the beginning of each interview, the worker was given these twenty-five cards as well as four IBM cards with a response category printed on each ("Very Important," "Somewhat Important," "Not Too Important," and "Not at All Important"). The question asked to elicit the importance ratings was: "The next question involves things a person may or may not look for in a job. Some of these things are on this set of cards. People differ a lot in terms of which of these things are more important to them. We'd like to know how important to *you* each of these things is. Please sort each card into one of the four groupings I have here, according to how *important* each thing is to *you*." The twenty-five items sorted under these instructions are listed in Table 1. After the four response cards were placed in front of the respondent, he was asked to put each of the descriptive statements on top of the response card that best indicated the importance to him of the condition described. No restriction was made as to how many cards could be put in each pile. Once the worker had finished sorting his cards, the four piles were assembled and submitted for direct computer scoring. This automatic card-sort technique was developed by Hunt, Schupp, and Cobb (1966).

At the end of the interview, the worker was asked to sort, under the same categories as the importance items, a set of twenty-five cards containing identical response statements under the instructions "I'd like you to put each card in the pile which best reflects *how true* you feel each is of *your* job." These instructions are referred to below as statements reflecting aspects of "Job Satisfaction."

The items that were rated in terms of their importance and satisfaction were scarcely new ones. Most had been appropriated from other measures of job satisfaction, particularly from the set of coding categories used in a prior national survey by Kilpatrick, Cummings, and Jennings (1964). In addition, the factor analytic studies of job satisfaction cited earlier were consulted to insure that job facets selected would represent most of the factors of job satisfaction that had been consistently identified in past research. However, since this was a national survey administered to workers in a wide range of occupational settings, there were two prominent omissions and one addition.

A frequently identified factor in job-satisfaction studies is satisfaction with "Company and Management." No items touching upon this aspect of job satisfaction were included, for three reasons. First, such questions would obviously have been meaningless to the 13.4 percent of the sample who were self-employed. Second, it was difficult to select from among the phrases "your employer," "your company," or "the management of your company" a term that would have had a common type of referent for workers in different types of establishments.

A second major omission was of any items referring to workers' jobs in terms of their usefulness or importance to society. Although several such items were included in the early pretests of the present survey, none of these "social relevance" items exhibited sufficient variance to warrant their inclusion in the final stages of data collection. Major additions to the item pool were items concerning the adequacy of the resources the worker received for doing his job.

Most studies of job satisfaction have ignored the question of resource adequacy. Kahn and Quinn (1970) have noted that even completely clear and conflict-free expectations about one's job behavior may be a source of stress if the role occupant does not have at his disposal adequate resources with which to comply with these expectations. Two major points of origin of such resources are cited by Kahn and Quinn: the role occupant himself and his organizational environment. Four general categories of organizational resources were included in the pool of items to be rated in the present study: technical information, facilities, power, and time.

Procedures. In order to identify dimensions which might underlie the importance ratings of the twenty-five job facets, the intercorrelations among the items were factor-analyzed. Several factor analyses were conducted with data from random subsamples of various sizes as well as with data from subsamples defined by the demographic characteristics of age, sex, race, and education. All factor analyses employed the principal axes method, with initial communalities estimated by squared multiple correlations. Kaiser's criterion and an orthogonal rotation principle were used.

Most of the questions answered below involved comparisons among factor structures based upon data obtained from different subsamples of workers. Factor comparisons were made through the use of a computer program derived from the Burt, Tucker, and Wrigley statistical paradigm for assessing factor similarity (Harmon, 1960). Given two factor matrices based on identical input variables, the program computes Coefficients of Interfactor Similarity (CIFSs) between all possible pairs of factors. These CIFSs range from −1.00 to 1.00. While it is tempting to think of CIFSs in correlational terms, they are in fact index scores, and the same standards of statistical significance that apply to Pearson *r*s do not apply to the CIFSs. Tucker (1951) suggests accepting CIFSs of .94 or greater as indicating congruent factors.

Results

Identifying the Basic Factor Structure. The Basic Factor Structure (BFS) was based on a factor analysis of the intercorrelations among the twenty-five importance ratings obtained from a random half-sample (*N* = 767) of respondents. The results of this factor analysis are presented in Table 1.

Table 1. Loadings of Importance Ratings of 25 Job Facets on Five Factors

	Factor				
	I	II	III	IV	V
				Relations with	
Job Facet	Comfort	Challenge	Pay	Co-workers	Resources
I have enough time to get the job done.	50	17	11	−01	42
The hours are good.	59	−08	16	17	11
Travel to and from work is convenient.	41	07	17	18	12
Physical surroundings are pleasant.	51	18	15	23	14
I am free from conflicting demands that other people make of me.	56	26	10	03	17
I can forget about my personal problems.	55	33	−07	18	05
I am not asked to do excessive amounts of work.	47	−05	11	−01	10
The work is interesting.	−06	51	28	30	18
I have enough authority to do my job.	17	50	12	07	36
I have an opportunity to develop my special abilities.	−12	56	12	22	20
I can see the results of my work.	24	50	02	24	22
I am given a chance to do the things I do best.	21	54	23	04	18
I am given a lot of freedom to decide how I do my work.	10	64	13	−01	09
The problems I am asked to solve are hard enough.	15	60	03	08	04
The pay is good.	14	16	60	10	17
The job security is good.	30	11	51	10	16
My fringe benefits are good.	36	10	58	08	15
My co-workers are friendly and helpful.	19	24	17	56	24
I am given a lot of chances to make friends.	23	08	13	51	06
I receive enough help and equipment to get the job done.	16	15	20	06	56
I have enough information to get the job done.	17	28	20	14	45
My responsibilities are clearly defined.	33	19	18	20	46
My supervisor is competent in doing his job.	22	21	04	30	46
My supervisor is very concerned about the welfare of those under him.	38	21	10	34	29
The chances for promotion are good.	−04	28	37	24	03

Note: Decimal points have been omitted.

Factor I of the BFS, the Comfort factor, described a worker's desire for a job which provided solid creature comfort and which presented no problems for him. There was no indication that a worker endorsing the items on this factor wished his job to be exciting, interesting, or challenging—only serene and easy—in short, a "soft" job. Factor II, Challenge, reflected a worker's desire to be stimulated and challenged by his job and to be able to exercise his acquired skills in his work. This factor corresponded somewhat to what in other factor analytic studies of job satisfaction had been identified as a "type of work" factor. Factors I and II, viewed in opposition to each other, corresponded to some degree to the conceptual distinction between extrinsic and intrinsic sources of job satisfaction. The Challenge factor was certainly akin to intrinsic satisfaction; Comfort, however, was not simply another name for extrinsic satisfaction, since it excluded such matters as pay, fringe benefits, and job security—all of which are traditionally regarded as extrinsic characteristics. Pay, fringe benefits, and job security comprised instead a factor of their own, which was orthogonal to the Comfort factor; this factor, Factor III, is not surprisingly labeled in later tables as Financial Rewards. Factor IV contained only two items, both of which concerned Relations with Co-workers. This factor had appeared frequently in factor analyses of job satisfaction in other studies. The fifth and final factor, Resources, represented workers' wishes for adequate resources with which to do their jobs well—help, equipment, information, and competent supervision.

Replicability of the Basic Factor Structure on a Comparable Sample. The reliability of the BFS was estimated through an attempted replication of the BFS employing the second random half-sample of 755 workers; that is, all those who had not been included in the random half-sample whose importance ratings initially determined the BFS. Five factors emerged in the analysis of importance ratings obtained from this second random half-sample of workers. The CIFSs in Table 2 indicated that there was substantial congruence, defined by CIFSs of .94 or greater, between the BFS and its attempted replication on the presumably equivalent second half-sample.

The one conspicuous exception occurred with regard to the Relations with Co-workers factor, for which the CIFS was only .88. As a whole, Table 2 shows, the Relations with Co-workers factor was by far the least stable of the five factors of the BFS.

Comparison of Factor Analyses Based on Importance and Satisfaction Ratings. Although the selection of job facets to be rated by workers in terms of their importance was in part determined by a review of previous factor analytic studies of job satisfaction, the factor analytic investigation in the present study was directed to the importance ratings of these facets rather than to their satisfaction ratings. Would the BFS of these job facets have been the same had the satisfaction ratings rather than the importance ones been factor-analyzed? To answer this question, a factor analysis was performed on the intercorrelations among the same set of twenty-five job facets that had been rated by each worker under the "job-satisfaction" instructions. This factor analysis produced six factors; and five of these could be identified as corresponding to the five factors of the BFS. The sixth factor was a Quality of Supervision factor, and its salient items and their loadings were: "My supervisor is competent in doing his job," factor loading = .64, and "My supervisor is very concerned about the welfare of those under him," factor loading = .77.

According to Table 2, only two of the factors of the BFS were statistically congruent with those obtained in the analysis of the satisfaction ratings. Both the Challenge factor and the Relations with Co-workers factor had CIFSs of .94. While the congruence between the Financial Rewards factor identified in the importance and satisfaction ratings (CIFS = .92) was below the minimal acceptable level, the items that were salient on

Table 2. Coefficients of Interfactor Similarity

Groups Compared	N	Comfort	Chal- lenge	Finan- cial Rewards	Relations with Co- workers	Resources
First random half-sample (BFS)	767					
Second random half- sample	755	.98	.98	.94	.88	.97
First random half-sample (BFS)	767					
First random half-sample (satisfaction items)	754	.82	.94	.92	.94	.86
First random half-sample (BFS)	767	.98	.99	.96	.90	.97
Random sample of 600	600					
First random half-sample (BFS)	767	.97	.95	.92	.80	.93
Random sample of 300	300					
First random half-sample (BFS)	767	.93	.89	.78	.82	.90
Random sample of 100	100					
Men	980	.96	.99	.93	.79	.96
Women	529					
Whites	1,335	.85	.86	.79	.75	.88
Blacks	157					
High school education or less	1,072					
Some college education or more	460	.98	.92	.93	.88	.97
Under 45 years old	911	.97	.93	.96	.80	.96
45 years old or older	593					

the two factors were identical. If identity of salient items is regarded as indicating factor congruence, the two Financial Rewards factors can be regarded as congruent in spite of their CIFSs of .92.

Conclusion

The pivotal factor analysis, based upon data obtained from a random half-sample of workers, indicated that the twenty-five facets of jobs that had been rated by workers in terms of their importance to them could be represented adequately by five dimensions. The five orthogonal factors that emerged in this analysis were readily interpretable and were provisionally designated as referring to Comfort, Challenge, Financial Rewards, Relations with Co-workers, and Resources. Comparisons of factor analyses based on two randomly selected half-samples of workers further indicated that four of these factors were highly replicable. The one factor that fell below the acceptable level of statistically defined replicability was the two-item factor concerning Relations with Co-workers. The lower replicability of this factor may have been due to its containing a "double-barreled" question, that which referred to one's co-workers as being "friendly" *and* "helpful."

The factor analysis of the *satisfaction* ratings yielded not five but six factors, the sixth defined by two items: "My supervisor is competent in doing his job" and "My supervisor is concerned about the welfare of those under him." This supervision factor did not, however, appear in the factor analysis of importance ratings. In the analysis of importance ratings, the item referring to the concern exhibited by one's supervisor was not a salient item on any of the five factors, and that referring to the competence of a worker's supervisor appeared as a part of the Resources factor. In terms of workers' desires, therefore, good supervision, or at least competent supervision, appeared to be just one "special case" of their general desires to be provided with the resources necessary for doing a good job.

The factor analysis that produced the BFS was the first such analysis to be performed with data obtained from a national probability sample of workers. Its prima facie generalizability was, therefore, greater than that of any analyses based upon data that could be obtained from workers in single companies or occupational situations.

The number and content of the factors identified in this study differed in several respects from those reported in previous factor analytic studies of questionnaire items or other materials relevant to job satisfaction. Several theories view work-related motivation or satisfaction in terms of dichotomies: economic versus noneconomic; intrinsic versus extrinsic; content versus context; motivation versus hygiene; satisfiers versus dissatisfiers. A perhaps overly literal application of any of these dichotomous or "two-factor" approaches to the present study's factor analysis might have predicted that the analysis would have uncovered only two factors, each of which corresponded to one term of the dichotomy. Instead, the analysis disclosed five factors. The present study was not alone in this regard, since previous factor analytic studies of job satisfaction have never, to the best of our knowledge, yielded any such neat "two-factor" brace of dimensions corresponding to the two terms of any of these dichotomies. Nor, according to many proponents of such dichotomies, should any factor analysis be expected to do so. These dichotomies, it is at times argued, correspond to "higher-order" levels of organization of work motivation and job satisfaction. The existence of, or at least the conceptual utility of, such dichotomous principles does not, according to some, require justification through factor analytic techniques.

Several points of correspondence were nevertheless recognizable between the importance factors identified in this study and those identified in previous factor analytic studies of job satisfaction. The clearest replication of a previously identified factor occurred with reference to this study's Financial Rewards factor. In addition to a Financial Rewards factor, the factors most successfully repeated from previous studies appeared to have been those concerning opportunities for advancement and attitudes toward supervision. Since only one question about promotional opportunities was asked in the present study, the emergence of a promotional opportunities factor was unlikely, and it did in fact fail to appear in the analysis of importance ratings. Herzberg and associates (1957), Vroom (1964), and Smith, Kendall, and Hulin (1969) also report the existence of factors that they describe respectively as "satisfaction with intrinsic aspects of the job," "attitudes toward job content," and attitudes concerning "the work itself." The Challenge factor was clearly in the same ballpark as these factors. At the same time, both the Comfort and Resources factors (especially the latter) also touched upon aspects of "the work itself."

References

Guilford, J. *Psychometric Methods.* New York: McGraw-Hill, 1954.

Harmon, H. *Modern Factor Analysis.* Chicago: University of Chicago Press, 1960.

Herzberg, F., and others. *Job Attitudes: Review of Research and Opinion.* Pittsburgh: Psychological Service of Pittsburgh, 1957.

Hunt, P., Schupp, D., and Cobb, S. *An Automated Self-Report Technique.* Ann Arbor: Survey Research Center, University of Michigan, 1966.

Kahn, R., and Quinn, R. "Role Stress: A Framework for Analysis." In A. McLean (Ed.), *Occupational Mental Health.* Chicago: Rand McNally, 1970.

Kilpatrick, F., Cummings, M., Jr., and Jennings, M. *Source Book of a Study of Occupational Values and the Image of the Federal Service.* Washington, D.C.: Brookings Institution, 1964.

Quinn, R. P., and others. *Survey of Working Conditions.* Document Number 2916-0001. Washington, D.C.: U.S. Government Printing Office, 1971.

Robinson, J., Athanasiou, R., and Head, K. *Measures of Occupational Attitudes and Occupational Characteristics.* Ann Arbor: Survey Research Center, University of Michigan, 1969.

Smith, P., Kendall, L., and Hulin, C. *The Measurement of Satisfaction in Work and Retirement: A Strategy for the Study of Attitudes.* Chicago: Rand McNally, 1969.

Tucker, L. *A Method for Synthesis of Factor Analysis Studies.* Personnel Research Section Report, No. 984. Washington, D.C.: Department of the Army, 1951.

Vroom, V. *Work and Motivation.* New York: Wiley, 1964.

21

Autonomy and Participation at Work

Bertil Gardell

Theoretical Aspects and Definition

The question of the relationships between job design and job involvement and their bearing on industrial democracy has been highlighted by the experiments with "autonomous groups" that have been conducted in Norway by Thorsrud (Thorsrud and Emery, 1969). One of the fundamental ideas here seems to be that an active orientation toward working life and the demand for worker participation in company affairs are generally favored by autonomy and the right to determine activities in one's own job. Hypotheses to this effect have also been formulated by Dahlström (1969). In a study of the human condition in large-scale highly mechanized industry in Sweden, the most important finding was that, at workplaces where production technology and organization restrict the individual's say in his own job performance, there arises a passive, alienative type of adjustment that stresses the instrumentality of work. In other words, the job is valued only as a means for the satisfaction of needs via different forms of consumption. The work itself is considered trivial and uninteresting, which in our terminology means that it will be assigned a low needs-satisfying value (Gardell, 1971a). The findings also show that these feelings of alienation go together with generally lower life satisfactions, with lower self-confidence, and with a higher degree of anxiety. Given the value judgments implicit in the study, we hold these relationships to indicate that the alienative adjustment model makes a poor mechanism for resolving conflicts between the efficiency demanded by the industrial production system and the individual's need for autonomy and the full realization of his human resources.

It is now relevant to ask: Does the passive, alienative adjustment model, and the lower self-confidence that flows from it, also lower aspirations to influence decisions in the firm ("participative management")? In other words, we want to know whether the prospects for involving broader groups in the work organization's decision-making processes—and hence in a change of their own situation in the job world—are influenced by production technology and work design and by the interest or lack of interest in work that is generated thereby. The experiments made by Thorsrud and his colleagues in Norway have apparently not been evaluated from this aspect, even though he operates with a

Reprinted from *Human Relations,* 1977, *30* (6), 515-533, with permission of the author and Plenum Publishing Corporation.

hypothesis of this nature; on the contrary, Thorsrud seems to have confined himself to certain attempts to evaluate the connection between increased autonomy, on the one hand, and work commitment and productivity, on the other hand. The foregoing also seems to hold true of most experiments with job enrichment and other types of organizational changes that strive toward greater autonomy, but in contrast with Thorsrud's work these experiments have usually not been fitted into the larger perspective of industrial democracy. However, the experiences gained to date—including our own findings—suggest that increased autonomy is accompanied by increased interest in work, from which it follows that these studies can be held to have confirmed Stage 1 of the hypothesis.

Our research material affords certain opportunities to study the relationship in a nonexperimental situation between objectively existing differences as regards autonomy at work, job involvement, and aspirations to influence, both for the individual and for the employees as a group. Consequently, it would be possible to test the second stage of the hypothesis; namely, that increased autonomy plus related greater commitment to work and increased self-confidence will intensify aspirations to exercise personal influence over decisions affecting not only the immediate job but also over higher-level decisions relating to the firm's management, finances, technological advance, and so forth. The assumption we are going to test may be schematically summarized in the following model:

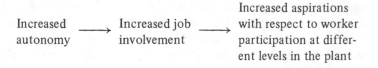

Even if one can never be quite confident about the meaning of cross-sectional relationships, we feel that there are certain methodological advantages in testing the assumption of a relationship between autonomy at work and aspirations to decision-making influence in a nonexperimental situation, since then we need not be apprehensive that any experimental effect will make it hard to interpret the relationship obtained. This risk of unintended experimental effects will always arise in a planned change situation, especially if the changes involve such sensitive issues as worker participation in management decisions. At the same time, of course, it is only by means of real-life experiments or changes that ideas can be subjected to practical application and testing. We feel that it may be easier to evaluate such experiments by having access at the same time to data from nonexperimental situations and that our study may be able to further understanding of how production technology affects the potentialities for getting broader groups committed to greater involvement in the decision processes of the employing firm.

Adapting a terminology introduced by Dahlström (1969, pp. 59-60), we have tried to uphold two distinctions. The first concerns the *form* of influence or participation, where we distinguish between (a) direct decision-making influence for oneself (that is, *personal level*) and (b) decision-making influence for the employees as a collective (that is, *group level*). The latter form refers to representative democracy at workplaces; that is, to participation of the kind that is looked after by the formal system of industrial relations. The other distinction refers to the *substance* of participation, where we distinguish between (a) autonomy over work performance (that is, *job level*), (b) decision-making influence over the personal work situation (that is, *team/department level*), and (c) decision-making influence over general management policy (that is, *plant level*).

As to the strength and diffusion of worker demands, we assume that these will vary with the actual existing opportunities for participation. The picture we therefore envisage is one where personal aspirations to decision-making influence at job and team levels will be more widespread than personal aspirations to influence decisions at plant level. The actual state of affairs, of course, is for the workers to have most to say about doing their own jobs and least about how their company is run, so any aspirations in the latter respect should reasonably be expected to be adjusted to square with this reality. As to aspirations on the part of employees to exercise influence as a collective, we proceed on the following tentative assumption. Since Sweden has long had national agreements on collaboration and worker participation, thereby serving to institutionalize this form of influence in our system of collective bargaining, the individual employees will translate part of their aspirations to influence plant-level decision processes to this system of representative democracy. Accordingly, we expect personal aspirations to direct influence at plant level to be lower than aspirations to influence the same decision processes through the medium of employee representatives. We assume, however, that such aspirations, both for oneself and for the employees as a group, will intensify with growing autonomy in the individual job. These problems will be dealt with in the next section.

At the same time, we expect *the degree of success for representative democracy* to affect the individual worker's aspiration to greater personal influence. This problem will be discussed in the section headed "Aspirations to Increased Collective Influence."

The opportunities open to us are to proceed from the actual differences among jobs with respect to autonomy, as expressed by our overall measure of job content, called "the level of *discretion and skill* (*D-S level*)," associated with the particular job. This measure contains a series of relevant work characteristics, such as the exercise of *discretion* as regards working pace, working method, impact on production quality, and so forth, and requirements with respect to manual and social *skills*. Measures of job involvement and different aspects of job satisfaction as well as demands for increased worker participation have been collected through questionnaires and interviews with workers in different types of jobs. (For a more detailed description of the D-S level, as well as attitude measures used, see Gardell, 1971a, p. 150.)

The material is drawn from two paper and pulp plants (process industry) and two metalworking industries with a mixture of mass-production and batch characteristics. Within each industry the two plants belong to the same company, and all plants are located in small industrial towns. In all, the material consists of 339 workers from process industry distributed among 131 different jobs, and 640 metalworkers distributed among 128 different jobs.

Relationship Between Autonomy and Involvement in Present Work and the Desire for More Decision-Making Influence

Our aim in this section will be to test the question that most directly bears upon our main problem; namely, whether the degree of autonomy over work performance and its influence on work commitment are related to the individual's aspiration to influence *at job and plant level.* Such an assumption will be found in the experimental studies carried out by Thorsrud and Emery (1969).

It has not been possible in the present study to measure in depth employee aspirations to participate in different types of decisions. We have measured the aspirations with a couple of direct, generally worded questions by which we sought to obtain an expression for a general emotional readiness or interest in increasing personal influence over decisions at job and plant level. It goes without saying that results based on such simple measuring methods should be interpreted with caution. It is also important to observe that answers to questions of this type are likely to be highly sensitive to the state of opinion in the domain that these questions touch upon. Data were collected from 1966 to 1968; that is, before the Swedish debate on work environment and industrial democracy entered a more intensive phase and before the political parties had spelled out a proper policy on these issues. That in itself is all to the good, since the results might otherwise have been influenced by this public debate. Were the same questions to be put today, a different set of responses would probably be obtained. For this reason, any conclusions as to the *absolute level* of the decision-making aspirations that we obtain through our questions should be interpreted with the utmost caution. On the other hand, it seems feasible to use the answers to draw *relative* comparisons between groups that diverge in various respects. Our primary interest, then, is in the *direction* taken by the relationships between job content and aspirations to worker participation in the plant.

Autonomy and Aspirations Toward Increased Influence. If we first look at the relationship between *degree of autonomy in present work* and the desire for more personal influence, we can draw upon our job content measure relating to the discretion and skill level of the job (D-S level). The relationships between D-S level of present job and the desire for more decision-making influence are set out in Table 1 by type of industry. This table may be read off as follows:

Table 1. Association Between D-S Level of Present Job and
Desire to Increase Decision-Making Influence[a]

D-S Level of Present Job		Desire to Increase Personal Influence over Decisions at Plant Level	Desire to Increase Personal Influence over Decisions at Team/Department Level
		Pulp and paper	
Low	($N = $ 90)	3.44	2.07
Medium	($N = $ 157)	3.16	1.82
High	($N = $ 92)	2.87	1.75
		$p(t)$ 1-3 = 0.000	$p(t)$ 1-3 = 0.024
		Engineering industry	
Low	($N = $ 228)	3.34	2.20
Medium	($N = $ 201)	3.46	2.23
High	($N = $ 211)	3.31	2.15
		NS	NS

[a]Five-point scale, low values = strong desire to increase decision-making influence.

1. The desire for greater personal influence at team/department level is more widespread than the desire for personal influence at the plant level. This finding is valid for both the industrial types investigated. In an earlier publication, we presented figures from five more firms, together with figures from those firms included in the present study (Gardell, 1969, p. 87). This series of responses shows a very uniform picture: 15-35 percent want to exercise greater influence at plant level, whereas 68-81 percent would like to have more personal influence over the immediate job situation.

The primary concern of workers with matters affecting their own jobs is natural enough, especially when one considers that the firms investigated are of middle or large size. The actual opportunities available to individuals in large organizations for bringing greater influence to bear on overall management policies are, as we all know, very small.

Obviously, this does not preclude the existence of a widespread desire to obtain greater influence *for the employees as a group* over decisions at plant level. Of the workers employed with the forestry and engineering companies we studied, no more than 13-17 percent are of the opinion that the employees as a group have an adequate say in management decisions; a similar opinion was held by 30-35 percent of the workers employed in flow-process plants. These figures may be interpreted as signifying the presence of a widespread desire to increase influence in the firm for the employees as a group.

2. Workers in *pulp and paper mills* who enjoy substantial autonomy (high D-S level) in their present work have *higher* aspirations to greater personal influence over decisions both at plant level and team/department level. This relationship between job content and demand for increased worker participation is especially clearcut with respect to demands for participation at plant level.

3. By contrast, the results from the engineering industry lend no support to these ideas, but then again they do not point to the movement of any correlations in the opposite direction. Although it is hard to say anything with certainty about what the differences among different types of industry might be due to, it seems reasonable to invoke differences of integration and continuity of production, signifying that process workers assigned to skilled tasks are quite unlike their craft-based counterparts in engineering in their dependence on the production flow and their ability to grasp its total structure.

In our material most of the highly skilled engineering workers are toolmakers and deal with a well-defined task that is more or less detached from the rest of the production flow, from which it may be inferred that they enjoy a higher degree of autonomy over performance compared with the skilled process workers. The latter are brought into a highly integrated production chain, where planning flaws or errors at an earlier stage in the process noticeably affect their ability to perform their own work satisfactorily. It may safely be assumed that not only are the process workers aware of these shortcomings, but that they also have ideas about setting them aright, provided only they were permitted a greater role in the work planning.

We consider that this state of affairs may well explain the higher aspirations to influence over work planning among the process workers, which also makes it reasonable to suggest that these aspirations extend to more general decision processes at plant level because of the more tangible link between these and the process workers' own working situation. Obviously, the same kind of link exists in batch manufacturing, but it does not have the same degree of visibility as in a highly integrated flow process. Besides, it appears as though vertical contacts are more pronounced in the process industry, indicating that process workers already have some ingrained habits of communicating face to face with technical experts and line superiors—a fact that no doubt in its turn makes them aspire more to influencing management decisions. Then, too, skilled process workers—and here they contrast sharply with their counterparts in engineering—can imagine being promoted upward on the hierarchical ladder (Gardell, 1971b, p. 311).

However, any attempt to extend this interpretation would require follow-up analyses of a kind beyond our present means, so we present our interpretation here as no more than an interesting possibility.

Job Involvement and Aspiration Toward Increased Influence. The second main question in this section is to find out whether subjectively felt job involvement relates in any way to interest in increased decision-making influence. This question becomes relevant in the light of what we know about a generally positive relationship between autonomy and job involvement, and also in the light of the theory that a more widespread interest among workers in participating in management decisions is encouraged by high autonomy, high interest in work, and involvement in problems of the workplace. However, we also know that a smaller group reacts to work as interesting and motivating *despite* low autonomy and low D-S level of the job. We shall therefore keep this group separate from the larger group that has a high D-S level and high job involvement. This concurrent breakdown by D-S level and job involvement is shown in Table 2 and Table 3.

Table 2. Desire for Increased Influence at Plant Level Among Groups with High Job Involvement and Low or High D-S Level in Present Work[a]

	Pulp and Paper	*Engineering*
Low D-S level	$N = 26$	$N = 51$
High job involvement	3.46	3.80
High D-S level	$N = 46$	$N = 118$
High job involvement	2.89	3.46

[a]Five-point scale, low values = strong desire for increased influence.

Table 3. Desire for Increased Influence at Team/Department Level Among Groups with High Job Involvement and Low or High D-S Level in Present Work[a]

	Pulp and Paper	*Engineering*
Low D-S level	$N = 26$	$N = 51$
High job involvement	2.15	2.94
High D-S level	$N = 46$	$N = 118$
High job involvement	1.80	2.32

[a]Five-point scale, low values = strong desire for increased influence.

The first thing to notice in these tables is that both industries contain roughly twice as many individuals in those groups that attach interest to jobs of high D-S level, compared with those working in jobs of low D-S level. Second, the tables show—and this is the central point—that *wider aspirations to increased decision-making influence are more common among those individuals who are involved in high-D-S-level jobs.* This relation holds for both industrial types and for decisions both at team level and plant level. By contrast, a monotonous and unskilled job felt to be interesting and involving does not combine with more elaborate aspirations to increased decision-making influence to such a great extent. In the latter case the attitude to work should probably be interpreted as manifesting generally low aspirations. Hence, it is not the attitude to work per se that seems to be most crucial; rather, it is not until high involvement can be seen as flowing from greater autonomy and more highly skilled tasks that we can expect a process that also leads to higher aspirations to influence decisions over the immediate job and over management policies.

These findings are important because they stress the necessity of structural changes in work organization and job design for instilling a more active orientation toward decision processes at different levels in the plant. It is not until job involvement has its counterpart in objective properties of job content, here embodied by discretionary factors and skill requirements, that the psychological processes leading to a more active orientation toward higher-level decision processes will be triggered off.

At the same time, the results show a clearer relationship within the process industry, and it is possible that increased autonomy over the immediate job unrelated to production as a whole will not intensify interest in participating in higher-level decision processes to the same extent as when production processes are more integrated. As we see it, these relationships between technology, work content, and aspirations to decision-making influence, both at team and plant levels, deserve attention for purposes of projects seeking to extend industrial democracy.

Aspirations to Increased Collective Influence and Its Relationship to Skill Level, Autonomy of Tasks, and Success of Representative Democracy

When, by way of introduction, we referred to the system of collective bargaining and the agreements governing industrial relations that have long existed in Sweden, we suggested that the consequence was for the employees to express their aspirations to influence over management policies by way of representative democracy in the firms. Given the established forms of collaboration that have long been operating in the Swedish working life, it is reasonable to expect that aspirations to influence via the representative system would be higher than aspirations to influence for oneself over higher-level decisions. At the same time, it is plausible to imagine, *first,* that the demands of individual employees to greater collective influence over management policies will grow with higher degree of autonomy over the immediate job in the same way as has been shown earlier for aspirations to increased influence for oneself; *second*, that the degree of success for *representative democracy* in the firm will intensify individual aspirations to *direct democracy* —that is, increase the aspirations to exercise more personal influence at plant level.

These questions seem to be well worth testing, not least in view of two contentions put forward in the debate on industrial democracy—*first,* that increased autonomy at work will lessen the interest in influence by way of representative democracy; and, *second,* that a successful representative democracy lessens the opportunities for, and hence the aspirations of, individual employees to exercise personal influence in the firm. Obviously, we do not lay claim to being able to exhaust these vital issues, but we nevertheless feel that our material opens up some intriguing possibilities.

The first question—that is, whether demands to increased influence for the employees as a group grow with greater autonomy—was tested with one question put in the pulp and paper industry and three questions put in the engineering industry. Here we proceeded from subjectively perceived decision-making influence, reckoning that those who are unhappy about influence for the employees as a group will express a desire to exercise more such influence. Our hope was that this indirect method of measuring the level of aspirations to collective influence would better reflect the individual's attitude than a more direct question, in which case the answers might well have been biased because of official ideology or made socially desirable for other reasons.

Respondents in both industrial types were asked about influence for the employees at plant level. Two additional questions were put in the engineering industry about employee influence over the firm's future planning and personnel policy.

The results may be read from Table 4, which for both industrial types shows that aspirations to greater influence at plant level for the workers as a group rise in tandem with rising skill and autonomy in one's own job. The two questions exclusively confined to the engineering industry strengthen the tendency taken by the correlations. Hence, it may safely be concluded that there is great interest among the more highly skilled workers in increased collective influence in working life. Our data lend no support to the view that increased autonomy and its related variable, increased job involvement, would *lessen*

Table 4. Association Between D-S Level and Aspirations for the Employees
as a Group to Influence Decisions at Plant Level[a]

D-S Level	Desires Increased Collective Influence over Corporate Management in General	Desires Increased Collective Influence over Firm's Future Plans	Desires Increased Collective Influence over Firm's Personnel Policy
Engineering industry			
Low ($N = 228$)	2.53	2.49	2.50
High ($N = 211$)	2.34	2.26	2.33
	$p(t) = 0.068$ N.S.	$p(t) = 0.020$	$p(t) = 0.086$ N.S.
Pulp and paper			
Low ($N = 90$)	3.00		
High ($N = 92$)	2.62		
	$p(t) = 0.020$		

[a]Five-point scale, low values = high aspirations to influence for the employees as a group.

the interest among individual workers to exercise influence by way of representative democracy.

The central result, however, is that all the relationships found are weak. This suggests that the aspirations to greater influence for the employees as a group essentially derive from other factors, presumably of a more macro and ideological nature, and are not very much influenced by those psychological motivation mechanisms that are bound up with job content.

As to the second question—whether success for the system of representative democracy in the firm will raise individual aspirations to exercise personal influence at plant level—we elected to test it with reference to the results we obtained in the present study as well as through data collected in five additional firms, where the same questions were asked. The matter at issue is whether subjectively perceived success for the employee representatives will increase personal aspirations to influence in the firm; or, conversely, whether successful representative democracy lessens interest in direct democracy.

If we proceed from the ratings of perceived influence, the enterprises in our studies can be divided into three categories: (1) the insurance company, (2) the process industries, and (3) the engineering and forestry companies. These three categories depict a falling scale of perceived success for the representatives of employees in terms of their influence in the firm. For each of these levels of success, one can then study the answers to the question about desiring enlarged decision-making influence in the firm for *oneself*. This has been done in Table 5, which shows in the main that the different levels of success for the employee representatives are accompanied by commensurate differences of aspirations to increased personal influence.

The following tentative inference may be drawn from Table 5. In firms where the employees feel that representative democracy gives them relatively great influence (the insurance company and the process industries), the aspirations to enlarge influence for oneself will be relatively great, whereas in those firms where the employees as a group are felt by the workers to exert slight influence (engineering plants and forestry companies), the demands for personal influence will be weak. In other words, there appears to be no contradiction between a successful representative democracy and aspirations to direct

Table 5. **Relation Between Perceived Influence by Local Union and Aspirations to Increased Personal Participation at Plant Level**

	Insurance Company N = 280 %	Pulp & Paper I N = 230 %	Pulp & Paper II N = 184 %	Chemical Products N = 87 %	Engi- neering Plant I N = 255 %	Engi- neering Plant II N = 398 %	Forestry Company I N = 129 %	Forestry Company II N = 128 %	Forestry Company III N = 118 %
Thinks local union has sufficient in- fluence at plant level	48	30	33	35	13	15	17	16	16
Interested in increased personal par- ticipation at plant level	35	31	27	35	26	22	25	15	20

democracy; on the contrary, it may be possible that a strong representative democracy stimulates the individuals to develop aspirations and interest in direct personal participation in decision processes at plant level.

Relationships Between Perceived Influence and Different Criteria of Job Satisfaction

In the previous sections we have dealt with fairly complex and elusive relationships between technology, job involvement, and aspirations to decision-making influence, and have sought to demonstrate how a more active orientation toward the firm's decision processes is concurrently dependent upon technology and job content and the status of representative democracy. This active orientation toward work deriving from increased autonomy, more highly skilled jobs, and a well-functioning representative democracy is something we regard in two ways: first, as a valuable goal in itself, permitting the expression of greater self-esteem and greater job satisfaction; and, second, as a condition to be met before a more widespread interest in the firm's decision processes can be developed, which in its turn must necessarily precede the further development of industrial democracy.

It follows that the efforts to develop industrial democracy operate with an assumption that greater influence for the employees will increase job satisfaction. If the trend toward a more democratic working life is to make any sense to the individual employee, it should also be possible for him to see and feel that his day-to-day working conditions are being improved in various respects.

One approach to a study of this assumption is to find out whether persons who differ on the influence criterion also differ in their job satisfaction.

Concerning the relationships between *autonomy* over immediate work performance and job satisfaction, these were accounted for at the first WHO Symposium on "Society, Stress and Disease," where it was particularly shown that feelings of alienation from work diminished with rising degree of autonomy at work (Gardell, 1971a, pp. 155 ff).

No equivalent objective measure of decision-making influence at the team/department and plant levels is at our disposal; in this case we shall have to proceed from *subjectively perceived decision-making influence.*

In the present section, we propose to take up the question of how perceived decision-making influence at the team/department level and the plant level relates not only to feelings of alienation from work but also to other criteria of job satisfaction. In line with the distinctions drawn earlier (Theoretical Aspects and Definition), we shall now distinguish between (1) *perceived personal influence over the immediate work situation* (personal level, team/department level); and (2) *perceived decision-making influence for the employees as a group over general management policies* (group level, plant level). The answers to the questions on perceived decision-making influence were treated to impute satisfactory influence to those who provided any of the "yes" alternatives and unsatisfactory decision-making influence to those who provided any of the "no" alternatives. Persons who answered neither "yes" nor "no" to the question of whether they feel their influence is large enough were excluded from the analysis. These expressions of perceived decision-making influence formed the independent variable, which was then tested against different criteria of job satisfaction. The results may be read as set out in Figures 1-4.

1. The facilities for discussing and affecting the immediate work situation are thought to be greater in the engineering industry compared with the pulp and paper

Figure 1. Relation Between Perceived Influence over Decisions at
Team/Department Level and Different Criteria of Job Satisfaction

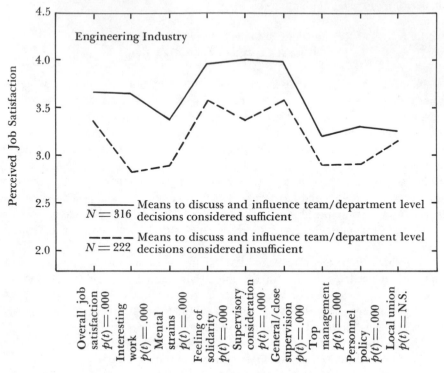

Note: Five-point scale. low values = low job satisfaction.

industry, which is plausible enough considering the technology and low degree of integration embodied in the manufacturing process. However, the differences of perceived personal influence over the immediate work situation are related to expressions of job satisfaction in a similar way in both types of industry. Those who feel they already exercise sufficient influence over the immediate work show consistently higher job satisfaction on all criteria (Figures 1, 2).

2. There is a tendency in both industries for the biggest job-satisfaction differences between groups who feel either satisfactory or unsatisfactory *personal influence over their work situation* to arise with respect to job involvement and attitudes to foremen and top managers (Figures 1, 2). A reasonable interpretation of this finding is that respondents will tend to react to matters of personal participation in decisions concerning the immediate work situation as being subject to the attitudes held and the methods used by members of line management. Any superior who encourages his subordinates to participate in decision processes is felt to be a good manager. Yet another consequence of these variations in supervisory technique will be for greater personal influence over the immediate work situation to make the work more interesting. It is important to bear this in mind alongside the variations in autonomy conferred by production technology considered in a narrower sense.

3. The groups who feel that employees do not exercise enough collective influence over corporate management show poorer job satisfaction on all criteria, both in the

Figure 2. Relation Between Perceived Influence over Decisions at
Team/Department Level and Different Criteria of Job Satisfaction

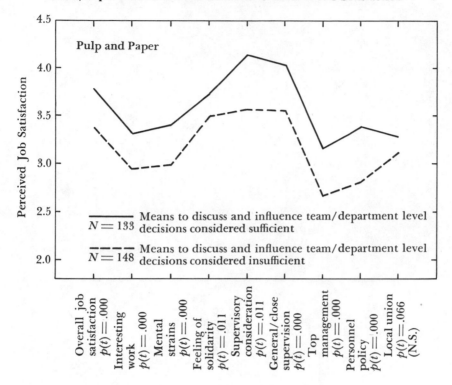

Note: Five-point scale, low values = low job satisfaction.

engineering plants and the pulp and paper mills. Especially noticeable is the difference of
attitude to top management and to the firm's personnel policy, where for both types of
industry the critical attitude is decidedly more pronounced in those groups who feel that
the employees as a group have too small influence in the firm (Figures 2-4).

4. In the engineering plants, the feeling of insufficient influence in the firm for its
employees is associated with a strongly critical attitude, not only of top management but
also of the local trade union (Figure 3).

A significant difference in this respect also applies to the pulp and paper mills, but
it is not of the same magnitude as in the engineering plants (Figure 4). The fact that men
who sit on *both sides* of the collective bargaining table are criticized is important, since it
connotes feelings of powerlessness not only in relation to the employing firm but also to
the trade union, which is supposed to speak for the employees. It should be pointed out
that we investigated the engineering plants over a period covering late 1967 and early
1968; that is, *before* the Swedish economy had recovered from the recession then prevailing and *before* the public debate and union activities concerning work environment and
industrial democracy had been triggered off. So it is not likely that any temporary external factors have been operating on our data. The results, rather, should be seen as an
expression of a serious trend taking place in organizational life; namely, that the individual, when unable to make his voice heard in a satisfactory manner, is coming to look

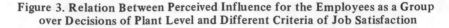

Figure 3. Relation Between Perceived Influence for the Employees as a Group
over Decisions of Plant Level and Different Criteria of Job Satisfaction

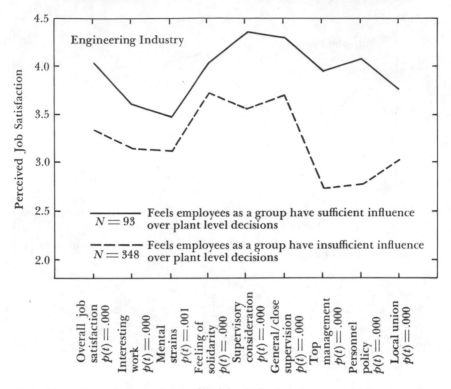

Note: Five-point scale, low values = low job satisfaction.

more and more on his trade union as an integral part of the managerial control system as opposed to a representative of the employees.

Conclusions

The data presented here lend support to the idea that worker interest in company affairs is favored by a design of jobs that allows for high autonomy and high demands on skill and cooperation. However, this seems to be more true in integrated production processes, where the socialization of workers is not confined to a craft-based and self-sufficient organization of work. The alienation of mass-production workers with repetitive and unskilled tasks seems to imply not only lack of interest in the job *but also a withdrawal from interest in those change processes that might lead to more autonomous tasks and to increased worker influence in working life.* This is true also for mass-production workers who are satisfied with repetitive and unskilled tasks. This is an important observation, since it implies that it is not until high involvement can be seen as derived from greater autonomy and more skilled tasks that we can expect a psychological process to start that leads to a more widespread interest for worker participation in higher-level decision making in working life.

Systems of representative democracy seem incapable by themselves of coping with the powerlessness of individual workers in mass-production industry; rather, when they

Figure 4. Relation Between Perceived Influence for the Employees as a Group over Decisions at Plant Level and Different Criteria of Job Satisfaction

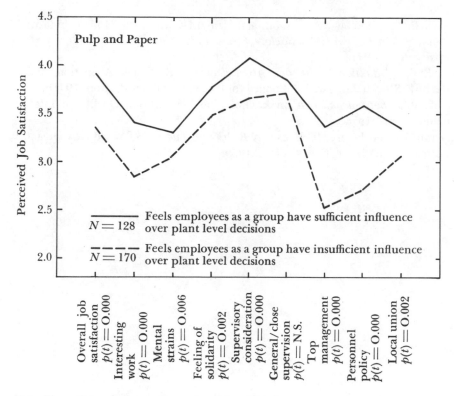

Note: Five-point scale, low values = low job satisfaction.

are perceived as not providing the opportunities to influence, they risk being regarded as part of the control system of the plant. On the other hand, there is no inevitable conflict between representative democracy and direct democracy; on the contrary, an effective system of representative democracy or collective bargaining seems to increase the demands among the workers for personal influence in company matters. The crucial factors, however, in coping with worker alienation seem to be related to technology and job content. Increased autonomy and increased requirements on manual and social skills are not only favorable to job involvement but seem also to favor aspirations toward increased worker participation, both at the personal level and for the workers as a group. The system of industrial relations in Sweden is now changing through a new set of laws providing the employees with legal rights to participate in decisions at all levels in the plant. If this development is going to involve the individual workers and carry meaning in their everyday lives, it seems necessary that management and unions involve themselves in a systematic way in the abolishment of the "robot jobs" so prevalent in today's industrial life.

References

Dahlström, E. *Fördjupad Företagsdemokrati* [Toward Industrial Democracy]. Stockholm: Prisma, 1969.

Gardell, B. *Skogsarbetarnas Arbetsanpassning* [Job Satisfaction and Mental Health Among Forest Workers]. Stockholm: Swedish Council for Personnel Administration, 1969.

Gardell, B. "Technology, Alienation, and Mental Health in the Modern Industrial Environment." In L. Levi (Ed.), *Society, Stress, and Disease.* Vol. 1. London: Oxford University Press, 1971a.

Gardell, B. *Produktionsteknik och Arbetsglädje* [Technology, Alienation, and Mental Health]. Stockholm: Swedish Council for Personnel Administration, 1971b.

Gardell, B. *Arbetsinnehåll och Livskvalitet* [Job Content and Quality of Life]. Stockholm: Prisma, 1976.

Thorsrud, E., and Emery, F. *Mot en ny Bedriftsorganiasjon* [Toward New Organizational Forms in Enterprise]. Oslo: Taunus, 1969.

PART V

∽∾ Communication

Organizational inputs are, as Miller (1978) has pointed out, of two types: *energic* and *informational.* The first type includes labor power and physical forms of energy, or materials to be transformed into energy. The second type deals with knowledge about the environment, from specific items of client demand to general accounts of trends in the outside world. Communication is the name given to the general process of information exchange, and it applies both to intercourse with the environment and to internal exchanges about the job to be done and the organizational machinery for achieving its objectives. Since organizations are constantly interacting with their environments in importing and exporting goods and services, they are in a position to keep informed about their impact and their performances. Communication of this sort is known as feedback, and organizations vary in the devices they use for measuring various aspects of their operations. Evaluation research, the term used for systematic feedback measures for programs, calls attention to the need for built-in procedures to assess the effectiveness of organizational action.

This section focuses on various internal problems of communication: coordination of task activities (*Hage, Aiken,* and *Marrett*); direction of information flow (*Bacharach* and *Aiken*); distortion of information (*O'Reilly*); and actual communication networks, including informal patterns (*Schwartz* and *Jacobson*).

Hage, Aiken, and *Marrett* take off from the theoretical assumption of March and Simon (1958) that coordination in organizations is achieved either through programming or through feedback; that is, by formalized communication or by feedback from performance and informal communication. Obviously, organizations employ both procedures, but there may be greater emphasis on formalization of plans for some tasks than for others and for some organizations rather than others. *Hage, Aiken,* and *Marrett* theorize that degree of complexity of the organization is positively related to the rate of task communication, but that formalization is negatively related to the rate of task communication—in other words, a test of the March-Simon hypothesis. They also predict that the greater the complexity, the greater the proportion of horizontal communication; and the greater the formalization, the higher the proportion of vertical task communication. In other words, there will be more communication among peers in complex organizations and greater communication up and down the line in organizations where communication is highly formalized. Finally, they hypothesize that with greater centralization there will be higher rates of vertical task communication.

They gathered data from sixteen social welfare organizations and, as a measure of formalization, took the completeness of the individual's job description and the specificity of procedures for handling all aspects and contingencies of the job. There was some support for the prediction that formalization would be negatively related to rate of task communication, as well as for the other hypotheses. The more complex the organization —that is, the more diversified its occupational structure—the greater the communication flow and the greater the horizontal communication. As organizations become diversified, they need to supplement programming with a system of reciprocal information flows. In brief, the investigators not only show the relationship between programming and feedback, but they specify the type of organization in which emphasis is placed on feedback rather than programming. They suggest an important role for future research in investigating the relative effectiveness of organizations that emphasize one type of coordination rather than the other.

Bacharach and *Aiken* also concentrate on organizational rather than individual or interpersonal variables in studying the frequency of communication in organizations. They first establish that position in the organization, whether department head or subordinate, is associated with direction of information flow, with department heads showing greater overall communication than subordinates. Subordinates, however, do show more lateral communication than department heads. Only two organizational constraints —namely, boundary spanning (number of outside contacts) and decentralization—affect the amount of communication of department heads. For subordinates, two additional factors—size and organizational width (number of departments in organization)—are important. In this study organizational variables explained as much as 50 percent of the variance in frequency of communication among subordinates, but little of the variance for department heads. This is a striking finding and suggests that organizational or structural constraints may account for much of the behavior of the rank and file in a system but that interpersonal variables need careful study when one is looking at the leadership. This hypothesis needs further investigation in a number of organizations and for various types of behavior. This study was limited to forty-four local government bureaucracies in Belgian cities and to the frequency of oral communications.

The *O'Reilly* paper is unusual in two respects. In the first place, it reports both laboratory and field studies bearing on essentially the same hypotheses concerning the distortion of information in organizational communication. In the second place, it uses both levels of concepts in determining distortion effects—the system level in dealing with the organizational direction of information flow upward, downward, or lateral; and the interpersonal level of trust in the receiver and perceived influence of the receiver. In addition, distortion was studied as it related to job satisfaction and job performance. The combination of the two approaches demonstrates the ideal strategy for studying organizational phenomena. The laboratory method led to a sharpening of concepts and more specifications for the measures to be employed in the field, and the field investigation provided the grounds for generalizing from the laboratory to the organizational setting. Directionality of communication was related to distortion, but only slightly, in that there was a tendency for individuals to be less informative when passing messages up the line. There was also evidence that information is lost in lateral communication and does not move up the line as might be expected. The only interpersonal variable that affected suppression of information was trust in the receiver. *O'Reilly* closes with an elaboration of his model that could be very useful for further research. It specifies the structural and personal variables that should be studied as they interact, so that an investigator can determine their effects on the accuracy of the communication process.

Schwartz and Jacobson provide a method for analyzing communication networks in organizations by working out sociometric patterns of mutual contacts among organizational members pertaining to informational matters. They use this method in a midwestern college to identify the role of the liaison person—the individual who has reciprocal contacts with members of two other groups besides his own. Such liaison persons were found more frequently among full professors than other ranks, among administrators, and among committee members. Moreover, liaison persons served more frequently as the first source of organization-related information than did nonliaisons. Without formal designation as leaders of their groups, liaison persons provide a linking role in the communication process. The methodology of the investigators can be applied to analyzing other properties of communication networks, such as extensity, redundance, and feedback loops, in relation to characteristics of the organization.

Attention is called to the descriptive study by Keegan (1974) (not included in this volume), which breaks new ground in the study of the information-seeking activities of organizations. Fifty executives responsible for international relations were asked to recall specific instances in which they personally obtained or received external information important to their job or to their company. Human sources were found to be more important than documentary sources, consistent with the old thesis that a key intelligence skill consists not of knowing a great deal of information but of knowing whom to consult. The most likely source of information is the corporation's own staff abroad and generally in the same functional area as the inquiring executive. In the entire sample, information storage was found only once outside of human memory. Comprehensive computerized information systems in many organizations are heavily concerned with internal information and not with a scanning of the broad environment. The organizational field sorely needs studies of the Keegan type, which would show how organizations acquire relevant information, what gaps and biases are likely to occur, and what the mechanisms are for the effective utilization of information about the environment. The bulk of research on the acquisition and utilization of information in organizations has been undertaken by investigators of research and development systems (see, for example, Allen, 1966; Fischer, 1979; Frost and Whitley, 1971; Rosenbloom and Wolek, 1970).

References

Allen, T. J. "Performance of Information Channels in the Transfer of Technology." *Industrial Management Review,* 1966, *8,* 87-98.

Fischer, W. A. "The Acquisition of Technical Information by R&D Managers for Problem Solving in Nonroutine Contingency Situations." *IEEE Transactions on Engineering Management,* 1979, *EM-26,* 8-14.

Frost, P. A., and Whitley, R. "Communication Patterns in a Research Laboratory." *R&D Management,* 1971, *1,* 71-79.

Keegan, W. J. "Multinational Scanning: A Study of the Information Sources Utilized by Headquarters Executives in Multinational Companies." *Administrative Science Quarterly,* 1974, *19* (3), 411-421.

March, J. G., and Simon, H. A. *Organizations.* New York: Wiley, 1958.

Miller, J. G. *Living Systems.* New York: McGraw-Hill, 1978.

Rosenbloom, R., and Wolek, F. W. *Technology and Information Transfer.* Boston: Division of Research, Graduate School of Business Administration, Harvard University, 1970.

22

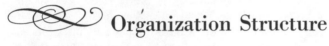 Organization Structure
and Communications

Jerald Hage
Michael Aiken
Cora B. Marrett

Internal communications in organizations have been the subject of considerable discussion in the literature on organizations, yet empirical studies which attempt to measure various aspects of organizational communications in organizations are scarce, Landsberger's (1961) article being a notable exception. In this paper we shall provide a framework for relating communication patterns to organizational structure and discuss some results of a test of this framework in sixteen health and welfare organizations.

Usually, communications have been related to only one aspect or dimension of organizational structure. For example, Thompson (1961), building upon an earlier study by Dalton (1950), showed the relationship between communication patterns and the degree of specialization within the organization. In their summary of a number of studies, Blau and Scott (1962) noted the relationship between communication patterns and status in an organization. Still other studies have related communication patterns to rules (Gross, 1953; Blau, 1955) and to power (McCleery, 1957; Smith, 1966). However, attempts to weave together all these aspects of organizational structure and the process of internal communications into a single framework are largely absent. In this paper, we first suggest a set of premises and hypotheses for relating various dimensions of organizational structure—complexity (the degree of personal specialization), centralization (the distribution of power), and formalization (the emphasis on rules and regulations)—to organizational communications. Second, we present findings about the relationship between aspects of social structure and organization communication patterns.

Theoretical Framework

In a few insightful pages March and Simon (1958, pp. 158-169) suggest that there are two basic ways in which organizations can be coordinated: feedback and plan. Coor-

Reprinted from *American Sociological Review*, Oct. 1971, *36*, 860-871, with permission of the authors and the American Sociological Association.

dination is here defined as the degree to which there are adequate linkages among organizational parts—that is, specific task roles as well as subunits of the organization—so that organizational objectives can be accomplished. Coordination by plan is based on preestablished schedules, while coordination by feedback involves the transmission of new information. (Thompson, 1967, distinguishes three types of coordination: standardization, plan, and mutual adjustment; however, the first appears to be an aspect of coordination through planning.) The point here is that there seem to be two major types of linkage mechanisms in organizations: linkages through preestablished rules, routines, blueprints, or schedules (coordination by standardization, plan, and programming) and linkages through the transmission of new information (coordination by feedback or mutual adjustment). The basic question with which each type of coordination is concerned is how these task roles and/or organizational subunits are articulated into a coherent whole, so that organizational objectives can be accomplished.

In a different context, Parsons (1951) has noted that social control over individuals can be maintained either by socialization or by sanctions. In the application of these ideas to professional organizations, Blau and Scott (1962) noted that professionals conform to organizational norms either because of peer pressures or because of certain rewards and punishments. Social control, however, is not the same as coordination; the first refers to the adequacy of achieving conformity with expectations of behavior and standards of work, while the latter refers to the method by which task roles are articulated together to accomplish a given set of tasks. At the same time, there does seem to be some consistency between these ideas; that is, coordination through planning or programming is more likely to imply use of sanctions to achieve social control; coordination through feedback is more likely to rely on socialization. Of course, we do not want to suggest that there is an identity here, since there are many other mechanisms of social control—such as performance records, reliance on hierarchy, or recruitment practices—that are also used to ensure predictability of performance in organizations.

Both feedback and programming involve the articulation of a variety of task jobs and their occupants in a division of labor in which each fulfills his respective tasks. Both mechanisms are intended to achieve the same result—the integration of the task roles; but the question remains as to how this is accomplished. Implicit in all of these writings is the premise that all organizations need coordination. This becomes our first assumption in our theory of organizational structure and communications. (See chart.)

Premises and Hypotheses About Organizational Control

Premises
  I. All organizations need coordination.
 II. There are two basic mechanisms for achieving coordination: programming with emphasis on sanctions and feedback with emphasis on socialization.
III. The greater the diversity of organizational structure, the greater the emphasis on coordination through feedback.
 IV. The greater the differences in status and power in an organization, the greater the emphasis on coordination through planning.

Derived Hypotheses
  1. The greater the degree of complexity, the greater the rate of task communications.
  2. The greater the degree of complexity, the greater the proportion of horizontal task communication.
  3. The greater the degree of formalization, the less the rate of task communications.

4. The greater the degree of formalization, the higher the proportion of vertical task communication.
5. The greater the degree of centralization, the less the rate of task communication.
6. The greater the degree of centralization, the higher the proportion of vertical task communication.

Our second assumption, following March and Simon (1958) and Thompson (1967), is that coordination can be achieved in two basic ways: (1) The activities of each job occupant can be programmed, and then a system of rewards and punishments can be utilized to ensure conformity to the basic organizational scheme. A clear blueprint of action would make departures from the plan immediately obvious, and a system of rewards would provide the force behind the basic plan. Standards would leave little ambiguity about whom to punish and whom to reward. (2) Organizations can rely more upon continuous flows of information (feedback or mutual adjustment) as a method for coordinating the organization. Under this system, errors, when detected, are often seen as a problem of improper socialization or training; one method of correcting this situation is through the provision of new information. Also implied in this approach is that pressure comes not so much from formal sanctions, in the strict sense of the term, but more from peer pressures and inner standards of quality developed through socialization. The first approach relies upon external control, whereas the latter is more concerned with internal control, or what is called self-control.

Thus, two basic processes to achieve coordination can be distinguished: feedback and programming. In practice, most organizations would use some mixture of the two mechanisms. For us, the most interesting as well as most important question is the specification of the organizational circumstances under which one or the other of these two mechanisms will be emphasized. March and Simon (1958) provide no suggestions about the structural concomitants of these mechanisms of coordination, although they do suggest that the uncertainty of the task may affect the choice. However, Thompson (1967) does suggest some structural concomitants of various types of interdependencies and coordination. The internal structure of an organization should have an important relationship to the form of coordination that is most dominant and, hence, to the way in which communications are designed.

We assume that there are two major structural factors that affect the patterns of internal verbal communication: diversity and the distribution of power and status. These are basic axes of organization structure that Thompson (1961) and others have noted. As the diversity of an organization increases, it becomes more difficult to plan a successful blueprint for the organization. As the variety of tasks in an organization increases, the number of potential connections among parts increases even more rapidly, and the articulation of organizational parts by a set of predetermined rules becomes more complicated. Moreover, the application of sanctions becomes more difficult because each of the jobs may require a different set of standards. The decision makers in such organizations are likely to be forced to rely more upon feedback mechanisms than upon rigidly programmed mechanisms of communication. This whole process is further intensified if the nature of most jobs in the structure is complex and involves a variety of activities (often the case with professionals). Here, we are suggesting that the variety of tasks, as well as the degree of uncertainty, is an important determinant of the degree of communications (March and Simon, 1958; Thompson, 1967; Perrow, 1967; Hage and Aiken, 1969).

In addition, differences in power and status among job occupants in an organization are likely to inhibit the rate of feedback communications. As social distance between organizational levels increases, the free flow of information is reduced (Barnard, 1964). Similarly, the threat of sanctions from the top discourages the frank discussion of problems, and, therefore, organizational decision makers are unlikely to learn of problems until a crisis has developed, as Blau and Scott (1962) have suggested and as Barnard (1964) explicitly argued.

The degree of organizational diversity propels the organization toward attempts to coordinate through information feedback while status and power differences propel the organization toward attempts to coordinate through programming. Together they influence the probabilities of the adoption of either programming or feedback—or, more precisely, the particular combination, since each of these factors can be operative at the same time. We assume that organizational elites attempt to program some interaction in the form of regular reports. Even where they have made a conscious decision to rely only upon a feedback mechanism of coordination, there will always be some feeble attempts to rationalize parts of the organization. What is critical here is the differential emphasis on coordination through feedback and coordination through planning or blueprints.

Although it is plausible that internal structure affects the type of coordination, one may logically ask what factors affect or determine internal structure. A number of recent writings have suggested that technology or task structure is a major determinant of variations in internal structure (March and Simon, 1958; Thompson, 1967; Perrow, 1967). A recent study by Hage and Aiken (1969) did find that routine technology was highly related to the centralization of decision making. Environmental characteristics such as stability, homogeneity, and certainty have also been suggested as important determinants of internal structural variation (Thompson, 1967; Lawrence and Lorsch, 1967b). Blau and Schoenherr (1971) have argued that size has pervasive effects on internal structural arrangements. Pugh and associates (1969) show that a combination of technology and size is an important predictor of the structure of organizations, although Hall, Haas, and Johnson (1967) report some negative findings regarding size. Others have suggested the importance of ecological pattern (Festinger, 1950; Rosengren and DeVault, 1963). These and many other variables may indeed determine organizational structure, and ultimately the choice of coordination mechanisms and the volume and intensity of communications in an organization. Here our concern is limited to exploring the relationship between dimensions of internal structure and communications, although it is possible, even probable, that other factors may condition these relationships.

A number of testable hypotheses can be deduced from our theoretical framework, but, before discussing them, we should note that feedback is itself an involved and complicated concept. For us, the simplest way of understanding feedback is to see it as a high volume of communication of information relevant to the work of the organization. One would not want to include gossip, rumors, jokes, and other forms of expressive communication. In addition, feedback carries the notion that it is information coming from different parts of the organization. Thus, direction, as well as volume, is a critical factor. Traditionally, the literature has tended to distinguish between the sheer rate of communication and its direction. The latter is frequently broken down into horizontal and vertical communication (Landsberger, 1961; Guetzkow, 1965; Price, 1967). For these reasons, the volume of task communication and the direction of task communication become two excellent derivations from the broader idea of feedback.

Diversity of organizational structure can be interpreted in different ways. For us, the major idea is the complexity of occupations; that is, their sheer number. The idea here is that of personal specialization as contrasted to the microdivision of labor implied by task specialization (Thompson, 1961). A secondary idea is that as occupations become more complex—that is, more professional—one can say that the organizational structure is more diverse. This leads to the following hypotheses:

1. The greater the degree of complexity, the greater the rate of task communications.
2. The greater the degree of complexity, the greater the proportion of horizontal task communications.

The key idea here is that greater diversity of occupations internally, as well as greater professional activism among the incumbents of these roles, is likely to mean greater reciprocal interdependence, and thus coordination through feedback, which should be reflected in a greater volume of communications overall as well as heightened horizontal communications.

The concept of programming may be caught by the idea of formalization; that is, the importance of job descriptions and the specificity of their content. If our reasoning is correct, a formalized set of jobs should reduce the need for communications between the different parts of the organization. This supplies two additional hypotheses:

3. The greater the degree of formalization, the less the rate of task communications.
4. The greater the degree of formalization, the higher the proportion of vertical task communication.

Social distance is created by concentration of power (or centralization) in an organization. There is less need for feedback when power is concentrated at the top of the organizational hierarchy, since the role of subordinates is to implement decisions rather than to participate in the shaping of those decisions. Therefore, as the concentration of power becomes greater, and consequently as the degree of participation in decision making by lower participants becomes less, we would expect inhibitions on communications in an organization (Crozier, 1964; Ronken and Lawrence, 1952). Therefore, the following hypotheses are additionally suggested:

5. The greater the degree of centralization, the less the rate of task communication.
6. The greater the degree of centralization, the higher the proportion of vertical task communication.

One could also logically derive hypotheses regarding the relationship between frequency of communication and the degree of stratification, but since we did not measure this variable, we do not include such hypotheses here.

Methodology

Research Design. The data upon which this study is based were gathered in sixteen social welfare and rehabilitation organizations located in a large Midwest metropolis in 1967. These agencies were all the larger welfare organizations that provide psychiatric and rehabilitation services as defined by the directory of the Community Chest. There are three mental hospitals, three residential treatment homes, three rehabilitation centers, six case-work agencies, and a department of special education in the public schools. Ten of these organizations are private, and six are publicly supported.

Respondents within each organization were selected by the following criteria: (1) all executive directors and department heads; (2) in departments of less than ten members, half of the staff was selected randomly; (3) in departments of ten or more members, one third of the staff was selected randomly.

Nonsupervisory administrative and maintenance personnel were not interviewed. The procedures used in aggregating individual data in order to develop measures of organizational characteristics have been described elsewhere (Aiken and Hage, 1968; Hage and Aiken, 1969).

Measurement of Communications. The measures of organizational communications in this analysis are limited to verbal interactions about tasks; that is, to interactions that are most immediately involved in the achievement of organizational goals. We do not include written communications, nor have we measured the content of these communications, although we make reference to their probable content. We phrased our questions so that respondents would exclude all purely expressive communications, such as camaraderie among friends or the exchange of gossip. Of course, this distinction may seem somewhat artificial, since effective task communications usually involve some expressive elements like jokes or pleasantries. We asked respondents to exclude only those communications that were completely expressive and which were in no way related to the accomplishment of some work objective.

We have separated task communications into two major types. The first includes the more routinized, usually planned communications, such as staff or committee meetings; the second includes less routine, often unplanned communications, such as informal, impromptu conferences between two staff members about a client's situation or the consultation between colleagues about a newly instituted organizational activity. We refer to the former as *scheduled* and the latter as *unscheduled* communications.

There is a variety of scheduled task communications in an organization. We found it helpful to distinguish between organizational committees, which involve members from different departments and occupational groups and are usually concerned with specific problems (such as personnel, finance, social, and so forth), from departmental or unit meetings, which involve members from the same department. The former is an example of horizontal communication, and the latter is an illustration of vertical communication. Both allow for feedback. In contrast, staff meetings and treatment meetings are less likely to have this characteristic. Staff meetings are used primarily to make announcements and were infrequently held in these organizations. Treatment meetings or production meetings are frequently held, but their content has little to do with the problems of *organizational* coordination.

Information about scheduled communications was obtained by asking each respondent the following question: "Now we would like to find out something about the committee and staff meetings in (organization name). Please list all staff committees or meetings in (organization name) of which you are a member."

For each committee or meeting reported, the following two questions were then asked: "How many times per month does (name of committee or meeting) meet?" "On the average, how many hours per month do you spend in meetings of (name of committee or meeting)?"

To aid in the classification of each response, we obtained a list of all the permanent committees and departments of the organization from the head of each organization and compared this list with the answers of respondents. In this way, we were able to classify responses into the fourfold classification of staff, organization-wide committee, departmental, and treatment (or production) meetings.

From these responses, several measures were constructed. The most important measure is the average frequency of attendance in both committee meetings and department meetings, since this taps the sheer rate of scheduled task communication and standardizes it for the varying number of respondents in each organization. We also constructed a measure of the average number of hours spent in these two kinds of meetings, but since the pattern of findings is the same, we do not report those results here. By distinguishing between organization-wide committees and department meetings, we can see if horizontal or vertical scheduled communications are most likely to be emphasized in organizations with given structural characteristics.

Unlike scheduled communications, unscheduled task communications are categorized by the level and department to which they are directed. (See Table 1.) In this way we can determine the degree to which communications flow in both horizontal and vertical directions.

Table 1. Means, Standard Deviations, and Ranges of the Intensity and Proportion Measures of Scheduled and Unscheduled Organizational Communications

	Mean	Standard Deviation	Range Low	High
A. Organization-wide committees				
1. Average number of committee meetings per month	.96	.53	0.0	1.91
2. Proportion of all staff members who participate in committee meetings per month	34%	6%	0%	60%
B. Departmental meetings				
1. Average number of departmental meetings per month	1.41	1.10	.18	4.00
2. Proportion of all staff members who participate in departmental meetings per month	41%	24%	6%	80%
C. Frequency of unscheduled communications				
1. Interdepartmental, higher level	3.74	2.83	.24	9.24
2. Interdepartmental, same level	4.98	3.70	.14	11.24
3. Interdepartmental, lower level	5.98	5.37	.00	17.14
4. Intradepartmental, higher level	6.38	4.25	.80	14.00
5. Intradepartmental, same level	7.05	4.17	.76	15.73
6. Intradepartmental, lower level	15.86	10.60	1.90	36.33
7. All unscheduled communications	26.84	13.91	6.50	61.79

Information about these more spontaneous and informal communications was obtained by asking each respondent the following questions: "In every position, it is sometimes necessary in fulfilling one's job to confer with other people. How many times in a typical week do you confer with people here in the organization other than at committee meetings?" "What are the names of these people?" "What are their job titles?" "How many times in a typical week do you confer with each of these persons?"

Two types of information were obtained from these questions: (1) the number of different persons in the organization with whom communications occur and (2) the frequency of these contacts. To simplify the presentation of the data, we only include here the latter, which is a measure of the intensity of information flow among members of the organization.

In order to determine whether a communication was intradepartmental or interdepartmental, we obtained a complete membership list of each department of each organization. We were thus able to locate the departmental affiliation of each person mentioned. The level within a department was determined by asking a series of questions at the outset of each interview about a respondent's job title, his major activity, names and titles of persons in the organization reporting to him, and names and titles of persons in the organization to whom hc reported. Since we had included most supervisors in our study, we were able to construct an "operative" organizational chart, which proved to be more useful than the formal organizational chart, which, if one existed, was often either outdated or inaccurate, or both. Thus, we were able to classify each unscheduled communication mentioned in one of the following categories: (1) interdepartmental, higher status level or upward communication; (2) interdepartmental, same status level or horizontal communication; (3) interdepartmental, lower status level or downward communication; (4) intradepartmental, higher status level or upward communication; (5) intradepartmental, same status level or horizontal communication; (6) intradepartmental, lower status level or downward communication; (7) all unscheduled communications, a summary of all informal communication.

Since organizations varied in size of staff, we standardized organizational scores by calculating the average frequency of unscheduled communications for each person in these organizations for each of the above categories. This was done by dividing the total frequency of communications in each category by the number of persons in the organizations for whom that type of communication was possible. It was logically impossible for some individuals to have particular types of communications. For example, those at the bottom of the chain of command could hardly communicate with someone lower down. The number of respondents used in the denominator therefore varied by category. Further, the information flow between the executive director and his subordinates was excluded in calculating organizational scores because such communications could not be classified as being in the same or a different department. Persons were given missing data scores for illogical types of communications, and final computations of organizational scores were based only on available data. In calculating the measure of "overall unscheduled communications," there were no missing data, since all respondents could logically have some kind of communications. This measure was constructed by dividing the total frequency of all unscheduled communications by the total number of respondents in each organization (excluding the organization head). These precautions hopefully allowed us to compute accurate rates of communication per organizational member, eliminating the biases created by different distributions of people among departments and status levels. As shown in Table 1, there is considerable variation among our organizations for these measures.

One might ask if scheduled and unscheduled communication scores are highly related to one another. In general, they are not. However, the greater the average frequency of committee meetings, the greater the horizontal unscheduled communications between departments. Thus, scheduled horizontal communication tends to be associated with unscheduled horizontal communication. On the other hand, the higher the proportion of people involved in departmental meetings, the less there are unscheduled intradepartmental communications. In other words, there seem to be alternative mechanisms for departments to achieve coordination.

Complexity and Communication Findings. Two measures of organizational complexity are used—the number of occupational specialties and the degree of professional activity. (See the Appendix for a description of measurement procedures for each variable.) The first is simply the number of specific occupational specialties that exist in each organization. The second reflects the degree to which staff members are active in professional activities outside the organization. The first two empirical hypotheses are (1) that the intensity of communications will vary directly with the number of occupational specialties and the degree of professional activity and (2) that these factors are most likely to be associated with communications in a horizontal direction.

Looking just at the relationships between occupational diversity and the intensity of communication, we note that the more diversified the occupational structure of an organization, the higher the intensity of overall unscheduled communications ($r = .51$) and the greater the involvement in organization-wide committees ($r = .66$), as shown in Panels C7 and A1 of Table 2. The relationship between the diversity of the occupational

Table 2. Pearsonian Correlation Coefficients Between Indicators of Complexity, Formalization, and Decentralization, and Measures of Scheduled and Unscheduled Communications

Communi-cation[a]	Complexity[b]		Formalization[b]		Decentrali-zation[b]
	Occ. Spe-cialties	Prof. Activity	Presence Job Descrip.	Index Job Specif.	
A1	.66[e]	.32	−.30	−.31	.60[d]
A2	.31	.20	−.40	−.29	.61[d]
B1	.20	.25	−.09	−.57[d]	.45[c]
B2	.13	.30	−.06	−.30	.37
C1	.34	.52[c]	−.41	−.08	.51[c]
C2	.67[e]	.62[d]	−.61[d]	−.20	.53[d]
C3	.40	.19	−.45[c]	−.42	.42
C4	.29	.26	−.15	.28	.18
C5	−.04	−.36	.15	.30	−.36
C6	−.19	−.31	−.52[c]	−.33	−.24
C7	.51[c]	.42	−.50[c]	−.12	.36

[a]See Table 1 for meaning of symbols.

[b]See the Appendix for a description of the construction of measures.

[c]$p < .10$.

[d]$p < .05$.

[e]$p < .01$.

structure and the frequency of attending departmental meetings is in the predicted direction but quite weak, as shown in Panel B1 ($r = .20$), indicating that while complexity is positively associated with the overall rate of scheduled communications it is more strongly associated with horizontal communications—that is, organization-wide committee meetings—than with vertical communications; that is, departmental meetings.

Professionalism was measured by the degree to which staff members were involved in professional associations, including number of associations, frequency of attendance, number of offices held, and number of papers given. This measure has weak relationships with most of the intensity of communication measures, although each is in the predicted direction; in the case of the intensity of overall unscheduled communications, the relationship is quite high, as shown in Panel C7 of Table 2 ($r = .42$).

To the extent that organization-wide committee meetings provide opportunities for horizontal communications, the second hypothesis above is supported. However, it requires some interpretation. Horizontal communications, as suggested earlier, can mean at least two things. (1) It can simply mean communications across departmental boundaries. But (2) it can mean communications with someone at the same status level, regardless of whether the communication is in the same or a different department. If we ask, however, whether such interdepartmental interactions are with someone at the same level, at a higher level, or at a lower level, we find that the frequency of such interdepartmental communications is greatest with others at the same status level for both the number of occupational levels ($r = .67$) and for the degree of professional activity ($r = .62$), although there is some suggestion that it can also be upward ($r = .34$ and $.52$, respectively) in other departments as well.

The conclusion we reach is that complexity—as measured both by the number of occupational specialties and professional activism—tends to be positively associated with the intensity of organizational communications, both organization-wide committees as well as all unscheduled communications. Looking more closely at this latter relationship, however, we find that it is the flow of communications with people *on the same status level in different departments* that is most highly associated with these two measures of complexity. Horizontal relationships with people in the same department are actually inversely related to the two measures of complexity. Thus, the word *horizontal* in our hypothesis should be modified to mean interdepartmental communications with persons on the same status level. However, this is exactly the intent of our original premise regarding the meaning of feedback. In particular, communication between departments is more likely to be of this kind. Regardless of this interpretation, it is clear that the volume of communications is higher in more complex organizations; and this is especially true of communications between departments, both scheduled and unscheduled.

Formalization and Communication. The measures of formalization included here are (1) the degree to which—as reported by respondents—there is a complete job description for their job and (2) the degree of job specificity. The latter measure was an index which included a number of additional items reflecting the programming of jobs, such as the existence of specific procedures for various contingencies, written records of job performance, and well-defined communication channels. The hypothesis here is that the greater the degree of formalization, the lower the rate of communications; and the direction is likely to be upward and downward within the same department, not between departments.

In general, we find that the correlations between formalization and measures of both the scheduled and unscheduled communications are not as strong as those between measures of complexity and communication rates. The existence of job descriptions tends to be negatively associated with the average frequency of participation in organization committees ($r = -.30$), as shown in Panels A1 and A2 of Table 2, middle column. However, the existence of job descriptions has no relationship with the intensity of participation in departmental meetings. Job specificity also has weak negative relationships with these same measures of communications. On the other hand, job specificity has a strong negative relationship with the frequency of attending departmental meetings; that is, the greater the degree to which jobs are programmed, the less frequently staff members attend departmental meetings, which also reflects in part that there are fewer departmental meetings in such organizations. The greater the degree to which there are job descriptions in an organization, the fewer the overall unscheduled interactions ($r = -.50$), although there is no relationship between job specificity and this measure of communication ($r = -.12$). The small size of these correlations, especially between the measures of formalization and scheduled communication, may reflect that we have poor measures of the degree of planning of the work flow. Both of our measures are specific to individual tasks, and neither reflects the degree of programming or coordination. This may explain why our measures work better with unscheduled communication than scheduled communication, since unscheduled communications are more likely to reflect discussions about particular jobs than organization-wide coordination.

Looking more closely at the categories of unscheduled communication, we see that the presence of job descriptions is negatively related to the frequency of interaction in each category, with the exception of communications on the same status level within the same department. The presence of job descriptions is especially strongly related (in a negative direction) in the case of communications between individuals at the same status level in different departments ($r = -.61$). Similarly, job specificity tends to affect the frequency of communications, although there are positive relationships between intradepartmental communications with superiors and colleagues on the same status level.

Centralization and Communication. The measure of centralization utilized here is the Index of Participation in Decision Making. It reflects the degree to which organizational members report their participation in (1) decisions about the hiring of personnel, (2) the promotion of personnel, (3) the adoption of new organizational policies, and (4) the adoption of new programs or services. A high score on this measure reflects the degree to which strategic organizational decisions, in contrast to decisions about work assignments and the like, are decentralized. Conversely, a low score on this measure means that there is a high degree of centralization in such organizations. Our hypotheses are that participation in decision making is positively related to the intensity of communications and that there are more horizontal communications in such organizations.

The degree of participation in these strategic organizational decisions was found to have strong positive relationships with the frequency of communications (see Table 2, last column). There is a strong positive relationship between the degree of participation in these strategic organization decisions and the frequency of attending both committee meetings ($r = .60$) and departmental meetings ($r = .45$). The relationship between participation in these decisions and the frequency of unscheduled interactions is in the predicted direction ($r = .36$), but not strong.

Looking more closely at the relationship between the index of participation in decision making and each category of unscheduled interaction, we note first that organizations with wide participation in decision making have a higher degree of interdepartmental communication. This is true for information flows upward, on the same level, and downward ($r = .51, .53,$ and $.42$, respectively). In decentralized organizations, there is greater interdepartmental communication in all directions—that is, at a higher level, the same level, and at a lower level in the chain of command; and this is generally true for staff members on all organizational levels. In decentralized organizations, there are fewer intradepartmental communications on the same level and downward.

Other Measures of Unscheduled Communication Volume and Direction. Although we have explored a number of measures of both scheduled and unscheduled communications, there are still others that one might consider. One could—and indeed we did—compute a proportional measure for unscheduled communications; that is, what percent of the flow is between departments at each relative status level, and what percent is within departments at each relative level. The advantage of this measure is that it provides the most stringent test regarding communication direction. In general, the pattern of findings is changed very little except to reduce the size of the correlations somewhat. In other words, complexity and decentralization not only positively affect the total volume of unscheduled communications but they increase the *proportion* and the frequency between departments per organizational members as well. Similarly, formalization reduces the *proportion* between departments as well as the volume. However, this effect is not as strong.

Still another way of computing unscheduled communications is to be concerned with level-specific communication rates, as opposed to our measures, which are not computed by level. For example, one can compute the frequency with which department heads confer with other department heads. However, preliminary analysis indicates that the same basic pattern of findings emerges when level-specific rates are substituted. Similarly, the level-specific rates indicate that it is not only the department heads and intermediate supervisors that are conferring between departments but other levels as well, suggesting again a pattern of coordination.

Discussion

Together these findings suggest that, as organizational structure becomes more diversified and, in particular, as personal specialization increases, the volume of communication increases because of the necessity of coordinating the diverse occupational specialists. The major direction of this increased flow of information is horizontal, especially cross-departmental communications at the same status levels. In this sense, committee meetings represent a greater emphasis on horizontal information flows than do departmental meetings because the former involve other departments. But there is also an increased horizontal flow of unscheduled task communication. Conversely, insofar as organizational leaders attempt to coordinate the organization via programming, as reflected in job descriptions and specified task procedures, the necessity for interaction declines. The interaction that exists is probably concerned with the interpretation of a particular regulation. Concomitantly, if power is dispersed in the organization, not only does the volume of communication increase, but the flow of communications across departmental boundaries is also increased. Similarly, organization-wide committees and departmental meetings (both scheduled mechanisms of interaction) are likely to be increased as well. As organizations have more and more of a sharp status pyramid, upward communication tends to be considerably inhibited, just as it is when the power is concentrated in the hands of a small elite.

If one accepts our theoretical framework, then there are some interesting implications of our findings. These findings suggest that, as organizations become more diversified, more specialized (personal specialization, not task specialization), and more differentiated, they have to rely less on a system of programmed interactions to achieve the necessary linkages between parts of the organization and more on a system of reciprocal information flows to achieve coordination. We have also suggested that such organizations would more likely rely on socialization rather than use of sanctions as a key mechanism of social control.

It may well be that findings such as ours are greatly affected by the nature of the technology in the organization or characteristics of the environment. That is, we might expect that an organization with a nonroutine technology would have a more diversified, more specialized (that is, more reliance on knowledge), and more differentiated structure, would more likely achieve coordination through feedback or mutual adjustment, and consequently would have a greater volume of communications (see Perrow, 1967). Similarly, we might expect that the consequences of an organization's having an environment that was unstable, heterogeneous, and characterized by uncertainty would be similar (see Thompson, 1967; Lawrence and Lorsch, 1967a). If this were true, it would suggest that the processes described here are only part of a larger system of interrelated forces. Future work might also explore the relative effectiveness of organizations using feedback as opposed to programming to achieve organizational goals, given similar structural characteristics. In these ways, the approach here might be extended and made more complete.

Appendix

Number of Occupational Specialties. The number of occupational specialties was based on questions with individual respondents, not on a count of number of specific titles. Each respondent was asked what he did, and then this was coded according to the kind of professional specialty. This procedure was considered to be more appropriate, since it permitted comparability across organizations and since it avoided the problem of task specialization in which one activity might be divided into many specific and separate tasks (see Thompson, 1961).

Professional Activity. The index of professional activity ranged from 0 to 3 points and was constructed as follows: (a) 1 point for belonging to one or more professional organizations; (b) 1 point for attending at least two-thirds of the previous six meetings of any professional organization; (c) 1 point for the presentation of a paper or holding any office in any professional organization.

Job Descriptions. The presence of job descriptions was determined by asking each respondent whether the following statement was definitely true, more true than false, more false than true, or definitely false: "There is a complete written job description for my job." Replies to these questions were scored from 1 (definitely false) to 4 (definitely true), and then the organizational score was computed using the aggregation procedure previously described (Aiken and Hage, 1968). A high score means the presence of job descriptions.

Job Specificity. The index of specificity of job was based on responses to the following six statements: (1) Whatever situation arises, we have procedures to follow in dealing with it. (2) Everyone has a specific job to do. (3) Going through the proper channel is constantly stressed. (4) The organization keeps a written record of everyone's job performance. (5) We are to follow strict operating procedures at all times. (6) Whenever we have a problem, we are supposed to go to the same person for an answer. Replies to these questions were scored and aggregated in the same way as job descriptions.

Participation in Decision Making. The index of participation in decision making was based on the following four questions: (1) How frequently do you usually participate in the decision to hire new staff? (2) How frequently do you usually participate in the decisions on the promotion of any of the professional staff? (3) How frequently do you participate in decisions on the adoption of new policies? (4) How frequently do you participate in the decision on the adoption of new programs? Respondents were assigned numerical scores from 1 (low participation) to 5 (high participation), depending on whether they answered "never," "seldom," "sometimes," "often," or "always," respectively, to these questions. An average score on these questions was computed for each respondent, and then the data were aggregated into organizational scores. A high number reflects a high degree of participation in decision making.

References

Aiken, M., and Hage, J. "Organizational Interdependence and Intraorganizational Structure." *American Sociological Review,* 1968, *33,* 912-930.

Barnard, C. "Functions and Pathology of Status Systems in Formal Organizations." In W. F. Whyte (Ed.), *Industry and Society.* New York: McGraw-Hill, 1964.

Blau, P. *The Dynamics of Bureaucracy.* Chicago: University of Chicago Press, 1955.

Blau, P., and Schoenherr, R. A. *The Structure of Organizations.* New York: Basic Books, 1971.

Blau, P., and Scott, W. R. *Formal Organizations.* San Francisco: Chandler, 1962.

Burns, T., and Stalker, G. M. *The Management of Innovation.* London: Tavistock, 1961.

Crozier, M. *The Bureaucratic Phenomenon.* Chicago: University of Chicago Press, 1964.

Dalton, M. "Conflicts Between Staff and Line Managerial Officers." *American Sociological Review,* 1950, *15,* 342-351.

Durkheim, E. *The Division of Labor in Society.* (G. Simpson, Trans.) New York: Free Press, 1933.

Festinger, L. *Social Pressures in Informal Groups: A Study of Human Factors in Housing.* New York: Harper & Row, 1950.

Gross, E. "Some Functional Consequences of Primary Controls in Formal Work Organizations." *American Sociological Review,* 1953, *18,* 368-373.

Guetzkow, H. "Communications in Organizations." In J. March (Ed.), *The Handbook of Organizations.* Chicago: Rand McNally, 1965.

Hage, J., and Aiken, M. "Routine Technology, Social Structure, and Organizational Goals." *Administrative Science Quarterly,* 1969, *14,* 366-378.

Hall, R. H., Haas, J. E., and Johnson, N. J. "Organizational Size, Complexity, and Formalization." *American Sociological Review,* 1967, *32,* 903-911.

Landsberger, H. A. "The Horizontal Dimension in Bureaucracy." *Administrative Science Quarterly,* 1961, *6,* 299-322.

Lawrence, P., and Lorsch, J. "Differentiation and Integration in Complex Organizations." *Administrative Science Quarterly,* 1967a, *12,* 1-47.

Lawrence, P., and Lorsch, J. *Organization and Environment.* Boston: Graduate School of Business Administration, Harvard University, 1967b.

McCleery, R. *Policy Change in Prison Management.* East Lansing: Government Research Bureau, Michigan State University, 1957.

March, J., and Simon, H. A. *Organizations.* New York: Wiley 1958.

Parsons, T. *The Social System.* New York: Free Press, 1951.

Parsons, T. *Societies: Evolutionary and Comparative Perspectives.* Englewood Cliffs, N.J.: Prentice-Hall, 1966.

Perrow, C. "A Framework for the Comparative Analysis of Organizations." *American Sociological Review,* 1967, *32,* 194-208.

Price, J. *Organizational Effectiveness.* Homewood, Ill.: Dorsey Press, 1967.

Pugh, D. S., and others. "The Context of Organization Structure." *Administrative Science Quarterly,* 1969, *14,* 91-115.

Ronken, H., and Lawrence, P. *Administering Change: A Case Study of Human Relations in a Factory.* Boston: Graduate School of Business Administration, Harvard University, 1952.

Rosengren, W. R., and DeVault, S. "The Sociology of Time and Space in an Obstetrical Hospital." In E. Friedsen (Ed.), *The Hospital in Modern Society.* New York: Free Press, 1963.

Smith, C. "A Comparative Analysis of Some Conditions and Consequences of Intraorganizational Conflict." *Administrative Science Quarterly,* 1966, *10,* 504-529.

Thompson, J. *Organizations in Action.* New York: McGraw-Hill, 1967.

Thompson, V. *Modern Organization.* New York: Knopf, 1961.

23

Communication in Administrative Bureaucracies

Samuel B. Bacharach
Michael Aiken

Much of the daily routine of organizations entails information exchange and coordination. To the extent that both these activities are dependent upon communication networks, communication thus becomes a plausible focus for comparative organizational analysis. However, while communication has been a recurrent theme in organizational theory (March and Simon, 1958; Blau and Scott, 1962; Barnard, 1938), there has been little empirical research dealing with organizational constraints on communication. For example, seldom have researchers studied how organizational size, shape, and technology affect communication. As Porter and Roberts (1976) have observed, what research has been done has been confined to such limited aspects of communication as the interactions between superiors and subordinates.

A review of the various comparative organizational studies undertaken in the last ten years reveals a lack of empirical research on organizational constraints on communication (see, for example, the works of Blau, 1968; Child, 1972; Pugh and others, 1968). This void is especially conspicuous since many of these studies have been concerned with control, decentralization, and decision making—all processes which are inextricably linked to the flow of communication. Indeed, it may be argued that, in most comparative organizational research, communication has been treated epiphenomenally. This tendency is exemplified by Blau's research on authority, for, as Brewer (1971) has observed, Blau makes several allusions to communication but neglects to examine its significance empirically.

Hage, Aiken, and Marrett (1971) conducted one of the few studies which examined the effect of organizational constraints on communication. Using a sample of sixteen health and welfare organizations, they investigated the effect of such organizational factors as complexity, formalization, and centralization. Generally, they discovered that in less complex, less formal, and more decentralized organizations, communication was greater than in complex, formal, centralized organizations. In operationalizing the fre-

Reprinted from *Academy of Management Journal*, 1977, *20* (3), 365-377, with permission of the authors and the Academy of Management.

quency of communication within organizations, Hage, Aiken, and Marrett (1971) derived a mean score for all organizational actors. However, actors are members of different subgroups in the organizations; consequently, organizational contraints may differentially affect the frequency of their communication depending on their location in specific subgroups.

While many subgroups are susceptible to empirical study, in the case of communication, status groups may prove most fruitful. Indeed, as Porter and Roberts (1976) have observed, previous research has shown variations in the nature of communication across organizational hierarchies. For example, Gerard (1957) found that in an experimental situation those subjects who were asked to assume the role of "boss" sent more messages to the "clerks" on the four-man teams. Similarly, two sets of findings indicate that the specific location in the organizational hierarchy affects communication patterns; Barnlund and Harland (1962) and Allen and Cohen (1969) found that high-status individuals communicate more with each other than with low-status individuals and that low-status individuals are also more likely to attempt to communicate with high-status individuals than with low-status individuals. In this context, this study will attempt to predict what effect organizational constraints have on the direction and the frequency of communication of two echelons in each of forty-four administrative bureaucracies.

Within these forty-four administrative bureaucracies, the study will be concerned with verbal communication, as opposed to written communication. Verbal communication is the most spontaneous and common form of communication in organizations and, therefore, provides the most sensitive measure for tapping daily interactions in these bureaucracies. It is through verbal interaction that important information is most frequently transmitted, such as the exchange of ideas, the specification of regulations, the discussion of organizational politics, or the planning of the monthly soccer game. This paper will concentrate on the frequency and the direction of verbal communication, confining its focus to the frequency of downward, upward, and lateral communication.

Sample

This study is based on data that were gathered in forty-four local administrative bureaucracies in Belgian cities in the size range of 15,000 to 100,000. These cities were selected on the basis of a 50 percent stratified random sample of the sixteen cities in the Brussels agglomeration, twenty-five cities in Wallonia, and fifty-five cities in Flanders as of December 31, 1968. Five cities in the original sample—four in Flanders and one in Wallonia—are not included because of either lack of cooperation from city officials or too low a response rate from members of the administrative units.

Within each city, the mayor and municipal secretary were interviewed, and a sample of members of the city administration was given a questionnaire. All department heads (that is, the head of departments or services who reported directly to the mayor, an alderman, and/or the municipal secretary) were automatically selected in the sample. Within each department a simple random sample of subordinates (that is, those responsible to department heads) was selected. The sampling ratio varied according to the size of the department as follows: In departments with less than ten members, one-half of the department members were selected; in departments with ten to nineteen members, one-third of the members were selected; and in departments with twenty or more members, one-fourth were selected. Only administrative personnel were included in the study. Workers, police, and fire-fighting personnel were excluded.

Of the 1,005 questionnaires distributed in these forty-four city administrations,

85.9 percent were returned, and approximately 82 percent were usable. There was no difference in the response rate of department heads and their subordinates.

Dependent Variable

In this study, a series of questions were asked about communication in the organization. Respondents were asked to report the number of contacts either in face-to-face meetings or by telephone with persons at the *same* level, at a *lower* level, and at a *higher* level in the organization in a typical week. Scores for each of the forty-four organizations were computed for both department heads and subordinates for the three dimensions of communication. For each, organizational scores for department heads were computed by averaging the responses of all department heads; likewise, organizational scores for subordinates were computed by averaging responses of all subordinates. The means, standard deviations, and range of communication scores are shown in Table 1.

Table 1. Means, Standard Deviations, and Range of Communication Scores by Level (N = 44)

	Mean	Standard Deviation	Range High	Range Low
Department head				
Upward communications	8.34	8.90	45.33	0.50
Lateral communications	3.45	3.15	15.25	0.00
Downward communications	17.91	13.13	51.00	1.20
All communications	9.60	7.28	36.00	0.58
Subordinate				
Upward communications	7.42	3.65	19.10	1.00
Lateral communications	6.08	3.86	18.90	0.00
Downward communications	6.71	3.93	22.00	0.00
All communications	6.55	3.31	19.99	0.33

As has been argued above, the analysis of communication patterns in organizations should take into account differences in patterns across status groups. Table 1 lends support to this position. Generally, department heads are found to engage in more communication than subordinates. Only for lateral communication does the mean for subordinates exceed the mean for department heads (6.08 versus 3.45). Using a t test for differences of means, we find that, with the exception of upward communication, all the mean scores are significantly different at the .05 level or greater. Porter and Roberts (1976) have suggested that a higher proportion of management communication will occur on the vertical axis, while a higher proportion of rank-and-file communication will occur on the horizontal axis. Indeed, we find that lateral communication constitutes a higher proportion of subordinate communication than it does of department head communication; on the average, 30 percent of subordinate communication is lateral, while 12 percent of department head communication is lateral.

Correlating department head communication with subordinate communication, we find no significant relationship (r = .02 between upward communication of department heads and upward communication of subordinates, r = .08 between lateral communication of department heads and lateral communication of subordinates, r = .17 between downward communication of department heads and downward communication of subordinates, and r = .12 between total communication of department heads and total communication of subordinates). Given the differences in communication patterns across levels, it becomes apparent that any analysis of organizational constraints on communication must take into consideration differences in communication patterns across the organizational hierarchy.

Hypotheses

In examining the various organizational constraints on communication of department heads and subordinates, the following independent variables will be considered: organizational size, administrative complexity, routineness of technology, decentralization of authority, and organizational permeability.

Organizational Size. Porter and Roberts (1976) claimed that the relationship of organizational size to communication has been virtually overlooked. In their extensive review of the literature, they cite only one study (Donald, 1959) which maintained that an increase in organizational size decreased vertical communication but left lateral communication unaffected. It may be argued that in larger organizations the need for control, coordination, and exchange of information is acute, necessitating greater frequency of communication. Consequently, *the first hypothesis speculates that in larger organizations both department heads and subordinates would engage in greater vertical and lateral communication.*

The measure of organizational size is the number of members in the local administrative bureaucracy. Even though city population size ranged from 15,000 to 100,000, the size of these administrative bureaucracies varied from 44 to 1,530. The mean number of members was 245.7, and the standard deviation was 271.4, indicating considerable skew in this variable. Therefore, it was transformed into its natural logarithm prior to statistical analysis.

Organizational Shape. Porter and Roberts (1976) also point out that there has been no research which is directly concerned with the relationship of the shape of the organization to communication within it. Two measures of structural complexity were used to tap the shape of the organization—width and vertical differentiation.

Width was measured by the number of departments in the organization. A department was defined as any unit having at least two persons and two levels, the head of which reported to the mayor, administrator, or an alderman. The organizations in this study varied from three to twelve departments; the mean was 7.16, and the standard deviation was 2.22.

Vertical differentiation or height was measured by counting the number of levels in each department from the department head to the lowest-level worker and then calculating the average for all departments. Organizational scores ranged from 2.50 to 6.0; the mean was 3.64, and the standard deviation was .87.

Generally, two interpretations may be offered as to how structural complexity affects frequency of communication. On the one hand, one can argue that, to the degree that structural complexity is indicative of high differentiation, it would reduce the need for constant communication, for such differentiation delineates the division of labor, making the usual communication associated with delegation of work unnecessary. On the other hand, it may be argued that such distinct differentiation, nonetheless, requires coordination, which, in turn, entails a high level of communication. Stressing the latter interpretation, *the second hypothesis posits a positive relationship between organizational structural complexity and the frequency of department head and subordinate communication.*

Routineness of Technology. In recent years, technology has come to be viewed as a primary constraint on organizational structure and behavior (Perrow, 1967; Woodward, 1965; Hickson, Pugh, and Pheysey, 1969; Hage and Aiken, 1969). But again, as Porter and Roberts (1976, p. 1570) point out, we have relatively little sound information as to the relationship between technology and communication. While there is an ongoing debate in the literature as to how technology is to be measured (Lynch, 1974), the measure of technology used here reflects the orientation of Hage and Aiken (1969) and Perrow (1967), which locates technology at the level of individual tasks. To the degree that a primary dimension of technology is the routinization of the work activity, workers were asked specific questions as to the nature of their tasks. The degree of routinization of work processes was based on six questionnaire items, which were coded (1) "definitely true," (2) "more true than false," (3) "more false than true," and (4) "definitely false," unless otherwise stated. The six questionnaire items included:

1. "There is something different to do here every day." (reversed)
2. "People here do the same job in the same way every day."
3. "In my bureau we need to learn more than one job."
4. "The same steps must be followed in processing every piece of work." (reversed)
5. "For almost every job there is something new happening almost every day."
6. "Would you say your work here is very routine (coded as 4), routine (coded as 3), nonroutine (coded as 2), or very nonroutine (coded as 1)?" (reversed)

For the above index, the department head scores varied from a low routinization score of 1.33 to a high routinization score of 2.71; the mean was 1.87, and the standard deviation was .264. The subordinate scores varied from a low routinization score of 1.57 to a high routinization score of 2.65, with a mean of 2.17 and a standard deviation of .233. To test the reliability of the measures of routinization, Cronbach's alpha was calculated. Its value for department head routinization was .70, and its value for subordinate routinization was .73.

The third hypothesis posits that in organizations where department heads and subordinates report their work as more routine, the less the communication in which they will engage. A number of justifications may be offered for this hypothesis. First, highly routine work does not require frequent communication to specify division of labor. Second, highly routine work does not require a high degree of communication to achieve coordination. Finally, highly routine work does not require communication for the sake of supervision; however, nonroutine work, owing to its unpredictability, would require communication for the sake of supervision and coordination.

Decentralization of Authority. Hage, Aiken, and Marrett (1971) found a strong relationship between decentralization of authority and a high degree of communication. The concentration of authority was held to diminish the participation of actors in the decision-making process, thereby decreasing their communication. Within the context of these findings, *it is also hypothesized that the more decentralized the organization, the greater the frequency of department head and subordinate communication.* Decentralization of authority was measured by examining the reported authority of organizational actors in making eighteen strategic decisions. Strategic decisions refer to those decisions which were concerned with policy matters. Included in the list of strategic decisions are such decision areas as budget, promotion, personnel, and publications. Department heads and their subordinates were asked whether they could not or could make decisions in these areas.

The specific decision areas included:

1. The promotion of lowest-level supervisors
2. Promotion of nonsupervisory personnel
3. Sanctioning of lowest-level supervisors
4. Sanctioning of nonsupervisory personnel
5. Decisions about whether or not people work overtime
6. Procedures used in personnel selection
7. Determination of the number of lowest-level supervisory positions
8. Determination of the number of nonsupervisory positions
9. Decisions about budget allocation of this township
10. Determination of the budget for your service
11. Determination of new programs and activities
12. Determination of new objectives and projects
13. Creation of new subbureau or division
14. Creation of new position
15. Handling public relations outside the local administration
16. Giving official information to someone or a group outside the local administration
17. Choosing suppliers for materials
18. Decisions about accounting procedures

Department heads' scores on decentralization varied from a low of .06 to a high of .63, and the mean and standard deviation were .30 and .14, respectively. Subordinates' scores on decentralization varied from a low of .00 to a high of .32, with a mean of .15 and standard deviation of .07. To test the reliability of the index of decentralization. Cronbach's alpha was computed, yielding a .8981 score for department heads and a .8687 for subordinates.

Boundary Spanning. Traditionally, organizational permeability has been defined as boundary-spanning activity. Thompson (1967) has referred to this relationship between an organization and its environment as "boundary-spanning roles"; other terms—such as boundary positions (Kahn and others, 1964), liaison role (Evan and Levin, 1966), and linking pin (Organ, 1971)—have also been used to refer to the same phenomenon. The authors define such boundary-spanning roles as "those roles which link the focal organizations in a social system and which are directly relevant for the goal attainment of the focal organization" (see Kahn and others, 1964; Organ, 1971).

In operationalizing boundary spanning, each respondent was asked to report the number of contacts with persons in other public services during a typical week as well as the number of contacts with persons outside the public sector during a typical week. These were summed for each person, and then level-specific boundary-spanning scores were constructed by taking the average for all department heads and the average for all subordinates. The range of boundary-spanning scores for department heads varied from a low of .25 to a high of 17.5. The mean was 4.8, and the standard deviation was 4.3. The range of boundary-spanning scores for subordinates varied from a low of 0.0 to a high of 11.0, and the mean and standard deviation were 3.0 and 2.0, respectively. To test the reliability of the index of boundary spanning, Cronbach's alpha was computed, yielding a .7812 score for department heads and a .5484 for subordinates.

The fifth hypothesis postulates that *the greater the degree of organizational boundary-spanning activity, the greater the frequency of department head and subordinate communication.* There are two explanations for this hypothesis. First, boundary-spanning activity assures access to unique information which needs to be exchanged in the organization, thus increasing the interaction rates. Second, it may be that where boundary-spanning activity occurs, a high degree of internal control and coordination are necessary. Thus, to the degree that the frequency of communication is indicative of information exchange and internal control, we would expect greater communication in permeable organizations.

Findings

Table 2 presents the relationship between size, width, and height and department and subordinate communication. Regarding department heads, the major finding is the lack of effect of these structural dimensions upon the frequency of department head communication. Neither the measures of shape (that is, width and height) nor size accurately predict the frequency of department head communication.

Unlike the case of department head communication, the measures of size and shape do appear to predict subordinate communication. In the zero-order correlation, the average number of levels and organizational size are positively correlated with each of the measures of communication. However, in the multiple regression model, width and size appear as the primary predictors of the frequency of communication. In the multiple regression model, width has a consistently negative effect upon the frequency of subordinate communication (beta = $-.44$ for upward communication of subordinates, beta = $-.43$ for lateral communication of subordinates, beta = $-.28$ for downward communication of subordinates, and beta = $-.41$ for total communication of subordinates). Organizational size has a consistently positive effect on the frequency of subordinate communication (beta = .46 for upward communication, beta = .67 for lateral communication, beta = .64 for downward communication, and beta = .62 for total communication). Clearly, the pattern represented in the regression model is different than the pattern represented in the zero-order correlation. It is important to note that the zero-order correlation between width and size was .55, and the zero-order correlation between average level and size was .64, while the zero-order correlation between average number of levels and width was .11. In the zero-order correlation presented in Table 2, size is obviously suppressing the negative effect of width on communication. It is only when we control for the effect of size in the multiple regression that the importance of width emerges. Average number of levels, however, loses any impact in the multiple regression model due to its high correlation with size.

Operationalized as the number of departments in the organization, width reflects organizational segmentation, which is a different phenomenon than either vertical differentiation or size. Segmentation implies a clustering of roles on the basis of common goals and objectives. Indeed, departmentalization is, in Thompson's (1967, p. 57) sense, a mode of homogenizing organizational positions and components, implying an underlying consensus as to goals, objectives, and work processes. Hence, communication for the sake of defining goals and objectives and specifying work processes may not be required when organizations are internally segmented.

Size by itself is neither a measure of differentiation nor of segmentation; rather, it is simply a measure of the number of individuals in the organization. This distinction is important if the above results are to be interpreted properly. If there are a large number of organizational actors whose relationships have not been specified, either by segmentation or by differentiation, there is a greater need for frequent communication. As the above results indicate, when organizations are highly segmented, the need for communica-

Table 2. Frequency of Department Head and Subordinate Communication with Shape and Size of the Organization
(N = 44)

Shape and Size	Upward Communication of Subordinates		Lateral Communication of Subordinates		Downward Communication of Subordinates		Total Communication of Subordinates		Upward Communication of Department Heads		Lateral Communication of Department Heads		Downward Communication of Department Heads		Total Communication of Department Heads	
	r^a	$beta^b$	r	beta	r	beta	r	beta	r	beta	r	beta	r	beta	r	beta
Width	−.17	−.44[d]	−.05	−.43[d]	.09	−.28	−.05	−.41[d]	−.05	.08	.03	.11	.00	−.17	−.01	−.05
Average number of levels	.31[d]	.06	.24[c]	−.15	.43[e]	.04	.36[e]	.00	−.07	.09	.21[c]	.33	.18	.00	.10	.07
Organizational size logged	.25[c]	.46[c]	.33[d]	.67[e]	.51[e]	.64[e]	.39[e]	.62[e]	−.16	−.26	.07	−.21	.21[c]	.32	.07	.05
	$R^2 = .21$		$R^2 = .21$		$R^2 = .32$		$R^2 = .27$		$R^2 = .03$		$R^2 = .06$		$R^2 = .07$		$R^2 = .01$	

[a] r = zero-order correlation (one-tailed test).
[b] beta = standardized regression coefficient.
[c] $p \leq .10$.
[d] $p \leq .05$.
[e] $p \leq .01$.

tion may prove to be minimal. However, when such specificity does not exist and the organization has a large number of members, frequent communication is necessary to achieve some definition of task and to achieve consensus as to subgroup goals and objectives.

Table 3 presents the findings regarding the relationship between routinization, boundary spanning, decentralization, and frequency of communication. For both department heads and subordinates, we find boundary spanning and decentralization to be positively associated with the frequency of communication. Routinization, however, fails to emerge as a significant factor. In the multiple regression model, boundary spanning is significantly related to all the measures of communication with the exception of downward communication of department heads. This finding would suggest that in organizations where department heads and subordinates have greater contact with the organizational environment, they will engage in more frequent internal communication.

As suggested earlier, a number of explanations may account for this finding. First, boundary-spanning activity provides access to unique information which needs to be distributed within the organization, thus increasing the level of internal communication. Second, perhaps where boundary-spanning activity occurs, a high level of internal control and coordination is necessary to channel the information generated by this activity. Thus, to the degree that frequency of communication is a form of internal control and coordination, it should increase in open organizations.

The final hypothesis speculated that the more decentralized an organization, the more likely the organizational members will engage in frequent communications. Examining the zero correlations in Table 3, we find decentralization to be associated with the frequency of subordinate and department head communication. In organizations where subordinates and department heads report themselves to have a high level of authority, they will also tend to engage in more frequent communication. However, examining the multiple regression model presented in Table 3, it is clear that, for most patterns of communication, boundary spanning is a stronger direct predictor of subordinate and department head communication than decentralization. A possible explanation of this finding is that open organizations will often tend to be decentralized; consequently, for some patterns of communication, the positive zero-order relationship between decentralization and communication is due to the strong relationship between decentralization and boundary spanning. Therefore, in some instances, the relationship between decentralization and frequency of communication drops out of the regression model.

Only two variables have emerged as predictors of the frequency of department head communication—boundary spanning and decentralization. For subordinates, four variables emerge as important—organizational size, organizational width, boundary spanning, and decentralization. Table 4 attempts to discover which of these remains the most significant. Examining the multiple regression models in Table 4, we discover the same pattern as that which emerges in the zero-order correlations. However, only the betas for boundary spanning and organizational size remain consistently strong in the multiple regression model, suggesting that, in order to understand the frequency of subordinate communication in these bureaucracies, the effects of openness and size on their inner workings need to be examined.

Summary and Conclusion

This paper began by maintaining that not enough research has focused on organizational factors that constrain the frequency of communication. Within this context, it

Table 3. Frequency of Department Head and Subordinate Communication with Routinization, Boundary Spanning, and Decentralization (N = 44)

Independent Variables	Upward Communication of Subordinates		Lateral Communication of Subordinates		Downward Communication of Subordinates		Total Communication of Subordinates		Upward Communication of Department Heads		Lateral Communication of Department Heads		Downward Communication of Department Heads		Total Communication of Department Heads	
	r^a	$beta^b$	r	beta	r	beta	r	beta	r	beta	r	beta	r	beta	r	beta
Routinization of work activity	$-.16$	$-.00$	$-.17$	$.04$	$-.22$	$-.02$	$-.23^c$	$-.02$	$-.23^c$	$-.10$	$-.26^d$	$-.17$	$-.26^d$	$-.17$	$-.28^d$	$-.17$
Boundary spanning	$.43^e$	$.36^d$	$.57^e$	$.52^e$	$.51^e$	$.41^e$	$.57^e$	$.47^e$	$.43^e$	$.29^d$	$.42^e$	$.36^e$	$.29$	$-.18$	$.41^d$	$.28^e$
Decentralization	$.34^d$	$.23$	$.39^e$	$.25^c$	$.47^e$	$.35^e$	$.44^d$	$.31^d$	$.45^e$	$.32^e$	$.21^e$	$.05$	$.29$	$.19$	$.38^d$	$.25^c$
	$R^2 = .23$		$R^2 = .39$		$R^2 = .38$		$R^2 = .41$		$R^2 = .29$		$R^2 = .21$		$R^2 = .16$		$R^2 = .26$	

[a] r = zero-order correlation (one-tailed test).

[b] beta = standardized regression coefficient.

[c] $p \leq .10$.

[d] $p \leq .05$.

[e] $p \leq .01$.

Table 4. Integrated Model for Subordinate Communication ($N = 44$)

Independent Variables	Upward Communication of Subordinates		Lateral Communication of Subordinates		Downward Communication of Subordinates		Total Communication of Subordinates	
	r[a]	beta[b]	r	beta	r	beta	r	beta
Width	−.17	−.33[d]	−.05	−.17	.09	−.11	−.05	−.22
Boundary spanning	.43[e]	.30[d]	.57[e]	.47[e]	.51[e]	.40[d]	.57[e]	.44[d]
Decentralization	.34[d]	.16	.39[e]	.16	.47[e]	.23	.44[e]	.21
Organizational size logged	.25[c]	.39[d]	.33[d]	.36[d]	.51[e]	.50[e]	.39[e]	.44[e]
	$R^2 = .33$		$R^2 = .46$		$R^2 = .56$		$R^2 = .52$	

[a]r = zero-order correlation (one-tailed test).

[b]beta = standardized regression coefficient.

[c]$p \leqq .10$.

[d]$p \leqq .05$.

[e]$p \leqq .01$.

has been demonstrated that the effects of organizational factors on the frequency of communication depend on which level of the organizational hierarchy is being examined. Indeed, for department heads, with the exception of boundary spanning and, to a lesser degree, decentralization, the organizational dimensions made little or no difference. For subordinates, however, the organizational constraints appear to be consequential; boundary spanning and organizational size had the most impact. In general, organizational variables explained as much as 50 percent of the variance in the frequency of subordinate communication but little of the variance in the frequency of department head communication.

The findings clearly suggest that organizational constraints are more important in predicting the frequency of communication among lower-level bureaucrats than they are in predicting the frequency of communication among middle-level bureaucrats. Thus, it may be inferred that, while subordinate communication is demonstrably influenced by structural determinants, department head communication may be more susceptible to psychological influences such as leadership and motivation. In conclusion, this research has not only sought to explain subordinate and department head communication, it has also demonstrated the value of level-specific analysis for examining organizational processes such as communication.

References

Allen, T. J., and Cohen, S. I. "Information Flow in Research and Development Laboratories." *Administrative Science Quarterly*, 1969, *14*, 12-20.

Barnard, C. I. *The Functions of the Executive.* Cambridge, Mass.: Harvard University Press, 1938.

Barnlund, D. C., and Harland, C. "Propinquity and Prestige as Determinants of Communication Networks." *Sociometry*, 1962, *26*, 467-479.

Blau, P. M. "The Hierarchy of Authority in Organizations." *American Journal of Sociology*, 1968, *73*, 453-467.

Blau, P. M., and Scott, W. R. *Formal Organizations.* San Francisco: Chandler, 1962.

Brewer, J. "Flow of Communications, Expert Qualifications, and Organizational Authority Structures." *American Sociological Review,* 1971, *36,* 475-484.

Child, J. "Organization Structure and Strategies of Control." *Administrative Science Quarterly,* 1972, *17,* 163-177.

Donald, M. N. "Some Concomitants of Varying Patterns of Communication in a Large Organization." Unpublished doctoral dissertation, University of Michigan, 1959.

Evan, W. M., and Levin, E. G. "Status-Set and Role-Set Conflicts of Stockbrokers." *Social Forces,* 1966, *45,* 73-83.

Gerard, H. B. "Some Effects of Status, Role Clarity, and Group Goal Clarity upon the Individual's Relations to Group Process." *Journal of Personality,* 1957, *25,* 475-588.

Hage, J., and Aiken, M. "Routine Technology, Social Structure, and Organizational Goals." *Administrative Science Quarterly,* 1969, *14,* 366-376.

Hage, J., Aiken, M., and Marrett, C. B. "Organization Structure and Communications." *American Sociological Review,* 1971, *36,* 860-871.

Hickson, D. J., Pugh, D. S., and Pheysey, D. C. "Operations Technology and Organization Structure: An Empirical Reappraisal." *Administrative Science Quarterly,* 1969, *14,* 378-397.

Kahn, R. L., and others. *Organizational Stress: Studies in Role Conflict and Ambiguity.* New York: Wiley, 1964.

Katz, D., and Kahn, R. L. *The Social Psychology of Organizations.* New York: Wiley, 1966.

Lynch, B. P. "An Empirical Assessment of Perrow's Technology Construct." *Administrative Science Quarterly,* 1974, *19,* 338-356.

March, J., and Simon, H. *Organizations.* New York: Wiley, 1958.

Organ, D. "Linking Pins Between Organizations and Environment." *Business Horizons,* 1971, *14* (6), 73-80.

Perrow, C. "A Framework for the Comparative Analysis of Organizations." *American Sociological Review,* 1967, *32,* 194-208.

Porter, L. W., and Roberts, K. H. "Communication in Organizations." In M. D. Dunnette (Ed.), *Handbook of Industrial and Organizational Psychology.* Chicago: Rand McNally, 1976.

Pugh, D. S., and others. "Dimensions of Organizational Structure." *Administrative Science Quarterly,* 1968, *13,* 65-105.

Thompson, J. D. *Organizations in Action.* New York: McGraw-Hill, 1967.

Woodward, J. *Industrial Organization: Theory and Practice.* London: Oxford University Press, 1965.

24

The Intentional Distortion of Information in Organizational Communication: A Laboratory and Field Investigation

Charles A. O'Reilly III

There exists considerable evidence confirming the notion that information is often blocked or distorted as it travels in organizational communication networks. Authors such as Downs (1967), Halberstam (1972), Janis (1972), Kaufman (1973), Wilensky (1967), and others have provided retrospective accounts documenting organizational dysfunctions attributed to failures in information flow and decision making. The specific causes and mechanisms of information distortion, however, have not been well explicated or understood.

At an organizational level of analysis, Wilensky (1967) postulates three structural conditions which, in his view, increase the probability that information in an organizational communication network will fail to reach the appropriate decision maker. These three are (1) *hierarchy,* which restricts the free flow of information; (2) *specialization,* which acts to reduce communication among subunits; and (3) *centralization,* which can result in decision makers being too far removed from reality to function effectively. Janis (1972) proposes that group cohesiveness or pressures toward *group conformity* may also operate to suppress the free flow of accurate information. Kaufman (1973) proposes a similar effect stemming from official rewards and sanctions rather than informal group norms.

At an individual level of analysis, March and Simon (1958) call attention to the phenomenon of "uncertainty absorption," which occurs when a sender draws inferences from a body of evidence and transmits the inferences rather than the data. Campbell (1958) reviews twenty-one mechanisms through which information transmitted by human links in a communication network can be distorted.

Still at the individual level of analysis, researchers have examined three interpersonal variables which have been shown to have a consistent impact on the transmission

Reprinted from *Human Relations,* 1978, *31* (2), 173-193, with permission of the author and Plenum Publishing Corporation.

of information in organizational hierarchies: (1) the sender's *trust* in the receiver of the message (see, for example, Giffin, 1967; Read, 1962; Zand, 1972); (2) the sender's perception of the receiver's *influence* over the sender (see, for example, Alkire and others, 1968; Watson and Bromberg, 1965); and (3) the sender's *mobility aspirations* (see, for example, Athanassiades, 1973; Lawler, Porter, and Tenenbaum, 1968; Read, 1962). In general, these three variables have not been investigated as they simultaneously affect communication behavior, nor have they been investigated as antecedents to specific distortion-producing mechanisms.

Based on these foundations, a sender-receiver paradigm linking the proposed antecedent variables to information distortion is proposed in Figure 1. The organizational

**Figure 1. Structural and Interpersonal Antecedents to the
Distortion of Information in Organizational Communication**

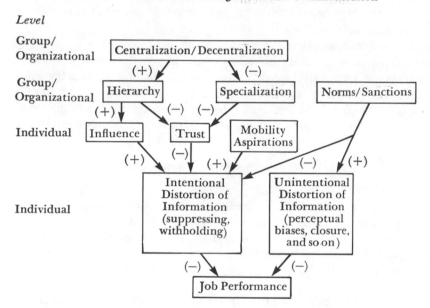

variables proposed by Wilensky (1967), Janis (1972), and Kaufman (1973) are seen as operating at the individual level through the three interpersonal variables researchers have shown to be consistently related to a variety of communication outcomes. These individual-level variables are postulated to result in propensities either toward intentional, or conscious, alteration of information or toward unintentional, or unconscious, distortion.

For the purposes of this research, information distortion is defined as the incorrect reproduction of objectively correct information and can result from either conscious or deliberate alteration or unconscious manipulation. The former is of primary interest here. The specific mechanisms investigated are those frequently referred to in descriptions of information failures and include (1) the blockage or omission of information, (2) summarization or condensation, (3) changing the form of a message, and (4) expanding or emphasizing certain details. These mechanisms may contribute to the "sharpening" or selective retention of certain details in a message or the "leveling" or selective omission of other details (Allport and Postman, 1947; Berkowitz, 1971; Shibutani, 1966).

Two situational variables are postulated to increase the likelihood that a sender will distort a message: (1) the type of information being transmitted and (2) the directionality of information flow. In the first instance, information which reflects either favorably or unfavorably on the sender, or information which is perceived as important or unimportant to the receiver, may be singled out for sharpening or leveling by the sender (Argyris, 1953; Simon, 1957). In the second instance, there exists some empirical evidence which suggests that information being transmitted upward in a hierarchy is perceived and perhaps treated differently than information flowing laterally or downward (Davis, 1968; Julian, 1966; Lawler, Porter, and Tenenbaum, 1968).

With this background, the study reported here focuses on testing a reduced set of the relationships proposed in Figure 1. Specifically, this investigation examines the impact of the three interpersonal variables (trust of the sender in the receiver, perceived influence of the receiver over the sender, and mobility aspirations of the sender) on the sender's propensity to sharpen or level information being transmitted upward in the organizational hierarchy. The focus is on the individual as an information transmitter and those intentional information-processing behaviors which may result in message distortion during transmission.

To examine adequately the antecedents to and mechanisms for information distortion, this research uses both laboratory and field investigations. The former concentrate on the interpersonal antecedents and specific distortion-producing mechanisms, while the latter, guided by laboratory findings, establish external validity for the laboratory results and examine the relationship between perceptions of information distortion and important organizational outcomes such as performance and job satisfaction.

General Hypotheses

The algebraic signs shown on the links among variables in Figure 1 suggest a set of hypotheses. In the aggregate, the general exploratory hypothesis is that the three interpersonal variables will be related in a nonrandom fashion to the sharpening and leveling of information being sent by subordinates to their superiors. The following subset of hypotheses is proposed:

1. *Trust in superior.* Under conditions in which the sender (subordinate) expresses high trust in the receiver (superior), more information is passed than under conditions of low trust.
2. *Influence of the superior.* Under conditions in which the sender perceives the receiver to have high influence, more total information will be passed than under conditions of low influence.
3. *Mobility aspirations of the sender.* Under conditions in which the sender has high mobility aspirations, less information will be passed than under conditions of low mobility aspirations.

In turn, the intentional alteration (sharpening-leveling) of information is postulated to be associated with work attitudes and job performance in the following manner:

4. *Job satisfaction.* Under conditions in which less information is passed (high leveling of information), job satisfaction will be lower than when information is not leveled.
5. *Job performance.* Under conditions in which less information is passed (high leveling), job performance will be lower than when more information is passed.

Method

Laboratory Experiment No. 1 (O'Reilly and Roberts, 1974b)

Objective. The purpose of the first experiments was to examine the impact of two interpersonal variables (trust, influence) on the sender's propensity to withhold or omit from transmission four types of information (favorable, unfavorable, important, unimportant) from a receiver (superior, subordinate, peer).

Hypotheses. Based upon the existing evidence about directionality of information flows in organizations and the impact of trust and influence on these flows, two sets of hypotheses were developed.

Directionality of information flow and filtration:
1. Less total information is passed upward than laterally or downward.
2. More information favorable to the sender is transmitted upward than laterally or downward.
3. More information unfavorable to the sender is passed downward than upward or laterally.

Effects of trust and influence on information filtration:
4. Under conditions in which the sender has high trust in the receiver:
   (a) more total information is transmitted than under conditions of low trust.
   (b) more unfavorable information is transmitted than under conditions of low trust.
   (c) more important information is transmitted than under conditions of low trust.
   (d) more unfavorable and important information is transmitted than under conditions of low trust.
5. Under conditions in which the sender perceives the receiver to have high influence over his future:
   (a) more total information is passed than under conditions of low influence.
   (b) more favorable information is passed than under conditions of low influence.

Subjects. Subjects, randomly assigned across the three experimental conditions, were 171 graduate and undergraduate students at the University of California, Berkeley. Over 88 percent of the subjects had previous work experience in formal organizations. Their average age was 24.2 years.

Information Coding. Twenty-four independent raters categorized 110 information items contained in an initial pool. Each judge was given the general and specific problem description later used in the experiment and instructions to code items presented to him into important and unimportant categories based on whether the item was considered directly relevant to the problem ("important") or not directly relevant ("unimportant"). Each judge then coded all items into favorable-neutral-unfavorable categories. Favorable items were those which reflected favorably on the sender's performance of his duties; unfavorable items were those which reflected unfavorably on his performance. Neutral items were eliminated.

Only fifty-eight items clearly judged as favorable or unfavorable and/or important or unimportant were retained for the experiment. The distribution of items included twenty items judged as favorable, twenty as unfavorable, twenty as important, and twenty as unimportant. Within this set, six items were clearly judged as both favorable and important, six as favorable-unimportant, six as unfavorable-important, and six as unfavorable-unimportant.

Procedure. The experiment was conducted in the Management Science Laboratories of the University of California. In each of the three experimental conditions (upward, downward, and lateral), subjects were placed in cubicles containing a table, chairs, and a videotape monitor. Each subject had an envelope containing instructions, written materials pertinent to the experiment, and fifty-eight items of information (randomly ordered). Using an intercom system, the experimenter directed subjects to open their packets and follow the instructions therein.

Experiments. Subjects were asked to role-play positions as subordinates, superiors, or peers (depending on the directionality of information flow) in an organizational hierarchy. They were told they would make some decisions about a business problem to be presented. They were then given written accounts of the general organizational situation in which they were operating, description of their duties, a biographical sketch of the person to whom they would be sending information (superior, subordinate, or peer), and a specific problem requiring their attention. This problem was concerned with corporate hiring policies and was constructed so that it required no special business skills or prior training.

The instructions in the packet then directed the subjects' attention to a video monitor. Using a central control, a two-minute tape was played in which the superior, subordinate, or peer (an actor in each case) requested information from the sender (subject). Subjects then read a memorandum outlining the information requested, examined the fifty-eight precoded information items, selected from the total set those items to be passed to the receiver, placed them in a separate envelope, and were debriefed.

Manipulation of the Independent Variables. "Trust," generally regarded as an expectancy held by an individual or group that the word or promise of another individual or group can be relied upon (Giffin, 1967), was dichotomized into high and low conditions, and manipulated to create a mental set on the part of the subject toward either high or low trust in the information recipient. For example, twice in the statement of the general job situation the receiver is described as either worthy or unworthy of the subject's trust. In one case he is characterized as "a highly ambitious man who doesn't mind using others to advance himself" or as a "fair man who always takes the needs and recommendations of others into consideration before making a decision." In the biographical sketch of the receiver, anecdotal accounts of his past performance portray either the high- or low-trust condition.

Receiver influence is based on the concept of legitimate reward power rather than on coercion or expertise (Raven and French, 1958). The receiver was portrayed as either possessing or lacking autonomy and as having the ability to affect the sender's promotional opportunities. Influence was dichotomized into a high and low condition and referenced in three places during the experiment. For example, on the instruction sheet subjects were informed that the receiver was either of low influence, "his evaluation of whether or not you do a good job will have little influence on whether or not you get promoted," or of high influence, "you need to be well thought of by him in order to be promoted."

Measurement of the Dependent Variables. Using the fifty-eight precoded items, nine measures of information filtration were obtained by counting the number of items passed by subjects in the following categories: (1) total, (2) favorable, (3) unfavorable, (4) important, (5) unimportant, (6) favorable-important, (7) favorable-unimportant, (8) unfavorable-important, and (9) unfavorable-unimportant. The last four measures are a subset of the first five.

Postexperimental Questionnaires. A twenty-item questionnaire was completed by all subjects to verify the success of the experimental manipulation. The questionnaire included items validated in previous research and used to assess interpersonal trust in the receiver of a message, influence of the receiver over the sender, and mobility aspirations of the sender (Roberts and O'Reilly, 1974b).

Laboratory Experiment No. 2

Objective. Based on findings from the first series of experiments, the experimental conditions were modified to examine the impact of interpersonal trust and directionality of information flow on several intentional information-altering mechanisms thought to result in information distortion (Berkowitz, 1971; Davis, 1968; Holzman and Gardner, 1960). Perceptions of the receiver's influence over the sender were not manipulated in these trials, because results of the first set of experiments suggested that influence was not a significant factor or could not be adequately manipulated in the laboratory setting.

Hypotheses. Two sets of hypotheses were advanced.

1. Under conditions in which the sender has high trust in the receiver:
   (a) more favorable-unimportant information will be leveled or suppressed than under conditions of low trust.
   (b) more unfavorable-important information will be sharpened than under conditions of low trust.
2. Under conditions in which the information flow is upward:
   (a) more favorable-unimportant information will be sharpened than when the information flow is lateral or downward.
   (b) more unfavorable-important information will be leveled than when information flow is lateral or downward.

The first set of hypotheses is based on the assumption that, when a sender trusts a receiver, (a) attempts will be made to eliminate irrelevant information and avoid overload and (b) information which is important will be emphasized, even if the information reflects unfavorably on the sender. Or, the converse, when the sender does *not* trust the receiver, unfavorable information will be leveled, even if that information is also important to the receiver. The second set of hypotheses is predicated upon a belief that favorable information will be channeled upward while unfavorable information is generally suppressed, even if it is important.

Subjects. Forty-seven respondents were drawn from graduate and undergraduate business courses. Of this total sample, thirty-seven (approximately 79 percent) had prior work experience in formal organizations. Average age was 24.9 years.

Information Coding. From the precoded item pool described in the first series of experiments, twenty-four items were selected which had been unanimously rated by the judges as either favorable-important, favorable-unimportant, unfavorable-important, or unfavorable-unimportant. Six items were chosen for each of the four categories of information.

Information Distortion Mechanism. To obtain a measure of sharpening-leveling for this experiment, six potential sharpening-leveling mechanisms were selected, based on a review of the literature (Porter and Roberts, 1976). These mechanisms, ranging from most sharpening to most leveling, included (1) expansion of information, (2) search for more information, (3) no change, transmit information intact, (4) minor changes in form, (5) summarize to reduce impact, and (6) omit or suppress completely.

Twenty-five independent raters were provided with the definitions of sharpening and leveling as used in this experiment and asked to rank-order the set of distortion mechanisms from most sharpening to most leveling. A 1 × 6 analysis of variance was computed on the rank ordering and found to be significant at beyond the $p < .001$ level. A Scheffé test at the $p < .10$ level demonstrated that the mean values for the following five change mechanisms were significantly different from each other: (1) expand, (2) search, (3) no change-minor change, (4) summarize, and (5) omit. This ordering was then used to form an index ranging from a low score, indicating high sharpening, through a high score, indicating high leveling.

Procedure. Subjects were again provided with an envelope containing instructions, written materials pertinent to the experiment, and the twenty-four precoded information items presented in one of two alternate orderings. The experimenter directed the subjects to open their packets and follow the instructions therein.

Experiment. Subjects participated in the same experimental scenario described in Experiment No. 1 with the following changes: (1) a videotape monitor was not used to reinforce the trust manipulation; (2) no manipulation of influence was attempted, and previous descriptions of the receiver's influence were deleted from the scenario; (3) as indicated, twenty-four items rather than fifty-eight were used; and (4) each respondent, rather than choosing to send or not send information to the receiver, was required to indicate how each of the twenty-four items was to be presented in a final report to be forwarded to the receiver. Hence, the respondent examined each of the twenty-four pre-coded items and indicated for each of the items if it was to be expanded upon, searched further, unchanged, summarized, or omitted completely from the final report.

Manipulation of the Independent Variables. "Trust" was again dichotomized and manipulated through written descriptions and anecdotes about the receiver. Directionality of information flow was again manipulated by altering the position of the receiver in the organizational hierarchy relative to the sender.

Measurement of the Dependent Variables. Since each respondent assigned a score ranging from sharpening (low) to leveling (high) to each item, it was possible to compute a total sharpening-leveling score for each of the four categories of information (favorable-important, and so forth). Hypotheses could then be tested by observing the amount of sharpening-leveling for the types of information associated with each of the independent variables (trust × directionality).

Postexperimental Questionnaire. Following the experiment, each subject again completed a questionnaire to verify the experimental manipulation (Roberts and O'Reilly, 1974b).

Field Investigations

Objective. The general intent of the field replication of the laboratory findings was to establish the external validity of prior results and to relate intentional distortion to attitudes and performance. Specifically, the impact of three interpersonal variables (trust, influence, and mobility) was examined on a sender's propensity to sharpen or level information being transmitted upward in the organizational hierarchy. The decision to focus on upward information flow was based on findings from the laboratory studies, which strongly suggest that the interpersonal variable effects were concentrated in the upward direction.

Subjects. The primary field data collection focused on three military organizations, with data being collected at two points in time. The first collection obtained usable questionnaire responses from 579 subjects (an 81 percent response rate). The second data collection, a year later, obtained 814 usable responses (an 80 percent response rate). Subjects surveyed were from all hierarchical levels and all job functions (from the lowest-ranking enlisted personnel through commanding officers). The three organizations all were high-technology fighter squadrons performing similar missions and located in the same physical complex.

Procedure. Prior to administration of the questionnaires, full cooperation of the commanding officers of the participating units was obtained, a pilot study was conducted in a similar navy organization, and announcements of the forthcoming survey and its confidential nature were made to all potential participants. Survey packets were administered and collected by university researchers. Performance data in the form of superiors' ratings were also obtained for both surveys.

Measurement of the Variables. The instrument package for the two data collections included two measures of job satisfaction assessing both overall satisfaction (Kunin, 1955) and satisfaction with five aspects of work—the job itself, pay, promotion, supervision, and co-workers (Smith, Kendall, and Hulin, 1969); two measures of performance (Mott, 1972; Robertson, Royle, and James, 1972); and measures of a number of interpersonal and perceptual communication variables (Roberts and O'Reilly, 1974b). Assessment of the respondent's sharpening and leveling of information transmitted upward was predicated on the laboratory distortion index developed in laboratory experiment No. 2. Recall the independent sample of raters' rank-ordered six potential mechanisms thought to result in the sharpening and leveling of information. Using this ordering as a guide, five questions assessing the same or similar mechanisms were drawn from a previously developed communication questionnaire (Roberts and O'Reilly, 1974b) and were summed to form an index score, so that a high score indicated a propensity on the part of the sender to level or suppress information being sent upward in the hierarchy.

Test-retest reliability for a four-item version of the index for forty-two managers over a three-week period was $r = .42$. Cronbach alphas for the two samples used in this study were $\alpha = .46$. Because the distortion index includes items drawn from five distinct communication indices developed by Roberts and O'Reilly (1974b), the internal consistency of the index was not expected to be high. However, each of the five items forming the index had been shown in previous research to be associated with other aspects of open (sharpening) or closed (leveling) communication (O'Reilly and Roberts, 1974a; Roberts and O'Reilly, 1974a). Hence, while reliability and validity are seen as mediocre, the results are considered to be sufficient for an exploratory investigation and allow for corroboration of the laboratory findings.

Results

Laboratory Experiment No. 1

To determine the effects of directionality of flow on respondent information behavior, a one-way analysis of variance was computed for each of the nine dependent variables (type of information), using each of the three directions of information flow (replications of the experiment) as independent variables. Table 1 presents the results.

Only hypothesis No. 2 was partially supported. That is, more favorable information is passed upward than downward ($F = 3, 86, p < .05$). While more favorable information is also passed upward than laterally, a Scheffé test indicated that this difference is not significant. The tendency to pass favorable information upward is further substan-

Table 1. Analysis of Variance for the Effects of Directionality of
Information Flow on Types of Information Filtered

Dependent Variables: Types of Information Being Transmitted	Independent Variables: Direction of Information Flow						F Ratio $(df = 2, 169)$	ω^2
	Upward $(N = 72)$		Lateral $(N = 46)$		Downward $(N = 52)$			
	$\overline{X}$	SD	$\overline{X}$	SD	$\overline{X}$	SD		
1. Favorable	13.6	3.0	12.8	3.2	11.8	4.1	3.86[a]	.03
2. Unfavorable	8.8	5.0	10.7	4.0	8.7	5.0	2.78	
3. Important	14.4	3.6	15.1	3.6	13.4	4.8	2.21	
4. Unimportant	4.9	3.6	5.1	3.8	4.5	3.4	0.38	
5. Total	42.4	9.7	44.6	12.1	39.2	13.6	2.68	
6. Favorable-important	5.6	0.8	5.1	0.9	4.5	1.5	17.72[b]	.16
7. Favorable-unimportant	1.9	1.6	1.8	1.4	1.8	1.5	0.14	
8. Unfavorable-important	3.2	2.0	4.0	1.5	3.7	2.0	3.32[a]	.03
9. Unfavorable-unimportant	1.4	1.4	1.9	1.5	1.1	1.3	3.54[a]	.03

[a] $p < .05$.

[b] $p < .01$.

tiated by observing the results for the favorable-important category ($F = 17, 72, p < .01$). Significantly more unfavorable-important ($F = 3, 32, p < .05$) and unfavorable-unimportant ($F = 3, 54, p < .05$) information is transmitted laterally than either upward or downward. It appears that unfavorable but important information is often denied to higher-level decision makers, who may be dependent upon hierarchical communication flows.

Results for each of the experimental replications (directionality of information flow) demonstrate the predominant impact of trust on information filtration. This effect was observed in the upward, downward, and lateral flow directions, but was most pronounced when information was passed to a superior-receiver. Table 2 presents the results of a 2 × 2 analysis of variance, with trust and influence as independent variables and each of the nine types of information as dependent variables.

The results clearly support the four hypotheses postulating the effects of trust in the receiver on attempts to alter information being sent to superiors. Under conditions of high trust, subjects passed significantly more total information ($p < .05$, $\omega^2 = .10$) and more unfavorable-important information ($p < .01$, $\omega^2 = .22$). Under conditions of low trust, subordinates passed significantly more favorable items ($p < .01$, $\omega^2 = .10$) and more favorable-unimportant items ($p < .05$, $\omega^2 = .05$).

Only one of the two influence hypotheses was supported. Under conditions in which subordinates perceived superiors to possess high influence, subordinates passed more favorable information ($p < .05$, $\omega^2 = .05$).

The two questions assessing the sender's trust in the superior and the two measuring the sender's perceptions of the influence of the receiver, included on the postexperimental questionnaire to verify the manipulation, demonstrated that subjects in the experimental conditions calling for high trust or influence expressed significantly higher perceptions of trust or influence than did subjects in the low-trust or low-influence conditions ($p < .001$).

Laboratory Experiment No. 2

Results of the second set of laboratory experiments, which examined the impact of trust in the receiver and directionality of information flow on the sharpening-leveling

Table 2. Summary of Two-Factor Analysis of Variance for Upward
Information Flow: Trust in Superior and Perceived Influence of the Superior
(N = 72)

Source	df	MS	F	ω^2
Information passed which was:				
1. Favorable:				
Trust (A)	1	73.9	9.6[b]	.10
Influence (B)	1	42.1	5.5[a]	.05
A × B	1	1.9	.3	
Within (error)	69	7.7		
2. Unfavorable:				
Trust (A)	1	395.1	20.5[b]	.22
Influence (B)	1	34.0	1.8	
A × B	1	35.6	1.9	
Within (error)	69	19.2		
3. Important:				
Trust (A)	1	127.4	10.6[b]	.12
Influence (B)	1	1.0	0.1	
A × B	1	13.2	1.1	
Within (error)	69	12.0		
4. Unimportant:				
Trust (A)	1	0.1	0.0	
Influence (B)	1	0.1	0.0	
A × B	1	5.5	0.4	
Within (error)	69	13.8		
5. Favorable-important:				
Trust (A)	1	2.1	3.7	
Influence (B)	1	0.6	1.0	
A × B	1	0.9	1.5	
Within (error)	69	0.6		
6. Favorable-unimportant:				
Trust (A)	1	11.6	4.7[a]	.05
Influence (B)	1	2.3	0.9	
A × B	1	1.5	0.6	
Within (error)	69	2.5		
7. Unfavorable-important:				
Trust (A)	1	67.5	21.9[b]	.22
Influence (B)	1	0.2	0.1	
A × B	1	4.0	1.3	
Within (error)	69	3.1		
8. Unfavorable-unimportant:				
Trust (A)	1	8.1	4.6[a]	.05
Influence (B)	1	4.6	2.6	
A × B	1	0.0	0.0	
Within (error)	69	1.8		
9. Total:				
Trust (A)	1	539.5	5.9[a]	.06
Influence (B)	1	0.6	0.0	
A × B	1	28.7	0.3	
Within (error)	69	91.6		

[a] $p < .05$.

[b] $p < .01$.

of four types of information (favorable-important, unfavorable-important, and so forth), are shown in Table 3. No significant interactions were found.

The findings presented in Table 3 confirm the two hypotheses relating inter-

Table 3. ANOVA Results for Trust and Directionality, with Type
of Information Leveled the Dependent Variable ($N = 47$)

Source	df	MS	F	ω^2
Information passed which was				
1. Favorable-important				
Trust (A)	1	3.0	0.2	
Directionality (B)	2	10.6	0.7	
A × B	2	17.9	1.2	
Within (error)	41	15.4		
2. Favorable-unimportant				
Trust (A)	1	87.7	4.7[a]	.07
Directionality (B)	2	38.5	2.1	
A × B	2	19.5	1.0	
Within (error)	41	18.7		
3. Unfavorable-important				
Trust (A)	1	55.7	4.9[a]	.07
Directionality (B)	2	54.2	5.1[a]	.07
A × B	2	10.0	0.9	
Within (error)	41	11.0		
4. Unfavorable-unimportant				
Trust (A)	1	5.6	0.3	
Directionality (B)	2	0.0	0.0	
A × B	2	6.2	0.4	
Within (error)	41	17.1		

[a] $p < .05$.

personal trust to the intentional distortion of information. Under conditions in which the sender evinces high trust in the receiver, (1) favorable-unimportant information is leveled ($\omega^2 = .07$) and (2) unfavorable-important information is sharpened ($\omega^2 = .07$). The first finding represents an attempt on the part of the high-trust sender to eliminate from transmission unimportant or irrelevant information. The second result indicates that senders who express low trust in the receiver are comparatively more willing to transmit favorable-unimportant information, undoubtedly reflecting an attempt on their part to appear in a more favorable light with the receiver.

Of the two directionality hypotheses, only one received partial support. Regardless of trust in the receiver, there exists a tendency for senders to level unfavorable-important information when transmitting it upward and laterally ($\omega^2 = .07$). Thus, independent of the impact of trust, there exists a bias against passing unfavorable information upward, even if that information is important (relevant to the problem faced by the superior).

Postexperimental checks again confirmed the trust manipulation. A check on the ordering of the precoded information items revealed no significant differences in responses attributable to the order of presentation.

Field Investigations

Intercorrelations between the distortion index and the three interpersonal variables are shown in Table 4. High trust in the receiver (immediate superior) and perceptions of the receiver as having high influence are significantly and inversely related, in both samples, to the leveling or suppression of information. Respondents with high mobility aspirations are also shown to be less likely to level information being sent to superiors.

Table 4. Correlations of Three Interpersonal Variables and the
Distortion Index for Two Field Samples

Interpersonal Variable	Distortion Index	
	Sample 1 (N = 579)	Sample 2 (N = 814)
1. Trust	−.38[b]	−.35[b]
2. Influence	−.15[b]	−.23[b]
3. Mobility aspirations	−.13[a]	−.21[b]

[a] $p < .01$.

[b] $p < .001$.

To establish the external validity of the laboratory findings and to examine the impact of respondent mobility aspirations, a median split was computed for each of the three interpersonal variables and a three-way analysis of variance run, using the distortion index as the dependent variable. Results for both samples are presented in Table 5.

Table 5. Three-Way ANOVA Results for Two Field Samples:
Dependent Variable Is Distortion Index

Source	Sample 1				Sample 2			
	df	MS	F	ω^2	df	MS	F	ω^2
(1) Trust (A)	1	841	52.2[c]	.08	1	793	51.7[c]	.06
(2) Influence (B)	1	0.1	0.0		1	95.2	6.2[b]	.01
(3) Mobility (C)	1	80.8	5.0[a]	.01	1	225	14.7[c]	.02
(4) A × B	1	0.1	0.0		1	1.1	0.1	
(5) A × C	1	13.2	0.8		1	44.7	2.9	
(6) B × C	1	14.6	0.9		1	1.7	0.1	
(7) A × B × C	1	34.7	2.2		1	2.1	0.1	
Within (error)	569				797			

[a] $p < .05$.

[b] $p < .01$.

[c] $p < .001$.

Significant main effects for trust and mobility aspirations were replicated across samples. Tests for strength of relationships confirm the predominant impact of trust. The results restate the correlational evidence showing that high trust in the superior, high perceived influence, and high respondent mobility aspirations are associated with less distortion of information being sent by the subordinate to the superior. Using the distortion index as the dependent variable, the R^2 for the three interpersonal variables for sample No. 1 equals .15 and for sample No. 2, $R^2 = .13$.

Comparison of laboratory and field results confirms the external validity of the findings, showing trust as highly related to the use of distortion-producing mechanisms by senders. Similarly, the comparison suggests that influence of the receiver over the sender is not a major determinant of information distortion as measured here. Using data from the second sample ($N = 814$), correlations between the distortion index and measures of job satisfaction (Kunin, 1955; Smith, Kendall, and Hulin, 1969) reveal that low satisfaction with work itself, with supervision, and with co-workers, and low overall satisfaction are associated with more intentional distortion of information. Partial correlations among trust in the superior, overall job satisfaction, and the distortion index are significant at beyond the $p < .001$ level, suggesting that low job satisfaction is independently related to distortion of information and not an artifact of the sender's lack of trust.

Associations between distortion and two measures of job performance are also statistically significant. The correlation between a measure of perceived group effectiveness (Mott, 1972) and the distortion index is $r = -.30$ ($p < .001$). The correlation between the supervisor's performance rating and the distortion index is $r = -.23$ ($p < .001$). Both of these relationships indicate that high information distortion is associated with lower performance. Both relationships remain significant when the effects of the three interpersonal variables are held constant. The evidence suggests that distortion of information is in part caused by a lack of trust in the receiver, and once the distortion has occurred, it is then independently associated with lower performance.

Directionality of Information Flow

Because of empirical evidence demonstrating that messages in organizational communication networks may be distorted when flowing in lateral or downward directions (Davis, 1968; Julian, 1966), the initial laboratory investigations included directionality of information flow (upward, downward, and lateral) as an independent variable. Results of the laboratory experiments confirmed a tendency for senders to level or suppress unfavorable-important items sent to superiors. Overall, the evidence demonstrates that, independent of the effects of the three interpersonal variables investigated here, there exists a significant bias toward screening unfavorable and sharpening favorable information sent upward by senders in an organizational hierarchy.

This bias is not necessarily dysfunctional. Ackoff (1967), Downs (1967), Kaufman (1973), and others have pointed out the need for lower-level participants to screen information before sending it upward to avoid upper-echelon overload. However, this bias can have deleterious effects when important or relevant information which reflects unfavorably upon the sender is systematically leveled, while irrelevant but favorable information is passed. Under these circumstances, decision makers may lose the ability to discriminate between relevant and irrelevant stimuli, with a consequent decrement in decision-making performance (Chervany and Dickson, 1974).

Impact of Interpersonal Variables

Trust. The findings reported here offer strong support for previous studies attesting to the importance of trust as a moderator of interaction among people in organizational settings (Friedlander, 1970; O'Reilly and Roberts, 1976; Zand, 1972). The results of this investigation clearly demonstrate that lack of trust by a subordinate (sender) in a superior (receiver) results in the blockage or leveling of unfavorable and the sharpening of favorable items. The twin effects of denial of unfavorable-important information and the presence of favorable-unimportant information may easily result in impaired decision making of the type reported by Wilensky (1967), Janis (1972), and others.

Influence. Intuitively, the idea that a receiver who is perceived as having high influence might be one to whom communication is guarded seems reasonable. Results of this study, however, offer little support for this notion. Previous research on the impact of influence on communication in hierarchies (see, for example, Kelley, 1951) focused on the transmission upward of criticism by the subordinate of the superior. While these results indicated that perceived influence may act to dampen the transmission of criticism upward, the present study suggests that perceptions of influence do not have any significant impact in explaining the intentional distortion of information as measured here.

Mobility. The results of this research show highly mobile respondents to engage in less intentional distortion of information than respondents with low mobility aspirations. This is in contrast to previous studies, which found upwardly mobile subjects to report less accurate information to superiors (see, for example, Athanassiades, 1973; Read, 1962). In previous studies, however, the dependent variable was not a measure of information distortion but inferred measures of accuracy. Read (1962) used mutual agreement on problems faced by the subordinate as a measure of communication accuracy, while Athanassiades (1973) used a revealed versus a hidden personality profile completed by the subordinate. In both cases highly mobile subordinates were less accurately perceived by superiors than less mobile types. While these findings indicate that subordinates may be misunderstood by superiors in terms of problems or personality, they do not indicate that subordinates intentionally distort information of the type likely to affect decision making. Instead, these findings may reflect either differing frames of reference with respect to problems, or attempts by subordinates to ingratiate themselves by presenting a favorable image.

A second explanation for the contradictory findings may stem from the nature of the sample used in the field portion of this study. Navy personnel with high mobility aspirations are those committed to the organization. These respondents may transmit information accurately because of a belief in the purpose of the organization. In other organizational samples, high mobility aspirations may not reflect a commitment to the organization but a commitment to self, with a concomitant willingness to alter information to achieve personal ends.

Overall, however, the impact of mobility aspirations on intentional distortion appears to be of little importance. As with the impact of influence, the amount of variance explained is trivial.

Correlates of Information Distortion in Organizations

Correlations between the distortion index and both job satisfaction and performance may be of practical and theoretical significance. Since the field study used respondents from all levels of the organizational hierarchy and from all job functions, the performance-distortion and satisfaction-distortion associations are seen as the most general case. Inherent in many of the jobs sampled is the little requirement or opportunity to affect information (for example, cooks, building guards). Distortion of information on the part of respondents in these jobs would have little impact on organizational functioning when compared to the critical effects which might result if distortion occurs in information flows emanating from positions which are critical links in communication networks. Similarly, the importance of the satisfaction and performance associations with intentional distortion might be magnified when aggregated over several hierarchical levels. Clearly, the evidence confirms that information distortion as measured here is related in a nonrandom way to important organizational outcomes. The precise form of these associations is a matter worthy of future research.

Conclusions and Future Research Directions

Results of this research clarify and extend the results of a number of previous studies of communication in organizations and suggest a revision and extension of the model presented in Figure 1. Figure 2 provides this revision and extension.

Besides eliminating two interpersonal variables (influence and mobility aspirations), the revised model incorporates the findings reported here to more precisely de-

Figure 2. Impact of Organizational Variables on Communication

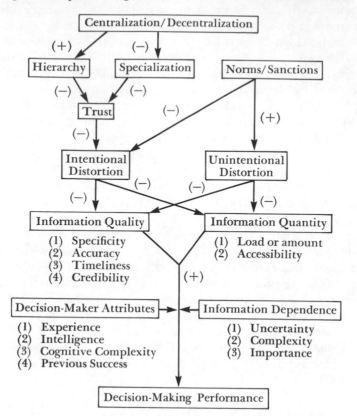

fined outcome variables. Thus, the impact of the organizational variables is mediated by sender-receiver trust and reflected in the intentional and unintentional distortion of information (other antecedents to interpersonal trust can be proposed but are not included here). Information distortion, in turn, is seen as affecting the quantity and quality of information available to a decision maker. Previous research has demonstrated the impact of information quantity and quality on decision-making performance.

Based on this paradigm, additional research is needed which (1) tests the impact of the organizational-level variables postulated in Figure 2, with particular emphasis on the influence of norms, sanctions, and counterbiasing mechanisms; (2) broadens and refines measures of the mechanisms through which information can be distorted in organizational communication, especially the combined impact of both intentional and unintentional distortion; (3) examines more closely the nature of the relationships between information distortion and job satisfaction and performance, with particular attention to (a) the aggregate impacts within and across hierarchical levels and (b) the effects for tasks which are seen as critical in terms of the organizational communication network.

References

Ackoff, R. "Management Misinformation Systems." *Management Science,* 1967, *14,* 147-156.

Alkire, A., and others. "Information Exchange and Accuracy of Verbal Behavior Under

Social Power Conditions." *Journal of Personality and Social Psychology,* 1968, *9,* 301-308.

Allport, G., and Postman, L. *The Psychology of Rumor.* New York: Holt, Rinehart and Winston, 1947.

Argyris, C. *Executive Leadership.* New York: Harper & Row, 1953.

Athanassiades, J. "The Distortion of Upward Communication in Hierarchial Organizations." *Academy of Management Journal,* 1973, *16,* 207-226.

Berkowitz, L. "Reporting an Experiment: A Case Study in Levelling, Sharpening, and Assimilation." *Journal of Experimental Social Psychology,* 1971, *7,* 237-243.

Campbell, D. T. "Systematic Error on the Part of Human Links in Communication Systems." *Information and Control,* 1958, *1,* 334-369.

Chervany, N., and Dickson, G. "An Experimental Evaluation of Information Overload in a Production Environment." *Management Science,* 1974, *20,* 1335-1344.

Davis, K. "Success of Chain-of-Command Oral Communication in a Manufacturing Management Group." *Academy of Management Journal,* 1968, *11,* 379-387.

Downs, A. *Inside Bureaucracy.* Boston: Little, Brown, 1967.

Friedlander, F. "The Primacy of Trust as a Facilitator of Further Group Accomplishment." *Journal of Applied Behavioral Science,* 1970, *6,* 387-400.

Giffin, K. "Interpersonal Trust in Small Group Communication." *Quarterly Journal of Speech,* 1967, *53,* 224-234.

Halberstam, D. *The Best and the Brightest.* New York: Random House, 1972.

Holzman, P., and Gardner, R. "Levelling-Sharpening and Memory Organization." *Journal of Abnormal and Social Psychology,* 1960, *61,* 176-180.

Janis, I. *Victims of Groupthink.* Boston: Houghton Mifflin, 1972.

Julian, J. "Compliance Patterns and Communication Blocks in Complex Organizations." *American Sociological Review,* 1966, *31,* 382-387.

Kaufman, H. *Administrative Feedback.* Washington, D.C.: Brookings Institution, 1973.

Kelley, H. "Communication in Experimentally Created Hierarchies." *Human Relations,* 1951, *4,* 39-56.

Kunin, T. "The Construction of a New Type of Attitude Measure." *Personnel Psychology,* 1955, *8,* 65-78.

Lawler, E., Porter, L., and Tenenbaum, A. "Managers' Attitudes Toward Interaction Episodes." *Journal of Applied Psychology,* 1968, *52,* 432-439.

March, J., and Simon, H. *Organizations.* New York: Wiley, 1958.

Mott, P. *The Characteristics of Effective Organizations.* New York: Harper & Row, 1972.

O'Reilly, C., and Roberts, K. H. "Communication: A Way of Viewing Organizations." Paper presented at annual meeting of the Academy of Management, Seattle, Washington, Aug, 1974a.

O'Reilly, C., and Roberts, K. H. "Information Filtration in Organizations: Three Experiments." *Organizational Behavior and Human Performance,* 1974b, *11,* 253-265.

O'Reilly, C., and Roberts, K. H. "Credibility and Communication in Work Units." *Journal of Applied Psychology,* 1976, *61,* 99-102.

Porter, L. W., and Roberts, K. H. "Communication in Organizations." In M. D. Dunnette (Ed.), *Handbook of Industrial and Organizational Psychology.* Chicago: Rand McNally, 1976.

Raven, B., and French, J. "Legitimate Power, Coercive Power, and Observability in Social Influence." *Sociometry,* 1958, *21,* 83-97.

Read, W. "Upward Communication in Industrial Hierarchies." *Human Relations,* 1962, *15,* 3-16.

Roberts, K. H., and O'Reilly, C. "Failures in Upward Communication in Organizations: Three Possible Culprits." *Academy of Management Journal,* 1974a, *17,* 205-215.

Roberts, K. H., and O'Reilly, C. "Measuring Organizational Communication." *Journal of Applied Psychology,* 1974b, *59,* 321-326.

Robertson, D., Royle, M., and James, J. *Design and Fleet Trial of Automated Performance Evaluation Forms for Two Pay-Grade Groups: E5-E6 and E1-E4.* Research Report SSR 73-11. San Diego, Calif.: Naval Personnel and Training Research Laboratory, Nov. 1972.

Shibutani, T. *Improvised News: A Sociological Study of Rumor.* Indianapolis: Bobbs-Merrill, 1966.

Simon, H. *Administrative Behavior.* New York: Free Press, 1957.

Smith, P., Kendall, L., and Hulin, C. *The Measurement of Satisfaction in Work and Retirement.* Chicago: Rand McNally, 1969.

Watson, D., and Bromberg, B. "Power, Communication, and Position Satisfaction." *Journal of Personality and Social Psychology,* 1965, *2,* 859-864.

Wilensky, H. *Organizational Intelligence.* New York: Free Press, 1967.

Zand, D. E. "Trust and Managerial Problem Solving." *Administrative Science Quarterly,* 1972, *17,* 229-240.

25

Organizational Communication Network Analysis: The Liaison Communication Role

Donald F. Schwartz
Eugene Jacobson

Network approaches to the study of interpersonal communication in complex organizations are found infrequently in the research literature. There are several reasons for this. One is that methods for efficient manipulation of large sets of network or sociometric data are just being developed. Second, there have been relatively few successful attempts to identify structural concepts that can be used, unambiguously, to classify network elements in complex organizations. Third, the empirical and theoretical correlates of network characteristics remain to be explored.

Some beginnings were made two decades ago, when Jacobson and Seashore (1951) and Weiss and Jacobson (1955) presented a methodology and a set of structural concepts that were intended to provide some solutions to the first two problems. Although the procedure they used was cumbersome and time consuming, they were able to produce an example of how a 200-person government agency could be described sociometrically.

With development of greater computer capability, interest in this method has been rekindled. The study reported here, on the liaison role in complex organizations, represents an elaboration of the descriptive analysis of complex organizations from a network perspective, examining the correlates of one of the strategic structural elements identified in the earlier research.

Network Analysis

In the Jacobson and Seashore article (1951), it was proposed that the structure of an organization can be conceptualized and described in terms of the regular, work-related, interpersonal communication patterns that are established between pairs of individuals. The organization is conceived of as a bounded social system in which there is a relatively

Reprinted from *Organizational Behavior and Human Performance*, 1977, *18*, 158-174, with permission of the authors and the publisher. Copyright © 1977 by Academic Press, Inc.

stable network of interpersonal linkages through which messages flow that affect the productivity and maintenance of the system. To some extent, these dyadic links are prescribed by and reflect the formal structure, but the formal structure does not define the sociometric structure. In collecting and analyzing data, the formal structure is disregarded and information about dyadic communication linkage is obtained directly from network members. This information provides a record of message transactions between pairs of members. When assembled from all members, these topological maps take the form of a total organizational sociogram and permit locating each member at the focal point of a unique set of information vectors (Thayer, 1967); that is, the set of previous message transactions with other members of the organization. These inclusive structural maps are, of course, reified and static. They represent the history of a process.

The important point is that the conceptual approach is more inclusive than either studies of formally prescribed relations (superior-subordinate and other structured relationships) or the informal communication structure (nonprescribed but regular communication contacts). The objective is to trace the actual functional communication system of the organization.

The methodology for the approach and a set of structural concepts for classifying network data are described in detail by Weiss and Jacobson (1955) in a report on an application of the procedure in a government agency. Briefly, the first step is to obtain a record of regular dyadic linkages by asking members to list names of persons in the organization with whom they work most closely (other sources of interaction histories are obviously possible, as are various interaction criteria such as frequency and content—see, for example, Burns, 1954; Conrath, 1973; Davis, 1953; Hinrichs, 1964). Next the reported contacts are compared against each other in a matrix to determine reciprocation of contact (mutual choice) among respondents. Only reciprocated contacts, with an exception for nonrespondents explained later, are used to define the communication network. The reciprocated contacts are then arrayed along the diagonal of a matrix, grouping individuals, as much as possible, adjacent to others with whom they have contact. The resulting graphic representation has clusters of reciprocated contacts along the diagonal and scattered contacts for some individuals throughout the matrix. The latter tentatively represent regular contact between individuals in separate groups. The last step in the process, using carefully prescribed, objective procedures (Weiss, 1956, pp. 88-108), allows one to separate out the groups and to classify all members of the organization into one of the following role types: group member, liaison role, and isolate. Further distinctions include group member with bridge contact, liaison person with group membership, and liaison individual with no group membership.

The liaison person was defined by Weiss and Jacobson (1955) as an individual who had contact with others in at least two groups other than his own, or, if he was a liaison individual, with persons in two or more separate groups. Isolates were individuals who had no reciprocated contacts with others in the organization. When a linkage between only two members of two separate groups existed, it was termed a bridge contact. A group was defined as a set of individuals whose relationships were primarily with each other and not with members of other groups except for bridge and liaison contacts. It is important to note that these groups are emergent or *extant* groups, not formally prescribed task units. They may be congruent with the formal structure, cut across the formal structure, or be subsets of a formal unit.

The liaison role is an analog to the articulation point in graph theory, the bridge contact to the bridge, and the group to the component.

Importance of Liaison Role

The basic procedure for classifying elements of the network in the last step of matrix analysis involves identifying and removing liaison persons from the matrix to isolate the separate groups. When the analysis is complete, the critical location of the liaison within the static picture of the network is clear—with the exception of a few bridge contacts, there are no regular working relationships among the separate extant groups. As Ross and Harary (1955) emphasize, "liaisons are essential to creating the total organizational structure; their removal destroys the connected unity of the organization."

It was primarily for this reason that the liaison role was selected as the focal concept for examination in the present study. The concept is a key to the method of network analysis. Evidence of characteristics showing consistent relationships with the role would tend to confirm the legitimacy of the concept and the strength of the operations. Because the liaison role has obvious practical implications for organizational information flow and influence, these characteristics also would be important in giving a more systematic understanding of the liaison role and its organizational functions.

A field study was designed to examine selected demographic, interactional, and functional attributes of the liaison communication role. Variables were selected which derived logically from the implied dynamics of the role. Since there is no exact analog to this structural concept in the literature, simple statements about expected relations were developed rather than formal hypotheses.

Expected Relationships

Demographic. Because diverse organizational contacts might reflect the status of a more established individual, it was expected liaisons would be older, have longer organizational tenure, and have higher professional status. Administrators serve a linking role between formal task units in the formal structure, so a higher proportion of administrators were expected among liaisons than among nonliaisons. Committee membership and activity was expected to be higher among liaisons because service on committees was anticipated to be related to diversified contacts among organization members.

Interactional. Because the occupant of the liaison role was defined as having contacts with persons in at least two groups other than his own, we expected that the data would demonstrate that liaisons would have a broader span of reciprocated contacts than nonliaison group members. Previous work (Weiss, 1956) supports this expectation.

The balance of the interactional data and the functional data to be discussed later were obtained from perceptions of liaison persons by nonliaison group members who had a regular working relationship with the liaison person. These data were compared with perceptions of nonliaison group members by other nonliaisons with whom there was a regular working relationship.

One question was whether those in contact with liaisons are aware of the actual structural diversity and span of contact of their work partner. It was expected that liaisons would be correctly seen as having greater diversity and span of contacts than would nonliaisons.

The fact that the contacts of liaisons are more structurally diverse within the network suggests that the initiation of message transactions would require more effort and, hence, would more frequently be planned or sought in liaison-nonliaison dyads. Further, it was predicted that, among the set of purposively initiated transactions, the ratio of the number of times each member of the dyad initiated transactions would be more nearly equal within nonliaison dyads than within liaison-nonliaison dyads.

Functional. Several aspects of the perception of liaison function were explored. They include (1) serving as first source of information, (2) providing credible information, (3) providing communication linkage to powerful people, (4) exerting influence in the power structure, (5) being persuasive, and (6) exerting opinion leadership in the dyad. These perceived functions are discussed briefly in the following paragraphs.

The location of the liaison role in the static network clearly implies a gatekeeper function for the groups to which they are connected. Katz and Lazarsfeld (1955, pp. 113, 119) distinguish between the information transmission function and the influence function of a gatekeeper. Focusing on one aspect of the information transmission function, it was expected that liaisons would be more likely to serve as first sources of organizational "news" for their contacts than would nonliaisons. Support for this expectation comes from Wager's (1962) study of rumor transmission in an organization and studies of network centrality in problem-solving small groups (see, for example, Leavitt, 1951), which indicate information relay leadership is a natural by-product of a strategic network location (liaisons are central among their contact groups, although they may not be central within their group).

The first of the variables related to influence functions examined was source credibility, which consistently has been found positively related to acceptance of information and to attitude change (Mortenson, 1972, pp. 145-147). The maintenance of a person in a liaison role might mean his contacts attribute greater credibility to him than do the contacts of nonliaisons. There is also evidence that attributed leadership is positively related to perceived competence (see, for example, Katz, 1957, p. 73). Hence, we expected liaisons to have higher ratings on the competence and trustworthiness dimensions of source credibility than nonliaisons.

Four aspects of organizational opinion leadership (Rogers and Shoemaker, 1971) were examined. The first was linkages to knowledgeable and powerful people in the organization. This involved the expectation that liaisons would be more likely to be perceived by their contacts to have such linkages than would nonliaisons. A related expectation was that liaisons would be perceived to be more influential in the organizational power structure than would nonliaisons. And it was predicted that liaisons would be seen as more persuasive with all their other contacts than would nonliaisons. The last area, dyadic opinion leadership, related to influence patterns within the dyad reported on by the respondents. Information on gatekeepers' influence with their groups (Katz and Lazarsfeld, 1955, p. 123) and preferential information access as a source of power (Leavitt, 1964, p. 238) led to the prediction that liaisons would tend to dominate the liaison-nonliaison dyads as opinion leaders while nonliaison-nonliaison dyads would report an approximately equal opinion leadership balance.

Methods

Setting

The organization selected for this study was a professional college within a large midwestern university. All of the faculty and academic administrators who had the rank of instructor or higher and who were officed in the main college building served as the study population. All 142 employees who met these criteria received questionnaire packets.

Instruments

The questionnaire packet administered to the respondents included the following three instruments:

Personal Contact Checklist. Patterned on the Jacobson and Seashore instrument, subjects received the following instructions for reporting work-related contacts: "Now go back over the past two or three months and think of the professional people in the college *with whom you have worked most closely.* We would like to have you list below the names of the people in the college with whom you work most closely."

Additional instructions defined "professional people" as faculty or college administrators and "work most closely" as having at least one contact per week on college matters or on teaching, research, or consulting. Blanks for listing names followed the instructions, and four columns were provided for checking the frequency of contact with each person listed (several times daily, about once per day, two or three times per week, about once per week). This questionnaire provided the data for network description and analysis.

Personal Contact Questionnaire. For each individual listed on the Personal Contact Checklist as a daily or several times daily contact, respondents were asked to complete a Personal Contact Questionnaire (PCQ). Two to five items were used for each of six variables to which respondents reacted on Likert-type seven-point response alternatives ranging from "agree very strongly" to "disagree very strongly" (for example, *first source of information,* "As new developments occur in the college, I usually get the word from someone other than this person"; *influence in the power structure,* "Those individuals who have a lot to say about what goes on in the college respect the suggestions this person makes.") Most of the items in these scales were adapted from responses Walton (1962) obtained from open-ended questions asking reasons for seeking information from fellow organizational members.

Dyadic opinion leadership was measured by five items adapted from self-designating opinion leadership scales developed by Rogers and Cartano (1962) and Troldahl and Van Dam (1965). For example, one of the five items was: "Considering the relationship I have with this person, when it comes to advice on matters related to teaching, research, or consulting, I depend on him/her [a seven-point response alternative, ranging from a lot more to a lot less] than he/she depends on me." Semantic differential scales were used to measure the competency (for example, qualified-unqualified, informed-uninformed) and trustworthiness (for example, honest-dishonest, safe-unsafe) dimensions of source credibility (Berlo, Lemert, and Mertz, 1969-70). Direction and deliberateness of interaction initiation in the dyad were estimated on the basis of the proportion of a hypothetical 100 contacts.

This and the other instruments were pretested among a faculty sample from a comparable college in the same university. Pretest and main study PCQ scale items were analyzed for unidimensionality using cluster analysis (McQuitty, 1957). The number of pretest scale items was reduced from thirty-seven to twenty-one.

Biographical Questionnaire. Items in this instrument sought information on personal attributes of the respondents which might help explain network position: age, committee work, highest attained degree, academic rank, administrative assignment, publication rate, and length of employment at the university. This questionnaire and the PCQ produced data not analyzed in this report. For a complete analysis and a full discussion of the development of the instruments see Schwartz (1968).

Procedures

Members of the study population were identified from a college directory and supplemental information from the dean's office. The sequence of data collection procedures included (1) distribution of an entry letter from a well-known faculty member in the college, (2) telephone contact with each person to enlist cooperation and make an appointment for delivery and pickup of the questionnaire packet, (3) personal delivery of the packet, and (4) personal pickup of the completed packet. Data were collected during the third (spring) quarter of the academic year. Ninety-eight percent of the packets were delivered within a six-day period and 86 percent were returned within the next five days, 97 percent within 10 days. Only one of the 142 employees refused to accept a packet, and two additional individuals refused to complete any part of a packet after receiving it.

Of the study population, 127 (89 percent) members completed a Personal Contact Checklist. A total of 895 reported contacts were compared against each other in a matrix to determine reciprocation of contact (mutual choice) among the respondents; 450 (50.3 percent) were reciprocated. Reciprocation was assumed for any of the nonrespondents listed as a daily contact. Only reciprocated contacts were used to define the organizational network.

The reciprocated contacts were then cast into a sociomatrix and, using procedures described by Weiss (1956, pp. 88-108), analyzed to yield identification of 23 liaison-role persons, 18 isolates, and 101 nonliaison persons who had membership in twenty-nine extant work groups varying in size from two to eight members. The resulting sociogram of the total communication structure is shown in Figure 1. Figure 2 clearly illustrates the breakdown of the communication structure when all liaison contacts between groups are deleted.

Figure 1. Extant Communication Structure of the Organization

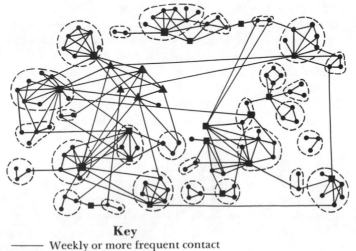

Key

———— Weekly or more frequent contact
-- -- -- Extant work groups
■ Liaison-role persons
▲ Liaison-set members
● Nonliaison persons

**Figure 2. Extant Communication Structure of the Organization
with Intergroup Contacts of Liaisons Removed**

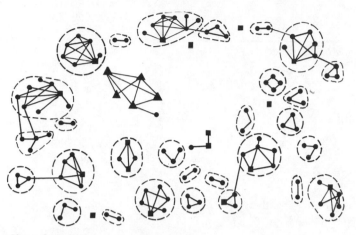

Note: Only bridge contacts remain between extant groups.

Respondents

Twenty-two of the 23 liaisons, 95 of the 101 nonliaisons, and 12 isolates completed the biographic questionnaire, a 91 percent response rate.

A total of 270 daily contacts, each of which was to require a PCQ, was reported by 96 respondents; 224 (83 percent) PCQs were completed. Of these, 166 were completed on one or both members of a reciprocated dyad, 31 by nonliaisons on liaisons, and 71 by nonliaisons on other nonliaison group members. These 102 questionnaires form the main data base for this study. A nonliaison member in each case was reporting his perceptions of relations with or other activities of persons with whom he has direct, daily contact. To use Barnes' (1968) terminology, if the person on whom a PCQ was completed is called "Alpha," it is one of his primary, or first-order, contacts who serves as the source of information about "Alpha."

Results

Liaisons were found to differ from nonliaisons in span of communication contacts, administrative activity, and committee work. They were perceived by their contacts to differ on diversity and span of contacts, one aspect of information relaying, and several dimensions of interpersonal influence.

Demographics

A summary of selected demographic information from 129 respondents to the biographic questionnaire is presented in Tables 1 and 2.

Considering the usual categories of academic rank, a high proportion of liaisons were full professors while nonliaisons were more evenly distributed among the ranks. It was apparent that administrators were strongly represented among liaisons. Liaisons also reported devoting more time to administration and less time to teaching than did non-

Table 1. Characteristics of Liaison and Nonliaison Persons

Variable	Liaisons[a] a. Mean b. SD	Nonliaisons[b] a. Mean b. SD
Percentage of time allotted:		
1. Teaching[e]	a. 26.5 b. 32.2	a. 47.4 b. 31.9
2. Research	a. 17.1 b. 30.2	a. 21.8 b. 26.0
3. Consulting	a. 6.9 b. 7.2	a. 7.4 b. 13.8
4. Administrative duty[e]	a. 39.3 b. 37.5	a. 17.0 b. 29.9
5. Committee work	a. 10.5 b. 21.9	a. 5.5 b. 8.4
Number of committee memberships:		
1. Departmental level	a. 2.0 b. 1.6	a. 1.6 b. 1.6
2. College level[c]	a. 1.1 b. 1.5	a. 0.6 b. 0.8
3. University level[e]	a. 1.0 b. 1.2	a. 0.3 b. 0.8
Total number of committee memberships[d]	a. 4.0 b. 2.6	a. 2.5 b. 2.3
Number of committee meetings in a typical month[d]	a. 7.4 b. 4.8	a. 4.4 b. 5.1

Note: t tests for independent means, $df = 115$.

[a]$N = 22$.

[b]$N = 95$.

[c]$p < .05$.

[d]$p < .02$.

[e]$p < .01$.

liaisons. But while 64 percent of the liaisons were administrators, only 30 percent of the administrators in the organization were liaisons.

The expectation that service on committees would be related to the role received strong support from the data. Liaisons reported an average proportion of time devoted to committees nearly double that reported by nonliaisons, a larger number of committee memberships, and nearly twice as many committee meetings in a typical month. There was also an apparent tendency for liaisons to have membership on a proportionately larger number of committees as the administrative level of the committees went from departmental level to university level.

Nonsignificant differences existed between liaisons and nonliaisons on age (46 versus 43), time devoted to research and consulting, publication rate, highest degree held (91 percent versus 84 percent doctorates), and length of employment at the university (9.6 versus 7.4 years).

Interactional

The Personal Contact Checklist (PCC), in addition to being the basis for the network analysis, provided information on communication contact distributions. The 127

Table 2. Characteristics of Liaison and Nonliaison Persons

	Liaisons		Nonliaisons	
Variable	N	%	N	%
Academic rank[b]				
1. Instructor or equal	1	4.5	17	17.9
2. Assistant professor	4	18.2	25	26.3
3. Associate professor	3	13.6	24	25.3
4. Professor	14	63.6	29	30.5
		99.9[a]		100.0
Administrative title[c]				
1. Head or assistant head of academic or research unit	10	45.5	11	11.6
2. Head or assistant head of special units or projects	4	18.2	22	23.2
3. None	5	22.7	49	51.6
4. No response	3	13.6	13	13.7
		100.0		100.1[a]

Note: Chi-square test, $df = 3$.

[a]Rounding error.

[b]$p < .05$.

[c]$p < .01$.

PCC respondents listed a total of 895 contacts, a mean of 7.1 per respondent (*SD* 3.4, range 0-16, median 6.6). Weiss and Jacobson (1955, p. 663) found an average span of twelve reported contacts per respondent but used a frequency criterion as low as several times yearly, while the lower limit in this study was once per week. Matching choices against each other to determine reciprocation yielded a mean number of reciprocated contacts of 3.2 (*SD* 2.6, range 0-13, median 3.2).

Partitioning the above data by structural type revealed that liaisons listed nearly twice the mean number of contacts as nonliaisons (11.7 versus 6.2) and received more than twice the mean number of choices (12.1 versus 5.8). No liaison person received fewer than five choices while 45.1 percent of the nonliaisons received less than five. Considering only reciprocated contacts, liaisons had a mean of 7.1 against 2.8 for nonliaisons. The range of reciprocated contacts for liaisons was two to thirteen, and for nonliaisons it was one to seven.

The isolates listed a mean of 5.4 contacts and received a mean of 1.9 choices, none of which, of course, were reciprocated.

Data for each of ten variables related to the perceptions of liaisons and nonliaisons are presented in Table 3. As predicted, liaisons were correctly perceived by their contacts to have both a more diverse and a larger number of contacts than were nonliaisons by their contacts. The expectation that liaison-nonliaison dyads would deliberately initiate message transactions more often than would nonliaison dyads and that message transaction initiation would be more disproportionate in the former dyad than in the latter was not supported by the data. Both types of dyads deliberately initiate approximately 88 percent of their transactions, and within these transactions roughly 42 percent are initiated by one member and 58 percent by the other.

Functional

There was strong support for the prediction that liaisons would more frequently serve as the first source of organization-related information for their contacts than non-

Table 3. Mean Scale Values and Standard Deviations for
Perceptions of Liaison and Nonliaison Persons

Variable	Liaisons[a] a. Mean b. SD	Nonliaisons[b] a. Mean b. SD	a. Possible Scale Range b. Scale Mid- point
1. Structural diversity[d]	a. 15.58 b. 3.57	a. 13.18 b. 4.45	a. 3-21 b. 12
2. Number of contacts[d]	a. 10.74 b. 2.58	a. 8.66 b. ⸴3.37	a. 2-14 b. 8
3. Transaction initiation deliberateness	a. 87.58 b. 17.46	a. 88.73 b. 17.19	a. 0-100
4. Transaction initiation disproportionate- ness	a. 0.739 b. 0.290	a. 0.737 b. 0.267	a. 0.0-1.00
5. First source of information[e]	a. 9.39 b. 2.87	a. 7.15 b. 2.91	a. 2-14 b. 8
6. Source credibility—competence	a. 31.10 b. 4.53	a. 31.17 b. 3.85	a. 5-35 b. 20
7. Source credibility—trustworthiness	a. 31.97 b. 3.35	a. 31.49 b. 4.25	a. 5-35 b. 20
8. Importance of other contacts[e]	a. 17.65 b. 3.25	a. 14.24 b. 3.77	a. 3-21 b. 12
9. Influence in power structure[e]	a. 15.94 b. 3.79	a. 12.96 b. 4.00	a. 3-21 b. 12
10. General persuasiveness[c]	a. 11.65 b. 2.39	a. 10.41 b. 2.58	a. 2-14 b. 8
11. Dyadic opinion leadership[c]	a. 23.35 b. 4.56	a. 20.82 b. 5.56	a. 5-35 b. 20

Note: t tests for independent means, $df = 100$.

[a]$N = 31$.

[b]$N = 71$.

[c]$p < .05$.

[d]$p < .01$.

[e]$p < .001$.

liaisons would for theirs, establishing one facet of the liaison's information relay function in the network.

Regarding interpersonal influence functions, there were no differences between liaisons and nonliaisons on their contacts' perceptions of the competence and trustworthiness dimensions of source credibility. But liaisons were perceived as having more links to individuals with access to the organizational power structure and who were knowledgeable about activities in the organization. Liaisons also were seen as more influential within the power structure and were rated more persuasive with all other of their direct contacts than were nonliaisons. Finally, liaisons were more frequently found to be opinion leaders for their nonliaison contacts than nonliaisons were for their nonliaison contacts. Of thirty-one liaison dyads, twenty-four (77 percent) were dominated by the liaison member of the dyad, and seven (23 percent) were equal to or dominated by the respondent non-liaison member. The seventy-one nonliaison-nonliaison dyads were more evenly split, with thirty-six dominated by the respondent nonliaison and thirty-five dominated by the contact nonliaison ($\chi^2 = 5.893$, $df = 1$, $p < .02$).

Discussion

The purposes of this study were to demonstrate the utility of a procedure for identifying certain roles in inclusive organizational communication networks, to test the validity of a key network concept called the liaison role, and to characterize liaison-role incumbents and some of their interpersonal communication functions. The liaison role is important because its identification is central to the network analysis procedure and because its location in the static structure of an organization argues for the dynamics of the role.

The utility of the conceptual schema and the methodology receives strong support from this study. The method did identify the specified role concepts in an unambiguous manner. We have demonstrated a means by which inclusive networks of communication in an organization can be described and manipulated for analysis. The analysis in this case focused on a significant property of the network itself. Other network properties may be explored in future research, as well as examining relations between extant and formal network roles. The development of refined computer methods for manipulation of sociometric data in short time periods will open the way for systemic process analyses.

The fact that there were several predicted differences between liaison and non-liaison members of the study organization provides empirical validation for the legitimacy of the role concepts and the operations for classifying people into the roles. The findings clearly indicate the liaison role, as defined, has meaning beyond its static location in the network structure of the organization.

The nature of the differences found between liaisons and nonliaisons provides an initial understanding of some of the dynamics of the liaison role and the characteristics of its incumbents. A combination of characteristics suggests liaisons are individuals who have achieved higher status designations than nonliaisons: there are more full professors and administrators among liaisons, they spend more time on administrative duties, and have more memberships on higher-level organizational committees. Because of their location in the formal structure, one might expect all, or at least most, administrators to emerge as liaisons, but these data, and findings reported by Jacobson and Seashore (1951), do not support the expectation. Being an administrator is not a necessary condition for assuming a liaison communication role.

That liaisons devote more time to committee work, have more committee memberships, and attend more committee meetings may suggest that committee work serves to diversify one's contacts among members of separate groups, thus creating a liaison role. But it is also possible that having diverse liaison contacts makes one more visible to those who create the committees.

This study, Jacobson and Seashore (1951), and MacDonald (1970) found liaisons have a broader span of contact than nonliaisons. Our data demonstrate that individuals linked to liaisons are aware of this extended span of contact and of the liaison's more organizationally diverse contact pattern, even though these characteristics are not objectively visible in the course of day-to-day relations. The finding is consistent with small-group network studies showing that members of problem-solving groups, where structured channel patterns are not known to them, soon become aware of which member is in a central information control position (Bavelas, 1950; Leavitt, 1951).

Evidence for the dynamic properties of the liaison role is most important because the greatest theoretic and pragmatic utility of studying this network role will result from knowledge of its contribution to information relay and influence functions in the organization. The information relay potential appears obvious from the static location of the role, and our data confirm it, at least for organizationally related news such as changes or proposed changes. The finding suggests that liaisons are early knowers who provide early dissemination of certain information through the organizational network.

Given the findings of this study, especially in regard to the influence functions of liaisons, it might seem surprising that liaisons are not accorded higher source credibility than nonliaisons. But as can be seen in Table 3, it is not that liaisons do not rate high on credibility but that nonliaisons are also highly rated. Homans (1950) asserted that the more frequently individuals interact, the more nearly alike they become in the norms and expectations they hold. The members of each dyad in this study interacted frequently (once or more per day) in a close working relationship, suggesting the high probability of a friendship bond. With high trust and mutual respect for professional competence between closely associated individuals, source credibility differentials, if any, may be very specific to certain types of information or to singular messages.

Regarding the influence function of liaison persons, Katz (1957, p. 74) asserted an individual may be valued by a group not only for what he knows but also for whom he knows outside of the group. Our findings both support and extend the assertion. Liaisons are known by their contacts to have structurally diverse (that is, out-of-group) linkages, and these linkages are with important people. Jacobson and Seashore (1951) found liaisons and their reciprocated contacts generally report each other as important contacts. Our findings lead one to speculate that the liaison's contact may consider him important because his *other* contacts are considered important, *and* because he has influence with them, particularly those in the power structure. The related finding that liaisons are perceived as generally more persuasive with all their contacts than nonliaisons are with theirs may have implications for who becomes a liaison.

Finally, the liaison's emergence as a dyadic opinion leader for nonliaison group members emphasizes the critical potential of this gatekeeper role in influencing the formation and change of organizational and job attitudes. The static location clearly presents this possibility, and our finding supports it. What remains is research tracing exact differential influences within and among the separate work groups.

Our tests of transaction initiation deliberateness and proportionality sought evidence which might shed light on how liaison roles are established. Are liaisons simply gregarious individuals? Or are they passive "magnetic centers" (Walton, 1962) who attract information seekers to them? The present data provide no clues to answer these questions.

Nor do these data provide a broad base for generalization. However, studies using comparable methods, referred to in this report, are supportive. They include the original Jacobson, Weiss, and Seashore study and the more recent works of MacDonald (1970), Jacobs (1971), and Farace and MacDonald (1974).

References

Barnes, J. A. "Networks and Political Process." In M. J. Swartz (Ed.), *Local-Level Politics.* Chicago: Aldine, 1968.

Bavelas, A. "Communication Patterns in Task-Oriented Groups." *Journal of the Acoustical Society of America,* 1950, *22*, 725-730.

Berlo, D. K., Lemert, J. B., and Mertz, R. J. "Dimensions for Evaluating the Acceptability of Message Sources." *Public Opinion Quarterly,* 1969-70, *33*, 563-576.

Burns, T. "The Directions of Activity and Communication in a Departmental Executive

Group: A Quantitative Study in a British Engineering Factory with a Self-Recording Activity." *Human Relations,* 1954, *7,* 73-97.

Conrath, D. W. "Communications Environment and Its Relationship to Organizational Structure." *Management Science,* 1973, *20,* 586-603.

Davis, K. "A Method of Studying Communication Patterns in Organizations." *Personnel Psychology,* 1953, *6,* 301-312.

Farace, R. V., and MacDonald, D. "New Directions in the Study of Organizational Communication." *Personnel Psychology,* 1974, *27,* 1-19.

Gold, D. "Statistical Tests and Substantive Significance." *American Sociologist,* 1969, *4,* 42-46.

Hinrichs, J. R. "Communication Activity of Industrial Research Personnel." *Personnel Psychology,* 1964, *17,* 193-204.

Homans, G. C. *The Human Group.* New York: Harcourt Brace Jovanovich, 1950.

Jacobs, M. A. "The Structure and Functions of Internal Communication in Three Religious Communities." Unpublished doctoral dissertation, Michigan State University, 1971. (University Microfilms, No. 72-22, 237.)

Jacobson, E., and Seashore, S. E. "Communication Practices in Complex Organizations." *Journal of Social Issues,* 1951, *7,* 28-40.

Katz, E. "The Two-Step Flow of Communication: An Up-to-Date Report of an Hypothesis." *Public Opinion Quarterly,* 1957, *21,* 62-78.

Katz, E., and Lazarsfeld, P. F. *Personal Influence: The Part Played by People in the Flow of Mass Communications.* New York: Free Press, 1955.

Leavitt, H. J. "Some Effects of Certain Communication Patterns on Group Performance." *Journal of Abnormal and Social Psychology,* 1951, *46,* 38-50.

Leavitt, H. J. *Managerial Psychology.* Chicago: University of Chicago Press, 1964.

MacDonald, D. "Communication Roles and Communication Content in a Bureaucratic Setting." Unpublished doctoral dissertation, Michigan State University, 1970. (University Microfilms No. 71-23, 212.)

McQuitty, L. L. "Elementary Linkage Analysis for Isolating Orthogonal and Oblique Types and Typal Relevancies." *Educational and Psychological Measurement,* 1957, *17,* 207-229.

Morrison, D. E., and Henkel, R. E. "Significance Tests Reconsidered." *American Sociologist,* 1969, *4,* 131-140.

Mortenson, C. D. *Communication: The Study of Human Interaction.* New York: McGraw-Hill, 1972.

Richards, W. A. *A Manual for Network Analysis (Using the Negopy Network Analysis Program).* Palo Alto, Calif.: Institute for Communication Research, Stanford University, 1975.

Rogers, E. M., and Cartano, D. G. "Methods of Measuring Opinion Leadership." *Public Opinion Quarterly,* 1962, *26,* 435-441.

Rogers, E. M., and Shoemaker, F. F. *Communication of Innovations.* New York: Free Press, 1971.

Ross, I. C., and Harary, F. "Identification of the Liaison Persons of an Organization Using the Structure Matrix." *Management Science,* 1955, *1,* 251-258.

Schwartz, D. F. "Liaison Communication Roles in a Formal Organization." Unpublished doctoral dissertation, Michigan State University, 1968. (University Microfilms No. 69-11, 162.)

Thayer, L. "Communication and Organizational Theory." In F. E. Dance (Ed.), *Human Communication Theory.* New York: Holt, Rinehart and Winston, 1967.

Troldahl, V. C., and Van Dam, R. "A New Scale for Identifying Public-Affairs Opinion Leaders." *Journalism Quarterly,* 1965, *42* (4), 655-657.

Wager, L. W. "Interpersonal and Mass Communication in an Organizational Setting." *Sociological Inquiry,* 1962, *32* (1), 88-107.

Walton, E. *A Magnetic Theory of Organizational Communication.* China Lake, Calif.: U.S. Naval Ordinance Test Station, 1962.

Weiss, R. S. *Processes of Organization.* Ann Arbor: Institute for Social Research, University of Michigan, 1956.

Weiss, R. S., and Jacobson, E. "A Method for the Analysis of the Structure of Complex Organizations." *American Sociological Review,* 1955, *20,* 661-668.

PART VI

✑ Leadership and Decision Making

Leadership research has shifted greatly over the years, from a concern with the personal qualities of leaders to an emphasis on the processes and procedures of leadership. The early emphasis on the personality of the leader is occasionally revived, as in attention to the charisma of the person who makes things happen. But for the most part we now think of leadership as an influence process rather than a personality syndrome. Once the emphasis shifts from person to process, recognition of group and organizational variables follows. These variables help to determine the procedures effective for different settings and different tasks. Thus, a contingency approach, which calls for some knowledge of the contingent conditions under which an influence process will work, has become popular. Many of the contingencies studied thus far are mediating perceptual variables and not organizational factors, but the trend is toward the inclusion of system variables.

The contingency approach led to a symposium at Southern Illinois University in 1973. In their paper in this symposium, Bass and Valenzi (1974) propose that contingent conditions may account for the conflicting findings about the relative effectiveness of participative and directive leadership. These conditions are (1) the manager's own history, values, and goals; (2) the subordinate's history, values, and goals; (3) the external environment of the organization; (4) specific attributes of top management; (5) organizational climate and structure; and (6) task requirements. In the same volume Korman (1974) points out that a statement of contingency should include an account of the mechanism by which the intervening variable has a mediating effect on the independent variable. Without such understanding, we have inadequate theory and limited application.

Some of these contingent conditions, in Bennis's (1976) view, have contributed to "the erosion of institutional autonomy," which he regards as a consequence of organizational size and complexity. As president of a university, he notes that 50 percent of his contacts were with external people. The pressures from without and the stresses from within (there were over 500 organized pressure groups in Bennis's university) make it difficult for the leader to do much more than managing or confining himself to routine administrative tasks. Bold acts of innovative, charismatic leadership are, moreover, easier in a growing, expanding economy than in a period of setting limits.

If leadership is viewed as methods of influence within an organizational context, it overlaps in subject matter with policy formulation and decision making, which are essential parts of the leadership process. As participative practices grow, there is more sharing of the influence process. That may be one of the reasons for the decline in leadership research as the study of personality. In fact, the central problem in leadership may become the knowledge of how to delegate, when to delegate, and how to involve subordinates in various levels of decision making. This is the point of departure for the Vroom-Yetton model presently to be discussed.

The traditional model of leadership was a two-factor model, in which task direction and socioemotional support of group members were the basic components (Bales, 1958). Any given leader did not have to possess both qualities as long as a subordinate or some informal leader could carry out the function that the formal leader lacked. This conception was productive of much research, and the Ohio State studies of supervisory satisfaction were based on the related concepts of initiation of structure (task orientation) and consideration (socioemotional support). Fiedler (1967) has added a number of contingent variables—such as task structure, power of the leader, and acceptance of the leader by the group—to the Bales concepts. His investigations, employing field and laboratory experiments, are still the most complete series of studies available, in that measures of performance were used and conditions were experimentally manipulated. His findings indicate that task-oriented leaders do better than supportive leaders when leaders are accepted by the group, with one exception. Where the task is unstructured and the power position of the leader is weak, the supportive leaders do better. Where the leader-member relationship is good, there is less need of support from above for effective performance.

Since Fiedler's work, the field, like social psychology, has gone subjective. House (1971), however, has elaborated a cognitive mode that includes objective and subjective elements. According to this path-goal model, the strategic function of leadership is to enhance psychological states that lead to increased motivation. This is done (1) by arousing subordinates' needs over which the leader has some control, (2) by increasing payoffs to subordinates for goal attainment, (3) by coaching and direction to make the paths to these payoffs easier of access, (4) by helping subordinates clarify expectancies, (5) by reducing frustrating barriers, and (6) by increasing the opportunities for personal satisfaction contingent on effective performance. To channel behavior, it is necessary to have people realize how their actions can increase their rewards.

It is difficult to quarrel with the theory, for people do move to satisfy their needs when the needs are aroused and the paths for their satisfaction are clear. The question is, however, how much more information is added by such a circular statement. From a scientific point of view, we do not know a great deal more; but from a practical point of view, it is helpful because leaders in organizations do not always enhance goal states or clarify paths to goals. Moreover, House and Dessler (1974) have related this model to the contingency factor of task structure. They hypothesized that task structure would have a negative moderating effect on the relationship between task direction and performance and satisfaction. Task direction has to do with the leader's clarifying expectations, assigning specific tasks, and specifying procedures. With high task structure, such instrumental leadership would be less important than with low task structure—a negative moderating effect. They further hypothesized that task structure would have a positive moderating effect on the relationship between supportive leadership and performance and satisfaction of subordinates. High task structure is assumed to have frustrating effects because of its rigidity, and this thwarting will be compensated by supportive leadership. The hypotheses were tested by means of questionnaires in two firms and received some, but not overwhelming, support. The great weakness in the study is the lack of hard data on performance. Subjects reported on expectancies, and there were no measures of actual performance.

Oldham (1976) has also moved in the direction of specifying the activities of supervisors in motivating employees. In place of the global measures of initiation (task orientation) and consideration (supportiveness), he has proposed seven motivational strategies that leaders may use: personally rewarding actions, personally punishing, setting goals, designing feedback systems, placing personnel, designing job systems, and designing reward systems. His categories are closer to the actual behavior of the supervisor in the work situation than are many of the attempts to characterize leadership style. These latter efforts resemble the personality approach in seeking for personal qualities in the individual leader. In testing his theory, Oldham studied the middle managers in ten stores of a national retail chain and obtained data from them and from their subordinates and the store managers as well. Of six strategies investigated, only the personally punishing technique was not significantly related to motivational effectiveness as rated by subordinates and supervisor. This finding is congruent with the literature on punishment in that negative reactions to sanctions affect other behavior than the penalized act. Though all the strategies studied, except punishment, related positively to the rated motivation of the manager, there was no attempt made at some form of multiple or partial correlation. Multivariate analysis would yield information on the independent contributions of these various strategies.

The ratings of subordinate performance were not as consistently related to motivational strategies as were the ratings on motivational effectiveness. Again we are not dealing with hard data, and the measure of motivational strategy is a composite of reactions from the three levels of superior, focal person, and subordinate, and so includes some of the same individuals as those in the effectiveness ratings. Hence, there is the possibility of a halo effect. Methodologically, more independently generated measures for the two variables would have been preferable. The investigator also used the standard measures of initiation and consideration, and they did not relate to motivation ratings as strongly as did the motivational strategies. What is needed are follow-up studies with hard data on performance to bolster the hypothesis about the importance of specific motivational tactics.

One aspect of leadership that emerges clearly in organizational settings is the ability of the leader to handle the constraints imposed by his or her position in the hierarchical structure. Despite Bennis's emphasis on constraints at the top, the latitude for action generally increases as one ascends the organizational ladder. The area of freedom at any given level is determined in part by the ability to deal effectively with the next level. If first-line supervisors can influence their boss, they can accomplish things for their own subordinates more than colleagues who do not relate as well to their superiors. This representative function of leadership was highlighted some three decades ago in the Detroit Edison study of Pelz (1951). It was not enough, Pelz found, for supervisors to possess human-relations skills in dealing with their subordinates. To be regarded as good leaders, these supervisors had to be perceived as going to bat for their subordinates with higher levels of management. This promising line of research was not followed up for some time, but Wager (1965) has shown the necessity for considering other variables, such as the blue-collar versus white-collar population of the organization, in the representative function.

More recently, Graen and his colleagues (1977) have revived interest in the problem by investigating what effects the linkages between supervisors and their superiors have on subordinates. In this research, the linking-pin concept of Likert is employed. Likert (1961) theorized that the relationships between levels can be facilitated through the supervisor or manager who is the leader of his or her own group and a member of a higher-echelon group, including his or her coordinates and their boss. Ideally, Likert saw group process occurring at both levels, with the linking-pin person the integrator. In their work, however, Graen and his colleagues reduce the linking-pin role to a dyadic relationship, in which every supervisor has a one-on-one relationship with every subordinate. Nevertheless, they found that the quality of the linking-pin relationship has definite effects on subordinates' perceptions and attitudes, such that more exchanges of information and influence in the upper dyad are accompanied by more exchange in the lower dyad. Likert's linking-pin theory has had some impact on experiments in organizational change, as in the work of Marrow, Bowers, and Seashore (1967), but the actual linkages in ongoing organizations have been inadequately studied. One practical approach, limited though it may be, is through a study of the representative function in nondemocratic structures.

No theme has occupied the attention of organizational theorists in recent years in dealing with leadership as has the concept of participation in the influence process. For McGregor (1960), encouragement or discouragement of participation depends on the personality of the leader. He distinguished between the open, supportive, and consultative type of leader (Manager Y) and the rigid, authoritarian, and punitive type of leader (Manager X). Blake and Mouton (1968) make the degree of consultative and participatory practices more a matter of management style. Likert calls for participation by the group in decisions at their own group level and representation by their supervisor at the next level in the hierarchy. Some Scandinavian exponents of reform have pushed the notion of representative democracy as appropriate for industry.

The motivational assumptions of McGregor and Likert are consistent with Maslow's (1954) need hierarchy, with its concern for self-actualization, and with Herzberg's (1966) distinction between hygiene factors (negative) and motivating factors (positive). Herzberg would distinguish between a lower-level need, such as satisfaction with working conditions, and a higher-level need, such as self-development.

Hall and *Donnell* point out that, in spite of much agreement in behavioral science about the appeal of participatory practices to a wide range of motives, there has been no investigation of the extent to which managers are actually committed to the newer philosophers. *Hall* and *Donnell* boldly attack this problem in a series of five separate studies involving over 12,000 managers. Even more significant, they relate these managerial practices to managerial achievement. They employed an objective index or hard criterion for their purpose; namely, the ratio of number of years in service to number of promotions. They also used an independent measure of managerial techniques by asking subordinates about their superiors. In general, their results show that managers whose philosophies and practices are congruent with modern concepts of motivation and participation are higher in achievement in the sense of moving up the organizational ladder. For example, high achievers were less likely to follow the philosophy of McGregor's Type X, the authoritarian personality. There is concordance, then, between the values of organizational leaders and the teaching of present-day social science. How much of this is due to changed academic doctrine and how much to more general culture change is not known. Nor is it clear from the *Hall-Donnell* investigations whether the newer philosophies are actually productive of higher group performance. The inference is that they are if one assumes that there is some correlation between promotion and the performance of subordinates.

To move from general conceptions of participative democracy to the specifics of wise decision making under given conditions requires an empirically oriented model. Vroom and Yetton (1973) furnish one that spells out five types of decision processes, ranging from authoritarian through consultative to democratic. They further examine the kinds of problems that suggest rules or criteria for decision making. For example, if quality of decision is important and the leader lacks adequate information, then the authoritarian procedure is eliminated. Or, again, if subordinates do not share organizational goals, then group decision will not ensure quality outcomes.

In a test of this model, *Vroom* and *Jago* asked ninety-six managers in management development programs to describe two cases of actual decision-making situations from their own experience and to code the relevant dimensions according to the Vroom-Yetton model. They were also asked to rate the decision on its effectiveness, quality of chosen alternative, and its acceptance by subordinates. In general, where the decision followed the proposed rules, the outcomes were favorable. For the most part, participative practices were favored, as would be expected from other research and the *Hall-Donnell* findings. But the model did somewhat better than uniform predictions based on participative democracy. In some situations—for instance, in the case of incongruent goals—these investigators found that group decisions were not effective processes.

There are contingent conditions for the exercise of small-group democracy, and the surprising aspect of the Vroom-Yetton model is that it inquires into so few of them. But the theory does give us a beginning in the use of contingencies and is valuable in looking at the particular ways in which problems arise and constraints occur. One difficulty with it in its present development is the circular character of some of its rules. We are told that where subordinates do not accept organizational goals, group decision will not be better qualitatively than the decision of the manager. This has to be the case, and the real issue is the degree to which subordinates do accept organizational goals. Similarly, the rule that if the manager lacks information or expertise, his method of decision making should involve seeking more information adds little to our theoretical knowledge. Finally, the method of relying completely on what managers can recall is fine for a pilot study, but it needs to be followed up by observation, by peer reports, and by reports of superiors and subordinates. The investigators, however, have opened the doors by theoretical precept and example.

The Vroom-Yetton framework for decision making, like other models, assumes a rational model of human behavior and applies it to leadership in organizations. Organizations, however, contribute their own variables to the determination and implementation of policymaking. Cyert and March (1963) point out that subgroups within a structure often have competing and even incompatible goals, and decisions are often the result of conflicts and compromises within the system. The jockeying for power and the formation of coalitions are behind the decision-making process. This organizational context for policy determination has often been neglected, but *Pfeffer* and *Salancik* have studied the budget-making process in a university with respect to the power of various departments. As a measure of the power of departments, two devices were employed: interviews with the twenty-nine departmental heads and the recording of membership on major university committees. With work load of the department controlled, the measures of departmental power were significantly related to the proportion of the budget received. The more powerful the department, the less likely were its allocated resources to be based on student demand for its courses. The authors' conclusion is similar to that of Cyert and March: that organizational decisions can reflect the interplay of subunit power rather than what is optimal for the organization as a whole. Not only do *Pfeffer* and *Salancik* bring some organizational reality into decision making; they also illustrate the value of an unobtrusive measure of subunit power. Their use of important committee memberships avoids the difficulty of direct obtrusive interviewing, yet correlates well with it.

In large organizations decisions often involve groups of leaders and do not follow a simple paradigm of a supervisor and his or her workers. Committees of vice-presidents, sessions of department heads, and group meetings of various sorts contribute to decision making. Policy formulation and implementation are thus subject to both the benefits of group problem solving and the distortions of groupthink. *Groupthink* is the term popularized by Janis (1972), who uses it "to refer to the mode of thinking that persons engage in when concurrence seeking becomes so dominant in a cohesive ingroup that it tends to override realistic appraisal of alternative courses of action" (p. 237). Experiments have conclusively demonstrated the strength of group pressures in affecting individual judgment. The weaknesses of the individual in reaching rational decisions can be greatly magnified in group settings. Janis urges breaking up the circle of social reinforcement through institutionalizing devices for obtaining independent opinions and for receiving feedback from actual operations.

Relatively early feedback is required about the working out of procedures in actual practice, as well as systematic information about environmental conditions. Not every piece of negative information need be responded to, since some continuity in policy is desirable. The Bennis-Slater (1968) model of a temporary system, completely flexible to changing winds, is the opposite extreme of rigid fixation on outmoded goals and goes too far in encouraging anarchy of policy. The common risk, however, is rigidity reinforced by groupthink. Mechanisms to counteract groupthink and to change old unworkable policies are, therefore, critical for organizational survival. Feedback procedures and research evaluation are the answer. Some organizations use the occasion of budget preparation for systematic review of the activities of various programs and projects. Outside evaluation is another device, but it tends to come too often as a measure to help public relations. There are few organizations which would not be strengthened by research subsystems for both their internal functioning and their external impact.

References

Bales, R. F. "Task Roles and Social Roles in Problem-Solving Groups." In E. Maccoby, T. M. Newcomb, and E. L. Hartley (Eds.), *Readings in Social Psychology.* (3rd ed.) New York: Holt, Rinehart and Winston, 1958.

Bass, B. M., and Valenzi, E. R. "Contingent Aspect of Effective Management Styles." In J. G. Hunt and L. L. Larson (Eds.), *Contingency Approaches to Leadership.* Carbondale: Southern Illinois University Press, 1974.

Bennis, W. G. "Leadership: A Beleaguered Species?" *Organizational Dynamics,* 1976, *5,* 1, 36.

Bennis, W. G., and Slater, P. E. *The Temporary Society.* New York: Harper & Row, 1968.

Blake, R. R., and Mouton, J. S. *Corporate Excellence Through Grid Organizational Development.* Houston: Gulf, 1968.

Cyert, R. M., and March, J. G. *A Behavioral Theory of the Firm.* Englewood Cliffs, N.J.: Prentice-Hall, 1963.

Fiedler, F. E. *A Theory of Leadership Effectiveness.* New York: McGraw-Hill, 1967.

Graen, G., and others. "Effects of Linking-Pin Quality on the Quality of Working Life of Lower Participants." *Administrative Science Quarterly,* 1977, *22,* 491-504.

Herzberg, F. *Work and the Nature of Man.* New York: World, 1966.

House, R. J. "A Path-Goal Theory of Leadership Effectiveness." *Administrative Science Quarterly,* 1971, *16,* 321-338.

House, R. J., and Dessler, G. "The Path-Goal Theory of Leadership: Some Post Hoc and A Priori Tests." In J. G. Hunt and L. L. Larson (Eds.), *Contingency Approaches to Leadership.* Carbondale: Southern Illinois University Press, 1974.

Hunt, J. G., and Larson, L. L. (Eds.). *Contingency Approaches to Leadership.* Carbondale: Southern Illinois University Press, 1974.

Janis, I. L. *Victims of Groupthink.* Boston: Houghton Mifflin, 1972.

Korman, A. K. "Contingency Approaches to Leadership: an Overview." In J. G. Hunt and L. L. Larson (Eds.), *Contingency Approaches to Leadership.* Carbondale: Southern Illinois University Press, 1974.

Likert, R. *New Patterns of Management.* New York: McGraw-Hill, 1961.

McGregor, D. *The Human Side of Enterprise.* New York: McGraw-Hill, 1960.

Marrow, A. J., Bowers, D. G., and Seashore, S. E. *Management by Participation.* New York: Harper & Row, 1967.

Maslow, A. H. *Motivation and Personality.* New York: Harper & Row, 1954.

Oldham, G. R. "The Motivational Strategies Used by Supervisors: Relationships to Effectiveness Indicators." *Organizational Behavior and Human Performances,* 1976, *15,* 66-86.

Pelz, D. C. "Leadership Within a Hierarchical Organization." *Journal of Social Issues,* 1951, *7,* 49-55.

Vroom, V. H., and Yetton, P. W. *Leadership and Decision-Making.* Pittsburgh: University of Pittsburgh Press, 1973.

Wager, L. V. "Leadership Style, Hierarchical Influence, and Supervising Roles Obligations." *Administrative Science Quarterly,* 1965, *9,* 391-420.

26

Managerial Achievement: The Personal Side of Behavioral Theory

Jay Hall
Susan M. Donnell

In a National Industrial Conference Board survey of five hundred organizations (Rush, 1969), over 79 percent of the respondents professed an interest in the implications of behavioral science for their organizations. And they seemed knowledgeable about the topic. Some 202 theorists were cited; the six most frequently mentioned contributions were the work of Douglas McGregor (1960) on managerial perceptions and beliefs, Frederick Herzberg's (1966) motivation-hygiene theory, Likert's (1961, 1967) analysis of management systems and linking-pin concepts, Maslow's (1954, 1965) ideas on motivational dynamics, and the managerial style treatment of Blake and Mouton (1964). It appears that the works of our more prominent applied scientists have indeed found their organizational mark.

But, commenting upon the NICB results and the status of applied behavioral science in general, Weisbord (1970) points out that only one manager of every four queried listed Douglas McGregor as having personally influenced him, while McGregor was named far and away more frequently than any of the other contributors cited. Weisbord concludes (1970, p. 5) that "A vast gap exists between the glib use of names like McGregor, Likert, and Herzberg . . . and the creative use of science-based theories to improve the way companies are managed."

Why this should be—why, as Marrow (1972) claims, there is a twenty-five-year gap between the discovery of new evidence in support of behavioral theory and its general application; why, again in Marrow's view, the present generation of executives is unwilling to learn new managerial systems to replace dying traditions—should be a major concern for a science that is both applied and normative.

Levinson (1972) has observed that most executives are people of ambition, powerfully motivated by distant goals of success, who prefer to guide and direct and are reluctant to rest their fate on people whose actions they cannot predict. Ambiguity threatens them; control procedures and well-defined organizational structures reassure them. And all the while, the essential thrust of behavioral science tenets is in the direction of greater

Reprinted from *Human Relations,* 1979, *32* (1), 77-101, with permission of the authors and Plenum Publishing Corporation.

366

reliance on internal rather than external controls, on less sheer conformity and more employee participation, and on an integration of individual and organizational goals rather than a subordination of one to the other.

The gap between paying homage to theorists and actually incorporating their principles in management, the gap between discovery and application—these may be due to a third gap, that of credibility. The normative and value-centered nature of social-industrial psychology and sociology, although consistent with empirical evidence, runs counter to both the intuitive precepts and personal motives of many a practicing manager. Like Ignaz Semmelweis laboring to convince his fellow physicians in Vienna to wash their hands rather than wipe them on their smocks—ignoring the status value of the oft-smeared surgical mantle—behavioral scientists have prescribed practices which, although touted as means to increased productivity and organizational renewal, ignore the manager's dreams and apprehensions about personal success. Where is the *personal* credibility of the behavioral sciences?

Only Blake and Mouton (1964), among theorists most familiar to managers, have addressed the personal implications of behavioral science contributions for managers and their careers—and then only via the issue of managerial style. Otherwise, a review of the literature reveals little scientific inquiry into the presence or lack of congruence between managerial practices and behavioral premises; it addresses not at all the relationship of such theories to managerial accomplishment. Yet, it is the executive—the middle manager, the first-line supervisor—who decides individually whether or not to apply the teachings of any applied discipline. As people who work daily with such decision makers, we are convinced that gaps of application and theory vis-à-vis practice will persist so long as executives are unsure of the consequences for themselves and their own achievement.

In our view, information about the relationship of managerial achievement to the use of science-based principles in management is needed if applied behavioral science is ever to enjoy the credibility of the physical sciences among managers. Organizations are founded on, and reflect in their processes, basic technologies; most managers link career achievement to technological expertise. If our theories are to have personal validity, needed in addition is a social technology of managerial achievement.

The present series of studies, constituting an Achieving Manager Research Project, seeks to remedy the research deficit in the area of applied social-industrial psychology by systematically assessing the practices of managers of varying degrees of accomplishment according to the provisions inherent in several normative models. In addition, these studies offer an alternative to trait approaches in that the level of analysis involves specified and standardized behavioral options as independent variables according to which the dependent variable of managerial achievement may be investigated. Both managerial self-reports and assessments by those they manage are included in the design. Over 17,000 managers were studied in the Achieving Manager Research Project, and, on the basis of five separate studies, the relationship of managerial achievement to values, motivational dynamics, participative methods, interpersonal competence, and managerial style is examined. Although our research posture was essentially exploratory, in the obtained results may be found the basis for a more personal and social technology of managerial achievement, consistent with the major provisions of applied behavioral science.

The Achieving Manager Research Project

The Achieving Manager Research Project focused on five major areas of the management process: (1) managers' values and beliefs regarding the nature of those they manage; (2) managerial and subordinate motivational phenomena; (3) managers' use of

participative practices and their related involvement effects, as reported by their subordinates; (4) the issue of interpersonal competence, as reported by managers themselves and
judged by their subordinates; and (5) managerial style, that cluster of behaviors resulting
from all the former. These were taken as a basis for a social technology of management as
it has been developed in the literature. Instrumentation involved the use of eight standardized and validated paper-and-pencil surveys, each based on a prominent behavioral
science model of managerial and human functioning.

Pilot studies with over 5,000 male managers were conducted, and the present investigation involved 12,000 more. All organizational levels, the full range of pertinent
ages, and over fifty actual organizations—ranging from automotive, retail, and drug firms
to the federal government, nonprofit social agencies, and research and development types
—are represented. Blind sampling procedures were used, with most of the data collected
and supplied by the organizations' own personnel, and statistical analyses were conducted
by an independent third party—steps designed to minimize the effects of researcher bias.
In each research instance, managers were assigned to high, average, or low managerial
achievement groups after assessment and on the basis of an objective and standardized
grouping formula.

Identifying the Achieving Manager

Attempts at measuring managerial achievement evoke the perennial criterion problem. Whereas Ghiselli (1963) presented a good case for the use of subjective criteria, we
desired a more objective index which incidentally incorporated those criteria subjectively
used as reference points by managers themselves. A straightforward exemplary-case criterion, for example, was rejected because, although quite objective in a post facto sense,
to study only those of high organizational rank would obscure potential for achievement
while saying nothing to questions regarding the low achiever and his possible use of
counterproductive behaviors. Purely subjective appraisals, on the other hand, often reflect
cultural biases which might or might not relate to achievement in a generic sense. A broad
yet rigorous and culture-free index of managerial achievement was needed.

A Formula for Measuring Achievement. For our measure of managerial achievement, we chose a variation of the formula developed by Dr. Benjamin Rhodes and used
by Blake and Mouton (1964) in their study of managerial style as related to career accomplishment. The Rhodes Managerial Achievement Quotient (MAQ) affords an evaluation of
an individual's career progress in light of his chronological age, taking into account the
number of career moves necessary to reach the top of a typical organization and the age
span most germane to career planning.

Whereas Blake and Mouton conducted their study in a single organization and
were able to specify eight different levels of organizational rank, such precision seemed
unfeasible in a study involving a wide range of organizations. Therefore, broadness of
managerial representation and cultural range was purchased at the expense of precision by
lowering the number of rank discriminations in the Rhodes index. As a generic index of
managerial achievement, the following formula was used:

$$\text{MAQ} = \frac{5(6 - \text{Rank})}{\text{Age}} \times 100$$

In the numerator, the number 5 is a constant progression factor representing the
time in grade per number of career moves available if one were to spend his forty-year

work life in an eight-level organization and reflecting potential mobility upward in the absence of any other forces, such as politics, seniority, chance, and so forth. Also in the numerator, the quantity (6 − Rank) amounts to a rank index obtained by assigning numerical values of 1 to 5 to organizational levels ranging from top (L1) to nonmanagement (L5) and subtracting from the correction factor of 6. In the denominator, Age (20 to 50 years) represents a seniority index: the time, given a standard entry age of 20 and an upper cutoff of 50 beyond which age is not a factor, in which an individual might advance from lowest to highest organizational level if advancement were purely mechanical. Finally, the constant multiplier of 100 is used to eliminate decimals.

Normative Data Base for the MAQ. So that there might be confidence in both the selection mechanism and the cutoff points chosen to differentiate individuals of high, average, and low managerial achievement, demographic data necessary for computing the MAQ were collected on a base sample of 5,451 male managers. All organizational levels, from nonmanagement supervisory personnel to chief executive officer, ages from 19 to 64, and twenty-six different types of organizations were represented. MAQ raw scores ranged from 9 to 109.15. The average manager in this base sample had an MAQ of 39.4; he was approximately 38 years old and occupied a middle-management (L3) position.

Raw scores were transformed to normalized standard scores with a mean of 50 and a standard deviation of 10 (Veldman, 1967), affording a control for bias and allowing us to categorize managers with standardized MAQs of 60 or above as high achievers, 41 to 59 as average achievers, and those with 40 or below as low achievers. Finally, a number of pilot studies were conducted to determine the sensitivity and discriminant power of the index, and their results confirmed the standardized MAQ as a robust and reliable indicator of managerial achievement.

Study I: Managerial Achievement and Personal Beliefs

An appropriate point of departure in assessing the relationship of managerial achievement to the various technologies enunciated by social-industrial theorists would seem to be the work of Douglas McGregor (1960) on personal belief structures. McGregor has maintained that every managerial act rests on fundamental assumptions, generalizations, and hypotheses about the nature of the people who populate the world of work. The personal assumptions or "cosmologies" management holds about controlling its human resources determine the whole character of the enterprise. McGregor posits two views for comparative emphasis: Theory X and Theory Y, examples of a pessimistic and reductive view of those human resources under the manager's purview as compared to a set of developmental and integrative beliefs.

Insofar as managerial achievement is concerned, it is McGregor's position that management philosophically based in Theory Y addresses itself to the dynamic potentials for growth and internal control of personnel, facilitating better accomplishment of organizational objectives and encouraging the growth of subordinates at the same time; on the other hand, subscription to a Theory X view is evinced in mechanistic thinking and a preoccupation with the use of external controls which limit growth and reduce organizational potential. If this is a valid position and if the manager's subscription to a reductive vis-à-vis a developmental set of beliefs about the nature of his human resources does indeed affect the quality of his management, achievers should be found to differ from nonachievers along the dimension of managerial belief. Study I was undertaken to investigate the relevance of personal belief systems for managerial achievement.

Subject and Instrumentation. The Managerial Philosophies Scale (Jacoby and

Terborg, 1975b) was employed to ascertain the strength of managers' subscriptions to Theory X and Theory Y generalizations about the nature of the human resources comprising their organizations. Based on McGregor's (1960) description of X-Y belief content, the MPS has been found to have a test-retest reliability of .68 and .59 and internal coefficients of .85 and .77 for X and Y scales, respectively. Support for the construct validity of the MPS lies primarily in the significant covariation of X scale scores with measures of general authoritarianism (Jacoby and Terborg, 1975a). The MPS was administered to 676 managers, representing the full range of organizational rank from fourteen different types of organizations. Subjects were then assigned to achievement groups on the basis of their standardized MAQ scores: 156 low achievers, 421 average achievers, and 99 high-achieving managers.

Results and Discussion. As in all the studies comprising the Achieving Manager Project, the nature of the variables of interest was best suited to a multivariate treatment; multiple discriminant function analysis was deemed most appropriate for detecting both the areas of maximum difference between groups and the structural nature of those differences (Kerlinger and Pedhazur, 1973). Group membership served as our dependent variable, and, in this instance, scores from the X and Y scales of the MPS were the independent variables.

A significant overall discrimination was detected ($F = 2.685$, $df = 4$ and 672, $p <$ .03). A single discriminant root was extracted, accounting for 88 percent of the between-group variance; with $\chi^2 = 9.414$ ($df = 3$), this function was significant beyond the .02 level of confidence.

The univariate F tests for the two independent variables revealed that only scores from the Theory X scale significantly differed for the three MAQ groups ($F = 3.891$, $p <$ .02), and this was reflected in the discriminant weights obtained; the resulting function emerged as a fairly pure index of an individual's strength of subscription to Theory X propositions. The three achievement groups were ordered on this dimension, as evidenced by their centroid scores, in an inverse manner to their level of achievement. That is, strong subscription to Theory X beliefs appeared to be a major characteristic of low-achieving managers, with such beliefs decreasing in strength from low- through average- to high-achieving groups.

The linear nature of the relationship between belief in reductive propositions regarding an organization's human resources and the level of managerial achievement attained is portrayed graphically in Figure 1. As the plot of centroid scores reveals, high-achieving managers differ from their average- and low-achieving colleagues primarily in terms of their relative lack of subscription to Theory X and, it is inferred, allegiance to alternative beliefs. In brief, the results best serve to illustrate the counterproductive impact of reductive views on managerial achievement; as McGregor would have us expect, adherence to Theory X suppositions regarding those who populate one's work environment is associated with lower levels of managerial achievement.

Of some interest is the fact that the obverse proposition, to the effect that reliance on a Theory Y view facilitates managerial accomplishment, fails to receive support. Managerial achievement appears in the present instance to be a negatively accelerated function of strength of subscription to the reductive and delimiting beliefs comprising Theory X and not much else. This may be an oversimplification of the results, however.

McGregor (1967) made explicit his view that X and Y are independent cosmologies, not polar opposites, and that one does not become an advocate of Theory Y simply by moving away from Theory X. The total profile requires analysis. It would appear from our results that the X to Y ratio holds some diagnostic merit. In the present case, an

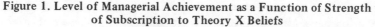

Figure 1. Level of Managerial Achievement as a Function of Strength
of Subscription to Theory X Beliefs

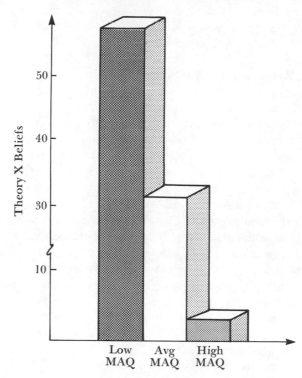

inspection of the X and Y means reveals that the high-achieving group falls well below the standardized mean for Theory X subscription while scoring equally above the mean for its Theory Y orientation. No such clear preference was evident among average and low achievers. Indeed, from our results, low and average achievers display something akin to what Meyers (1964) has called a traditional view: Theory X tempered by human relations training or, perhaps, social desirability effects. Thus, the present results appear more suggestive than definitive; they point up the significant negative relationship between a Theory X subscription and managerial achievement, and they suggest, moreover, that a more critical consideration might well be the degree of subordination of Theory X beliefs to Theory Y assumptions as a precursor to achievement.

We might say that the results of Study I reveal more about failure to achieve than they do about achievement per se. Nevertheless, our results indicate that managerial cosmologies, as a part of the existing social technology of management, do distinguish among managers of differing achievement. And, consistent with McGregor's position, it may be expected that managers of differing achievement will be found as well to embrace different approaches to the interaction components of management.

Study II: Managerial Achievement and Motivational Phenomena

McGregor (1960) particularly felt that managerial cosmologies influence one's approach to motivation; Study II addresses this facet of managerial achievement. A comprehensive study of motivational phenomena in the organizational setting is, of necessity, tripartite. Likert's (1961) interaction-influence paradigm would lead us to expect that simultaneously involved are (1) the motivational profiles of the managers themselves, (2) the managers' emphases in administering the motivational process, and (3) the ostensible consequences of the former as exhibited in the motivational profiles of subordinate personnel. Three separate studies were undertaken to explore such considerations as they relate to the issue of managerial achievement.

Differential Work Motivation Among Managers

The theoretical basis of our motivational studies lay with the work of Herzberg (1966), Maslow (1954, 1965), and Meyers (1964, 1966). Although these authors have all addressed the issue of motivation in the workplace, their primary emphasis has been on nonmanagement personnel. Yet, given differences in managerial achievement and the previously noted subscriptions to different managerial values, one might expect managers to differ as well in their needs, goals, and personal aspirations. We assessed the motivational profiles of managers of varying achievement to test this assumption.

Subjects and Instrumentation. The Hall and Williams (1967b) Work Motivation Inventory (WMI) was administered to 1,265 management personnel from twenty-three different types of organizations. The instrument is based on a synthesis of Maslow's need-hierarchy concept (1954) and Herzberg's motivation-hygiene theory (1966). Designed to assess the factors most important to an individual in work-related situations, the WMI generates five scores: basic creature comfort, safety, belongingness, ego status, and self-actualization. Its median test-retest correlation has been established as .70, and construct validity is high. Pilot studies have revealed that the factor structure of the WMI is composed of two bipolar dimensions: (1) a social dimension, encompassing self-centered vis-à-vis other-directed concerns, and (2) a work incentives dimension, defined by hygiene-maintenance vis-à-vis motivator considerations.

Creature comfort and safety needs, for example, underlie a preoccupation with hygiene or maintenance incentives, whereas ego status and actualization needs are linked to motivator incentives. Similarly, belonging and actualization tend to compete with ego and security considerations in social encounters. Thus, the WMI yields a two-dimensional profile according to which managers may be assessed.

The data were divided by MAQ scores into three groups: 556 low achievers, 622 average achievers, and 87 high achievers.

Results. The data were submitted to a multiple discriminant analysis; in this instance, the five WMI scores were the independent variables. An overall significant discrimination was obtained ($F = 4.546, df = 10$ and $2,516, p < .0001$), with two significant roots accounting for all of the between-group variance. The univariate F ratios revealed that the nature of the discrimination between groups was particularly influenced by differences in scores on the basic, safety, and actualization scales.

Root I, accounting for 73 percent of the between-achievement variance, yielded a χ^2 of 32.98 ($df = 6, p < .0001$) and, in light of the WMI-by-discriminant-root correlations, is best interpreted as a bipolar work incentives dimension negatively defined by hygiene-maintenance needs and positively defined by actualization concerns. The second dimension, Root II, accounting for the remaining between-group variance, yielded a χ^2 of 12.18 ($df = 4, p < .02$) and also emerged as bipolar—negatively defined by egocentric, self-centered values and positively defined by altruistic, other-directed considerations; it is taken as a social incentives dimension.

An inspection of the group mean scores showed that the need for self-actualization is the dominant motivational influence for high achievers, whereas average achievers are most driven by ego-status needs; both groups emerge as motivator seekers (Meyers, 1964). Low achievers are preoccupied with creature comfort and ego-status needs, signifying a motivational crisis in which neither hygiene nor motivator needs are being well met; conditions for a counterproductive response competition exist, and lower-order needs very likely inhibit the effective expression of higher-order considerations. These findings, of course, conflict with those of Haire, Ghiselli, and Porter (1963) to the effect that self-realization and autonomy are universally more important to managers than are lower-level needs. When achievement status is controlled for, such commonalities disappear.

We will return momentarily, for a more telling look at its implications, to the issue of differential work motivation among managers; for the present, it may be said that one's achievement level is significantly linked to his motivational profile.

Managerial Achievement and the Management of Motives

The fact that managers differing in achievement have markedly different motivational profiles, pursue different incentives, and adhere to different working assumptions regarding the makeup of those they manage suggests that high-, average-, and low-achieving managers may also be characterized by different approaches to employee motivation. To test this possibility, a study of managers' personal theories of employee motivation and consequent biases in administering the motivational process was conducted.

Subjects and Instrumentation. Hall's (1968) Management of Motives Index (MMI) was administered to 664 managers. The three MAQ groups identified consisted of 190 low achievers, 442 average achievers, and 32 high achievers. As a companion piece for the WMI and based on the same motivation-hygiene need-hierarchy synthesis, the MMI also yields five scores, tapping the manager's personal theory of what motivates others. Each score is an index of how much the manager emphasizes that particular need in administering the motivational process. The median coefficient of stability for the MMI has been established as .71 over a six-week time span.

Results. The multivariate analysis of group data yielded an overall significant discrimination, as indicated by an F ratio of 3.335 (df = 10 and 1,314, $p < .0005$) with the independent variables being the five MMI scales. The univariate F ratios revealed that the three achievement groups differ significantly ($p < .001$) in their management of all needs except belongingness.

One significant root, accounting for 77 percent of the variance ($x^2 = 25.51, df = 6, p < .0006$), emerged as a negatively defined bipolar dimension on which highest-scoring managers were those attending primarily to hygiene-maintenance needs among employees while low scorers attached greater emphasis to social, ego-status, and actualization concerns. The dimension appeared to reflect a fairly straightforward hygiene-motivator assumption. Resulting centroid scores were ordered consistently with MAQ group membership: high MAQ = 112.57, average MAQ = 113.57, and low MAQ = 116.31.

High achievers place major emphasis on motivator incentives: actualization, belonging, and ego status; they pay average attention, according to MMI norms, to hygiene factors. Average achievers stress ego status while adequately attending to subordinates' actualization needs, also promoting essentially motivator seeking. Low achievers practically ignore motivators, stressing hygiene incentives, especially safety and security issues.

A comparison of the manner in which high, average, and low achievers mediate reality for their subordinates with the three groups' own motivational profiles found in the preceding section reveals that managers apparently manage the motivational process for others as a function of their own needs.

Managerial Achievement and Subordinate Motivation

Given the finding that managerial achievement is linked significantly with the type of motivational climate promoted for subordinates as well as with the nature of personal striving, a question arises of whether or not a manager's achievement status is associated as well with the need profiles of his subordinates. To explore this possibility, a study of subordinate motivation was conducted in light of the managerial achievement status of their managers.

Subjects and Instrumentation. The WMI (Hall and Williams, 1967b) was administered to more than 3,500 subordinates of 1,291 managers. The mean subordinate score for each manager was computed, used as a measure for that manager, and assigned to him. The data were then separated according to the managers' MAQs, yielding the following groups: 365 mean subordinate scores for low achievers, 772 for average achievers, and 154 for high achievers.

Results. A multiple discriminant analysis yielded an overall significant function (F = 3.661, df = 10 and 2,568, $p < .0003$), indicating qualitative differences between MAQ groups with respect to subordinate need systems and consequent work motivation. The nature of the differences was further revealed by the extraction of two significant roots.

Root I accounted for 60.65 percent of the variance (χ^2 = 22.07, df = 6, $p < .0002$) and emerged as a bipolar dimension reflecting subordinate preoccupation with altruistic, other-directed needs vis-à-vis egocentric, self-centered concerns: a social incentives index. Root II, accounting for 39.35 percent of the variance, was significant at the .007 level (χ^2 = 14.364, df = 4) and emerged as a bipolar index of subordinate preoccupation with hygiene-maintenance considerations vis-à-vis advancement and growth concerns: a work incentives index. An inspection of group means indicated significant ($p < .01$) univariate differences between the need profiles of high achievers' subordinates and those of both average and low achievers on four of the five need systems of interest.

Discussion and Synthesis

The two roots emerging from the analysis of subordinate data closely parallel those characterizing the managers' profiles in the first section of our study of motivational phenomena. Although reversed in terms of percentage of variance accounted for, this congruence of work and social incentives dimensions makes it possible, when both are low-score deviated, to superimpose the centroid scores for the three subordinate MAQ groups over the managers' centroid scores for a graphic evaluation of their relationship, as in Figure 2.

The dimensions emerging from the analyses are best interpreted as indicating the degree to which managers and their subordinates are (1) maintenance seeking or motivator seeking and (2) either self-centered or other-directed. Two generalizations are suggested by the centroid plots in Figure 2: First, individuals of different levels of managerial achievement are characterized by significantly different motivational dynamics; and, second, the subordinates of each achievement grouping appear to adopt as their own their manager's motivational profile. As portrayed in Figure 2, low achievers are self-centered maintenance seekers, and their subordinates display the same, presumably conditioned, characteristics. High achievers, on the other hand, are other-directed motivator seekers

Figure 2. Comparison of Manager and Subordinate Motivational Profiles for
Groups Identified According to Level of Managerial Achievement

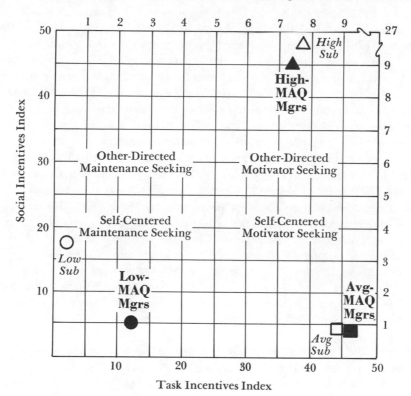

Note: Centroid scale values of managers' data plots designated by boldface type;
those of subordinates' designated by italics.

and so are their subordinates. Average achievers, while also motivator seekers, pursue
their goals in a self-centered fashion as do their subordinates.

In summary, it would appear that not only does his personal motivation affect the
manager's achievement level, so, as well, does his management of the motivational
process. Moreover, his achievement is directly linked to the motivational profile of his
subordinates in the same, apparently causal, fashion, and thus are motivational prophesies
fulfilled.

Study III: Managerial Achievement and Participative Management

The findings of Study II have further implications. The motivational assumptions
of low achievers are consistent with the reductive Theory X view of working man which
we found to characterize such managers in Study I, whereas those of high achievers are
consistent with a developmental Theory Y. Average achievers, falling in between both
motivationally and philosophically, continue to exemplify Meyers' previously explained
traditional view. Considering the control issues which McGregor (1960) has identified as
implicit in the kinds of combined motivational Theory X-Theory Y postures revealed, it
follows that the view a manager holds of his subordinates and their motivational makeup
probably influences his choice of managerial options, particularly as regards subordinate
participation in the making of work-related decisions.

Employment of participative practices has long been considered a point of departure among managers of differing persuasions as well as among management theorists. And whereas the efficacy of the participative approach vis-à-vis organizational effectiveness has been demonstrated (Coch and French, 1948; Marrow, 1972; Marrow, Bowers, and Seashore, 1967), no apparent attempt has been made to link reliance on such an approach to managerial achievement or career accomplishment. Theory lends itself to an implicit hypothesis that achievement and reliance on participative management might well covary significantly; to test this notion, a study was made of subordinate perceptions of and reactions to managers' participative or nonparticipative practices.

Subjects and Instrumentation. The assumption was made in this study that it is the subordinate who is best equipped to report on his manager's use of participative practices and his own resulting feelings. Therefore, the Personal Reaction Index (Hall, 1971) was administered to over 2,000 subordinates of 731 managers in eighteen types of organizations. The PRI assesses the degree to which the manager allows a subordinate to participate in making and encourages him to influence work-related decisions. It also gauges the feelings flowing from such opportunities: affectual factors such as job satisfaction, sense of personal responsibility, commitment, pride in work, and frustration level, which, when combined, reflect the kind of work climate the manager creates. The Spearman-Brown item-test estimate of reliability for this participation-involvement index has been found to be .68. In the present study, the mean subordinate score for each manager was used as a measure for that manager, and the data were separated into three MAQ groups: 214 mean subordinate scores for low achievers, 417 for average achievers, and 100 for high achievers.

Results and Discussion. Once again, a multiple discriminant analysis yielded an overall significant discrimination ($F = 2.222$, $df = 12$ and $1,446$, $p < .01$). Univariate tests revealed that a major portion of the discrimination occurred on the participation, related satisfaction, commitment, and perceived quality of decision scales. As reflected in a single significant root accounting for 84.13 percent of the variance, this discriminant function, with $\chi^2 = 22.29$ and $df = 7$, was significant at the .003 level of confidence.

In Figure 3 are plotted the centroid scores of the three MAQ groups, and, as reference will reveal, subordinates perceive dramatic differences among managers of varying achievement in their use of participative methods. Low achievers, according to their subordinates, offer very few opportunities to participate, and average achievers offer only slightly more. However, high achievers are reported to employ participative practices to such a greater extent that participative management may be said to be a major characteristic of the high-achieving group.

The pattern of root correlations and discriminant weights indicates that the significant dimension comprises both participative opportunity and feeling data; it is best interpreted as an index of total ego involvement. In this light, only the subordinates of high achievers may be found to enjoy the satisfaction and commitment that characterize a healthy organizational climate. Low achievers, and to some extent average achievers, are reported by their subordinates to employ practices which repress and frustrate subordinate personnel. And so the manager's use of participative practices also emerges as a significant factor in managerial achievement, with noteworthy implications for organizational well-being as well.

Study IV: Managerial Achievement via Interpersonal Competence

The findings in Study III do not stand alone any more than did those of the first two. According to Marrow, the effectiveness of participative management may be ex-

Figure 3. Relative Employment of Participative Practices by Managers of High, Average, and Low Achievement as Reported by Their Subordinates

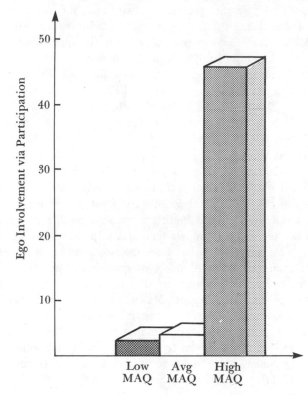

pected to vary with the amount of mutual confidence found in the manager-subordinate relationship (Marrow, Bowers, and Seashore, 1967). A conducive climate must be prepared, the nature of which is determined by the skill with which face-to-face relationships are managed; that is, by the level of authenticity and interpersonal competence brought to the relationship by the manager (Argyris, 1962). Managerial achievement may therefore be expected to be affected by the manager's level of interpersonal competence, defined as the ability to (1) own up to and accept responsibility for one's own ideas and attitudes, (2) be open to one's own ideas and attitudes and those of others, (3) experiment with new ideas and attitudes, and (4) help and encourage others to accomplish all of the former (Argyris, 1962; Hall, 1973, 1974). To explore the career implications of interpersonal competence, a study was conducted with both managers and subordinates to determine the relationship of such competence to achievement.

Subjects and Instrumentation. The Hall and Williams (1967a) Personnel Relations Survey (PRS) was administered to 1,691 managers. As a measure of competence in interpersonal encounters, the three-part instrument is based on the Luft-Ingham (1969) Johari Window model and generates six scores reflecting the extent to which the manager discloses personal intellective and emotional data to and solicits comparable feedback from subordinates, colleagues, and superiors. The PRS coefficient of stability has a median value of .67, and construct validity is well established (Hall, 1973, 1974). The MAQ groups sampled included 418 low-achieving managers, 857 average achievers, and 416 high achievers.

A PRS companion piece with comparable reliability, the two-part Management

Relations Survey (Hall and Williams, 1970), was administered to 1,884 subordinates for comparative purposes. Based on the same model, the MRS requires that the subordinate appraise his manager's interpersonal practices in Part I and, in Part II, reveal his own consequent exposure and feedback solicitation in relating to his manager, thereby generating four scores. The MRS scores were grouped according to the appropriate manager's MAQ: 475 low achievers, 1,218 average, and 191 high achievers.

Results and Discussion. Managers' self-report and subordinate data were treated separately. The multivariate analysis of managers' PRS data yielded a significant overall discrimination ($F = 3.327$, $df = 12$ and $3,366$, $p < .002$). The univariate F ratios indicated significant ($p < .005$) differences between MAQ groups on all six subscales. Two significant roots were extracted. Root I, accounting for 70.58 percent of the variance, yielded a χ^2 of 28.04, which, with seven degrees of freedom, was significant at the .0004 level; Root II, with $\chi^2 = 11.74$ ($df = 5$, $p < .04$), accounted for the remainder of the discriminated variance. Root I was interpreted as an index of overall interpersonal competence, whereas the pattern of correlations and weights for Root II was such that no meaningful interpretation was apparent. Of prime importance was the finding that, for managers, the centroid scores resulting from self-reports on the interpersonal competence dimension were ordered in a like manner to the same managers' ranking in achievement. Achievement, it may be said, varies directly with one's interpersonal competence.

Groups composed of the subordinates of low, average, and high achievers provide concurrent validation in their MRS reports. Manager ratings and reports of personal practices with those managers were analyzed separately. For Part I data, ratings of managers' practices, there was a significant overall discrimination ($F = 8.273$, $df = 4$ and $1,880$, $p < .001$), and the emergent root was similar to that found with the managers' PRS: Root I, defined overall interpersonal competence, accounted for 88.73 percent of the variance and, with $\chi^2 = 29.12$ ($df = 3$), was significant at the .0001 level of confidence. Again, although significant ($\chi^2 = 3.73$, $df = 1$, $p < .05$), Root II was not interpretable. Analysis of the subordinates' ratings of their own practices, Part II of the MRS, yielded comparable results, albeit in a single significant root. The F ratio of the significant overall discriminant function was 8.98 ($df = 4$ and $1,880$, $p < .0001$), and this root, accounting for 98.21 percent of the variance ($\chi^2 = 43.99$, $df = 3$, $p < .0001$), also emerged as an index of overall interpersonal competence.

Plots of centroid scores in Figure 4 portray both the substantial differences in interpersonal competence levels between the three managerial groups and, moreover, how subordinate appraisals tend to confirm those provided by managers themselves. Apparently, achievement not only varies with competence but in ways readily recognized by others as well. In addition, although not included in the portrayal of results, centroid scores reflecting subordinates' practices in relating to their managers were found essentially to duplicate those of the subordinates' ratings of their managers.

Thus, interpersonal competence appears directly bound to managerial achievement; subordinates confirm the fact and report that their own interpersonal competence varies as a function of their managers'. Hall (1974) has reported the tendency of subordinates to reflect the interpersonal practices of their managers. Now, as with motivational dynamics, it appears that the competence of one's subordinates is a direct reflection of his level of managerial achievement as well. Summarily, as Argyris (1962) has suggested, the manager's interpersonal competence has a normative influence on the type and quality of relationships which will characterize the organization. And it affects as well the achievement status of the manager and those he supervises.

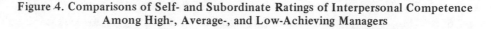

Figure 4. Comparisons of Self- and Subordinate Ratings of Interpersonal Competence
Among High-, Average-, and Low-Achieving Managers

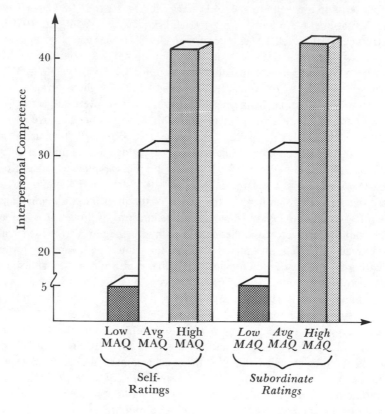

Study V: Managerial Achievement and Managerial Style

Argyris (1962) has stressed interpersonal competence primarily as it relates to organizational effectiveness; questions regarding the possible link between competence and the effective management of production-centered, as well as interpersonal, facets of the organization naturally arise. Studies by Hall (1973) have confirmed a relationship between level of interpersonal competence and preferred manner for managing the people-production interface within the organization, and Blake and Mouton (1964) have reported that managerial style may also be linked to managerial achievement. In the Blake and Mouton study, however, no information was given regarding statistical procedures or levels of confidence, and, since the study involved the ratings of co-members of seminar groups within a single organization, we have no assurance that the results are not merely cultural artifacts.

To achieve a more generic and realistic treatment, therefore, a multivariate study of managerial style as it relates to achievement was conducted with both managers and their subordinates in twenty-three types of organizations.

Subjects and Instrumentation. The Hall, Harvey, and Williams (1963) Styles of Management Inventory (SMI) was administered to 1,878 managers. The SMI is based on the Blake-Mouton managerial grid model; it generates five scores—one per style—and measures the manager's strength of emphasis on and responsiveness to task demands vis-à-vis social concerns. The median test-retest coefficient of the SMI has been found to range from .69 to .74 over a six-week period. The managerial SMI data were divided into three groups as follows: 445 low achievers, 1,243 average achievers, and 190 high achievers.

The Management Appraisal Survey (Hall, Harvey, and Williams, 1970), a companion instrument with reliability comparable to the SMIs wherein subordinates rate the style practices of their managers, was administered to 2,024 subordinates. MAS scores were assigned to the appropriate manager for grouping by MAQ, yielding 505 subordinates of low achievers, 1,197 of average achievers, and 322 of high achievers.

Results and Discussion. Manager and subordinate data were subjected to separate analyses. The multivariate analysis of managers' SMI data produced an overall significant discrimination ($F = 3.813$, $df = 10$ and 3,742, $p < .0002$), with two significant roots accounting for total between-group variance. Root I yielded a chi square of 28.564 ($df = 6$, $p < .0003$) and accounted for 75.22 percent of the variance, whereas Root II accounted for 24.78 percent of the variance, with $\chi^2 = 9.45$ ($df = 4$, $p < .05$).

Despite its attained significance, the nature of the discrimination among managers' SMI self-reports was more suggestive than definitive in terms of preferences and aversions. The results from univariate tests implied an antipathy on the part of the high achiever for a low-risk, bureaucratic, defensive management style of the type favored by low achievers while indicating an integrative preference and equal concern for task and social issues. There were also indications of the average achievers' aversion to any style devoted primarily to maintaining the human system, but no clear depiction of a most preferred style. Analysis of the subordinate appraisals (MAS) proved more definitive.

The multiple discriminant analysis of subordinate appraisals from the MAS yielded an overall significant discrimination ($F = 5.32$, $df = 10$ and 4,034, $p < .0001$). The univariate F ratios revealed that the three achievement groups were seen by their subordinates as differing significantly on all five measures of style preference ($p < .03$). The multivariate nature of these differences was reflected in two significant roots. Root I, accounting for 64.12 percent of the variance ($\chi^2 = 33.894$, $df = 6$, $p < .0001$), emerged as a bipolar dimension best interpreted as reflecting the manager's attendance to task demands. Root II ($\chi^2 = 19.003$, $df = 6$, $p < .002$) accounted for 35.88 percent of the variance and emerged as an index of concern for the quality of manager-subordinate relationships.

The existence of independent task and social dimensions makes it possible to plot the centroid scores of subordinate appraisals in a two-dimensional format. In Figure 5 we have defined four general regions or styles of management: low task-low relationship, high task-low relationship, low task-high relationship, and high task-high relationship. Our labels are qualitative, capturing the general focus of a given cluster of practices; whether or not such a style corresponds to a Blake 9,9 or a Likert System 2, for example, is far less important than the significant differences found in the manner in which high, average, and low achievers are perceived to approach management dynamics.

In essence, as the subordinate centroids graphically capture, subordinates and their managers tend to agree: a collaborative, participative high-task—high-relationship managerial style typifies high achievers, who integrate maximum concern for task and relationship demands; average achievers, too preoccupied with production goals to adequately attend to people problems, appear to favor high-task-low-relationship practices, which are directive and self-authorizing; the low achiever's mechanical, prescriptive approach to the management process—evinced as low task-low relationship—makes sense in light of his motivational profile and social competencies.

These results tend to replicate those obtained by Blake and Mouton (1964) inso-

Figure 5. Managerial Styles of High-, Average-, and Low-Achieving Managers
as Reported by Their Subordinates

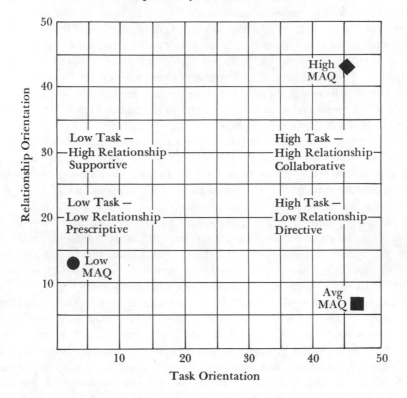

far as their overall implications are concerned; choice of management style does covary significantly with achievement status. The significance of specific styles, whether as dominant or back-up strategies, is less clear, since the two-dimensional structure which emerged does not correspond to the Blake grid. Indeed, it is the multivariate interplay of styles which is captured in the present study, and the implications of this are best appreciated against a backdrop of the managerial beliefs, motivational phenomena, interpersonal competencies, and so forth, portrayed in earlier sections. Style per se, it would appear, does not stand alone very well as a meaningful predictor of achievement any more than, say, participative practices. At issue is what the person does who is oriented to a high-task-high-relationship or some other posture, and this question is best answered in reference to the first four studies. Style treatments, therefore, serve primarily as summary statements of a complex of sentiments, predilections, and practices which covary in determining one's level of managerial achievement.

Discussion

Combined, the results of the five studies reported support the normative implications of the models employed at a personal level. The intent here has not been the usual one of testing the applicability of social-industrial constructs to total systems. Our aim was to explore the relationship of those behavioral science values and practices typically aimed at organizational dynamics to the very personal and individual issue of managerial achievement. Our results suggest rather strongly that the teachings of Argyris (1957,

1962), Blake and Mouton (1964), Herzberg (1966), Likert (1961, 1967), Marrow (1967, 1972), Maslow (1954, 1965), and McGregor (1960) do apply at the individual level and are worthy of credibility among managers concerned with their own career progress. Although few of the theorists upon whose work our studies are based have ventured opinions about the personal significance of their theories for career growth, it would appear that those who achieve are in fact doing in their management essentially what applied behavioral thought would prescribe. Conversely, those who fail to achieve are found in the present studies to violate most of the same tenets. The major import of this series of studies, therefore, would seem to be neither one of alternative discovery nor theory validation so much as a refinement of applicability.

For example, prevailing intervention theory—and any applied science must rely heavily for its success on its intervention strategy—holds that we must view and treat organizations as *systems,* enlarged versions of man with overlapping, reinforcing, and interrelated components in which a change in any one component may be expected to trigger off changes in others. A corollary is that dealing with isolated factors results in minimal payoff. By and large, the systems view has proved out. But it has produced a neglect of those individuals, often themselves seen as "isolated factors," who not only comprise the system but also decide whether interventions will be incorporated into systemic practice. Often, we suspect, individuals cannot help but ask "What's in this for me?" Our results suggest an answer in terms of personal achievement.

Finally, our review of managerial practices leading to achievement has not been exhaustive. There are certainly many other factors which may very well distinguish achievers from nonachievers. We have avoided the trait approach, such as that reported by Ghiselli (1963) in his Walter Van Dyke Bingham Lecture on managerial talent, in favor of a more behavioral treatment. But personal traits very likely influence the ease and efficacy with which the achieving practices identified might be employed. We cannot generalize our results to the increasing number of female executives because our sample was composed entirely of male managers; an informed guess is that the same practices will be found to distinguish female achievers from their nonachieving colleagues—both male and female—but we will not know this until additional data can be collected for study. Such studies are already under way. At best the present studies should be taken as indicating new directions for applied behavioral research. For example, given the amount of variance accounted for in each study and the discreteness of the samples, we cannot yet deal in predictions regarding managerial achievement. But we have narrowed the field of focus somewhat and, in the process, afforded a basis for including the individual manager concerned about his accomplishments within our theories of organizational excellence.

References

Argyris, C. *Personality and Organization.* New York: Harper & Row, 1957.

Argyris, C. *Interpersonal Competence and Organizational Effectiveness.* Homewood, Ill.: Dorsey Press, 1962.

Blake, R. R., and Mouton, J. S. *The Managerial Grid.* Houston: Gulf, 1964.

Coch, L., and French, J. R. P. "Overcoming Resistance to Change." *Human Relations,* 1948, *1* (4), 512-532.

Ghiselli, E. E. "Managerial Talent." *American Psychologist,* 1963, *18* (10), 631-642.

Haire, M., Ghiselli, E. E., and Porter, L. W. "Cultural Patterns in the Role of the Manager." *Industrial Relations,* 1963, *2,* 95-117.

Hall, J. *Management of Motives Index.* Conroe, Texas: Teleometrics, 1968.

Hall, J. *Personal Reaction Index.* Conroe, Texas: Teleometrics, 1971.

Hall, J. "Communication Revisited." *California Management Review,* 1973, *15* (3), 56-67.

Hall, J. "Interpersonal Style and the Communication Dilemma. I: Managerial Implications of the Johari Awareness Model." *Human Relations,* 1974, *27* (4), 381-399.

Hall, J., Harvey, J. B., and Williams, M. S. *Styles of Management Inventory.* Conroe, Texas: Teleometrics, 1963.

Hall, J., Harvey, J. B., and Williams, M. S. *Management Appraisal Survey.* Conroe, Texas: Teleometrics, 1970.

Hall, J., and Williams, M. S. *Personnel Relations Survey.* Conroe, Texas: Teleometrics, 1967a.

Hall, J., and Williams, M. S. *Work Motivation Inventory.* Conroe, Texas: Teleometrics, 1967b.

Hall, J., and Williams, M. S. *Management Relations Survey.* Conroe, Texas: Teleometrics, 1970.

Herzberg, F. *Work and the Nature of Man.* New York: Wiley, 1966.

Jacoby, J., and Terborg, J. R. *Development and Validation of Theory X and Y Scales for Assessing McGregor's Managerial Philosophies.* Conroe, Texas: Teleometrics, 1975a.

Jacoby, J., and Terborg, J. R. *Managerial Philosophies Scale.* Conroe, Texas: Teleometrics, 1975b.

Kerlinger, F. N., and Pedhazur, E. J. *Multiple Regression in Behavioral Research.* New York: Holt, Rinehart and Winston, 1973.

Levinson, H. "Problems That Worry Executives." In A. J. Marrow (Ed.), *The Failure of Success.* New York: AMACOM, 1972.

Likert, R. *New Patterns of Management.* New York: McGraw-Hill, 1961.

Likert, R. *The Human Organization.* New York: McGraw-Hill, 1967.

Luft, J. *Of Human Interaction.* Palo Alto, Calif.: National Press Books, 1969.

McGregor, D. *The Human Side of Enterprise.* New York: McGraw-Hill, 1960.

McGregor, D. *The Professional Manager.* New York: McGraw-Hill, 1967.

Marrow, A. J. (Ed.). *The Failure of Success.* New York: AMACOM, 1972.

Marrow, A. J., Bowers, D. G., and Seashore, S. E. *Management by Participation.* New York: Harper & Row, 1967.

Maslow, A. *Personality and Motivation.* New York: Harper & Row, 1954.

Maslow, A. *Eupsychian Management.* Homewood, Ill.: Dorsey Press, 1965.

Meyers, M. S. "Who Are Your Motivated Workers?" *Harvard Business Review,* 1964, *42,* 73-88.

Meyers, M. S. "Conditions for Manager Motivation." *Harvard Business Review,* 1966, *44,* 58-71.

Rush, H. M. F. *Behavioral Science Concepts and Management Application.* New York: Conference Board, 1969.

Veldman, D. J. *Fortran Programming for the Behavioral Sciences.* New York: Holt, Rinehart and Winston, 1967.

Weisbord, M. R. "What, Not Again! Manage People Better?" *Think,* 1970, *36* (1), 2-9.

27

On the Validity of the Vroom-Yetton Model

Victor H. Vroom
Arthur G. Jago

Several years ago, Vroom and Yetton (1973) introduced a new contingency model of leader behavior. The model purported to specify the nature of the decision process that should be employed by the leader, based on a diagnosis of situational demands. The model used the decision processes shown in Table 1, which vary in the extent to which

Table 1. Taxonomy of Decision Processes

AI	You solve the problem or make the decision yourself using the information available to you at the present time.
AII	You obtain any necessary information from subordinates, then decide on a solution to the problem yourself. You may or may not tell subordinates the purpose of your questions or give information about the problem or decision you are working on. The input provided by them is clearly in response to your request for specific information. They do not play a role in the definition of the problem or in generating or evaluating alternative solutions.
CI	You share the problem with the relevant subordinates individually, getting their ideas and suggestions without bringing them together as a group. Then *you* make the decision. This decision may or may not reflect your subordinates' influence.
CII	You share the problem with your subordinates in a group meeting. In this meeting you obtain their ideas and suggestions. Then *you* make the decision, which may or may not reflect your subordinates' influence.
GII	You share the problem with your subordinates as a group. Together you generate and evaluate alternatives and attempt to reach agreement (consensus) on a solution. Your role is much like that of chairman, coordinating the discussion, keeping it focused on the problem, and making sure that the critical issues are discussed. You can provide the group with information or ideas that you have, but you do not try to "press" them to adopt "your" solution and are willing to accept and implement any solution that has the support of the entire group.

subordinates are given an opportunity to participate in decision making. To determine the process (or processes) prescribed for a particular problem or decision, the leader must first diagnose the status of that problem or decision on seven problem attributes corresponding to situational variables believed to influence the effectiveness of the five processes.

Yes-no responses to questions pertaining to the seven problem attributes determine the problem type, which in turn specifies one or more decision processes as feasible to that problem or decision. This "feasible set" constitutes the processes that remain after a set of seven rules (Table 2) have been applied, each of which eliminates methods deemed inapplicable to particular types of problems.

The rules are of two different types. The first three rules are intended to protect the quality of the resulting decision by eliminating methods with a substantial probability of resulting in decisions that are technically unsound. The remaining four rules are intended to protect the acceptance of decision by subordinates, eliminating methods that have a substantial probability of proving ineffective due to the resistance of subordinates or the lack of needed support from them during implementation.

These rules eliminate all but one process for certain types of problems or decisions, thereby prescribing a unique solution. For other problems, however, from two to five processes remain in the feasible set after application of the rules. Choice among such processes should be made by the leader, based on considerations not represented in the problem attributes, such as time pressure (dictating a choice of the most autocratic alternative within the feasible set) or concern with development of subordinates (dictating a choice of the most participative alternative within the feasible set). The former is termed Model A and has been described as a short-term or time-efficient model; the latter is termed Model B, which has been described as long term and developmental.

At the moment, the validity of the normative model rests largely on the validity of its underlying assumptions, particularly the rules that define the feasible set. Vroom and Yetton (1973) argue that these rules are consistent with available empirical evidence but correctly point out that this evidence is far from complete and that their particular rules are not the only ones that could have been formulated based on existing evidence.

What is needed is evidence that decisions made in accordance with the model are more effective than those that are not made in accordance with the model. Vroom and Yetton (1973, pp. 182-184) described an investigation directed toward this end. They asked a set of managers, each unacquainted with the model and without any prior familiarity with the underlying concepts, to describe in written form a problem that they had recently encountered in carrying out their managerial responsibilities. Each manager was also asked to (1) judge the problem on each of the problem attributes, (2) specify the process employed in solving the problem, and (3) evaluate on seven-point scales the effectiveness, technical quality, and subordinate acceptance of the resulting solution or decision.

It was hypothesized that decisions in which the managers' behavior violated one or more of the rules underlying the model would be judged less effective than decisions not violating these rules.

The difference was in the predicted direction but did not satisfy acceptable criteria for statistical significance. Vroom and Yetton attribute these results to limited variance in the dependent variables. In choosing a problem or decision to describe, most managers chose a "success experience." The modal response on the seven-point scales used to measure decision effectiveness was 6; only one decision was judged to have less than adequate acceptance (a response of 3 or below), and only three were judged to have less than adequate quality.

Table 2. Rules Underlying the Model

Rules to Protect the Quality of the Decision

1. The Leader Information Rule

    If the quality of the decision is important and the leader does not possess enough information or expertise to solve the problem by himself, then AI is eliminated from the feasible set.

2. The Goal Congruence Rule

    If the quality of the decision is important and subordinates are not likely to pursue the organization goals in their efforts to solve this problem, then GII is eliminated from the feasible set.

3. The Unstructured Problem Rule

    In decisions in which the quality of the decision is important, if the leader lacks the necessary information or expertise to solve the problem by himself, and if the problem is unstructured, the method of solving the problem should provide for interaction among subordinates likely to possess relevant information. Accordingly, AI, AII, and CI are eliminated from the feasible set.

Rules to Protect the Acceptance of the Decision

4. The Acceptance Rule

    If the acceptance of the decision by subordinates is critical to effective implementation and if it is not certain that an autocratic decision will be accepted, AI and AII are eliminated from the feasible set.

5. The Conflict Rule

    If the acceptance of the decision is critical, an autocratic decision is not certain to be accepted, and disagreement among subordinates in methods of attaining the organizational goal is likely, the methods used in solving the problem should enable those in disagreement to resolve their differences with full knowledge of the problem. Accordingly, under these conditions, AI, AII, and CI, which permit no interaction among subordinates and therefore provide no opportunity for those in conflict to resolve their differences, are eliminated from the feasible set. Their use runs the risk of leaving some of the subordinates with less than the needed commitment to the final decision.

6. The Fairness Rule

    If the quality of the decision is unimportant but acceptance of the decision is critical and not certain to result from an autocratic decision, it is important that the decision process used generate the needed acceptance. The decision process used should permit the subordinates to interact with one another and negotiate over the fair method of resolving any differences with full responsibility on them for determining what is fair and equitable. Accordingly, under these circumstances, AI, AII, CI, and CII are eliminated from the feasible set.

7. The Acceptance Priority Rule

    If acceptance is critical, not certain to result from an autocratic decision, and if subordinates are motivated to pursue the organizational goals represented in the problem, then methods that provide equal partnership in the decision-making process can provide greater acceptance without risking decision quality. Accordingly, AI, AII, CI, and CII are eliminated from the feasible set.

Note: See Table 1 for a description of AI, AII, CI, CII, and GII.

The purpose of the present investigation is to provide additional empirical evidence relevant to the validity of the Vroom-Yetton model. The design deficiencies in the earlier investigation are remedied in an effort to determine whether these deficiencies constitute the cause of lack of empirical support or whether the cause resides in weaknesses inherent in the model itself.

Method

The subjects of the investigation were ninety-six managers, all participants in management development programs. The majority of these managers were employed in a variety of private-sector organizations in such industries as manufacturing, travel, and banking. A small proportion were engaged in public service, including the military. Their positions ranged from first-level supervisor to president, with the largest number engaged in middle-level management positions.

Data collection was an integral part of the management training program. Data were collected from managers at two different points in time, separated by a time interval that ranged from one to four days. To overcome difficulties in the previous study stemming from the complexity of the judgments required of subjects, each data collection period was preceded by training aimed at increasing the competence of subjects in making the kinds of judgments required. The following ordering of training and data collection activities was followed for each manager.

Training: Phase 1. The purpose of this phase was to develop an understanding on the part of subjects of the taxonomy of decision processes shown in Table 1 and the distinction between attributes of decision quality and decision acceptance. Each manager attended a lecture describing the essential differences among the five processes, witnessed and discussed films exhibiting different processes being used in making the same decision, and responded to a set of thirty cases specifying the decision process they would employ if faced with each case. In addition, most managers read an article which explained the difference between decision quality and decision acceptance (Maier, 1963, chap. 1).

Data Collection: Phase 1. Each participant was then asked to select two decision-making situations that the manager had personally experienced in his or her own managerial role. Both situations were to represent decisions that fell within his or her own area of freedom or discretion in the organization and that had potential effects on at least two immediate subordinates. Within these broad limits, the following guidelines were provided as the basis for case selection: "One of these should be a success experience; that is, one in which the action chosen worked out well and was successful from an organizational standpoint. The other should be the opposite, that is, one in which the decision was unsuccessful from an organizational standpoint."

Once selected, these two cases were described in written form by each manager. For each case, the manager then (1) specified (from the list shown in Table 1) the actual decision process used in solving the problem or making the decision and (2) rated, on seven-point scales, the overall effectiveness of the outcome, the quality (for example, rationality or technical adequacy) of the decision, and the degree to which the affected subordinates accepted (that is, were committed to) the decision or solution achieved.

Training: Phase 2. The objective of this phase was to develop in subjects an understanding of the problem attributes (for example, existence of a quality requirement, degree to which problem is structured) used in the normative model and an ability to analyze cases using these problem attributes. Each manager attended a lecture on the problem attributes, with illustrative examples of cases representing the presence and the absence of each attribute. Subsequently, each manager coded from four to ten written cases and received feedback on the correctness of these codings.

Data Collection: Phase 2. Each manager was then given two copies of a flow chart identical in structure to one used to represent the normative model (Vroom, 1976) but different in that model prescriptions were replaced on the chart by numbers representing problem type. One of these flow charts was labeled *successful outcome,* and the other, *unsuccessful outcome.* The following instructions accompanied the flow charts:

> Now that you have been exposed to the model and have applied it to some typical situations within the problem set, you can now begin to apply it to problems from your own experience. First, reread the first of the two problem situa-

tions you wrote earlier (the decision with the successful outcome). On the flow chart provided, apply the decision model to this problem by asking yourself each relevant question in the decision flow chart. Please circle the answer you chose for each question as well as the number indicating the "problem type" once you reach the end of the chart. Then repeat the process for the second (that is, unsuccessful) situation. Be sure to consider your problem descriptions only when you apply the decision model. Your answers to the various questions should not be influenced by the decision style you chose or by its success or failure in the situation.

Results

From the ninety-six managers, 181 written cases were collected. They covered an extremely wide range of managerial decisions, including international investment, hiring and firing of key subordinates, and weapons procurement (from a navy admiral). Of the 181 cases, 94 dealt with decisions that the managers identified as having successful outcomes, and 87 were identified as having unsuccessful outcomes. (The unequal number resulted from eleven respondents who provided only one case rather than the two that were requested.)

In addition to labeling the problem as successful or unsuccessful, each respondent was asked to rate the outcome of each decision on three seven-point criteria: overall effectiveness ($M = 4.45$, $SD = 2.29$), quality of the chosen alternative ($M = 4.56$, $SD = 1.97$), and acceptance of the decision by subordinates ($M = 4.62$, $SD = 2.09$). Regressing ratings of overall effectiveness on decision quality and decision acceptance produces partial regression coefficients (β) of .44 and .47, respectively (multiple $R = .80$). Although the method of selecting successful and unsuccessful decisions ensured some degree of correlation between ratings of quality and acceptance ($r = .51$, $p < .01$), neither dimension appears substantially more important than the other in determining managers' perceptions of the ultimate effectiveness of a decision.

Feasible Set Behavior and Decision Outcomes. For each case, the manager's report of the method of dealing with the problem (obtained in data collection, Phase I) was compared with the processes prescribed by the model (obtained from the coding of problem attributes in data collection, Phase 2). In 117 of the cases (65 percent), the manager's behavior fell within the feasible set of methods prescribed by the model. This result is surprisingly close to the values of 68 percent and 69 percent reported by Vroom and Yetton (1973) for behavior in recalled and standardized problems, respectively.

Of course, the central question is whether agreement with the feasible set is associated with decision success. Table 3 addresses this question. By examining the row marginals (which can be treated as a 2 × 2 contingency table), it is evident that of the 117 decisions in which the manager's behavior agreed with the feasible set, 80 (or 68 percent) were successful. On the other hand, in the 64 cases in which the manager's behavior disagreed with the feasible set, only 14 (or 22 percent) were successful. The relationship between these two dichotomous variables reaches statistical significance, $\chi^2(1) = 34.00$, $p < .01$, and is strong ($\phi = .43$).

Although these data support the proposition that behavior conforming to the Vroom-Yetton model is likely to be successful, it could also be argued that Table 3 supports a more parsimonious model. If one ignores agreement with the feasible set and merely considers differences in the frequency of successful and unsuccessful decisions among the five columns in Table 3, it becomes apparent that the decision process em-

Table 3. Relationship Between Feasible Set Agreement and Decision Outcome
for Each Decision-Making Process

Feasible Set Status and Decision Outcome	Decision Process					
	AI	AII	CI	CII	GII	Total
Choice in agreement with feasible set						
Successful	9	7	13	27	24	80
Unsuccessful	6	0	14	9	8	37
Choice outside feasible set						
Successful	1	1	7	4	1	14
Unsuccessful	26	6	10	2	6	50
χ^2		13.89^a	7.29^a	.02	.01	6.75^a	34.00^a
ϕ		.58	.72	.02	.01	.42	.43

Note: Each column chi square is computed for the 2 × 2 (Status × Outcome) contingency table and is corrected for continuity (*df* = 1). See Table 1 for a description of AI, AII, CI, CII, and GII.

[a]$p < .01$.

ployed can also predict decision success. CII and GII appear to be comparatively effective processes overall (74 percent and 64 percent success rates, respectively), whereas A1 and C1 appear to be comparatively ineffective overall (24 percent and 45 percent success rates, respectively). These results lend some support for the view of many behavioral scientists, including Likert (1961), Blake and Mouton (1964), and Maier (1963), who emphasize the utility of participative management per se without paying explicit attention to situational moderator variables such as those in the Vroom-Yetton model.

Because participative processes are substantially more likely to be within the feasible set than autocratic ones, the relationship between agreement with the feasible set and success could simply reflect the correlation of both variables with participation. Such potential spuriousness is controlled, however, in analyses performed *within* each of the five decision processes. Separate chi-square tests for the relationship between agreement with the feasible set and decision success were computed for each of the five columns in Table 3. Three of these tests reveal statistically significant relationships, each of which is in a direction that further supports the validity of the specific Vroom-Yetton prescriptions. Although the noncontingent models of other theorists can account for the frequent superiority of participative approaches, the data clearly suggest that the Vroom-Yetton model has the additional capability of predicting those instances in which certain autocratic processes will be successful and in which certain participative processes will fail.

The same issues can be explored with more analytical power by substituting the seven-point ratings of decision outcomes (overall effectiveness, decision quality, and subordinate acceptance) for the dichotomous dependent variable of success and failure. Two-way analyses of variance employing these criteria were performed using the hierarchical (step-down) regression procedure of Overall and Spiegel (1969). Decision process (a nominal independent variable having five levels) was given priority in the partition of variance because of the parsimony of its expected relationships with the criteria. Agreement with the feasible set (yes versus no) was then introduced as a potential predictor of residual variance not explained by process alone.

Table 4 contains the cell means produced by the 5 × 2 classification. The analyses offer some basis for the noncontingent theories of participation in that the chosen

Table 4. Dependence of Decision Outcomes on Process Choice and
Agreement with Feasible Set (AgFS)

| Group | N | Decision Outcomes[a] | | |
		Overall Effectiveness	Decision Quality	Decision Acceptance
AI process				
AgFS–yes	15	5.13	4.87	4.80
AgFS–no	27	2.22	3.33	2.11
AII process				
AgFS–yes	7	6.43	5.57	5.86
AgFS–no	7	3.43	3.57	2.57
CI process				
AgFS–yes	27	4.56	4.30	5.19
AgFS–no	17	3.94	4.65	3.82
CII process				
AgFS–yes	34	5.44	5.35	5.44
AgFS–no	6	5.00	5.50	5.50
GII process				
AgFS–yes	32	5.22	5.03	5.75
AgFS–no	7	2.57	2.57	4.57

Note: See Table 1 for a description of AI, AII, CI, CII, and GII.

[a]Decision outcomes are measured on seven-point scales. Higher values represent greater effectiveness, quality, or acceptance.

process (df = 4) does account for a significant amount of variance in overall effectiveness (F = 6.31, p < .01), decision quality (F = 3.46, p < .01), and decision acceptance (F = 14.46, p < .01). These trends are largely linear and consistent with the view that the use of participative decision processes tends to enhance both the quality and acceptance of decisions and their ultimate effectiveness.

The amount of variance in decision criteria accounted for by process, however, is small in comparison with the total amount of variance accounted for by the use of both predictors. After the influence of process has been removed as an explanatory variable, a main effect for agreement with the feasible set (df = 1) accounts for substantial additional variance in overall effectiveness (F = 28.36, p < .01), decision quality (F = 8.54, p < .01), and decision acceptance (F = 34.70, p < .01). A process by agreement with feasible set interaction (df = 4) is also statistically significant for all three criteria (F = 2.83, p < .05; F = 3.26, p < .05; F = 3.25, p < .05, respectively). An examination of cell means suggests that this interaction may be attributable to a greater effect of agreement with the feasible set at extreme levels of participation (that is, AI, AII, and GII) than at the less extreme levels (that is, CI and CII).

When the hierarchical ordering of predictors is reversed and agreement with the feasible set is given priority and introduced first in the step-down procedure, the analyses of variance produce different F values for the main effects. Agreement with feasible set remains significant in the analyses of overall effectiveness, $F(1)$ = 44.62, p < .01; decision quality, $F(1)$ = 15.75, p < .01; and decision acceptance, $F(1)$ = 70.75, p < .01. However, for the first two of these criteria, the variance attributable to process is reduced to non-significance, $F(1)$ = 2.25, *ns;* F = 1.66, *ns.* In addition to its unique effect, agreement with the feasible set is, therefore, also able to account for the variance previously attributed to process. For the acceptance criterion, however, a similar conclusion cannot be reached. Decision process remains a significant predictor of subordinate acceptance even after the variance explainable by agreement with feasible set is removed, $F(4) = 5.45, p < .01$.

Rule Violations and Decision Outcomes. So far, we have treated agreement with the feasible set as a dichotomous variable. It is true that a manager's method of dealing with a particular problem either falls within or outside the feasible set. For those that fall outside that set, however, finer discriminations can be made, since such processes can violate up to five of the rules shown in Table 2. A further indication of the model's validity could be obtained by investigating a possible relationship between the number of rules violated by a manager's method of dealing with a particular case and criteria of decision effectiveness.

Of the 64 cases in which the manager's behavior fell outside the feasible set, there were 29 cases in which only one rule was violated, 29 cases in which two rules were violated, and 6 cases in which three or four rules were violated. Table 5 shows mean

**Table 5. Relationships Between Number of Rules Violated and Ratings
on Three Criteria**

	No. Rules Violated					
Criterion	*0*	*1*	*2*	*3 or 4*	*F*	*F Linear*
Overall effectiveness	5.19	3.90	2.69	1.33	17.99[a]	53.96[a]
Quality	4.97	4.45	3.28	3.50	6.99[a]	19.32[a]
Acceptance	5.41	4.41	2.38	1.33	33.51[a]	98.35[a]
N	115	29	29	6		

[a]$p < .01$.

ratings of the three decision criteria for each of these sets of cases. It is clear that the manager's ratings relevant to the success of the decision decline as the number of rule violations increases. This linear trend is apparent for all three decision criteria but is strongest for acceptance ($r = -.60$) and overall effectiveness ($r = -.49$) and weakest for quality ($r = -.31$).

In explaining the structure of the model, a distinction was made between rules designed to protect decision quality (Rules 1-3 in Table 2) and those designed to protect decision acceptance (Rules 4-7 in Table 2). An inspection of the nature of the rule violations in this population reveals sixty-nine instances of acceptance rule violation and thirty-seven instances of quality rule violation. The fact that acceptance rules are more likely to be violated than quality rules has been reported previously by Vroom and Yetton (1973, p. 147) and, in the present context, suggests that the weaker relationship between total rule violation and decision quality reported in Table 5 may reflect the fact that the violations that did occur were largely of acceptance rules.

Further analyses (see Table 6) separate violations of the two types of rules by examining the relationship between ratings of decision quality and violation of quality rules and the relationship between ratings of decision acceptance and violation of acceptance rules. To ensure that one set of rules does not spuriously cause a relationship in the other set, each trend is evaluated controlling for the violations of the other type of rule. The analyses suggest that both sets of rules work in the manner intended. In terms of strength of effect, however, ratings of decision acceptance appear more closely related to

Table 6. Relationship Between Ratings of Decision Quality and
Acceptance and Number of Relevant Rules Violated

| Criterion | No. Relevant Rules Violated | | | F | F Linear |
	0	1	2		
Decision quality					
M	4.75	3.89	2.64	5.39[a]	10.65[a]
N	148	25	6		
Decision acceptance					
M	5.21	3.97	1.88	42.22[a]	83.38[a]
N	134	21	24		

Note: Cell means are adjusted for any effect of nonrelevant rules. Rules 1-3 are relevant to decision quality. Rules 4-7 are relevant to decision acceptance.

[a] $p < .01$.

the number of acceptance violations (partial $r = -.57$) than ratings of decision quality are to quality violations (partial $r = -.24$). Apparently, the validity of the model rests somewhat more on its ability to account for the acceptance rather than the quality of decisions.

Instead of treating rules in accordance with their type (quality or acceptance), it is possible to analyze the contribution of each rule individually to the validity of the model. It is conceivable that some rules are contributing nothing to model validity or even acting to decrease that validity. Table 7 shows the mean differences in ratings of overall decision

Table 7. Judged Overall Effectiveness on Problems with
Violated Versus Nonviolated Rules

| Rule | Rule Applicable and | | t |
	Not Violated	Violated	
1	4.65 (77)	1.92 (12)	7.57[b]
2	3.86 (43)	2.57 (7)	1.54
3	5.20 (20)	3.22 (18)	2.79[b]
4	4.75 (51)	2.36 (28)	5.17[b]
5	4.50 (2)	2.00 (8)	.96
6	5.00 (7)	2.56 (9)	2.05[a]
7	5.56 (16)	3.75 (24)	2.70[b]

Note: t test (one-tailed) was computed using separate variance estimate. N in each cell is in parentheses.

[a] $p < .05$.
[b] $p < .01$.

effectiveness between decisions in which the rule was violated and those in which it was not violated. Only a subset of the 181 cases are used in each comparison. Those cases in which the rule is not "applicable" (that is, the configuration of problem attributes is such that the rule is not invoked) are excluded.

Significant differences in the predicted direction were obtained for five rules (1, 3, 4, 6, and 7), thereby supporting their individual validity. Of the remaining two rules, Rule 5 exhibits a large mean difference between cases of violation and nonviolation, but the very small number prevents statistical significance from being achieved. Rule 2 has a larger number but exhibits the smallest mean difference of the group of seven rules.

A more reliable assessment of the validity of Rule 5 awaits more data. For Rule 2, however, additional analyses are available to examine its effects further. Designed to protect decision quality, this rule eliminates the use of GII for problems possessing a quality requirement and in which the goals of subordinates are incongruent with those of the organization. It is unique in the model because it is the only rule in which violations may reasonably be expected to optimize one criterion (subordinate acceptance) but minimize another (decision quality). To explore whether managers' ratings of these two components of decision effectiveness reflected this fact, mean differences on these criteria were computed for the forty-three cases of rule nonviolation and the seven cases of rule violation. For nonviolations, the mean quality rating was 4.53, compared with 2.57 for violations ($t = 2.42$, $p < .05$). Thus, the rule appears to be performing its intended function to protect against low-quality decisions. However, the means of acceptance ratings were 3.88 for nonviolations and 4.57 for violations ($t = -.74$, ns). Though not statistically significant, the direction of this latter difference is consistent with expectation and suggests greater subordinate acceptance of GII decisions even when such a process violates Rule 2. Use of GII on problems with a strong quality requirement but low goal congruence appears to produce lower-quality decisions that perhaps gain more subordinate acceptance. The small (and nonsignificant) mean difference in overall effectiveness reported in Table 7 may reflect these opposing forces.

As is the case with Rule 5, more evidence may be required before the validity of Rule 2 can be fully accepted. These analyses, however, have strengthened the case for the construct validity of the ratings of quality and acceptance. The fact that the ratings made by managers of these two decision criteria revealed differences opposite in sign but equally consistent with theory reinforces the view that the subjects in the investigation were able to discriminate appropriately between these two criteria.

Discussion

Methodological Issues. This investigation was designed to avoid the methodological deficiencies of the previous attempt at validating the Vroom-Yetton model. We believe the methods used here to be a clear improvement over earlier efforts, but by no means are they perfect or free from potential error and bias. In this section, we intend to examine some of the principal sources of error and try to assess their implications for the internal validity of the research design. In the second part of the discussion, we will return to substantive considerations involving the implications of findings for the validity of the Vroom-Yetton model.

No measures of behavioral variables are free from measurement error. Despite the elaborate steps taken to train the subjects in this investigation to be sophisticated observers of the phenomena they were describing, it would be naive to assume that their ratings of decision outcomes, their coding of problem attributes, or even their reports of their own decision-making processes were free from the influence of either systematic or random errors. Random errors of measurement (that is, those which are uncorrelated across variables) would only attenuate the obtained relationships and do not constitute a threat to the internal validity of the findings reported. The consequences of systematic errors, correlated across variables within subjects, are potentially more serious. Because the measurement of all variables is based on self-reports provided by the same subjects, there exists the possibility that reported correlations among variables could in part reflect such correlated errors.

Fortunately, many of the most likely sources of systematic error could, like random error, only be expected to attenuate obtained relationships. For example, the response tendency to view one's own behavior as more participative than others view that behavior (Jago and Vroom, 1975) would equally affect reports for both successful and unsuccessful decisions and could not contribute to different relationships within these two categories. Demand characteristics also fail to account for the results. Because the normative model prescribes behavior on the basis of several complicated interactions among several problem attributes and five decision processes, subjects could not be expected to "guess" the hypotheses to be tested and supply supporting data. In fact, managers' familiarity with the ubiquitous participative prescriptions of human relations theorists would suggest that any subjects so motivated in this investigation would be more likely to add support to the alternative model of leadership against which the validity of the Vroom-Yetton model is compared.

There is, however, one quite complex line of argument dealing with systematic measurement errors that could conceivably account for all or a substantial portion of the explained variance in this investigation. This argument rests on the fact that the codings of problem attributes were obtained after the effectiveness of the decision had been determined and not at the time the decision was made. To borrow from the language of test validation, we have demonstrated concurrent validity for the model rather than predictive validity. Just as the test scores of a job applicant (for example, on a test of job skills) may change with experience on the job, so the codings by managers of problem attributes may change with knowledge of the success or failure of the decision.

It is possible that a successful decision could enhance the probability that a manager would code the problem as structured or as one in which he possessed the necessary information or one in which his subordinates shared the organizational goals. Similarly, it is possible that an unsuccessful decision would increase the likelihood that the manager would code the problem as one in which acceptance by subordinates was important and one in which he lacked the power to sell his own decision. Each of these effects would increase the size of the feasible set for successful decisions and decrease it for unsuccessful decisions. Because the odds that even a randomly selected decision process would fall within the feasible set are a function of the set's size, it is possible that the present findings could be explained by the operation of such postdecision mechanisms.

To address the efficacy of such an explanation, an analysis of the size of the feasible set of successful and unsuccessful decisions was performed. The results reveal only a modest difference in mean feasible set size (successful = 2.98; unsuccessful = 2.31), a difference not nearly large enough to account for the observed differences in agreement with the feasible set. Furthermore, such an argument cannot account for the differences in decision outcomes for situations in which specific rules while applicable were violated versus not violated. In the analyses reported in Table 7, problem type and hence size of feasible set were controlled. Finally, the difference in size of feasible sets for successful and unsuccessful decisions can be explained, perhaps more simply, by the assumption that problem types with larger feasible sets are "easier" and less subject to managerial error.

Those who conduct future research to assess the validity of the Vroom-Yetton model would do well to obtain independent estimates of the decision process used, problem characteristics, and decision outcomes. If managerial perceptions are to be used, it would be highly desirable to conduct a longitudinal study in which perceptions are measured prior to the resolution of the problem and before information concerning decision effectiveness is available. Use of this procedure, essentially that of predictive validation, would require a substantial time lag between before and after measurements but would completely remove any possibility of confounding.

Theoretical Issues. In all of the analyses, the relationships between a manager's behavior and the effectiveness of his decision were consistent with the model and with the rules on which it is based. Moreover, this contingency model was shown to be superior to a simpler, situation-independent model offered by other theorists, which asserts that participative methods should always result in more effective decisions than more autocratic methods.

The model, however, is certainly not perfect. Behaviors consistent with its prescriptions appear to increase the probability of successful decision outcomes but in no way guarantee that success. Similarly, behaviors that are inconsistent with its prescriptions appear to decrease the probability of success but in no way guarantee failure.

Apart from measurement errors, there are several possible explanations for the occurrence of these "off-diagonal elements." The most obvious ones pertain to the structure of the model itself. We have noted in the presentation of results, for example, the absence of conclusive evidence that Rules 2 and 5 individually contribute to overall effectiveness. Other deficiencies of the model may result from the treatment of both agreement with the feasible set and problem attributes as dichotomous (for example, good versus bad, high versus low) rather than continuous (for example, good to bad, high to low) variables. Although simplifying the design of research, the implied discontinuities seem theoretically unjustified (Vroom and Yetton, 1973, pp. 195-196). The greater ability of the model to account for differences in decision acceptance than in decision quality may also signal a further deficiency. Conceivably, other attributes, such as those discussed by Janis and Mann (1977), will need to be developed to better account for the differences in the technical adequacy or rationality of decisions resulting from the use of different decision processes.

Although the Vroom-Yetton model attempts to prescribe the social arrangements conducive to effective decision making, Janis and Mann's criteria specify the cognitive information-processing activities that should be performed. If decision quality is indeed closely related to such cognitive processes and if decision acceptance is closely related to the social arrangements, the fact that the Vroom-Yetton model is a better predictor of decision acceptance than it is a predictor of decision quality would not be unexpected. The fact that the Vroom-Yetton model accounts for any of the variance in decision quality may only suggest that the social processes specified by this model to some degree constrain the type of informative processing likely to occur during decision-making deliberations.

Finally, we might consider whether it will ever be possible to formulate a model of decision process that will be perfectly predictive of decision outcomes. Is it ever possible for a perfect process to result in an unsatisfactory outcome or for an imperfect process to result in a satisfactory outcome? On logical grounds, the answer would appear to be a resounding "yes." Insofar as organizations are "open systems" and decisions made within them are made under conditions of risk and uncertainty, the effectiveness of decisions will be influenced by exogenous variables, the effect of which could not be anticipated at the time the decision was made.

Despite its possible deficiencies, it is tempting to conclude that substantial improvements in the effectiveness of decisions could result from the model's use even in its present form. Estimates from a variety of sources (Vroom and Jago, 1974; Vroom and Yetton, 1973), including the present investigation, place the number of decisions made that are inconsistent with the feasible set of the model at around one third. Using the data collected in this investigation, we can estimate that agreement with the model in all cases would have increased the number of successful decisions from 52 percent to 68 percent in our sample and increased the overall effectiveness of decisions from 4.45 to 5.19 (on a seven-point scale). The latter effect is due more to the usefulness of the model in enhancing decision acceptance (where the expected increase would be from 4.62 to 5.41) as opposed to decision quality (from 4.56 to 4.97). It is of course as difficult to translate these estimates into economic terms as it is to know how to increase the model's use and the costs of so doing.

We can conclude that the evidence for the validity of the Vroom-Yetton model no longer rests solely on the plausibility of its assumptions and on scattered empirical evidence for its component rules. Although the use of the model is no guarantee of an effective decision and evidence obtained has already suggested avenues for its improvement, its use even in its present form can be expected to reduce many of the errors to be found in current managerial practice.

References

Blake, R., and Mouton, J. *The Managerial Grid.* Houston: Gulf, 1964.

Jago, A. G., and Vroom, V. H. "Perceptions of Leadership Style: Superior and Subordinate Descriptions of Decision Making Behavior." In L. Larson and I. G. Hunt (Eds.), *Leadership Frontiers.* Kent, Ohio: Kent State University Press, 1975.

Janis, I., and Mann, L. *Decision Making: A Psychological Analysis of Conflict, Choice and Commitment.* New York: Free Press, 1977.

Likert, R. *New Patterns of Management.* New York: McGraw-Hill, 1961.

Maier, N. R. F. *Problem-Solving Discussions and Conferences: Leadership Methods and Skills.* New York: McGraw-Hill, 1963.

Overall, J. E., and Spiegel, D. K. "Concerning Least Squares Analysis of Experimental Data." *Psychological Bulletin,* 1969, *72,* 311-322.

Vroom, V. H. "Can Leaders Learn to Lead?" *Organizational Dynamics,* 1976, pp. 17-28.

Vroom, V. H., and Jago, A. G. "Decision Making as a Social Process: Normative and Descriptive Models of Leader Behavior." *Decision Sciences,* 1974, *5,* 743-769.

Vroom, V. H., and Yetton, P. W. *Leadership and Decision-Making.* Pittsburgh: University of Pittsburgh Press, 1973.

28

Organizational Decision Making as a Political Process: The Case of a University Budget

Jeffrey Pfeffer
Gerald R. Salancik

Analysis of organizations from the perspective of decision making is well established in the study of organizations (March and Simon, 1958). Yet, "in spite of the obvious importance of decision making as an organizational process, there has been only a limited amount of empirical research on the subject" (Yukl and Wexley, 1971, p. 104). All social systems face the important task of allocating scarce resources. While economists and political scientists have treated resource allocation processes occurring between organizations, there has been no systematic study of resource allocations within organizations. As Pondy has noted, "although sociologists have devoted considerably more attention to studying the structure and behavior of formal organizations than other social scientists, they have tended not to focus on the resource allocation problem" (1970, p. 271).

This article examines organizational decision making by analyzing the allocation of budget resources to subunits within an organization. First, a paradigm and analytical strategy for examining organizational decision making is presented. Second, budget allocations at a university are examined quantitatively to illustrate the political nature of organizational decision making (March, 1962; Cyert and March, 1963). Third, unobtrusive measures based on an analysis of archival records are employed to indicate how organizational political systems can be diagnosed without utilizing more direct, but socially reactive, techniques involving questionnaires or direct interviewing. Unobtrusive measurement is applicable for those who want to diagnose organizational politics without running the risk of offending or arousing organizational participants.

Decision Premises and Models of Organizations

In studies of organizational decision making, different models of organizations represent different variables relevant to the decision process. The bureaucratic model of organizations specifies a well-defined authority structure and well-defined objectives for

Reprinted from *Administrative Science Quarterly*, 1974, *19* (1), 135-151, with permission of the authors and the publisher.

the organization, which tend to result in the use of a computational, optimizing, or more rational type of decision strategy. On the other hand, the coalition model of organizations (Cyert and March, 1963) views participants as having divergent values and objectives. A computational strategy is not likely to be employed. When there is disagreement over objectives or over the relationships between actions and desired results or outcomes, strategies of compromise or judgment are likely to be employed (Thompson and Tuden, 1959).

In criticizing the bureaucratic model as a description of reality, Cyert, Simon, and Trow (1956) have noted that the rational choice model is lacking in the following respects: (1) alternatives are not given but must be sought, (2) information as to what consequences stem from which alternatives must also be sought, (3) comparisons among alternatives are usually made along many dimensions, and (4) the identification of the problem itself is a problem. In a subsequent article, Cyert, Dill, and March (1958), examining four business decisions in three firms, concluded that expectations or forecasts were developed to justify the decision that was desired, rather than having the decision based on the forecasts.

Baldridge (1971) has described three organizational archetypes. One is the bureaucratic model of organizations, with its emphasis on universalistic criteria, formalization of rules and procedures, a hierarchy of authority, well-defined channels of communication, and concern with efficiency and goals attainment. The second model is that of a group of professionals organized on a collegial basis. This model stresses the interpersonal context and the making of decisions through processes of consultation rather than by recourse to formal authority. The third model, and the one that Baldridge used in his study of New York University, is the political model. In this, the organization is viewed as a coalition; there is conflict among participants, and the answer to what decisions will be made is to be found in examining who has power to apply in a particular decision context. Thus, power, rather than what is optimal for achieving some organizational objective, becomes an important decision variable.

Power, especially horizontal subunit power (Perrow, 1970), is emphasized in the political model of organizations as contrasted with the bureaucratic. In the bureaucratic model, universalistic criteria are used for decision making (Perrow, 1972); subunit interests are presumed to be subordinated to overall organizational objectives. Although the models are conceptually distinct, it may be difficult to distinguish them empirically. The universalistic criteria implied by the bureaucratic model may be determined as a result of power. Political power, in addition to being used to obtain organizational resources, may be used more subtly to obtain the use of universalistic criteria that happen to favor one subunit's position. Few subunits would rank equally regardless of what criterion is used, and thus one use of power is to ensure that a criterion favoring the particular subunit is employed.

Baldridge has argued that a political model is frequently a more accurate description of reality. There is some empirical support for this position. In a survey of 217 executives in 109 companies, Stagner found that the executives believed that "strong divisions within the company may get their way without regard to the welfare of the whole" (1969, p. 12). He also found no support for the hypothesis that a vigorous personality may win a decision against opposition with a stronger power base. In other words, power within the organization was a characteristic of a given role rather than a consequence of personal attributes. Perrow (1970), in a sample of twelve firms, examined perceptions of power in industrial firms and found that the marketing department was almost always perceived to be the most powerful. Hickson and colleagues (1971) developed a theory attempting to account for variations in subunit power in organizations based on the idea that power accrued to those subunits which could best deal with critical organizational uncertainty (Crozier, 1964; Thompson, 1967).

Building upon the ideas advanced by Baldridge and Cyert and March, it is argued here that organizations operate as coalitions in many decisions, with subunits contending for resources and with resource allocations being shaped by considerations of relative political strength as well as by more bureaucratic, universalistic criteria. Baldridge tested the political model of organizational functioning using three separate cases at New York University. The present study develops and uses a quantitative method for assessing which variables most affect organizational decisions—in this instance, budget allocations. Thus, the relative importance of various decision criteria can be more precisely measured, and the way is opened for comparative studies of the use of various decision criteria in different organizations.

A Paradigm for Analyzing Organizational Decisions

The critical issue raised by the present analysis is what criteria are used in making organizational decisions? If the relative importance of various criteria for allocating resources in a single organization can be assessed, it should be possible to develop comparative studies of organizational decision making and specify the conditions affecting premises for decision making and resource allocation within organizations.

The paradigm used for analyzing organizational decisions is borrowed from the extensive literature on individual decision making and judgment (Slovic and Lichtenstein, 1971). One important line of research in the empirical study of individual decision making has been the analysis of the relative weighting of factors used to arrive at some judgment. The paradigm proceeds typically as follows. A subject or group of subjects is given a set of stimulus objects which vary according to some specified attributes. For example, the object may be an application for graduate school and the attributes may be college grades, scores on admission tests, and recommendations (Dawes, 1971). The judge ranks or rates the objects or makes some decision concerning them. He may admit or not admit the student, for example. The researcher infers the criteria utilized in the decision by regressing the scores of the attributes on the decision made; this analysis may be performed either within or between subjects to estimate the variance of the decision associated with each attribute.

The procedure has been called a paramorphic representation of individual judgment or decision making (Hoffman, 1960) and has been used to study clinical diagnoses (Goldberg, 1970), admissions decisions (Dawes, 1971), ratings of common stocks (Slovic, Fleissner, and Bauman, 1972), and judgments of personality characteristics (Hammond, Hursch, and Todd, 1964; Knox and Hoffman, 1962). The important feature of this paradigm is that the determination of attribute weights is made by statistical analysis of actual decisions and not by obtaining protocols of the decision process or by asking the individuals involved in the task what they think are the decision criteria. Asking persons the criteria they use for decisions may provide misleading results because the persons will tell the researcher what they think he wants to hear or what is normatively valued. This statistical representation of the weighting of decision criteria is complemented by simulations of individual cognitive processes, such as Clarkson's (1962) simulation of the investment behavior of trust officers. Similarly, the present extension of this form of analysis to organizational decision making is complementary to simulations of organizational decision making (Gerwin, 1969; Crecine, 1967).

With the exception of the inability to obtain experimental control over the stimulus attributes, the paradigm used so extensively for analyzing the individual decision making can be directly extended to the analysis of organizational decisions. It is possible to observe decisions and also the values of those variables believed to be influencing the decisions. Using essentially similar analytical procedures, the relative influence of each independent variable on the decision can be assessed. One danger in the uncontrolled field situation is that an important variable influencing the decision may be omitted. To the extent that the variables that are examined account for a large amount of the variance in decisions, however, it is less likely that there are important variables that have been overlooked.

Resource Allocation Within Organizations

One important decision made within virtually all organizations is the allocation of scarce resources to organizational subunits. Because of the pervasiveness of large organizations in contemporary society (Boulding, 1963), resource allocation decisions within organizations are important in understanding how resources are distributed to various activities within the larger society. As Pondy (1970) has pointed out, in a society dense with large organizations, many of the important allocating activities occur within, rather than among, organizations. Moreover, because resource allocation is a task confronted by most organizations, it serves as a basis for comparatively examining the importance of various types of variables in the decision-making process.

It is argued here that, conceptually at least, there are two classes of decision variables which can be employed in determining resource allocations. First, there are variables that represent universalistic or bureaucratic criteria. Second, there are those variables which represent particularistic or political criteria that are used in decision making. It is further argued that organizational decision making, particularly with respect to decisions that allocate resources within the organization, are political in nature and that to understand resource allocation within organizations considerations of relative power of the subunits, as well as of bureaucratic criteria, are necessary.

For this study of organizational decision making, the dependent variable is the allocation of the budget. As a dependent variable, the budget has some attractive pragmatic and theoretical features. Pragmatically, budgets at public organizations are visible and developed annually. Since they are found in all organizations, they provide opportunities for extending and replicating research results. Budgets are theoretically important because they represent decisions that are both critical and contested within most organizations. Because resources are scarce, organizational subunits compete for a share of these resources, with the total amount fixed in the short run. Resource commitments have been suggested (Etzioni, 1964, p. 6) as one way of measuring an organization's objectives. Cyert and March (1963) have noted that the budget represents the result of the bargaining process which goes on within the coalition that constitutes the organization. Wildavsky has written:

> For our purposes, we shall conceive of budgets as attempts to allocate financial resources through political processes. If politics is regarded as conflict over whose preferences are to prevail in the determination of policy, then the budget records the outcomes of this struggle. If one asks who gets what the (public or private) organization has to give, then the answers for a moment in time are recorded in the budget. If organizations are viewed as political coalitions, budgets

are mechanisms through which subunits bargain over conflicting goals, make side payments, and try to motivate one another to accomplish their objectives [1968, p. 193].

It is the hypothesis of this study that organizational decision making, and particularly resource allocation decision making, is a political process and can be explained by consideration of relative subunit power, as well as by consideration of possible bureaucratic criteria.

It is important to distinguish this study from those examinations of the budgeting process itself. In a classic study, Davis, Dempster, and Wildavsky (1966) found that the best predictor of this year's budget is last year's budget. Studying departments within the federal government, the authors developed linear models predicting budgets on the basis of last year's budget, the amount requested in the present year, and the proportion of an agency's request Congress usually granted. The distribution of resource shares is relatively stable in organizations. This stability may derive from the fact that relative power within the organization is stable, as well as from the possibility that, as Cyert and March (1963) have noted, precedent is important for organizations, since it enables them to resolve and avoid conflict, as well as avoid the uncertainty entailed in beginning the bargaining process anew each year. The fact, however, that budget shares are relatively stable does not address the question of what determines these proportional shares in the first place. It is the determination of those variables that appear to be associated with relative shares of resources within the organization that is the object of this study.

Empirical Setting

While March (1962) has argued that business organizations can be viewed as coalitions and Baldridge (1971) has developed a political model for analyzing universities, it is likely that most formal organizations have both elements of the bureaucratic and the political model. The development of knowledge that can predict when decisions will be more or less political or bureaucratic is one important task that remains for the development of models of organizational choice. The specific focus of this study is decisions on budget allocations at a single university, the University of Illinois at Urbana-Champaign, during the years 1958 to 1970.

The University of Illinois is a large land-grant institution with many programs that have earned high national ranking (Roose and Andersen, 1970). In 1972 the university had approximately 34,000 students, of which about 8,000 were graduate students. Its setting is likely to be typical of large state universities. As at many high-prestige universities, a strong emphasis is placed on graduate programs, graduate students, and research. In interviews with twenty-nine department heads at the university, graduate students were considered the most important resource departments provide to the university; national prestige was the second. When the department heads were asked to rank criteria by which general funds should be allocated to departments, the number of graduate students was ranked first and the national prestige of the department third, out of six items.

Dependent Variable. The principal dependent variable is the proportional allocation of discretionary resources to the various departments in the university. There are two classes of funds recognized in the budget, general and restricted. Restricted funds are largely, though not exclusively, funds from outside grants and contracts. General funds are those which are appropriated by the state legislature and approved by the governor. General funds are relatively more discretionary in terms of how they can be allocated to the departments. By focusing on proportional shares of the general funds budget, the effects of general university growth and inflation are removed. One can visualize the budget as a pie, representing 100 percent of the general funds budget. The variable, then, is what proportion of this pie each department receives in each year. Budget data were collected for the thirteen-year period.

In 1958 the sociology and anthropology departments were still combined as one, and in 1970 the budget for the chemistry department became part of a new school of life sciences. In these three instances, budget estimates were derived from curve-fitting the remaining data for each department separately. As the estimated data constitute only three of 377 data points (29 departments × 13 years), it is not likely that errors in the estimates have much consequence for the results.

Unit of Analysis. The unit of analysis is the department. Perrow (1970), Hickson and associates (1971), and Milburn (1972) have lamented the dearth of studies of horizontal subunit power within organizations. This study attempts to provide some evidence on the use of subunit power in organizational decision making. In universities subunits at the departmental level of analysis have, it appears, the most organizational meaning. Crucial decisions concerning promotions and salaries are made at the departmental level, and faculty identification is along departmental, disciplinary lines. Though the department is the primary unit of analysis, tests for the effects of college power are also reported in this article.

Because of the time required to collect data from an archive, the number of departments in the analysis was limited to twenty-nine. The departments were chosen to represent major fields of study and to cover most of the colleges within the university. The list of departments used in the analysis is presented in Table 1.

Measures of Subunit Power. Several measures of departmental power were developed. Because of the occasionally tenuous position of the concept of power in social science literature (March, 1966), it was useful to obtain several measures to ensure the validity of the measurement of the variable. There has also been criticism of the practice of obtaining almost all organizational data from questionnaires. The use of obtrusive, direct questioning is especially likely to create difficulties when the issues being explored are sensitive, such as the question of who possesses influence within an organization. Measures of power derived from archival data were therefore developed.

The first measure of power was obtained from interviews with the twenty-nine department heads of the departments included in the study. Each department head was asked to rate each of the departments, including his own, according to how much power he thought each department had within the university. If further clarification was requested, he was told that power was the ability of the department to affect decisions so that they conformed more closely to what the department wanted. All were asked to indicate their judgments by placing a check in one of the seven columns headed by labels ranging from a great deal of power to very little. An eighth column was provided in case the department head wanted to indicate that he was unfamiliar with one of the departments being rated. The departments were listed in random order on the page. The measure of power obtained corresponds to the measure obtained by Perrow (1970) in his study of industrial firms and is an estimate of subunit power as assessed by the department heads themselves.

In addition to the budget, functions and responsibilities are allocated within organizations (Cyert and March, 1963). Outcroppings of this allocation of functions, such as membership on major university committees, were considered an excellent unobtrusive measure of departmental power. Because some of the committees had control over the

Table 1. Departments and Committees Utilized in Study of University
Budget Allocations

Departments	Committees
Economics	Building program
History	Nonrecurring appropriations
Psychology	University research board
Anthropology	Budget
Political Science	Student affairs
Sociology	Senate coordinating council
Geography	Educational Policy
Electrical Engineering	
Mechanical Engineering	Executive committees of
Physics	College of Liberal Arts and Sciences
Chemistry	Agriculture
Mathematics	Engineering
Civil Engineering	Physical Education
Aeronautical and Astronautical Engineering	Fine and Applied Arts
Geology	Commerce and Business Adminis-
Computer Science	tration
Classics	
English	
Spanish and Italian	
French	
Germanic Languages	
Dairy Science	
Home Economics	
Accounting	
Finance	
Architecture and Fine Arts	
Health Education	
Business Administration	
Animal Science	

allocation of resources within colleges and within the university, a powerful unit would want to have representation on the committees. Moreover, membership on the committees would provide the subunit with some additional power. Whether the committee membership creates the power or whether membership on the committee merely reflects an outcropping of the true relative power of departments does not matter for this analysis. As long as committee membership is associated with subunit power, this variable can be used to assess the effects of political power on resource allocation decisions. The criteria used for selecting the committees were (1) that it be a recurring committee and (2) that it be a committee which had responsibility for allocating real resources or for dealing with matters of educational or student policy. The committees examined are listed in Table 1. The measure of power used included the relative representation of each department on the total of the thirteen committees and the proportional representation of each department on each of the thirteen committees individually. Since department members can be on the executive committee in their college only, this variable was transformed to the proportional representation on the college executive committee, adjusted for the number of contending departments in the sample.

If it is valid, the unobtrusive measure of power provides a historical record of subunit power. Such an accurate record is not possible using only questionnaire or interview techniques, since the ability of persons to recall relative departmental power in the past is not likely to be accurate.

Measures of Universalistic Criteria. Power has been defined as the ability of an actor A to influence an actor B over some period of time with respect to some set of activities (Dahl, 1957). Implicit in this definition is the ability to know what would have occurred in the absence of the exercise of power. It seems an impossible task to completely exhaust the list of possible bureaucratic criteria for budget allocations that might be proposed. Ridgway (1956), however, has noted that variables which are measured in an organization by that fact alone obtain attention and quantities which are unmeasured are unlikely to be used in decisions. Thus, the set of possible bureaucratic criteria which might be used in organizational decision making can be assumed to be those criteria that are measured in the organization. The effect of measurement in shaping behavior in organizations has been documented by Blau (1955), Berliner (1956), and Argyris (1952).

The single universalistic, rational, or bureaucratic criterion that might guide resource allocation and the one measured here is the instructional work load of the department. It is measured in several ways, including evaluating the number of graduate students and instructional units—IUs—both in total and for various levels of study. Instructional units are the number of students taught multiplied by the number of credit hours per course. Instructional units represent an imperfect measure of student demand for the departmental subject matter and also represent a measure of the department's work load. Instructional units per faculty member is almost perfectly correlated with the student-faculty ratio and is a well-known and frequently used quantity in budget discussions, both within the university and the state legislature. For this study, instructional units are measured on a proportional basis.

Results

Validation of Measures of Subunit Power. Multiple measures of the concept of subunit power were collected, including interview ratings from the department heads of the power of all the departments and ratings of departmental representation on thirteen major committees. The latter were obtained from the university archives. From the interview data, two measures of departmental power were developed. First, the assessments of all the department heads who rated a given department were averaged. Second, assuming that powerful departments were more likely to be visible on the campus and therefore that departments which were unfamiliar to the raters were consequently less powerful, a second measure of power was computed, including don't know responses as the smallest scale value for power. The committee membership variables were averaged over the thirteen-year period to provide an overall assessment of power. The correlations among the various measures of power are presented in Table 2. The results in Table 2 indicate that the measures of subunit power have construct validity because they are correlated with each other. Not only are the measures of power correlated with each other, but they are not correlated as highly with other organizational measures. The correlations of the proportion of total instructional units is .46 with the proportion of membership on the research board, .16 with membership on all committees, and .30 with the interview-based measure of power. The correlations of the proportion of full-time-equivalent teaching faculty are .56 with membership on the research board, .31 with membership on all committees, and .32 with the interview-based measure of power.

Of some importance is the fact that the unobtrusive measures of power, obtained from examining representation on major committees, significantly replicate the ratings of power as reported by the various department heads. This finding reinforces the possibility of using unobtrusive measures to assess organizational political systems.

Table 2. Correlations Among Measures of Subunit Power

	Power1	Power2	Resbd	#Com	Budget	Execcom
Power1		.96ᵃ	.62ᵃ	.61ᵃ	.46ᵇ	.60ᵃ
Power2			.66ᵃ	.54ᵇ	.42ᶜ	.53ᵇ
Resbd				.53ᵇ	.57ᵃ	.50ᵇ
#Com					.52ᵇ	.80ᵃ
Budget						.16

Power1 represents interview data with don't know responses omitted.

Power2 represents interview data with don't know responses included as very little power.

Resbd represents representation on the university research board.

#Com represents representation on sum of all committees.

Budget represents representation on the budget committee.

Execcom represents representation on the respective college executive committees.

$^a p < .001.$

$^b p < .01.$

$^c p < .05.$

Correlations are Spearman rank order, and tests of significance are one-tailed.

Prediction of General Funds Allocations. It has been hypothesized that organizational decision making, and specifically resource allocation decisions, results from a political process within organizations in which subunit power, as well as bureaucratic criteria, influences decisions. In the case of the university budget being examined, general funds budget allocations are explained as a function of (1) the proportion of instructional units taught, the bureaucratic criteria, and (2) the subunit's power in the organization.

There are two ways to perform cross-sectional analyses on the data. First, all 377 data points (twenty-nine departments providing thirteen years of observations) can be used to estimate the relationship between general funds and instructional units and power. This analysis shows that the correlation between the proportion of instructional units taught and the proportion of general funds received is .50 ($p < .001$), while the correlation between the proportion of general funds received and the proportional representation on the research board is .42 ($p < .001$); with proportional representation on the total set of thirteen committees, it is .33 ($p < .001$). As there is essentially no relationship between instructional units and membership on all the committees ($r = .14$) and a somewhat stronger relationship between instructional units and representation on the research board ($r = .42$), when the three variables are combined in a multiple regression, all three contribute significantly to accounting for the variation in general funds allocations.

$$GENFD = .0112 + .393 \, IU + .090 \, RESBD + .199 \, \#COM \qquad (1)$$
$$(9.10) \quad (4.46) \qquad (4.18)$$
$$R = .59,$$

where *GENFD* represents the proportion of the general funds budget received, *IU* represents the proportion of instructional units taught, *RESBD* represents the proportional representation on the research board, and *#COM* represents the proportional representation on all thirteen committees. The numbers in parentheses are the *t* values of the respective regression coefficients. With a sample of 377, all three coefficients are statistically significant at less than the .001 level of probability.

The analysis as reported contains two elements, the correlations between the variables cross sectionally and the correlation between the variables over time within single departments. An examination of the correlation matrices showing the relationship among the variables within a single department over the thirteen years indicated that there were large differences between the various departments. These correlations themselves then are used as dependent variables to control for some competing hypotheses and to test in another way the effect of power on allocation decisions. To eliminate this variance due to differences in the relationships among the variables within departments, a pooled estimate of the variables was developed by taking the average for each department on each variable over the thirteen years. This reduces the number of data points to twenty-nine, the number of departments. Reestimating equation 1, the result is

$$GENFD = .010 + .326 \, IU + .196 \, RESBD + .192 \, \#COM \qquad (2)$$
$$(3.93) \quad\;\; (3.33) \qquad\;\; (1.74)$$
$$R = .87,$$

where the variables are defined as above and, again, the numbers in parentheses are the t values of the respective regression coefficients.

Both analyses indicate a separate and significant effect of subunit power on resource allocation outcomes. The higher proportion of explained variance in the second equation is due partially to the effects of aggregation (Hannan, 1971) and partially to removal of the within-department variance in the relationships between instructional units and resources. There are two reasons for using the aggregated analysis. The measure of power based on representation on committees is likely to be more valid, assuming power distributions are relatively stable, when averaged over time because there are relatively few positions on committees. In any given year, this leads essentially to defining two classes of department members: those who are on and those who are not on the committee. Over time, there are more positions—the number on the committee multiplied by the number of years—which permits the development of a more continuous, refined measure of subunit power. Also, in order to use the interview-based measure of power, collected only at one point in time, only one estimate of the other variables can be used at that time. Both the aggregated and not aggregated results are displayed, however.

In Table 3 the set of correlations between the various committee and power measures and the proportional allocation of general funds is shown. Here, membership on the university research board accounts for more variance than either instructional units or the interview-derived measure of power. It is also evident in that table that we can proceed to use only the research board and total number of all committee variables, as well as the interview-based measure of power, without considering the other committee memberships individually.

The university research board is not actually involved in allocating the budget. It closely represents the strength in the graduate college, however, and apparently, in a research and graduate education-oriented setting, also is an outcropping of relative departmental power. Both the bureaucratic criterion of instructional units and the measures of subunit power contribute to explaining variance in budget allocations. The formulation is able to explain a substantial amount of the variation in budget allocations.

Size as an Alternate Explanation. When confronted with a relatively large proportion of explained variance—equation 2 accounts for 76 percent of the variation in the allocation of general funds, averaged over the thirteen-year period—there is the possibility that the results are tautological. The variables all may be measuring the same thing, such

Table 3. Correlations Between Explanatory Variables of Instructional Units and Subunit Power Measures with Proportional Allocation of General Funds

Variable	Correlation	Level of Significance[a]
Membership on research board	.77	.001
Instructional units	.68	.001
Power, as measured by interviews	.58	.001
Number of persons on total committees	.53	.002
Proportion of persons on budget committee	.27	.10
Proportion of persons on college executive committee	.31	.10
Proportion of persons on student affairs committee	.01	not significant
Proportion of persons on educational policy committee	.30	.10
Proportion of persons on senate coordinating council	−.10	not significant
Proportion of persons on building program committee	.40	.05
Proportion of persons on nonrecurring appropriations committee	.25	.10

[a]One-tailed test.

as the size of the department. Alternatively, the perceived power of the departments or, more particularly, representation on major committees might be a function of the size of the department. Thus, the relationship is really between size and the budget. This alternative was tested as follows. Four measures of departmental size were obtained. They were the proportion of (1) the total number of instructional units taught, (2) the number of advanced graduate instructional units taught, (3) the full-time-equivalent (FTE) teaching faculty, and (4) the number of full-time-equivalent faculty supported by research or other restricted funds. Size is then measured by two variables of instructional work load and two variables of faculty size. Partial correlations were computed between the three power measures and the allocation of general funds, controlling for each of the four measures of subunit size. The results of this analysis are displayed in Table 4.

Table 4. Partial Correlations of Power with Resource Allocation, Controlling for Measures of Subunit Size

	Correlations of Power Measure with Allocation of General Funds, Controlling for			
Power Measure	Total Instructional Units	Advanced Graduate Instructional Units	FTE Teaching Faculty	FTE Faculty Supported by Restricted Funds
Research board membership	.69[a]	.53[b]	.64[a]	.54[b]
Membership on all committees	.57[a]	.54[b]	.48[b]	.35[c]
Power, from interviews	.55[b]	.28[d]	.57[a]	.17

[a]$p < .001$.

[b]$p < .01$.

[c]$p < .05$.

[d]$p < .10$.

Note: All tests of significance are one-tailed.

The results shown in Table 4 are robust across all four measures of subunit size. Out of the twelve correlations, only one is not significant at the .10 level of probability, and that correlation uses the interview-based measure of subunit power. Table 4 represents substantial evidence that the results obtained are not due to the fact that the variables are all measuring the same thing or that the variables are all surrogate measures of subunit size. There is theoretical justification for making the argument that one of the uses of power is to increase subunit size. Katz and Kahn (1966) spoke of a growth dynamic and noted that organizational subunits frequently seek expansion. Downs (1967) has dealt with the growth of subunits in even greater detail. He also argued that subunit growth is a desired objective and that subunits within bureaucracies will pursue expansion by a variety of means, which would certainly include the use of subunit power.

The Effect of National Rank. Another explanation for the results concerns the national reputation of the various departments. The argument could be made that some departments will obtain more than their proportional share of the budget justified by strict consideration of the work load, but this increased budget is justified by their national prominence and not by their position of political power within the organization. A variant of this argument might be that departments acquire power because of their national reputations. In a sense, national rank, though not measured for all university departments, may be considered as another universalistic criterion.

To explore this hypothesis, the 1964 and 1969 national rankings of the departments were obtained from Roose and Andersen (1970) and Cartter (1966). Since the probability of obtaining a high rank is affected by the number of contenders, the number of total departments ranked in 1964 and 1969 was also obtained. The American Council on Education does not rank every university discipline, and of the twenty-nine departments, only seventeen could be approximated in the ACE rankings. Partial correlations for these seventeen departments can be computed, controlling for the relative national rank of the department; however, since there are different numbers of departments being ranked in each field, the probability of being ranked first or in any other position is not equal across fields. To equalize the probability, the rank of the department is divided by the number of departments ranked in its field. This new measure of rank is referred to as the relative rank of the department. These correlations are displayed in Table 5. It is

Table 5. Partial Correlations of Measures of Power with Allocations of
General Funds, Controlling for National Rank

Variable Pair	*Correlation*	*Level of Significance*
Membership on research board with general funds	.76	.001
Interview-derived measure of departmental power with general funds	.72	.001
Membership on all committees with general funds	.58	.01

evident in that table that national rank does not account for the findings of an effect of subunit power on the resource allocation process. This is further illustrated when national rank is added in the multiple regression equation:

$$GENFD = .027 + .208 \, RESBD + .317 \, IU - .037 \, RANK69 \qquad (3)$$
$$(3.48) \qquad (2.51) \qquad (1.72)$$
$$R = .89,$$

where the lower the number of *RANK*69, the better the department's rank in 1969.

Variations in Correlations Within Departments Over Time. An additional set of variables can be defined which will test the effect of subunit power even more clearly, thus eliminating some additional alternate explanations for the results.

One explanation for the results presented here is that instructional cost per student varies widely in different departments and the results showing a relationship between the power measures and the proportion of budget obtained are spurious, due to the omission of this relative cost of instruction factor.

Second, while an association between proportion of general funds received and subunit power has been shown, an association which is robust against some competing explanations, it is still possible that the measures of power are caused by the relative proportion of general funds received rather than the reverse as it has been argued.

For each of the twenty-nine departments, the correlations over the thirteen-year period between the proportion of general funds received and the proportion of instructional units taught and the correlation between instructional units and full-time-equivalent teaching faculty can be computed. If resource allocations are changing in response to student demand or departmental work load, as measured by instructional units, these correlations should be high and positive, regardless of the differences between departments in the relative cost of instruction. Further, the correlation between instructional units and general funds is independent of the size of the department and presents a strict test of the concept of subunit power as a basis for allocation. The correlation between instructional units and general funds over time within departments is correlated at only $r = .02$ with total instructional units and at only $-.16$ with full-time-equivalent teaching faculty.

Power is the ability to influence outcomes, changing what might have been in the absence of the use of power. Since it might be assumed that, in the absence of other criteria, budgets and work load and faculty and work load would vary together, the extent to which they do not provides a measure of the use of departmental power.

The hypothesis, then, is that to the extent a subunit has power within the organization, the department has an advantage in obtaining resources regardless of its work load. It is hypothesized, therefore, that there will be a negative relationship between the power of the department and the correlation over the period between instructional units and general funds and between instructional units and teaching faculty.

The hypothesis is generally supported by the data. The department's average representation on all committees is correlated $r = -.38$ $(p < .05)$ with the correlation within the department between instructional units and general funds and $r = -.24$ $(p < .10)$ with the correlation between instructional units and full-time-equivalent teaching faculty. Membership on the research board is correlated $-.18$ $(p < .20)$ with the correlation between instructional units and general funds and $-.40$ $(p < .05)$ with the correlation between instructional units and full-time-equivalent teaching faculty. The interview-based measure of power performs worst in this analysis, being correlated only $-.11$ with the correlation between general funds and instructional units and $.03$ with the correlation between instructional units and teaching faculty. Out of the six correlations, five are in the expected direction, indicating that the more power the department has, the more its change in resources over time is independent of its change over time in work load or student demand. This analysis over time supports the argument that subunit power affects the allocation of resources within the organization.

This argument can be illustrated with an example. One powerful department had a correlation of $-.60$ over the thirteen-year period between the proportion of the budget received and the proportion of instructional units taught. This indicates that the department's resource allocations were not only independent of changes in work load but were actually negatively related to changes in teaching demands over the period. Conversely, a less powerful department had a correlation of +.92 between the proportion of the budget received and the proportion of instructional units taught over the period.

The Effect of the College. Only departments have been discussed thus far, yet departments are also a part of colleges. It is possible, therefore, that there is a college effect on resource allocations, so that, for example, a weak department in a strong college might fare better than a strong department in a weak college. To test whether or not there was an effect of the department's college on resource allocations, three dummy variables were defined. In the sample, there were fourteen departments in the College of Liberal Arts and Sciences, five departments in the College of Engineering, and four departments in the College of Commerce and Business Administration. The remaining departments were distributed among several other colleges. The three dummy variables defined were coded 0 or 1, depending upon whether or not the department was in the College of Liberal Arts and Sciences, Engineering, or Commerce, respectively. Using simple correlations, only two of the variables were promising enough to include in a multiple regression. The estimated equation was:

$$GENFD = .015 + .230\ RESBD + .328\ IU + .011\ ENGIN - .0086\ COMMERCE \quad (4)$$
$$(4.62) (4.00) (1.68) (1.22)$$
$$R = .88,$$

where, as before, the numbers in parentheses are the *t* values of the respective regression coefficients and *COMMERCE* is the dummy variable for whether or not the department was in the College of Commerce and *ENGIN* the variable for whether or not it was in the College of Engineering. Considering either the significance of the coefficients or the amount of variance explained compared with equation 2, which does not include the college variables, it is clear that there is not a significant college effect on the resource allocation process. This is surprising, since the college supposedly intervenes between the university and the department in the dispersal of funds. Moreover, the college dummy variables are not correlated with the measure of power, membership on the research board. What is likely is that, since so much attention and focus is placed on the departmental unit, this unit is the one that is salient in both discussions of power and in the allocation of resources within the organization.

Discussion

The use of subunit power in organizational decision making—and particularly resource allocations, which have been the focus of this study—is not unconstrained. Resource allocations to organizational subunits may be influenced, for instance, by other organizations in the particular organization's environment. State legislatures or other government agencies may constrain the allocation of resources within the organization. Banks, creditors, suppliers, or trade unions may be interested in organizational decisions and therefore exert influence and constraint on the focal organization. It is plausible to hypothesize that subunit power will influence organizational decisions only to the extent that such decisions are not otherwise constrained. In addition to external constraints on organizational actions, the use of subunit power is constrained by internal realities of organizational life. Organizational subunits are interdependent, at least to the extent that they share pooled interdependence (Thompson, 1967). One subunit, therefore, cannot contend with another for resources without this struggle having some consequences for itself. In the present instance, while each subunit might want more budget for itself, it is also likely to be true that each would not want to take over all the resources and become the only subunit in the organization. Internal interdependence among subunits and external constraints and contingencies, then, limit the utilization of subunit power in organizational decision making.

Focusing on universities, it is likely that there will be more external constraint on public rather than private universities and on those universities which are newer or less prestigious and therefore have less power relative to external agencies, such as boards of administrators or legislatures. Further, there is more likely to be a greater use of political power in decision making in those universities that have relatively more flexibility because they have discretionary resources to allocate. Since extra funds are often provided by grants or contracts, one might predict that the higher the proportion of outside funding and money, the more power would be used in resource allocation. In all organizations, competition for resources may constrain the organization's behavior (Thompson and McEwen, 1958). Therefore, it may be predicted that there will be more use of power in resource allocations and organizational decision making to the extent that the organization is in a less competitive, less threatening environment.

The fact that organizational decision making has elements of political power involved has implications for the understanding of organizational behavior. To the extent that decisions are based on considerations of subunit power, theories of organizational choice which focus on what is optimal from the point of view of the organization as a whole are likely to have limited predictive utility.

References

Argyris, C. *The Impact of Budgets on People.* Ithaca, N.Y.: School of Business and Public Administration, Cornell University, 1952.

Baldridge, J. V. *Power and Conflict in the University.* New York: Wiley, 1971.

Berliner, J. S. "A Problem in Soviet Business Management." *Administrative Science Quarterly,* 1956, *1,* 86-101.

Blau, P. M. *The Dynamics of Bureaucracy.* Chicago: University of Chicago Press, 1955.

Boulding, K. E. *The Organizational Revolution.* New York: Harper & Row, 1963.

Cartter, A. M. *An Assessment of Quality in Graduate Education.* Washington, D.C.: American Council on Education, 1966.

Clarkson, G. P. E. *Portfolio Selection: A Simulation of Trust Investment.* Englewood Cliffs, N.J.: Prentice-Hall, 1962.

Crecine, J. P. "A Computer Simulation Model of Municipal Budgeting." *Management Science,* 1967, *13,* 786-815.

Crozier, M. *The Bureaucratic Phenomenon.* Chicago: University of Chicago Press, 1964.

Cyert, R. M., Dill, W. R., and March, J. G. "The Role of Expectations in Business Decision-Making." *Administrative Science Quarterly,* 1958, *3,* 307-340.

Cyert, R. M., and March, J. G. *A Behavioral Theory of the Firm.* Englewood Cliffs, N.J.: Prentice-Hall, 1963.

Cyert, R. M., Simon, H. A., and Trow, D. B. "Observation of a Business Decision." *Journal of Business,* 1956, *29,* 237-248.

Dahl, R. A. "The Concept of Power." *Behavioral Science,* 1957, *2,* 201-215.

Davis, O. A., Dempster, A. H., and Wildavsky, A. "A Theory of the Budgetary Process." *American Political Science Review,* 1966, *60,* 529-547.

Dawes, R. M. "A Case Study of Graduate Admissions: Application of Three Principles of Human Decision Making." *American Psychologist,* 1971, *26,* 180-188.

Downs, A. *Inside Bureaucracy.* Boston: Little, Brown, 1967.

Etzioni, A. *Modern Organizations.* Englewood Cliffs, N.J.: Prentice-Hall, 1964.

Gerwin, D. "A Process Model of Budgeting in a Public School System." *Management Science,* 1969, *15,* 338-361.

Goldberg, L. R. "Man Versus Model of Man: A Rationale plus Some Evidence for a Method of Improving on Clinical Inferences." *Psychological Bulletin,* 1970, *73,* 422-432.

Hammond, K. R., Hursch, C. J., and Todd, F. J. "Analyzing the Components of Clinical Inference." *Psychological Review,* 1964, *71,* 438-456.

Hannan, M. T. "Problems of Aggregation." In H. M. Blalock, Jr. (Ed.), *Causal Models in the Social Sciences.* Chicago: Aldine, 1971.

Hickson, D. J., and others. "A Strategic Contingencies Theory of Intraorganizational Power." *Administrative Science Quarterly,* 1971, *16,* 216-229.

Hoffman, P. J. "The Paramorphic Representation of Clinical Judgment." *Psychological Bulletin,* 1960, *57,* 116-131.

Katz, D., and Kahn, R. L. *The Social Psychology of Organizations.* New York: Wiley, 1966.

Knox, R. E., and Hoffman, P. J. "Effects of Variation of Profile Format on Intelligence and Sociability Judgments." *Journal of Applied Psychology,* 1962, *46,* 14-20.

March, J. G. "The Business Firm as a Political Coalition." *Journal of Politics,* 1962, *24,* 662-678.

March, J. G. "The Power of Power." In D. Easton (Ed.), *Varieties of Political Theory.* Englewood Cliffs, N.J.: Prentice-Hall, 1966.

March, J. G., and Simon, H. A. *Organizations.* New York: Wiley, 1958.

Milburn, T. W. "Buried Treasures, a Review of Conflict Resolution, Contributions of the Behavioral Sciences." *Contemporary Psychology,* 1972, *17,* 596-598.

Perrow, C. "Departmental Power and Perspective in Industrial Firms." In M. N. Zald (Ed.), *Power in Organizations.* Nashville: Vanderbilt University Press, 1970.

Perrow, C. *Complex Organizations: A Critical Essay.* Glenview, Ill.: Scott, Foresman, 1972.

Pondy, L. R. "Toward a Theory of Internal Resource-Allocation." In M. N. Zald (Ed.), *Power in Organizations.* Nashville: Vanderbilt University Press, 1970.

Ridgway, V. F. "Dysfunctional Consequences of Performance Measurements." *Administrative Science Quarterly,* 1956, *1,* 240-247.

Roose, K. D., and Andersen, C. J. *A Rating of Graduate Programs.* Washington, D.C.: American Council on Education, 1970.

Slovic, P., Fleissner, D., and Bauman, W. S. "Analyzing the Use of Information in Investment Decision Making: A Methodological Proposal." *Journal of Business,* 1972, *45,* 283-301.

Slovic, P., and Lichtenstein, S. "Comparison of Bayesian and Regression Approaches to the Study of Information Processing in Judgment." *Organizational Behavior and Human Performance,* 1971, *6,* 649-744.

Stagner, R. "Corporate Decision Making: An Empirical Study." *Journal of Applied Psychology,* 1969, *53,* 1-13.

Thompson, J. D. *Organizations in Action.* New York: McGraw-Hill, 1967.

Thompson, J. D., and McEwen, W. J. "Organizational Goals and Environment." *American Sociological Review,* 1958, *23,* 23-31.

Thompson, J. D., and Tuden, A. "Strategies, Structures, and Processes of Organizational Decision." In J. D. Thompson and others (Eds.), *Comparative Studies in Administration.* Pittsburgh: University of Pittsburgh Press, 1959.

Wildavsky, A. "Budgeting as a Political Process." In D. L. Sills (Ed.), *International Encyclopedia of the Social Sciences.* New York: Crowell, Collier and Macmillan, 1968.

Yukl, G. A., and Wexley, K. N. *Readings in Organizational and Industrial Psychology.* New York: Oxford University Press, 1971.

PART VII

❧ Work and Health

Unabridged dictionaries list dozens of meanings for *work,* a fact that suggests both familiarity and imprecision. The core idea, however, is instrumentality; work is activity with an external purpose, and its success is judged by external accomplishments. We count houses built, coal mined, parts stamped out, books written—the intended consequences of work. It has long been recognized, however, that work also affects the worker. Farmers and mathematicians, miners and violinists, government officials and factory workers encounter different work demands, live different lives, and in some degree become different people, physically and mentally.

Social science has been slow to comprehend the depth and complexity of the relationship between work and workers. It is admittedly a relationship full of contradictions. Many ideologies and some religions teach that work is ennobling, and most workers say that they would go on working even if they had no economic need to do so. Yet in most societies leisure is prized, and workers and their representatives persistently attempt to reduce the duration and effort of work. Although most workers say that they are satisfied with their present jobs, less than half would choose them again if they were "free to go into any type of job."

Whatever general resolution of these matters may be developed will require a great deal of qualification for individual cases. Jobs differ in their demands and opportunities, and people differ in their needs and abilities. One person's stress is another's welcome stimulus. At the most abstract level, the interaction of work and worker poses the great societal paradox: we create social institutions and are in turn created by them. At the level of the individual and the organization, the questions involve the initial goodness of fit between person and organization and the ramifying costs and benefits of that process.

Complementary to the more traditional domain of productivity and organizational effectiveness, then, there is a domain of theory and research that might be called "work and well-being." The traditional research questions, posed in many forms and varieties, have been concerned with the contributions of the member to the organization; in contrast, questions of work and well-being are concerned with the effects of organizational role on the individual—effects both positive and negative, intended and unintended.

Until recent years, this latter domain has been relatively unexplored except for two subareas: the measurement of self-reported satisfaction with work and the study of certain occupational hazards to physical health. Organizational psychologists have done a good deal of work on the measurement of satisfaction and some on its determinants. The effects of physical risks, toxic substances, and other noxious materials in the work situation have been studied mainly as a branch of medicine and public health.

Only within the last decade or so have we begun to see research publication from social scientists that takes its independent variables from organizational theory and its dependent variables from individual psychology, psychiatry, and physiology. Four examples of such research are presented in this section. *Kahn* traces the development of research on a single stressor, role conflict, and shows the refinement of that concept in a series of related studies. *House* and his associates are also concerned with stressors in the work situation and correlated measures of individual strain, but the variables that they have measured are considerably more extensive in range. *French* has investigated two additional issues in work-related stresses: the issue of individual differences and the "buffering" effect of social support. The research described by *Cobb* is unusual among studies of stress and work, primarily because he is concerned with the stresses of job loss rather than those of job performance. Let us consider these four research descriptions more closely.

The framework described by *Kahn* is useful for assessing all four articles. That framework proposes that the relationship of work to well-being be studied by means of six conceptual categories. Four of these—objective and corresponding subjective properties of the work environment, immediate responses (affective, physiological, and behavioral) of the worker, and health outcomes—represent a hypothesized causal sequence. The other two categories of variables—enduring properties of the person and of his or her interpersonal relationships—are of interest primarily for their hypothesized interactions at each step in that causal sequence.

None of the studies that *Kahn* reports gives full weight to all six of these categories, but there is some complementarity among them. The initial study of role conflict showed it to be associated with a number of negative psychological outcomes—feelings of tension, lower levels of satisfaction and confidence in the organization, and (relatively) negative attitudes toward other persons in the work situation. Many of these relationships were moderated by personality characteristics, and not always in expected ways; for example, people of flexible personality reported higher levels of tension in conflictual situations than did those of more rigid personality.

It was a strength of this study that role conflict was measured independent of self-report, by pooling data from members of a person's role set about ways in which they wanted that person to change his or her performance. The number of role sets studied in this fashion was small, however, and their representativeness doubtful. The paired study, which asked questions about role conflict of a national sample, is an interesting attempt at complementarity. It achieved representativeness and adequate numbers by sacrificing independence of measures; all data were self-reported. Its value lies partly in the replication of findings from the more intensive research and partly in its addition to descriptive data on the prevalence of reported role conflict.

One of the limitations of the paired studies was the lack of commensurability between the two measures of role conflict, objective and subjective. The two measures were related—that is, people subjected to role conflict were more likely to report intense conflict experience—but the interpretation of the relationship between external fact and experience was confounded by the lack of comparability between measures. Kraut's (1965) research solves this problem by using a rather specialized measure of objective role conflict, the amount of sales in dollars that a manager expected from a given salesman minus the amount that the salesman himself considered appropriate. Subjective role conflict was then measured as the amount the salesman said the manager expected minus the amount that the salesman himself considered appropriate. Kraut's study replicated the negative effects of role conflict in terms of self-reported affect and added an interesting point that deserves further attention: the tendency of people to underestimate the conflict to which they are subjected. In the circumstances this tendency to underestimate must be considered denial or distortion rather than coping. Its costs, benefits, and generality in other settings remain uninvestigated.

Sales' (1969) research must be credited with bringing about some change in the thinking about role conflict. He demonstrated that the correlations reported between role conflict and various negative self-reported outcomes were being generated largely by items having to do with work load. The reinterpretation of much role conflict as overload is not an assertion that work situations are conflict free; it is rather a specification of what most role conflict in work situations is about—quantity versus quality, time pressures, quotas, magnitude of assignments, and the like.

The subsequent work on overload by French and Caplan (1973) at installations of the National Aeronautics and Space Agency both replicated and extended the previous work. The extensions consisted partly in further refinement of the concept, especially the distinction between quantitative and qualitative overload, and partly in the demonstration of physiological as well as self-reported effects. The correlation of overload with heart rate and cholesterol levels, both of which have been considered risk factors in coronary heart disease, comes closer to fulfilling the full causal sequence that this group of research workers set for themselves—from objective properties of the work situation to criteria of health.

This set of studies by a group of associated research workers (French, Kahn, Caplan, Sales, Kraut, and others) is interesting for the replication of the basic findings about the negative correlates of role conflict and for the successive refinements of that concept. The concentration on a limited number of stressors, however, leaves unanswered the question of what the total stress pattern in work situations may be like, and the reliance on cross-sectional research designs leaves doubts about the direction of causality. These are aggravated in those cases where the information on both the stressor and the hypothesized effect comes from self-report.

House's research sheds considerable light on the first of these problems. He and his colleagues utilized a comprehensive battery of measures to deal with the multiple aspects of perceived occupational stress, of environmental exposure, and of self-reports of ill health in a single plant population of blue-collar workers in the rubber and chemical industry. In addition, a subsample of workers received medical examinations, so that hard data as well as psychological reports were available. The results extend earlier work in showing that many aspects of perceived stress, from role conflict to lack of challenge, are associated with symptoms of ill health. Moreover, the relationships found were not just a matter of consistent self-reporting, because perceived stress was also related to the findings of the medical examiners. And the effects of stress were greater for workers who reported exposure to potentially noxious physical-chemical agents.

The scope of the *House* investigation—its coverage of various aspects of stress, its use of established scales for measuring health symptoms, and its inclusion of objective medical data—marks an advance in research on industrial health problems. A further advance will be achieved where these procedures are employed within a longitudinal design to deal definitively with causal relationships.

French's research extends the work of *Kahn* and *House* in three important ways. It systematically attempts to relate the properties of the job to the needs and abilities of the person; it clarifies the relationship between stress and strain by introducing the concept of social support as a conditioning variable, and it includes a battery of physiological measures to mitigate the usual dependence on self-report. All of French's data come from a single population, employees of the National Aeronautics and Space Administration, and the physiological data were obtained from only a small part of that population. Such trade-offs of representativeness for more demanding measures are, of course, almost unavoidable.

The procedure that *French* uses for taking account of individual differences in strain responses is of considerable theoretical interest. For each major job dimension of hypothetical stress—work load, responsibility, role ambiguity, and the like—he attempts to create and measure an analogous dimension that characterizes a person's need or ability. Each person can then be located in terms of goodness of fit on each dimension—the extent to which his or her needs and the demands of the job coincide. The theory requires that the predictive power of these goodness-of-fit variables shall be greater than the power of the corresponding job characteristics themselves. The research results are encouraging without being definitive; the goodness-of-fit functions tend to be curvilinear and the evidence of strain is least where goodness-of-fit is perfect. However, the correlations are not large, nor are they always significant.

The findings involving social support are more impressive. The apparent effects of work load on a number of physiological measures of strain—systolic and diastolic blood pressure, and serum glucose—are strongly conditioned by supportive relationships with one's superiors, peers, and subordinates. Indeed, the stress-strain correlations are insignificant when these interpersonal relations are optimal. The possibilities of application, should such findings be widely upheld, are exciting. Stresses that cannot be prevented at work may nevertheless be made less costly if such natural "buffers" can be discovered and synthesized.

Cobb's study is of methodological as well as substantive interest. It belongs to the genre of natural experiments, a type of research more often honored in textbooks than conducted in the field. Like *French, Cobb* managed to combine physiological and self-reported measures of strain, but he also obtained such measures at five points in time over a two-year period. His study shares with the others in this section (*Kahn, House* and *French*) a focus on job-related stresses and their effects, but it differs in the stress under study. In choosing to study job loss in plant closings rather than stresses on the job, Cobb has a considerable methodological advantage. His entire population suffers the same objective stress at almost the same time, and the imposed stress is severe enough to evoke widespread evidence of strain. By including as a control or comparison group a set of similarly employed men in the same community in other plants that did not close, *Cobb* is able to assess the additional strains associated with job loss. The results are impressive but complex. The stress of job loss shows effects on a number of physiological indicators of strain—norepinephrine excretion, serum creatinine, serum uric acid, and serum cholesterol. These effects vary in time of onset and duration, and they are moderated in some cases by personality traits and by the presence of social support from family and friends.

References

French, J. R. P., Jr., and Caplan, R. D. "Organizational Stress and Individual Strain." In A. Marrow (Ed.), *The Failure of Success.* New York: American Management Association, 1973.

Kraut, A. I. "A Study of Role Conflicts and Their Relationships to Job Satisfaction, Tension and Performance." Unpublished doctoral dissertation, University of Michigan, 1965. (University Microfilms No. 67-8312.)

Sales, S. M. "Differences Among Individuals in Affective, Behavioral, Biochemical and Physiological Responses to Variations in Workload." Unpublished doctoral dissertation, University of Michigan, 1969. (University Microfilms No. 69-18098.)

29

Conflict, Ambiguity, and Overload: Three Elements in Job Stress

Robert L. Kahn

Large-scale organizations have become a subject of sustained interest to social scientists, and no wonder. Much of life is lived in organizations, and the quality of extraorganizational life is to a considerable extent organizationally determined. The gross national product is essentially an organizational product.

These facts correspond to two rather different lines of organizational research, theory, and application. One has to do with productivity. Research in this tradition looks for differences between effective and ineffective organizations, high-producing and low-producing work groups, successful and unsuccessful supervisors, "motivated" and "unmotivated" workers. Theories that direct or accrue from such research concentrate on the explanation of organizational effectiveness. Application centers on supervisory training, worker exhortation, and organizational development.

More recently, research has begun on the other major aspect of organizations—their human membership and the effects of organizational demands and opportunities on individual members. Research in this still embryonic tradition seeks to explain occupational and other role-related differences in health or illness, mental and physical. Similar research aims have also generated studies that identify some hypothesized form of stress in organizations and attempt to trace its effects on individuals.

Theory in this context is likely to take its criterion variables (effects) from medicine, psychiatry, or clinical psychology and its independent variables (causes) from sociology or organizational psychology. Application is at too primitive a stage to encourage generalization, but some practitioners of organizational development are attempting to synthesize the attainment of organizational effectiveness and individual well-being. The view of organizations as sociotechnical systems (Trist and Bamforth, 1951; Rice, 1958; Trist and others, 1963) and the recent emphasis on the humanization of work exemplify the growing concern with the effects of organizations on individuals.

That concern is at the core of our research program—Social Environment and Mental Health—now in its fourteenth year at the Institute for Social Research of the University of Michigan. The broad aims of the program are expressed in the explanatory

Reprinted from Alan McLean (Ed.), *Occupational Stress* (Springfield, Ill.: Thomas, 1974), pp. 47-61, with permission of the author and Charles C Thomas, Publisher.

framework shown as Figure 1. The figure specifies immediately the six sets of variables around which the program is constructed; they appear as the numbered boxes in the figure. The categories of relationships and hypotheses are represented by arrows, which also remind us of the directions of causality to be emphasized.

Figure 1. Theoretical Framework: Social Environment and Health

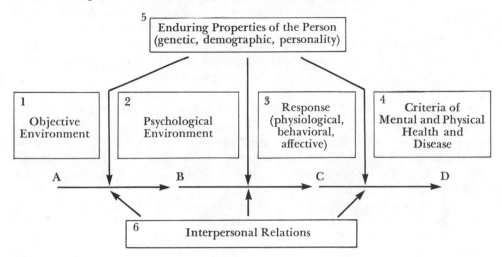

Thus, hypotheses of the A→B category have to do with the effects of the objective environment on the psychological environment (the environment as the individual experiences it). To take an example within the subject of job stress, we find that people whose jobs require them to engage in transactions across the organizational boundary (a fact in their objective environment) more often report that they are subjected to incompatible demands (a fact in their psychological environment). Hypotheses of the B→C category relate facts in the psychological environment to the immediate responses that are invoked in the person. For example, the perception that one is subject to persistent conflicting demands on the job is associated with feelings of tension. The C→D category deals with the effect of such responses on criteria of health and illness. The relationship of job tension to coronary heart disease illustrates the C→D category.

Finally, the categories of hypotheses just described must be qualified by an additional class, represented by the vertical arrows in the figure. This class of hypotheses states that relationships between objective and psychological environment, between psychological environment and response, and between response and criteria of health are modified by enduring characteristics of the individual and by interpersonal relations. For example, the extent to which a person experiences tension on being exposed to role conflict depends very much upon the personality characteristic of flexibility-rigidity; people who are flexible rather than rigid respond with greater tension to the experience of role conflict. In similar fashion, other properties of the person and his interpersonal relations act as conditioning variables in the hypotheses described above.

The research aims of our program are represented by all four of these categories of hypotheses, in combination. We are attempting to develop a theory of mental health as it is affected by the contemporary environment of the individual, taking into account the facts of genetic endowment and personality insofar as necessary to make sense of the environmental effects. Given this framework, it is clear what constitutes an adequate explanatory sequence—a chain of related hypotheses beginning with some characteristic of the objective environment, ending with some criterion of health, specifying the intervening variables in the psychological environment and response categories, and stating the ways in which this causal linkage is modified by the differing characteristics of individuals and their interpersonal relations. Such a causal chain we call a *theme.* We have attempted to state the aims of each research project in terms of one or more such themes, and to make the results of research projects additive by building toward the completion of such themes.

In conducting such thematic or programmatic research, we find that successive projects build on their predecessors in five main ways—by defining more precisely or differentiating concepts, by improving measures, by demonstrating more clearly (or extending further) some effect under study, by specifying more completely the relevant conditions or populations for which a given cause-and-effect relationship holds, and by extending the demonstrated relationships earlier into the causal sequence (discovering factors antecedent to those already known). This paper and that by Dr. French illustrate all these processes for a central concept in our program—job stress. We will be particularly concerned, however, to show the differentiation of the stress concept through a sequence of a dozen or more research projects.

I shall be referring to six of these projects and will describe them now; hereafter I will mention them only by name or convenient abbreviation:

1. *Conflict and Ambiguity, Intensive Study.* This study—by Kahn and associates (1964)—was built around fifty-three people, selected from several major corporations to represent the full range of jobs, from first-level supervisor to corporate officer. Data were collected by interview, written questionnaire, and personality test from each of the fifty-three. Interviews were also conducted with 381 other persons, who had been identified as members of the role sets of the fifty-three "focal persons." These 381 people held jobs that made them functionally interdependent with the fifty-three focal persons. In a sense, therefore, the expectations and demands of the 381 defined the roles of the fifty-three. Our purpose was to explore the degree of conflict or harmony, ambiguity or clarity in the role requirements confronted by the fifty-three focal persons and to discover some of the organizational causes and individual consequences.

2. *Conflict and Ambiguity, National Survey.* This study (Kahn and others, 1964), done in conjunction with the study or role sets just described, was an interview survey of about 1,500 respondents. Each of them was treated as a focal person and responded to the same basic questions about his work role as did the fifty-three focal persons in the intensive study. The main contribution of the national survey, of course, was information about the prevalence of role conflict and ambiguity in the work situation and replication of some of the findings of the intensive study on a representative population. The obvious methodological limitation of the national survey was the reporting of both causes and effects by individual respondents; no data were obtainable from members of their role sets, the people with whom they interacted on the job.

3. *Sales Office Study* (Kraut, 1965). This study was conducted in the sales department of a large corporation with a decentralized nationwide structure of sales offices. In each of 151 such offices, data were obtained from written questionnaires filled by the sales manager and a sample of salesmen, 823 of whom were included in the research. This study not only replicated major findings from the first intensive study of conflict and ambiguity but also allowed the collection of quantitative data (in terms of dollars of sales) indicating the magnitude of disagreements and their effects on performance.

4. *Secondary Analysis of Role Conflict Data* (Sales, 1969). Several related studies

were conducted by Sales, one involving secondary analysis of the earliest study in this series for the purpose of differentiating the concept of role conflict. This analysis concerns us directly. Sales followed this analysis with several experimental studies, with students and with engineers, scientists, and administrators at the National Aeronautics and Space Administration. About eighty-four NASA employees and 150 students were involved.

5. *Goddard Space Flight Center Study* (Caplan, 1971). This study, which included 205 scientists, engineers, and administrators at the Goddard Center (NASA), was designed to press further with overload as a particular form of role conflict and a particular source of stress in certain jobs. The locus of the study and the remarkable cooperation of NASA staff also permitted the collection of individual physiological data not available in any of the previous research.

6. *Kennedy Space Center Study* (French and Vickers). This study was designated primarily as a replication of the work at Goddard Space Flight Center. It also includes more intensive measures of strain and is longitudinal in design. The population consists of about 150 engineers and administrators, for whom there have now been two collections of data. Let us now turn to things learned about role stress from this series of studies:

Role Stress: A Global Concept

Although we consider the notion of stress important, we use the word as a generic term and have from the beginning sought more specific concepts for our research. In this respect we benefited from, but did not follow, the leading work of Selye (1956), who defines stress as the reactions of an organism to damaging stimuli. We have adopted instead what Lazarus (1966) has called "the engineering analogy," which regards stress as any force directed at an object, defines strain as the effects of stress, and measures such effects in terms of deflection or some other structural change. To make the metaphor useful, however, we have chosen to study certain specific environmental stresses and equally specific criteria of individual strain.

Role Conflict. The first of these was role conflict, which we thought of initially as consisting of logically incompatible demands made upon an individual by two or more persons whose jobs were functionally interdependent with his own. In the intensive study of role conflict (Study #1), each member of the fifty-three role sets was asked to indicate, for each major job activity of the relevant focal person, the extent to which he wanted the focal person's behavior to change. Four component scores were developed, reflecting responses in terms of amount of change wanted, number of activities involved, changes in time allocation wanted, and changes in behavioral style wanted. These scores, summed for the members of a person's role set, constituted the index of role conflict for him. We regard them as describing a fact in his objective environment, since they represent the views of his role senders rather than his own perceptions; in that sense they are a measure of objective role conflict.

The main effects of such conflict were measured in terms of the responses of the fifty-three focal persons, thus linking panels 1 and 3 in our programmatic schema (Figure 1). The effects of role conflict, so measured, are varied in form but consistently negative in their implications for the focal person. Persons subjected to high role conflict report greater job-related tensions, lower job satisfaction, less confidence in the organization itself, and more intense experience of conflict (Table 1); these might be considered some of the emotional costs of role conflict.

Similar analyses show that role conflict is also associated with poor interpersonal

Table 1. Emotional Reactions to Role Conflict (from Intensive Study)

| Emotional Reaction | Degree of Role Conflict | | p |
	High	Low	
(a) Intensity of experienced conflict	3.3	1.9	< .07
(b) Job-related tensions	5.1	4.0	< .03
(c) Job satisfaction	4.4	5.6	< .02
(d) Confidence in organization	5.7	7.3	< .001
N	(27)	(26)	

relations; in comparison to persons subjected to little or no role conflict, persons subjected to high role conflict report that they trust members of their role sets less, respect them less, like them less, and communicate with them less (Tables 2 and 3).

Table 2. Interpersonal Consequences of Role Conflict (from Intensive Study)

| Interpersonal Bond | Degree of Role Conflict | | p |
	High	Low	
Trust in senders	4.5	5.8	< .01
Respect for senders	4.2	5.9	< .001
Liking for senders	4.8	5.2	< .05
N	(27)	(26)	

Table 3. Interactional Consequences of Role Conflict

| Interaction Variable | Degree of Role Conflict | | p |
	High	Low	
Communication frequency	3.9	5.8	< .001
Power attributed to others	3.8	5.6	< .001
N	(27)	(26)	

All these represent findings of the A →C pattern in our schema. People who were in high-conflict situations were, naturally enough, more likely to report intense experience of conflict, a finding of the A→B pattern. However, a strong link between objective and subjective role conflict could not be established, because we had no measure of subjective conflict that was commensurate with our measure of objective conflict. The potential link between the focal person's responses and his health was also missing, because in this study we had no adequate measures of health.

We were, however, able to extend in other ways the findings between objective conflict and individual responses, even in this initial study. One such extension reached further into the objective environment, identifying the kinds of positions that were most likely to be characterized by conflicting expectations among role senders. These included positions that required the "crossing" of an organizational boundary—dealing simultaneously with people inside and outside the organization. Positions involving creative problem solving, in contrast to routine, were also more likely to be conflict ridden. Positions in supervision and management were more often conflict laden than were nonsupervisory positions.

The responses of individuals to role conflict were not uniform, however; they were mediated or "conditioned" by the personality of the focal person and by the quality of his interpersonal relations. Under high-conflict conditions, people who tended to be anxiety prone experienced the conflict as more intense and reacted to it with greater tension than people who were not anxiety prone (Figures 2 and 3). Similarly, introverts

**Figure 2. Intensity of Experienced Conflict in Relation to Role Conflict
and Neurotic Anxiety**

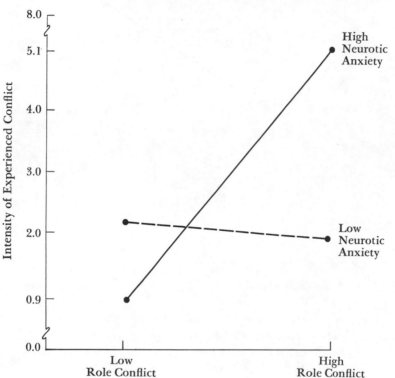

reacted more negatively to role conflict than did extroverts; they (introverts) suffered more tension and reported more deteriorated interpersonal relations. The personality dimension of flexibility-rigidity mediates still more strongly the relationship between role conflict and tension, with the flexible people accounting for almost the entire effect of role conflict and the rigid people reporting virtually no greater tension in the high-conflict situation than in the low (Figure 4).

The relationships between role conflict and various responses indicating strain are mediated by the interpersonal context in much the same way as by the personality characteristics of the focal person. The more frequent the communication between role senders and focal person, the greater the functional dependence of the focal person on the role set, and the greater the power of the role set over the focal person—the more signs of strain he shows when role conflict occurs. For example, he is more likely to experience a sharp reduction in job satisfaction, a sense of futility, and a negative change in affect for his role set.

The study of fifty-three role sets told us a great deal about the dynamics of role conflict but very little about its prevalence. The national survey (Study #2) was designed to complement the intensive study by concentrating on the task of description. It re-

Figure 3. Tension in Relation to Role Conflict and Neurotic Anxiety

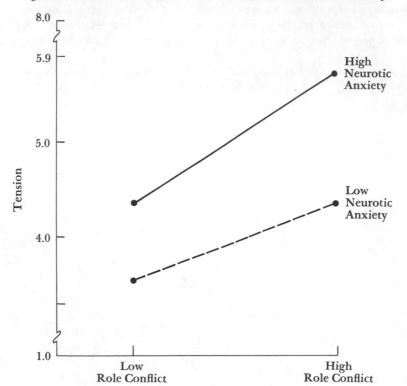

vealed that the experience of role conflict is common indeed in the work situation. Almost half of all respondents reported being "caught in the middle" between two conflicting persons or factions, more or less frequently. Most of these conflicts are hierarchical; nine out of ten of the people involved in conflicts reported that at least one of the parties to the conflict was above them in the organization. Somewhat less than half said that one of the conflicting parties was outside the organization.

These things were not unexpected. We were surprised, however, that one of the more dominant forms of conflict reported did not involve logically or morally incompatible demands, but rather temporally incompatible demands. People complained of overload—willingness to meet the demands and expectations of others, even to acknowledge them as separately legitimate and reasonable, but inability to meet them simultaneously or within the prescribed time limits.

Two of our colleagues, Allen Kraut and Stephen Sales, undertook to extend these research findings, especially by improving and refining the concept of role conflict itself. Kraut's (1965) study, utilizing a population of 823 salesmen and their managers in 151 offices, obtained commensurate measures of objective and subjective role conflict. For example, he measured in dollars the amount of sales that the manager expected from a salesman and the amount that the salesman himself considered appropriate; the difference between the two was taken as an objective measure of conflict. But Kraut also asked each salesman what he thought the manager expected of him; the difference between this amount and the salesman's own estimate of appropriate performance was taken as a measure of subjective conflict. Objective and subjective conflict are significantly correlated, as one would expect; the salesmen were not in a state of delusion. However, they did show a

Figure 4. Tension in Relation to Role Conflict and Flexibility-Rigidity

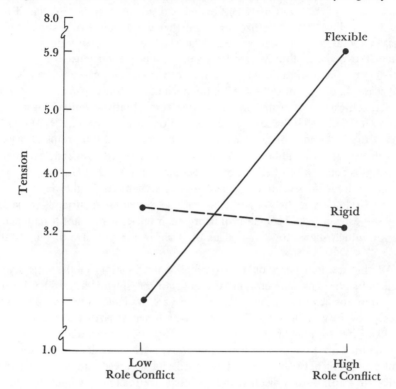

very general tendency to underestimate the manager's expectations, and thus to perceive their supervisors as nearer their own positions than was in fact the case. The effect of this distortion was to understate the conflict; subjective conflict was significantly less than objective conflict. Such distortion can be viewed as a way of coping with conflict, perhaps reducing its tension-evoking effects. It does nothing to resolve the objective problem, and its long-run success in reducing tension must therefore be suspect. Better methods of coping and conflict resolution can be taught.

Role Overload. Stephen Sales (1969) was intrigued by the frequency with which respondents in the first study of role conflict talked about overload when they were asked to discuss the nature of the conflict. He improvised an index of overload from three items from that study—the amount of pressure felt to do more work, the feeling of not being able to finish one's work in an ordinary day, and the feeling that the amount of work interferes with "how well it gets done." He found that these items correlated .6 with job-related tension and explain much of the effects that we had ascribed to role conflict in general.

In subsequent studies at Goddard and Kennedy Space Centers, we concentrated more explicitly on the process of overload and developed separate measures of quantitative load (a continuum running from "having too little to do" to "having too much to do") and qualitative load (a continuum running from "having work that is too easy to do" to "having work that is too difficult to do"). In order to obtain information independent of the person's own perceptions, we supplemented the usual interviews and questionnaires with observations and records of numbers of meetings, office visits, telephone calls, and hours worked.

The distinction between qualitative and quantitative work load had been developed in a study of 122 university professors and administrators (French, Tupper, and Mueller, 1965). Factor analysis had indicated that these were two distinct and separate variables, and that they showed some similar and some disparate effects. For example, both quantitative and qualitative overload were related to job tension ($r = .4$ and $.6$, respectively), but their relationships to self-esteem were more specialized. Quantitative overload was related to low self-esteem among administrators ($r = .7$) but not among professors. The self-esteem of professors was related to qualitative overload, however ($r = .3$).

The research at Goddard and Kennedy (French and Caplan, 1973) replicated the findings on the prevalence of overload and on the associated symptoms of psychological strain; it also investigated indicators of physiological strain. In general, overload in these work settings is common; 73 percent of the people interviewed at Goddard reported overload, compared to 44 percent of male white-collar workers in the nation as a whole. Among the Goddard scientists, when this overload is qualitative, it tends to be associated with low self-esteem ($r = .3$). Like professors, their self-esteem is not threatened by mere quantity, although they show other signs of strain in the presence of quantitative overload.

All this research bears on relationships among factors in the objective environment, the subjective environment, and responses of the individual. Less has been done on explicit criteria of health and illness. Some data are available, however, on physiological responses to overload (Caplan, 1971). Twenty-two men at NASA were observed at work for periods of two to three hours on three days. Their heart rates were recorded telemetrically during the same periods, and their cholesterol levels were determined daily. Findings indicated agreement between reported overload and observed numbers of telephone calls and visitors ($r = .6$). Both subjective and objective overload were related to heart rate ($r = .7$ and $.4$) and to cholesterol ($r = .4$).

In short, we find that conflict often occurs as overload, that the fact and experience of overload are common in the work situation, that qualitative and quantitative overload must be differentiated, and that these forms of overload are clearly associated with symptoms of psychological and physiological strain.

Role Ambiguity. Role ambiguity is conceived as the discrepancy between the amount of information a person has and the amount he requires to perform his role adequately. When we asked people about such matters in the national survey (Study #2), 35 percent said they were unclear about their responsibilities and were disturbed by that fact, and about equal numbers expressed similar feelings of unclarity and disturbance about what their co-workers expected of them, how their supervisors evaluated them, and what their opportunities for advancement might be. Moreover, the experience of ambiguity was correlated with job-related tension ($r = .5$), with job dissatisfaction ($r = .3$), with a sense of futility ($r = .4$), and with low self-confidence ($r = .3$). It was also associated with low trust and low liking for co-workers. These relationships, reasonably enough, were conditioned by individual differences—especially the individual's need for structure.

At Goddard (Caplan, 1971), the findings on ambiguity as related to dissatisfaction with the job were replicated ($r = .4$), and ambiguity was also found to be related to feelings of job-related threat, to mental and physical well-being ($r = .4$), and to lack of utilization of intellectual skills and knowledge ($r = .5$). Moreover, the ambiguity experience at Goddard was relatively common; it was reported by 60 percent of the men in that organization.

More recently, at Kennedy Space Flight Center (French and Caplan, 1973), we are attempting to look more deeply at the strains associated with ambiguity and to differentiate forms and aspects of ambiguity. In that study we find role ambiguity to be associated, as before, with dissatisfaction with the job ($r = .4$), with job-related threat ($r = .5$), and slightly with low self-esteem ($r = .2$). But we also find it to be related to anxiety ($r = .3$) and to a four-item scale of somatic symptoms of depression ($r = .5$).

Our efforts to differentiate the ambiguity concept are modest thus far, but it seems worth distinguishing between ambiguity about the present role and ambiguity about one's future prospects. Future ambiguity, as measured in the Kennedy study, explains most of the relationship between the overall ambiguity index and such variables as dissatisfaction with the job, job-related threat, and affective depression.

Conclusion

To attempt a concluding statement to this paper is inappropriate in at least two respects: The processes that it describes are still at an early stage. Moreover, even the present story line has only begun with this paper; Dr. Cobb and Dr. French will complete it. In doing so, they will draw on the programmatic framework described above and continue the development already sketched—from role stress to role conflict and ambiguity, from conflict to role overload and "underload," from overload in general to quantitative and qualitative overload, and from ambiguity in general to present and future ambiguity. Such differentiation, we are convinced, is as necessary for understanding as for solving the pragmatic problems of job stress.

References

Caplan, R. D. "Organizational Stress and Individual Strain: A Social-Psychological Study of Risk Factors in Coronary Heart Disease Among Administrators, Engineers and Scientists." Unpublished doctoral dissertation, University of Michigan, 1971.

French, J. R. P., Jr., and Caplan, R. D. "Organizational Stress and Individual Strain." In A. J. Marrow (Ed.), *The Failure of Success*. New York: American Management Association, 1973.

French, J. R. P., Jr., Tupper, C. J., and Mueller, E. F. *Work Load of University Professors*. Cooperative Research Project No. 2171. Ann Arbor: University of Michigan, 1965.

Kahn, R. L. "Work Modules." *Psychology Today,* Feb. 1973, *6,* 35-39, 94-95.

Kahn, R. L., and others. *Organizational Stress: Studies in Role Conflict and Ambiguity.* New York: Wiley, 1964.

Kraut, A. I. "A Study of Role Conflicts and Their Relationships to Job Satisfaction, Tension and Performance." Unpublished doctoral dissertation, University of Michigan, 1965.

Lazarus, R. S. *Psychological Stress and the Coping Process.* New York: McGraw-Hill, 1966.

Rice, A. K. *Productivity and Social Organization: The Ahmedabad Experiment.* London: Tavistock, 1958.

Sales, S. M. "Differences Among Individuals in Affective, Behavioral, Biochemical and Physiological Responses to Variations in Work Load." Unpublished doctoral dissertation, University of Michigan, 1969.

Selye, H. *The Stress of Life.* New York: McGraw-Hill, 1956.

Trist, E. L., and Bamforth, K. W. "Some Social and Psychological Consequences of the Long-Wall Methods of Coal-Getting." *Human Relations,* 1951, *4,* 3-38.

Trist, E. L., and others. *Organizational Choice.* London: Tavistock, 1963.

Work in America: Report of a Special Task Force to the Secretary of Health, Education and Welfare. Cambridge, Mass.: M.I.T. Press, 1973.

30

Occupational Stress and Health Among Factory Workers

James S. House
Anthony J. McMichael
James A. Wells
Berton H. Kaplan
Lawrence R. Landerman

Psychosocial forms of occupational stress have been increasingly implicated in the etiology of poor mental health and psychosomatic disease (House, 1974a, 1974b; Jenkins, 1971, 1976; Kasl, 1974, 1978). Although there is growing evidence that psychosocial job stress may impair the health of blue-collar, as well as white-collar, workers (see Kasl, 1978), discussions of "blue-collar stressors" are not infrequently limited to physical-chemical hazards, such as noise, heat, dust, and fumes (Poulton, 1978). There is thus a continuing need for research on the relation of psychosocial, as well as physical-chemical, stressors to the health of blue-collar workers. More importantly, Ashford (1976, pp. 124-126) has emphasized the need for research that simultaneously considers the relation to health of psychosocial job stress and physical-chemical hazards, both because apparent effects of occupational stress might really be due to physical-chemical hazards and because the effects of stress and physical-chemical hazards may be interactive. That is, psychosocial stress may make persons more susceptible to the effects of noxious physical, chemical, or biological agents in the environment, thus playing a role in the etiology of many diseases, not just those traditionally considered psychosomatic.

Although a variety of authors have argued that psychosocial stress may be an etiological factor in almost all diseases (see, for example, Cassel, 1970, 1976; Syme, 1967, 1974), much theory and research have focused on the relation of one or a few psychosocial stresses to a single disease (for example, the relation of job dissatisfaction or the Type A behavior pattern to coronary heart disease). To adequately understand the full

Excerpted from *Journal of Health and Social Behavior,* Nov. 1979, *20,* 139-160, with permission of the authors and the American Sociological Association.

range of health problems that may be affected by a given form of psychosocial stress and
to understand the mechanisms through which such effects occur, however, it is essential
to study the relation of multiple indicators of stress to multiple health outcomes in conjunction with other physical, chemical, and biological factors that might induce these
health outcomes. In sum, research is needed (1) to further document the impact of
psychosocial job stress, as well as physical-chemical hazards, on the health of blue-collar
workers; (2) to consider explicitly how psychosocial stress and physical-chemical hazards
combine both additively and interactively in predicting health; and (3) to begin to eluci-
date how wide a range of health outcomes is affected by stress and how these effects are
produced.

The present study addresses each of these issues by examining the relation of perceived occupational stress to self-reported symptoms and medically diagnosed signs of a
range of health outcomes among nonsupervisory blue-collar workers in a tire, rubber,
plastics, and chemicals manufacturing plant. Specifically, we examine the relation of perceived job pressures (for example, excessive work load, responsibility pressure, role conflict, or other stresses that stem from demands straining workers' abilities) and perceived
deprivations or dissatisfactions (for example, lack of intrinsic or extrinsic rewards, general
job dissatisfaction, or other stresses stemming from lack of gratification of workers'
needs) to self-reported symptoms of angina pectoris, gastrointestinal ulcers, neurosis or
poor mental health, itch and rash on skin, and persistent cough and phlegm, and to medical evidence of hypertension, heart disease risk, dermatitis, and respiratory signs from
stethoscopy and lung function tests. In all cases, the effects of perceived stress are
assessed in conjunction with those of both self-reported and objectively assessed exposure
to potentially noxious physical-chemical agents in the environment.

Methods

Source of the Data. The study population was the entire hourly (nonmanagerial)
work force of a large tire, rubber, plastics, and chemicals manufacturing plant in a small
city in the Northeast (U.S.), which included a wide range of blue-collar occupations, from
skilled craftsmen and technicians to relatively unskilled laborers. As part of a larger study
of the effects of working conditions on health in the rubber industry, a self-administered
questionnaire concerning perceived job stresses, health, and exposure to physical-chemical
hazards was mailed to all 2,856 hourly workers in late April 1974. Repeated follow-ups
over eight months resulted in a 70 percent response rate (N = 1,809) among white males,
the group used in the present analysis (see House and others, 1977, for details of data
collection procedures). The small numbers and relatively poor response rates of blacks
and women in the plant precluded using their data in this analysis. Extensive analyses
comparing questionnaire respondents and nonrespondents, and also early versus later
responders, suggest that respondents were somewhat older than nonrespondents; otherwise, the two groups differ little once age is controlled (detailed report available from the
first author). Age is controlled in all analyses in this study.

A nonrandom subset of 447 workers from the same population received medical
examinations and tests in October 1974; of these, 353 were white males who had also
returned questionnaires. These examinations were done to assess effects of long-term
exposure to vinyl chloride among chemical and plastic workers (with a small control
group of rubber workers). Though the examinations focused on bodily systems presumably more affected by vinyl chloride, some of the resulting data were relevant for the
present study. Comparisons of the questionnaire responses (and correlations among these

responses) of workers who did and did not receive medical examinations revealed few differences between the two groups (detailed report available from the first author) aside from their different occupational composition.

In this study we examine the relation of perceived stress (1) to self-reported health outcomes in the total set of 1,809 white male questionnaire respondents and (2) to medical conditions in the subset of 353 of those men who also received medical examinations.

Measures of Stress. The perceived occupational stress measures are all multi-item questionnaire indices, which derive from previous research (see, for example, Caplan and others, 1975; House, 1972) but have been adapted in content and wording to the present study population. Five types of job pressure are assessed, each by a three-item index: (1) *responsibility pressure*—having too much responsibility for people, process, or products and insufficient human or material assistance; (2) *quality concern*—having concern about not being able to do as good work as one could or should; (3) *role conflict*—receiving ambiguous and/or conflicting expectations from others at work; (4) *job versus nonjob conflict*—feeling that the job interferes with nonwork (for example, family) life; and (5) *work load*—reporting a large quantity of work and frequent time pressure. We have also examined the association with health of a measure of the *Type A behavior pattern*—a five-item index excerpted from nine items selected by Caplan and associates (1975) from an original pool of seventy-two items, developed by Sales (1969), that correlated quite highly (see Sales, 1969, p. 50) with the Jenkins Activity Survey (Jenkins, Rosenman, and Friedman, 1967). The Jenkins survey, in turn, has substantial construct validity and criterion validity against the clinical ratings of Friedman and Rosenman (Jenkins, 1975). The Type A pattern reflects a strong sense of occupational pressure, though our items emphasize stable attributes of the person rather than immediate situational pressures.

The study includes six measures of self-reported job deprivations or dissatisfactions (or the lack thereof, since high scores on our measures indicate satisfaction or lack of deprivation). These measures derive from ones previously used by House (1972) and Quinn and Shepherd (1974). Four measures assess the different types of perceived rewards or gratifications in the job: (1) *intrinsic rewards* (eight items assessing the degree to which work is interesting, challenging, varied, and so forth); (2) *extrinsic rewards* (four items assessing the degree to which the worker's job pays well, is secure, and has good fringe benefits and working conditions); (3) *importance rewards* (five items assessing the degree to which the worker's job is important, prestigious, and influential); and (4) *control rewards* (three items assessing the degree to which the work pace is not excessively rapid and is subject to worker control). The other two measures assess the worker's general satisfaction with his job and with himself: *job satisfaction* (five items) and *occupational self-esteem* (three items).

All of these measures have adequate to very good reliability, reasonable face validity, good convergent validity, and satisfactory discriminant validity, though intercorrelations between different indices are occasionally higher than might be desired (see Campbell and Fiske, 1959). In almost all cases, previous studies with very similar, if not identical, indices provide evidence of construct validity as well (Cronbach and Meehl, 1955).

Health Outcome Measures. In this study health was assessed by self-reports and medical examination, each data source having unique strengths and weaknesses. Data from the self-report measures of health, which were designed for the purposes of this study, are available for all study respondents. These measures include, first, self-reported symptoms of three health outcomes previously associated with the types of occupational stresses of interest in this study: (1) angina (House, 1974a, 1974b; Jenkins, 1971, 1976; Kasl, 1978), (2) peptic ulcer (Kahn and French, 1970; Susser, 1967), and (3) neurosis or poor mental health (Kasl, 1974, 1978; Kornhauser, 1965). Second, they include two health outcomes expected by physicians and industrial hygienists associated with this research to be especially affected by the environmental conditions of the rubber industry: (1) itch and rash on skin and (2) persistent cough and phlegm. Hence, they allow us to determine for a large blue-collar population whether psychosocial job stress is related to a wide range of health outcomes, and how these relations change when stress is analyzed in additive and interactive combination with exposure to physical-chemical hazards. However, owing to their self-report nature, the association of these health outcomes with perceived stress may be spuriously produced by general tendencies to report or not report undesirable symptoms and feelings about work. This problem will be further considered below.

In contrast, the medical assessments of health status are based on physicians' observations and/or laboratory tests and are quite independent of workers' self-reports. Although such assessments are, of course, not without error, the errors involved are very unlikely to produce spurious associations between perceived stress and these health outcomes. Unfortunately, however, the medical data available to us were collected for other purposes and on only a small subset ($N = 353$) of the full group of study respondents ($N = 1,809$). Although, as noted above, the medical examination subgroup is not notably different from other questionnaire respondents on the questionnaire indices used here, they are quite unrepresentative of the occupational composition of the plant. The medical examination also dealt only incidentally and somewhat casually with the medical conditions of interest in our study—diseases traditionally considered psychosomatic and other health outcomes (for example, itching skin and rash and persistent cough and phlegm) that might be affected over a short or medium term by the most pervasive environmental hazards in the plant. Blood pressure and other heart disease risk factors are the only major psychosomatic conditions previously linked with job stress (House, 1974a; Jenkins, 1971, 1976; Kasl, 1978) that were assessed in the medical examination. Selected physicians' diagnoses of dermatological and respiratory problems seem most likely to reflect the effects of environmental exposure (considered alone or in conjunction with stress).

The following specific diagnoses from the medical examination were used in our analysis: (1) *hypertension* (systolic blood pressure $\geqslant$ 150 mm Hg, based on a single reading in sitting position); (2) *high coronary heart disease (CHD) risk*—defined as having elevated levels of *two* of three major CHD risk factors (Gordon, Sorlie, and Kannel, 1971): cigarette smoking (here reporting current smoking of one pack or more per day), high systolic blood pressure (here $\geqslant$ 150), and high serum cholesterol (here $\geqslant$ 280 mg/100 ml based on a single automated analysis); (3) physician's diagnosis of "*dermatitis* or eczema" from observation; (4) physician's diagnosis of "*diminished breath sounds* diffusely" from stethoscopy; and (5) *impaired lung function* (a forced expiratory volume in one second, or FEV_1, that is 79 percent or less of the normal value for the person's age and weight).

The major limitation of self-report health measures for our purposes is their potential for spurious association with perceived stress because of common self-reporting tendencies or biases. To reduce this potential as much as possible, the medical staff of the study chose self-report questions that had, according to available evidence, the greatest sensitivity and specificity against related medical diagnoses and subsequent morbidity or mortality. Further, we have dichotomized these measures so as to maximize their specificity (even at some slight loss of sensitivity), since lower specificity (that is, more false positives vis-à-vis medical diagnoses) is the more important potential contributor to spurious associations between perceived stress and self-report health measures.

Environmental Exposure to Physical-Chemical Agents. Workers in the plant were exposed to a variety of environmental hazards, especially talc and carbon black dust, numerous chemicals and solvents, and fumes from these chemicals and reactions involving them, such as tire curing. These various physical-chemical agents in the environment seemed very likely to irritate or obstruct the skin and/or respiratory tract. Ideally, we would like to have objectively monitored the exposure of *each* worker to a variety of such agents. Instead, we again have two types of data, each with certain strengths and weaknesses. The available objective measures are industrial hygienists' assessments of levels of respirable particulates in broad environmental areas of the plant, with workers reporting on the questionnaire the area in which they worked. These measures do not take account of substantial individual variation in exposure within work areas and provided only a rough classification of areas as high, medium, or low in particulate or dust exposure. The other measure, used more extensively in our analysis, combines self-reports of exposure to dust, fumes, and chemicals into an index of *self-reported exposure to physical-chemical agents.* These different agents were combined into a single index both for economy of presentation and because their separate referents are not very specific, they often occur together in the plant, and analysis indicated they had similar effects on our health measures. This index provides an independent assessment of exposure for each individual but may exhibit spurious associations with other self-report measures of stress or health.

Data Analysis Procedures. Since all dependent variables in this study are dichotomies with fewer than 20 percent of the cases in the "positive" category, the data were analyzed via multiple-logistic-function analysis using maximum-likelihood-estimation procedures (Hanushek and Jackson, 1977; Nerlove and Press, 1973; Truett, Cornfield, and Kannel, 1974). The procedure estimates the probability (P) of a positive response or diagnosis on the dependent variable as a function of a set of interval-level independent variables (X_1 to X_K):

$$P = 1/(1 + e^{-B_0 + B_1 X_1 \ldots B_K X_K}).$$

The model becomes linear when the dependent variable is the logit (or log of the conditional odds) of P:

$$ln(P/1 - P) = B_0 + B_1 X_1 + \ldots B_K X_K.$$

Maximum likelihood estimation of a logistic response model avoids the two major problems of using dichotomous dependent variables in ordinary least squares (OLS) regression: (1) heteroskedasticity of the conditional distributions of the dependent variable and (2) estimated coefficients that yield predicted values of P outside the range of 0-1.

We have analyzed the effect of each of the twelve stress measures reviewed above on each of our five self-report health indices and five diagnoses from medical exams or tests. All analyses controlled for the confounding effects of any of the following variables that had a significant impact on a dependent variable: (1) *age* (in years), (2) *education* (n years), (3) amount of *cigarette smoking* per day, (4) *self-reported exposure to* potentially noxious *physical-chemical agents,* (5) *obesity*—Quetelet ratio or weight in pounds/height in inches, and (6) a five-point company rating of the amount of *physical effort required by the worker's job* (a measure of physical activity).

Results

Tables 1 and 2 present the logistic coefficients for all significant associations between stress and health, net of the appropriate confounding variables. Since logistic coefficients do not have a simple interpretation (they represent increases in the log of the odds of a "positive" response for each unit increase of the independent variable), we also present for each significant association the predicted proportions of persons "sick" (that is, manifesting positive symptoms of that health outcome) at the maximum and minimum values (for example, 12 and 0 for each job pressure) of each stress variable. The ratio of the two predicted proportions suggests the relative risks of workers experiencing very high versus very low stress. In deriving these predicted proportions, we set the relevant control variables equal to the approximately "average values" in our sample. Thus, for example, the predicted proportions in the upper left-hand cell of Table 1 (that is, 3.2 percent versus 8.4 percent) can be viewed as expected probabilities of self-reported angina symptoms for workers scoring 0 (low) versus 12 (high) on the responsibility pressure scale who are 42 years old, have some high school education, smoke ten to twenty cigarettes a day, report potentially hazardous exposure to one physical-chemical agent (dust *or* fumes *or* chemicals), have an average Quetelet ratio (3.7), and have jobs rated as requiring average physical effort.

Self-Reported Health Outcomes. The results on the left sides of Tables 1 and 2 reveal a pervasive association of perceived occupational stress with self-reported symptoms. Every self-reported health outcome is at least marginally associated ($p < .05$, two-tailed) with three or more of the twelve measures of stress in Tables 1 and 2—substantially more than would be expected by chance—after controlling for six potential confounding variables, including exposure to hazardous physical-chemical agents. All but a few of these associations are highly statistically significant ($p < .01$, two-tailed). The magnitude of these associations is not trivial—the expected proportion of workers with self-reported symptoms of ill health is at least two to three times greater at the highest levels of stress than at the lowest levels, even for the more marginal associations.

The pervasive impact of stress across all self-reported health outcomes is consistent with the hypothesis that stress increases the susceptibility of blue-collar workers to a wide range of health problems and diseases. Our measure of the Type A coronary-prone behavior pattern, for example, has a quite substantial association with angina, but it is also related to neurotic symptoms and cough and phlegm. Neurotic symptoms are significantly increased by all job pressures and the lack of all job gratifications, while symptoms of itch and rash are only slightly less strongly and pervasively associated with perceived stress. Persistent cough and phlegm are significantly associated with five of six job pressures and two of six gratifications—a pattern slightly less pervasive and strong than that manifested in relation to itch and rash. Thus, these three health outcomes seem to be affected by a wide range of occupational stresses, though cough and phlegm may be affected more by pressures than by rewards.

However, the results for the self-reported health outcomes in Tables 1 and 2 also manifest some interesting "specificities." Angina and ulcers are affected by only a limited number of stress factors, but these form a pattern that is quite consistent with prior theory and research. Ulcers are associated with two job pressure measures (role conflict and job-nonjob conflict) indicative of interpersonal conflict and tension (with others at work or outside of work) and also with self-esteem—results consistent with prior research and theoretical formulations linking ulcers with interpersonal conflict and low self-esteem (Kahn and French, 1970; Susser, 1967). Job satisfaction is the only other stress variable

Table 1. Multiple-Logistic-Function Estimates of Relationships Between Job Pressures and Health, Controlling Confounding Variables

Stress Variables	Self-Reported Symptoms					Medical Diagnoses				
	Angina	Ulcers	Neurosis	Itch and Rash	Cough and Phlegm	Hypertension	High CHD Risk	Diminished Breath Sounds	Diminished FEV_1	Dermatitis
Responsibility pressure										
Logistic coefficient	.089[b]	—	.092[a]	.094[a]	—	—	—	—	—	—
Predicted } Low stress	3.2%		9.9%	8.2%						
% "sick" } High stress	8.4%		23.0%	20.3%						
Role conflict										
Logistic coefficient	—	.086[b]	.177[a]	.100[a]	.115[a]	.167[b]	—	—	—	—
Predicted } Low stress		9.9%	7.5%	8.5%	6.1%	4.9%				
% "sick" } High stress		21.8%	38.5%	22.0%	19.6%	27.5%				
Work load										
Logistic coefficient	—	—	.104[a]	.114[a]	.086[a]	.128[b]	—	—	—	—
Predicted } Low stress			7.2%	5.8%	5.2%	3.2%				
% "sick" } High stress			20.2%	18.4%	12.8%	13.3%				
Quality concern										
Logistic coefficient	.100[b]	—	.147[a]	.119[a]	.081[a]	—	—	—	—	—
Predicted } Low stress	2.9%		7.3%	7.1%	6.6%					
% "sick" } High stress	8.8%		30.1%	22.7%	14.8%					
Job vs. nonjob conflict										
Logistic coefficient	—	.071[a]	.171[a]	.118[a]	.058[b]	.107[c]	—	—	—	—
Predicted } Low stress		10.8%	9.0%	8.3%	8.7%	7.2%				
% "sick" } High stress		20.2%	41.2%	25.5%	15.0%	16.5%				
Type A										
Logistic coefficient	.057[a]	—	.034[a]	—	.024[b]	-.042[c]	—	—	—	—
Predicted } Low stress	1.9%		8.7%		6.3%	12.9%				
% "sick" } High stress	9.4%		19.5%		11.5%	8.2%				

Note: Entries are the logistic coefficient and the percentage predicted to be "sick" on the basis of the logistic coefficient at the *highest* and *lowest* values of each stress variable at the means of the control variables. Coefficients are omitted for self-reported symptoms if $p > .05$ and for medical diagnoses if $p > .10$. (Tests are two-tailed for self-reported diagnoses, one-tailed for medical diagnoses.)

[a] $p < .01$.
[b] $p < .05$.
[c] $p < .10$.

Table 2. Multiple-Logistic-Function Estimates of Relationships Between Job Gratifications and Health, Controlling Confounding Variables

	Self-Reported Symptoms					Medical Diagnoses				
Stress Variables	Angina	Ulcers	Neurosis	Itch and Rash	Cough and Phlegm	Hypertension	High CHD Risk	Diminished Breath Sounds	Diminished FEV_1	Dermatitis
Job satisfaction										
Logistic coefficient	—	-.058[b]	-.235[a]	-.118[a]	-.102[a]	-.151[b]	-.098	—	—	.088[c]
Predicted } Low stress		9.8%	4.9%	7.0%	5.8%	3.5%	16.0%			17.3%
% "sick" } High stress		19.4%	53.9%	24.5%	17.0%	14.4%	33.6%			8.0%
Occupational self-esteem										
Logistic coefficient	—	-.055[a]	-.084[a]	-.051[a]	—	-.061[c]	—	.172[c]	—	—
Predicted } Low stress		10.1%	9.9%	9.4%		6.7%		4.8%		
% "sick" } High stress		30.2%	49.9%	26.2%		13.0%		2.3%		
Intrinsic rewards										
Logistic coefficient	—	—	-.050[a]	-.029[a]	—	-.084[a]	-.077[a]	—	—	.043[b]
Predicted } Low stress			7.2%	7.9%		2.6%	10.2%			19.2%
% "sick" } High stress			25.8%	17.3%		16.9%	41.8%			7.8%
Extrinsic rewards										
Logistic coefficient	—	—	-.115[a]	-.098[a]	-.064[b]	-.198[a]	-.186[a]	—	—	—
Predicted } Low stress			6.5%	5.5%	5.9%	2.1%	7.6%			
% "sick" } High stress			27.9%	18.7%	13.4%	19.1%	43.4%			
Importance rewards										
Logistic coefficient	—	—	-.034[b]	—	—	—	-.068[c]	—	—	—
Predicted } Low stress			9.9%				13.7%			
% "sick" } High stress			18.3%				30.7%			
Control rewards										
Logistic coefficient	—	—	-.098[a]	—	—	—	—	—	—	—
Predicted } Low stress			9.5%							
% "sick" } High stress			25.3%							

Note: Entries are the logistic coefficient and the percentage predicted to be "sick" on the basis of the logistic coefficient at the *highest* and *lowest* values of each stress variable at the means of the control variables. Coefficients are omitted if $p > .05$ and for medical diagnoses if $p > .10$. (Tests are two-tailed for self-reported diagnoses, one-tailed for medical diagnoses.)

[a] $p < .01$.
[b] $p < .05$.
[c] $p < .10$.

significantly related to ulcers. In contrast, angina is significantly correlated only with variables indicative of task-oriented and achievement concerns (responsibility, quality concern, and Type A), again consistent with much prior theory and research on CHD (Jenkins, 1971, 1976).

In sum, our self-report data show neurotic, dermatological, and probably respiratory symptoms to be associated with almost all types of occupational stress, whereas angina and ulcers appear to be related only to certain types of stress—interpersonal ones in the case of ulcers and task-oriented ones in the case of angina. This patterning suggests hypotheses about the mechanisms through which various diseases may be affected by stress. However, some or all of the observed associations in the left-hand panels of Tables 1 and 2 may be a spurious product of the self-report nature of both the stress and health variables. We shall return to this issue after considering the associations between stress and medical conditions assessed by examination or laboratory tests.

Medical Health Outcomes. The results in the right-hand panels of Tables 1 and 2 with respect to our medical outcomes reveal further associations between occupational stress and health, but the pattern of results is neither as strong nor as pervasive as that for the self-reported health outcomes. Although the relationships are not always strong and significant, major coronary heart disease risk factors, except smoking, are consistently related to stress in the predicted direction. The strongest pattern of results appears in the case of systolic hypertension (≥ 150), as shown in the leftmost column of the medical diagnoses panel of Tables 1 and 2. Eight of twelve relationships are significant ($p \leq .10$, one-tailed), and only one of these (involving Type A) is not in the predicted direction. Four of the twelve relationships between stress and the general measure of CHD risk (combining systolic blood pressure, cholesterol, and smoking) are significant in the predicted direction (all involving gratifications in Table 2), while four relationships between CHD risk and job pressures (not shown in Table 1) are nearly significant in the predicted direction. The predicted proportions in Table 2 show the rates of heart disease risk to be two to six times greater at the highest versus lowest levels of stress, net of all confounding variables.

In contrast to the results for heart disease risk, the three "significant" associations between perceived stress and dermatological or respiratory medical conditions shown in Tables 1 and 2 could easily have occurred by chance (and all are in the opposite direction from our expectations). Even using a quite liberal standard of statistical significance, we find no evidence in the medical data for a generalized effect of occupational stress on health (if anything, the pattern of significant and nonsignificant results runs counter to the pattern of the self-report findings). There is thus a major discrepancy between our results using self-reported symptoms and our results based on medical conditions, a subject that we explore more fully below.

Stress as Exacerbator of the Effects of Environmental Agents. Both our self-report and medical health data show that occupational stress is associated with increased risk of diseases traditionally considered wholly or partly psychogenic—self-reported symptoms of angina, ulcers, and neurosis and medical examination assessments of high blood pressure and other coronary disease risk factors. Such effects could be produced exclusively by the heightened responses of the central nervous, cardiovascular, and gastrointestinal systems in the face of stress. Our self-report data also indicate that occupational stress may contribute to the development of dermatological and respiratory problems as well, but the medical data reveal no evidence of such effects. Although it is possible that occupational stress per se might affect dermatological or respiratory functioning, it is more likely that such symptoms are stimulated by physical, chemical, or biological irritants and that stress acts primarily to exacerbate the reactions to such irritants. If this hypothesis is true, it implies two things. First, the associations of stress with self-reported dermatological and respiratory symptoms apparent in Tables 1 and 2 should be partly or wholly due to an interaction between stress and exposure to physical-chemical irritants. Second, the explanation for the lack of association between stress and medically diagnosed dermatological and respiratory conditions in Tables 1 and 2 may be that workers in the medical examination group were on the average not sufficiently exposed to appropriate irritating agents. Interactions between stress and exposure to agents might still have been present in that group. Thus, it is crucial to test for interactive (synergistic) effects of stress and exposure to agents in relation to health.

Our operational procedure was first to determine whether the effects of stress on health varied across levels of agents in a manner that was both significantly different from what might occur by chance and theoretically expected and meaningful. If there was evidence of such statistically significant and theoretically meaningful interaction between stress and exposure to agents in predicting a particular health outcome, we then examined in detail how the effects of each stress on that health outcome varied across levels of exposure to agents by simply performing separate analyses of the effects of each stress on that health outcome at various levels of exposure to agents. The results shown in Table 3 derive from these latter analyses. But first let us review the procedure and results of our initial tests for evidence of interaction between stress and exposure to agents in predicting each health outcome. (Note: Results of these initial analyses discussed below are not presented in tabular form in the paper.)

A theoretically expected and meaningful interaction between stress and exposure to agents would be synergistic: the effects of stress on health should increase as exposure to agents increases; and, similarly, the effects of agents on health should increase as stress increases. A multiplicative interaction term provides a theoretically appropriate test for such interaction, and one which proved statistically more powerful than merely testing for any and all differences in the effects of stress on health across levels of exposure to agents. Therefore, we created a series of interaction terms by multiplying each perceived stress variable by our index of self-reported exposure to dust, fumes, and chemicals. We then estimated the effects and tested the significance of these interaction variables (net of their main effects and appropriate confounding variables) in multiple logistic (and regression) equations predicting each major self-reported and medical health outcome. The more positive the logistic (or regression) coefficients for such an interaction term, the more the effects of stress on health tend to increase as exposure to agents increases. The significance level of each such coefficient provided a test for differences in the effects of stress on health across levels of exposure to agents.

The results of these analyses for our self-report health measures strongly suggest that stress interacts synergistically with exposure to agents in producing symptoms of persistent cough and phlegm and probably itch and rash as well, while no such interaction is evident with respect to angina, ulcers, or neurotic symptoms. Both the initial logistic function and regression analyses showed four perceived stress variables—role conflict, quality concern, job-nonjob conflict, and (lack of) extrinsic rewards—to interact significantly ($p < .05$, two-tailed) and as expected with exposure to agents in equations predicting persistent cough and phlegm. That is, stress was essentially unrelated to persistent cough and phlegm symptoms among workers reporting no exposure to hazardous physical-chemical agents, but was increasingly strongly related to these symptoms as reported hazardous exposure increased. Though not statistically significant, interaction trends of the same type appeared for all but one other perceived stress variable in relation to persistent cough and phlegm.

Table 3. Multiple Logistic Coefficients for Relationships Between Perceived Stress and Self-Reported Respiratory and Dermatological Symptoms for Workers Reporting Exposure to 0 ($N = 503$), 1 ($N = 545$), 2 ($N = 408$), or 3 ($N = 353$) Physical-Chemical Agents

| | Persistent Cough and Phlegm | | | | | | Itch and Rash | | | | | |
| | No. of Agents to Which Exposed | | | | Predicted % Sick Exposed to 3 Agents | | No. of Agents to Which Exposed | | | | Predicted % Sick Exposed to 3 Agents | |
Stress Variable	0	1	2	3	Low Stress	High Stress	0	1	2	3	Low Stress	High Stress
Responsibility pressure	.020	.042	.067	.107[c]	8.7%	25.6%	-.016	.098[c]	.120[b]	.111[b]	14.8%	39.7%
Role conflict	-.011	.073	.101	.244[a]	5.8%	53.9%	.042	.137[a]	.061	.113[b]	16.3%	43.2%
Work load	.024	.120[b]	.022	.142[b]	6.3%	26.8%	-.024	.139[a]	.094[c]	.182[a]	7.6%	42.0%
Quality concern	.007	.075	.041	.161[a]	7.3%	35.2%	.080	.116[b]	.131[b]	.126[b]	13.8%	42.0%
Job-nonjob conflict	-.033	-.011	.078	.124[b]	10.1%	33.2%	-.029	.117[b]	.116[b]	.155[a]	13.9%	50.9%
Type A	-.002	.025	.024	.042[c]	8.3%	24.0%	.003	.032	.030	-.010	9.6%	7.3%
Job satisfaction	-.110	-.113[c]	-.067	-.138[b]	8.9%	28.0%	-.013	-.071	-.169[a]	-.161[a]	12.0%	59.3%
Occup. self-esteem	-.032	-.021	-.083[c]	-.021	20.3%	27.1%	-.160[a]	-.041	-.016	-.047	24.6%	43.2%
Intrinsic rewards	.012	-.042	.034	-.052[b]	9.0%	25.5%	-.047	-.014	.028	-.039[c]	16.2%	32.8%
Extrinsic rewards	.025	-.126	.057	-.200[a]	4.2%	32.4%	-.170[b]	-.081	-.070	-.107[b]	12.7%	34.3%
Importance rewards	.071	-.061	.024	.017	18.3%	14.7%	-.074	-.038	-.045	-.032	19.5%	28.0%
Control rewards	.114	-.132[c]	-.052	-.120[c]	10.9%	26.5%	-.001	-.040	-.041	-.094	18.5%	34.6%

Note: Entries are the logistic coefficient and the percentage predicted to be "sick" on the basis of the logistic coefficient at the *highest* and *lowest* values of each stress variable at the means of the control variables. All tests are two-tailed.

[a] $p < .01$.

[b] $p < .05$.

[c] $p < .10$.

Similar, though somewhat weaker, results were obtained with respect to self-reports of dermatological symptoms, though the regression and initial logistic function analyses disagreed as to the statistical significance of the interaction between agents and stress. Regression analyses revealed four significant ($p < .05$, two-tailed) interactions (involving work load, quality concern, job versus nonjob conflict, and extrinsic rewards), but none of these interactions attained significance in our logistic analyses—this was the only time we observed a notable discrepancy between results of logistic function and regression analyses. Interaction terms involving several other perceived stresses were in the expected direction, but were not statistically significant in either the regression or logistic analyses.

In contrast to the results for cough and phlegm and itch and rash, both the regression and initial logistic analyses revealed no more significant interactions between agents and perceived stress in predicting self-reported angina, ulcers, and neurotic symptoms than would be expected by chance. Synergistic interactions between stress and agents in predicting health thus do *not* occur for all self-report measures of health, only for those symptoms most likely to be produced by exposure to dust, fumes, or chemicals.

Perceived Stress and Traditional Psychosomatic Disorders. Although the validity of any particular association may be open to dispute, the overall pattern of our results indicates that perceived occupational stress is positively associated with disorders traditionally considered psychological and psychosomatic. We find clear evidence of associations between perceived stress and blood pressure and other medically assessed CHD risk factors, after controlling a range of confounding variables. Perceived stress is also associated with self-reported symptoms of angina, ulcers, and neurosis, again after controls for a range of confounding variables. Whether these latter associations involve underlying medical conditions is, of course, open to question. Undoubtedly, the observed associations substantially reflect symptom-reporting tendencies, but a number of factors suggest that these associations may also involve underlying medical conditions.

Prior research discussed above suggests that the angina and neurotic symptom measures have substantial validity against medical diagnoses, though our ulcer index is somewhat problematic in this regard. The relatively low correlations (.06-.32) among all of the self-reported symptom measures suggest that only a small portion of the variance in each reflects any very general tendency to experience and/or report symptoms. Finally, as noted above, the pattern of results with respect to the angina, ulcer, and neurotic symptom measures in Tables 1 and 2 is notably consistent with prior theory and research on psychosocial factors in these diseases. Angina symptoms are significantly associated almost exclusively with stresses involving performance and achievement, whereas ulcer symptoms relate primarily to interpersonal tensions and self-esteem, and neurotic symptoms correlate with a broad range of stresses, most notably with job satisfaction and self-esteem.

In sum, Tables 1 and 2 may overstate the magnitude of the association that would obtain between perceived stress and independent medical diagnoses of angina, ulcers, and neurosis, but stress would likely be associated with such diagnoses, except perhaps in the case of ulcers. Combined with the associations of stress with medically diagnosed CHD risk factors, these results suggest a consequential association between psychosocial job stress and psychosomatic disorders among blue-collar workers.

Conclusion

The present study provides substantial further evidence that psychosocial job stress is significantly associated with psychological and psychosomatic disorders among blue-collar workers, while also suggesting that such stress may pose an additional hazard to blue-collar workers by making them more susceptible to the effects of noxious environmental agents on dermatological and, especially, respiratory functioning. Future research is needed, however, that relies less on self-report measures of health and environmental exposure and that examines these relationships in a longitudinal design allowing clear causal inferences. Our experience suggests that such research will be challenging to design and analyze, but that it also has great potential for increasing our understanding of the etiology of health and illness.

References

Ashford, N. A. *Crisis in the Workplace: Occupational Disease and Injury.* Cambridge, Mass.: M.I.T. Press, 1976.

British Medical Research Council, Committee on Etiology of Chronic Bronchitis. "Standardized Questionnaire on Respiratory Symptoms." *British Medical Journal,* 1960, *2,* 1665.

Campbell, D. T., and Fiske, D. W. "Convergent and Discriminant Validation by the Multitrait-Multimethod Matrix." *Psychological Bulletin,* 1959, *56,* 81-105.

Caplan, R., and others. *Job Demands and Work Health: Main Effects and Occupational Differences.* Washington, D.C.: U.S. Government Printing Office, 1975.

Cassel, J. "Physical Illness in Response to Stress." In S. Levine and N. Scotch (Eds.), *Social Stress.* Chicago: Aldine, 1970.

Cassel, J. "The Contribution of the Social Environment to Host Resistance." *American Journal of Epidemiology,* 1976, *104,* 107-123.

Cederlof, R., Jonsson, E., and Lundman, T. "On the Validity of Mailed Questionnaires in Diagnosing 'Angina Pectoris' and 'Bronchitis.' " *Archives of Environmental Health,* 1966, *13,* 738-742.

Cronbach, L. J., and Meehl, P. E. "Construct Validity in Psychological Tests." *Psychological Bulletin,* 1955, *52,* 281-302.

Dohrenwend, B. P. "Sociocultural and Social-Psychological Factors in the Genesis of Mental Disorders." *Journal of Health and Social Behavior,* 1975, *16,* 365-392.

Dunn, J. P., and Cobb, S. "Frequency of Peptic Ulcer Among Executives, Craftsmen, and Foremen." *Journal of Occupational Medicine,* 1962, *4,* 343-348.

Epstein, L. M. "Validity of a Questionnaire for Diagnosis of Peptic Ulcer in an Ethnically Heterogeneous Population." *Journal of Chronic Diseases,* 1969, *22,* 49-55.

Gordon, T., Sorlie, P., and Kannel, W. B. "Coronary Heart Disease, Atherothrombotic Brain Infarction, Intermittent Claudication—A Multivariate Analysis of Some Factors Related to Their Incidence: Framingham Study, 16-Year Follow-Up." Section 27 of the Framingham Study. Washington, D.C.: U.S. Government Printing Office, 1971.

Hanushek, E. A., and Jackson, J. E. *Statistical Methods for the Social Sciences.* New York: Academic Press, 1977.

House, J. S. "The Relationship of Intrinsic and Extrinsic Work Motivations to Occupational Stress and Coronary Heart Disease Risk." Unpublished doctoral dissertation, University of Michigan, 1972.

House, J. S. "Occupational Stress and Coronary Heart Disease: A Review and Theoretical Integration." *Journal of Health and Social Behavior,* 1974a, *15,* 12-27.

House, J. S. "Occupational Stress and Physical Health." In J. O'Toole (Ed.), *Work and the Quality of Life: Resource Papers for Work in America.* Cambridge, Mass.: M.I.T. Press, 1974b.

House, J. S., Gerber, W., and McMichael, A. J. "Increasing Mail Questionnaire

Response: A Controlled Replication and Extension." *Public Opinion Quarterly,* 1977, *41,* 95-99.

Jenkins, C. D. "Psychologic and Social Precursors of Coronary Disease." *New England Journal of Medicine,* 1971, *284,* 244-255, 307-317.

Jenkins, C. D. "The Coronary-Prone Personality." In W. D. Gentry and R. B. Williams, Jr. (Eds.), *Psychological Aspects of Myocardial Infarction and Coronary Care.* St. Louis: Mosby, 1975.

Jenkins, C. D. "Recent Evidence Supporting Psychologic and Social Precursors of Coronary Disease." *New England Journal of Medicine,* 1976, *294,* 987-994.

Jenkins, C. D., Rosenman, R. H., and Friedman, M. "Development of an Objective Psychological Test for the Determination of the Coronary-Prone Behavior Pattern." *Journal of Chronic Diseases,* 1967, *20,* 371-379.

Kahn, R. L., and French, J. R. P., Jr. "Status and Conflict: Two Themes in the Study of Stress." In J. McGrath (Ed.), *Social and Psychological Factors in Stress.* New York: Holt, Rinehart and Winston, 1970.

Kasl, S. V. "Work and Mental Health." In J. O'Toole (Ed.), *Work and the Quality of Life.* Cambridge, Mass.: M.I.T. Press, 1974.

Kasl, S. V. "Epidemiological Contributions to the Study of Work Stress." In C. L. Cooper and R. Payne (Eds.), *Stress at Work.* New York: Wiley, 1978.

Kornhauser, A. *The Mental Health of the Industrial Worker.* New York: Wiley, 1965.

Leighton, D. C., and others. *The Character of Danger.* New York: Basic Books, 1963.

Nerlove, M., and Press, S. J. *Univariate and Multivariate Log-Linear and Logistic Models.* Santa Monica, Calif.: Rand, 1973.

Popeila, T., and others. "Validity of Questionnaire Criteria in Mass Screening for the Diagnosis of Peptic Ulcer." *International Journal of Epidemiology,* 1976, *5,* 251-253.

Poulton, E. C. "Blue Collar Stressors." In C. L. Cooper and R. Payne (Eds.), *Stress at Work.* New York: Wiley, 1978.

Quinn, R. P., and Shepherd, L. J. *The 1972-73 Quality of Employment Survey.* Ann Arbor: Survey Research Center, University of Michigan, 1974.

Rose, G. A. "Chest Pain Questionnaire." *Milbank Memorial Fund Quarterly,* 1965, *43* (Part 2), 32-39.

Rose, G. A. "Predicting CHD from Minor Symptoms and Electrocardiographic Findings." *British Journal of Preventive and Social Medicine,* 1971, *25,* 94-96.

Rose, G. A., and Blackburn, H. *Cardiovascular Survey Methods.* Geneva: World Health Organization, 1968.

Rose, G., McCartney, P., and Reid, D. D. "Self-Administration of a Questionnaire for Chest Pain and Intermittent Claudication." *British Journal of Preventive and Social Medicine,* 1977, *31,* 42-48.

Sales, S. M. "Differences Among Individuals in Affective, Behavioral, Biochemical and Physiological Responses to Variations in Workload." Unpublished doctoral dissertation, University of Michigan, 1969.

Susser, M. "Causes of Peptic Ulcer: A Selective Epidemiologic Review." *Journal of Chronic Diseases,* 1967, *20,* 435-456.

Syme, S. L. "Implications and Future Prospects." *Milbank Memorial Fund Quarterly,* 1967, *45* (Pt. 2), 175-180.

Syme, S. L. "Behavioral Factors Associated with the Etiology of Physical Disease: A Social Epidemiological Approach." *American Journal of Public Health,* 1974, *64,* 1043-1045.

Truett, J., Cornfield, J., and Kannel, W. "A Multivariate Analysis of the Risk of Coronary Heart Disease in Framingham." *Journal of Chronic Diseases,* 1974, *27,* 511-524.

Wells, J. A. "Social Support as a Buffer of Stressful Job Conditions." Unpublished doctoral dissertation, Duke University, 1979.

Winch, R. F., and Campbell, D. T. "Proof? No. Evidence? Yes. The Significance of Tests of Significance." *American Sociologist,* 1969, *4,* 140-143.

31

Person-Role Fit

John R. P. French, Jr.

The purpose of my paper is to refine and to qualify the findings on the main effects of job stress on individual strain. Dr. Kahn has already reported that the effects of organizational stresses on strain within the individual will vary depending upon the personality of the individual. I will focus on two additional conditioning variables: first, the goodness of fit between the environment and the person; and, second, the conditioning effects of social support.

First let me sketch very briefly a theory about person-environment fit, developed by French, Cobb, and Rodgers. One kind of fit between a man and his job environment is the degree to which his skills and abilities match the demands and requirements of the job. Another type of fit is the degree to which the needs of the man are supplied in his job environment; for example, the extent to which his need to utilize his best and highest abilities is satisfied by his current job. Our basic assumption is that both forms of misfit will cause job dissatisfaction, depression, physiological strains, and other symptoms of poor mental health. In order to be able to test this theory, we need to be able to measure quantitatively the goodness of fit between the man and the job. This we have done by asking the man to rate the quality of his job environment along a quantitative scale; for example, "the responsibility you have for the work of others." On the same scale, the person was then asked to rate "the responsibility you would *like to have* for the work of others." Then we derived a quantitative score of the goodness of fit, by subtracting the actual score for the job environment from the desired score on the same dimension of the job environment. A given individual might want more responsibility or less responsibility. Or there might be a perfect fit, with no discrepancy between what he has and what he wants. Figure 1 illustrates such a scale measuring the person-environment fit. The negative numbers represent a deficiency—the person wants more of the environmental variable than he has. The zero represents a perfect fit, and the positive numbers represent an excess. One hypothesis suggests that an increasing deficiency in supplies to meet a person's needs will lead to increasing strain, as shown in Curve A. According to this hypothesis, an excess of supplies to meet the need will make no difference. For example, a man who has completely satisfied his hunger will not be more satisfied with more food. The man will still show the same low level of strain as if he had a perfect fit. Another hypoth-

Reprinted from Alan McLean (Ed.), *Occupational Stress* (Springfield, Ill.: Thomas, 1974), pp. 71-79, with permission of the author and Charles C Thomas, Publisher.

Figure 1. Two Hypothetical P-E Fit Curves

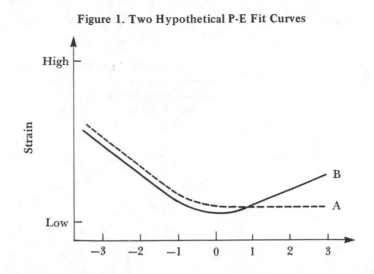

esis, shown in Curve B, assumes that an excess may also result in increased strain. This seems reasonable, for example, when we think about responsibility for other people. Too much responsibility may be more than a person can bear easily, whereas too little responsibility may mean that he has a low-level, uninteresting job. Both hypotheses seem reasonable, and we might expect Curve A for one type of environmental variable and Curve B for another type. In either case, our theory of person-environment fit should account for additional variance in mental health over and above the variance we can account for by the linear effects of job stresses and of personality variables.

Now let us look at some tests of these theories. I would like to report findings from two different studies, one conducted at Goddard Space Flight Center and the other at Kennedy Space Center. In both studies, we measured the actual state of the job environment along about a dozen different dimensions. Then we measured the desired state of the environment along those same dimensions. The measures of both the actual and the desired state were constructed from several questionnaire items. Thus, we could derive quantitative measures of the goodness of fit between the man and his job environment.

Figure 2 shows the results for a sample of managers, engineers, and scientists at Goddard Space Flight Center. We have plotted job satisfaction against person-environment fit, so we should expect the highest satisfaction at zero, where there is a perfect fit between what a man has in his job environment and what we wants.

Looking first at the curve for goodness of fit with respect to role ambiguity, we see that the curve is displaced to the right, indicating that most people want less role ambiguity than they actually have. Given this distribution, the curve shows the expected inverted "U" shape, with the highest satisfaction where there is a perfect match between the amount of role ambiguity experienced and the amount desired; for those who want either less role ambiguity or more, there is lower job satisfaction.

The measure of relations with subordinates deals primarily with quantity and quality of work they expect their superior to require from them. As we can see from the curve, there is generally good fit between the perceived expectations and the desired expectations. As predicted, job satisfaction is highest when the fit is perfect, and falls off with either a positive or a negative discrepancy.

The curve for goodness of fit with respect to the responsibility for persons shows

Figure 2. Data from 206 Men at Goddard Space Flight Center

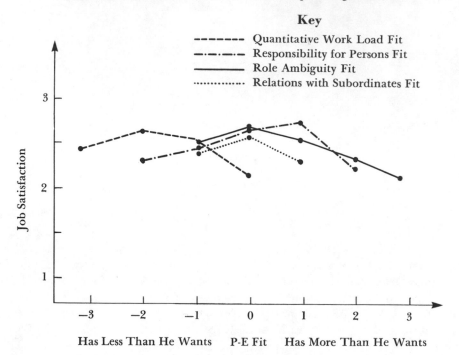

Key

------- Quantitative Work Load Fit
—·—·— Responsibility for Persons Fit
——— Role Ambiguity Fit
············ Relations with Subordinates Fit

Has Less Than He Wants   P-E Fit   Has More Than He Wants

Note: The Ns at the ends of the curves are typically from 4 to 13.

the generally expected shape, but the maximum satisfaction does not occur among men with a perfect fit, but instead among men who have slightly more responsibility for others than they would like to have. Other data show that this same group had the lowest level of cholesterol. Perhaps the stressful effects of a slight excess in responsibility for other people is offset by a better fit with respect to utilization of one's best abilities and participation in decision making.

Finally, Figure 2 shows that these men generally want more quantitative work load than they have, a rather surprising fact, since the reported levels of work load at Goddard are higher than in our national samples. Again, the curve shows the expected shape, but now there is a large displacement to the left. It is the eager beavers who show the highest job satisfaction. Perhaps the direction of causation is reversed here: high satisfaction with work causes a person to want more of it.

There were similar significant relations between job satisfaction and person-environment fit with respect to five other dimensions of the work environment: namely, participation, responsibility for things, qualitative work load, the utilization of abilities, and the opportunities for advancement. In sum, nine out of eleven dimensions of job stress showed significant relations between person-environment fit and job satisfaction.

The same dimensions of person-environment fit were correlated with a measure of job-related threat which probed the extent to which various kinds of job stress posed a threat to perceived health and well-being. The results were similar to the findings we have just reported for job satisfaction. For eight out of eleven dimensions, poor fit is associated with high job-related threat. Frequently, the relationship is curvilinear, conforming to one or the other of the theoretically predicted curves.

Now let us turn to the findings from Kennedy Space Center. In this study, we developed measures of person-environment fit with respect to six job stresses: role ambiguity, subjective work load, participation, responsibility for things, responsibility for people, and underload. We correlated these measures of goodness of fit with five measures of psychological strain, including job satisfaction, job-related threat, anxiety, work-related depression, and somatic depression. The two measures of depression were factors derived from the Zung scale for depression. Sixteen out of the thirty measures of curvilinear correlation were significant. When these same measures were administered six months later, there was a good replication of the findings that person-environment fit is significantly related to psychological strain.

Of the sixteen significant correlations between goodness of fit and psychological strain on the first questionnaire, twelve were linear and four were significantly curvilinear. These four are shown in Figure 3. Again, we notice that most men want less role ambi-

Figure 3. Data from 165 Men at Kennedy Space Center

Key

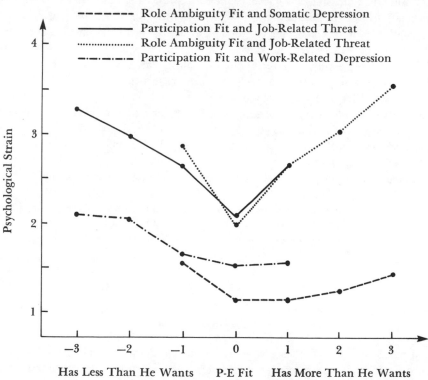

guity than they have, and we can now add that most men would like more participation than they have. As predicted, all four curves showed the lowest strain where person-environment fit is perfect. As in Figure 2, the number of cases at the extreme ends of the curves is quite small; nevertheless, there is a significant departure from a linear relation.

Our measures of person-environment fit are only rarely related to physiological measures, and then the correlations are quite low and inconsistent. However, we have found significant correlations with cholesterol, systolic blood pressure, and glucose. All of these physiological measures are related to person-environment fit in the expected direction.

We may summarize our findings on person-environment fit by saying that many dimensions of fit are related quite strongly and in the predicted direction to a variety of measures of psychological strain. Many of these relations between fit and psychological strain show the forms of curvilinearity predicted by the theory. Only a few of our measures of fit are related, but then quite weakly and in the predicted direction, to our measures of physiological strain. Our tests of the hypotheses tend to be weak because (1) we have too few cases where there is a strong discrepancy between what a person has and what he wants; (2) the measures of fit, like other measures of discrepancy scores, tend to be unreliable; (3) the measures are probably biased by wishful thinking and dissonance reduction; and (4) there are some unsolved problems of analysis. Considering the methodological difficulties, the empirical results we have obtained show about as strong support for our theory of person-environment fit as we could expect. An unequivocal test of the theory will require an improvement in methods.

Now let us look at the conditioning effects of social support on the relationship between job stress and individual strain. Our conceptions and our measures of good, supportive relationships are taken from the work of Rensis Likert and others at the Institute for Social Research. The measure on good relationships with the immediate supervisor included items on "the extent to which your superior is willing to listen to your problems," "the extent to which your superior has confidence in you and trusts you," "the extent to which you can trust your superior and have confidence in him." The items measuring relationships to the work group included "the extent to which persons in your work group are friendly and easy to approach," and "the extent to which persons in your work group are willing to listen to your problems," and "the degree of cooperation in the group." The measure of relations with subordinates included similar items, and also items on mutual expectations with regard to the quantity and quality of work.

Table 1 shows how the effect of role ambiguity on serum cortisol varies with rela-

**Table 1. The Effect of Relations with Subordinates on the Correlation
Between Role Ambiguity and Serum Cortisol**

Relations with Subordinates	r	$p <$	N
Poor	.35[a]	.01	60
Medium	.26	.05	57
Good	.06[a]	ns	76

[a]The difference between these two correlations is significant at $p < .05$.

tions with subordinates. For men who have poor relationships with their subordinates, there is a significant positive correlation between role ambiguity and cortisol; but for men who have good relations, there is no such correlation. This pattern of findings is not obtained when relations with one's immediate superior is used as a conditioning variable.

Table 2 shows that the effects of quantitative work load on several physiological variables vary depending on the quality of relationships with the superior, the work group, and subordinates. Diastolic blood pressure is related to work load, but only among those who have poor relationships with their immediate superiors. Serum glucose is related to work load, but again only among those who have poor relationships with their work groups. Relations with subordinates have even stronger conditioning effects on systolic blood pressure, on diastolic blood pressure, and on serum glucose. Thus, good

Table 2. The Effect of Relations with Others on the Correlation Between
Work Load and Physiological Strain

Relations with Strain	Quality of Relations		
	Poor	Medium	Good
Immediate Superior			
Diastolic blood pressure	.33[a]	−.06	.06
Work Group			
Serum glucose	.31[a]	.03	−.01
Subordinates			
Systolic blood pressure	.24	.22	−.09
Diastolic blood pressure	.31[a]	.19	−.13
Serum glucose	.36[a]	.06	.04

[a]$p < .01$. The correlations for those with poor relations are always significantly higher than the correlations for those with good relations at $p < .05$.

relations with others, especially with one's subordinates, serve as a buffer between the stress of quantitative work load and the physiological strains which may result. We do not obtain similar findings when we use other measures of work load or other measures of physiological strain. More surprising, supportive relations with others do not seem to condition the effects of job stress on psychological strain.

Table 3 shows that the quality of relations with one's superior does condition the

Table 3. The Effect of Relations with the Immediate Superior on the Correlation
Between Subjective Work Load and Number of Cigarettes Smoked[a]

Subjective Work Load Measure	Relations with Superior		Poor	Good
	Poor N = 24	Good N = 28	$p <$	
Number per week of:				
Outgoing phone calls	.36	−.26	.025	
Incoming phone calls	.32	−.06	.10	
Office visits	.06	−.26	ns	
Self-initiated meetings	.30	−.34	.025	
Other-initiated meetings	.09	−.44[b]	.05	
Total activities	.36	−.17	.05	

[a]Smokers only.

[b]$p < .05$ (two-tailed).

effects of work load on smoking. For half a dozen different measures of work load, such as number of phone calls, number of office visits, and number of meetings, there is a positive correlation between work load and smoking among those men who have poor relations with their superior, whereas there is a negative correlation among those men who have good relations with their superior. When we use relationships with the work group or with subordinates as the conditioning variable, we find similar but weaker relations.

Finally, we find that the amount of stress reported coming from other parts of the organization—for example, the amount of stress coming from other branches—is positively related to pulse rate, but again only in those men who have poor relations with their subordinates. The relations with one's superior and with one's work group have similar conditioning effects on the effect of stress from other parts of the organization on pulse rate. In all cases, good relationships act as a buffer between stress and strain.

To summarize, in many cases we have found that the effect of job stresses on individual strain is eliminated by the buffering effect of good supportive relations with one's superior, one's work group, and one's subordinates. However, in many other cases, especially when we are dealing with psychological strain, we do not find such buffering effects. Additional analyses of the effect of supportive relationships at Kennedy Space Center are now in progress, and it is hoped that they may further clarify some of these relationships. However, it will probably be necessary to do additional studies in which we examine in more detail the *processes* by which supportive relationships prevent strain. Perhaps social support reduces the objective environmental stresses, or perhaps it only affects the perceived stresses, or perhaps it enables the person to cope more effectively with stresses which are there. These and other hypotheses require further research.

Now I would like to end by stating six general conclusions which I think can be drawn from the research reported by Dr. Kahn, Dr. Cobb, and myself.

1. Both our theoretical thinking and our empirical findings have led us to develop more differentiated concepts and measures for describing role stress. We have progressed, for example, from talking about a fairly global role conflict to distinguishing between conflict and overload; then we distinguished between quantitative and qualitative overload. Next we added responsibility for persons and responsibility for things, as more specialized aspects of the work load. Then we added underload as an additional role stress discovered at NASA. To date we have examined the effects of fourteen objectively measured job stresses and twenty subjectively measured job stresses.

2. As we have become more differentiated in our thinking about job stress, we have also improved the reliability and validity of our measures, not only by developing different measures for the different stresses but also by improving the measures by adding items, by eliminating unsatisfactory items, by decreasing response biases, and so forth.

3. These more differentiated and improved measures have paid off; they have yielded new findings which were previously masked. In general, our findings support the specificity hypothesis that specific kinds of job stress interacting with specific personality characteristics result in specific strains in the person, including psychological strains, physiological strains, and psychosomatic diseases.

4. The simple main effects of various role stresses have been further qualified by discovering many conditioning variables which permit us to explain more of the variance in strain. In addition to the conditioning effects of personality variables we have also found that the goodness of fit between the characteristics of the person and the characteristics of his job will influence the effects of job stresses. Finally, we are beginning to find that supportive relations with other people can often act as an effective buffer between job stress and strain, particularly physiological strain, within the person.

5. As our work has progressed, we have added new measures of psychological strains, of physiological strains, and of disease entities. These new measures have revealed ever more ubiquitous consequences of job stresses.

6. As we develop more refined and more empirically validated knowledge of the nature of role stresses and their effects, we will be better able to design intervention programs to prevent their undesired effects on mental and physical health. Currently we are in the middle of our first study of the feasibility of reducing the risk of coronary heart disease by altering role stresses. We hope that the kind of findings presented here can be applied in additional experiments on the prevention of strain.

32

Physiologic Changes in Men Whose Jobs Were Abolished

Sidney Cobb

This study was dedicated to the notion that one of the best ways to increase our understanding of human beings is to observe them through a period of stress. Likewise, one of
the best ways to evaluate the effect of potential social stressors is to look at the changes
that take place over time in relation to these stresses. There have of course been a great
many such studies done in the relative unreality of the laboratory. Fortunately, it is
agreed between experimenter and subject that laboratory experiments are always designed to have happy endings. Therefore, the maximum stress that one can induce in such
situations is limited. There are some studies of combat situations in which before, during,
and after data have been collected. Likewise, there are longitudinal studies of bereave-
ment, but most of these are limited to during and after. Beyond this, longitudinal studies
of the effects of social stress are quite rare. My colleagues and I considered it a real privi-
lege to be allowed to collect data on members of the United Automobile Workers Union
who were employed in plants about to be closed.

The men studied came from two companies that closed at the end of 1965 and of
1966, respectively, and from four companies for which there was no threat of termination. Company A was a paint plant in an urban area, and Company B was a plant manufacturing lightweight display fixtures in a small town. For comparison, men under no
threat of termination were sampled from the rolls of two urban and two small-town companies. The terminees were visited during the phase of anticipation, shortly after the closing, and six months, twelve months, and twenty-four months later. At each visit to the
man's home, a standardized set of physiological, psychological, social, and economic data
were collected by public health nurses. The controls were visited at similar intervals except that very few were followed beyond twelve months.

The men in the study were all blue-collar workers who had on the average completed tenth grade in school and were earning about three dollars an hour and had a mean
seniority of twenty years. They ranged in age from 35 to 62, with a mean of 49, and all
were married. Just over 10 percent of the total were black.

At each of the appointed times, blood and urine specimens were taken for analysis

Reprinted with permission from *Journal of Psychosomatic Research*, 1974, *17*,
1-14. Copyright 1974 Pergamon Press, Ltd.

in the laboratory. The specimens were iced immediately and returned to the laboratory within seven hours. On arrival in the laboratory, the blood specimens were centrifuged and the serum was removed and frozen in aliquots. The urines were obtained over a measured period of not less than ninety minutes. They were collected in acidified bottles and were also iced immediately. On return to the laboratory, the specimens were measured and aliquots were frozen. Of the various determinations made on these specimens, we will be concerned with the following.

Norepinephrine was determined fluorimetrically by a method slightly modified from that of von Euler and Lishajko (1961). The twenty-four recoveries average 96±7 percent; the test-retest correlation on sixteen duplicate determinations was .88; and fifty-five repeat determinations on four specimens suggested that 95 percent of repeat determinations would lie within ± 12 percent of the true value.

Creatinine, uric acid, and urea nitrogen were determined in both blood and urine in a Technicon auto-analyzer, using standard methods that gave thoroughly satisfactory reliability. Serum cholesterol was also determined in the auto-analyzer, using Technicon method N-24a.

Three measures in the psychological area are relevant. All are used as control or moderating variables. The first is a measure which we have presumed to call "psychological defense." This identified a man as well defended if he was in the extreme 12 percent of any of the following measures: (1) The rigid end of CPI Flexibility-Rigidity scale of Gough (1964); (2) The high end of the Need for Approval scale of Crowne and Marlowe (1964); (3) The high end of the Subtle Ego Resilience scale of Block (1965); (4) The oral end of the orality scale of Lazare, Klerman, and Armor (1966). (The three suggestibility items which did not hang together with the rest of the scale on factor analysis were deleted.) This provided an approximately equal division of the population into those with no defenses and those with one or more of the listed defenses. Only about 10 percent reported more than one defense, which is not much in excess of the random expectation. The justification for calling these defenses is that, at the extreme, each of these scales represents a retreat from the more common responses to real-life situations, whether this be extreme rigidity, extreme approval-seeking behavior, or extreme passive dependency. The ego resilience measure by its very nature implies competent psychological defense: For example, many of the items involve freedom from anxiety and guilt.

The second measure of concern was an ad hoc measure of social support. When the study was designed, we had a general interest in the issue, but we had not realized how important social support would turn out to be. Therefore, the measure had to be developed out of the available items that had face validity for the support area. The only test of the validity of this measure is provided by its success in correctly predicting that the men from plant B, who were living in the rural area, were more supported than those from plant A in the urban area.

The measure was made up of thirteen items covering the following components of supportive relationships: (1) the individual's perception of wife, friends, and relatives as supportive or unsupportive (eight items); (2) his reported frequency of activity outside the home with his wife, with friends, and with relatives (three items); (3) his perceived opportunity for engaging in social activities which are satisfying and which allow him to talk about his problems (two items). The men in the lowest population tertile were designated the unsupported or, more appropriately, the inadequately supported versus the men in the upper two thirds of the distribution, who may be considered well supported.

The third measure of concern is the measure of life events. This was collected in two ways. First, of course, detailed data were collected about employment changes. Then a subset of the items from the Social Readjustment Rating Questionnaire (Rahe, 1969) was used at the twelve-month visit to elicit changes in the family and social area. Only the items describing more severe events, such as deaths or serious illness in the family, were included, and personal illness and employment-related problems were excluded in order to avoid duplication. Since no predictive advantage accrued from using the weights assigned by Rahe and his colleagues, the events were merely counted. A median split for the terminees came between three and four events occurring during the year following termination. Less than 12 percent of the controls experienced four or more of these events.

At this point I would like to walk you through the average experience of the one hundred men whose jobs were abolished, so that you will have a picture of the nature of the stress involved. In the first place, it was obviously impossible to visit these men before they learned of the impending shutdown. We were, therefore, forced to settle for our first data collection during the phase of *anticipation.* As you can see from Figure 1, this came,

Figure 1. The Basic Design of the Longitudinal Study of Men Losing Their Jobs and the Schedule of Home Interviews by Public Health Nurses

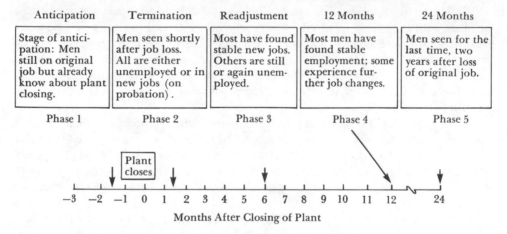

Anticipation	Termination	Readjustment	12 Months	24 Months
Stage of anticipation: Men still on original job but already know about plant closing.	Men seen shortly after job loss. All are either unemployed or in new jobs (on probation).	Most have found stable new jobs. Others are still or again unemployed.	Most men have found stable employment; some experience further job changes.	Men seen for the last time, two years after loss of original job.
Phase 1	Phase 2	Phase 3	Phase 4	Phase 5

Months After Closing of Plant

on the average, about six weeks before the closing. At this time the men were still on their old jobs but already knew that the plant would shortly be closed. Visits during the phase of *termination* average about six weeks after the closing. At this time the men were either unemployed or in the probationary period on a new job. At phase 3, *readjustment,* about six months after the closing, the men were mostly on new jobs in which they were to remain. Others were still unemployed, and a few had lost the first new job and were again unemployed. Phase 4 is twelve months after the closing; and phase 5 is twenty-four months post termination. There were relatively few job changes in the second year.

In a field situation like this, one is not able to produce a complete data set. There are always some people who are unable or unwilling to participate at any given time. In doing the analysis, we are then plagued by missing data, so means from one period to the next are not necessarily on the identical people. Therefore, whenever the pattern of changes over time is not obviously highly significant, I have checked the change scores to make sure that change from one time period to another in those people observed on both occasions is also statistically significant.

With regard to comparisons between the one hundred terminees and the seventy-four controls, it is important to note that with respect to forty-three variables, the two groups were found to be homogeneous. However, the terminees were about two years younger, slightly less well educated, and had less seniority and lower pay than the controls. Furthermore, the controls had substantially more health complaints, which suggests that some of the controls joined the study because they had a health problem about which they were concerned.

Before starting the analyses of any physiologic variable, we always checked to see that the controls did not show a sequence effect, as did, for example, our measure of anxiety. At each successive visit, the mean anxiety level of the controls was slightly lower. Only with regard to serum creatinine and urinary norepinephrine was there a suggestion of such an effect. Since the effects were small and statistically insignificant, it was decided to neglect them.

Second, we regularly looked for a systematic season variation. This was a serious problem with regard to certain reports of illness; but among the physiologic variables, only cholesterol showed a suggestion of seasonal variation. Since the pattern was not fully self-consistent nor quite the same as that reported in the literature, and since the pattern could not possibly account for the findings in the terminees, it was decided to neglect the effect in the further analysis of this variable.

The statistical analysis compared the mean value for the terminees at any particular phase with the overall mean value for the controls. One-tailed t tests were used whenever the results were in the hypothesized direction. Whenever differences were of borderline significance, the additional tests were applied to reassure us that we had not too readily accepted a chance finding. This means that we have very commonly examined the significance of the between-phase change scores for those men who provided specimens on both occasions.

In examining the results, it is convenient to begin with norepinephrine. First off, it was necessary to look for extraneous sources of variance. Six specimens on three men were rejected on the basis of drugs that would influence the results. Alcohol, tobacco, and extreme values of creatinine clearance did not introduce enough noise to justify rejecting additional specimens. The effect of caffeine-containing beverages will be discussed below.

All the specimens were collected between 10:00 A.M. and 10:00 P.M. There was a slight tendency for afternoon specimens to average higher than late-morning or early-evening specimens, but the differences were not significant and there was not any serious confounding of time of day with the variables of interest.

After thus clearing the decks, we felt prepared to go ahead with the analysis. Multiple specimens were analyzed on thirty-nine of the one hundred terminees, but there were some specimens missing at every phase except at the twenty-four-month visit. At that twenty-four-month visit, an additional set of specimens were analyzed to increase the power of the test of the hypothesis that by that time the terminees would have returned to normal. The mean for the added set was not significantly different from the mean for those who had several specimens analyzed. In fact, it was slightly higher. Finally, forty-nine specimens on twenty-three of the seventy-four controls were available for analysis. The subsetting for norepinephrine was not entirely random. Rather, there was a bias in favor of the more cooperative, who provided us with the most complete set of specimens.

Figure 2 shows that the mean rate of norepinephrine excretion was significantly elevated, for those whose jobs were abolished, before termination and for twelve months afterward. One star at the top of a column means that it is significantly different from the controls ($p < .05$), and a dagger indicates higher degrees of significance. By twenty-four months after termination, the mean rate had returned well within the expected range of the controls. Furthermore, the change scores from each of the earlier phases to twenty-four months are significantly different from a mean of zero.

Figure 2. Norepinephrine Excretion Rate in Gamma/Min by Phase of the Study

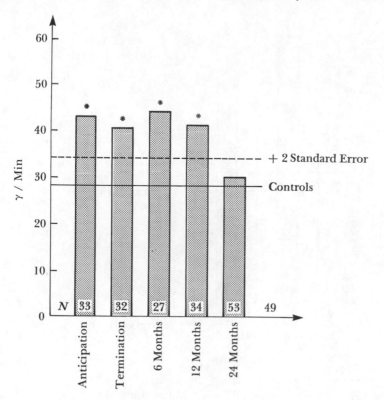

Since the interviews focused on the consequences of the termination, it is possible that some anamnestic response contributed to the long continued elevation. However, the nurses doing the interviews insisted that the men were not yet back to normal by twelve months.

In Figure 3 the phases of anticipation and termination have been collapsed, as have the six- and twelve-month visits. This provides approximately twice the number of observations and thus permits subdivision by relevant characteristics. Here it can be seen that the closing produced more norepinephrine in the urban environment than in the rural environment. At first, this gave some concern lest the heterogeneity should logically forbid collapsing across the companies. As will be seen later, much of the difference between the two companies can be explained by other variables of interest, and clearly by two years after the termination the two means were almost identical. For the earlier and the later phases of the study, the difference between companies is significant, but by twenty-four months the means for the two companies are both very similar to each other and to the controls. The change scores to twenty-four months are significantly different from a mean of zero for both companies.

It has been repeatedly pointed out that caffeine-containing beverages increase the excretion of catecholamines. Figure 4 is interesting because it indicates very clearly that there is an interaction effect between environmental stress and coffee (and other caffeine-containing beverages) on norepinephrine excretion. Clearly, both for the controls and for the terminees at twenty-four months, coffee makes no difference, but for the period of anticipation plus termination there is a highly significant difference ($p < .01$), and for six plus twelve months later there is a modest difference that is not statistically significant.

Figure 3. Norepinephrine Excretion Rate in Gamma/Min by Phase and Company Location

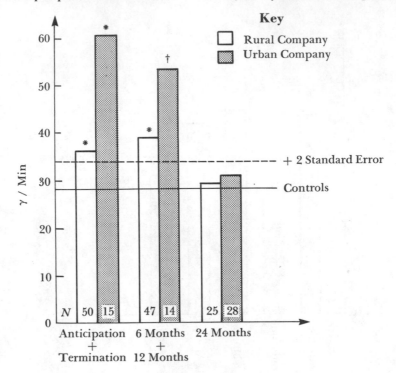

Figure 4. Norepinephrine Excretion Rate in Gamma/Min by Phase and by Whether or Not Coffee or Another Caffeine-Containing Beverage Was Taken in the Last Three Hours

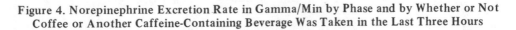

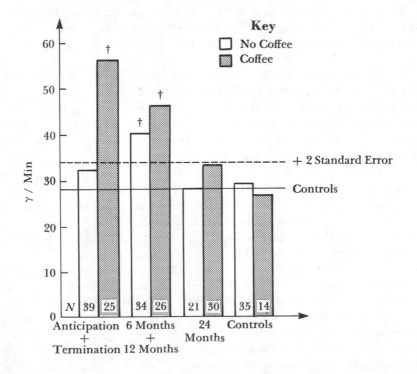

These data are interesting in a number of ways. First, when the coffee effect was taken out, there remained little in the way of a tobacco effect. This was because smoking and drinking coffee were strongly associated. Second, there was no coffee effect at all among the controls. Furthermore, this finding was replicated in that, at twenty-four months after termination, there was no effect of coffee among the terminees. This clearly suggests that when a man is relaxed at home, coffee does not raise his norepinephrine output. However, it would seem that when he is uncertain about the future as during the phases of anticipation and termination, coffee really makes a difference in his norepinephrine output.

This finding is reminiscent of Henry's observation on hypertension in mice (Henry and Cassel, 1969). Apparently, isolated mice had little or no rise in blood pressure when given coffee rather than water, while those mice boxed in groups of eight, so they had the opportunity to fight, had significantly greater rises if they were on coffee. When we put these findings together, we come to the conclusion drawn by some clinicians long ago that in overly aroused individuals it is wise to withdraw coffee.

At this point perhaps I should add a caveat to the effect that, though this interpretation seems obvious, there is at least one other possibility to be considered. That is the possibility that one kind of person drinks coffee under stress and has his norepinephrine output increased, while another kind of person drinks coffee primarily when relaxed and has no change in his output. This possibility cannot be ruled out because there were only four cases who drank coffee in the early phases and at twenty-four months. In all of these there was a drop from the early phase to twenty-four months (mean drop = 15 γ/min). This, of course, supports the original explanation.

In comparing our findings of interaction of coffee with stress to the reports of others that coffee simply raises the catecholamine output, there emerges a useful lesson. It is reasonable to assume that none of the experimental subjects in the earlier studies were fully relaxed but rather were experiencing the novelty effect of the laboratory situation. They were therefore in mildly stressful situations, and the effect was therefore detected. Perhaps we should do more of our research on people who are relaxing at home.

In Figure 5 is presented the effect of the number of life changes during the twelve months following termination. As indicated previously, most of the changes involved employment, as there were relatively few deaths of friends or relatives and few serious economic changes. From the figure it is clear that those with many (four or more) life changes had significantly higher norepinephrine outputs than did those with fewer life changes during the early phases of the study. However, by twenty-four months the two groups are almost identical. Therefore, it would seem not to be a difference between the men in the two groups but rather the difference between their experiences that accounts for the between-group variation.

It is particularly interesting that those who had the most life changes had elevated excretion rates before most of these changes had taken place. This suggests that those who had the worst time settling into new jobs anticipated their difficulty. In thinking about this, we hypothesized that the black men would probably anticipate greater difficulty than the white men. Unfortunately, the number of black men available for this analysis was too small (5) for them to be significantly different from the whites, even though their mean for the period of anticipation went to 73 γ/min compared to a mean of only 40 γ/min for the white men.

Figure 6 represents the effect of "psychological defense." As might be expected, strong psychological defenses helped significantly to keep the norepinephrine level low during anticipation and termination. But later on, when the stresses were of the nature of

Figure 5. Norepinephrine Excretion Rate in Gamma/Min by Phase and by
Number of Life Changes

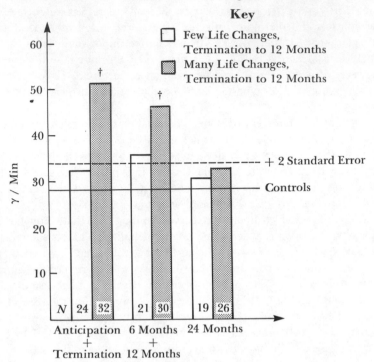

Figure 6. Norepinephrine Excretion Rate in Gamma/Min by Phase and
Level of Psychological Defense

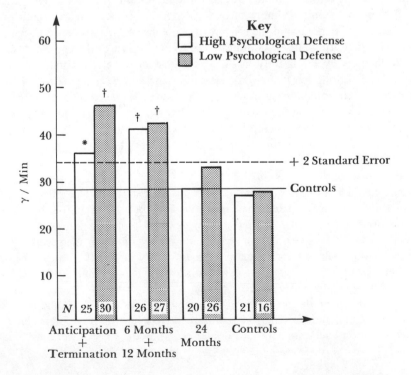

work overload and requirement for adaptation to a new environment, the defenses were not so useful. Again it is of importance to note that among the controls and when the stress was over for the terminees at twenty-four months, "psychological defense" did not make any difference.

We have seen that it is feasible, practical, and heuristically useful to measure norepinephrine output during the period of an interview. We have noted the effects of life change, of "psychological defense," and of coffee and have noted an urban-rural difference. The urban terminees differed from the rural counterparts in that a proportion of them were black, they drank more coffee, and experienced more life changes. When one adjusts for all three of these factors, most of the difference between the companies disappears. In retrospect, we can therefore feel comfortable about having combined the data from the two companies. An ideal analysis of a data set like this one should include a multivariate approach. Since the numbers are small and since the further collapse of the phases of the study is not logically justified, a full multivariate analysis is not possible. However, it is relevant to note that among the three major explanatory variables—number of life stresses, defenses, and coffee—there is almost complete independence. It is therefore reasonable to assume that the several effects observed are not the result of overlap between variables.

Having reviewed the findings on norepinephrine excretion in considerable detail, it is possible to present the findings on the other variables rather more rapidly. The same standards of analysis prevailed. The principal difference is that the following determinations were made on all specimens obtained, not just on a subset as was necessary for norepinephrine.

Serum creatinine is the next variable. The mean level shows a substantial peak during the period of readjustment, with a significant rise from phase 2 to 3 and a significant drop from phase 3 to 4. In contrast to norepinephrine excretion, the peak is significantly higher for the rural than for the urban residents, but life events and social support do not have significant control effects. In Figure 7 are shown the differences by phase between those with one or more of the measured psychological defenses as opposed to those with no defenses. This might be phrased as a cost of psychological defense if modest elevations of serum creatinine can be thought of as detrimental. Since this was a serendipitous finding, two-tailed t tests have been applied.

There are two ways that the serum level of creatinine might be raised. First, there might be a reduced excretion rate; and, second, there might be increased production. A look at the data on the rate of excretion of creatinine suggests that the latter is the case. Like the serum level, the excretion rate goes up during the phase of readjustment and again more strikingly for those who are well defended than for those who are undefended. Though the pattern is the same, the variances are large, so the changes are not significant. However, this consistency gives the whole creatinine picture rather more strength. The findings can hardly be accidental, though their meaning is not readily apparent. The elevation does not seem to be related to the number of life events during the period, so it must be related to some more subtle stress that is characteristic of the phase of readjustment. Creatinine would seem to be an interesting variable to pursue.

The effects with regard to serum uric acid are depicted in Figure 8. There is an elevation during the phase of anticipation, and this is more true for those with little social support than for those who are adequately supported. There is a borderline significant tendency for the mean level across all terminees to remain elevated through the twelve-month visit. This is again more striking for those low on social support. This effect of social support is particularly noticeable in examining the drop from phase 1 to 5 or the drop from phase 4 to 5. In each instance the drop is very much larger for those who are unsupported.

Figure 7. Serum Creatinine in mg/100 ml by Phase and Level of Psychological Defense

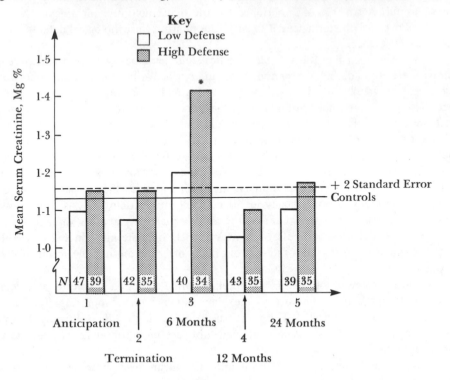

Figure 8. Serum Uric Acid in mg/100 ml by Phase and Level of Social Support

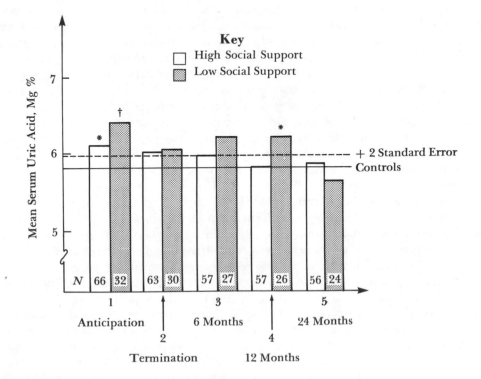

In a preliminary report Kasl and Cobb (1968) called attention to the fact that the key issue here seemed to be reemployment, as levels came down dramatically with reemployment. This finding is confirmed in the final analysis. By comparison, the effect of the number of life events in the year following termination is trivial. This suggests that there is some special characteristic of the anticipation of an experience of unemployment that raises the serum uric acid. Finally, psychological defenses are not protective; rather, there is an insignificant tendency for the levels to be higher in the well defended.

Asking the overproduction versus underexcretion question again, the data suggest a different answer from that for creatinine because when the excretion rates are going up the serum values are coming down. The conclusion that the effects are due to changes in the excretion rate is far from sure, but results are sufficiently suggestive to warrant further investigation.

The final variable for consideration is serum cholesterol. The relevant data are presented in Figure 9. Here the style of presentation is different for two reasons. First,

Figure 9. Serum Cholesterol in mg/100 ml by Phase and Employment Status and Level of Social Support

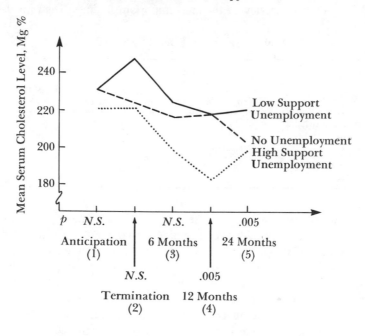

cholesterol is not as responsive a variable as the others with which we have been dealing; and, second, the between-persons variance is substantially larger than the within-persons variances. I am therefore presenting a more complex analysis. In this analysis the principal statistical testing is done on the change scores rather than on a comparison of the means for the terminees with the means for the controls. The first finding is that on an overall basis there is a significant drop in cholesterol level from the early visits, anticipation plus termination, to the later visits, twelve and twenty-four months after the closing. This is not a methodological artifact because no such trend is observed in the control data. Looking at the figure, we see three lines. The broken line in the middle represents the cholesterol changes for those who had little or no unemployment. For these men who experience rather less stress as a result of the termination, there is a significant downward trend

($p < .005$) and a drop from beginning to end of about 25 mg%. Turning to those who experienced unemployment but were well supported, the dotted line, we find a similar significant downward trend. However, this trend line contains a dip at twelve months which is only in part accounted for by those who are persistently unemployed. Furthermore, this dip is characteristic of both urban and rural members of this group.

Turning to those who had little support and unemployment, we see that there is no trend from beginning to end of the study and a small peak at the time of termination. This peak involves a mean within-persons rise of 30 mg% from anticipation to unemployment and a mean within-persons drop of 24 mg% from unemployment to employment approximately six months later. Both of these changes are significant ($p < .005$).

In looking over this set of data, one notes that the values are rather low; so one wishes that the observations could have been extended both further backward and further forward in time, so that the patterns could be better interpreted. One thing can be said with some certainty. The differences in pattern between those who were supported and those who were not are striking. If ultimate relative risk of coronary heart disease is related to the area between the curves, those who were well supported may live longer than those who were not.

Table 1 is a quick overview of the most important findings. The variables are listed

Table 1. Summary Effects by Variable

| | Effects in Controls | | Effects in Terminees | | |
	Sequence	Season	Phases	Psychol. Defense	Social Support
Norepinephrine excretion	–	–	1-4	+	–
Serum creatinine	±	–	3	+	–
Serum uric acid	–	–	1-2	–	+
Serum cholesterol	–	±	2	–	+
Serum urea nitrogen	–	–	0	–	–

in the order in which they have been presented. On the last line is a new variable, serum urea nitrogen. This has been added as a reminder that there are variables that do not respond to this kind of stress. The first two columns of the table are reminders that the controls were checked for sequence effects and for seasonal variation. In no instance were the effects important enough to warrant corrections.

With regard to norepinephrine, we noted that levels continued elevated through phase 4, twelve months after termination; that there was a close response relationship to number of life events; that there is an interaction of stress and coffee; and that strong psychological defenses, but not high social support, moderated the effects.

Serum creatinine was elevated only during the phase of readjustment, and then only among those with few defenses. A similar but not significant elevant of creatinine excretion rate was noted, suggesting that overproduction of creatinine was taking place. Uric acid presents another pattern—that is, elevation in the early phases, perhaps extending on to twelve months, especially in those who receive little social support. Here underexcretion rather than overproduction seemed to be the mechanism. Similarly, cholesterol levels drop from beginning to end of the study in those who are well supported but not in those with little social support. It is surely not clear why some variables are moderated by psychological defense and others by social support. This is an area that has only recently come to attention, and it is one that surely will require mapping before we start doing much in the way of interpretation. As a first thought, it would seem possible that different variables respond to different stimuli and are therefore moderated differently. Certainly there is no reason to believe that job termination is a unitary stress. Rather, it must contain components of future ambiguity; episodes of both work underload and work overload; and changes in responsibility, self-actualization, and autonomy. In another study such dimensions should be measured.

Finally, as sort of a savory, I would like to mention two other findings. There were six of the one hundred who resigned their jobs early. These men are interesting because they had high stable uric acid levels, averaging 7.1 mg%. The fact that the level remained high in this group instead of dropping off after the stressful period was over suggests that the pattern of causation might be the other way from that which we have been considering. Specifically, it suggests that those who have predetermined high levels may respond to a threatening situation more promptly and perhaps more vigorously than their fellows. Perhaps this is part of the reason why we find high levels of uric acid in executives.

Similarly, it turns out that those who had high levels of norepinephrine excretion during the phase of anticipation had significantly shorter periods of initial unemployment. This effect is seen in Table 2.

Table 2. The Effect of Norepinephrine Excretion Rate During Anticipation on the Subsequent Length of Initial Unemployment, for Those Who Did Not Drink Coffee

Norepinephrine γ/min Phase 1	Initial Unemployment (in weeks)			
	< 4	4-12	13+	Total
< 15			2	2
15-29	1	4	3	8
30-49	4	3		7
50+	2	1		3
Total	7	8	5	20

$\gamma = -.84, p < .01.$

The reason I bring in these last two almost trivial findings is that I want to remind you that physiological variables may modify or predict behavior as well as be caused by stressful events in the social environment.

In summary, it has been found that there are meaningful changes in norepinephrine excretion and in serum creatinine, serum uric acid, and serum cholesterol associated with the stress of job termination. No such changes took place with regard to serum urea nitrogen. The fact that two variables were moderated by psychological defense and two by social support raises some interesting questions for future research. The finding that stress and coffee interact in raising the excretion rate of norepinephrine is a useful reminder that for some purposes studies done at home have advantages over studies done in the laboratory. Finally, the observation that norepinephrine and uric acid elevations are associated with specific behaviors reminds us that the relationships in this field are complex.

References

Block, J. *The Challenge of Response Sets.* New York: Appleton-Century-Crofts, 1965.
Crowne, D. P., and Marlowe, D. *The Approval Motive.* New York: Wiley, 1964.

Gough, H. C. *California Psychological Inventory Manual.* Palo Alto, Calif.: Consulting Psychologists Press, 1964.

Henry, J. P., and Cassel, J. C. "Psychosocial Factors in Essential Hypertension: Recent Epidemiologic and Animal Experimental Evidence." *American Journal of Epidemiology,* 1969, *90,* 171-200.

Kasl, S. V., and Cobb, S. "Changes in Serum Uric Acid and Cholesterol Levels in Men Undergoing Job Loss." *Journal of the American Medical Association,* 1968, *206,* 1500-1507.

Lazare, A., Klerman, G. L., and Armor, D. J. "Oral, Obsessive and Hysterical Personality Patterns." *Archives of General Psychiatry,* 1966, *14,* 624-630.

Medical News. "Coffee + Crowds = Stress." *Journal of the American Medical Association,* 1970, *212,* 979, 982.

Rahe, R. H. "Multi-cultural Correlations of Life Change Scaling: America, Japan, Denmark and Sweden." *Journal of Psychosomatic Research,* 1969, *13,* 191-195.

von Euler, U. S., and Lishajko, F. "Improved Technique for the Fluorimetric Estimation of Catecholamines." *Acta Physiologica Scandinavica,* 1961, *51,* 348-355.

PART VIII

Conflict and Change

Although few theories are explicit about the relatedness of conflict and change, they are necessarily related. It is almost axiomatic that every change in an organization (or a multi-organizational set) involves some conflict, and most organizational conflicts involve issues of change or defense against change. Conflict and change can be defined independently of each other, but organizational life brings them inevitably together.

Katz and Kahn (1978, p. 613) define conflict as the direct interactive behavior of two or more parties (persons, groups, organizations, nations) such that "the actions of one tend to prevent or compel some outcome against the resistance of the other." The "outcome" may be either an altered state of affairs or the maintenance of the previous state. In the former case, change has occurred despite conflict to prevent it or, as the more familiar phrase puts it, despite resistance to change. The latter case may be described as an unsuccessful change attempt or a successful resistance, depending on the narrator's frame of reference; in fact, it is both. One can, of course, readily call to mind organizational conflicts in which both parties want change but disagree about its nature, extent, or means. When neither party wants change, however, conflict—although logically possible—seems quite unlikely.

The assertion that every attempt at organizational change involves resistance is perhaps less than obvious, but it is derived from the essential nature of human organizations. Organizations are characterized by orderly, recurring patterns of behavior; an array of people whose behavior shows no such interdependent patterning and recurrence we call unorganized. These persisting behavior patterns imply a quality of organizational inertia; organizations tend to keep on doing what they are doing. Were there no such inertial tendency, every random trivial event, internal or external, would alter the organizational structure or course and change the pattern; the defining properties of order and recurrence would never be attained. The resistance of organizations to change can be wise or foolish, constructive or destructive, peaceful or violent. The point is that some resistance is inherent, and the forms of that resistance are often conflictful.

Perhaps the theoretical statement that comes nearest to integrating conflict and change is that of Dahrendorf (1959). Dahrendorf criticizes Parsons and other "structural-functional" sociologists for neglecting conflict and change and for making only consensual or Utopian assumptions about human organizations and societies. He sums up their point of view in terms of four assumptions:

1. Every society is a relatively persistent stable structure of elements.
2. Every society is a well-integrated structure of elements.

3. Every element has a function; that is, it contributes to the maintenance of the system.
4. Every functioning structure is based on a consensus of values.

Against these he poses the opposite assumptions of a conflict model:

1. Change is ubiquitous.
2. Social conflict is ubiquitous.
3. Every element contributes to disintegration and change.
4. Every society is based on coercion.

Dahrendorf's emphasis is on the conflict model. Ours is on the complementarity of the two sets of assumptions. Both state truths about human organizations and their characteristic pattern of persistence and change. Neither is complete without the other.

Admittedly, the state of theory is less than ideal when two seemingly incompatible sets of assumptions are necessary to comprehend the observed phenomena. Physicists have endured a more celebrated and sophisticated paradox of this type, however, and have chosen to accept the seeming incompatibility until they develop a single theory that resolves it. In using both the corpuscular and the wave theories for explaining the propagation of light, they remain truer to their data and include more of them than would otherwise be possible.

So it is with the two sets of assumptions we have cited. Organizations are persistent and stable in significant degree, or they would not *be* organizations; and yet they do change, always and everywhere. Those that attempt to refuse all change suffer the greatest change of all; they do not endure. Every organization consists of interdependent elements and subsystems, each with its own function; yet each has distinctive interests and perceptions, and therefore distinctive preferred states for the organizations as a whole. An organization exists and functions as a whole, and thus expresses a kind of consensual agreement, but it is an agreement born of compromise, bargaining, and the exercise of power. To the extent that power implies coercion, potential or actual, organizations are coercive.

The six articles included in this section do not resolve the theoretical problems of conflict and change, but they emphasize the relatedness of these two domains and they increase our knowledge of both.

The first three articles (by *Bernardin* and *Alvares; Bigoness;* and *Lind* and his associates) can be thought of as attacking a series of increasingly complex questions about organizational conflict. *Bernardin* and *Alvares* are concerned with modes of conflict resolution within organizations. They concentrate on three such modes, all of them involving only the two parties to the conflict: *forcing, compromise,* and *confrontation. Bigoness* is not concerned with two-party modes of conflict resolution. He tends to classify all of them as bargaining, and his interests are concentrated on the effects of different forms of third-party intervention: *mediation, voluntary arbitration,* and *compulsory arbitration. Lind* and his colleagues concentrate on a special category of compulsory arbitration, the process of *legal adjudication,* in which the formalities of the court take control of the conflict and its resolution.

Bowers, Pasmore, and *Bragg* and *Andrews* are interested in organizational change and the means of achieving it. None of them deals explicitly with conflict and resistance to change; in evaluating the success or failure of change attempts, they do not differentiate the components of opposition. All of them, however, muster experimental evidence for change, and two of them (*Bowers* and *Pasmore*) offer that rarest of organizational information: comparative data on different approaches to creating change. Between them, they cover seven of the best known of such approaches: *survey feedback, interpersonal process consultation, task process consultation, "laboratory" training, "data handback," sociotechnical intervention,* and *job redesign.* Let us consider all six articles more closely and more critically.

The basic data with which *Bernardin* and *Alvares* work consist of responses to four fixed-alternative questions. Each question poses a hypothetical situation of role conflict, in which a foreman's own supervisor and one of his subordinates make directly contradictory and incompatible demands on him. The fixed alternatives consist of three "strategies," corresponding to the three modes of forcing, compromise, and confrontation. The respondents included general foremen, foremen, and nonsupervisory workers in a single manufacturing company.

The main response pattern is hierarchical, with rank-and-file employees most in favor of confrontation (in which all parties convene to work out their differences directly) and least in favor of forcing; the tendency is reversed among second-level supervisors; and the foremen (once again) are in the middle. These discrepant preferences are not equally characteristic of all triads (worker, foreman who supervises that worker, and general foreman who supervises that foreman). Moreover, the fewer the discrepancies about how conflicts should be resolved, the higher the effectiveness rating of the foreman by the workers.

It is not clear whether responses to these four hypothetical situations of role conflict can be taken as valid indicators of what first-level supervisors would actually do under those circumstances, or even what their supervisors and subordinates would urge them to do. The implications for understanding conflict in organizations, however, are that people at different hierarchical levels differ predictably in their evaluation of actual behavior (effectiveness ratings) and in their expressed values about what should be done in specific situations. Thus, the signs of incipient hierarchical conflict are visible. Moreover, the observed differences in perceptions and beliefs had to do with conflict-resolving strategies; hence, we would predict conflict about how to manage conflict, as well as conflict over the adequacy of other aspects of supervisory behavior.

Bigoness does not attempt to replicate any of the Bernardin and Alvares findings, but his work extends theirs in several respects. It deals with the more complex circumstances of third-party interventions in conflict resolution, and with the relative effectiveness of four different intervention modes under two different initial behavior patterns ("soft" or "tough") on the part of either party to the conflict. His resulting factorial design ($2 \times 2 \times 4$) is quite elegant, and he pays a price for such control; the unions and managements in the experiment are really undergraduate dyads, the stakes are modest ($3.30 to zero), and the negotiations are brief (fifteen minutes).

Bigoness's findings contradict some of his hypotheses in ways that are counterintuitive and of considerable interest both theoretically and pragmatically. For example, he expected that the success of a third-party intervention would increase with its strength. In fact, more contracts were settled and fewer issues left unresolved under the bargaining mode (no third-party intervention) than under any of the other three experimental modes (mediation, voluntary arbitration, and compulsory arbitration). Compulsory arbitration was second most effective, however. A possible interpretation would be that direct negotiation by the principal parties to a conflict is to be preferred, but that third-party intervention, when it is necessary, should be in strength (compulsory arbitration).

No recipe seems to fit all cases, however; the effectiveness of third-party interventions also depends on the initial management position. When the initial management position is tough, arbitration works better than other modes; when the initial management position is soft, bargaining seems to be more successful. Moreover, concessions were greater from a soft position than from a tough initial position, contrary to the folk wisdom of starting with an unrealistic set of demands so that there will be "room" for negotiation.

Most of all, we need field studies and field experiments to assess the external validity of these findings. We need to know whether they hold when the stakes are high, the negotiations protracted, the history of conflict long, and the behavior of representatives at the bargaining table much under the control of their constituents and their organizational roles.

Of all the contexts that shape social behavior, national norms are perhaps the most difficult to study in quantitative terms. To make the national context visible, it must be compared with other such contexts, and multinational studies are difficult to design and accomplish. They are especially difficult when the topic under discussion is sensitive, as interesting topics so often are. *Lind* and his colleagues have managed a four-nation study of preferences for different procedural models of adjudicative conflict resolution. The four models represent points on a theoretical continuum of "adversariness," a term that refers primarily to the amount of control that the original parties to the conflict retain over the adjudicative procedure. Each subject in the experiment answered questionnaires that required ranking the four judicial procedures in hypothetical cases in which the subject was supposed to take the role of either the defendant or the plaintiff.

The research shows that people prefer models according to their "adversariness"—ranking them, in decreasing order of preference, adversary model, double-investigator model, single-investigator model, and inquisitorial model. Moreover, these preferences are largely independent of the country in which the experiment was performed, which means that people are not merely expressing a preference for the adjudicative procedures of their own country. *Lind* and his colleagues offer the plausible interpretation that people prefer procedures that allow them to remain active and influential in the judicial process.

These findings fit with those of the preceding two studies. In combination they offer evidence for a sequence of preference and effectiveness that begins with bargaining —in the general sense of active effort at settlement by the principals to the conflict themselves. Only as bargaining fails and the failure is acknowledged by the two parties themselves do procedures of third-party intervention seem wanted, and at that point the intervention probably should be in the form of compulsory arbitration—binding on the parties at conflict. And even when a third party is in the role of decision maker in the conflict, the preference is for procedures that recognize the original adversary relationship and allow the adversaries to continue active and influential within the framework of adjudicative procedure. If all this is supported by further research, in the field and in real-life contests as well as in hypothetical cases, and with representative populations of adults as well as undergraduate experimental subjects, the implications for organizational change would be very great. They would include the teaching of conflict-resolving behavior under adversary circumstances—confrontation and problem solving as well as compromise and bargaining in its more limited sense. They would also include the modification of judicial procedures of trial and defense to maximize the constructive participation of the adversaries themselves.

Studies of organizational change have not often dealt explicitly with such issues. Most approaches to organizational change proposed and evaluated by social scientists, if they involve conflict at all, take conflict reduction as their implicit or explicit purpose. Some such approaches—"T groups," for example—assume or invite a period of heightened

overt conflict, as previously suppressed issues are made discussable, as techniques of confrontation are taught, or as some equalization of power between contestants is attained.
The main purpose of social science approaches to organizational change, however, has
been to increase organizational effectiveness or individual satisfaction, or both. Studies of
such attempts at change have a characteristic set of weaknesses; they are usually limited
to a single mode of change, to a short time span, to a single organization, and to limited
subjective indicators of change. In addition, they seldom include control or comparison
groups, and they often present little in the way of quantitative evidence for change.

The three studies of change included here were selected in part because they avoid
many of these weaknesses. *Bowers'* research is perhaps the prime example in these respects. It involves four "experimental" and two "control" treatments, twenty-three
organizations, 14,000 individuals, and the use of a standard questionnaire (the Survey of
Organizations or SOO) as the means of assessing change. Although the implications of the
research findings are open to argument, the raw data are themselves unequivocal. *Survey
feedback*—a combination of group discussion and coaching based on questionnaire responses of the group itself, in comparison with larger organizational units—generated
favorable change on eleven of sixteen criterion indices and unfavorable change on none.
The main control groups (*no-treatment* groups) and the *laboratory training* groups (T
groups) showed negative changes, and the rest showed mixed results.

Bowers offers a series of statistical analyses to rule out some of the more plausible
alternative interpretations of these data, and acknowledges the importance of organizational climate as a mediating or conditioning factor. Certainly some advocates of T-group
approaches or variants thereof (for example, Argyris, 1971) have emphasized the fact that
not all management or organizations are ready and able to benefit from these methods.
We badly need replication and extension of *Bowers'* work, in order to see whether the
results hold under less favorable circumstances and whether the subjective data can be
strengthened with objective criteria. *Bowers* and some of his colleagues at the Institute
for Social Research (University of Michigan) are committed to organizational change
through the approach of survey feedback. The Survey of Organizations (questionnaire
and indexes) was designed for use as a feedback instrument and was also used as the
means of evaluating change; the people who introduced the other methods of change in
Bowers' experiment, while they were following their own preferences, might have felt,
nevertheless, that their mode of work was somehow less facilitated in the ISR setting.
Bowers invited such experimental work in his article, but there have been too few responses.

Bowers did not deal explicitly with the effects of technostructural interventions as
compared with survey feedback. *Pasmore* made such a direct comparison in a company in
which one unit received reorganization affecting its sociotechnical structure as well as
survey feedback and another unit received only survey feedback in the first stages of the
experiment. Both units showed improved satisfaction scores, but only the first unit
showed significant increases in productivity. *Pasmore* believes that the critical factor in
the production scores was the sociotechnical intervention, but additional research in
which only this intervention occurs is needed to clinch the point. His emphasis on technostructural changes as against human process interventions is sound, however. It harks back
to the importance of structural factors as in the early experimentation of the Tavistock
group (Rice, 1958) and the hierarchical changes in the old Morse-Reimer (1956) experiment. It is consistent with the theory of Katz and Kahn (1978) that the central target for
organizational change is not the individual or interpersonal relations but organizational
structure.

Bragg and *Andrews* have carried out a field experiment that is strong in some respects that Bowers' data are not. The minutes of twenty-eight meetings provide a detailed account of what was discussed and decided in the name of introducing Participative Decision Making (PDM). Attitudinal data were minimal, but data on absence and productivity are highly specific. The results indicate a substantial success for the experiment; the workers liked it, and management was rewarded with increased productivity.

The question of whether gains in productivity were to be shared in some degree with the employees seems not to have arisen during the eighteen months of the experiment, although experience with the Scanlon Plan suggests that it is a potential source of conflict. The foreman of the hospital laundry workers in the experiment "was able to state in all honesty that the basic purpose of the program was to make jobs more interesting." Yet the investigators' hypotheses included the prediction of gains in productivity and attendance.

The investigators also tell us that the situation was particularly favorable for the introduction of participative decision making, and they mention another situation in the hospital where a similar attempt was less than successful. It would be interesting to compare such situations with respect to conflict and resistance to the attempted intervention, and thus to bring into the same empirical research the twin topics of conflict and change.

References

Argyris, C. *Management and Organizational Development.* New York: McGraw-Hill, 1971.

Dahrendorf, R. *Class and Class Conflict in Industrial Society.* Stanford, Calif.: Stanford University Press, 1959.

Katz, D., and Kahn, R. L. *The Social Psychology of Organizations.* (2nd ed.) New York: Wiley, 1978.

Morse, N., and Reimer, E. "The Experimental Change of a Major Organizational Variable." *Journal of Abnormal and Social Psychology,* 1956, *52,* 120-129.

Rice, A. K. *Productivity and Social Organization: The Ahmedabad Experiment.* London: Tavistock, 1958.

33

The Effects of Organizational Level on Perceptions of Role-Conflict Resolution Strategy

H. John Bernardin
Kenneth M. Alvares

Numerous studies have reported discrepancies in ratings of the first-line supervisor from organizational levels above and below him (Fleishman, Harris, and Burtt, 1956; Rambo, 1958; Besco and Lawshe, 1959). These studies seem to imply that there is very little relationship between ratings of the first-line supervisor by superiors and by subordinates, regardless of the type of occupation sampled.

House, Filley, and Kerr (1971) propose a simple explanation for this finding. Superiors, they say, evaluate a "structured" leadership style more highly than a "considerate" style while subordinates prefer the "considerate" style. Thus, a particular leadership style is perceived quite differently as a function of organizational level, and this explains the rating discrepancies.

This explanation, however, is confuted by the lack of evidence that subordinates in all occupations prefer a "considerate" type while superiors prefer the "structured" type. In fact, several studies have shown preferences for a particular style to be a function of the type of occupation (Filley and Grimes, 1967; Patchen, 1960; Pelz and Andrews, 1966; Wigdor, 1969). Thus, employees above and below a supervisor do not necessarily prefer one leadership style over another.

There are, of course, other possible explanations for these discrepant perceptions of leadership style. Besco and Lawshe (1959), in a study of twenty-nine production foremen, found no relationship between subordinate and superior ratings of the leadership behavior of the same group of foremen. These authors used a scale developed by Rambo (1958) to measure the leadership dimensions "consideration" and "initiating structure" (Fleishman and Harris, 1962). They offered two competing explanations for their findings without offering a means of choosing between them. The first of these suggests that there could be real differences in perceptions of the same supervisory behaviors as a func-

Reprinted from *Organizational Behavior and Human Performance*, 1975, *14*, 1-9, with permission of the authors and the publisher. Copyright © 1975 by Academic Press, Inc.

tion of organizational level. Similarly, it could also have been possible that the supervisors participating in this study actually exhibited different behavior patterns to their superiors than they did to their subordinates. If this were the case, differences in perceptions would only be an accurate reflection of the actual supervisor behavior. A third alternative, which was not suggested by these authors, is a combination of the previous two. It could be that supervisors behaved differently to their superiors than they did to their subordinates and that these behaviors were also perceived differently as a function of organizational level. Besco and Lawshe suggest that by investigating perceptions of specific behaviors important to the job instead of constructs such as "consideration" and "initiating structure," these alternative explanations could be tested directly.

Among the behaviors that are generally considered to be very important to a first-line supervisor's effectiveness are those involving role-conflict situations (Gardner and Whyte, 1945). Kahn and his associates (1964) define role conflict as the "simultaneous occurrence of two (or more) sets of pressures such that compliance with one would make more difficult the compliance with the other" (p. 18). Such situations are quite common to the role of the first-line supervisor, and resolving these conflicts is crucial to his performance as a leader (Roethlisberger, 1945).

Kahn and his associates (1964) identified two types of role conflict common to the first-line supervisor: (1) intersender conflict—when pressures from one role sender (for example, subordinates) oppose pressures from one or more other senders (superiors); (2) person-role conflict—when role requirements violate personal values.

Blake and Mouton (1964) identify five behavioral strategies for dealing with such conflicts. They are withdrawing, smoothing, compromising, forcing, and confrontation. Burke (1969) identified forcing, compromise, and confrontation as the most often utilized strategies in organizational role conflict situations. Forcing is a behavior utilized by a "task management orientation" (Blake, Mouton, and Bidwell, 1962, p. 12). Basically, this orientation assumes that man is a commodity like a machine and conflict or disagreement is intolerable and insubordinate. Thus, when conflict arises, a supervisor with this orientation would simply suppress it.

Compromise is the behavior used by the "dampened pendulum" (Blake, Mouton, and Bidwell, 1962, p. 12). This involves seeking a middle ground or "splitting the difference" (Blake and Mouton, 1964, p. 122), regardless of what is the best solution. Thus, the supervisor would seek to compromise the pressures from the opposing role senders.

Confrontation is the conflict behavior of the "team management orientation" (Blake, Mouton, and Bidwell, 1962, p. 13), whereby production is facilitated by the integration of task and human requirements. Confrontation involves rooting out the causes of the conflict. A supervisor with this type of orientation would meet with his subordinates and superiors to discuss the area of conflict and work through the problems.

It was the purpose of this study to examine perceptions of forcing, compromise, and confrontation behavioral strategies of the first-line supervisor in role-conflict situations common to his position. It was predicted that perceptions of these behaviors will differ as a function of organizational level. This difference would be used to help explain the discrepant ratings of first-line supervisory effectiveness from levels above and below him.

Method

Subjects. One hundred twenty-nine employees of a large midwestern manufacturing company participated in the study. Of those receiving requests to participate, 41 out of 50 general foremen, 46 out of 55 first-line supervisors, and 42 out of 73 subordinates returned usable questionnaires.

Procedure. All participants were given a folder with a cover letter explaining that the study was to be a brief survey of employee attitudes. One section of the folder consisted of four conflict situations (two intersender and two person-role). Each conflict situation was followed by a description of three behavioral strategies for dealing with the conflict. Participants were asked to rate each description on a seven-point scale, from extremely ineffective to extremely effective in terms of that particular conflict. The conflict situations were randomly ordered across subjects, and behavioral strategies were randomly ordered within subjects.

The four role-conflict situations were critical incidents written by the first author, based on his personal experiences with this sample of supervisors. Classification of the conflict examples into the two role-conflict categories was done initially by the authors and then verified by means of a preliminary study using an 85 percent correct placement criterion.

The following is an example of a conflict situation and the three strategies of dealing with it:

> A foreman's supervisor wants an individual assigned to a particularly difficult and generally disgusting job as a form of "unwritten punishment" for previous misbehavior. After a few days of this assignment, the individual begins to complain rather loudly and by this time the foreman feels rightfully so. What should the foreman do?
>
> Strategies: (Forcing) He makes what *he* himself feels is the appropriate decision and emphasizes that the workers have no choice but to abide by it. (Compromise) He looks for a compromise. He tries to find some sort of middle ground and attempts to please everyone. (Confrontation) He organizes a meeting of all interested parties, providing them with an opportunity to work out their differences.

In addition to the ratings of the conflict behaviors, participants also completed supervisory effectiveness ratings. Each scale consisted of five behavioral statements to be applied to the appropriate person and rated on a six-point scale, from never to always.

Results

Discrepant Ratings of Effectiveness. Ratings on the five statements of leadership effectiveness were summed for an overall effectiveness rating for the first-line supervisor. Discrepant ratings of leadership effectiveness were tested by a *t* test for related measures. General foremen and subordinates differed significantly ($t = 3.58$, $df < 26$, $p < .01$) in their ratings of the same first-line supervisors. Thus, results corroborate earlier findings of discrepant ratings of leadership effectiveness from positions immediately above and below the first-line supervisor.

Organizational-Level Effects. The design of the analysis was a $3 \times 2 \times 3$ factorial design with repeated measures on the last two factors. There were three organization levels, two role-conflict types (intersender and person-role), and three role-conflict behavioral strategies (forcing, compromise, and confrontation).

Results of the $3 \times 2 \times 3$ analysis of variance are presented in Table 1. For purposes of analysis, ratings of strategies were summed across the two examples of each conflict type.

Table 1. Analysis of Variance of Resolution Strategy Ratings

Source	df	MS	F
Organizational level (A)	2	43.16	6.16[a] [b]
Ss within groups	126	7.01	
Conflict type (B)	1	9.12	10.99[a]
A × B	2	.44	.55
B × Ss within groups	126	.83	
Resolution strategy (C)	2	105.68	26.68[a]
A × C	4	33.15	8.37[a]
C × Ss within groups	252	3.96	
B × C	2	1.30	2.79
A × B × C	4	4.78	10.02[a]
BC × Ss within groups	252	.48	

[a] $p < .01$.
[b] $\omega^2 = .08$.

The main effect of organizational level was found to be statistically significant ($F = 6.16$, $df = 2,126$, $p < .01$; $\omega^2 = .08$). Additionally, a significant level × strategy interaction was found ($F = 8.37$, $df = 4,252$, $p < .01$). Table 2 presents mean ratings as a function of organizational level and conflict type.

Table 2. Mean Ratings of Resolution Strategies as a Function of Conflict Type and Organizational Level

Organizational Level	Resolution Strategy					
	Forcing		Compromise		Confrontation	
	Inter-sender	Person-Role	Inter-sender	Person-Role	Inter-sender	Person-Role
Superiors ($N = 41$)	9.16	9.00	9.58	9.08	9.82	9.92
First-line supervisors ($N = 46$)	8.88	8.08	8.96	8.60	8.78	8.82
Subordinates ($N = 42$)	8.00	7.96	9.48	9.60	10.98	10.42

Note: The larger the average mean value, the more favorable the rating. Means are based on sums across two examples of each conflict type.

Post hoc comparisons (Duncan multiple range for nearly equal numbers) were made on the mean ratings of superiors and subordinates. Significant differences were found between superiors and subordinates on the "forcing" and the "confrontation" resolution strategies for both conflict types and on the "compromise" strategy within the person-role type conflict.

In summary, the results showed ratings of role-conflict resolution differed as a function of organizational level. More specifically, superiors and subordinates differed in their ratings of all three resolution strategies within certain role-conflict situations.

Relationship of Resolution-Rating Discrepancies and Effectiveness Ratings. In order to further investigate the relationship between ratings of role-conflict strategies and ratings of a first-line supervisor's effectiveness, discrepancy scores were computed for each of three organizational-level combinations. Absolute differences between ratings of resolution strategies for each conflict situation were summed to reveal one absolute discrepancy score for each of the following: (1) superior-subordinate combination with a common first-line supervisor; (2) each subordinate with his respective first-line supervisor;

and (3) each first-line supervisor with his respective supervisor. Table 3 presents the mean discrepancy values for these three combinations.

Table 3. Mean Discrepancy Values for Ratings of Resolution Strategies

	Discrepancy	
Level Combination	Mean	SD
Subordinate-superior	10.96	2.42
Subordinate-first-line	12.32	2.59
First-line-superior	8.46	1.86

Ratings on the five "effectiveness" statements were summed for an overall "effectiveness" rating for each first-line supervisor from his superior and his subordinates. For the superior-subordinate combinations with the same first-line supervisor, an "effectiveness" difference score was also calculated for each first-line supervisor. Table 4 presents mean effectiveness ratings of the first-line supervisors from superiors and subordinates and the mean difference value between their ratings for the same first-line supervisor.

Table 4. Mean Effectiveness Ratings and Difference Value for
First-Line Supervisors

	Rating	
Source of Rating	Mean	SD
Subordinate	14.76	2.06
Superior	17.38	2.79
Difference value	2.98	.87

To measure the relationship between discrepancy scores and effectiveness ratings, the following correlations were performed: (1) discrepancy scores between superiors and subordinates with the same first-line supervisor were correlated with the effectiveness rating difference scores between superiors and subordinates; (2) discrepancy scores between subordinates and first-line supervisors on strategies were correlated with ratings of effectiveness for the first-line supervisor from subordinates; and (3) discrepancy scores between superiors and first-line supervisors were correlated with effectiveness ratings of the first-line supervisors from the superiors.

Regarding (1) above, if, as Besco and Lawshe hypothesize, differences in what was perceived as a function of organizational level accounts for differences in effectiveness ratings, then there should be a significant positive correlation between strategy-rating discrepancies and effectiveness-rating difference.

Results of a Spearman product-moment correlation revealed a significant relationship between absolute discrepancies between superiors and subordinates and their ratings of the same first-line supervisors ($r = .38$, $p < .05$).

For (2) above, a Spearman product-moment correlation revealed a significant relationship between absolute discrepancies in ratings of resolution strategies and ratings of effectiveness for the subordinate-first-line supervisor combinations ($r = -.43$, $p < .01$). The correlation coefficient between discrepancy scores and ratings of effectiveness for the superior-first-line-supervisor combinations, however, revealed a nonsignificant relationship ($r = -.17$, ns).

Discussion

As in previous studies, discrepancies in ratings of leadership effectiveness existed in this sample of supervisors and subordinates. The difference in ratings of resolution strategy as a function of organizational level helps to explain this discrepancy. Besco and Lawshe (1959) posit that the discrepancy they observed in their study of first-line supervisors could be due to either (1) real differences in what was perceived from two levels in the organization; or (2) that first-line supervisors exhibit different behavioral patterns to their superiors and to their subordinates. It has been shown that subordinates and superiors differ in their ratings of particular conflict resolution strategies (forcing, confrontation, and compromise). If we can assume that these ratings reflected perceptions of behavior, it would therefore follow that superiors and subordinates would differ in their perceptions (favorable or unfavorable, for example) of related behaviors by the same person.

As shown in Table 2, subordinates rate the forcing resolution strategy as less effective than superiors, while ratings are reversed for the confrontation style. The differences in rated effectiveness of the forcing alternative could be expected because subordinates usually bear the brunt of such a supervisory style. The confrontation difference may be a function of superior experience with the strategy and the realization that such tactics, while conducive to greater subordinate satisfaction, are not necessarily an effective means of dealing with conflict.

The significant correlation ($r = .38$) between strategy-rating discrepancy scores and differences in effectiveness ratings between superiors and subordinates further corroborates the first Besco and Lawshe hypothesis. Here again, if it can be assumed ratings reflect perceptions, differences in perception did account for 14 percent of the variance in rating differences between superiors and subordinates.

Of course, the hypothesis that the first-line supervisor exhibits different behaviors to personnel above and below him is still feasible. In fact, in lieu of the 86 percent unaccounted variance in the correlation of discrepant strategy ratings and effectiveness ratings and the low ω^2 calculated on the ANOVA level effect ($\omega^2 = .08$), we have indirect support for such a hypothesis.

This study does identify specific differences in perceptions of first-line supervisory behavior. With conflict situations common to this sample, and alternative behavioral strategies, superiors and subordinates perceived the strategies differently in terms of their effectiveness for resolving such conflicts.

The significant correlation between effectiveness ratings and resolution strategy discrepancies also illustrates the crucial nature of role-conflict behavior for the first-line supervisor. Perceptions of his behavior in these situations will have a substantial effect on his overall effectiveness as a leader.

These results illustrate the need to investigate the relationship between important behaviors elicited by a leader and perceptions of those behaviors from positions above and below him. Rather than studying hypothetical constructs, such as "consideration" and "structure," to explain leader behavior, dealing with behaviors in situations common to the samples involved will result in more useful and generalizable information.

The significant conflict *type* effect and level × strategy interaction also accentuate the complexity of the relationship between perceptions of behavior with situational variables. Thus, the well-documented finding of discrepant perceptions of effectiveness cannot be explained away simply by different perceptions of a particular leadership style.

References

Besco, R. O., and Lawshe, C. H. "Foremen Leadership as Perceived by Superiors and Subordinates." *Personnel Psychology,* 1959, *12,* 573-582.

Blake, R. R., and Mouton, J. S. *The Managerial Grid.* Houston: Gulf, 1964.

Blake, R. R., Mouton, J. S., and Bidwell, A. C. "Managerial Grid." *Advanced Management,* Sept. 1962, pp. 12-15.

Burke, R. J. "Methods of Resolving Interpersonal Conflict." *Personnel Administration,* 1969, *32,* 48-55.

Filley, A. C., and Grimes, A. J. "The Bases of Power in Decision Processes." Unpublished manuscript, University of Wisconsin, 1967.

Fleishman, E. A., and Harris, E. F. "Patterns of Leadership Behavior Related to Employee Grievances and Turnover." *Personnel Psychology,* 1962, *15,* 43-56.

Fleishman, E. A., Harris, E. F., and Burtt, H. E. *Leadership and Supervision in Industry.* Columbus: Bureau of Business Research, Ohio State University, 1956.

Gardner, B. B., and Whyte, W. F. "The Man in the Middle: Positions and Problems of the Foreman." *Applied Anthropology,* 1945, *4,* 1-28.

House, R. J., Filley, A. C., and Kerr, S. "Relation of Leader Consideration and Initiating Structure to R & D Subordinates' Satisfaction." *Administrative Science Quarterly,* 1971, *16,* 19-30.

Kahn, R. L., and others. *Organizational Stress: Studies in Role Conflict and Ambiguity.* New York: Wiley, 1964.

Patchen, M. "Absence and Employee Feeling About Fair Treatment." *Personnel Psychology,* 1960, *13,* 349-360.

Pelz, D. C., and Andrews, F. M. *Scientists in Organizations.* New York: Wiley, 1966.

Rambo, W. W. "The Construction and Analysis of a Leadership Behavior Checklist for Industrial Managers." *Journal of Applied Psychology,* 1958, *42,* 409-415.

Roethlisberger, F. "The Foreman: Master and Victim of Double Talk." *Harvard Business Review,* 1945, *23,* 283-298.

Wigdor, L. A. "Effectiveness of Various Management and Organizational Characteristics of Employee Satisfaction and Performance as a Function of the Employee's Need for Independence." Unpublished doctoral dissertation, City University of New York, 1969.

34

The Impact of Initial Bargaining
Position and Alternative Modes
of Third-Party Intervention
in Resolving Bargaining Impasses

William J. Bigoness

The expansion of strife and conflict within numerous spheres of contemporary society during the past decade has caused social scientists to devote renewed attention and energies to the study of conflict and conflict resolution strategies (Coser, 1956; Schelling, 1960; Pondy, 1967; Walton, 1969). Among the most fruitful strategies frequently employed in resolving conflict is the intervention of a third party who is not a direct participant to the immediate conflict. Blake, Shepard, and Mouton (1964) have argued that conditions for a third-party resolution exist when two disagreeing parties have reached an impasse, and it is assumed that no further interaction can produce a change in the disagreement. The present study investigates the effect of alternative modes of third-party intervention in resolving bargaining impasses under conditions of high and low conflict.

The extent to which a third party is successful in resolving bargaining impasses is often determined, in part, according to the power granted the third party by the principal contestants. On a continuum of increasing power, third-party intervention is characteristically classified (Bok and Dunlop, 1970; Chamberlain and Cullen, 1971) into one of the following categories: (1) mediation, (2) voluntary arbitration, and (3) compulsory arbitration. Mediation involves those responses by a third party aimed at bringing about agreement or compromise. Under conditions of mediation, the decision-making responsibility regarding mutual accommodation remains internalized within the bargaining dyad. Arbitration entails a third party's entrance into the conflict and its final determination regarding the terms of the settlement. Under a system of voluntary arbitration, parties must mutually agree to the intervention of a third party regarding any specific bargaining impasse. Compulsory arbitration differs from voluntary arbitration in that a superior power, in relation to the bargaining parties, may dictate that, should an impasse occur, the dispute will be submitted to compulsory arbitration. Therefore, decision making under an

Reprinted from *Organizational Behavior and Human Performance*, 1976, *17*, 185-198, with permission of the author and the publisher. Copyright © by Academic Press, Inc.

arbitration system, in terms of closure, is granted to the third party and thus externalized beyond the dyad.

Which of the preceding modes of third-party intervention is most effective and under what conditions has remained an issue of considerable controversy. Northrup (1966) contends that when closure by arbitration is available, the incentive for the bargainers to agree declines sharply, even to the point where bargainers will force intervention. Bok and Dunlop (1970) have argued that compulsory arbitration, even within a few industries, tends to undermine an important ingredient in productive labor-management relations; namely, the willingness of the parties to bargain conscientiously over their differences. Reuther (1965), however, contended that the threat of government intervention often fosters a greater sense of urgency for the bargainers to settle their disputes. Stevens (1966) has stated that the contention that the availability of a strike is an essential part of collective bargaining may not be as self-evident as most proponents believe.

Researchers have sought to investigate the effectiveness of alternative modes of third-party intervention. Podell and Knapp (1969) found that suggested concessions attributable to a mediator were more readily accepted by subjects than comparable concessions offered by the subjects' opponent. Pruitt and Johnson (1970) reported that subjects who have encountered a bargaining impasse would accept a suggestion by a mediator of a point of settlement halfway between the positions of the two negotiators. Urban (1973) examined the effect of three alternative modes of third-party intervention (no arbitration, voluntary arbitration, and compulsory arbitration) upon bargaining behavior. He found that bargainers anticipating voluntary arbitration requested the least initial profit, concluded negotiations in the least amount of time, and exchanged the least number of bids.

Based on earlier field studies by Landsburger (1955), Vidmar (1971) demonstrated that conflict intensity may serve as a moderator of mediation effectiveness. Vidmar reported that mediators tended to improve significantly the performance of negotiation groups while not significantly enhancing the performance of discussion groups. Johnson and Pruitt (1972) found that negotiators faced with a binding decision (arbitration) made larger and more frequent concessions than those faced with nonbinding (mediation) decision.

Johnson and Tullar (1972) sought to investigate four forms of third-party intervention—no third-party intervention (control), nonbinding suggestion (mediation), selection of the best of the bargainers' own proposals (govplan), and binding decision (arbitration)—under conditions of both high and low need to save face. Under a condition of high need to save face, dyads expecting the govplan form of intervention were far from agreement, while those not expecting any intervention were close to agreement. Those anticipating mediation and arbitration were at a moderate distance from agreement. In the low face-saving condition, those expecting arbitration had all reached agreement while those anticipating mediation were farthest from agreement. After intervention, those who received a suggestion for settlement were no more likely to reach agreement than were those who did not receive a suggestion.

Although need to save face should not be equated as a direct corollary of conflict intensity, it does appear logical that some correlation between the two phenomena is plausible. If this is the case, Johnson and Tullar's findings are of particular importance. Their findings imply, at least indirectly, that bargainers confronted by the most difficult bargaining situations bargain least effectively when confronted by binding arbitration. Such a conclusion tends to support Northrup's impressions drawn from field experience while at the same time contradicting earlier research by Johnson and Pruitt. The ineffectiveness of mediation reported by Johnson and Tullar challenges results of earlier studies (Podell and Knapp, 1969; Pruitt and Johnson, 1970; Vidmar, 1971).

The present study was designed to test three related hypotheses. First, it was hypothesized that bargainers assuming tough initial bargaining positions would reach fewer settlements than bargainers assuming soft initial bargaining positions. Second, it was hypothesized that subjects anticipating stronger modes of third-party intervention would reach more settlements than subjects anticipating weaker forms of third-party intervention. Finally, a significant interaction effect between initial position and mode of intervention was predicted, such that stronger modes of third-party intervention would result in significantly more settlements under a tough initial position, while stronger modes of third-party intervention would result in fewer settlements under a soft initial position.

Currently, no study has attempted to evaluate the impact of the three most commonly utilized styles of third-party intervention (mediation, voluntary arbitration, and compulsory arbitration) as well as including a control group within the context of a single study. To date, only two studies (Vidmar, 1971; Johnson and Tullar, 1972) have attempted to weigh the impact of moderating variables upon third-party intervention.

Method

Experimental Design. A 2 × 2 × 4 factorial design with fixed effects and equal cell sizes was employed in this study. Factor A was initial management position, "soft" or "tough." Initial union position, "soft" or "tough," constituted Factor B. Modes of third-party intervention—bargaining (no third-party intervention), mediation, voluntary arbitration, and compulsory arbitration—represent the four levels of the third factor (C). This experimental design was expanded by adding a fourth factor, role within the bargaining dyad (management role or union role), in cases where the individual subject's responses rather than the bargaining dyad served as the unit of analysis.

The expanded experimental design therefore was a 2 × 2 × 4 × 2 factorial design with repeated measures analysis on the last variable. There were five dyads (ten subjects) in each of the sixteen cells of the experimental design. The 160 subjects were undergraduate male business and psychology students at Michigan State University who volunteered to participate in this study. At the time of recruitment, the subjects were told they would participate in a collective bargaining exercise where they would have the opportunity to earn some money.

Procedures. A simulated collective bargaining game originally developed by Campbell (1960), and significantly modified for the purposes of this study, was utilized. The task involved face-to-face bargaining between two subjects in a dyad. Subjects bargained over three issues: wages, hospital and medical plans, and a cost-of-living clause. Each bargaining issue was presented on an individual scale indicating various potential points of settlement. Each bargaining scale also included scales informing the bargainers of "points" they would receive should a settlement be reached at any designated location. Subjects were informed that their earnings in the collective bargaining game were contingent upon the points they earned. Payoff schedules for each issue were asymmetrical, thereby prohibiting parties from simply splitting the difference. Subjects were informed that they could bargain each issue separately or make offers on all three issues at the same time. Subjects were requested to record each of their bids on sheets provided for each issue under negotiation and to indicate when an agreement was reached on each issue. Potential earnings ranged from $3.30 to zero if subjects failed to reach agreement on any issues under negotiation.

All subjects received an instructional sheet providing general background information regarding the company-union relationship. Management representatives also received additional information pertaining to the company position. Correspondingly, union representatives were provided with further information explaining the union position. Subjects also received an instructional sheet outlining the procedures which would be followed in the event of a bargaining impasse. These sheets stated that if a negotiated settlement was not reached fifteen minutes after negotiations had begun, negotiations would stop. The remainder of the instructions were different, depending upon mode of third-party intervention.

To encourage subjects to reach a settlement prior to intervention and thereby simulate costs similar to those incurred when bargainers fail to reach collective bargaining settlements without strikes, subjects were instructed that should they be unable to reach a contract settlement within the specified time (fifteen minutes) their earnings, based upon points accumulated, would be reduced by 20 percent. Subjects received ten cents for every point earned when a contract was settled within the specified time. Subjects requiring more than the specified time to reach an agreement received eight cents for every point earned until twenty-five minutes of bargaining time had elapsed, after which they received no payments.

After subjects had finished reading their instructions, the experimenter discussed the instructions with them and answered questions. Great care was taken to ensure that each subject was totally familiar with the process before negotiations began. When the instructions were completely understood, the negotiations began. The experimenter would exit the room and leave the door open so that he could observe the bargaining process.

Two classrooms were used in this study. Subjects were randomly assigned to one of five dyads in each of sixteen treatment conditions. Each room contained tables and chairs arranged so that the subjects faced each other across a table. Only dyads under the same experimental condition bargained within the same room. Clocks were also provided in each room, so that subjects had knowledge of the negotiating time remaining. Five dyads bargained per negotiating session. Negotiation sessions were conducted on four consecutive evenings.

Independent Variables. There were four independent variables in this study. The first and second independent variables were initial management bargaining position and initial union bargaining position. Each of these two independent variables consisted of two levels, "soft" or "tough." A "soft" initial position was manipulated by assigning subjects to a treatment condition where their initial bargaining demand was low; that is, not very demanding. A "tough" initial position was manipulated by assigning subjects to a treatment condition where their initial bargaining demand was high; that is, very demanding. The extent to which a subject's initial demand was high or low was controlled by instructing subjects to initiate bargaining with a soft or tough opening offer. The appropriate initial offers appeared above each bargaining scale to ensure that subjects commenced negotiations at the proper positions. Table 1 presents initial management and union bargaining positions for all three issues under negotiation.

The mode of third-party intervention constituted the third independent variable and was manipulated by means of different instructional sheets. Under each mode of third-party intervention, the remainder of the message was different. Under bargaining (no third-party intervention), subjects were instructed to cease discussion with their opponent and to reevaluate their bargaining strategy. After they had thought things over for a few minutes, it was indicated that negotiations would resume. Subjects under mediation were instructed that a person unrelated to the experiment but knowledgeable in the

Table 1. Initial Bargaining Positions

Issues Under Negotiation	Initial Management Position		Initial Union Position	
	Soft	Tough	Soft	Tough
Wages	Management offers 6-cent increase	Management offers 2-cent increase	Union demands 16-cent increase	Union demands 20-cent increase
Hospital and medical plan	Management offers to pay 4/12 of plan	Management offers to pay 2/12 of plan	Union demands company pay 9/12 of plan	Union demands company pay 11/12 of plan
Cost-of-living clause	Management offers to pay 32% of cost-of-living increases	Management offers to pay 16% of cost-of-living increases	Union demands that company pay 72% of cost-of-living increases	Union demands that company pay 88% of cost-of-living increases

field of industrial relations and who had earlier studied these bargaining issues would present to them his proposal for a settlement. This proposal, it was stressed, was to be considered a suggested settlement, and subjects were free to act or not act on his suggestion. After the mediator's suggested settlement was presented, subjects were informed that negotiations would resume. Under voluntary arbitration, subjects were informed that should a bargaining impasse arise they could elect to submit their impasse to a neutral third party knowledgeable in the field of industrial relations who had earlier studied these bargaining issues and arrived at a proposed settlement. This individual's settlement would be binding upon the parties. However, such third-party intervention would occur only upon the joint request of the subjects. Subjects under compulsory arbitration were informed that should they be unable to reach a settlement within fifteen minutes, a third party knowledgeable in the field of industrial relations who had earlier studied these issues and arrived at a proposed settlement would intervene and render a binding settlement. The mediator's suggested settlement and the arbitrator's dictated settlement were identical and are presented in Table 2.

Table 2. Mediator's Suggested/Arbitrator's Dictated Settlement Points

Wages	A 12-cent/hr increase
Hospital and medical plan	Company pays 6/12 of plan
Cost-of-living clause	Company pays 56% of cost-of-living increases

The fourth independent variable was the subject's role nested within the dyad: management role and union role. Role was determined by randomly assigning subjects to represent either the management position or the union position.

Dependent Variables. Three behavioral dependent variables were collected during this study. The dependent variables under examination in each treatment condition, as operationally defined, included (1) *number of contracts settled* (a contract was regarded settled only if subjects reached agreement on all three issues under negotiation during the initial fifteen-minute bargaining session), (2) *number of issues left unresolved* (issues under negotiation not settled during the initial fifteen-minute bargaining session were regarded as unresolved), (3) *total amount conceded* (the total amount conceded by subjects as a percentage of the maximum they could have conceded, based on all three issues under negotiations during the initial fifteen-minute bargaining session).

Results

Contracts Settled. It was predicted that the stronger the anticipated mode of third-party intervention, the greater would be the number of contracts settled. Table 3 presents the results of the analysis of contracts settled.

Table 3. Chi-Square Analysis of "Contracts Settled"[a]

Contracts	Bargaining	Mediation	Voluntary Arbitration	Compulsory Arbitration
Settled	11	2	7	10
Unsettled	9	18	13	10

[a] $\chi^2 = 6.52, p < .10$.

These results did not confirm the hypothesis. Dyads bargaining under voluntary arbitration reached more contract settlements than those negotiating under mediation. Further, dyads bargaining under compulsory arbitration reached more settlements than subjects under either mediation or voluntary arbitration. Surprisingly, the greatest number of contract settlements occurred under bargaining. A second unexpected finding was the small number of contracts settled under mediation.

Issues Left Unresolved. To examine further the impact of alternative modes of third party intervention, in addition to including initial management position and initial union position within the analysis, a $2 \times 2 \times 4$ ANOVA was conducted to analyze the dependent variable, the number of issues left unresolved.

Significant main effects based on initial position and mode of intervention were expected. Specifically, it was hypothesized that more issues would be left unresolved under a tough rather than a soft initial position. It was predicted further that the stronger the anticipated mode of third-party intervention, the fewer the number of issues which would remain unresolved. Finally, a significant interaction effect between initial position and mode of intervention was predicted, specifically that stronger modes of third-party intervention would result in fewer unresolved issues under a tough initial position, while stronger modes of third-party intervention would result in more unresolved issues under a soft initial position. Table 4 presents an analysis of issues left unresolved.

The findings presented in Table 4 reveal, as predicted, that significantly fewer issues were left unresolved under a soft as compared to a tough initial management position. Mode of third-party intervention was also found to affect significantly the number of issues left unresolved. Fewest issues were left unresolved under bargaining, followed by compulsory arbitration, voluntary arbitration, and mediation. A significant interaction effect was found between initial management position and mode of third-party intervention. Tests of simple effects revealed that issues left unresolved did differ significantly under different modes of third-party intervention for both soft ($F = 2.93, p < .05$) and tough ($F = 3.94, p < .05$) initial management positions. Under a soft initial management position, compulsory arbitration and voluntary arbitration were superior to bargaining and mediation, while bargaining alone was found to be superior to all other modes of intervention under a tough initial management position ($p < .05$ by Newman-Keuls tests).

Total Amount Conceded. It was predicted that subjects confronting a higher conflictual situation, as determined by initial positions, would make greater concessions in an attempt to reach settlements prior to third-party intervention. It was further hypothesized that the stronger the anticipated third-party intervention, the greater would be the total amount conceded. Finally, a significant interaction was expected between initial

Table 4. Means, Standard Deviations, and Summary of Analysis of Variance
of the "Number of Issues Left Unresolved"

Initial Management Position		Initial Union Position							
		Soft				Tough			
		BAR[a]	MED	V.A.	C.A.	BAR	MED	V.A.	C.A.
Soft	M	1.60	1.40	1.00	.60	.80	2.00	.20	.20
	SD	1.14	.55	1.00	1.34	1.30	1.23	.45	.45
Tough	M	.20	1.80	2.00	1.60	.80	2.00	1.80	2.00
	SD	.45	1.10	1.41	1.34	1.30	1.00	1.30	1.23

Source of Variance	df	MS	F	p <
Management position (A)	1	6.07	5.07	.03
Union position (B)	1	.05	< 1	ns
Mode (C)	3	3.23	2.71	.05
AB	1	1.80	1.51	ns
AC	3	4.95	4.15	.01
BC	3	.68	< 1	ns
ABC	3	.70	< 1	ns
Error	64	1.19		

[a]BAR, bargaining; MED, mediation; V.A., voluntary arbitration; C.A., compulsory arbitration.

position and mode of third-party intervention, such that stronger modes of third-party intervention would result in a greater total concession under a tough initial position, while stronger modes of intervention were expected to lead to a smaller total concession under a soft initial position.

Contrary to expectation, Table 5 shows that subjects negotiating under a tough initial management position conceded significantly less than subjects negotiating under a soft initial management position. A significant interaction was found between initial union position and role. There was a marginally significant interaction between initial management position and role. Additional analysis of the interaction of initial union position by role failed to show significant differences in total amount conceded based upon role under soft or tough initial position. Simple effects analysis of initial management position by role showed that union representatives conceded significantly more under a soft initial management position. No significant difference in total amount conceded was found among management representatives based on initial management position.

One limitation of the above findings is that the dependent variable *total amount conceded* was derived by simply summing over the three issues. Therefore, a dyad that had reached agreement on two issues but was far apart on the third issue could conceivably report the same total amount conceded as a dyad which was close to agreement on all three issues but had not reached any final settlements.

Discussion

Findings reveal that initial position significantly affected the number of issues left unresolved and the total amount conceded. The effects of initial position were generally as predicted. Significantly fewer issues were left unresolved when management assumed a soft as opposed to a tough initial position. Contrary to expectation, a tough initial man-

Table 5. Means, Standard Deviations, and Summary of Analysis of Variance
of "Total Amount Conceded"

Initial Management Position		Initial Union Position							
		Bargaining		Mediation		Voluntary Arbitration		Compulsory Arbitration	
		M	U	M	U	M	U	M	U
		Soft							
Soft	M	24.00	22.40	22.80	26.80	28.20	26.60	36.00	28.00
	SD	14.11	17.37	15.47	19.01	13.52	19.55	22.78	16.57
Tough	M	23.00	18.20	27.80	20.00	12.00	15.40	25.20	21.60
	SD	16.45	12.19	25.14	6.52	16.43	21.90	23.35	16.61
		Tough							
Soft	M	26.60	39.00	5.00	4.80	24.00	35.20	25.80	33.40
	SD	7.96	17.56	5.00	5.72	10.51	16.35	14.46	15.76
Tough	M	20.80	20.80	15.60	13.40	10.80	16.40	15.40	10.60
	SD	15.02	16.90	20.02	14.43	12.77	11.06	9.10	7.77

Source of Variance	df	MS	F	$p <$
Between				
Management position (A)	1	2,310.40	5.30	.03
Union position (B)	1	570.03	1.31	ns
Mode (C)	3	494.71	1.14	ns
AB	1	52.90	< 1	ns
AC	3	734.85	1.69	ns
BC	3	745.64	1.72	ns
ABC	3	205.62	< 1	ns
Error	64	435.86		
Within				
Role (D)	1	14.40	< 1	ns
AD	1	225.63	3.58	.06
BD	1	384.40	6.10	.02
CD	3	98.92	1.57	ns
ABD	1	112.23	1.78	ns
ACD	3	28.58	< 1	ns
BCD	3	35.98	< 1	ns
ABCD	3	82.44	1.31	ns
Error	64	62.97		

Note: Cell means represent the percentage of total amount conceded.

agement position resulted in a significantly smaller total concession than a soft initial position.

Dyads under bargaining were found to be most successful in reaching contract settlements, followed by dyads under compulsory arbitration, voluntary arbitration, and mediation. Similar findings were found when analyzing issues left unresolved. Fewest issues were left unresolved by dyads under bargaining, followed by dyads under compulsory arbitration, voluntary arbitration, and mediation. Contrary to stated predictions, these findings imply that subjects anticipating no outside assistance in resolving a bargaining impasse were most successful in reaching bargaining settlements. Almost equally successful were subjects anticipating compulsory arbitration. Surprisingly, mediation was found to be a highly ineffective mode of third-party intervention.

These findings lend partial support to the observations of Northrup (1966) and Bok and Dunlop (1970), who contend that collective bargaining is most successful when parties negotiate free from outside intervention. However, these results fail to support their contention that compulsory arbitration seriously undermines collective bargaining.

A plausible explanation of these findings is that dyads bargaining in the absence of any form of third-party intervention view themselves as solely responsible for the success of negotiations and thereby strive to reach a settlement. Failure to reach a settlement cannot be transferred to any party outside the dyad. In situations where third-party intervention is present, compulsory arbitration is most conducive to settlement because subjects seek settlements in an attempt to avoid a binding decision over which they have no control. Under voluntary arbitration, subjects maintain the right to reject third-party intervention and thereby reduce the threat of outside intervention. Mediation, where failure to reach an agreement results in a third party merely suggesting a settlement, is viewed as least threatening and, therefore, provides little stimulus to reach an agreement. Subjects under mediation may, in fact, await the mediator's suggested solution prior to reaching an accord.

A major interest to the present investigation was the possible interaction effect of initial position with third-party intervention. Vidmar's (1971) and Johnson and Tullar's (1972) findings have suggested such a possibility. The principal interaction predicted in this study was that stronger modes of third-party intervention would be significantly more effective under tough as opposed to soft initial positions. This hypothesis was based on field observations reported by Landsburger (1955) and Vidmar's (1971) experimental findings.

A significant interaction was found to affect issues left unresolved. However, the interaction effects were not as anticipated. Compulsory arbitration and voluntary arbitration resulted in significantly fewer unresolved issues under a soft initial management position than either bargaining or mediation. However, under a tough initial management position, bargaining was superior to all other modes of third-party intervention. These findings support Johnson and Tullar's (1972) results that under conditions of high need to "save face," subjects bargained most successfully in the absence of third-party intervention. Conversely, in situations of low need to save face, compulsory arbitration was found to be the most successful style of third-party intervention.

In general, it can be argued that the results of this study suggest caution to individuals and parties advocating the introduction of arbitration into additional spheres of contemporary society. Supporters of such legislation argue that the threat of outside intervention will encourage parties to reach mutual agreements. The results of this study only partially support such a contention. Arbitration was found to facilitate agreements only under conditions of low conflict. The threat of any form of outside intervention in instances of high conflict was found to prove detrimental to the bargaining process. These findings suggest that parties are most successful in resolving difficult bargaining issues when they do not perceive the availability of outside alternatives. Researchers and policy-makers who believe that collective bargaining settlements reached by the parties themselves are more broadly accepted and result in greater industrial peace would be advised, on the basis of this research, to oppose the passage of legislation requiring arbitration.

The effectiveness of mediation reported by earlier researchers appears seriously challenged by this study's findings. Earlier studies citing mediation effectiveness often foreclosed the possibility of contract settlements prior to the mediator's suggested settlement and thereby considerably enhanced mediation effectiveness. The present study was specifically designed to overcome such limitations, and mediation was found to be the least effective strategy of third-party interventions.

It is important to note, however, that the present study presented subjects with only the anticipation of a mediator's intervention. Anticipation of a suggestion from a qualified mediator may have, in fact, encouraged subjects to refrain from concluding a settlement prior to the mediator's suggestion. Mediation is perhaps most successful when it is introduced only after the parties have been unable to reach an agreement themselves.

The findings with respect to initial position strongly demonstrate that parties who enter negotiations with less disparity between their initial demands are more successful in reaching collective bargaining agreements. These findings tend to offer indirect support and encouragement for the efforts by several leading corporations and unions who have instituted "continuous bargaining" in an attempt to resolve or to narrow the differences between their respective positions prior to the commencement of formal collective bargaining negotiations.

References

Blake, R. R., Shepard, H. A., and Mouton, J. S. *Managing Intergroup Conflict in Industry.* Houston: Gulf, 1964.

Bok, D. C., and Dunlop, J. T. *Labor and the American Community.* New York: Simon and Schuster, 1970.

Campbell, R. J. *Originality in Group Productivity. III: Partisan Commitment and Productive Independence in a Collective Bargaining Situation.* Columbus: Ohio State University Research Foundation, 1960.

Chamberlain, N. W., and Cullen, D. E. *The Labor Sector.* (2nd ed.) New York: McGraw-Hill, 1971.

Coser, L. *The Functions of Social Conflict.* New York: Free Press, 1956.

Johnson, D. F., and Pruitt, D. G. "Preintervention Effects of Mediation Versus Arbitration." *Journal of Applied Psychology,* 1972, *56,* 1-10.

Johnson, D. F., and Tullar, W. L. "Style of Third Party Intervention, Face Saving, and Bargaining Behavior." *Journal of Experimental Social Psychology,* 1972, *8,* 319-330.

Komorita, S. S., and Brenner, A. R. "Bargaining and Concession-Making Under Bilateral Monopoly." *Journal of Personality and Social Psychology,* 1967, *6,* 349-353.

Landsburger, H. A. "Interim Report of a Research Project on Mediation." *Labor Law Journal,* 1955, *6,* 552-560.

Northrup, H. R. *Compulsory Arbitration and Government Intervention in Labor Disputes.* Washington, D.C.: Labor Policy Association, 1966.

Podell, J. E., and Knapp, W. M. "The Effect of Mediation on Perceived Firmness of the Opponent." *Journal of Conflict Resolution,* 1969, *13,* 511-520.

Pondy, L. R. "Organizational Conflict: Concepts and Models." *Administrative Science Quarterly,* 1967, *12,* 296-320.

Pruitt, D. G., and Johnson, D. F. "Mediation as an Aid to Face Saving in Negotiations." *Journal of Personality and Social Psychology,* 1970, *14,* 239-246.

Reuther, W. Quoted in N. W. Chamberlain, *The Labor Sector.* New York: McGraw-Hill, 1965.

Schelling, T. *The Strategy of Conflict.* Cambridge, Mass.: Harvard University Press, 1960.

Stevens, C. M. "Is Compulsory Arbitration Compatible with Bargaining?" *Industrial Relations,* 1966, *5,* 38-52.

Urban, T. F. "The Influence of Intervention Mode and Experience upon Bargaining Behavior." Paper presented at Midwest AIDS Conference, Michigan State University, 1973.

Vidmar, N. "Effects of Representational Roles and Mediators on Negotiation Effectiveness." *Journal of Personality and Social Psychology,* 1971, *17,* 48-58.

Walton, R. E. *Interpersonal Peacemaking: Confrontations and Third Party Consultations.* Reading, Mass.: Addison-Wesley, 1969.

35

⊸⊸ Reactions to Procedural Models for Adjudicative Conflict Resolution

E. Allan Lind
Bonnie E. Erickson
Nehemia Friedland
Michael Dickenberger

Adjudication, the resolution of conflict through the binding judgment of an impartial decision maker, is a common technique for the settlement of interpersonal and intergroup disputes. Adjudications may occur in a variety of settings, but perhaps the most salient examples of this form of conflict resolution are the decisions rendered by law courts. Although adjudication was long neglected as a topic of study in social science research on conflict resolution, recent years have seen a considerable expansion of the research literature concerning this technique for resolving disputes. Investigators have shown increasing interest both in examining the relation of adjudication to other forms of conflict resolution (see, for example, LaTour and others, 1976a, 1976b) and in identifying specific social processes influencing the behavior and perceptions of those involved in adjudications (see, for example, Lind, 1975; Thibaut, Walker, and Lind, 1972; Walker and others, 1974).

One approach to the study of adjudication has been the experimental investigation of the effects of various procedures which might be used in adjudications (Thibaut, LaTour, and Houlden, 1974; Walker and others, 1974). An overall dimension of procedural variation is the "procedural model" specified for the adjudication—the structuring principle of the conflict-resolving group. Legal scholars have engaged in much debate and speculative discussion regarding the relative merits of various procedural models (see, for example, Adams, 1973; Ehrenzweig, 1971). Although the distinctions among various extant and ideal procedural models have been made in terms of variables familiar to social

The original version of this article appeared under the title "Reactions to Procedural Models for Adjudicative Conflict Resolution: A Cross-National Study," by E. Allan Lind, Bonnie E. Erickson, Nehemia Friedland, and Michael Dickenberger, published in *Journal of Conflict Resolution*, Vol. 22, No. 2 (June 1978), pp. 318-341, and is reprinted herewith by permission of the publisher, Sage Publications, Inc.

scientists (for example, the presence or absence of particular roles in the adjudicative group and the permitted information and outcome dependence among various roles), systematic empirical studies of procedural models have begun only recently (see Thibaut and Walker, 1975, for a presentation of some of the studies on this topic). These studies have produced considerable information of value to the understanding of adjudicative conflict resolution. However, one disadvantage of this research is that virtually all of these investigations have been conducted in one country, the United States, using experimental subjects who are, in all probability, aware that their national legal system is based on one particular procedural model, the adversary model. The present study sought to remedy this situation by examining reactions to a variety of procedural models among individuals from several nations, including some nations that endorse procedural models other than the adversary.

The four procedural models examined in the present study are termed the "inquisitorial," "single-investigator," "double-investigator," and "adversary" models (see Figure 1). These four models were chosen for examination because they represent differ-

Figure 1. Four Procedural Models for Adjudication

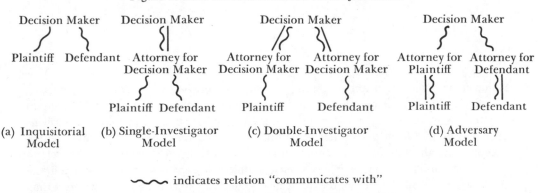

ent points on a conceptual continuum of systemic "adversariness," a dimension which has been of much concern to legal theorists and lawmakers (for example, Fuller, 1961) and which is related to national differences in legal procedures. At one end of this dimension is the adversary model (Figure 1d), an avowed goal of many specific procedures in American and British courts (see Cound, Friedenthal, and Miller, 1974). The adversary model permits each disputant in the conflict to exercise a great deal of control over the substance of the adjudicative hearing through the actions of his attorney, whom the disputant has chosen to be responsible for advancing his interests. In the adversary model the role of the adjudicative decision maker is essentially passive. It is the adversary attorneys (not the decision maker) who investigate the case in conflict, and it is the attorneys who control the flow of information to the decision maker in an effort to secure a decision favorable to the disputant with whom their outcomes are aligned. At the other end of the continuum is the inquisitorial model (Figure 1a). The inquisitorial model is characterized primarily by the fact that control over most of the substance of the adjudicative hearing lies in the hands of the legal decision maker. The inquisitorial decision maker himself accumulates information during the hearing of the conflict through personal interrogation of the disputants and witnesses.

Between these two extremes lie the single- and double-investigator models (Figures 1b and 1c). In these two procedural models one or two court-aligned investigators accumulate evidence about the dispute and, during the hearing of the case, relay this information to the decision maker. Neither the decision maker nor the disputants have complete control over the substance of the hearing. Of these two models, the double investigator may be supposed to be the more adversary, since the assignment of a different investigator to collect and present evidence for each disputant is a major element of the adversary model (see Thibaut, Walker, and Lind, 1972).

Although the procedural models examined in this study are best considered as "pure types" constructed from conceptual variables relevant to adjudicative conflict resolution, there are important approximations of each model in natural conflict resolution settings. As noted above, the adversary model is the basis of American and British legal procedures. In contrast, the civil and criminal law of many of the nations of continental Europe specifies the use of elements of both the inquisitorial and single-investigator models. For example, the presiding judge at a French legal hearing himself interrogates the disputants and witnesses to the case in order to supplement the information he obtains from an investigating official (Herzog, 1967; Pugh, 1962). A similar nonadversary procedure is used in the courts of West Germany, where the court and its agents conduct most of the fact-finding investigations and interrogations (Kaplan, von Mehren, and Schaeffer, 1958). The role relations in the United States court-martial resemble to some extent those specified in the double-investigator model, with the defense and prosecuting attorneys employed by the same organization which employs the decision maker (see Thibaut and Walker, 1975, ch. 4, for further discussion of these issues).

The inquisitorial-to-adversary dimension along which the four procedural models range may be construed as a continuum defined by increasing control over the substance of the case by the disputants and decreasing control by the decision maker. Thibaut and Walker (1975) have suggested that the perceived distribution of control between the decision maker and the disputants is a major determinant of the preference or satisfaction of the disputants with any particular procedural model. Specifically, Thibaut and Walker propose that models which are perceived to be high in disputant control and low in decision maker control are seen as characterized by procedural fairness and that the perception of procedural fairness leads to greater preference among disputants for using the model. This proposition has been supported by a number of studies that have demonstrated, among American subjects, a general preference for more adversary (disputant-controlled) over more inquisitorial (decision maker-controlled) procedural models (LaTour, 1974; Thibaut, LaTour, and Houlden, 1974; Walker and others, 1974).

As noted above, however, all of the previous studies of disputant preferences for procedural models have used American subjects. It is possible that these subjects were responding favorably to the adversary model because they were more familiar with adversary procedures or because the adversary model receives extensive endorsement in the legal institutions of the United States, rather than because of some intrinsic positive characteristic of the model. Quite different patterns of preference might have been observed had the studies been conducted in continental Europe, where societal prescriptions call for inquisitorial models. Lind (1974) found, for example, that French and American subjects differed in their reactions to adjudicator behavioral styles within an adversary model and suggested that at least some of these cross-national differences could be attributed to different societal prescriptions for adjudicator behavior. The present study tested the generality of the Thibaut and Walker proposal relating preference to the distribution of control in procedural models. This was done by examining preferences for the four procedural models in countries which endorse more inquisitorial models (France and West

Germany) as well as in countries which endorse more adversary models of adjudication (Britain and the United States). If the Thibaut and Walker proposal is generally correct, one would expect to observe greater preferences in all four nations for more adversary models. On the other hand, if the apparent preference for more adversary models found in previous studies is largely a result of national endorsement of those models, one would expect the French and West German subjects to show greater preference for inquisitorial than for adversary models.

Because previous research (Thibaut, LaTour, and Houlden, 1974; Walker and others, 1974) had shown that an individual's expected position in an adjudicated conflict may influence his evaluation of procedural models, approximately half the subjects in each nation were asked to evaluate the models from the perspective of the plaintiffs in a personal-injury case, while the remaining subjects were asked to adopt the perspective of the defendant in such a case. In an attempt to generate information not only about preferences for the models but also about international similarities and differences in the psychological concomitants of these preferences, the subjects were asked both to rate their preference for using each model and to rate each model on a number of dimensions which previous studies had shown to be important in describing the social characteristics of procedural models.

Method

Subjects and Sites. One hundred and seventy-eight subjects took part in the study. In the United States, sixty-two introductory psychology students participated in the study in partial fulfillment of a course requirement. Forty French university students participated for monetary payment (four of these subjects did not complete the entire questionnaire and were therefore omitted from all analyses of the data). In West Germany, thirty university students and young professionals participated in the experiment. The British subjects were forty-six university students. The study was conducted in Chapel Hill, North Carolina, USA; Paris, France; Cambridge, England; and Mannheim, West Germany. At each site, approximately half the subjects were randomly assigned to the plaintiff role condition; and the remainder were assigned to the defendant role condition.

Procedure. (The following procedure is that used in France. Essentially the same procedure was used at all four sites.) Subjects reported to the experiment one to four at a time. They were met by a native French-speaking experimenter, shown to a library, and seated at some distance from each other. The experimenter gave each subject two booklets containing all the materials to be used in the experiment. The subjects' attention was directed to the first of these booklets, which contained an instruction page, descriptions of the four procedural models, and a rating scale asking for the subjects' preferences among the four models. The experimenter asked the subjects to complete this booklet before continuing to the second booklet, which contained four pages of additional rating scales—one page for each of the models. The subjects were told to work through the two booklets at their own speed and were asked to return both booklets to the experimenter when they had finished. When all subjects had completed both booklets, the experimenter answered any questions concerning the study and paid the subjects for their participation in the experiment.

Materials. The subjects received written instructions (including the manipulation of the role factor) on the first page of the experimental booklet. The instructions for subjects in the defendant role conditions were as follows:

Imagine that you have been accused by another person of having wrongfully done injury to him, of having harmed him with malicious intent. Suppose further that, as defendant, you have some choice in deciding how the issue will be resolved; that is, which of several types of hearing procedures will be used to decide whether the charges against you are justified and hence whether you will have to pay damages to the plaintiff. Read over the following four types of hearing procedures and indicate your evaluations of them as ways of deciding whether the charges against you are justified.

Each subject in the plaintiff role conditions was asked in a similar manner to assume that he had charged another with having done wrongful injury to him.

Following these instructions were descriptions of the four procedural models discussed above. The models, labeled "Hearing Procedures," were identified only with the letters A-D to avoid any evaluative implications of specific titles. The models were presented in completely neutral terms, using only a simple statement of the roles included in the model and of the relationships among these roles. For example, the following is the English text of "Hearing Procedure C," the double-investigator model.

(1) *Decision Maker*—Under this procedure a decision maker will in turn appoint two investigators. One investigator will be assigned to present facts favorable to the plaintiff; the other, those facts favorable to the defendant. When the investigators have concluded their presentations, the decision maker will close the hearing, deliberate, and announce his decision.

(2) *Investigators or Representatives*—Two investigators, appointed by decision maker, are assigned to obtain the facts of the case. One investigator is assigned to each disputant, but the investigators are representatives of the decision maker and not of either plaintiff or defendant. During the hearing, the investigators may ask questions about the facts presented by the other investigator.

(3) *Disputants*—Prior to the hearing, plaintiff and defendant will furnish the facts requested by the investigator assigned to present their side of the case.

After studying the four models, the subjects were asked to rate their preferences among the models. Preference ratings of the four models were made on a nineteen-point scale, with the constraint that no two models could receive exactly the same rating on this scale. The scales in the second booklet solicited ratings of the extent to which each model was perceived to favor the subject himself, and to favor his opponent; the opportunity of each party to present evidence; the fairness of each model; and the degree to which the decision maker, the subject himself, and the subject's opponent were thought to have control over who won the dispute.

The same English version of the experimental materials was used in Chapel Hill and Cambridge. For use in Paris and Mannheim, the materials were translated by native French and German speakers and were back-translated to English to verify essential equivalence of meaning.

Design and Analyses of the Study. The data of the study were analyzed as a 4 (site) × 2 (plaintiff versus defendant role) × 4 (procedural model) complete factorial design with one within-subjects factor (that is, the procedural model factor). To avoid the necessity of making assumptions concerning the equality of variance-covariance matrices, the analyses used multivariate analyses of variance of contrast scores generated from the within-subjects factor (Bock, 1975; McCall and Appelbaum, 1973). These contrast scores were based on pairwise contrasts of the procedural models adjacent on the inquisitorial-to-adversary dimension (that is, inquisitorial versus single investigator, single investigator versus double investigator, and double investigator versus adversary). Analyses of covariance were used to provide "stepdown" tests of each contrast in order to avoid any inflation of significance as a result of the nonindependence of these contrasts (see Bock, 1975, ch. 7). This technique of analysis permitted conservative testing of the general ANOVA effects and assessment, via the specific difference contrasts, of the locus of these general effects.

All statistical analyses used least squares solutions to assure accuracy of the results in spite of the unequal number of subjects in various cells of the between-subjects design.

Results

Preference Ratings. The results of the analysis of subjects' preference ratings of the four procedural models are presented in Table 1. Of the several significant effects

Table 1. ANOVA of Preference Ratings of the Four Procedural Models

Source	df	F
Between-subjects		
Site (S)	3,166	1.75
Role (R)	1,166	1.88
S × R	3,166	< 1.0
Within-subjects		
Procedural model (M)	3,164	96.80[c]
Single investigator vs. inquisitorial (B-A)	1,164	76.84[c]
Double investigator vs. single investigator (C-B)	1,164	177.01[c]
Adversary vs. double investigator (D-C)	1,164	56.02[c]
S × M	9,399	2.14[b]
S × (B-A)	3,164	3.39[b]
S × (C-B)	3,164	1.97
S × (D-C)	3,164	2.49
R × M	3,164	3.12[a]
R × (B-A)	1,164	3.20
R × (C-B)	1,164	< 1.0
R × (D-C)	1,164	3.71
S × R × M	9,399	< 1.0
S × R × (B-A)	3,164	< 1.0
S × R × (C-B)	3,164	< 1.0
S × R × (D-C)	3,164	< 1.0

[a] $p < .05$.

[b] $p < .025$.

[c] $p < .005$.

observed on these ratings, the most striking is the main effect for the procedural model being rated. The marginal means for this effect, averaging across all sites and role conditions, are −4.91 for the inquisitorial model, −2.85 for the single-investigator model, +2.06 for the double-investigator model, and +4.87 for the adversary model. (On the preference scale, the endpoint "−9" was labeled "strongly prefer not to use this procedure"; the midpoint "0," "no preference one way or the other"; and the endpoint "+9," "strongly prefer to use this procedure.") The F values of the specific contrasts (see Table 1) confirm the pattern of responses evident from the above means. In terms of the conceptual dimension of interest, within each contrast the more adversary model is significantly preferred to the more inquisitorial model.

The significant site × model and role × model interactions are not due to any reversal of this general preference for more adversary models, but indicate instead local or role-specific variation in the relative difference between preferences for particular models. The site × model interaction, graphed in Figure 2, is the result of only a very slight pref-

Figure 2. Mean Preference Ratings of the Four Models at the Four Sites of Experimentation (Site × Model Interaction)

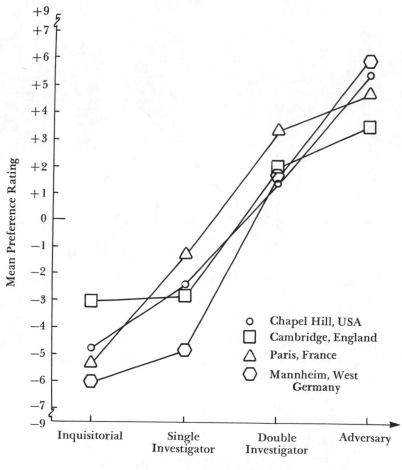

erence for the single-investigator over the inquisitorial model among British subjects and a more substantial difference in preferences for these two models among subjects at the other sites. (That this interactive effect is confined to ratings of the single-investigator and inquisitorial models is indicated by the fact that only the contrast testing this portion of the interaction is significant; see Table 1.) It should be noted that all subjects—including the British—much preferred the double-investigator to the single-investigator and inquisitorial models and preferred the adversary model to any of the other three.

The role × model interaction on preference ratings is graphed in Figure 3, which presents the mean preference ratings of the four models by plaintiff and defendant sub-

Figure 3. Mean Preference Ratings of the Four Models by Defendant and Plaintiff Role Subjects (Role × Model Interaction)

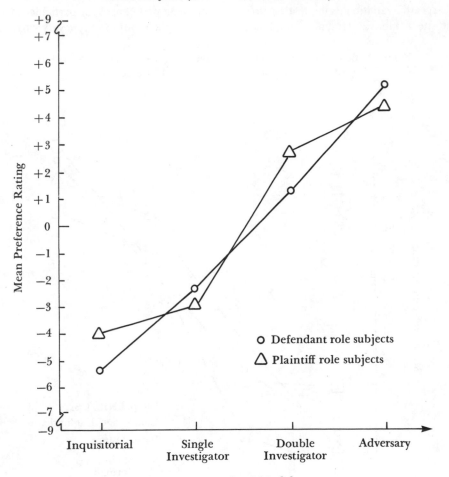

jects. The pattern of means and the specific contrast tests indicate that this interaction is due to relatively greater preference by defendant than plaintiff subjects for the more ad-versary procedure in the single-investigator versus inquisitorial and in the adversary versus double-investigator model contrasts (although the contrast interactions fall just short of significance: $F(1,164) = 3.20, p < .08$ and $F(1,164) = 3.71, p < .06$, respectively). That is, although both plaintiff and defendant subjects preferred the single-investigator to the inquisitorial model and the adversary to the double-investigator model, this differential preference was more pronounced with defendant role subjects. The preference for the double-investigator over the single-investigator model was substantial and did not vary with the subjects' role.

Other Questionnaire Items. In order to examine the subjects' perceptions of the characteristics of the four procedural models, responses to the eight items in the questionnaire booklet were subjected to analyses similar to that just reported for the preference ratings. Two other indices, generated from combinations of the questionnaire items, were also analyzed. One of these indices, labeled "total control," was the sum of the subjects' ratings on the three questionnaire items assessing the degree to which the decision maker, the subject himself, and the subject's opponent were perceived to control the outcome of the conflict. The second index, labeled "percent decision maker control," was the decision maker control rating expressed as a percentage of the total control index. The results of these analyses are reported in Table 2.

As indicated in Table 2, all ten dependent variables showed strong main effects for the procedural model factor. Marginal means for this main effect, averaging across sites and roles, are presented in Table 3. The subjects' ratings of the fairness of the model, the degree to which the model provided the subject and the subject's opponent the opportunity to present evidence, and the degree to which the model favored the subject showed model main effects very similar to that observed on the preference ratings. That is, on each of these measures each pairwise specific contrast was significant, indicating that the subjects felt that the more adversary model in each pair exhibited these qualities to a greater extent than did the more inquisitorial model. The ratings of the decision maker's control over the outcome of the conflict and the percentage index of this control dimension showed significant decreases across the inquisitorial-to-adversary dimension: for each pairwise contrast, the more inquisitorial model was seen as involving more decision maker control. The remaining four measures (ratings of the subject's and his opponent's control over the outcome, ratings of the degree to which the model favored the opponent, and the total control index) showed either no increase in or a significant decrease between the inquisitorial and single-investigator models and significant increases along the remainder of the inquisitorial-to-adversary dimension.

Significant site × model interactions were observed on two of the ten dependent variables under consideration (see Table 2). The interaction on ratings of the fairness of the models seems to be due to the fact that the American and West German subjects rated the adversary model as substantially more fair than the double-investigator model, while the French and British subjects gave nearly equivalent fairness ratings to these two models (F (3,164) = 2.55, $p < .058$ for the specific contrast interaction testing this locus of the overall interaction). A site × model interaction was also observed on the total control index. While subjects at all four sites felt that the total control of three primary roles in the adjudication was less in the single-investigator than in the inquisitorial model, this difference was most strongly evident for the British subjects (although the specific contrast interaction is not strictly significant; F (3,164) = 2.17, $p < .10$).

A significant role × model interaction was observed on the ratings of the degree to which each model would favor the subject himself. Specific contrast tests within this interaction revealed that defendant role subjects, to a greater degree than plaintiff role subjects, felt they would be more favored by the single-investigator than the inquisitorial model (F (1,164) = 4.38, $p < .04$) and more favored by the adversary than the double-investigator model (F (1,164) = 5.27, $p < .03$). This is the same interaction pattern as that revealed by the role × model interaction on the preference ratings.

The two scales assessing perceptions of disputant control (that is, those asking the degree to which the subject and his opponent would control the outcome of the case) showed site main effects. Higher ratings of disputant control were observed for the French subjects than for the subjects at the other three sites. (These effects in turn produced site main effects on the percent decision maker control and total control indices, which were based in part on these control ratings.)

Table 2. ANOVAs of Subjects' Responses to Questionnaire Items and Indices

	Source						
	Between-Subjects			Within-Subjects			
Item	Site (S)	Role (R)	S × R	Model (M)	S × M	R × M	R × S × M
Model is fair	1.15[a]	—	1.80	55.95[d]	2.01[c]	1.29	—
Decision maker controls conflict resolution	2.12	—	1.06	73.72[d]	1.37	—	—
Subject controls conflict resolution	2.90[c]	1.27	—	35.14[d]	1.37	1.50	—
Opponent controls conflict resolution	4.28[d]	—	—	36.38[d]	1.75	2.50	—
Subject's opportunity to present evidence	1.80	1.44	—	81.41[d]	1.80	—	—
Opponent's opportunity to present evidence	1.77	—	—	65.78[d]	1.89	—	—
Model favors subject	—	—	—	49.98[d]	1.80	2.85[c]	—
Model favors opponent	—	5.80[c]	—	35.73[d]	1.58	1.07	—
Total control[b]	4.62[d]	—	—	23.24[c]	2.20[c]	1.61	—
Percentage decision maker control[b]	3.02[c]	—	—	58.33[d]	1.33	2.06	—
Degrees of freedom	3,166	1,166	3,166	3,164	9,399	3,164	9,399

[a]Values entered in table are F ratios. No value is entered when the F is less than 1.0.

[b]See text for explanation of this index.

[c]$p < .05$.

[d]$p < .01$.

Table 3. Marginal Means for Main Effect of Procedural Model on
Questionnaire Items

Item	Procedural Model			
	Inquisi-torial	Single Investigator	Double Investigator	Adver-sary
Model is fair	3.33[b]	4.16	5.78	6.33
Decision maker controls conflict resolution	12.74[c]	10.40	9.65	8.62
Subject controls conflict resolution	5.03[c]	4.72	6.06	7.56
Opponent controls conflict resolution	5.84[c]	5.05	6.23	7.93
Subject's opportunity to present evidence	3.93[b]	4.32	5.88	7.10
Opponent's opportunity to present evidence	4.31[b]	4.47	5.72	6.93
Model favors subject	4.12[b]	4.54	4.88	5.63
Model favors opponent	4.61[b]	4.40	4.68	5.57
Total control[a]	23.60	20.18	21.94	24.11
Percentage decision maker control[a]	56.84	52.35	45.51	36.61

[a]See text for explanation of this index.

[b]Item rated on nine-point scale; higher values indicate ratings in the direction named.

[c]Item rated on fifteen-point scale; "1" = "too little," "8" = "right amount," "15" = "too much."

Finally, a significant main effect for the role factor revealed that defendant role subjects more than plaintiff role subjects thought that all four models would favor the subject's opponent.

Other Analyses. Because a major goal of this study was to determine which characteristics of the models were most closely associated with differential preferences, additional analyses were conducted to aid in this aspect of the interpretation of the results. "Pattern scores"—an index of association used by Thibaut, LaTour, and Houlden (1974) and Thibaut and Walker (1975)—were computed for each subject. These pattern scores indicate the degree to which a particular subject's response to the questionnaire items showed the same pattern across the four models as did his preference ratings. As is the case with traditional between-subject correlations, the absolute magnitude of the pattern score indicates the strength of the relation between the preference scale and the questionnaire scale, while the sign of the pattern score indicates whether the relation is direct or inverse.

The correlations on which these pattern scores were based were not computed in the traditional manner across subjects. Instead, a correlation coefficient was calculated for each subject across the four procedural models to represent the degree to which his preference ratings were linearly related to his ratings on a questionnaire item. Because the distribution of correlation coefficients is nonnormal, these within-subject correlation scores were transformed using the following formula, where r is the subject's correlation score:

$$\text{pattern score} = 1/2 \log_n ((1 + r) / (1 - r)).$$

Thus, if a particular subject's ratings of the fairness of the four models correlated .85 with his preference ratings, the resulting pattern score would be:

$$1.256 = 1/2 \log_n ((1 + .85) / (1 - .85)).$$

Unlike traditional correlation coefficients, pattern scores can have absolute values greater than 1.0. Pattern scores have the advantage, not found in traditional correlation coefficients, of permitting easy analysis of intersubject differences in the relationship between two scales.

In order to assess the effects of the role and site factors on concomitants of the preference ratings, these pattern scores were submitted to analyses of variance. Table 4

Table 4. Mean Pattern Scores Relating Preference Ratings and Questionnaire Items

Item	Site			
	Chapel Hill, USA	Cambridge, England	Paris, France	Mannheim, W. Germany
Model is fair	1.58[a]	1.40	1.12	1.95
Decision maker controls conflict resolution	−1.25	−.34	−.85	−.95
Subject controls conflict resolution	1.02	1.16	.74	1.46
Opponent controls conflict resolution	.85	.75	.20	1.36
Subject's opportunity to present evidence	1.35	1.14	1.33	1.10
Opponent's opportunity to present evidence	1.37	1.00	.99	.61

[a]See text for an explanation of this index.

shows the mean pattern scores relating the preference ratings to selected questionnaire ratings at each site of experimentation. The pattern scores reported here were chosen for presentation because of their relevance to previous thought about procedural preferences (see, for example, Thibaut and Walker, 1975) or because they showed interesting international differences.

Congruent with the Thibaut and Walker contention that the perception of procedural fairness leads to greater preference for a procedural model, all four sites showed high positive pattern scores relating the preference and fairness ratings of the models. Although there was a significant site main effect on these pattern scores ($F (3,166) = 4.09, p < .01$), at three of the four sites (that is, for the American, British, and German subjects) the fairness pattern score mean was the highest of any pattern score mean computed.

It should be noted that only the pattern scores using the ratings of decision maker control were negative, indicating that only this rating dimension showed an inverse relationship with the preference ratings. It is also noteworthy that the pattern scores relating the model preferences with the subjects' ratings of their own control over the conflict resolution and with the subjects' ratings of their own opportunity to present evidence were universally high and did not exhibit significant between-site variation ($F (3,166) = 1.96$, ns, and $F (3,166) < 1.0$ for the two dimensions, respectively).

Site main effects were observed on three sets of pattern scores in addition to those pertaining to the fairness-preference relationship. The British subjects' preference ratings appear to be less closely related to their perceptions of decision maker control than was the case with the American, French, and German subjects ($F (3,166) = 6.05, p < .001$). On the pattern scores relating model preferences to perceptions of the opponent's control, the relatively low mean of the French subjects seems to be responsible for the site main effect (F (3,166) = 6.10, $p < .001$). Finally, on the pattern scores relating the preference ratings to ratings of the opponent's opportunity to present evidence, the mean of the German subjects was distinctively lower than the mean of the other subjects (F (3,166) = 4.67, $p < .01$).

Discussion

The most striking effect observed in the present study was the tendency of subjects at all four sites and in both role conditions to order the four procedural models, on a number of dependent variables, as the models are ordered on the theoretical inquisitorial-to-adversary dimension. That this ordering was observed on the subjects' preference ratings, with only minor variations in mean values among the four sites of experimentation, provides considerable evidence that there is some quality of more adversary procedures that is generally desired. This general preference for more adversarial procedural models, even among subjects whose own legal systems are based on inquisitorial models, indicates that model preferences are not due primarily to such factors as familiarity or national endorsement of particular models. The analyses of the questionnaire items and their pattern scores with the preference ratings suggest a cluster of variables which may be important in explaining the preference results obtained. (It must be noted, however, that the pattern scores, like any correlational index, can only suggest, but never confirm, causal relationships.)

We noted earlier that the questionnaire items concerning the subjects' perceptions of fairness and their perceptions of their own influence capacity over the adjudicative process (that is, the ratings of their own opportunity to present evidence and of their own control over the resolution of the conflict) exhibited strong positive pattern scores with the preference ratings. The close relationships between these three questionnaire items and the preference ratings are congruent with the Thibaut and Walker (1975) suggestion that procedures that induce perceptions of high disputant control over the conflict resolution process lead to perceptions of fairness and to the preference for and satisfaction with the procedure. It is particularly noteworthy that perceived personal control was closely related to model preferences not only in the United States and Great Britain but also in France and West Germany, where inquisitorial, decision maker-controlled procedures are more common. This leads us to believe that there exists (at least in Western societies) a general desire for high personal control over the adjudicative process, a desire which is not dependent on the societal specification of models designed to maximize this variable.

In light of the apparent importance of perceptions of personal control in determining preferences for models of adjudication, it is interesting to note that related variables have been shown to have considerable influence on the reactions of individuals to a variety of situations other than adjudication. For example, recent studies by Glass and Singer (1972) on the effects of environmental stressors have indicated that the provision of mechanisms which are alleged to render the stressor controllable by a subject results in the reduction of negative aftereffects of the stressor (see also Schulz, 1976). Similarly, it is a common finding in studies which have assessed reactions to communication networks that subjects are more satisfied with more central positions in the networks than with peripheral positions (see Collins and Raven, 1969, for a review of these studies). Central positions in communication networks certainly involve more actual control over the group's goal attainment, and it seems likely that subjects recognize this. That variables related to the perception of personal control over outcomes are associated with positive reactions to situations as diverse as these, together with the absence in the present study of any national differences in the relationship between such perceptions and preferences among adjudicative models, suggests that perceived personal control is a variable of major importance and of great generality in the understanding of reactions to social structures and events.

Our previous remarks about cross-national similarities in reactions to the procedural models notwithstanding, the significant site × model interaction on the preference ratings shows that there were some differences among subjects in different nations in their evaluations of the models. It will be recalled that this interaction was due to the British subjects showing less preference for the single-investigator model over the inquisitorial model than was the case for subjects at the other three sites. We propose, however, that this finding can also be explained by control considerations, although it is necessary to expand our theoretical examination to include the control perceived to be vested in other roles in the adjudicative group. Thibaut and Walker have suggested recently (Houlden and others, forthcoming) that the desire of disputants for high control over the adjudicative process is the result of the perception that there is greater likelihood that the particular facts in the case under adjudication will be presented if there is high disputant control and low decision maker control. High disputant control is thought to be associated with consideration of the particular circumstances in the case and with consideration of the relation of these circumstances to concepts of distributive justice or equity (see Adams, 1965; Homans, 1961). High decision maker control, on the other hand, is thought to be associated with a more "legalistic" conflict resolution process, which may neglect the particulars of the case.

If the British subjects, more than the subjects in the other three nations, saw the single-investigator model as involving the transfer of control to the investigative official, and if the British subjects thought that this official would focus on legalistic rather than equity concerns, their reactions to the inquisitorial and single-investigator models can be explained. There is little reason to prefer a powerful investigator to a powerful judge if one believes that neither will focus on the particular circumstances of the case. Although it is not possible with the present data to test the proposition that the British subjects saw the single investigator as oriented toward legalistic concerns, there is some evidence that the transfer of control to the investigator was especially salient to the British subjects. Specifically, the site × model interaction on the total control index revealed that, more than the subjects at the other three sites, the British saw the single-investigator model as leading to less control by the decision maker and the disputants than did the inquisitorial model.

The role × model interaction on the preference ratings, due to the somewhat greater preference of defendant subjects than of plaintiff subjects for more adversary models, may also be explained in terms of the distribution of control over the adjudicative process and the implications of this control for the presentation of the particular circumstances in the case. More commonly than plaintiffs, defendants in personal-injury cases (such as that used in the present study) base their evidence and arguments on protestations that the particular facts in the case do not fit the legal rules under which the suit is brought. Subjects in the defendant role thus may have more strongly preferred more adversary models because they feared that these important particulars of the case would not emerge under more decision maker-controlled, inquisitorial models. This is not to say that the presentation of the particular circumstances of the case would be unimportant to plaintiffs; this issue is assumed simply to be of even greater concern to defendants.

Some limitations of the present study require comment. The subjects at all four sites were for the most part university students and were, of course, not entirely representative of the national populations from which they were drawn. Since the major purpose of the study was to provide a test of the control distribution hypothesis against the hypothesis that previous findings had resulted from national endorsement and familiarity with particular models, this nonrepresentativeness was not considered a serious problem. It was assumed that university students in each nation would be well aware of the procedural model characteristics of their nation's legal system, and would thus provide an adequate opportunity to test these hypotheses. Nevertheless, it is noteworthy that several recent studies using different subject groups have replicated the finding that procedures are more preferred when disputant control is high and decision maker control over the adjudicative process is low. These studies include an experiment by Houlden and associates (forthcoming) using undergraduate students, law students, and military judges as subjects and an experiment by LaTour and associates (1976b) using German and American undergraduate and law students. Another study asked posttrial prisoners in an American military prison to judge a number of procedural models in a fashion much like that used in the present study and produced results very similar to those presented here.

A second limitation of the present study is that the subjects were asked to role-play defendants and plaintiffs in a conflict and did not, of course, actually expect to make use of the procedural models they evaluated. It is possible that their reactions would have been different had they actually been involved in a conflict resolution situation. The method used here was chosen because of its practicality and economy of use at the several sites of experimentation. However, this limitation may be at least partially discounted in view of the fact that the results reported here are very similar to those obtained in a number of studies in which subjects in actual conflict resolution situations evaluated these or similar procedural models (see, for example, LaTour and others, 1976b; LaTour, 1974; Thibaut, LaTour, and Houlden, 1974; Walker and others, 1974).

Finally, it is important to note that the present study was designed to test the generality of previous empirical findings and the theoretical proposals advanced to explain those findings. Any application of the above results to policy evaluations of actual adjudicative procedures is hazardous, not only because of the usual problems attending the generalization of laboratory results to other situations but also because there are many factors other than disputant preference (for example, judicial accuracy, efficiency, and economy) which must be considered in such evaluations.

The primary value of this study resides in its confirmation of the importance of control relationships in determining reactions to adjudicative conflict resolution and in the demonstration that this psychological process seems to transcend national boundaries. The present data have permitted us to make some suggestions about similarities and differences between nations in the perception of procedural justice. There remains, of course, considerable need for further studies of this topic. It is desirable, for example, to extend the study of adjudication to include other subject populations and to examine adjudicative situations which more closely approximate the complex contexts of formal adjudications. Further, if preference for procedures is indeed the result of perceptions about the distribution of control and the implications of these control perceptions for equity versus legalistic considerations, additional research may show that preferences for adversary models might be decreased if for some reason disputants feel a loss of control or perceive that the adversary adjudication is taking a more legalistic orientation than they desire. Similarly, it may be found that inquisitorial models may be rendered more acceptable if they include some salient, standard provision for disputant input concerning the particular circumstances of the case. In any event, it is from such further study that a greater understanding of procedural justice will be achieved and that suggestions may be offered with confidence concerning the likelihood that existing procedures will provide equitable and satisfactory outcomes from interpersonal and intergroup conflicts.

References

Adams, G. W. "The Small Claims Court and the Adversary Process: More Problems of Function and Form." *Canadian Bar Review,* 1973, *51,* 583-616.

Adams, J. S. "Inequity in Social Exchange." In L. Berkowitz (Ed.), *Advances in Experimental Social Psychology.* Vol. 2. New York: Academic Press, 1965.

Bock, R. D. *Multivariate Statistical Methods in Behavioral Research.* New York: McGraw-Hill, 1975.

Collins, B. E., and Raven, B. H. "Group Structure: Attraction, Coalitions, Communication, and Power." In G. Lindzey and E. Aronson (Eds.), *The Handbook of Social Psychology.* Vol. 4. Reading, Mass.: Addison-Wesley, 1969.

Cound, J. J., Friedenthal, J. H., and Miller, A. R. *Civil Procedure: Cases and Materials.* St. Paul, Minn.: West, 1974.

Ehrenzweig, A. A. *Psychoanalytic Jurisprudence.* Dobbs Ferry, N.Y.: Oceana, 1971.

Fuller, L. "The Adversary System." In H. Berman (Ed.), *Talks on American Law.* New York: Vintage Books, 1961.

Glass, D. C., and Singer, J. E. *Urban Stress.* New York: Academic Press, 1972.

Herzog, P. *Civil Procedure in France.* The Hague: Martinus Nijhoff, 1967.

Homans, G. C. *Social Behavior: Its Elementary Forms.* New York: Harcourt Brace Jovanovich, 1961.

Houlden, P., and others. "Preference for Modes of Dispute Resolution as a Function of Process and Decision Control." *Journal of Experimental Social Psychology* (forthcoming).

Kaplan, B., von Mehren, A. T., and Schaeffer, R. "Phases of German Civil Procedure." *Harvard Law Review,* 1958, *71,* 1193-1268, 1443-1472.

LaTour, S. "Determinants of Satisfaction with Adversary and Inquisitorial Modes of Adjudication." Unpublished master's thesis, University of North Carolina, 1974.

LaTour, S., and others. "Some Determinants of Preference for Modes of Conflict Resolution." *Journal of Conflict Resolution,* 1976a, *20,* 319-356.

LaTour, S., and others. "Procedure: Transnational Perspectives and Preferences." *Yale Law Journal,* 1976b, *86,* 258-290.

Lind, E. A. "Reactions of Participants to Adjudicated Conflict Resolution: A Cross-Cultural, Experimental Study." Unpublished doctoral dissertation, University of North Carolina, 1974.

Lind, E. A. "The Exercise of Information Influence in Legal Advocacy." *Journal of Applied Social Psychology,* 1975, *5,* 127-143.

McCall, R. B., and Appelbaum, M. I. "Bias in the Analysis of Repeated-Measures Designs: Some Alternative Approaches." *Child Development,* 1973, *41,* 401-415.

Pugh, G. W. "Administration of Criminal Justice in France: An Introductory Analysis." *Louisiana Law Review,* 1962, *23,* 1-28.

Schulz, R. "Effects of Control and Predictability on the Physical and Psychological Well-Being of the Institutionalized Aged." *Journal of Personality and Social Psychology,* 1976, *33,* 563-573.

Thibaut, J., LaTour, S., and Houlden, P. "Procedural Justice as Fairness." *Stanford Law Review,* 1974, *26,* 1271-1289.

Thibaut, J., and Walker, L. *Procedural Justice: A Psychological Analysis.* Hillsdale, N.J.: Erlbaum, 1975.

Thibaut, J., Walker, L., and Lind, E. A. "Adversary Presentation and Bias in Legal Decisionmaking." *Harvard Law Review,* 1972, *86,* 386-401.

Walker, L., and others. "Reactions of Participants and Observers to Modes of Adjudication." *Journal of Applied Social Psychology,* 1974, *4,* 295-310.

36

OD Techniques and Their Results in Twenty-Three Organizations: The Michigan ICL Study

David G. Bowers

In 1966 staff members of the University of Michigan's Institute for Social Research launched a five-year program of organizational projects, the Inter-Company Longitudinal Study (ICLS). This ambitious undertaking addressed itself to a number of substantive questions of organizational behavior and change research within a framework containing the following features:

1. *Continuity of site* (over a period of one or more years).
2. *Use of a common survey instrument* (as a benchmark measure of the functioning of the human organization).
3. *Organizational development as a beneficial tool* (to increase payoff to participating firms and to ensure the presence of constructive movement for research purposes).
4. *Research on organizational change techniques* (to permit the acquisition of systematic knowledge about the comparative effect of a number of possible interventions).

After an initial year of instrument development, staff acquisition, and pilot projects, the main phase of the study began. The hopes and aims sketched in the four precepts listed above were in varying degrees brought to fulfillment. Continuity of site proved to be greater than has been the case in the great majority of previous studies. Most organizations remained committed to and involved in an ICLS project for at least two years. They did not, however, endure for the full five years (although some may well ultimately do so).

A common instrument, the Survey of Organizations questionnaire, was developed and refined. It has been used, in one of its editions, in each site and data collection wave. Most participating organizations underwent at least two measurement waves using that instrument, with some form of change, development, or intervention occurring in the interval between the two; some had as many as five successive measurements. Rele-

Reproduced from the *Journal of Applied Behavioral Science,* 1973, *9* (1), 21-43, by special permission from the author and the NTL Institute for Applied Behavioral Science.

vant portions of this instrument generated the substance of the data examined in this article.

All organizations, with the exception of a very few in which no action plan was intended and in which none evolved, undertook some program of organizational development; as we shall see, the specific nature of the activity varied from one site to another.

Organizational change research is an uncharted territory in many aspects, and the research staff has had, of necessity, to feel its way along quite gradually. Many of the findings are only now slowly entering into the professional purview. As the reader can imagine, content analysis of five years of documents and multivariate analysis of a mountain of quantitative data is a lengthy, difficult task. I wish to forewarn the reader who anticipates a detailed chronicling of intervention strategies that I will present less of that than he (or I) might wish. Instead, my present purpose is an overview of results from this study's large number of cases and their possibilities for comparative analysis.

At the end of five years, work in some form has been under way in thirty-one organizations (plants or separate marketing regions) in fifteen companies. Data from twenty-three of these organizations in ten companies are included in the present analysis. Six organizations, in four companies, were excluded because no repeat measurements have as yet been obtained. One company was excluded because it was primarily involved in an ancillary activity unrelated to organizational research and change of the kind considered here.

The twenty-three organizations comprise 14,812 persons, in white-collar and blue-collar positions, and constitute a wide array of industries—paper, chemicals, petroleum refining, aluminum, automobiles, household products, and insurance, in the areas of continuous-process manufacturing, assembly-line manufacturing, components fabrication, marketing, and research and development.

Change Treatments to Be Compared

Six forms of intervention can be identified as having occurred in one or more of the twenty-three organizations. For the most part, they are not "pure" treatments, since nearly all involved at least some form of return of tabulated survey data. Nevertheless, they are sufficiently different from one another to have been the source of conflicts between the change agents who used them and to have been regarded as different by the client systems who experienced them.

Survey Feedback. No authoritative volume has as yet been written about this development technique, although a number of article-length references exist (Bowers and Franklin, 1972, for example).

Many persons mistakenly believe that survey feedback consists of a rather superficial handing back of tabulated numbers and percentages, and little else. On the contrary, when employed with skill and experience, it becomes a sophisticated tool for using the data as a springboard to development. In the sites classified as having received *survey feedback* as a change treatment, this treatment formed the principal substance of the intervention. Data were tabulated for each group engaged in the project, as well as for each combination of groups that represented an area of responsibility in the organizational pyramid. Data appeared in the format shown in Figure 1.

Each supervisor and manager received a tabulation of this sort containing data from the responses of his own immediate subordinates; the measures, descriptions of their basis, and meaning; and suggestions concerning their interpretation and use. A resource person, from ISR or the client system's own staff, usually counseled privately with the

Figure 1. Typical Format of Survey Feedback Tabulation

GROUP NUMBER 99999

Item	Percentage Distribution (1)	(2)	(3)	(4)	(5)	Mean	Std. Dev.	N
7 CO USES NEW WK METHODS	8	0	17	42	25	3.82	1.11	11
8 CO INTEREST IN WELFARE	8	8	17	25	33	3.73	1.29	11
22 DISAGREEMTS WKED THRU	0	8	50	17	8	3.30	0.78	10
38 OBJECTIVS SET JOINTLY	17	8	25	17	17	3.10	1.37	10

supervisor-recipient about the contents of the package and then arranged a time when the supervisor could meet with his subordinates to discuss the findings and their implications. The resource person ordinarily agreed to attend that meeting in order to help the participants with the technical aspects of the tabulations and the process aspects of the discussion.

Feedback procedures typically vary from site to site, and did so within the ICLS sites that received this treatment. In certain instances, a "waterfall" pattern, in which the feedback process is substantially completed at superordinate levels before moving to subordinate groups, was adopted. In other instances, feedback to all groups and echelons was more or less simultaneous.

Time and space do not permit a lengthy discussion of the various forms which feedback may take. It should be stated, however, that an effective survey feedback operation helps an organization's groups move from a discussion of the tabulated perceptions, through a cataloging of their implications, to commitment to solutions to the problems identified and defined by the discussion.

This technique has long been associated with organizational development and change work conducted by the Institute for Social Research and was considered at the outset of this study as likely to constitute a more or less standard tool. That it was not as universally employed as this statement might suggest forms the basis for its identification as a distinct treatment.

Interpersonal Process Consultation. This treatment bears at least some resemblance to what Schein (1969) has termed "process consultation." The change agent most closely identified with this treatment attaches great importance to developing, within the client groups themselves, a capacity for forming and implementing their own change program. Considerable importance is attached to the change agent's establishing himself from the outset as a trustworthy, helpful adjunct to the group's own process. A great deal of effort and emphasis is placed on his catalyzing a process of surfacing data in areas customarily not plumbed in work organizations (attitudes, feelings, individual needs, reasons for conflict, informal processes, and so on). In behavioral specifics, the change agent employs the posing of questions to group members; process analysis periods; feedback of observations or feelings; agenda-setting, review, and appropriateness-testing procedures; and occasional conceptual inputs on interpersonal topics. Work is sometimes undertaken with members singly, but more often in natural work groupings. Human, rather than technical, processes are generally assumed to have primacy for organizational effectiveness.

Task Process Consultation. This treatment is oriented very closely to task objectives and the specific interpersonal processes associated with them. A change agent who adheres to this pattern typically begins by analyzing a client unit's work-task situation privately, after extensive interviews concerning its objectives, potential resources, and the organizational forces blocking its progress. He consults privately with the supervisor at frequent intervals to establish rapport and to gain commitment to objectives and desired future courses of action. He sets the stage for client group discussions by introducing select bits of data or by having another person do so. He encourages group discussion and serves as a process observer, but also uses role playing, some substantive inputs at timely points, as well as nondirective counseling techniques, to guide the discussion toward commitment to desired courses of action.

Laboratory Training. As practiced within ICLS projects, this intervention technique more nearly approximates the interpersonal relations laboratory than the intrapsychic or personal-growth session. A "family group" design was followed almost exclusively, with the entire laboratory lasting from three days to two weeks, depending upon circumstances and organizational schedule requirements. Sessions were ordinarily conducted at a motel or resort away from the usual work place. Experiential exercises (for example, the NASA Game or "Moon Problem," the Ten-Dollar Exercise, the Tower-Building Problem) were interspersed with unstructured discussion time. During the years of the study, a number of terms were used by those conducting the training to describe it. Initially it was referred to as "T-group training"; in later years it was termed "team development training," or simply "team training." The content, however, remained relatively constant in kind, if not in exact substance. The change agents who conducted the training were not novices; on the contrary, they had had many years of experience in conducting it and were judged by those familiar with their work to be competent.

Data Handback. Not truly a change treatment, this forms instead a control or comparison condition. In certain sites no real survey feedback work was conducted. Data were tabulated and returned in envelopes to the appropriate supervisors, but no effort was made to encourage group problem-solving discussions concerning those data. Nor did any other treatment occur in these sites.

No Treatment. In a few sites, data were tabulated and returned to the appropriate top or staff manager but were not shared by him with relevant managers and supervisors. They were instead filed away in a cabinet. Since no other development activities were undertaken in these sites, it seems justifiable to classify them as having had no treatment at all.

Survey feedback was earlier described as the "principal substance of the intervention" in sites labeled as such in the study. It was also stated that some form of tabulated survey data was returned to someone in all sites. Both statements are true. A system is classified in this article as having received survey feedback as its treatment when survey feedback, *and that alone,* was used, both with capstone groups (those groups at the top management rungs of the organizational ladder) and with all groups below them which were involved in the project. Where interpersonal process consultation, task process consultation, or laboratory training are the reported treatments, the principal intervention *with the capstone groups* consisted of that particular treatment. These groups, along with all other participating groups in their organization, also received tabulated data and ordinarily spent a varying amount of time discussing it. Change agents who used these treatments characteristically placed survey feedback work in a distinctly secondary role. In some instances, after a few brief and sometimes superficial sessions, groups were encouraged to move on to the "real" change activity; in other instances, the nonfeedback activity began before survey data were made available, and the data were used only occasionally (perhaps by the change agent himself) to underscore a point or a development. Data feedback, to the extent that it went on at all, was often left in these sites to partially trained, and normally overloaded, internal resource persons, who were often more attracted to the more glamorous activities modeled by the external change agent.

Thus, events, schedules, and the personal style preference of the change agents combined to produce a contrast between sites in which survey feedback was truly and thoroughly conducted at all levels and without other treatments, and sites in which a rather half-hearted effort at data discussion was overshadowed by other treatments with capstone groups.

Finally, a word must be said about the way in which organizations came to receive different treatments. In a true experiment, assignment to treatment category is random. No pretense can be made that a purely random assignment procedure was employed in this multicompany study. Still, if not random, it appears to have been less than systematic. Change treatment was determined on a basis having little, if anything, to do with the nature of the client system; it was instead determined by change agent preference—that is, by the preferred and customary techniques of the change agent assigned to the site. In short, treatment was determined by change agent selection, which was in turn determined by sheer availability at the time of contract.

Measurement and Analysis Procedures

The dependent variables in the analyses reported below are measures of organizational functioning obtained from repeated administrations (ordinarily one year apart) of the Survey of Organizations questionnaire (Taylor and Bowers, 1972), particularly the sixteen critical indices that constitute the core of that instrument. The content of this instrument was originally developed from the many studies which ISR had conducted over the years prior to 1966. Subsequently, the content of this questionnaire has been subjected to a number of analyses, employing both smallest-space analysis and hierarchical cluster analysis, which suggest that the total may really comprise the limited number of multi-item indices employed in this present study. Six are measures of the organizational conditions that surround any particular focal group to form the environment within which it must live. These conditions, outside and especially above a particular manager's group, are really nothing more than the perceived accumulated effects of the ways in which other groups function. Helpful or harmful policies, for example, are the output of higher-echelon groups with good or poor leadership, respectively. We call these accumulated effects *organizational climate* and attach to that term essentially the same meaning given it by Evan (1968); that is, a concrete phenomenon reflecting a social-psychological reality, shared by people related to the organization, and having its impact on organizational behavior. We do *not* imply by the term the alternative meaning sometimes given it, that of a general flow of behavior and feeling within a group (see Halpin, 1966).

Four other indices measure managerial leadership behavior of an interpersonal (support and interaction facilitation) and task (goal emphasis and work facilitation) nature. Four similar measures tap the peer leadership area, and together these eight measures reflect what has come to be called the "four-factor" theory of leadership (Bowers and Seashore, 1966; Taylor and Bowers, 1972). The remaining two measures tap group process and satisfaction, respectively.

High scores on these sixteen measures, for any organization or group, are considered to be reasonably reflective of a general state of organizational effectiveness; lower scores, of a less effective state. The content of the measures, like their place in a conceptual scheme, is based upon the Likert "metatheory" of the human organization as a social system (Likert, 1961, 1967), which itself represents an integration of a large array of empirical findings. The questionnaire has been subjected to extensive analyses, and the healthy and inquisitive skeptic is directed to Taylor and Bowers (1972), where both reliability and validity data are presented in considerable detail. For present purposes, a brief summary of content and reliability is presented in Table 1. Evidence concerning validity

Table 1. Summary of Content and Reliability of Sixteen Indices of
the Survey of Organizations Questionnaire

Area–Measure	Description	No. of Items	Internal Consistency Reliability Coefficient
Organizational climate			
Human resources primacy	Whether the climate indicates that people, their talents, skills, and motivation are considered to be one of the organization's most important assets.	3	.80
Communication flow	Whether information flows effectively upward, downward, and laterally in the organization.	3	.78
Motivational climate	Whether conditions and relationships in the environment are generally encouraging or discouraging to effective work.	3	.80
Decision-making practices	How decisions are made in the organization: whether they are made effectively, at the right levels, and based upon all the available information.	4	.79
Technological readiness	Whether the equipment and resources are up to date, efficient, and well maintained.	2	.58
Lower-level influence	Whether lowest-level supervisors and employees feel they have influence on what goes on in their department.	2	.70
Managerial leadership			
Support	Behavior toward subordinates that lets them know they are worthwhile persons doing useful work.	3	.94
Interaction facilitation	Team building, behavior that encourages subordinates to develop close, cooperative working relationships with one another.	2	.89
Goal emphasis	Behavior that stimulates a contagious enthusiasm for doing a good job (*not* pressure).	2	.85
Work facilitation	Behavior that removes roadblocks to doing a good job.	3	.88
Peer leadership			
Support	Behavior by subordinates toward one another that enhances their mutual feeling of being worthwhile persons doing useful work.	3	.87

(continued on next page)

Table 1 *(Continued)*

Area–Measure	Description	No. of Items	Internal Consistency Reliability Coefficient
Interaction facilitation	Behavior by subordinates toward one another that encourages the development of close, cooperative working relationships.	3	.90
Goal emphasis	Behavior by subordinates toward one another that stimulates a mutually contagious enthusiasm for doing a good job.	2	.70
Work facilitation	Behavior that is mutually helpful; helping each other remove roadblocks to doing a good job.	3	.89
Group process	How the group functions; does it plan and coordinate its efforts, make decisions and solve problems, know how to do its job, share information; is it motivated to meet its objectives, is it adaptable, is there confidence and trust among its members?	7	.94
Satisfaction	Whether employees are satisfied with economic and related rewards, adequacy of their immediate supervisor, effectiveness of the organization, compatibility with fellow employees, present and future progress within the organization, and their job as a whole.	7	.87

is perhaps best summarized by the following statement, taken from the basic reference: "Fairly clear evidence exists that the Survey of Organizations measures relate appropriately to both efficiency and attendance criteria. Relationships to efficiency extend across all four time periods and reach levels as high as .80. Relationships to attendance attain only slightly lower levels and, where data are available, show every sign of extending across all time periods. Relationships to other criteria present patterns which are far less definitive. In the case of product quality, no clear pattern emerges at all. In the human cost area, organizational climate seems to have appropriate and significant relationships to all three measures available for analysis: minor injuries, physical health, and grievance rate" (Taylor and Bowers, 1972).

Two successive measures are considered simultaneously for the analyses to be reported here: those preceding and following (a year later) the occurrence of a particular change treatment. In certain instances, index measures for the premeasure or the postmeasure are considered separately, and are therefore reported as arithmetic means on a five-point Likert scale (high score = desirable condition, low score = undesirable condition). In other instances, change itself is the focal concern; for these purposes, the first (or pre-) measures have been subtracted from the second (or post-) measures. Thus, a "positive" change score indicates enhanced effectiveness; a "negative" score, deterioration.

The balance of the article considers findings which, within the confines of the

ICLS setting, help answer the following research questions: (1) *Were the treatments differentially effective in producing change in organizational functioning, as measured by the Survey of Organizations questionnaire?* (2) *What is the relationship between change in organizational climate and the effects of these various treatments?*

Results

We begin with a consideration of change or gain scores for each of the sixteen critical indices for each treatment, presented in Table 2. The reader may note that, for each treatment, two sets of scores are given for each variable category. One comparison is labeled "Whole Systems" and refers to grand response mean gain scores for all respondents combined within organizations receiving that treatment for the first and second waves of measurement (ordinarily one year apart). The other comparison is labeled "Capstone Groups" and refers, within the interpersonal process consultation, task process consultation, and laboratory training treatments, to persons in groups that actually received that particular treatment. For comparison purposes, persons in groups of a similar nature (ordinarily the top-management groups) are presented for the survey feedback, data handback, and no-treatment clusters.

The findings presented in Table 2 may be summarized as follows:

1. *Laboratory training* is associated with negative change in organizational climate for both capstone groups and systems as a whole. Although group process improves at both levels, peer support declines for capstone groups, and both peer and managerial support decline for the systems in which these groups are located, as does overall satisfaction.

2. *Interpersonal process consultation* contains so few cases within capstone groups, and the changes are of such a (low) magnitude, that firm conclusions cannot be drawn. For their systems *in toto,* however, seven of the sixteen measures reflect significant, positive changes, largely in the managerial and peer leadership areas. Organizational climate, group process, and satisfaction measures change scarcely at all.

3. *Task process consultation* is associated with little significant change among capstone groups; only two measures (decision-making practices, satisfaction) change, both in a positive direction. For whole systems, however, all significant changes are negative, and a majority of them occur in the area of organizational climate. Considering that the two measures of support (managerial and peer) also show a significant decline, the pattern shows at least some resemblance to that observed in conjunction with laboratory training.

4. *Survey feedback* reflects positive and significant changes for capstone groups in every area except managerial leadership. For whole systems, eleven of the sixteen measures show positive, statistically significant change. No measure, for either capstone groups or whole systems, reflects negative change.

5. *Data handback* is associated in capstone groups with improved communication flow but a decline in the amount of influence attributed to lower organizational levels. Managerial leadership generally improves in these groups; all other measures show essentially no change. For their systems *in toto,* organizational climate is viewed as becoming worse, while peer leadership and some aspects of managerial leadership improve.

6. *No treatment,* as a "treatment," is associated with general negative change for capstone groups and whole systems.

Table 2. Changes in Questionnaire Indices, from First to Second Survey Waves, by Variable and Change Treatment

| | Treatment | | | | | | | | | | | |
| | Laboratory Training | | Interpersonal Process Cons. | | Task Process Cons. | | Survey Feedback | | Data Handback | | No Treatment | |
Area—Measure	Caps. Gps (N=116)	Whole Sys. (N=3,417)	Caps. Gps (N=12)	Whole Sys. (N=3,788)	Caps. Gps (N=38)	Whole Sys. (N=1,847)	Caps. Gps (N=85)	Whole Sys. (N=3,893)	Caps. Gps (N=55)	Whole Sys. (N=932)	Caps. Gps (N=51)	Whole Sys. (N=935)
Organizational climate												
Hum. resources prim.	−.42[a]	−.18[a]	+.10	−.02	−.04	−.17[a]	+.35[a]	+.15[a]	+.13	−.05	−.59[a]	−.61[a]
Communication flow	−.19[a]	−.12[a]	+.10	+.12[a]	+.16	−.06	+.22[a]	+.15[a]	+.23[a]	−.12[a]	−.02	−.06
Motiv'l conditions	−.13[a]	−.12[a]	−.22	+.02	+.03	−.04	+.24[a]	+.01	+.04	−.16[a]	−.09	−.09
Dec-making prac's	−.15[a]	−.13[a]	−.17	+.03	+.21[a]	−.14[a]	+.30[a]	+.17[a]	+.04	.00	−.32[a]	−.52[a]
Tech. readiness	−.01	+.13[a]	−.25	−.07	+.02	−.11[a]	+.39[a]	+.05	+.02	−.08	NA[b]	NA[b]
Lower-level infl.	+.03	−.10[a]	−.23	+.05	+.11	+.03	+.26[a]	+.01	−.33[a]	−.18[a]	−.47[a]	−.23[a]
Managerial leadership												
Support	−.10	−.11[a]	+.31	+.11[a]	−.11	−.19[a]	+.07	+.18[a]	+.18	+.01	−.16	−.32[a]
Inter. facilitation	−.04	+.02	−.05	+.20[a]	+.07	.00	+.11	+.36[a]	+.27[a]	+.15[a]	+.21[a]	.00
Goal emphasis	+.11	−.06	−.13	+.08	+.09	−.06	.00	+.17[a]	+.21[a]	+.06	−.11	−.11[a]
Work facilitation	+.12	−.08	+.29	+.21[a]	−.09	−.05	+.17	+.27[a]	+.33[a]	+.15[a]	−.09	−.16[a]
Peer leadership												
Support	−.20[a]	−.11[a]	−.24	+.02	+.17	−.13[a]	+.29[a]	+.06	−.01	+.03	−.19[a]	−.23[a]
Inter. facilitation	+.09	−.04	−.07	+.12[a]	+.08	−.06	+.30[a]	+.20[a]	+.06	+.20[a]	−.04	−.11[a]
Goal emphasis	−.05	.00	+.08	+.12[a]	+.22	−.02	+.21[a]	+.14[a]	+.15	+.12[a]	+.04	−.12[a]
Work facilitation	+.07	+.03	−.17	+.15[a]	+.04	−.03	+.36[a]	+.19[a]	+.09	+.20[a]	−.02	−.08
Group process	+.20[a]	+.27[a]	−.05	+.01	−.03	−.06	+.28[a]	+.21[a]	−.14	−.21[a]	NA[b]	NA[b]
Satisfaction	−.09	−.15[a]	−.04	+.04	+.32[a]	−.03	+.17[a]	+.09	+.07	−.02	−.07	−.23[a]

[a] Change large enough to be statistically significant at or beyond .05 level of confidence.

[b] Measures omitted in edition of questionnaire used in these sites.

There are, therefore, clear differences in reported change among treatment categories. It would be premature, however, to discuss substantive implications of these results before considering the possible impact of several methodological or situational factors.

Regression Toward the Mean. One such factor is the familiar argument concerning "regression toward the mean." Although clients were assigned on a staff-availability basis, it is conceivable that client systems were assigned to change agents (and therefore to treatments) in a way which coincided with their initial positions on the characteristics measured. If so, and if regression toward the mean accounts for the observed results, we would expect those initially below the mean to exhibit positive change (toward the mean) and those initially above the mean to exhibit negative change (also toward the mean). We would also expect them to reflect significant differences at the outset; that is, to have been different from one another in the premeasure in ways congruent with a regression explanation. Table 3 presents an analysis of variance test of the differences among treatment categories at the time of the premeasure, and Table 4 shows a simple categorization of significant changes in terms of their consistency or inconsistency with a regression hypothesis.

There are clearly significant differences at the outset. Inspection of the treatment means shows that these differences do not, however, coincide with what would be expected if some form of regression toward the mean were to account for the contrasting results obtained with the various treatments. Task process consultation sites, which began the effort around mid-range of the comparative distribution, show scarcely any change, and that which does occur is mixed as to its possible regression effects. Interpersonal process consultation and data handback treatment sites did, in fact, begin the change process from a somewhat lower scale point. Although capstone groups in data handback reflect a pattern in Table 4 that might suggest consistency with a regression hypothesis, the pattern for whole systems in this treatment is mixed, and that for whole systems in interpersonal process consultation is clearly contrary to the hypothesis.

The contrary pattern presented by both laboratory training and survey feedback is even stronger. Laboratory training, which began below the mean of the array and which would therefore be expected to show improvement, in fact declined. Survey feedback, which started above the array mean and would be expected on a "regression toward the mean" hypothesis to decline, showed improvement.

Only in the case of whole systems experiencing no treatment is there some substantial evidence for the regression hypothesis. In terms of the most striking differences in changes associated with various treatments, it therefore seems reasonable to reject the hypothesis that they represent regression toward the mean, methodological artifacts.

Organizational Climate as a Mediating Factor. Still another possible explanation of the findings centers around the role played by organizational climate in conjunction with attempts at intervention. A quite plausible argument can be made (and indeed was made at the time, particularly by individuals connected with the laboratory training sites) that basically autocratic and punitive practices and policies contribute to an organizational climate that masks the true effects of the change treatment. Thus, the argument goes, if organizational climate could be controlled, the effects of the treatment on group member leadership behavior would show themselves to be positive.

What could not be controlled in the course of the projects can be controlled at least reasonably well by an analytic strategy employing multiple classification analysis, which produces estimates of the effect of each of several predictors alone, after controlling for the effects of all others (Andrews, Morgan, and Sonquist, 1967). Table 5 shows

Table 3. Intertreatment Differences in Premeasures

| | | | | Treatments—Capstone Groups (df = 5,350) | | | | |
Area—Measure	F	p	Lab. Training	Interpersonal Process Consult.	Task Process Consult.	Survey Feedback	Data Handback	No Treatment
Organizational climate								
Hum. resources prim.	10.97	.001	4.00	3.46	3.92	3.80	3.46	4.46
Communication flow	4.94	.001	3.74	3.28	3.74	3.75	3.33	3.93
Motiv'l conditions	6.83	.001	3.92	3.64	3.98	3.86	3.47	4.20
Dec-making prac's	6.94	.001	3.28	3.11	3.49	3.53	2.90	3.60
Tech. readiness	2.09	ns	3.64	4.50	3.86	3.69	3.64	NA
Lower-level infl.	3.34	.01	2.96	2.54	2.97	2.96	2.86	3.43
Managerial leadership								
Support	5.02	.001	4.17	4.05	4.26	4.45	3.85	4.42
Inter. facilitation	8.93	.001	3.99	3.49	4.12	4.11	3.25	3.90
Goal emphasis	5.73	.001	4.14	4.08	4.41	4.49	3.85	4.40
Work facilitation	6.53	.001	3.38	3.21	3.68	3.70	3.10	3.79
Peer leadership								
Support	5.34	.001	4.09	4.06	3.76	3.91	3.87	4.38
Inter. facilitation	2.55	.05	3.45	3.17	3.31	3.53	3.16	3.71
Goal emphasis	1.70	ns	3.63	3.46	3.38	3.61	3.44	3.78
Work facilitation	1.69	ns	3.00	3.19	3.14	3.21	2.96	3.32
Group process	5.54	.001	3.52	4.00	3.74	4.00	3.63	NA
Satisfaction	4.68	.001	3.99	3.88	3.99	4.22	3.78	4.32

Treatments—Whole Systems (df = 5, inf.)

Organizational climate							
Hum. resources prim.	236.78	.001	3.00	3.28	3.65	3.17	2.93	4.01
Communication flow	110.09	.001	2.94	2.98	3.27	2.94	2.96	3.57
Motiv'l conditions	99.25	.001	3.23	3.31	3.56	3.25	3.10	3.77
Dec-making prac's	164.16	.001	2.73	2.84	3.13	2.68	2.47	3.38
Tech. readiness	342.60	.001	2.80	3.47	3.70	3.37	3.53	*NA*
Lower-level infl.	61.81	.001	2.56	2.48	2.68	2.50	2.37	3.01
Managerial leadership							
Support	83.15	.001	3.78	3.84	4.04	3.82	3.77	4.44
Inter. facilitation	33.44	.001	3.20	3.20	3.37	3.11	2.98	3.48
Goal emphasis	50.52	.001	3.72	3.75	3.86	3.66	3.57	4.16
Work facilitation	75.13	.001	3.15	3.19	3.32	3.17	2.99	3.74
Peer leadership							
Support	51.97	.001	3.84	3.83	3.89	3.73	3.80	4.20
Inter. facilitation	44.98	.001	3.16	3.18	3.19	2.96	2.91	3.40
Goal emphasis	41.19	.001	3.30	3.36	3.36	3.21	3.15	3.60
Work facilitation	34.65	.001	3.10	3.20	3.12	2.98	2.85	3.22
Group process	95.33	.001	3.28	3.56	3.59	3.63	3.56	*NA*
Satisfaction	61.65	.001	3.60	3.73	3.74	3.68	3.51	4.07

Table 4. Consistency of Significant Changes with a Regression Hypothesis,
by Change Treatment

Treatment	No. Consistent with Regression Hypothesis	No. Inconsistent with Regression Hypothesis
Laboratory training		
Capstone	1	5
Whole systems	1	9
Interpersonal process consult.		
Capstone	0	0
Whole systems	0	7
Task process consult.		
Capstone	0	2
Whole systems	3	2
Survey feedback		
Capstone	0	12
Whole systems	0	11
Data handback		
Capstone	4	1
Whole systems	5	4
No treatment		
Capstone	1	4
Whole systems	10	0

change scores for the eight leadership indices, adjusted to remove the effects of organizational climate change.

The results indicate considerable merit to the argument that the impact of a treatment is in part contingent upon the organizational climate in which it occurs, particularly in the case of laboratory training. The significant decline in managerial support present in the unadjusted scores disappears when adjustment is made for organizational climate, and the changes for managerial interaction facilitation and work facilitation, as well as for peer work facilitation, become positive. Only peer support remains significant and negative, although a decline in magnitude is apparent there as well.

Data handback also benefits somewhat from controlling for level of organizational climate, with previously significant, positive changes increasing slightly in magnitude, and one additional measure attaining significance.

The remaining treatments (interpersonal and task process consultation, survey feedback, and no treatment) show slight reduction in effects as a result of controlling for the effects of organizational climate.

Spurious Effects in Survey Feedback. An additional issue potentially affecting interpretation must be at least acknowledged before discussion of the overall implications of the findings. As an intervention technique, survey feedback usually employs the same instrument as a development tool that it uses to measure changes in the dependent variables. Therefore, the argument may be made, the results are likely to be confounded.

On reflection, this question breaks down into two separate issues: (1) the possibility that the feedback process subtly teaches organizational members how to respond to the questionnaire and (2) the greater likelihood that issues tapped by the instrument will receive more attention during the work or change activities which intervene between pre- and postmeasures than will other issues.

The "subtle education" issue seems plausible on the surface but with close examination proves less reasonable in the present setting. First, at least as employed within

Table 5. Mean Work Group Change Scores, Adjusted to Remove Effects of Organizational Climate Change, by Leadership Measure, by Treatment

	Treatment											
	Lab. Training (N = 167)		Interpersonal Process Consult. (N = 298)		Task Process Consult. (N = 109)		Survey Feedback (N = 112)		Data Handbook (N = 98)		No Treatment (N = 104)	
Area–Measure	Unadj.	Adj.	Unadj.	Adj.	Unadj.	Adj.	Unadj.	Adj.	Unadj.	Adj.	Unadj.	Adj.
Managerial leadership												
Support	−.15[a]	−.04	+.12[a]	+.04	−.25[a]	−.22	+.13	+.05	+.03	+.07	−.25[a]	−.18[a]
Inter. facilitation	+.07	+.20[a]	+.23[a]	+.13[a]	+.03	+.07	+.43[a]	+.33[a]	+.14	+.18[a]	+.05	+.14[a]
Goal emphasis	−.02	+.09	+.13[a]	+.05	−.09	−.06	+.14	+.06	+.06	+.09	−.08	−.01
Work facilitation	−.01	+.11[a]	+.22[a]	+.13[a]	−.09	−.05	+.24[a]	+.15	+.16[a]	+.21[a]	−.13[a]	−.05
Peer leadership												
Support	−.17[a]	−.11[a]	+.06	+.01	−.18[a]	−.17[a]	.00	−.06	+.07	+.08	−.22[a]	−.17[a]
Inter. facilitation	−.01	+.11	+.16[a]	+.06	−.09	−.06	+.17[a]	+.08	+.20[a]	+.24[a]	−.12	−.03
Goal emphasis	−.04	+.05	+.15[a]	+.08[a]	−.06	−.04	+.10	+.04	+.16[a]	+.20[a]	−.10	−.03
Work facilitation	+.05	+.15[a]	+.24[a]	+.16[a]	−.10	−.08	+.25[a]	+.18[a]	+.22[a]	+.26[a]	−.05	+.02

[a]Statistically significant at .01 level of confidence.

ICLS, questionnaires were administered by members of the ISR project staff, who literally took them to the sites and returned them to Ann Arbor. Large stocks of questionnaires left for scrutiny, memorization, or "boning up" were not available to member-participants. Second, the questionnaire contains over one hundred items, and only a shorthand identification of the question stems appears on the computer printout employed in feedback. Third, the tabulation sheets for any group or organization show considerable variation in response among members, as well as variation among the responses of any single respondent. Fourth, organizations of the type included in this study undergo a great deal of member rotation and turnover. Fifth, a substantial amount of evidence (not reported here) obtained from more detailed analyses within organizations reflects the construct validity of the measured changes. Changes in questionnaire indices relate differentially to one another in ways congruent with chronicled events in the project's history, with reports of change agents and top managers (obtained by content-analyzed interviews), and with performance measures from the operating records of the firm.

All in all, then, in order for the observed effects in the present study to represent a "subtle education" in how to respond, either an educative capability that would make organizational development itself obsolete or a conspiracy of organizational members so large and complex as to be mind boggling would have had to occur. Consider: the invisible hand guiding such a process would have had to build into the memory banks of hundreds—often thousands—of persons (many of them relatively uneducated) exactly that correct combination of responses which would square with all or most of the appropriate comparisons internal to the data themselves, with data from operating records, and with events during the interim which had been flagged by project staff members. It would have had to accomplish this without inducing an undifferentiated, across-the-board rise in response positiveness, while taking into account a large percentage of members who were new to the setting. Finally, it would have had to arrange all of this some six to eight months after the overwhelming majority of persons within the organization had seen the instrument or any data tabulated from it!

The second problem, that greater attention is likely to be paid during the intervention to issues reflected in the survey rather than to issues not reflected in the survey, is not to be denied, but rather acknowledged. In its most basic form, this is not a "problem" (in the sense of something which distorts or obfuscates). Instead, it is the heart of the change process for any system attempting to adapt to changes in its environment by a process of information inputs concerning the effect of mid-course corrections. This so-called problem appears in any change treatment and any evaluation or self-monitoring system geared to corrective input short of ultimate survival or destruction.

Having said this, we must also acknowledge that a measuring instrument fails to the extent that it is parochial in content. It may well be, for example, that the questionnaire used in this study omits content areas of great significance for organizational effectiveness—areas which are targeted by non-survey feedback treatments. If that is the case, however, it becomes an error of omission, not of commission. Errors of commission only appear if the instrument or the metatheory on which they are based is itself invalid. To the extent that the questionnaire taps what it purports to tap, and to the extent that those characteristics *do* relate to valid outcomes, its use as an assessment device is appropriate.

Thoughts About the Implications of These Findings

Although these findings emphasize the differences present among the several treatments, all the application methods used in the present study appear to be quite climate impacted. If the organizational climate is not changing positively, none of the treatments show any likelihood of substantially enhancing supportive behavior, whether by managers or by peers, or of enhancing goal emphasis by managers. Similarly, the problem-solving behavioral combination of interaction facilitation and work facilitation, as well as mutual goal emphasis by peers, seems climate prone, in the sense that it is enhanced by positive shifts in climate and harmed by negative shifts.

In the sites and projects included in the present study, laboratory training clearly suffers from an organizational climate that is *becoming* harsher and more barren. This may, in fact, explain the discrepancy between findings in the present study and findings reported elsewhere: it may be that laboratory-like, experiential learning is successful in organizations whose climate is, or is becoming, positive (for example, a Harwood or a TRW; see Marrow, Bowers, and Seashore, 1967; or Davis, 1967), but unsuccessful in organizations whose superstructure is, or is becoming, more autocratic and punitive.

Survey feedback, on the other hand, is the only treatment in the present study associated with large, across-the-board, positive changes in organizational climate. Controlling for these changes tends to *reduce* the raw, significant, and positive change observed in survey feedback sites for managerial and peer leadership variables. By way of contrast, data handback shows an increase, not a decrease, in positive change in managerial and peer variables when change in organizational climate is controlled statistically. In both treatments, the data format, content of the tabulation, and nature of the recipients are the same. Why, then, do we find a difference? The reason may be that the survey feedback process, in combination with the data, produces an attention to those issues related to organizational climate that must change if the system itself is to change. In fact, considering the intrinsic nature of the other treatments, it seems at least plausible that survey feedback is the only treatment of those considered which is likely to attend to these system-level issues in anything like a comprehensive form. Although the issue whether treatment itself effects climate change remains truly unanswered within these present data, a technical report (Bowers, 1971) investigates this particular problem and produces evidence to suggest that it does. In any event, more research on this question is needed; if treatments do not affect organizational climate positively or if other ways of accomplishing that end are not available, the present findings suggest that one would be best off following the rather barren practice of simply tabulating the data and handing them back!

Little more can be added at this point by way of interpreting the present findings. At the very least, they indicate that the different intervention strategies employed in ICLS had somewhat different outcomes. Beyond this, however, they add a degree of credence to the argument advanced by some that organizational change is a complex, systems-level problem in organizational adaptation, not merely an additive end-product of participation in particular development activities.

References

Andrews, F., Morgan, J., and Sonquist, J. *Multiple Classification Analysis.* Ann Arbor: Institute for Social Research, University of Michigan, 1967.

Bowers, D. *Development Techniques and Organizational Climate: An Evaluation of the Comparative Importance of Two Potential Forces for Organizational Change.* Washington, D.C.: Office of Naval Research, 1971.

Bowers, D., and Franklin, J. "Survey-Guided Development: Using Human Resources Measurement in Organizational Change." *Journal of Contemporary Business,* 1972, *1,* 43-55.

Bowers, D., and Seashore, S. "Predicting Organizational Effectiveness with a Four-Factor Theory of Leadership." *Administrative Science Quarterly,* 1966, *11,* 238-263.

Davis, S. "An Organic Problem-Solving Method of Organizational Change." *Journal of Applied Behavioral Science,* 1967, *3,* 3-21.

Evan, W. "A Systems Model of Organizational Climate." In R. Tagiuri and G. Litwin (Eds.), *Organizational Climate.* Cambridge, Mass.: Harvard University Press, 1968.

Halpin, A. W. *Theory and Research in Administration.* New York: Macmillan, 1966.

Likert, R. *New Patterns of Management.* New York: McGraw-Hill, 1961.

Likert, R. *The Human Organization.* New York: McGraw-Hill, 1967.

Marrow, A., Bowers, D., and Seashore, S. *Management by Participation.* New York: Harper & Row, 1967.

Schein, E. "Process Consultation: Its Role in Organization Development." In E. Schein, W. Bennis, and R. Beckhard (Eds.), *Organization Development.* Reading, Mass.: Addison-Wesley, 1969.

Taylor, J., and Bowers, D. *The Survey of Organizations: A Machine-Scored Standardized Questionnaire Instrument.* Ann Arbor: Institute for Social Research, University of Michigan, 1972.

37

∾∾∾ The Comparative Impacts
of Sociotechnical System, Job-Redesign,
and Survey-Feedback Interventions

William A. Pasmore

From time to time, most organizations have an opportunity to change the ways in which employees perform organizational tasks. At times, these opportunities are welcomed as signs of progress; new facilities are constructed or older ones are revamped. At other times, opportunities for change come up in the form of problems—strikes, mechanical breakdowns, and layoffs. Whatever the causes of organizational change, managers turn to the behavioral sciences for suggestions and solutions. Unfortunately, what many find are not single, widely accepted solutions to their problems but a myriad of techniques, all of which supposedly provide answers to organizational concerns. It is not surprising, therefore, that managers opt for the technique that is the current fad or is best advertised. To date, only a handful of studies have compared the effectiveness of different types of intervention techniques, and their findings have not always been clear.

Without additional comparative research, even recommendations by experts about which techniques a manager should use tend to be less than scientific, if not heavily colored by personal bias. Consequently, some managers report success and others may not; the result is that the behavioral sciences are seen as unreliable for providing organizational assistance.

The aim of this paper is to help managers and experts alike make more informed choices about what intervention techniques to apply. The effectiveness of sociotechnical system, job-redesign, and survey-feedback methods will be studied in comparable units of a single organization. Both attitudinal and productivity measures will be used to assess the comparative effectiveness of these methods. It will be evident that, in terms of improving employee attitudes, the technique chosen makes little difference; in terms of improving productivity, however, the method used appears critical.

A Brief Description of the Intervention Techniques

Friedlander and Brown (1974) have classified interventions into two categories: human process and technostructural. The survey-feedback technique is representative of

Reprinted from W. A. Pasmore and J. J. Sherwood (Eds.), *Sociotechnical Systems: A Sourcebook* (San Diego, Calif.: University Associates, 1978), pp. 291-301. Used with permission.

the former type; job redesign and sociotechnical system interventions fall into the latter classification.

Human-process interventions "value human fulfillment highly and expect improved organizational performance to follow on improved human functioning and processes" (Friedlander and Brown, 1974, p. 325). The survey-feedback technique begins with a survey of employee attitudes and organizational characteristics. This information is tabulated and shared by each supervisor with his or her employees, who are asked to make suggestions for improvement; whenever possible, the suggestions are implemented. Although employees may suggest changes in technology or work content, we have found that instead they usually suggest changes in work methods or conditions *given their present jobs,* degree of responsibility, and so forth. This distinction between human-process and technostructural approaches to organizational change is important.

Technostructural interventions, in contrast to human-process interventions, "affect work content and method and affect the sets of relationships among workers" (Friedlander and Brown, 1974, p. 320). Technostructural techniques are based on the premise that increased employee responsibility and improved work methods will lead to greater satisfaction and higher performance.

Although both job-redesign and sociotechnical system interventions are technostructural in nature, job redesign is aimed at motivating individual employees by adding more variety, autonomy, responsibility, and feedback to their jobs. Generally, job-redesign interventions do not affect the technology used to produce outputs. Sociotechnical system interventions, on the other hand, have traditionally been focused on tasks performed by groups of employees and may actually alter the technology to provide better social relationships and production methods. These distinctions are important because, to the extent that levels of output are constrained by technological or group forces, changes in these variables may be required to bring about significant improvements in productivity.

Reviews of the literature by Friedlander and Brown (1974), Kahn (1974), and Srivastva and associates (1975) indicate both human process and technostructural techniques have been fairly successful in improving employee attitudes. The reviewers concluded that technostructural interventions were more often associated with improvements in quality and productivity. In more detailed comparisons of the technostructural methods, the reviewers noted that job redesign interventions were often associated with improvements in quality but not productivity, and sociotechnical system interventions were associated with improvements in both. Based on these reviews of the literature, the following hypothesis could be posited: Employee attitudes will improve following either human process or technostructural interventions; however, productivity will improve only after sociotechnical intervention.

The Study

To provide comparative data to test this hypothesis, in 1974 the author became part of a research team commissioned to evaluate the start-up of a new unit at a midwestern production facility of a large food-processing corporation. The facility employed approximately two hundred unionized hourly workers in two separate plants (Units "I" and "II"). The units were devoted to the processing of different products, although both were controlled by the same site-management group. The technologies employed in both units were highly sophisticated, requiring high levels of skill on the part of many operators. The work force consisted of nearly equal numbers of men and women.

The research team was commissioned after a decision was made by the home office of the corporation to revamp a major portion of the production facilities in Unit I due to changing market demands. Although the original employees would remain after the redesign, their work conditions would be quite different. The corporation decided to utilize sociotechnical system design principles in reconstructing the unit due to the success of such interventions elsewhere in the corporation. In addition to the substantial reconstruction of Unit I, a new first-level management group was hired to supervise its operation. Although the top management group and the supervisors of Unit II remained the same, it was considered necessary to hire and train new managers for the Unit I operation to support the increased employee responsibility called for by the design. Although traditional management techniques had been successful at the site, management had stressed technology concerns and production control and had a fairly hard-nosed approach to labor relations.

Naturally, there was some initial friction between the old and new management groups. The existing Unit I management group suspected that the corporation and other employees would pressure them to become less traditional in their approach to management and more like the new supervisors. The new supervisors, on the other hand, felt constrained by existing labor contracts and informal agreements. The site manager recognized these concerns and commissioned the research team to evaluate the start-up and the impact it had on the operation of the total site. He wanted the researchers to use whatever data they collected to improve the start-up and the functioning of the total site. This led the researchers to use survey-feedback techniques, which could provide data about the start-up and also be used for organizational improvement.

As a result of the start-up of the new unit and the survey-feedback interventions that took place, a job-redesign program was eventually undertaken in Unit II.

Thus, the research team was given an opportunity to compare the impacts of survey-feedback, job-redesign, and sociotechnical system interventions on employee satisfaction and productivity. The design of the study is shown in Figure 1.

Figure 1. Experimental Design

Unit I	O_1	X_1	X_2	O_2	X_3		O_3
Unit II	O_1	X_1		O_2	X_3	X_4	O_3

Time 1	Time 2	Time 3
1974	1975	1976

Key

$O_{1\,2\,3}$ = Survey Research Measures
X_1 = Survey Feedback (waterfall method)
X_2 = Sociotechnical System Redesign of Unit I to Process Product T
X_3 = Survey Feedback (bottom-up method)
X_4 = Job Redesign in Unit II

During the first time period, the research team administered surveys in both units. At that time, employees who were to staff the redesigned unit were still in their old jobs at the site, working under the traditional system of management.

The second period began with the feedback of the data to site personnel. Beginning with the site manager, each supervisor met with his or her subordinates to share the data and solicit suggestions for improvement. The researchers were present throughout the feedback process to answer questions about the data and to facilitate discussion.

The sociotechnical system redesign of Unit I also took place during the second time period. The design of the unit incorporated many of the key features mentioned by Walton (1972), including autonomous (self-directing) work groups, integrated support functions, challenging job assignments, job mobility, facilitative leadership, managerial decision information for operators, and opportunities for continuous learning and evolution. The design of the production process itself called for several production stages, each separated by technologies for storing buffer inventories. Each stage of the process was to be operated by an autonomous work group in which all group members would eventually become skilled at all of the tasks in their areas. In addition, these groups would perform periodic maintenance, quality control, training, and employee-selection functions. To encourage team effort, all employees received a single pay rate. The second period ended with the administration of another survey measure.

The third period began with the feedback of the data from the second survey, this time beginning at the lowest level of the organization. Each supervisor and his or her subordinates discussed the data and formulated action proposals to be considered by the next level of management. Through this process, top management eventually received a list of employee-initiated suggestions for consideration and action.

A short time later, as a result of the redesign of Unit I and the survey-feedback process, a job-redesign program was undertaken in Unit II that resulted in greater variety and responsibility for a number of employees. A rotational process was begun in some areas, and some of the most repetitive jobs were eliminated through automation or divided among a number of employees.

Unlike in Unit I, there were no efforts in Unit II to form autonomous work groups, alter the existing technology, or change the style of management. Individual operators were given responsibility for the performance of some maintenance and quality-control functions, and a small pay raise was granted to equalize conditions across the site. The study was concluded with the administration of a third survey measure in both units.

A comparison of time 1 versus time 2 data in Figure 1 indicates the effects of the sociotechnical system and survey-feedback interventions that occurred in Unit I versus the survey-feedback intervention alone that occurred in Unit II. Similarly, a comparison of time 2 versus time 3 data reveals the effects of the second survey-feedback intervention in Unit I versus the survey-feedback and job-redesign interventions that occurred in Unit II. Finally, a comparison of time 1 versus time 3 data contrasts the effects of the overall combined interventions in both units.

Results of the Study

Both attitudinal and productivity measures were used to evaluate the impacts of the interventions. At each survey administration, a full sampling of the hourly population was sought, although completion of the surveys was voluntary. Company time was provided for survey completion, and employees were assured that their responses would be completely anonymous. In all, 195 employees and supervisors completed the first survey, 209 the second, and 184 the third. Although the number of persons at the site fluctuated over time, at least 90 percent of the available hourly population completed each survey.

Because the research was concerned with employee responses to the interventions, supervisory data were excluded from the analysis. Also, some surveys were not usable due to substantial missing information. This left 175 first surveys, 128 second surveys, and 154 third surveys for analysis.

A complete description of the survey measures is provided in Pasmore (1976). Ten measures of employee attitudes were included in the surveys: general job satisfaction, alienation (Blauner, 1964), job involvement (Lodahl and Kejner, 1965), intrinsic motivation (Hackman and Lawler, 1971), need strength (Hackman and Lawler, 1971), task attributes of employee jobs (Turner and Lawrence, 1965; Hackman and Oldham, 1974), measures of satisfaction with specific aspects of working conditions, supervisory consideration (Fleishman, 1960), organization structure (Friedlander, 1973), and intergroup relations. The average internal consistency reliability coefficients for these measures across the three survey administrations ranged from .53 to .89, with an average of .70.

In addition to the survey measures, records of productivity, start-up costs, absenteeism, and on-site observations were kept during the study.

The effect of the intervention on the means of the survey variables in each unit over time is presented in Table 1. Univariate and multivariate analyses of variance performed on the data indicated that overall interventions in both units affected a number of employee attitudes positively and significantly (Pasmore, 1976). Significant ($p < .01$) increases were noted in the levels of general job satisfaction, intrinsic motivation, and job involvement; alienation decreased markedly ($p < .01$). Job design was reported to be more complex ($p < .01$), and the organization was perceived to have acquired a more flexible structure ($p < .01$).

Thus, the hypothesis was supported, as both human-process and technostructural interventions did result in improvements in employee attitudes. It is interesting to note the different trends in employee attitudes in each unit. In Unit I, the initial combined sociotechnical system and survey-feedback intervention resulted in greatly improved employee attitudes. The survey-feedback intervention that occurred later in Unit I did little to further improve employee attitudes. In Unit II, on the other hand, the initial survey-feedback intervention alone resulted in improved employee attitudes, and the later combined survey-feedback and job-redesign interventions resulted in further improvements. Thus, it seems that *combined* human-process and technostructural interventions have a somewhat greater impact on employee attitudes than human-process interventions alone.

In Unit I, the effects of the sociotechnical system and survey-feedback interventions on the planned versus actual productivity of the operation were quite dramatic. Based upon start-ups of similar facilities elsewhere in the corporation, the original cumulative start-up production volume for Unit I was set at 1,093,600 units. By the end of the start-up period, approximately 1,450,000 units had been produced, or 133 percent of that originally planned. Despite the increased volume and corresponding raw material costs, the start-up cost was less than predicted. Instead of an estimated eleven-month operating cost of $931,800, the cost was approximately $860,000, a savings of $71,800, or 7.7 percent of the planned amount. The major saving achieved during the start-up was in terms of labor cost due to the sociotechnical system design of the unit. Industrial-engineered standards called for a crew of between 126 and 129 employees to operate the facility, while the actual number required under the new design was 104. A conservative estimate places the annual fixed labor expense savings at $264,000. It should be noted that these results were achieved with a unionized labor force and by adapting the optimal design of the unit to fit the existing facilities at the site.

The impact of the survey-feedback and job-redesign interventions in Unit II was not as impressive. Although the productivity of the two units could not be compared directly because they were processing different products, data obtained from the company records indicated no significant changes in productivity that could be attributed to the interventions in Unit II. It should be noted that the technology of the Unit II operation was complex and constrained the rate of productivity. Perhaps because the technol-

Table 1. Means and Standard Deviations of Survey Variables by Unit over Time

Variable	Time 1		Time 2		Time 3	
	Unit I (N = 61)	Unit II (N = 114)	Unit I (N = 42)	Unit II (N = 86)	Unit I (N = 56)	Unit II (N = 98)
General job satisfaction	4.164[a] (1.734)[b]	4.272 (1.821)	5.643 (1.495)	4.744 (2.019)	5.482 (1.250)	4.980 (1.250)
Specific job satisfactions	3.736 (1.195)	3.735 (1.186)	4.301 (.860)	3.487 (1.144)	3.937 (.854)	3.947 (.911)
Alienation	3.235 (1.118)	3.298 (1.105)	1.500 (1.358)	1.942 (1.577)	1.589 (1.255)	1.758 (1.429)
Job involvement	3.650 (1.517)	3.544 (1.307)	4.738 (1.726)	4.767 (2.027)	4.875 (1.926)	4.765 (1.827)
Intrinsic motivation	5.585 (1.186)	5.526 (1.225)	6.000 (1.249)	5.733 (1.718)	5.964 (1.464)	5.908 (1.437)
Intergroup relations	3.574 (1.283)	3.789 (1.065)	3.764 (1.213)	3.708 (1.256)	3.482 (1.073)	3.506 (1.051)
Organic structure	2.658 (1.239)	2.759 (1.103)	4.678 (1.034)	4.139 (1.040)	4.357 (.794)	4.290 (.994)
Supervisory consideration	3.951 (1.374)	4.250 (1.268)	4.282 (1.397)	3.446 (1.540)	3.708 (.912)	3.571 (1.184)
Job design	4.121 (.936)	4.116 (.824)	4.963 (1.020)	4.733 (1.086)	4.701 (.903)	4.735 (.936)
Absenteeism	2.033 (1.402)	3.509 (2.465)	2.095 (4.762)	2.663 (5.233)	2.750 (2.158)	3.102 (3.892)
Need strength	5.708 (.855)	5.700 (.849)	NA	NA	5.116 (.975)	5.463 (.943)

Note: 1 = low, 7 = high.

[a]The first figure reported is the mean.

[b]The second figure (in parentheses) is the standard deviation.

ogy in Unit II was not affected greatly by the job-redesign or survey-feedback interventions, no improvement in productivity could have taken place. Other operating data collected by the Unit II supervisors indicated an improvement from time 2 to time 3 in terms of equipment downtime ($t = 4.61; p < .01; df = 33$; two-tailed test) and an increase in the time spent in meetings with employees ($t = 2.57; p < .05; df = 30$). There was no significant change in the number of cases of product that had to be reworked, a measure of quality. The job-redesign intervention did reduce the number of employees needed to operate the facility (by approximately six out of eighty). Thus, Unit II was able to maintain its production levels with fewer employees, despite the fact that more time was spent in meetings.

In summary, although the interventions had similar effects in terms of improving employee attitudes, only the sociotechnical system intervention was associated with significant improvements in productivity and cost savings.

Discussion

In interpreting these findings, it would be easy to jump to the conclusion that sociotechnical system interventions should be applied in all organizations and other techniques should be abandoned. This certainly is not the case. Even in this capital-intensive setting, the value of the human-process/survey-feedback intervention was apparent to the research team. Not only did it offer the means to collect important information regarding employee sentiments at the site, but it also became a vehicle for building trust between labor and management. Prior to the study, relationships between union and management at the site were typically adversarial, and there was some question in the minds of both the managers and researchers about the role the union would play in the study. It was not surprising to find that the union resisted the study and the improvement program at the site initially. Union members claimed that the improvement program was another effort by management to "get more work out of employees for the same pay" and that the research study was being conducted to back up the actions taken by management. These rumors were dispelled only after long hours of discussion in survey-feedback meetings and subsequent demonstrations by management of their good faith in responding to employee concerns.

Although the sociotechnical system method is intended to provide better working conditions for employees as well as greater productivity, in practice it easily could be perceived by employees as another management gimmick.

To dispel this notion, it is essential that employees have an active part in shaping their work environment, and it is here that human-process interventions are most useful. In retrospect, it would seem that combined human-process and technostructural interventions present the most balanced and potentially effective approach to organizational change in this type of setting. Managers and experts need to overcome the temptation to apply a neat and quick technique. If the results of this study can be generalized, as we believe they can, organizational improvement will be the result of a concerted effort to change the actual jobs of employees, with their participation, through changes in the technology. One-sided efforts aimed either at smoothing over employee attitudes or simply altering technological arrangements will probably meet with resistance and do more harm than good.

In other settings that do not involve capital-intensive technologies, such as hospitals, universities, or government agencies, human-process interventions may have more impact than technostructural techniques. To date, sociotechnical system and job-redesign theorists have not offered much guidance for change in this type of setting. We would expect that even limited technostructural interventions would produce more positive effects when combined with human-process methods in such settings than would human-process interventions alone. Simply changing employee attitudes is probably *not* enough to improve productivity. More comparative studies are necessary to determine the most effective combinations of interventions.

References

Blauner, R. *Alienation and Freedom.* Chicago: University of Chicago Press, 1964.

Cronbach, L. "Coefficient Alpha and the Internal Structure." *Psychometrika,* 1951, *16,* 297-334.

Fleishman, E. *Manual for the Leadership Opinion Questionnaire.* Chicago: Science Research Associates, 1960.

Friedlander, F. *Organization Structure Inventory.* Cleveland: School of Management, Case Western Reserve University, 1973.

Friedlander, F., and Brown, L. D. "Organization Development." *Annual Review of Psychology,* 1974, *25,* 313-341.

Hackman, J. R., and Lawler, E. "Employee Reactions to Job Characteristics." *Journal of Applied Psychology,* 1971, *55,* 259-286.

Hackman, J. R., and Oldham, G. *The Job Diagnostic Survey: An Instrument for the Diagnosis of Jobs and Evaluation of Job Redesign Projects.* New Haven, Conn.: Department of Administrative Sciences, Yale University, 1974.

Kahn, R. "Organization Development: Some Problems and Proposals." *Journal of Applied Behavioral Science,* 1974, *10,* 485-502.

Lodahl, T., and Kejner, M. "The Definition and Measurement of Job Involvement." *Journal of Applied Psychology,* 1965, *49,* 24-33.

Pasmore, W. "Understanding Organizational Change: A Longitudinal Investigation of the Effects of Sociotechnical System, Job Redesign, and Survey Feedback Interventions on Organizational Task Accomplishment and Human Fulfillment." Unpublished doctoral thesis, Purdue University, 1976.

Srivastva, S., and others. *Job Satisfaction and Productivity.* Cleveland: School of Management, Case Western Reserve University, 1975.

Turner, A., and Lawrence, P. *Industrial Jobs and the Worker: An Investigation of Response to Task Attributes.* Boston: Graduate School of Business Administration, Harvard University, 1965.

Walton, R. E. "How to Counter Alienation in the Plant." *Harvard Business Review,* 1972, *50,* 70-81.

38

Participative Decision Making: An Experimental Study in a Hospital

J. E. Bragg
I. Robert Andrews

Since several excellent summaries of previous work on participative decision making (PDM) are already available (see, for example, Bucklow, 1966; Campbell and others, 1970; Lowin, 1968), this report will not include the usual literature survey. In general, the experimental design and analyses in this study were most influenced by Lowin's (1968) theoretical model, which defines PDM as "a mode of organizational operation in which decisions as to activities are arrived at by the very persons who are to execute those decisions," and by his prescriptions for PDM research. Stated quite simply, our hypotheses predicted that the introduction of participative decision making into a particular hospital laundry would improve employee attitudes, reduce absenteeism, and increase productivity.

Method

In his section on "Experimental Studies in Organizations," Lowin (1968) specified six standards which such an experiment must meet. In addition, his theoretical definition of participative decision making implies a seventh standard. Each of these standards will be considered in turn as they apply to the present study.

Standards

1. "A determined effort must be made to unfreeze the system in preparation for the PDM program." In the present study, the attitudes and values of the chief nonmedical administrator were modified by three behavioral science courses in an executive M.B.A. program. According to the administrator, his experiences in the courses sharpened and intensified an already favorable feeling about a participative management style.

Reproduced from the *Journal of Applied Behavioral Science,* 1973, *9* (6), 727-733, by special permission from the authors and the NTL Institute for Applied Behavioral Science.

Another key figure, the foreman in charge of the laundry, had already established himself as a highly effective supervisor, with a driving, authoritarian style of management. When first approached by the chief administrator about the possibility of trying a participative management style, the foreman was dubious and negative. It was not until six months after the first discussion that the foreman elected to accept the challenge of trying a new management style. A key factor in his acceptance of the challenge was his own very positive response to the high degree of decision-making autonomy which he had been given by the chief administrator. Another important factor was his participation in a weekend sensitivity-training workshop with nonmedical management personnel.

In anticipation of PDM, the foreman prepared a list of eighteen problems that might be encountered during the changeover. He also restated the goals of his department to make them consistent with the PDM philosophy.

When PDM was introduced to the thirty-two laundry workers, the foreman was able to state in all honesty that the basic purpose of the program was to make jobs more interesting. The workers were told that PDM sometimes does result in higher productivity but that this was unimportant to top management because their current level of productivity was already excellent. They were also told that they would have the right to discontinue PDM if they found it unsatisfactory.

One other important factor in the total system was the union leadership. Because of previously established trust and respect (without love, it might be added) for top management, it was fairly easy to obtain union approval for the tentative introduction of PDM. Active support for the program, however, was not offered.

Finally, the unfreezing process was greatly expedited by the results of the first two PDM meetings. One of the key employee suggestions in these early meetings was the revision of work hours to begin and end two hours earlier. Because the laundry unit was completely isolated from other subsystems in the hospital, there was no reason for not acting immediately upon that suggestion. In the following week the work hours were changed, and PDM was off to a good start.

2. "Attitudinal data should be collected to document the adaptation to PDM or its rejection." At the end of every two-month period in our study, a seven-item questionnaire was completed by all thirty-two laundry workers. Included were such questions as "Should we continue with PDM?" and "Do suggestions get a fair trial?" The data from these questionnaire responses are reported in the Results section.
3. "Similar changes in organization behavior should be recorded." Most closely related to the attitudinal data would be the data on absenteeism, which are reported in the Results section. Less closely related to the attitudinal data are changes in rate of productivity, also reported in the Results section.
4. "Appropriate control groups must be utilized." Two other hospital laundries in the same city were used as comparison groups for evaluating changes in productivity. Strictly speaking, these were not "control groups," since the workers in the comparison laundries were not aware that their performance data were of interest to persons outside their own organization. It is also true, however, that postexperimental interviews with PDM employees showed that they were not aware that they were subjects in an experiment. They knew only that, for the first three months of PDM, the chief administrator seemed to be interested in what they were doing.

During the period studied, there was only one technical innovation to confound the productivity data. Fortunately, it was possible to correct the data for this one factor (the introduction of some polyester fabrics into the linen supply).

Since the comparison hospitals were not able to provide suitable data on absenteeism, results for the PDM group were compared with absence data for other nonmedical staff in the PDM hospital. Neither the PDM nor the comparison groups were aware that their absence records were being monitored in other than routine ways.

In the first three or four months of the study, any differences between the experimental and comparison groups could have been confounded by a strong Hawthorne effect (in the usual sense of "increased attention, novelty"). However, it is highly unlikely that such an effect could have lasted over the eighteen months of the study. Active interest and participation by the chief nonmedical administrator ceased after the first three months. As stated above, the PDM workers were not aware at any time that they were subjects in an experiment.

5. "Long-term research is essential." The eighteen-month time period of the study provided ample time for worker adjustment to PDM and reduced the likelihood that any observed differences were due either to random fluctuations or to a Hawthorne effect. Moreover, both attitudinal and behavioral data showed gradual improvement throughout the study period. It is unlikely that some extraneous factor stabilized behavior at an improved level and continued to do so throughout the study.

6. "The validity of organization records should be checked." The basic record-keeping procedures for absenteeism and productivity were constant throughout the study period, and throughout the period preceding. The absentee record-keeping procedures were identical for the PDM group and the comparison group (other nonmedical employees who worked in the same hospital). With regard to productivity data, the inclusion of pre- and postmeasures for the PDM group and the comparison hospital laundries reduced the likelihood that any differences would be an artifact of record-keeping procedures.

7. In defining PDM (as quoted above), Lowin continues: "The PDM process shifts the locus of some decisions downward—from superior to subordinate." In the present study, decision-making power was transferred from the laundry foreman to a committee composed of all the laundry employees. Any and all aspects of managing the laundry could be considered by the committee. It was agreed, however, that union matters and personal gripes would not be discussed in the meetings.

Role of the Foreman

In the initial PDM meeting, the laundry foreman was elected to serve as a discussion moderator. By the fifth meeting, the role of discussion moderator was taken over by several of the laundry employees, with the foreman's main tasks reduced to agenda setting and the scheduling of meetings. During the meetings, the foreman refused to be active as a task expert, even in cases where the group's decision was, in his opinion, incorrect. Once the group reached a decision, the foreman did what he could to assist the particular employees charged with the responsibility of implementing the changes agreed upon. Because the foreman himself was operating with a very high degree of autonomy, there was seldom need to obtain approval from higher management before taking action. This made it possible to implement most of the proposed changes within one or two weeks of the date of the committee's decision.

It was agreed that meetings should be restricted in length to thirty or forty minutes, and that they should be called only when there were specific proposals to discuss. From this it is clear that most of the PDM work was accomplished outside of the formal meetings. Throughout each working day, the foreman tried to make himself easily available to individual employees (or groups of employees) who wanted to discuss new ideas or problems. In these informal meetings, the foreman concentrated on being a good listener—on acting as a sounding board so employees could develop their own ideas with a minimal amount of help from him. Also, whenever it seemed appropriate, the foreman attempted to transfer his task expertise to the employees, thereby reducing their dependence on him. Lastly, because the overall climate in the laundry became supportive and cooperative, even shy employees were able to develop, present, and gain acceptance for their ideas.

Results

PDM Group Meetings. The laundry foreman kept a record of the twenty-eight meetings which occurred during the first fifteen months of PDM. An analysis of his minutes revealed that 147 employee suggestions were discussed. Of these, eleven involved hours of work and working conditions, ninety had to do with the work flow (process and methods), forty-four involved minor equipment modifications, and two were concerned with safety. No record was kept of the innumerable additional ideas discussed on the shop floor between meetings.

Attitudes Toward PDM. It was anticipated that some of the older workers would react negatively to PDM, while younger workers would be more receptive. As it turned out, however, the only strong negative reactions came from three younger workers, who objected to the transfer of decision-making power from the foreman to the laundry committee. Fortunately, their attempts to sabotage participative decision making were overcome by the enthusiastic supporters of it; eventually their resistance changed to active support.

For each of the seven items on the employee attitude questionnaire, an employee could write in "yes," "no," or "?" For scoring purposes, the "?" responses were added to the "no" responses, and this total was compared with the number of "yes" responses. The following percentages of "yes" responses are reported by two-month intervals for the first fourteen months of the study: 62, 64, 75, 71, 79, 84, 90. As is apparent from these data, the employees' initial uncertainty about PDM gave way to a positive attitude by the end of the first two months. From that point, there was almost a steady climb to a highly favorable attitude toward PDM.

Absenteeism. In the thirty-eight reporting periods which immediately *preceded* the introduction of PDM, the absence rate for the laundry group was less than the overall hospital absence rate twenty-three out of thirty-eight times. In the thirty-eight reporting periods *after* the introduction of PDM, the absence rate for the laundry group was less than the overall hospital absence rate thirty-two out of thirty-eight times. This shift in proportions, from .61 to .80, was highly significant ($Z = 1.9$, $p < .03$). Thus, an already superior absence record became substantially better after the introduction of PDM. It is of possible interest that, immediately after PDM began, the absence rate for the laundry group was worse than the overall hospital rate in five out of eight reporting periods. After that unimpressive beginning, the absence rate for the laundry group was lower than the overall hospital rate in twenty-nine out of thirty reporting periods. Expressing that remarkable record in different terms, the absence rate for the laundry group averaged 2.95 percent before PDM versus 1.77 percent with PDM. For other nonmedical staff, the rates were 2.80 percent before the study began versus 3.07 percent during the study. Expressed in yet another way, the 1,791 hours of sick time in the laundry group in the year before PDM fell to 1,194 hours in the first year of PDM. There were no long- or short-term trends in the hospital at large to account for this drop in absenteeism.

Productivity. In the year prior to the introduction of PDM, productivity in the experimental group averaged approximately 50 pounds of laundry processed per paid employee hour. In the first six months of PDM, production rose gradually to an average of approximately 61 pounds. In the second six-month period, production surged to 78 pounds, but this was followed by a slight drop in the third six-month period to 73 pounds per paid employee hour. As shown in Table 1, the productivity rate in the two compari-

Table 1. Productivity Rates[a] for the PDM Laundry
and for Two Comparison Laundries

	PDM Laundry[b]	Comparison A	Comparison B
12 months before study	50	47	39
18 months during study	71	45	37

[a]Pounds of laundry processed per paid employee hour, rounded to the nearest whole number.

[b]Figures corrected to allow for the introduction of some polyester fabrics into the linen supply.

son hospitals remained constant or perhaps even declined slightly during the year-and-a-half study period.

Since the rate of productivity in the experimental group was already higher than the rates for the two comparison hospitals, these initial differences in favor of the experimental group had to be discounted before testing for the significance of mean differences during the study period. After this adjustment, the mean difference between the experimental group and each of the comparison groups was 23 pounds per paid employee hour. For each of the two comparisons, this difference in mean productivity was significant ($t = 8.43$ for comparisons A and B respectively, $df = 34$, $p < .01$, two-tailed).

Though cost savings through increased productivity was not an important objective of the PDM program, significant economic benefits to the hospital were realized, equal to approximately $1,000 per employee per year.

Discussion

In this study, which attempted to adhere closely to Lowin's (1968) recommendations for PDM experiments in ongoing organizations, it was found that attitudes improved, absence declined, and productivity increased. No such changes were observed in the comparison groups. The differences between the experimental and comparison groups were statistically significant and in the direction hypothesized. Because of the long duration of the study and because the more substantial performance improvements were not realized in the early months of the PDM program, it seems highly improbable that the reported results can be explained in terms of a Hawthorne effect.

There were several factors in the subsystem studied which favored a successful PDM effort: the program was initiated and actively encouraged for three months by the hospital's chief nonmedical administrator; an already successful laundry foreman existed who felt secure enough in his position to experiment with a radical change in his management style and was able to effect PDM; the foreman had been given a high degree of decision-making autonomy well in advance of the PDM program; previously established trust and an already high level of productivity made it easier for the union leaders to believe management when they said that the primary objective of the PDM program was job improvement for the workers; the isolation of the laundry subsystem made it easier for management to comply with some of the initial employee suggestions about such things as hours of work, choice of holidays, and self-control over work breaks; and, lastly, the middle-class work values of several foreign-born immigrants in the work group might have facilitated the establishment of a group norm in favor of PDM.

At the time of this somewhat belated report, PDM has been in effect in the hospital laundry for over three years. Neither the foreman nor the workers have expressed any desire to return to the old style of management. The foreman has said that it would be easy for him to revert to his old style of autocratic management, but he would "miss the satisfactions he derives from PDM." He has also mentioned that he has not had to reprimand a worker since PDM began.

The success of PDM in the laundry has encouraged other subsystems in the hospital to follow suit. In a medical records section where there was an adequate unfreezing of the system and strong support (but no involvement) by the chief nonmedical administrator, a serious turnover problem has been eliminated through PDM, and a high level of union grievances has been reduced to zero. With the nursing staff, on the other hand, a deficiency of unfreezing activities and substantial resistance by the head nurse caused PDM to flounder badly for the first six months. In fact, PDM was a dismal failure until the introduction of a new head nurse with a favorable attitude toward PDM, and until the chief nonmedical administrator found time for some involvement in the program. With these changes, the tide was turned, and after a year and a half the PDM program for nurses is still alive. However, continued resistance by some of the administrative medical personnel has kept PDM from flourishing in the nursing group.

In closing, it might be of value to ask why production increased when top management's main concern was job improvement for the laundry workers. Looking back at the foreman's record of PDM meetings, it can be seen that 90 percent of all employee suggestions involved technological modifications in the laundry subsystem. This suggests quite convincingly that the creation of a genuine PDM atmosphere led employees to adopt organizational goals as their own. Moreover, since there was no economic gain for employees' contribution of ideas for technological improvements, it is safe to assume that the underlying motivational force was higher-order need fulfillment. We thus believe that releasing this rich vein of heretofore untapped energy led to technological and attitudinal changes which substantially increased productivity. The relative impact of these two sources of productivity improvement should be tested in future research. For example, one group might experience PDM, and the technological changes they develop might be introduced into other groups by conventional managerial methods. This would enable distinguishing the productivity-raising effects of methods improvement as such from the attitudinal changes occurring in PDM.

References

Bucklow, M. "A New Role for the Work Group." *Administrative Science Quarterly,* 1966, *11,* 59-78.

Campbell, J. P., and others. *Managerial Behavior, Performance, and Effectiveness.* New York: McGraw-Hill, 1970.

Lowin, A. "Participative Decision Making: A Model, Literature Critique, and Prescriptions for Research." *Organizational Behavior and Human Performance,* 1968, *3,* 68-106.

~~~ Conclusion

Methodological Issues

Five issues must be met in the next decade if organizational psychology and organizational sociology are to make significant advances. These issues are at once methodological and theoretical. One is the amount of attention that needs to be given to organizational against individual variables. System variables can be studied through the use of organizational records and products, or through aggregated psychological measures. The second major problem is the use of independent measures to establish relationships—measures that do not come from the same source and do not have built-in correlations. The third is the tradeoff between internal and external validity—between the experimental laboratory and the field study. Another problem is the adequacy of the time span under study in relation to the natural cycle of events relevant to the investigation. The fifth is the use of the case study in supplementing quantitative techniques in the development of programmatic research.

Organizational Versus Individual Variables

The organizational field over the years has suffered from a preoccupation with the study of individual psychological variables. Organizations are recognized as the setting in which individual behavior occurs; but organizational variables—such factors as differentiation of structure, coordination, and degree of hierarchical control—have received little systematic study. These aspects of organization are seen as sociological conceptions and their empirical investigation as somehow not proper for the involvement of the psychologist. Yet, at the other border of their discipline, the biological, psychologists do not hesitate to interact with physiologists to advance the state of physiological psychology. This is, in part, due to the belief that the lower we go in the science hierarchy, the more basic the processes under scrutiny. But the social sciences can be more relevant in dealing with organizational problems than biology is in dealing with problems of learning and perception. The issue is not only a question of the choice of measures and the use of aggregation; it is also an issue in the conceptualization of human organizations. To what extent are organizations aggregations of individuals, and to what extent are they something more, something that must be understood at their own level?

The field of organizational behavior has two major aspects. One is the behavior of

individuals in organizational contexts. The other is the behavior of organizations as entities—for example, the productivity of systems in relation to internal characteristics (such
as control structure) or to external factors (such as the turbulence of the environment).
This second aspect clearly calls for theoretical concepts that go beyond individual psychology. But even the first aspect, the behavior of people in organizational settings, requires study of what these settings are. We cannot neglect the stimulus setting that pre-
cipitates behavior and conditions perceptions and attitudes. We cannot control and
manipulate organizational environment as we can the objective conditions of the laboratory, but we can at least try to measure the dimensions of the environmental field. Thus,
these two aspects need to be brought together, and one should not be reserved for sociologists and the other for psychologists.

A measure that is psychological—in the sense that it assesses attitudes, perceptions, or behavior of people—is not necessarily nonorganizational in nature. It can be
aggregated for members of a subsystem, so that we can speak of a high-producing section
or a low-morale department. Or the consensus of the perceptions, either of observers or
of participants, can be utilized in the study of systems. Aggregations of individual data,
while useful, are not necessarily identical with the corresponding organizational-level concepts and measures. Individual productivity may be summed to give a measure of organizational productivity; and, for some kinds of organizations, that may be sufficient. For
sophisticated and highly differentiated organizations, however, the additive model may
not be sufficient. What makes the measure organizational is its reference to some aspect
of the functioning or structure of social systems. If it is designed to get at some personality characteristic rather than some aspect of the social field, it is psychological rather than
organizational. When psychologists enter an organization, they can narrow their questions
to their previous theoretical orientation, or they can broaden their conceptions and take
account of system functioning. For example, if they merely ask how supportive a supervisor is of others, they are on the psychological level. If they also ask how much power
the supervisor has to get things done, they are on the organizational level. The conceptual
frame of reference determines the questions to be asked and hence the data to be gathered. Our contention is that, with the narrow frame of the individual psychologist, we
have not been asking a broad enough range of questions about the structure and functioning of social systems. Tajfel and Billig (1974) have made the same point with respect to
the study of race relations, and the Gurins and their colleagues (Gurin and Epps, 1975;
Gurin and others, 1969) have documented this departure in their work on the system and
individual orientations of underprivileged groups.

We should not, however, be restricted to the use of aggregated psychological measures for assessing organizational variables. Objective records—of group productivity,
growth and decline, profitability, resource allocation, group decisions, and so forth—also
can help us characterize various aspects of organizations. Similarly, the formal structure,
although not synonymous with actual organizational procedures, is easy to ascertain and
can yield valuable information in such areas as differentiation of structure, hierarchical
levels, the material reward system, prescribed feedback structures, and planned coordination.

Contingency theories are becoming popular, and they call attention to factors and
conditions that may mediate between the independent and dependent variables. But
often the emphasis is on an individual variable rather than an organizational characteristic. For example, increasing the challenge of a task supposedly will increase motivation
—at least for workers with needs for self-actualization. But it is also important to note
whether the challenge created by a change in job design is supported by a related change
in organizational design. Even studies of individual factors outside organizations are able

to explain a surprisingly small amount of variance (Sarason, Smith, and Dienet, 1975). Situational variables are somewhat better, though not a great improvement. Nor does their interaction do much more. In organizations, however, situational variables that take into account systemic or structural properties may be much more helpful. The contingency approach which seeks moderating variables has not yet paid off. It may well prove profitable if we define our moderating variables from an organizational rather than an individual point of view.

The implications of an emphasis on organizational variables for comparative study are clear. Most notably, multiorganizational investigations are called for. If we are to know how organizations adapt to their environments, we need to compare organizations in different environments. If we are to know how organizations' characteristics are related to one another, we need to study more than one structure. Comparative analysis can cover more than one concern in a single industry; it can cut across industries, it can also cut across types of organizations, or it can even be cross-cultural. Our knowledge of organizations will always be severely limited if we do not push ahead to comparative analysis.

Independence of Measures

A second methodological issue concerns the independence of the measures used to assess our independent and dependent variables. Measures can be objective indices of the stimulus situation; observations of behavior by trained observers; behavioral records; self-reports of behavior, attitudes, and motivation; or reports by other organizational members. If all measures come from one source, the investigation yields information of a limited and circular character—especially if the measures are confined to self-reports. Cognitive consistency may be operative, or a halo factor may color all the respondent's perceptions positively or negatively. The halo factor may result from the mood of the respondent, from the tendency to give socially desirable answers, or from the format of the questionnaire or interviewing instrument. An example of the latter point can be seen in factor analysis of attitude items in which factors emerge for questions asked in the same manner. A mediating variable of another self-report does not help. What is needed is a measure that will anchor the self-report to the stimulus situation on the one side or actual behavior on the other, and ideally to both.

Theoretically, if the behavior of individuals in organizations has causes that are structural (organizational level) and outcomes that are also organizational, self-report is inadequate in furnishing data on this whole causal process. Organizations may be unique in the extent to which their daily operations generate descriptive data at the collective level—profit, productivity, policy decisions, and so forth.

The critical point is the degree to which the data are contaminated by coming from the same type of measure or source, so that true relationships between variables are not established. Studies are often based on self-reports because of the relative ease of questionnaire devices. Observations of behavior by outside experts are costly and difficult. Productivity records which take account of comparable units of work for different individuals or groups are the exception rather than the rule, and setting up new productivity measures is a major undertaking.

Where we are forced to rely on participant perceptions, we can strengthen our investigations by using both self-reports and the reports of other organizational members. We can not only ask supervisors about their own behavior but can put related questions to their superiors and their subordinates.

Sets of self-reports can be profitably used in two ways. In the first place, they can be examined to see to what extent consensus or agreement exists. If the supervisors' description of their own behavior accords with the description of their superiors and their subordinates, we can assume that it possesses some validity. If there are discrepancies, however, we do not know whom to believe. We can also treat the agreement-disagreement gap as a variable. For example, the supervisor whose self-perceptional behavior agrees with the perceptions of his or her employees and whose report of their behavior is accurate is in different circumstances from one who disagrees on these dimensions. In the second place, we can relate the reported behavior of one group not to its perception by another group but to its hypothesized effect on another group. Thus, we can see what kinds of self-report items by supervisors produced effects on subordinates—effects such as commitment to the organization or acceptance of group goals. The second type of procedure can thus establish relationships between variables. It can also be used in connection with the consensus method to clarify the relationship reported.

Internal Versus External Validity

The tradeoff between experimental and field methods is such that both approaches need to be retained for the study of organizations. The great advantage of the experimental method is that it permits a measure of the independent variable—the condition manipulated—as it affects a dependent variable. Something is pushed and something happens, and we know what these things are. Thus, experimentation is directed at the heart of science, the discovery of the relationship between variables. Fortunately, we have seen the growth of laboratory experimentation both in simulation studies and in experiments dealing with isolated variables. The ingenuity of this work is a hopeful sign for the future of the field. If research is confined to self-reports, there is always the problem of interpretation of results. They may reflect the mood of the respondent, or the investigator's demands, or a relationship between two aspects of the same variable, or a true causal relationship. With experimentation the meaning of the results is clear. We know what given experimental conditions lead to certain outcomes. Thus, unlike most self-report studies, experiments are additive in character, permitting the accumulation of knowledge. The addition to knowledge from a single experiment may not be great, but it is an addition.

Although experiments are high on internal validity, they do not provide external validity or generalization to the real-life organizational world. That is, the experimental finding may be clear and valid within the laboratory setting but may have little relevance for the life situation. Experimentalists enthusiastic about internal validity may be too casual about external validity. After all, it is the organization setting about which we are trying to generalize (and perhaps even advise). The issue of external validity cannot be avoided or indefinitely postponed. All of this argues for complementarity in the use of experiment and field approaches.

There is a question, too, of reversible or symmetrical hypotheses in relationships. Some relationships are characterized by causal interaction or reciprocity rather than the one-way linear causality of the traditional experiment. Organizations are full of these types of relationships, and we are false to organizational phenomena if we think and test only one-way hypotheses.

Because of the problems of generalizing from the laboratory to the field setting, field experiments are a potent weapon in the armament of the researcher, since they afford some of the causal knowledge of the laboratory experiment without being as molecular in the variables under consideration. However, they lack the controls of the laboratory in that they operate in something of an open field; it is generally very difficult to rule out the differential effects of other variables save in a custodial setting. But the great disadvantage of the field experiment is its cost in time and effort and the poor power position of the researcher in establishing experimental conditions and controls. Field experiments, though providing some of the most interesting studies in our history, have thus given way to what is now known as evaluation research. The logic here is that of Campbell (1969), who has proposed that reforms be considered as experiments and that continuing measurements be taken before, during, and after the reform. Programs not instituted by the researcher can thus be monitored over time, and we have a renewal of the spirit of action research, with a bringing together of science and practice. The contribution of evaluation research depends on the adequacy of its measures of the program of action and the dependent outcomes.

Time Span of Investigation

Just as we need adequate samples in space for comparative study, so we need to consider what segment of a time cycle we have included in our investigation. In order to design research with time spans that are appropriate to the phenomena under study, we need theories about event sequences and their timing. Longitudinal studies and repeated measures help us to develop such time-specifying hypotheses, and the statement of hypotheses in terms that include the time dimension then helps us set the time parameters of our research.

Many studies of organizational intervention report results shortly after the intervention but fail to follow up and find out what happens in a subsequent time period. The work of Marrow, Bowers, and Seashore (1967) is an exception to this practice and also one of the few investigations reporting a sustained and diffusion effect. In drug experiments we would not stop our work after one or two dosages but would continue our scrutiny to look for cumulative effects and side effects. Every organizational act can be thought of as having effects that can be specified in time. For example, if a supervisor becomes more supportive in his behavior toward employees, it will take some time before they respond. Their response to the new supervisory style may increase to some maximum and then persist or drop off but not to the previous level. If we want to know the effects of the change in supervisory behavior, we have to tap employee responses at appropriate times. The time issue involves not only durability of change but also types of changes.

Moreover, sufficient time must be provided to identify feedback loops. In social interaction, a stimulus, A, which affects B, usually is itself affected by the feedback from B. In the real world of living organisms, such effects are the rule. A variable that is "independent" in the first phase of a cycle becomes "dependent" in the second phase, while the first-phase "dependent" variable becomes "independent" in the second. This extends to multiple variables, of course. Since there are lags in feedback effects, the time period of the investigation must be sufficient to permit them to operate; many months or more may be entailed, as in the case of policy decisions which are changed or revised after their initial effects become known. Also, long-range corporate strategies are altered as often as several times per year in the face of external events.

The organizational development movement was correct in seizing on the time dimension for improving organizations, but it failed to emphasize the role of research for the study of development. Just as psychology was late in its research on developmental processes, so too organizational psychology has been slow to study system processes over time. Theoretically, time studies could tell us a good deal about causality in natural settings. Practically, a continuing program of cooperation between some ongoing agency and a research facility is what is needed, as in the early Mayo studies.

Supplemental Case Studies

The case study needs to be revised and revitalized to furnish supplementary information for quantitative field studies. The field received major impetus from the old sociological case studies of Selznick's (1949) account of the Tennessee Valley Authority; Gouldner's (1954) study of a coal mine; Stanton and Schwartz's (1954) investigation of a hospital psychiatric ward; Blau's (1955) comparison of two government agencies; Lipset, Trow, and Coleman's (1956) description of a labor union; and Sykes' (1958) study of a prison. Somehow the method lost popularity, but its effectiveness came to light in the insightful work of Stotland and Kobler (1965) on the life and death of a mental hospital. An extensive library of case studies is maintained by the Intercollegiate Case Clearing House (Soldiers Field, Boston), which also provides useful models.

We need the qualitative description of the case-study approach for three purposes: (1) to help interpret quantitative findings, (2) to sharpen the questions for which data must be accumulated, and (3) to give a more adequate account of organizational processes over time. In other words, when field experiments and evaluation research are undertaken, we want to know more about the setting in which they take place. Quantitative surveys can document anthropological description. Although qualitative case studies and empirical measurement developed separately in the social sciences, there is no reason why they cannot be put together to advance the study of organizations. Each approach yields valuable information. We cannot afford to throw away knowledge because it comes from a given method. If, for example, we are considering a field experiment on decision making by rank-and-file workers, it is critical to know whether the plant is unionized and what areas of decision making are reserved by contract for labor-management negotiation. In their qualitative description of organizations where they carry out quantitative research, the Tavistock investigators (Rice, 1958; Trist and others, 1963) have furnished good models of the type of case study we are proposing. Comparative research is critical, but we should not give up the case study, which provides depth of understanding.

Research Problems

Our general consideration of methodological issues alerts us to difficulties and pitfalls in the prosecution of research. But we would call attention to the topics dealt with in this volume and raise some specific questions about the direction of future research efforts. What are some of the next steps that the investigator may want to take? In short, what needs to be done to move our discipline ahead as a research field. The following paragraphs list some of the lines of inquiry for our eight topics: environment and technology; types, characteristics, and roles; effectiveness and performance; motivation; communication; leadership and decision making; work and health; and conflict and change.

Environment and Technology

1. *To what extent do organizations of similar technologies tend to have similar structural characteristics?* This was the question with which Woodward (1965) began and which several others have addressed (Hickson, Pugh, and Pheysey, 1969; Blau and others,

1976). The work of Blau and his colleagues could be extended by an analysis of variance design, applied to a substantial sample of organizations, diverse in technology and structure. The basic question would be the extent to which each of a number of basic structural properties could be explained in terms of technology (between-group variance) and how much of the structural variance lies within technological groups.

2. *To what extent are the* central *structural tendencies in organizations of given technological characteristics also the* optimal *structural choices?* This question also derives from Woodward's work, although it has been neglected in the work of others. She emerged with a kind of Darwinian conclusion—that, for each technological level (batch, mass, process), most organizations operate with the structure best adapted to that technology. This finding has had remarkably uncritical acceptance, considering other lines of research (Likert, 1967; Argyris, 1971) that have been concerned with suboptimal managerial choices about structure and have demonstrated them to be widespread. To put it more succinctly and perhaps more constructively, what factors determine the choice of structure within a given technology?

3. *What technological characteristics are relevant for the prediction and understanding of organizational structure?* The issue here is the differentiation of the concept of technology. Social scientists who have considered technology at all have tended to treat it as a single variable, ranging from simplicity to complexity. But technologies can be compared on many other dimensions—for example, interdependence of components, extent of manual (operator) control versus machine control, cost of errors, length/time of feedback loop, duration of cycle. We can think in terms of a matrix of technological and structural properties, and the question then becomes one of searching out the pattern of relationships.

4. *What are the problems of technology transfer across organizations?* There are two issues here. One is the diffusion of technological advances within the type of industry in which they were developed. Research indicates that personal and informal communication can greatly aid the process. The second issue is the transfer across types of organizations—specifically, from industry to human service institutions. Should we facilitate or slow down the imitation of industry by government and education? What kinds of technology lend themselves to effective transfer across systems? How appropriate is the technology for the organization? For example, a mass-production method like the assembly line, which fractionates the purpose and process for the people involved, may be inappropriate for human services. In contrast, more technological developments, such as the typewriter and the computer, are inherently flexible and can be used in the interests of decentralization as well as centralization.

5. *As organizations grow, is there a constant ratio of members in various types of roles? Do organizations become top heavy? Do boundary roles proliferate more than production roles?* Haire (1959) found that there is a constant ratio of people inside the organization to those in boundary roles, but this finding needs confirmation and extension. Research results show a decrease in employees in direct production relative to nonproduction workers, but what groups of supportive personnel increase most rapidly has not been established. Parkinson's (1957) law about the growth of administrative personnel does not hold in general, but there may be conditions under which it does operate.

6. *What are the characteristics of organizations in a growth phase, a stable period, or a period of decline?* There is little research to test the popular notion that rapidly growing organizations are characterized by high morale, commitment, and motivation. Even less attention has been given to the processes by which organizations try to adapt to a contracting environment and diminishing resources.

Types, Characteristics, and Roles

1. *To what extent are the roles in an organization supported by normative codes of the organization?* People behave in roles because of the needs of the situation and the expectations of others. How much is such role behavior buttressed by explicitly formulated justifications of the organization's mission? How effective are such normative codes?

2. *How much conflict is created in the individual by discrepancies between role demands and personal and social values? What are the consequences of such conflicts?* Role conflicts of various kinds have been studied, but we know little about the stresses created by the variance between organization requirements and social values. Milgram (1974) found that people resolve the conflict by obeying the immediate authority, but at considerable psychological expense. In less extreme situations, how do individuals handle the stresses of organizational demands that run counter to their beliefs?

3. *Are organizational roles internalized or carried out because of external constraints?* Lieberman (1956) demonstrated several decades ago that people readily take on the norms of their roles. Workmen who became foremen acted like foremen and accepted their attitudes; similarly, workers who became union stewards soon assumed the behavior and norms of that role. But the reasons for their enactment of these roles was not clear. Was it an opportunistic adaptation to the external demands of the situation, or did the individual's self-image change to absorb the new role?

4. *How do boundary roles differ from other organizational roles in breadth of role perception, opportunity for role making, objective conflict, and experienced conflict?* The research of Adams (1976, 1979) and his students has shown the complexity of boundary roles as functional linkages between the organization and its environment. The boundary-role person is a member of two systems and is subject to both internal and external role sanctions; thus, feedback effects from two cycles crisscross in the boundary person. This exciting area of research can substantially advance our knowledge of organizations.

5. *What are the differences between private, public, and employee-owned organizations with respect to various characteristics, such as coordination, differentiation, efficiency, effectiveness, commitment to goals, and adaptability?* In spite of the many claims for private enterprise, few studies have compared private and public organizations on various organizational dimensions. Conte and Tannenbaum (1978) have begun an investigation of employee-owned firms but have not yet extended their work to a systematic comparison of these companies with private or public organizations. In a pioneering venture, Rushing (1976) found suggestive evidence of a stronger relationship between coordination and differentiation in profit than in nonprofit enterprises, presumably because profit organizations more clearly follow a rational model. This finding needs to be followed up by further research for definitive testing of the hypothesis.

6. *Do organizations involve one dominant form of power? Is such a dominant form more appropriate to a given organization than other forms?* The Etzioni (1975) theory is that one type of power tends to neutralize another; for example, coercion undermines the use of normative appeals. The effective organization is the one where there is congruence between type of commitment sought and type of power utilized. Franklin (1975) found that the more normative the power, the greater the commitment; but there has been no thorough empirical test of the theory.

Effectiveness and Performance

1. *Why is it difficult to obtain substantial correlations among various measures of effectiveness, such as turnover, absenteeism, productivity, profitability, and adaptability?*

One research study of thirty-two operating units of a nationwide service organization (Seashore, Indik, and Georgopoulis, 1960) showed low and even insignificant correlations for measures of unexcused absences, chargeable accidents, observed errors, productivity, and overall ratings of effectiveness. Factor analyses of seventy-six performance variables (Yuchtman and Seashore, 1967) generated ten different factors of considerable stability. Part of the problem is theoretical, and part of it is technical. Theoretically there has been little agreement on effectiveness criteria. Some writers have confused profitability, efficiency, and effectiveness. Argyris (1971) and Yuchtman and Seashore (1967) have achieved conceptual clarity in focusing on the relationship between inputs and outputs, but less has been done on the technical side in specifying the variables to be measured. Many of the measures used are of low reliability, restricted range, and questionable validity. A measure of absenteeism encounters problems of voluntary and involuntary absence and of restricted range. Moreover, the behavior under study varies in the degree to which it is under the control of the group members being studied. Hence, their performance may be satisfactory in those areas where controls are not in force. Such variation will lower correlations among the different criteria.

2. *Can service to clients furnish a criterion of organizational effectiveness?* Organizations that lack feedback from the marketplace need other types of feedback to know how well they are doing. The evaluation of their service can stem from the number of cases handled, percentages of cures, recidivism rates, or client satisfaction. In many instances, measures of client satisfaction can be readily employed and directed not at general feelings but at particular aspects of the service. Even where more objective measures are available, the reactions of the public served can be helpful, as in the case of hospital administration. From such research, generalizations about the relative importance of speed, effectiveness, and equity in the delivery of services could be derived.

3. *Can the contributions of an organization to the suprasystem, apart from its own specific objective, be assessed as a form of effectiveness?* Most considerations of effectiveness are within the frame of reference of the organization's own goal. But it may affect the larger society both positively and negatively. It may directly contribute to charitable causes, or it may not maximize profits in order to provide more employment. Public universities are often assumed to have more than the specific objective of turning out trained students, and many demands are placed on them in the public interest. The negative side of the picture is beginning to receive attention as organizational activities affect the environment and the health of people. Such secondary negative effects are a matter of increasing concern for the organization. If it alienates enough people, it will cut down its market. Legal suits against organizational excesses have become common. Automobile companies now call back defective models to guard against such lawsuits. Such actions mark an advance over a period where many organizations attempted to placate the public with high-pressure public relations.

4. *How much do organizations need to build in more systematic measures of feedback in their research and development departments?* A major interest in the organization's effectiveness lies within the organization itself. It has crude measures of its production as part of its operations, but the refinement of these measures, so that they can be comparable across various units, has not progressed much beyond time-and-motion study. Most large organizations have the possibilities of setting up comparable departments and divisions for natural experiments. Very few do. Research and development departments also need to concern themselves with measuring external impact—for instance, through studies of client satisfaction and long-range studies of the outcomes of given programs. Evaluation research is at the beginning, not the end, of a new phase of experimentation and research.

Motivation

1. *Is there a hierarchy of motives according to which lower-level needs must be satisfied before higher-level needs come into play?* There is no doubt about the plausibility or popularity of the Maslow (1954) need hierarchy, but it has received little empirical testing. In organizational settings, the question is whether ego rewards and opportunities for self-development will be effective when pay is at such a low level that people have difficulty in meeting sustenance and security needs. Before a company can effectively restructure jobs to make them more ego enriching, does a certain minimum wage level have to be reached?

2. *How generalized is the effect of rewards on behavior? Does it spread to more than the specific behavior being rewarded?* It is often assumed in organizations that good wages, fringe benefits, and fair treatment will give rise to various forms of behavior supportive of the organization. Laboratory experiments suggest, however, that the reinforcing effect of a reward is limited to behavior instrumental in securing the reward. If higher pay is not tied to piece rates, for example, it will not result in greater productivity. Human beings do generalize from their experiences, however, and there are transfers of affectivity. Are there any organizational conditions under which company rewards of a noncontingent character will lead to higher productivity? Will system rewards such as good fringe benefits produce a higher level of supportive actions in a munificent system than in a niggardly system—in other words, when the comparison is made across organizations and not within individuals in the same organization?

3. *Can the negative effects of aversive stimuli be restricted to proscribed behavior?* The use of punishment is often questioned because it may lead to withdrawal from, or hostility toward, the punishing agent. Avoidance occurs, but it may not be the avoidance anticipated. Nonetheless, we do learn to avoid harmful objects and to live in a hazardous world. How, then, can penalties be used so that their negative effects will be restricted to specific forms of behavior? Four conditions are apparently important: the objective or impersonal character of the punishment, its elicitation only for given actions, its acceptance as a legitimate norm, and its mild or nontraumatizing character.

4. *How important is clarity of expectations and structure in motivating people?* The literature on rewards and punishments and even on motivation gives scant attention to the need people have for clear structure. Chaotic and confused situations and conflicting demands are a source of frustration. McMahon and Ivancevich (1976) have been pioneers in the research on this issue and have demonstrated that people want to know who is in charge. More work on this problem could help account for considerable variance in predicting behavior.

5. *Are motives additive in producing given patterns of behavior, or do they interfere with one another in behavioral outcomes?* The debate on this question is between those who believe that extrinsic and intrinsic incentives are appropriate for different forms of behavior and those who regard them as additive. The one contention is that an appropriate reward may actually interfere with the desired outcome; the other contention is that different rewards are substitutable. Both sides can cite some experimental evidence, so the issue remains a research inquiry. What, specifically, are the incentives, what are the appropriate patterns of behavior, and what are the conditions of their addition or their interference?

6. *How is identification with a large organization and commitment to its goals achieved?* Theory suggests that participation produces involvement and that identification with larger structure is mediated through attachment to smaller groups. Both propositions need more empirical evidence than is presently available.

Communication

1. *Which mechanisms for handling information overload are adaptive, and which are maladaptive?* Miller (1960) has described the various reactions to information overload under seven headings: (1) omission, failure to process some of the information; (2) error, processing information incorrectly; (3) queuing; (4) filtering; (5) approximation; (6) employing multiple channels; and (7) escaping from the task. There has been little research, however, on the adaptive or maladaptive outcomes of these mechanisms and the ways in which some of them could be made adaptive. Filtering, queuing, and approximation can be either adaptive or maladaptive, depending on whether they follow established patterns of the organization or the ease of operation of the individual receiver. The organization, then, that plans for emergency situations can escape some of the deleterious effects of overload by the priorities and standards set up. Galbraith (1973) deals with overload in relation to decision-making structure and recommends a number of informal group structures, task groups, and vertical information-processing computers.

2. *Should authority and intelligence functions be structurally separated, so that instructions and commands are carried downward by one line and feedback upward by another line?* There are advantages and disadvantages in structural separation. With such separation, intelligence about organizational functioning and impact on environment is less likely to be controlled by line officers in data gathering, but there is still a problem about the utilization of information. Under some circumstances, there is an advantage to a structure that provides short circuits between information and authority, so that a lower-level officer can work in cooperation with an intelligence person. Information does not have to go all the way up the line and then all the way down to be utilized. The risk of corruption of information by the executive line is well known, but there is also the risk of intelligence taking over the authority function. In totalitarian systems, espionage groups may be leading subsystems. In our own society, the CIA has on occasion allowed its action tendencies to take precedence over its information role. We have seen little research in industrial organizations on the consequences of separating or consolidating authority and intelligence functions.

3. *Under what conditions will lateral communication in organizations increase?* Lateral communication may increase with a decline in vertical communication. What is the relation between the two? Do they increase and decrease together, or is one the reciprocal of the other? Does lateral communication increase under conditions of environmental uncertainty?

4. *How are the amount and type of communication related to job satisfaction and commitment to the organization?* Early studies suggested that adequacy of communication affects the motivation of employees, but we need more work in which communication is related to hard data such as productivity, absenteeism, and turnover.

5. *As organizations expand into social space, how necessary is it to expand informational networks?* The multinational character of some organizations and their dependence on world markets call for revolutionary changes in information gathering. Is there any relationship between organizational effectiveness and type of informational network employed? Huneycutt (1974) has shown that the availability of information from an independent external source influences decisions of managers whose internal gatekeepers may be biased.

6. *Can market research be profitably used as a guide to systemic and systematic study of communication feedback between environment and organization?* Market research, as the objective search for and analysis of information designed to reduce the uncertainty of organization decision makers, is an organized system of communication, or

feedback loop, from markets to organizations as diverse as industrial, commercial, voluntary, health, and government institutions (Green and Tull, 1975). Operating at the organization-environment interface, the research is systemic in nature and serves both organizational boundary and adaptive functions. It is also dynamic in that complex, changing markets (consumers, ideas, technology, products, services, resources, competitors) require continuous updating of information. Markets research therefore may be useful to students of organizations in two ways. First, the observation of the content of market research provides data on what external variables influence organization decisions. Second, insight into organization-environment feedback processes is provided.

Leadership and Decision Making

1. *What are the critical dimensions of leadership, and how are they interrelated?* Older research rightly emphasized the importance of task facilitation and socioemotional supportiveness. More discriminating analysis is needed, however, to move us ahead. We suggest three major dimensions for the leader: (1) involving subordinates in decision making, (2) representing their interests at higher levels in the system, and (3) showing understanding and affection.

2. *What are the techniques for involving and motivating subordinates?* French and Raven (1960) have called attention to five sources of power: reward, punishment, expert, legitimate, and referent. How does the utilization of these various sources affect motivation and performance? Incremental influence refers to the effects of expert and referent power over and above reward, punishment, and legitimate power. Student (1968) has shown that such incremental influence increased performance in an appliance factory. Additional research is needed in other organizations, both industrial and nonindustrial, to confirm this finding and to furnish specifications for the operation of incremental influence.

3. *How can supportive leadership be taught without institutionalizing it and thereby impairing it?* The interest and concern of the supervisor for his subordinates is conveyed by expressions of positive affect. But if such expression is perceived as a technique, it can be self-defeating. If it becomes bureaucratic in character, the behavior is there but the meaning is lost. Reinforcement theory does not address itself directly to this problem, nor does the human relations school.

4. *With the growth of technology, does expert power assume a larger role in developed organizations?* The concept of leading subsystem implies that a given substructure may exert heavy influence on the policy formulation and decision making of the larger system. In growing organizations, the technical groupings of the research and development department may be the leading subsystem. There is no arguing with technical expertise on technical matters; and, as the organization grows, its problems become increasingly technical.

5. *If group process is used for decision making, does the area of freedom for such decisions have to be redefined for the unit in question?* Group process, if it is not rigidly constrained, is a powerful force. But can it maintain its vitality if the old constraints and limitations of the traditional system prevail? Does not the whole structure have to be loosened up for group process to work? In other words, if group members are to become involved in the process, does not the group need to have meaningful decisions to make?

6. *Do leadership qualities vary for different levels in the organization and for different subsystems of the organization?* Cognitive skills may be more important as we ascend the hierarchy, and administrative skills may be of great importance at middle

levels. We need to know what breadth of the system perspective is optimal for leaders at different organizational levels. Moreover, the socioemotional supportiveness of the leader may change markedly for lower and higher levels. Charisma may be difficult to achieve for the first-line officer in direct contact with subordinates. Charisma may require some social distance if magical qualities are to be imputed to the leader.

7. *How far can contingency theory be pushed to furnish more information on leadership, and what types of contingent conditions should be studied?* Leadership is the area where contingency theory becomes the central issue. The universalistic approach is represented by Likert (1967), in his generalizations about supportiveness; the situational approach is represented by Fiedler (1967), with his contingency specifications. Vroom and Yetton (1973) have proposed a model that puts less emphasis on the objective contingencies and relies heavily on subjective self-reports of decision makers. Research has yet to establish the limits of the claims of either the Likert or the Fiedler school, and the Vroom-Yetton model needs to be supported by more objective evidence about the decision processes of leaders.

Work and Health

1. *What are the dimensions that describe the stress-relevant properties of jobs?* To provide a frame of reference for the researcher, there is need for an explicit set of variables concerned with job stress. One study might not attempt to measure all these variables, and all of them might not be involved in any particular work setting. But they would represent a theoretical development and a research agenda in terms of which the content of specific studies could be interpreted.

2. *What are the effects of different durations of exposure to stress?* There is a need to distinguish between chronic and acute stresses at work, to specify the duration of exposure to the stresses under study and the extent of change from some previous base. In short, the specifications that are routine in epidemiological and toxicological studies should be introduced into research on sociopsychological stress at work.

3. *What are the structural antecedents of different types of job stress?* Some research on occupational and positional differences has been done (see, for example, Adams, 1976, on the boundary role), but little has been done to investigate the effects of organizational size, shape, and structure on the generation of stress. Such research will require multiorganizational designs.

4. *What are the methods of coping with and defending against stress at work?* Coping behavior, by definition, is adaptive, whereas defense mechanisms often aggravate the problem. Defenses such as projection may create interpersonal problems; but do some defenses, such as denial and blocking, have adaptive value in defending against stress and holding the individual in role? When people underestimate the magnitude of role conflicts, they may be both coping and defending. Here again the basis for evaluation must have a time line. Today's successful denial may be tomorrow's disaster.

5. *What are the positive outcomes of work, and how are they related to job characteristics?* Research on work and health needs to look at the positive outcomes of work. As Cobb's (1974) research suggests, nonwork is often the more stressful condition. Hence, the positive findings of Weiner, Akabas, and Sommer (1973) in delivering health services to workers on the job need to be followed up. Jahoda (1958) long ago proposed the importance of positive criteria of mental health and suggested several. Some work has been done with measures of self-development and self-actualization, but an adequate set of positive outcome measures has not yet been created.

6. *What is the role of longitudinal studies in the field of health and work?* Natural experiments and field experiments that attempt stress-reducing or stress-buffering interventions are needed. House and associates (1979) state well the particular limitations of cross-sectional designs in research in this domain and use highly sophisticated analytic procedures to control statistically for some of the more plausible alternative explanations of their own data. Such analyses should be followed, however, with longitudinal designs to give definitive tests to the more important findings.

Conflict and Change

1. *What are the major causes of organizational conflict, as against individual conflict?* By organizational conflict is meant the clashes or potential clashes between organizational groupings; for example, labor versus management or sales personnel versus production people. Research has slighted the issue of the nature of conflict, its underlying basis, and its precipitating causes. How much are conflicts rooted in economic and power differentials, and how much in ideological difference? Differential returns to subgroups in organizations may be built-in sources of conflict in that dissatisfactions may arise among the less privileged. Thus the organizational reward structure may determine collective conflict along the lines of group interest. Dahrendorf (1959) has assumed that any hierarchical arrangement with respect to power will produce a conflictual relationship between superior and subordinate. The history of communist countries supports Dahrendorf's thesis in that the reduction of economic struggle between social strata has not meant the elimination of political conflict. Hence profit sharing alone might not reduce organizational conflict, but profit sharing and participation in decision making might. The effects of participative decision making on industrial peace warrant thorough study.

2. *How are modes of conflict resolution related to the nature and source of conflict?* Negotiation and compromise are more appropriate ways of dealing with economic than with ideological conflicts. Concessions and tradeoffs are the crux of industrial and political bargaining. But ideological principles go beyond opportunistic tactics and are resistant to compromise proposals. The strategy in conflict resolution is to avoid phrasing the issue in the language of ideological goals and to concentrate on pragmatic pawns that can be traded. Conditions that impede the trading process, as in open sessions of representatives of two conflicting groups can freeze the position of the contending parties. The general rule is to provide an area of freedom for the representatives of the two groups at odds with one another, so that they can negotiate without continual reference to their constituents. In this manner the negotiators can develop norms and practices of their own. The fascinating experients by Blake, Shepard, and Mouton (1964) on the roles of group representatives have been rigorously pursued by subsequent investigators (Rubin and Brown, 1975).

3. *Does the method of decreasing threat have significant application to reducing organizational conflict?* Conflicts escalate as each group feels threatened by the demands of its opponent and increases its own demands. Both parties get locked into a cycle of threats and counterthreats. To cut through this vicious cycle, two methods have been prepared. One is a cooperative move, with additional cooperation if the move is reciprocated (conditional cooperation). The other—the Osgood (1962) GRIT strategy—is unilateral concession (unconditional cooperation). Gaming experiments have found that conditional cooperation is more effective than unconditional cooperation (Swingle, 1970), but full exploration of a number of related variables and their parameters is needed. Where there is a history of mistrust and hard bargaining between parties, it may take more than a single conditional move to get cooperation under way.

4. *Do organizations have to reform their political structure to reduce intraorganizational conflict?* Worker representation in organizational decision making is gaining support in many quarters, but what form this participation should take and what the consequences are for conflict are open questions. What combinations of direct and indirect democracy are viable in nonpolitical organizations? What are the advantages and disadvantages of industrial unions, craft unions, labor-management committees, or some combination of these methods? What forms of representation are most effective in reducing conflict as well as contributing to member satisfaction? Questions of this sort have generally been raised for political systems, but they are also appropriate for other systems. Cross-national research involving experimenting European countries is necessary to cover the wide range of critical variables.

5. *Will attempts at organizational change fail over time if the changes do not spread through the organization?* The organization consists of interdependent subsystems. Hence, a modification in one part calls for an adjustment in other parts of the system. Either the new practices are echoed in the larger system or they have a short life. They are more likely to diffuse if they are introduced and legitimated at the highest levels in the hierarchical structure. They are also likely to spread if they are consistent with the dominant trends of slow change already under way in the organization. But if they call for revolutionary changes in one subsystem and hence do not diffuse, they will not last. This area for research needs to be approached first through case studies, as in Warwick's (1975) investigation of attempted reforms in the State Department.

6. *What kinds of intervention are most effective in changing productivity and member satisfaction: survey feedback, T-group training, structural change, or some combination?* Bowers (1973) found survey feedback superior to T-group training, and Pasmore (1978) found sociotechnical intervention superior to survey feedback. Pasmore believes, however, that a combination will yield the best results, since human process techniques will help secure the cooperation of the people involved. Pasmore also hypothesizes that settings like universities and government agencies, which do not involve capital-intensive technology, will respond more positively to survey feedback than to sociotechnical intervention. Comparative research across various types of organizations is thus indicated, but there needs to be more specification of the target of change—whether interpersonal relations, technology, political structure, or hierarchical level of the sociotechnical system.

7. *What kinds of research on the utilization of scientific knowledge help to ensure the application of research findings?* In spite of the widespread research agreement on the effectiveness of various types of participatory practices, the movement toward adopting these procedures has been modest. Although a more democratic restructuring gives a competitive advantage to the enterprise, organizations, supposedly committed to the goal of greater productivity, seem resistant to change. To solve this puzzle, three lines of work on research utilization are suggested. In the first place, we need a technology that would translate scientific findings into usable tools, as engineering does for physical science. The problem is more difficult for the social sciences because tools for dealing with people require more understanding of their functioning by the practitioner than machines for processing objects. Nonetheless, technology such as survey feedback needs to be made clearly visible, with clearly formulated objectives and explicit sets of instructions. In the second place, managers' resistances to change need to be explored. Are these resistances specific apprehensions about loss of control, about starting a dynamic process that cannot be halted? Is it a matter of reluctance to learn a new game by those who are effective masters of the established game? Do the necessary changes challenge vested interests? In the third place, the differences between organizations need to be studied as democratic

procedures are adopted to discover the conditions that make for successful participatory practices. Differences between countries can be similarly investigated. With respect to utilization, we can distinguish two kinds of errors: failure to use research findings that are applicable to existing problems (as we have just discussed) and actually using findings that are inapplicable or false. In the relationship between organizational research and organizational practice, we believe that errors of omission are more frequent than errors of commission. Nevertheless, managements have bought and continue to buy many programs and packages that purport to incorporate the findings of social science research. The claims are often not based on a rigorous program of research, and we suspect that many of them would fail such tests. To what extent the remedy lies in the increasing sophistication of managerial clients and to what extent in more formalized requirements for evaluation is itself debatable.

References

Adams, J. S. "The Structure and Dynamics of Behavior in Organizational Boundary Roles." In M. D. Dunnette (Ed.), *Handbook of Industrial and Organizational Psychology*. Chicago: Rand McNally, 1976.

Adams, J. S. "Interorganizational Processes and Organizational Boundary Activities." In B. M. Staw and L. Cummings (Eds.), *Research in Organizational Behavior*. Vol. 2. Greenwich, Conn.: JAI Press, 1979.

Argyris, C. *Management and Organizational Development*. New York: McGraw-Hill, 1971.

Blake, R. R., Shepard, H. A., and Mouton, J. S. *Managing Intergroup Conflict in Industry*. Houston: Gulf, 1964.

Blau, P. M. *The Dynamics of Bureaucracy*. Chicago: University of Chicago Press, 1955.

Blau, P., and others. "Technology and Organization in Manufacturing." *Administrative Science Quarterly*, 1976, *21*, 20-40.

Bowers, D. G. "OD Techniques and Their Results in Twenty-Three Organizations: The Michigan ICL Study." *Journal of Applied Behavioral Science*, 1973, *9* (1), 21-43.

Campbell, D. T. "Reforms As Experiments." *American Psychologist*, 1969, *24*, 409-429.

Cobb, S. "Physiological Changes in Men Whose Jobs Were Abolished." *Journal of Psychosomatic Research*, 1974, *18*, 245-258.

Conte, M., and Tannenbaum, A. S. "Employee-Owned Companies: Is the Difference Measurable?" *Monthly Labor Review*, July 1978, pp. 24-27.

Dahrendorf, R. *Class and Conflict in Industrial Society*. Stanford, Calif.: Stanford University Press, 1959.

Etzioni, A. *A Comparative Analysis of Complex Organizations*. (Rev. ed.) New York: Free Press, 1975.

Fiedler, F. E. *A Theory of Leadership Effectiveness*. New York: McGraw-Hill, 1967.

Franklin, J. L. "Power and Commitment: An Empirical Assessment." *Human Relations*, 1975, *28* (8), 737-753.

French, J. R. P., Jr., and Raven, B. H. "The Bases of Social Power." In D. Cartwright and A. Zander (Eds.), *Group Dynamics: Research and Theory*. (2nd ed.) New York: Harper & Row, 1960.

Galbraith, J. *Designing Complex Organizations*. Reading, Mass.: Addison-Wesley, 1973.

Gouldner, A. W. *Patterns of Industrial Bureaucracy*. New York: Free Press, 1954.

Green, P. E., and Tull, D. S. *Research for Marketing Decisions*. Englewood Cliffs, N.J.: Prentice-Hall, 1975.

Gurin, P., and Epps, E. *Black Consciousness, Identity and Achievement*. New York: Wiley, 1975.

Gurin, P., and others. "Internal-External Control in the Motivational Dynamics of Negro Youth." *Journal of Social Issues,* 1969, *25* (3), 29-53.

Haire, M. "Biological Models and Empirical Histories of the Growth of Organizations." In M. Haire (Ed.), *Modern Organization Theory.* New York: Wiley, 1959.

Hickson, D. J., Pugh, D. S., and Pheysey, D. "Operations Technology and Organization Structure: An Empirical Reappraisal." *Administrative Science Quarterly,* 1969, *14,* 378-397.

House, J. S., and others. "Occupational Stress and Health Among Factory Workers." *Journal of Health and Social Behavior,* 1979, *20,* 139-160.

Huneycutt, M. J. "Effects of Information Distortion, Personalized Opposition, and Defensiveness upon Decision Makers' Responses to Environmental Pressure." Unpublished doctoral dissertation, University of North Carolina at Chapel Hill, 1974.

Jahoda, M. *Current Concepts of Positive Mental Health.* New York: Basic Books, 1958.

Lieberman, S. "The Effects of Changes in Roles on the Attitudes of Role Occupants." *Human Relations,* 1956, *9,* 385-402.

Likert, R. *The Human Organization.* New York: McGraw-Hill, 1967.

Lipset, S. M., Trow, J. A., and Coleman, J. S. *Union Democracy.* New York: Free Press, 1956.

McMahon, J. T., and Ivancevich, J. M. "A Study of Control in a Manufacturing Organization: Managers and Nonmanagers." *Administrative Science Quarterly,* 1976, *21,* 66-83.

Marrow, A. J., Bowers, D. G., and Seashore, S. E. *Management by Participation.* New York: Harper & Row, 1967.

Maslow, A. H. *Motivation and Personality.* New York: Harper & Row, 1954.

Milgram, S. *Obedience to Authority: An Experimental View.* New York: Harper & Row, 1974.

Miller, J. G. "Information Input, Overload, and Psychopathology." *American Journal of Psychiatry,* 1960, *116,* 695-704.

Osgood, C. E. *An Alternative to War Is Surrender.* Urbana: University of Illinois Press, 1962.

Parkinson, C. N. *Parkinson's Law.* Boston: Houghton Mifflin, 1957.

Pasmore, W. A. "The Comparative Impacts of Sociotechnical System, Job-Redesign, and Survey-Feedback Interventions." In W. A. Pasmore and J. J. Sherwood (Eds.), *Socio-Technical Systems: A Sourcebook.* La Jolla, Calif.: University Associates, 1978.

Rice, A. K. *Productivity and Social Organization: The Ahmedabad Experiment.* London: Tavistock, 1958.

Rubin, J. Z., and Brown, B. R. *The Social Psychology of Bargaining and Negotiations.* New York: Academic Press, 1975.

Rushing, W. A. "Profit and Nonprofit Orientations and the Differentiations-Coordination Hypothesis for Organizations: A Study of Small General Hospitals." *American Sociological Review,* 1976, *41,* 676-691.

Sarason, I. G., Smith, R. E., and Dienet, E. "Personality Research: Components of Variance Attributable to the Person and the Situation." *Journal of Personality and Social Psychology,* 1975, *32* (2), 199-204.

Seashore, S. E., Indik, B. P., and Georgopoulos, B. S. "Relationships Among Criteria of Job Performance." *Journal of Applied Psychology,* 1960, *44,* 195-202.

Selznick, P. *TVA and the Grass Roots.* Berkeley: University of California Press, 1949.

Stanton, A., and Schwartz, M. *The Mental Hospital.* New York: Basic Books, 1954.

Stotland, E., and Kobler, A. L. *Life and Death of a Mental Hospital.* Seattle: University of Washington Press, 1965.

Student, K. "Supervisory Influence and Work-Group Performance." *Journal of Applied Psychology,* 1968, *52,* 188-194.

Swingle, P. (Ed.). *The Structure of Conflict.* New York: Academic Press, 1970.

Sykes, G. M. *The Society of Captives.* Princeton, N.J.: Princeton University Press, 1958.

Tajfel, H., and Billig, M. "Familiarity and Categorization in Intergroup Behavior." *Journal of Experimental Social Psychology,* 1974, *10,* 159-170.

Trist, E. L., and others. *Organizational Choice.* London: Tavistock, 1963.

Vroom, V. H., and Yetton, P. W. *Leadership and Decision-Making.* Pittsburgh: University of Pittsburgh Press, 1973.

Warwick, D. P. *A Theory of Public Bureaucracy: Politics, Personality and Organization in the State Department.* Cambridge, Mass.: Harvard University Press, 1975.

Weiner, H. J., Akabas, S. H., and Sommer, J. S. *Mental Health Care in the World of Work.* New York: Association Press, 1973.

Woodward, J. *Industrial Organization: Theory and Practice.* London: Oxford University Press, 1965.

Yuchtman, E., and Seashore, S. E. "A System Resource Approach to Organizational Effectiveness." *American Sociological Review,* 1967, *32,* 891-903.

~~~~ Name Index

Subject Index

A

Absenteeism, 172, 174; control policy toward, 211-217; and participative decision making, 534; work attitudes related to, 219-222, 224, 226-230

Achieving Manager Research Project, 367-382

Action research, 3

Adjudication, 466, 489-504

Administrative intensity, 11, 57, 201, 204, 208; and size, 43-44

Adversary model, of adjudication, 468, 489-504

Alienation: and organizational change, 527; from the work process, 284

Anxiety, and role conflict, 423

Arbitration. *See* Conflict resolution

Areas of freedom: of groups, 548; of leaders, 361

Aston group, 10, 14, 18

Attitudes: financial impact of, 224-232; and organizational change, 526-527, 529; and participative decision making, 534-536; as predictors of absenteeism, 219-222

Authoritarian management style, 532. *See also* Manager X and Manager Y philosophies; Managerial achievement; Managerial style

Autonomy: and aspirations toward more influence, 287-292; involvement in work, 286; and participative decision making, 535; and worker participation, 284-286

B

Bargaining. *See* Conflict resolution

Boundary activities: allocations to, 62-63; and communication, 300, 321, 324; and role conflict, 137, 144, 419; and roles, 75-76, 157, 543; and spanners, 152-153

Boundary role position, 157-170; evaluation of, 158; and obedience, 159, 160, 163, 168, 170; and outputting effectiveness, 158, 160, 163, 170; and outside receptiveness, 159, 160, 163

C

Case studies, 542

Centralization: and communication, 312, 320, 324, 328; and computers, 33, 35-39, 110; of decision making, 17, 312; of power, 235

Change: and conflict, 465-466; and diffusion, 551. *See also* Organizational change techniques, comparison of; Survey feedback; Sociotechnical intervention; T groups

Choice: and insufficient justification, 267-272; and motivation, 265-273

Clarity of structure, and motivation, 235, 546